THE ROUTLEDGE HANDBOOK OF ETHICS AND PUBLIC POLICY

What does it mean to do public policy ethics today? How should philosophers engage with ethical issues in policy-making when policy decisions are circumscribed by political and pragmatic concerns? How do ethical issues in public policy differ between areas such as foreign policy, criminal justice, or environmental policy?

The Routledge Handbook of Ethics and Public Policy addresses all these questions and more, and is the first handbook of its kind. It is composed of 41 chapters written by leading international contributors, and is organised into four clear sections covering the following key topics:

- Methodology: philosophical approaches to public policy, ethical expertise, knowledge, and public policy
- Democracy and public policy: identity, integration, and inclusion: voting, linguistic policy, discrimination, youth policy, religious toleration, and the family
- Public goods: defence and foreign policy, development and climate change, surveillance and internal security, ethics of welfare, health care and fair trade, sovereignty and territorial boundaries, and the ethics of nudging
- Public policy challenges: criminal justice, policing, taxation, poverty, disability, reparation, and ethics of death policies.

The Routledge Handbook of Ethics and Public Policy is essential reading for students and researchers in philosophy, politics, and social policy. It will be equally useful to those in related disciplines, such as economics and law, or professional fields, such as business administration or policy-making generally.

Annabelle Lever is Professeure des Universités à Sciences Po, Paris, France. She is the author of *On Privacy* (2012) and *A Democratic Conception of Privacy* (2014), the editor of *New Frontiers in the Philosophy of Intellectual Property* (2014), and the co-editor of *Ideas That Matter: Justice, Democracy, Rights* (2018).

Andrei Poama is Assistant Professor (with a focus on ethics and political philosophy) at the Faculty of Governance and Global Affairs, Institute of Public Administration, Leiden University, the Netherlands.

ROUTLEDGE HANDBOOKS IN APPLIED ETHICS

Applied ethics is one of the largest and most diverse fields in philosophy and is closely related to many other disciplines across the humanities, sciences, and social sciences. *Routledge Handbooks in Applied Ethics* are state-of-the-art surveys of important and emerging topics in applied ethics, providing accessible yet thorough assessments of key fields, themes, thinkers, and recent developments in research.

All chapters for each volume are specially commissioned, and written by leading scholars in the field. Carefully edited and organized, *Routledge Handbooks in Applied Ethics* provide indispensable reference tools for students and researchers seeking a comprehensive overview of new and exciting topics in applied ethics and related disciplines. They are also valuable teaching resources as accompaniments to textbooks, anthologies, and research-orientated publications.

Also available:

THE ROUTLEDGE HANDBOOK OF FOOD ETHICS
Edited by Mary Rawlinson and Caleb Ward

THE ROUTLEDGE HANDBOOK OF NEUROETHICS
Edited by L. Syd M Johnson, Karen S. Rommelfanger

THE ROUTLEDGE HANDBOOK OF THE ETHICS OF DISCRIMINATION
Edited by Kasper Lippert-Rasmussen

THE ROUTLEDGE HANDBOOK OF THE PHILOSOPHY OF PATERNALISM
Edited by Kalle Grill and Jason Hanna

THE ROUTLEDGE HANDBOOK OF THE ETHICS OF CONSENT
Edited by Peter Schaber and Andreas Müller

THE ROUTLEDGE HANDBOOK OF ETHICS AND PUBLIC POLICY
Edited by Annabelle Lever and Andrei Poama

For more information about this series, please visit: www.routledge.com/Routledge-Handbooks-in-Applied-Ethics/book-series/RHAE

THE ROUTLEDGE HANDBOOK OF ETHICS AND PUBLIC POLICY

Edited by Annabelle Lever and Andrei Poama

Routledge
Taylor & Francis Group

LONDON AND NEW YORK

First published 2019
by Routledge
2 Park Square, Milton Park, Abingdon, Oxon OX14 4RN

and by Routledge
52 Vanderbilt Avenue, New York, NY 10017

Routledge is an imprint of the Taylor & Francis Group, an informa business

British Library Cataloguing-in-Publication Data
A catalogue record for this book is available from the British Library

Library of Congress Cataloging-in-Publication Data
Names: Lever, Annabelle, editor. | Poama, Andrei, editor.
Title: The Routledge handbook of ethics and public policy / edited by Annabelle Lever and Andrei Poama.
Description: Abingdon, Oxon ; New York, NY : Routledge, 2019. | Series: Routledge handbooks in applied ethics | Includes bibliographical references and index.
Identifiers: LCCN 2018028489 | ISBN 9781138201279 (hardback : alk. paper) | ISBN 9781315461731 (e-book)
Subjects: LCSH: Policy sciences—Moral and ethical aspects. | Political planning—Moral and ethical aspects.
Classification: LCC H97 .R6774 2019 | DDC 172—dc23
LC record available at https://lccn.loc.gov/2018028489

ISBN: 978-1-138-20127-9 (hbk)
ISBN: 978-1-315-46173-1 (ebk)

Typeset in Bembo
by Apex CoVantage, LLC

Printed in the United Kingdom
by Henry Ling Limited

CONTENTS

Contents

CONTRIBUTORS

Albert Atkin (*albert.atkin@mq.edu.au*) is a philosopher based at Macquairie University. His research focuses on the philosophy of race and racism, with a particular interest in how the definition of "racism" impacts upon social, policy, and political questions. Dr Atkin has additional interest in the philosophy of language and pragmatism, especially when they intersect with applied questions in social and political philosophy.

Aurélia Bardon (*aurelia.bardon@uni-konstanz.de*) is Junior Professor in Political Theory at the University of Konstanz. Her research focuses on public justification, religion, secularism, and liberal neutrality. She recently co-edited *Religion in Liberal Political Philosophy* with Cécile Laborde (2017).

Juliana Bidadanure (*j.bidadanure@stanford.edu*) is Assistant Professor of Philosophy at Stanford University, where she also directs the Stanford Basic Income Lab. Her interests lie at the intersection of philosophy and public policy. She writes mainly on social egalitarianism and age-group justice. Her public policy interest has so far led her to study the basic income, basic capital, job guarantee, and youth quotas proposals.

Michael Blake (*miblake@uw.edu*) is Professor of Philosophy, Public Policy, and Governance at the University of Washington. Until 2016, he was Director of UW's Program on Values in Society. He received his bachelor's degree in philosophy and economics from the University of Toronto, and a PhD from Stanford University. He obtained some legal training at Yale Law School, before running away to become a philosopher.

Astrid von Busekist (*astrid.vonbusekist@sciencespo.fr*) is Professor of Political Theory at Sciences Po. She is chief editor of the journal *Raisons Politiques*. She has widely published on nationalism, language policies, and boundaries. Forthcoming (2018) with J. Cohen and A. Arato is *Forms of Pluralism and Democratic Constitutionalism*.

Giulia Cavaliere (*giulia.cavaliere@kcl.ac.uk*) is a PhD candidate in bioethics and society at the Department of Social Science, Health and Medicine of King's College, London. Her Wellcome Trust–sponsored project is titled 'Preimplantation Genetic Diagnosis and

Eugenics: A Social Moral Epistemology Approach'. Giulia's main research interests are in philosophical and sociological approaches in bioethics, with a focus on reproductive genetic technologies and the history of eugenics.

Emanuela Ceva (*emanuela.ceva@unipv.it*) is Associate Professor of Political Philosophy at the University of Pavia. She has held visiting fellowships at Harvard, Oxford, St Andrews, and Montreal. She works on value conflict, democracy, and corruption. She is the author of *Interactive Justice* (2016) and her most recent articles have appeared in *Social Theory and Practice* and *Politics, Philosophy & Economics*.

François Claveau (*francois.claveau@usherbrooke.ca*) is Canada Research Chair in Applied Epistemology and Assistant Professor in the Department of Philosophy and Applied Ethics at Université de Sherbrooke. His research involves conceptual and empirical work in the philosophy of the social sciences and in social epistemology. See *epistemopratique.org/en*.

Malcolm Dando (*M.R.Dando@bradford.ac.uk*) is Professor and Leverhulme Emeritus Fellow in the Division of Peace Studies, Faculty of Social Sciences, University of Bradford. Professor Dando is a biologist by original training and works on strengthening the chemical and biological non-proliferation regime. He is co-editor of *Preventing Chemical Weapons: Arms Control and Disarmament as the Sciences Converge*, published in 2018.

Peter Dietsch (*peter.dietsch@umontreal.ca*) is a philosopher and economist by training. Professor Dietsch's research focuses on questions of economic ethics. He is the author of *Catching Capital – The Ethics of Tax Competition* (2015) and co-author of *Do Central Banks Serve the People?* (2018).

Ezekiel J. Emanuel (*MEHPchair@upenn.edu*), MD, PhD, is Vice Provost for Global Initiatives and Chair of Medical Ethics and Health Policy at the University of Pennsylvania. He has served as a special advisor for health policy to the director of the Office of Management and Budget in the White House and is the former Chair of the Department of Bioethics at the National Institutes of Health.

Maria Paola Ferretti (*maria.ferretti@normativeorders.net*) is Senior Researcher in Political Theory at the Goethe University of Frankfurt on Main. Her research interests include contemporary liberalism, democratic participation, and the ethics of public policy, with a focus on risk regulation and political corruption. She has published in journals such as *Politics, Philosophy and Economics*, the *Journal of Applied Philosophy*, *Review of Policy Research*, and *Philosophy Compass*.

Clément Fontan (*clement.fontan@uclouvain.be*) obtained his PhD in political sciences from Sciences Po Grenoble in 2012. He is now Professor of European Economic Policies at the Université Catholique de Louvain and co-editor of the *Journal Politique Européenne*.

Anca Gheaus (*agheaus@gmail.com*) is a researcher at the Universitat Pompeu Fabra. She published articles on child-rearing and gender justice and has recently edited a special issue of the *Journal of Applied Philosophy* on the nature and value of childhood and co-edited *The Routledge Handbook of the Philosophy of Childhood and Children*.

Benjamin Goold (*goold@allard.ubc.ca*) is Professor at the Peter A. Allard School of Law at the University of British Columbia. His major research interests include privacy rights, the use of surveillance technologies by the police and intelligence communities, and the rhetoric and language of human rights.

John Harris (*john.harris@manchester.ac.uk*) is Lord Alliance Professor of Bioethics at the University of Manchester, and Director of the Institute for Science, Ethics, and Innovation, School of Law. Professor Harris's research interests are in the area of the ethics of science and applied philosophy; he is well known for his libertarian-consequentialist approach to bioethics, and is one of the foremost critics of paternalistic or restrictive approaches to the regulation of access to medical services and medical technology.

Teddy Harrison (*teddy.harrison@mail.utoronto.ca*) is a PhD candidate in political science at the University of Toronto. He is a former civil servant and holds an MPhil from the University of Oxford.

Søren Holm (*soren.holm@manchester.ac.uk*) is Professor of Bioethics at the University of Manchester. Professor Holm has been President of the European Society for the Philosophy of Medicine and Health Care, and President of the International Association of Bioethics. Professor Holm has a broad set of research interests in health care ethics and bioethics, the philosophy of medicine, and the intersection between bioethics, public policy, and law.

Iseult Honohan (*iseult.honohan@ucd.ie*) is Associate Professor Emeritus at the School of Politics and International Relations, University College Dublin, and a member of the Royal Irish Academy. Her current research focuses on civic republican political theory and its applications, particularly with respect to issues of citizenship, migration, and diversity.

Jeffrey Howard (*jeffrey.howard@ucl.ac.uk*) is Lecturer in Political Theory at University College London. He works on topics in contemporary political and legal philosophy, including criminal punishment, freedom of expression, and counter-terrorism. He has published in various journals, including *The Journal of Political Philosophy*, *The Journal of Applied Philosophy*, and *Law and Philosophy*.

James Johnson (*jd.johnson@rochester.edu*) teaches social and political theory at the University of Rochester, where he is Professor of Political Science. His research cuts across pragmatist political thought, democratic theory, philosophy of social science, and political economy.

John Kleinig (*jkleinig@jjay.cuny.edu*) is Professor Emeritus of Philosophy at John Jay College of Criminal Justice and the Graduate Center, City University of New York. He is also Adjunct Professor of Philosophy at Charles Sturt University. He is author/co-editor of 22 books in moral, social, and political philosophy.

Christopher Kutz (*ckutz@law.berkeley.edu*) is C. William Maxeiner Distinguished Professor of Law at UC Berkeley's Jurisprudence & Social Policy Program. Professor Kutz, who holds a law degree and PhD in philosophy, works in the area of moral, legal, and political philosophy, with special expertise in criminal law and international ethics.

David Lawrence (*david.lawrence@ncl.ac.uk*) is Research Excellence Academy Postdoctoral Fellow at the University of Newcastle Law School, and trained at the Institute for Science Ethics and Innovation in Manchester. His work centres around ethics, law, and consciousness in emerging technologies, particularly those which may produce new forms of intelligent life.

Robert Lepenies (*robert.lepenies@ufz.de*; *Robert.Lepenies@eui.eu*) is a research scientist at the Helmholtz Centre for Environmental Research and a member of the Global Young Academy. He works on the politics of nudging and on themes in the philosophy of the social sciences, international political economy, and public policy (particularly environmental policy).

Annabelle Lever (*annabelle.lever@sciencespo.fr*) is Professeure des Universités à Sciences Po, Paris. She is the author of *On Privacy* (2012) and *A Democratic Conception of Privacy* (2014), the editor of *New Frontiers in the Philosophy of Intellectual Property* (2014), and the co-editor of *Ideas That Matter: Justice, Democracy, Rights* (2018).

Ira K. Lindsay (*i.lindsay@surrey.ac.uk*) is Senior Lecturer in Finance Law and Ethics at the University of Surrey School of Law and Research Fellow at the Surrey Centre for Law and Philosophy. Dr Lindsay's research interests are in the areas of tax law, the ethics of taxation policies, property law, comparative law, and political philosophy.

Kasper Lippert-Rasmussen (*lippert@ps.au.dk*) is Professor in Political Theory at University of Aarhus and Professor II in Philosophy at UiT-University of Tromsø. Recent books include *Born Free and Equal: A Philosophical Inquiry into the Nature of Discrimination* (2013) and *Relational Egalitarianism: Living as Equals* (2018).

Magdalena Małecka (*magdalena.malecka@helsinki.fi*) is Academy of Finland Postdoctoral Researcher at the Centre for Philosophy of Social Science (TINT) at the University of Helsinki. She has published on a variety of topics in philosophy of economics, philosophy of social sciences, and legal theory. In her most recent project she analyses the contemporary transfers of scientific knowledge to policy contexts.

Matt Matravers (*matt.matravers@york.ac.uk*) is Professor of Law and Director of the Morrell Centre for Toleration at the University of York. He is the author of *Justice and Punishment* (2000) and *Responsibility and Justice* (Polity, 2007) and editor of seven books, most recently *Criminal Law and Cultural Diversity* (with Will Kymlicka and Claes Lernestedt, 2014) and *The Criminal Law's Person* (with Lernestedt, forthcoming).

Matthew S. McCoy (*mmcco@pennmedicine.upenn.edu*) is Assistant Professor in the Department of Medical Ethics and Health Policy at the University of Pennsylvania's Perelman School of Medicine and a Senior Fellow at the University of Pennsylvania's Leonard Davis Institute of Health Economics.

Darrel Moellendorf (*darrel.moellendorf@normativeorders.net*) is Cluster Professor of International Political Theory at the Excellence Cluster Normative Orders and Professor of Philosophy at Johann Wolfgang Universität Frankfurt. He is the author of *Cosmopolitan Justice* (2002), *Global Inequality Matters* (2009), and *The Moral Challenge of Dangerous Climate Change: Values, Poverty, and Policy* (2014).

Alasia Nuti (*alasia.nuti@york.ac.uk*) is Lecturer in Political Theory at the University of York. She is currently completing a manuscript entitled *Injustice and the Reproduction of History*, which is forthcoming. Alasia's research interests include historical injustice, gender inequality, structural injustice, memory, violence, immigration, and pluralism.

Susan Orr (*sorr@brockport.edu*) is Associate Professor of Political Science at College at Brockport, State University of New York. Her research traverses empirical and normative concerns related to political institutions and civic engagement. She is particularly interested in questions located at the intersection of politics and the workplace.

Jennifer M. Page (*jennifer.page@uzh.ch*) holds a postdoc at the Center for Ethics at the University of Zurich, and before that, held a postdoc at the Center for the Study of Slavery and Justice at Brown University. A political theorist by training, her research areas are reparations, historical injustice, and restorative justice. Her articles appear in *Raisons Politiques* and *Ethnic and Racial Studies*.

Andrei Poama (*a.poama@fgga.leidenuniv.nl*) is Assistant Professor (with a focus on political philosophy and the ethics of public policy) at Leiden University, the Faculty of Governance and Global Affairs, Institute of Public Administration. His major research interests include the philosophy of punishment, the ethics of public policy, democratic theory (with an emphasis on juries and jury decision-making), and experimental philosophy. Dr Poama is co-coordinator of the Centre for Public Values and Ethics, and a member of the Centre for Political Philosophy at Leiden University.

Daniel Putnam (*Daniel.M.Putnam@Dartmouth.edu*) is a postdoctoral fellow in philosophy and political economy at Dartmouth College. Before that, he was a postdoctoral research associate at Princeton University. He received his PhD in philosophy from Yale University in 2016.

Helder De Schutter (*helder.deschutter@kuleuven.be*) is Professor of Social and Political Philosophy at KU Leuven. He writes on issues of linguistic justice, federalism in multinational states, nationalism and nation-building, migration and citizenship, and the case for non-territorial authority. He currently serves as the director of RIPPLE, the Leuven research group in political philosophy.

David Steiner (*d.steiner@jhu.edu*) is Executive Director of the Johns Hopkins Institute for Education Policy and Professor of Education at Johns Hopkins University. He previously served as Commissioner of Education for New York State and as the Klara and Larry Silverstein Dean at the Hunter College School of Education.

Dennis F. Thompson (*dennis_thompson@harvard.edu*) is the Alfred North Whitehead Professor of Political Philosophy Emeritus at Harvard University, and the founding director of the university-wide Edmond J. Safra Center for Ethics. Professor Thompson is one of the leading initiators of the institutional approach to political ethics, and is particularly known for his books *Political Ethics and Public Office* (1987), *Ethics in Congress: From Individual to Institutional Corruption* (1995), and *Just Elections: Creating a Fair Electoral Process in the US* (2002), as well as the books he co-authored with Amy Guttmann, such as *Why Deliberative Democracy* (2004) or *The Spirit of Compromise: Why Governing Demands It and Campaigning Undermines It* (2012).

Jörg Tremmel (*joerg.tremmel@uni-tuebingen.de*) is Permanent Lecturer at Eberhard Karls University Tübingen. From 2010 to 2016, he was the incumbent of a Junior Professorship for Intergenerationally Just Policies at the Institute for Political Science of Tübingen University. His research interests lie mainly in political theory/political philosophy.

Pieter Vanhuysse (*vanhuysse@sam.sdu.dk*) is Professor of Comparative Welfare State Research at the University of Southern Denmark and researches the political sociology and political economy of public policies, generations, and population ageing. He has authored *Divide and Pacify* (2006) and co-edited *Aging Populations in Post-Industrial Democracies* (2012) and *Post-Communist Welfare Pathways* (2009). He has spoken at the White House (under President Obama), the European Commission, the Inter-Parliamentary Union at the Canadian Parliament, the International Social Security Association, and the Global Economic Symposium.

Alexandru Volacu (*alexandru.volacu@bcept.eu*) is Assistant Professor at SNSPA (Bucharest) and Postdoctoral Fellow at the Research Institute of the University of Bucharest. He is also Director of the Bucharest Center for Political Theory and co-editor in chief of the *Romanian Journal of Society and Politics*.

Bouke de Vries (*devries@mmg.mpg.de*) is a postdoctoral research fellow at the Max Planck Institute for the Study of Religious and Ethnic Diversity in Göttingen, Germany. His research interests include liberal toleration, state neutrality, multiculturalism, migration, conscientious accommodation, and, more recently, family ethics. He received his PhD from the European University Institute.

Ivo Wallimann-Helmer (*wallimann@philos.uzh.ch*) is Managing Director of the Program for Advanced Studies in Applied Ethics, University of Zurich. He specialises in normative research about climate justice, environmental justice, and democratic decision-making in the face of environmental challenges. He has published various articles on climate adaptation, loss, and damage, and waste disposal.

Andrew Walton (*andrew.walton@newcastle.ac.uk*) is Lecturer in Political Philosophy at Newcastle University. His research focuses on global justice, international trade, and economic ethics.

Albert Weale (*a.weale@ucl.ac.uk*) is Emeritus Professor of Political Theory and Public Policy, University College London. His research has concentrated on a wide range of issues of political theory and public policy. His latest book is *The Will of the People: A Modern Myth* (2018).

Simon Whitby (*s.whitby@bradford.ac.uk*) is Senior Lecturer at the University of Bradford. Dr Whitby works at the interface between the life sciences and national security communities to address the threat of deliberate disease and chemical warfare. He published the following chapter in June 2018: 'The Future of Chemical Weapons: Advances in Development of Anti-Plant Agents', in Michael Crowley, Malcolm Dando, and Lijun Shang (Eds), *Preventing Chemical Weapons: Arms Control and Disarmament as the Sciences Converge*.

Stuart White (*stuart.white@jesus.ox.ac.uk*) is Tutorial Fellow in Politics at Jesus College, Oxford. He is the author of *The Civic Minimum* (2003) and *Equality* (2006) and is currently working on a book provisionally titled *Democracy Over Wealth? Liberal Republican Political Economy*.

Melissa S. Williams (*melissa.williams@utoronto.ca*) is Professor of Political Science and Founding Director of the Centre for Ethics at the University of Toronto, where she teaches political theory. Her general research focus is on contemporary democratic theory, and addresses core concepts in political philosophy through the lens of group-structured inequality, social and political marginalisation, and cultural and religious diversity.

Jonathan Wolff (*jonathan.wolff@bsg.ox.ac.uk*) is Blavatnik Professor of Public Policy, Blavatnik School of Government, University of Oxford. His books include *Ethics and Public Policy* (2011) and (with Avner De-Shalit) *Disadvantage* (2007).

Bernardo Zacka (*nardoz@mit.edu*) is Assistant Professor of Political Science at MIT. His first book, *When the State Meets the Street*, examines the everyday moral life of street-level bureaucrats. He is also interested in the intersection of architecture and political theory and is co-editing a collection of essays on the topic.

ACKNOWLEDGEMENTS

We thank our authors, more than a few of whom have struggled with serious illness during the time that our collection came to life. Several authors kindly came on board at the last moment, agreeing to write and revise their chapters on extremely tight schedules, while maintaining the accelerated rhythm of teaching, research, and grant-writing that characterises life in our competitive, worldly, and global 'ivory tower'. Richard Bellamy, Jonathan Wolff, Albert Weale, and Dennis F. Thompson provided support throughout, and the former helped us with valuable comments that allowed us to revise our introduction. Our team of editors at Routledge – Tony Bruce and Adam Johnson – supported us through the many bumps that, we now know, are inevitable in such a big project. Yoann Della Croce and Mélis Pinar Akdag helped to prepare this huge manuscript for publication. Their contribution has been exceptional, as has their good humour and equanimity throughout. As editors as well as contributors, we have benefited from the support of our respective universities and research agencies – the Swiss National Science Foundation, the *Centre de Recherche en Éthique* in Montreal, the Max Weber Programme at the EUI, and Leiden University. We are very grateful to them all.

This *Handbook* is dedicated to Dennis F. Thompson, with gratitude and admiration. His book *Political Ethics and Public Office* (1987) remains one of the classics of the field, and the interdisciplinary ethics centre that he started and ran for many years at Harvard University has been an inspiration for numerous institutes, summer schools, books, articles, and courses ever since. His important work in democratic political theory and wide-ranging interests in public ethics have shaped our field, as well as our own work, as academics. We are happy to have been able to include his chapter on the ethics of electoral campaigns for this collection, a chapter that was originally written before all the recent revelations about the funding and manipulative tactics of Brexit and the 2016 US presidential election, but which remains timely for all that. It is a pleasure to be able to dedicate this volume to him.

INTRODUCTION

Annabelle Lever and Andrei Poama

Is public policy ethics possible and, if so, is it desirable? This twofold question can – and some-times does – elicit a smile or a frown. The smile implies that ethical theorising rests on a naïve idea of policy-making; the frown implies that there is something tasteless or incongruous in expecting philosophy to engage with problems of policy, and with the political bargaining and compromise that policy-making involves.[1] These reactions – familiar to many working in this academic discipline – point to the ways in which ethics and public policy have been taken to be separate areas of practical concern and theoretical inquiry.

For some philosophers, the very idea of public policy ethics rests on a category mistake, confusing proper reflection on moral ideals with thinking about what is practically feasible. Gerald Gaus's qualms that 'participation in public controversy masked as philosophy corrupts philosophy' captures this worry well, reflecting the anxiety that 'a sophisticated, rational, ideo-logical advocacy is conducted as if it were philosophy, giving the impression (both to ourselves and our students) that philosophy is merely an intellectual game in which you defend what you want to believe' (Gaus 2005: 67). Public policy ethics, on this account, diverts the moral philosopher from doing philosophically relevant work and downgrades ethical theorising to the level of wishy-washy opinion and rhetorical hot air.[2] The worry, of course, is that the only way for philosophers to gain the ear of policy-makers is to betray the commitment to the reasoned evaluation of abstract arguments that defines philosophical ethics in the first place. In short, public policy ethics is no *ethics* at all – or so the argument for policy-free ethics implies.

Other philosophers occasionally point to the fact that the rubber of ethical theory never quite meets the road of policy. The contention here is that proper ethical reflection rarely plays more than a minor or decorative role in the actual policy-making process. One of the reasons for this alleged disconnect between ethics and public policy is that moral philosophy is not the kind of material that typically matters for policy work. Jonathan Wolff (2011) comes close to this position when he notes that it is not so much the philosophical quality of an argument that informs policy as the philosopher's ability to play the language game of the policy *status quo*.[3] Wolff notes that 'it is very rare for a policy to have been introduced for clear and principled reasons', which means that 'to have any effect on immediate policy, philosophers will have to swallow hard and accept that the discussion will often have to take place within the terms and space set by political and pragmatic concerns' (80). Following this reading, rigorous ethical theorising as currently practised often fails to capture the real concerns of actual policy-makers, thus raising the spectre of irrelevance for public policy ethics as a distinct discipline.

Public policy experts have their own versions of these concerns. After all, if policy analysis is a scientific pursuit, with its own standards for success, philosophical analysis will seem at best like unnecessary hand-waving, and at worst, like a distraction from the work to be done. This might explain why, as Henry Shue remarked (2006: 709), experts in public policy often treat 'specialists on ethics or normative issues' as unfortunate additions to the main event, 'like the wilted salad that comes whether requested or not' with one's meal, or as matters of taste, to be taken or left, 'like the pepper that is entirely optional'. Worse still, philosophy can sometimes seem like a threat to public policy, encouraging us to focus on the desirable rather than the practicable, and, in a famous phrase, making 'the perfect the enemy of the good'. Hence, students are encouraged carefully to distinguish *policy analysis* – which is about 'learning why governments do what they do and what the consequences of their actions are' through 'the tools of systematic inquiry' – with *policy advocacy*, which is about 'saying what governments *ought* to do' using 'the skills of rhetoric, persuasion, organization and activism' (Dye 1981: 6–7). Since, by definition, ethics deals with *oughts*, this widely taught view of public policy tends to equate policy ethics with the promotion of partisan agendas and ideological advocacy. Thus, those working in ethics and public policy can feel like an unloved child, disparaged and disowned by its parents.

Other familiar concerns with public policy ethics reflect the fact that public policy is a political activity, and espouse the belief that politics is fundamentally amoral. Such a separation of ethics and policy draws on familiar images of politicians and public officials as Machiavellian creatures, who must be willing to set their moral scruples aside, and to 'dirty their hands', climbing 'the greasy pole' of power, in order to achieve their objectives. Couched in the language of Weber, rather than Machiavelli, good politicians and apt public officials must be concerned with the choice of means to given ends, and not with the evaluation of ends. It is not for them to 'turn the other cheek', nor to pursue the 'ethics of conviction',[4] however permissible, even admirable, such behaviour may be in private life.

Now, if politics were really amoral, there would be little point in examining the moral principles that should guide it, however enjoyable it might be to play a parlour game called 'imagining the good polity' or 'choosing principles of social justice'. Some moralists might relish arguing among themselves about where, how far, and why our actual world departs from the ideal. But were politics and, with it, policy-making, reducible to a scramble for power and influence, it is hard to see why most people should interest themselves in ethical arguments about policy. Perhaps morality might have a place in private life – or those spaces for personal choice and action that happen to be free from political struggles – but to suppose that public policy might be subject to ethical reflection, choice, and control would seem delusional at best, and manipulative and deceptive at worst.

However, many people reject such amoral views of politics as incoherent and reductive, and accept that a normative approach to politics can be helpful, and even desirable. Thus, there has been a veritable explosion in normative political philosophy since the 1970s and the pathbreaking work of analytic political philosophers, such as John Rawls, Robert Nozick, and Ronald Dworkin, of critical theorists, such as Jürgen Habermas and Axel Honneth, and feminist philosophers, such as Iris Marion Young, Nancy Fraser, and Anne Phillips.[5] Yet, until recently, this explosion had produced no systematic interest in ethics and public policy. Indeed, it is only very recently that a debate has started to take place on the distinctive methods, if any, of ethics and public policy, and the different approaches, styles, or ways in which it might be developed. However, to date, there is no collective publication – handbook or otherwise – on the current state of the discipline.[6]

It is not that moral, political, or legal philosophers do not engage in ethical discussions of public policy, or that they are never asked to participate in public inquiries on matters of controversy. On the contrary, we can think of the contributions of Bernard Williams on obscenity, Mary Warnock and Onora O'Neill on bioethics, Salvatore Veca on 'Feeding the Planet', or the contributions of Jürgen Habermas, Ronald Dworkin, Charles Taylor, and Amartya Sen to see that philosophers play an important public role.[7] Indeed, several contributors to this volume have been involved in public commissions, or in policy-making bodies concerned with public health, education, and security. Nonetheless, the dominant approach to ethics and public policy, until recently, has seemed to be more concerned with 'sex, drugs, and rock and roll' than with the ethics of public policy as most politicians, policy-makers, civil servants, and citizens understand or experience it. Thus, publications and teaching on ethics and policy would centre on popular controversy around prostitution, abortion, homosexuality, euthanasia, recreational drug use, pornography, and 'hate speech' – all seen, correctly, as meriting normative attention, but treated as though they had nothing much to do with more mundane and less contentious issues.

Interesting and important though such discussions have been, for philosophers as for other people, this traditional approach to ethics and public policy suffers from two problems. The first is that a focus on the more sensational issues reinforces the idea that 'ordinary' matters of policy raise no interesting or complex ethical questions in themselves, and none that need affect our approach to abortion, euthanasia, or free speech. But as feminists and disability activists have insisted, we cannot easily separate the assumptions about the value of life or the best way to distinguish public and private matters when it comes to the regulation of sexuality or speech from those that shape our practices of security, health care, education, and transport.[8] In addition, a focus on 'sexy' topics plays into an idea of public ethics as merely an extension, or application of, familiar moral theories, rather than as a subject which may lead us to rethink our moral categories, conceptual distinctions, and normative approaches.

Our collection, therefore, adopts a perspective on ethics and public policy which is at once broader, and narrower, than is usual. It is broader, because we wanted to bring together work on the ethical dimensions of public policy spanning issues of domestic and international politics, intergenerational politics, and such ordinary or technical, but nonetheless central, topics as the siting of nuclear waste, the ethics of taxation, and policies on disability and poverty. Ideally, we would have loved to have had chapters examining the ethical dimensions of every policy issue as instantiated in current governmental practice – but that, of course, would have been overwhelming, as well as impossible. So, instead, we tried to focus our attention on the breadth of work that is now being done in ethics and public policy in order to highlight the range and quality of research in the area, and to illuminate the ethical dimensions of public policy that many of us – the editors included – have never considered and have no idea how to handle.

Nevertheless, if our collection is very much broader in its conception of ethics and public policy than is usual, it is narrower in its focus on one important dimension. Following theorists such as Dennis F. Thompson, Jonathan Wolff, and Richard Bellamy, we take the political dimensions of policy-making to play an important role in determining the ethical content, dynamics, and types of justification that can be offered for public policy.[9] Moreover, because that content and those justifications will depend on whether we think of people as political equals, and on the forms of freedom, well-being, and opportunity which that equality requires, permits, or forbids, we focus explicitly on issues of ethics and public policy that arise as a result of democratic political struggles and ideals, and that can be resolved domestically and internationally in ways consistent with democratic government.

It is not that undemocratic governments are of no interest to us, nor that they cannot improve our understanding of morality and politics. Given that democratic societies are imperfect in many ways, as is our understanding of democratic values and institutions, it would be absurd to cut ourselves off from potential sources of knowledge based on current ideas about what is, and is not, democratic. However, for practical and for philosophical reasons, we believe it best to centre this collection on problems of ethics and public policy that arise in democracies, and on democratically-informed or democratically-sensitive principles, broadly conceived. Practically, we hope that this will give our collection a substantive coherence and a methodological focus that it might otherwise lack, given the breadth of its subject matter. We also hope that it might provide some consistency of factual and normative assumptions across chapters dealing with very different moral and political problems.

Philosophically, this selection on the basis of democratic considerations reflects our conviction that ethics and public policy can no more adopt 'the view from nowhere' than other branches of philosophy, but need not therefore be limited to the presentation and evaluation of 'the way we do things around here', to borrow a famous phrase from Richard Rorty.[10] Instead, we hope that combining the ethical evaluation of policy with democratic theory and practice, quite broadly understood, will enable our collection to speak to all those for whom the right to participate in the government of one's society is an essential right, and a defeasible constraint on the legitimacy of any government.[11]

Democracies are quite varied political arrangements, and the adjective 'democratic' can be applied to associations, individuals, institutions, and ideals. Nonetheless, democratic governments are committed to the belief that all citizens are, in principle, entitled to participate in government, and this makes democracies different from other forms of government, in which wealth, virtue, sex, religion, or parentage is thought to justify limiting political participation to a few, select, individuals. Importantly, for our purposes, it means that democracies cannot evaluate public policies purely on the assumption that citizens are the subjects of government, or the objects of government policy. In addition – and this is a distinctive implication of democratic government – ethical evaluation has to consider the effects of policy on citizens as governors, or potential governors, of their society and, therefore, the consequences of policy on people's ability to see themselves as active participants in government rather than passive beneficiaries of public policy.[12] Hence, democracies must find ways of selecting people for positions of power and influence that reflect democratic ideas about political ends and means, as opposed to theocratic, aristocratic, plutocratic, or epistocratic ones.

The ethics of public policy in a democratic society involves meeting at least two important constraints that other societies might avoid. The first is that, in its design and implementation, public policy must reflect "equal respect and concern" for citizen's well-being and rights, to borrow Ronald Dworkin's fortunate phrase.[13] The second is that it must also protect and foster people's capacities to share in the process of governing, however that process is conceived. Hence, as this collection shows, while democratic government comes in many forms, reflecting different political ideals, circumstances, and needs, the differences between democratic and undemocratic government provide a fruitful lens for envisaging the ethics of public policy and may, on occasion, be necessary, not merely useful.

Our aim is not to replace the currently contending moralities of utility, liberal rights, republican virtue, contractualist counterfactuals, or care relationships with a distinct (and presumably preferable) democratic ethics. Rather, we seek to show that it can be morally illuminating and politically helpful to understand the constraints that democracy places on public ethics, regardless of whether those constraints differ markedly from those suggested by alternative ethical perspectives. To put it in slightly more technical terms, we aim to investigate how democratic values, conceived as *pro tanto* or *prima facie* reasons for government action, might inform ethical reflection on public policy, bearing in mind that they may have little or no distinctive significance in some cases.

There is no one favoured view of democracy that unites the 41 chapters of this *Handbook*. Authors were not asked to take a particular 'line', and they were selected, as far as possible, not just for their obvious expertise but also to reflect the geographical, professional, and personal variety of scholars working in the field. Collections of this sort tend to be dominated by scholars who are already well known. However, much new work in ethics and public policy is being done by relatively young scholars, for whom public ethics is central to their academic work, rather than being of sporadic interest, or an outgrowth of the more traditional philosophical concerns with which they are principally occupied. Thus, while the chapters in each part complement each other and, we hope, provide an accessible introduction to recent work in ethics and public policy, they are written in different styles, and draw on the experience of different countries, and the ideas of different thinkers. Their effect is panoramic, as well as synthetic, in ways that defy simple summary.

Our refusal to commit to a specific view of democracy should hardly come as a surprise, given the extent of philosophical and political controversy about its nature and value. Even when different authors agree in their general normative positions about what democracy is, or ought to be, they nonetheless end up disagreeing on the exact implications that these positions have for particular public policies. Some of these disagreements emerge, we think, as a natural consequence of what Rawls calls the 'burdens of judgment' (Rawls 1996: 54),[14] an expression meant to capture the difficulties we confront in prioritising competing moral values and principles, the hard selection and weighing of complex evidential matters, or decisions about the least implausible instantiations of vague normative concepts. But disagreements will also arise because of the substantive variations across distinct policy areas and issues, even in cases where those areas and issues are contiguous or otherwise connected. As many of the chapters in this *Handbook* show, democratic commitments play out differently in different areas of policy – for example, in the area of warfare as compared to the field of foreign policy, and democracy does not direct us to the same kinds of decisions in the domain of waste disposal policies as it does when it comes to matters of climate change.[15] Hence, our *Handbook* comprises different perspectives on democracy, as well as different facets of public policy.

The absence of a unifying democratic view is furthermore motivated by theoretical considerations pertaining to the conceptual structure of democracy. Since the publication of Kenneth Arrow's *Social Choice and Individual Values* in 1951, a rich literature has demonstrated the logical impossibility for any decision-making system to be simultaneously fully inclusive and pluralistic, respectful of majoritarian preferences, and collectively rational, although these are all democratic values, which we may want our institutions to realise.[16] We have therefore encouraged our authors to focus on those democratic desiderata (if any) that seem most pertinent to the policy areas with which they are concerned. The result is a sequencing of the chapters that is meant to provide a helpful introduction to contemporary ethics and public policy, rather than tell a particular story about democracy.

Part I is dedicated to questions of methodology. It explores what it means to do public policy ethics today, raises questions about the contours and content of public policy ethics as a distinctive discipline, examines the ethical dimensions of cognate disciplines such as policy analysis and the place of policy ethics in the wider landscape of ethical theorising, and considers contrasting approaches to the place and role of philosophers in the public policy process, and the public arena more generally.

Parts II, III, and IV cover various substantive areas of public policy. The parts mirror a quasi-historical sequence in the theory and practice of public policy, starting from the basic idea that the public policy domain consists in whatever governments happen to be doing at any particular moment,[17] while at the same time reflecting the changes in democratic policies and modes of government since the Second World War.[18] Drawing on an analogy with Ian Hacking's notion of 'styles of reasoning', one could see these three parts of the *Handbook* as instantiating different *styles of governing*. For Hacking, it is characteristic of styles of reasoning that they 'introduce new ways of being a candidate for truth and for falsehood' (Hacking 1994: 42). Similarly, we take a style of governing to establish new dimensions whereby practical subject matters become matters of policy concern. Though styles of governing can change the substance or scope of various policy areas, styles are also about different *ways of doing government* that underlie, define, control, or revise what are considered to be the proper bounds and inner dynamic of the public policy domain.

Part II corresponds to a vision of government centred on the state's *de jure* monopolising of some basic domestic functions, such as the organisation of domestic security, criminal justice, and education; the mediation of economic interests; and the regulation of finance as well as of military security in the international realm. Intuitively, these are policy areas which seem inseparable from the contemporary idea of government, the *sine qua non* of public policy.

Part III is concerned with a more expansive conception of government than the first, taking us from a mode of government tightly associated with the *pouvoirs régaliens*, as the French helpfully describe them, to a vision of government as a privileged agent for securing the well-being of individuals, no matter the ascriptive and voluntary associations to which they otherwise belong. Government has a duty to prevent poverty and to help the poor but, beyond that, it has the responsibility to dismantle those social distinctions which keep people 'in their place' and make government the preserve of a privileged elite. Thus, the chapters in this third part are concerned with a mode of governing, as much as the content of actual policies – a mode which assumes that government has a special duty to foster social solidarity and inclusion, and to enable people to have an active say – for instance, *via* electoral participation – in the way that they are governed.

Part IV brings together a group of public policies concerned with both existential issues and questions of identity which, until recently, would have been the preserve of individuals, or of churches and other secondary associations, rather than of government. Thus, some of the policies in this part are concerned with the future existence, quality of life, and sustainability of future citizens, as instantiated in the chapters on intergenerational justice, youth policies, new reproductive technologies, behavioural nudges, climate change, and waste policies. Others are concerned with the responsibilities of government, faced with the inevitable, albeit often unintended, effects of government on the civic and cultural identities of citizens, and on the social standing and respect for minority ethnic, racial, and religious groups. The chapters on citizenship tests, family reunification programs, language policies, and policies on religious diversity and accommodation reflect this strand of contemporary public policy, with its concern for the nature and identity of citizens, and with the existential choices and threats that they face.

We hope that this sequencing of chapters will make the *Handbook* easier for readers, be they practitioners, academics, students, or simply citizens interested in particular policies. The four parts are not meant to deploy a precise historical narrative – which would in any case be impossible given the different political trajectories of contemporary democracies – and some chapters could fit in more than one part. For instance, the chapter on education could have been included in Part III, the chapter on privacy and surveillance or the chapter on death policies in

Part IV, and the chapter on language policies or the one on religious accommodations could have been inserted in Part II. However, we hope that this ordering of the 41 chapters that make up this *Handbook* will benefit readers and facilitate future scholarly debate.[19]

Notes

1 This is the position underlying much of the political realism about foreign policy defended by E.H. Carr or Hans Morgenthau. For an analysis of and reply to political realism, see Coady (2008).

2 The tenet that practical ethics (and, with it, public policy ethics) is not philosophy proper can be traced back to Bertrand Russell, who equates it with preaching. In a 1944 text where he defends his emotivist meta-ethics against Buchler's critique, Russell writes that "persuasion in ethical questions is necessarily different from persuasion in scientific matters. According to me, the person who judges that A is good is wishing others to feel certain desires. He will therefore, if not hindered by other activities, try to rouse these desires in other people if he thinks he knows how to do so. This is the purpose of preaching, and it was my purpose in the various books in which I have expressed ethical opinions"; in Russell (1999: 149).

3 Wolff (2011) does not believe that the gap between philosophy and politics makes public policy ethics non-sensical or pointless, as both his book and his chapter in this collection reveal.

4 Weber himself is more nuanced when he reflects on the relation between the "ethics of conviction" (which focuses on the morality of ends) and the "ethics of responsibility" (which concentrates on the morality of effective ends). In *Politics as a Vocation* he finds it 'immeasurably moving when a mature human being (. . .) who feels the responsibility he bears for the consequences of his own actions with his entire soul and who acts in harmony with an ethics of responsibility reaches the point where he says, 'Here I stand, I can do no other'''. That is authentically human and cannot fail to move us. For this is a situation that may befall any of us at some point, if we are not inwardly dead. In this sense an ethics of conviction and an ethics of responsibility are not absolute antitheses but are mutually complementary, and only when taken together do they constitute the authentic human being who is capable of having a 'vocation for politics'"; in Weber (2004: 92).

5 For an interesting attempt at carving out a *sui generis* moral space for public policy and political activity, see also Palumbo and Bellamy (2010).

6 There are, to be sure, quite a few public policy *analysis* handbooks, like the ones edited by Moran, Rein, and Goodin (2006), Peters and Pierre (2006), or Fischer, Miller, and Sidney (2007). Add to this the existence of a handbook that examines issues of administrative ethics (Cooper 2000, 2nd ed.), that of a handbook on the ethics of economics (Wilber 1997), that of a handbook of policy evaluation (Nagel 2002), that of a more general companion looking at global policy issues (Lawton, Van Der Wal, and Huberts 2015), and, finally, that of a collective publication that adopts a general philosophical approach to public policy (Gehring and Galston 2002). There is also a series of publications that focuses on the morality of particular public policy areas. These include: Aaron, Mann, and Taylor (1994); Preston and Sampford (2012); Little (2004); Kahn and Kasachkoff (2002); Bluhm and Heineman (2007); Stewart (2009); Boston, Bradstock, and Eng (2011); Bradstock, Eng, and Boston (2011); Wolff (2011); Weber (2011); Cohen (2014); Searing and Searing (2016). This indicates that public policy ethics is thriving, but in a state of disciplinary fragmentation that we wish to alleviate in and through this handbook.

7 An abridged version of Williams's report on obscenity and film censorship is available at https:// assets.cambridge.org/97811071/13770/frontmatter/9781107113770_frontmatter.pdf; a link to Mary Warnock's 1978 report on special educational needs can be found here: www.educationengland. org.uk/documents/warnock/, and the link to Warnock's 1984 Report on Human Fertilisation and Embryology is available here: https://embryo.asu.edu/pages/report-committee-inquiry-human-fertilisation-and-embryology-1984-mary-warnock-and-committee; the 2007 Bouchard-Taylor report on 'reasonable accommodation' can be found at www.mce.gouv.qc.ca/publications/CCPARDC/rapport-final-integral-en.pdf; the Report of the Stiglitz-Sen-Fitoussi Commission on the Measurement of Economic Performance and Social Progress is available at http://ec.europa.eu/eurostat/documents/118025/118123/Fitoussi+Commission+report.

8 See, in particular, MacKinnon (1997); Minow (1990); Roberts (1997; 2002), and Tremain (1999).

9 See Thompson (1987), Palumbo and Bellamy (2010), and Wolff (2011).

10 Rorty initially uses the phrase to deflate thick conceptions of objectivity and science, but he later extends it to (liberal) moral and political normativity as well. See Rorty (1991: 101). This comes close,

but differs from, Bernard Williams's contention that liberalism is the way we make sense of political legitimacy "now and around here"; in Williams (2005: 7–12).

11 Democratic legitimacy is defeasible in that there may be forms of undemocratic government which are properly considered legitimate. On this issue, see Rawls (2001b), Cohen (2009: 349–372), and Miller (2015: 177–192). Moreover, democratic governments may lose their legitimacy through such grave violations of human rights that citizens are released from their duty to obey. So even if it is reasonable to grant democracies a presumptive legitimacy that other forms of government lack, being democratic is neither necessary nor sufficient for legitimacy.

12 In this respect, we find ourselves concurring with democratic approaches to public policy analysis, like the one formulated by Schneider and Ingram (1997), who describe policies that fail to involve ordinary citizens as degenerative processes.

13 Dworkin (1977).

14 Rawls (1971, 2001a).

15 Thus, Christopher Kutz points to democracy working as a side-constraint on warfare, while Michael Blake focuses on equality and toleration as values that should be promoted *via* foreign policy.

16 See, in particular, List (2011).

17 On definitions of *public policy*, see, most notably, Dye (1972), and, for a useful recent discussion, Howlett and Cashore (2014).

18 We would like to thank Toon Kerkhoff, Frits van der Meer, Natascha van der Zwan, Alexandre Afonso, and Elena Bondarouk for useful discussions on this quasi-historical ordering.

19 Another advantage of this normatively non-committal ordering is that it lends itself to multiple scholarly interpretations. For instance, one could read it as deploying a narrative about the metamorphosis of the state's scope of action and intervention, moving from a watchman state (Part II) to a welfare state (Part III) to an enabling state (parts of Part III and Part IV). Alternatively, for those who might choose to assess the morality of public policy on the basis of a human rights standard, one could draw a rough parallel between our three parts and Karel Vasak's (1977) famous division of human rights into three generations (civil and political, social and economic, and developmental human rights) or connect our ordering to the lively debates prompted by T.H. Marshall (1949/1950) about the state's evolving responsibilities toward its citizens.

References

Aaron, Henry J.; Mann, Thomas E.; Taylor, Timothy T. (eds). 1994. *Values and Public Policy*. Washington, DC: Brookings Institution Press.

Bluhm, William; Heineman, Robert A. 2007. *Ethics and Public Policy: Method and Cases*. Upper Saddle River: Pearson.

Boston, Jonathan; Bradstock, Andrew; Eng, David. 2011. *Public Policy: Why Ethics Matters*. Canberra: ANU Press.

Bradstock, Andrew; Eng, David; Boston, Jonathan. 2011. *Ethics and Public Policy: Contemporary Issues*. Wellington: Victoria University Press.

Cahn, Steven M; Kasachkoff, Tsiporah. 2002. *Morality and Public Policy*. Pearson.

Coady, Cecil Anthony John. 2008. *Messy Morality: The Challenge of Politics*. Oxford: Clarendon Press.

Cohen, Andrew I. 2014. *Philosophy, Ethics, and Public Policy*. New York: Routledge.

Cohen, Joshua. 2009. *Philosophy, Politics, Democracy: Selected Essays*. Cambridge, MA: Harvard University Press.

Cooper, Terry L. (ed.). 2000. *Handbook of Administrative Ethics*. New York: Routledge.

Dworkin, Ronald. 1977. *Taking Rights Seriously*. Cambridge, MA: Harvard University Press.

Dye, Thomas. 1972. *Understanding Public Policy*, 1st edition. Englewood Cliffs: Prentice Hall.

Dye, Thomas. 1981. *Understanding Public Policy*, 4th edition. Englewood Cliffs: Prentice Hall.

Fischer, Frank; Miller, Gerald J.; Sidney, Mara S. 2007. *Handbook of Public Policy Analysis: Theory, Politics, and Methods*. London: CRC Press.

Gaus, Gerald. 2005. "Should Philosophers 'Apply Ethics?' " *Think* 3(9): 63–68.

Gehring, Verna V.; Galston, William A. 2002. *Philosophical Dimensions of Public Policy*. New York: Routledge.

Hacking, Ian. 1994. "Styles of Scientific Thinking or Reasoning: A New Analytical Tool for Historians and the Philosophers of Science" IN Gavroglu, Kostas; Christianidis, Jean; Nicolaidis, Efthymios. (eds). *Trends in the Historiography of Science*. Dordrecht: Springer: 31–48.

Howlett, Michael; Cashore, Ben. 2014. "Conceptualizing Public Policy" IN Engeli, Isabelle; Allison, Christine R. (eds). *Comparative Policy Studies: Conceptual and Methodological Challenges*. Basingstoke: Palgrave Macmillan: 17–33.

Lawton, Alan; Van Der Wal, Zeger; Huberts, Leo. 2015. *Ethics in Public Policy and Management: A Global Companion*. New York: Routledge.

List, Christian. 2011. "The Logical Space of Democracy" *Philosophy and Public Affairs* 39(3): 262–297.

Little, Ian M.D. 2004. *Ethics, Economics, and Politics: Principles of Public Policy*. Oxford: Oxford University Press.

MacKinnon, Catherine. 1997. *Feminism Unmodified: Discourses on Life and Law*. Cambridge, MA: Harvard University Press.

Marshall, Thomas H. 1950. *Citizenship and Social Class: And Other Essays*. Cambridge, UK: Cambridge University Press.

Miller, David. 2015. "Is There a Human Right to Democracy?" IN Celikates, Robin; Kreide, Regina; Wesche, Tilo. (eds). *Transformations of Democracy: Crisis, Protest and Legitimation*. London: Rowman and Littlefield: 177–192.

Minow, Martha. 1990. *Making All the Difference: Inclusion, Exclusion and American Law*. Ithaca, NY: Cornell University Press.

Moran, Michael; Rein, Martin; Goodin, Robert E. 2006. *The Oxford Handbook of Public Policy*. Oxford: Oxford University Press.

Nagel, Stuart S. 2002. *Handbook of Public Policy Evaluation*. London: Sage.

Palumbo, Antonino; Bellamy, Richard. 2010. *Public Ethics*. London & New York: Routledge.

Peters, B. Guy; Pierre, Jon. 2006. *Handbook of Public Policy*. London: Sage.

Preston, Noel; Sampford, Charles. (eds). 2012. *Public Sector Ethics: Finding and Implementing Values*. New York: Routledge.

Rawls, John. 1996. *Political Liberalism*. New York: Columbia University Press.

Roberts, Dorothy. 1997. *Killing the Black Body, Race, Reproduction and the Meaning of Liberty*. New York: Vintage.

Roberts, Dorothy. 2002. *Shattered Bonds: The Colour of Child Welfare*. Sydney, Australia: Basic Books.

Rorty, Richard. 1991. *Essays on Heidegger and Others: Philosophical Papers*, vol. 2. Cambridge: Cambridge University Press.

Russell, Betrand. 1999. *Russell on Ethics: Selections from the Writings of Bertrand Russell*, ed. Pigden, Charles R. London & New York: Routledge.

Schneider, Anne Larason; Ingram, Helen. 1997. *Policy Design for Democracy*. Lawrence: University Press of Kansas.

Searing, Elizabeth A.M.; Searing, Donald R. 2016. *Practicing Professional Ethics in Economics and Public Policy*. Dordrecht: Springer.

Shue, Henry. 2006. "Ethical Dimensions of Public Policy" IN Moran, Michael; Rein, Martin; Goodin, Robert E. (eds). *The Oxford Handbook of Public Policy*. Oxford: Oxford University Press: 709–728.

Stewart, Jenny. 2009. *Public Policy Values*. New York: Palgrave Macmillan.

Thompson, Dennis F. 1987. *Political Ethics and Public Office*. Cambridge, MA: Harvard University Press.

Tremain, Shelley. 1999. *Bodies of Knowledge: Critical Perspectives on Disablement and Disabled Women*. London: Women's Press.

Vasak, Karel. 1977. "A 30-Years Struggle: The Sustained Efforts to Give Force of Law to the Universal Declaration of Human Rights" *Unesco Courier.* 29, 32.

Weber, Eric Thomas. 2011. *Morality, Leadership, and Public Policy: On Experimentalism in Ethics*. London, New York: Continuum.

Weber, Max. 2004. *The Vocation Lectures*. Indianapolis: Hacket Publishing.

Wilber, Charles. 1997. *Economics, Ethics, and Public Policy*. New York: Rowman & Littlefield.

Williams, Bernard. 2005. *In the Beginning Was the Deed*. Princeton, NJ: Princeton University Press.

Wolff, Jonathan. 2011. *Ethics and Public Policy: A Philosophical Inquiry*. London & New York: Routledge.

PART I

Ethics for public policy

Models and methods

1

METHOD IN PHILOSOPHY AND PUBLIC POLICY

Applied philosophy versus engaged philosophy

Jonathan Wolff

The attractions of moral and political philosophy

Many moral and political philosophers, I assume, became interested in their subject initially through a concern with particular ethical or political questions. I can remember, for example, as a teenager worrying about the justification of punishment. Later I became interested in questions of inequality and social justice, and the justification of authority. Moral and political philosophy, I hoped, would help me think about, perhaps even solve, some of these questions.

The experience of studying moral and political philosophy took me, though, in a different direction. Mainstream moral philosophy, when I was an undergraduate in the early 1980s, was concerned largely with questions about the metaphysics of value, making connections with epistemology and philosophy of language. Political philosophy was dominated by the study of the crisply formulated theories of justice of Rawls and Nozick, albeit elaborated in great, sometimes laborious, detail. Essentially political philosophy, as it was taught to me (and it will have been different for others), was identified with the construction of abstract principles, and the provision of arguments for or (more often) against, primarily in the form of counter-examples. The options for a political philosopher were to defend or attack an existing grand theory, or, in a daunting flight of fancy, attempt to construct a new one. There was little attention to practical issues, with the exceptions of civil disobedience and freedom of speech, which were hangovers of the flurry of philosophical activity generated by the civil rights movement and the Vietnam War.[1]

This led to a type of anxiety regarding the role of political philosophers. While the injustice in the world around them attracted students to political philosophy, the state of the discipline meant that what made them successful was abandoning passion and protest, and replacing it with analytical precision and abstract thought. R.M. Hare captures this attitude by asserting that 'If philosophers are going to do good rather than harm in politics they must value clarity and rigour above excitement' (Hare 1989, p. 1). What mattered was pointing out that an important theorist had overlooked a distinction or was vulnerable to a counter-example. Papers of this nature filled the most prestigious journals. Yet, at the same time, there were counter-currents: rejections of the abstractions of political philosophy, such as to be found in the communitarian critics of liberalism who sometimes themselves fell short of doing much more than making criticisms, and thereby struggled to rise above the abstraction they opposed (Sandel 1982). But at least this work had the virtue of raising the question of how political philosophy can be brought into contact with the real world of public policy, and some communitarians also showed a rich understanding of history and politics (e.g., Walzer 1983).

Such criticisms reflected the feeling that the dominant voices in political philosophy had encouraged the pursuit of only one path out of many possibilities. A deep concern with the injustices of the world is displaced or hijacked into a professionalised discourse that has become removed from those initial motivations. But is there an alternative?

Applied political philosophy and its discontents

One, apparently plausible, answer, is to address real-world problems by working out how to solve them by 'applying' a moral or political theory, thereby providing 'philosophical founda-tions' for social and public policy. I shall call this the 'applied philosophy' approach. So, for example, those convinced by Rawls's theory of justice would seek to formulate policies that would move the basic structure of society closer to his principles of justice: equal basic liberties for all, fair equality of opportunity, and the difference principle, making the worst off as well off as possible. Laws would need to change, and taxes raised and redistributed, to bring us closer to Rawls's conception of a just society (Rawls 1999a [1971]). Similarly, those inspired by Nozick's libertarianism would set out steps that would strengthen property rights, reduce the sphere of government action, and lower taxes, again in the hope of moving society in a libertarian direc-tion (Nozick 1974). These, however, are largely aspirational projects, as far as philosophers are concerned, for notably Rawls and Nozick said very little about how their theories can be applied to current circumstance. Indeed, setting out the connective tissue between theory and policy has rarely been done in detail, at least in relation to the topic of distributive justice. Even a book with such a title as *Realizing Rawls* (Pogge 1989) delivers little by way of concrete policy recommendation. This is not to say that there is no role for such work (I will return to this) but rather that something else is also needed.

There are, however, philosophers who attempt to show in detail how their abstract philo-sophical theories can resolve particular policy issues. For example, in a series of volumes, Hare drew on his utilitarian moral theory to explore topics such as education, terrorism, slavery, punishment, and the environment (Hare 1972, 1989, 1996, 1998). These writings exemplify the idea of applied moral and political philosophy as the process of applying a theory to policy. This appears a reasonable, even obvious, way of proceeding. Yet there are difficulties.

The first is the most obvious; the apparent *dogmatism* of such an approach. Policy proposals derived from a particular moral or political theory are no more firmly based than the premises. Those who doubt the starting point will not be convinced. What happens next? Do we need to provide arguments for a philosophical theory as part of the policy debate? What are those arguments? Hare does not shirk this challenge, claiming that utilitarianism can be derived from an analysis of the logic of the moral concepts citing his other works where he has argued the point in detail. But, first, his arguments have convinced only a small number of other philoso-phers (Seanor and Fotion 1988), and second, even if sound, they need to be conveyed to people within the public policy process in a manner they understand. Yet if Hare's arguments are not strong enough to bring about a consensus within philosophy, what hope is there of convincing all relevant decision-makers in the policy process (cf. MacIntyre 1981)? Without compelling arguments, Hare is arguing from his own authority, or perhaps the authority of a tradition, and one of the first lessons in philosophy is that arguments from authority have no weight other than to suggest promising lines of enquiry. Others such as William MacAskill have claimed to be arguing from an 'ecumenical' starting point, which in his case is a form of consequentialism that, he suggests, can make room for values such as freedom and equality, but still the framework remains a maximising consequentialist one, perhaps within constraints (MacAskill 2015, n. 42). And there are many who deny that this outlook encompasses all that is relevantly at stake (Srinivasan 2015).

I have assumed that it is possible to move directly from a theory to a policy recommendation. A second difficulty is that theories often *under-determine* policy outcomes. For example, John Rawls suggests that his theory of justice is compatible with both 'property-owning democracy' and 'liberal socialism'. Hence those who agree on the philosophical theory can disagree about policy (Rawls 2001). In some cases disputes can be resolved by rejecting one approach on other grounds, such as what fits best with existing traditions, but not always. This leaves us unclear how to deal with remaining disagreements.

Even more significant, however, is the third problem of *implausibility of recommendations*. My first experience of policy work concerned a review of the law of gambling. Broadly, I had thought that I believed some version of John Stuart Mill's 'harm principle', giving adults in possession of their normal reasoning capacities the right to act as they wish, provided that they do not harm others (Mill 2003 [1859]). The obvious application is that gambling should be regulated according to the harm principle, from which it follows that anything should be permitted between informed, consenting adults, provided there are no significant third-party effects. Yet gambling has never been regulated on this basis. To take a mundane example, in the US a roulette wheel must have 36 numbers and two zeros (and hence the odds of winning any bet is 36/38), while in the UK and Europe a roulette wheel has 36 numbers and only one zero. A UK casino cannot try to compete by making the game more favourable to the customer by, say, having 40 numbers and only one zero, even if it were to make this advantage very clear to every customer. The regulation is a type of paternalistic intervention to ensure that the odds can be relatively easily understood, to minimise the possibility of unfairness. Yet is arguable whether it is compatible with the harm principle, which would seem to call for a liberalisation of the games on offer, as long as there is full disclosure of odds. For perhaps a clearer example, in the UK you cannot play on a slot machine by inserting your credit card and repeating play until your credit card limit is reached. I doubt that anyone objects to this law, but again its justification seems paternalistic. Some may reply that extensive borrowing could harm third parties, most notably dependents, but this is a general argument against credit cards, rather than specific to gambling (for discussion, see Wolff 2011, pp. 37–60). Hence, the harm principle, though widely supported and recited, is not a sound basis for policy on its own (see Feinberg 1984, 1985).

The problem, though, is not with the harm principle but the goal of applied philosophy to formulate concise philosophical principles that can directly determine policy. For another example, when I was working on the policy question of how invasive experiments on animals should be regulated Peter Singer and Peter Carruthers were the most prominent voices in the philosophical debate. Singer, famously, on the Benthamite basis that sentience is a critical factor, argued for animal liberation (Singer 1995). Although in his book of that name he did not discuss experiments for critical medical research, the obvious conclusion of his argument is that we are no more justified in experimenting on animals than we would be on humans without consent. Carruthers, by contrast, argued that we owe animals a lower level of concern than humans because of their limited cognitive capacities (Carruthers 1992). Strictly, it seems, Singer's view entails that no experiments on animals are permitted (unless they would also be permitted on humans), while Carruthers's position suggests that there are minimal moral limits to what humans can do to animals. But in their extremes neither view has any prospect of being adopted by policy-makers. Currently, experiments are permitted under licence for some purposes (human and animal health) on some animals (no great apes) under strict controls. The policy question is whether current regulations require adjustment, and suggestions of very radical change to fit a philosophical theory will make no impression (however, as I will argue later, philosophical theories are vital to the policy process on a longer arc).

The three problems for 'applied philosophy' mentioned so far are *dogmatism, under-determination,* and *implausibility of recommendations.* A fourth is that sometimes a theory requires several steps for implementation, but partial implementation could be worse than doing nothing. This is a version of the *theory of the second best.* Consider, for example, Ronald Dworkin's theory of equality of resources (1981). For Dworkin the just society combines background equality in distribution with respect for individual choice and ambition. People should receive the benefits and burdens of their freely made choices. Suppose a government seeks to put this theory into practice. Equalising background resources will be a very long, politically arduous programme, likely to meet a great deal of resistance. Moving towards a system in which people reap the costs and benefits of their choices seems more straightforward, leading to reduction of taxes on incomes and profits, and reducing the benefits of those who could work but choose not to. Suppose this 'responsibility for choice' element is introduced before background conditions are equalised. Unfortunately, rather than half-way to equality of resources, we would find ourselves in something like the 'everyday libertarianism' encouraged by Margaret Thatcher; few restrictions on property transfers, but taking existing property ownership for granted (cf. Murphy and Nagel 2002). Although there is no necessity that any theory is implemented as incompetently as described, it is natural to try to change the easy things first. Hence, at a minimum, it is something for which we should be on our guard.

The fifth problem is what we can call *blindspots.* This is well illustrated with Charles Mills's criticism of Rawls (Rawls 1999a [1971]; Pateman and Mills 2007). Suppose that US society transitions to become fully compliant with Rawls's theory of justice. Everyone has equal basic liberties, fair equality of opportunity, and the worst off have as much as any worst-off group could have. Mills asks whether we would, therefore, have eliminated race-based injustice. Perhaps surprisingly, he answers in the negative. The worst off in terms of income and wealth in the US are disproportionately Black and Hispanic. Suppose we greatly improve the fortunes of the worst off. Nevertheless, there is little reason to believe that the racial composition of the worst-off group would have changed. The worst-off group is still likely to be overwhelmingly Black and Hispanic. Other policies of compensation and rectification will be needed to eliminate racial difference in life fortune in order to overcome racial injustice.

Finally, I need to mention the problem of *conceptual inadequacy,* which can be illustrated with the example of disability. Although there is important work making a conceptual bridge between the concerns of philosophers and activists (see, e.g., Silvers et al. 1998; Kittay 1999; Barnes 2016), on the whole the abstract concepts of justice employed by philosophers provided no, or poor, policy proposals for the area. John Rawls, notoriously, assumes the problem away, at the most fundamental level (Rawls 1999a [1971], 1999b). Dworkin addressed disability by means of an ingenious hypothetical insurance market to set levels of redistribution (Dworkin 1981). However, this conceptualises the disadvantage experienced by people with disabilities in purely economic terms, with tax and transfer as the proposed solution. At a time when disability studies was gripped with the debate between the 'medical' model (repair the person) and the 'social' model (change the world so everyone can find their place), and in other disciplines academics engaged in participatory research with people with disabilities to understand their concerns (Shakespeare 2000), the dominant philosophical traditions had nothing to contribute to the policy debates. The reason for this is simply that the concepts in which the theories of justice were formulated did not map onto cutting edge policy questions as formulated by disabled people themselves, and activists on their behalf.

For another, more recent example, Amia Srinivasan has argued that William MacAskill's widely noted and discussed effective altruism, in concentrating on individual, primarily charitable, action

> does not address the deep sources of global misery – international trade and finance, debt, nationalism, imperialism, racial and genderbased subordination, war, environmental degradation, corruption, exploitation of labour – or the forces that ensure its reproduction. Effective altruism doesn't try to understand how power works, except to better align itself with it.
>
> *(Srinivasan 2015)*

Effective altruism appears to be a classic example of applied philosophy in the sense of starting with a theory and looking for problems to which to apply it. But that leaves open whether the particular problems it treats are best addressed with the conceptual resources of that theory.

Engaged political philosophy

What is the alternative? One, simply, is to try to navigate around the difficulties. But dogmatism, and the associated issue of implausibility of recommendations, will be hard to handle. At bottom the problem is that policy is rarely made in pursuit of a single theory or value. Pluralism, pragmatism, and compromise are the stuff of real life, and deducing policy conclusions from a philosophical theory can, at best, be just one input into the argument. The obvious alternative is to start at the other end: what is the problem in need of attention?[2] Consider Iris Marion Young's approach in *Justice and the Politics of Difference*, which attempts to ground political philosophy in the concerns of real social movements, rather than the philosopher's imagination (Young 1990). Amartya Sen, similarly, has approached political questions in this style very often throughout his career (e.g., Sen 1981, 1990), as has Elizabeth Anderson, especially in her most recent work (Anderson 2013, 2017). Hence in considering any policy issue, the first question is why has (or should) this particular issue come to public attention right now? And what are the positions in the debate and what drives people apart? From here an alternative methodology can then unfold. I shall call it 'engaged philosophy'. This methodology runs through a number of steps. In some cases the steps blur into each other, and in others one or more will not be needed, but schematically it will be helpful to set them out.

Step 1: identify the issue and current state of affairs

Sometimes an issue will have been rumbling on for a while, and then erupts to great public attention, and is therefore widely understood. Yet we should not naively assume that all policy dilemmas are easily graspable. In many cases, against backgrounds of established practice, it may take perception and skill to see, name, and explain a problem that should be of public concern even if it is not at the moment. An observation from Alison Jaggar brings this out beautifully:

> As a young woman . . . I was unable to articulate many vague and confused feelings and perceptions because the language necessary to do so had not yet been invented. The vocabulary I needed included such terms as "gender," . . . "sex role," "sexism," "sexual harassment," "the double day," "sexual objectification," "heterosexism," "the

male gaze," "marital, acquaintance, and date rape," "emotional work," "stalking," "hostile environment," "displaced home-maker" and "double standard of ageing."

(Jaggar 2000, p. 238)

Jaggar talks of a time when it was very difficult for women to express the many ways in which they experienced oppression and disadvantage. There is often work to be done – identification and articulation – to convert a situation that is taken for granted into a policy problem that needs to be addressed. Identification is typically the task of real movements and activists, including philosopher/activists.

However, even when a problem is well known, real understanding requires an appreciation of not just what is being publicised in the headlines but the underlying position regarding law and regulations, as well as facts of behaviour. Journalists will often simplify complex issues to bring out striking messages. Wilful or not, this will sometimes misrepresent how the facts are, or make ill-advised recommendations – for example, by calling for a law that already exists, or criticising a policy that doesn't require what is alleged, or arguing for criminalising a practice that barely ever happens. Understanding relevant facts, and how the situation is currently regulated, is a painstaking task. But it is critical, for without this background work, it is impossible to know what does and does not need to change in order to carry through some policy reform, and to be able to estimate what its effects are likely to be. This complex information-gathering exercise is also, of course, shot through with values, often partially revealed by what type of information is easily available and what is more difficult to access.

Step 2: identify the arguments and values

Once the issue is clear, or at least clearer, it is then necessary to identify the arguments on both sides, although sometimes, especially with a newly identified issue, one side is so overwhelmingly strong that there is no real debate. For example, when Amartya Sen identified the problem of millions of 'missing women' in the world, and explained that it was due to the relative neglect of young girls around the world, compared to their brothers, I doubt that there was much attempt to defend such practices (Sen 1990). In these cases, and the identification of marital rape may be another, philosophically little argument is needed, and the question moves directly to policy: what, if anything, can be done to mitigate or remove these evils?

In other cases, there are likely to be two sides. Consider the regulation of gambling. Gambling has rarely, if ever, been accepted as an ordinary commercial activity, like going to the cinema or even going to a bar. It is often regarded as somewhat disreputable, to be avoided (Chinn 2004). Even the young John Stuart Mill, in a letter to the medical journal *The Lancet*, claimed that it corrupted the human character (Mill 1986 [1832]). Corruption or not, it can lead to rapid loss of money, and sometimes to theft to pay off gambling debts, violence if they are not paid, imprisonment if theft is detected, and then divorce and even suicide. Such tragic stories are regularly reported in the press. Why, then, is gambling permitted? One answer is that in a country such as the UK, more than half the adult population gambles at some point in the year, if only to purchase a lottery ticket, and it brings excitement to many even when they lose. If there is anything to the idea that how you spend your money reveals your preferences then the amount of money spent on gambling each year shows that it yields a great deal of preference satisfaction, even if in some cases it is compulsive or immediately regretted. But it is also extremely difficult to suppress gambling, and so in practice our choice is between having a regulated legal industry, and an unregulated illegal one, with all the problems of crime, corruption, and blackmail that it may bring with it (Chinn 2004).

Hence there are two or more sides to the issue and here the skills and training of a philosopher can be particularly helpful. Philosophers can 'deepen the arguments and make them more rigorous, [and] question . . . assumptions' (Hare 1972, pp. 5–6). The forensic skills of the philosopher should help to take the debate apart, to understand the values – autonomy, utility, paternalism, protection of the vulnerable, fairness, and so forth – that are relevant to the debate, and understand how they figure in arguments for different positions. Gaps in the arguments, false assumptions, false dilemmas, and so on may all become exposed once the debate is dissected. This can be a lengthy and difficult task, and becomes even more difficult when inputs from social science are included. At this stage, however, the task is one of understanding, reconstruction, and correction of false inferences or pre-supposition, rather than settling the issue by argument or fiat, unless it turns out that the great weight of argument is on one side.

Step 3: history and comparisons

The first step, then, was to set out the problem and gather facts about regulation, law, and behaviour, and the second to draw out the underlying moral debate. It may seem that the natural next step could be to consider possible solutions, but this is often premature. It can be greatly facilitated by an intermediate phase of looking at examples of practice at other times and places. (And as the types of tasks involved multiply the advantages of multi-disciplinary team working become apparent.) To take the historical dimension first, it can be very important to understand how current policy came into being. Sometimes no explicit policy was ever formulated, or current policy was the first explicit attempt to do so. But sometimes a policy is introduced because of the failure of a previous policy. If that is not understood it may be that the next recommendation ends up repeating something that has been tried and failed. Of course it is unsafe to conclude that because something failed once it will fail again. But nevertheless, those circumstances should be studied. Otherwise we risk destructive 'policy cycles' of the sort that have been observed in foreign aid (Riddell 2007).

Seeking (negative) guidance from the past can usefully be combined with the experience of other jurisdictions. Most policy dilemmas have their counterpart elsewhere. Every country has to have a policy about gambling, or about animal experimentation, or about road safety, and seeking comparisons may help us see how limited our own national imagination has been.

Step 4: create a profile of possible solutions

With the insight of history and international comparison we can begin to construct a menu of options, adding others proposed by activists or politicians, with room for creative proposals that could provide a new solution. However, caution is needed. Policy change is always change from where we are. There is a very powerful, unavoidable, status quo bias in policy. First, if we don't agree a change we remain where we are. (Hence those who wish to defend the status quo may find their energies best spent in dividing the opposition rather than providing more direct support for the current situation.) Second, there is truth in the conservative position, articulated by Roger Scruton, that institutions take a great deal of time to establish, but can be destroyed very rapidly, and hence the burden of proof should be on those wishing to make a change (e.g., Scruton ND). Philosophically this status quo bias has been said to be unsupportable, and that all options should be appraised fairly and independently (Husak 1989). But in policy terms, some apparent options are simply out of reach, at least for the time being, and all we can aim at is incremental change. I will return to this later, as it may seem a disappointingly restrictive condition for philosophical engagement with the policy process.

Step 5: evaluation of options

At this point, with our menu of potentially reachable options, we arrive at the fifth, and most challenging, stage: how to decide which option to pursue. In some cases, it will be easy to eliminate options as being too restrictive of individual liberty, or being inferior to other options on key criteria, but very often we will be left with a variety of options supported by different value systems, with no obvious way of adjudication. It is in these difficult cases where it may seem that the 'applied philosophy' methodology, which I have rejected, seems strongest. It may appear that where there is disagreement on policy the appeal to a firm set of principles, established by a theory, promises a way out, and a form of resolution. But this is a false promise. Theories differ and what impartial method is there for determining which theory is right? Choice of methodology is just as disputed as choice of theory. Hence, we have returned to the problem of dogmatism in a new form: why accept the philosopher's theory about how to choose a theory, especially if you reject the conclusions it leads to?

There is no magic solution to the problem of deep disagreement. However, it is possible that the second stage outlined earlier, where the real basis of disagreement, underneath the surface debate, is identified, can help. Consider the controversy about the morality of abortion. As Ronald Dworkin has helpfully pointed out, it is often posed as the clash between a woman's right to choose and the foetus's right to life. But Dworkin claims this is misleading. Few believe in a woman's absolute right to choose, such as, for example, to choose to have an abortion just a few weeks before the baby is due. And relatively few people will insist on the foetus's right to life when the life, or even the health, of the mother is threatened. Rather the great majority on both sides accept that both the mother and the foetus have legitimate interests and the question is how to balance these interests, which changes as the pregnancy advances (Dworkin 1993).

This type of reframing of the debate can be very helpful in that it means that some, potentially very controversial, questions can be left to one side. But to reframe a debate, or even to narrow the difference, is not necessarily to solve it. Dworkin's argument does not tell us whether abortion should be permitted, and, if so, under what conditions. Indeed, some attempted reframings are little more than disguised attempts to win the debate by fiat.

However, as Daniel Weinstock has observed, it is very common at this point to try to solve a policy dilemma in a different way, by shifting away from explicitly moral argument to the issues of 'harm reduction' (Weinstock 2012). Recall the point that sometimes it is very difficult to enforce a particular regulation. Therefore we must always pay attention to 'second round' effects: how the world would react back to a new regulation. After all, many of us when confronted with a new regulation try to work out how we can carry on doing what we were doing before, with impunity. Sometimes we find a loophole, or carry on as before and hope either not to be detected or not to be punished even if detected. My example earlier in this chapter was gambling, where studies suggest that when off-track gambling in the UK was illegal, in the 1950s, in some towns a significant proportion of the adult population nevertheless illegally gambled on a regular basis (Chinn 2004). This led to a crisis in the criminal justice system with backlogs of cases, as well as blackmail, extortion, and theft, and corruption of the police. Eventually off-track gambling was legalised in a highly controlled way. The argument is that regardless of whether gambling is wrong in itself, banning gambling will lead to a series of harms that we would do better to avoid. Therefore, from the point of view of harm reduction, it is better to control gambling than to ban it.

The first critical move in this argument is to accept the limited power of law and regulation to change behaviour. If we pass a law to solve a problem and people don't obey the law, we now have two problems where once we had only one. Of course, restrictive policies do not always fail. People wear seat-belts in cars and helmets on motorbikes, and don't smoke in pubs. But it would be wrong to generalise in either direction. Returning to the case of abortion, what would actually happen if we banned abortion in the UK? Wealthy women would find access to safe abortions. But the less wealthy may resort to very dangerous procedures, at risk to their lives. An abortion ban may well lead to some reduction in the number of abortions, but it is also likely to lead to a higher rate of maternal mortality. Hence a harm-reduction approach suggests permitting abortion under controlled circumstances. Note that even those who oppose abortion on moral grounds can believe that it would be an even greater moral wrong to have a law against abortion, given the likely consequences. And similar harm reduction arguments are regularly made with relation to gambling and the regulation of drugs.

Philosophically, the harm reduction argument bears examination. I presented it as, in essence, a way of cutting through moral debate. The thought is that if a particular moral position leads to a law that is likely to be regularly broken, with harmful effects, it is wrong to insist on that moral position. But what sort of 'wrong' is that? Is it morally wrong to advocate a policy that, while reflecting your own moral position, is likely to lead to serious harm? Some will believe, conversely, that it is morally wrong to compromise in the way the harm reduction argument suggests, even if the effects of not compromising are problematic. After all, people can choose how they act. Or are we in some sort of 'tragic' position, where morality needs to be compromised for the sake of humanity?

Is the harm reduction argument a way of avoiding moral argument, or a way of substituting a different moral argument – one heavily weighted towards consequentialism – for those in dispute? And if it is the latter, how neutral is it between differing positions? Those who believe in religious or conservative moralities are likely to see their own position regularly 'trumped' by harm reduction arguments, and hence may reasonably suspect that harm reduction arguments are biased towards liberalism and individualism as well as consequentialism. The reply that harm reduction is simply humanitarianism in the light of predicted human behaviour may or may not convince. The most likely reply is that it is defeatist to take human behaviour for granted, and that law and regulation are a vitally important way of sending messages about what is, and is not, morally justified. This is especially so when government is trusted and held in high regard. Not even the harm reduction argument, therefore, can function as a trump card in debate, even though it can often help us to make significant progress.

Step 6: policy recommendation

Once the positions are evaluated a recommendation has to be made, even if it is to leave things as they are. The recommendation should also meet a number of conditions, including being supported by reasons that can be readily communicated. If it is to have a chance of adoption it must be capable of becoming part of a general political debate, rather than being regarded as the possession of a charismatic thinker who can personally make a compelling presentation. But the task need not end here, for at this stage the philosopher can become an activist. As Terrell Carver has put it, the activist needs to garner an audience, unite a movement, and proceed to a goal (Carver 2017). Who has the skills and appetite for this is another matter.

In the end, however, laws and regulations are enacted not by philosophers but by elected politicians. Philosophers can push their recommendations, but it will be for policy-makers to decide whether to follow those recommendations. And at this point they are likely also to be influenced by the response of the media, the practicalities of what is possible within a parliamentary timetable, and, most decisively of all, perhaps, what effect they expect a new measure will have on their prospects of re-election. Much UK regulation regarding recreational drugs, for example, can be seen in this light.

Conclusion: the role of the philosopher

The 'applied philosophy' approach supposes that it is possible to give the philosopher a distinctive, even privileged role in the policy process, as the formulator of the theory that provides a moral foundation for public policy. My arguments here, however, suggest that this is myth. On my alternative 'engaged' model, there are no foundations in this sense. The philosopher identifies relevant values, in the context of a problem, current facts, past history, and contemporary alternatives. There is a certain amount of sifting and balancing to articulate the moral dilemmas underlying the messy public debate, and then the identification and evaluation of possible solutions, before making recommendations, that may or may not have any effect on actual policy. I have also suggested that there is an inbuilt conservatism in the process, in that any proposals that are distant from the status quo are unlikely to be considered real possibilities, which also diminishes the role of the free-thinking philosopher.

At this point a certain concern may creep in that I am denying the philosopher any special role. After all, what I have described could be done by academics from many backgrounds, as well as civil servants and journalists. But I think this is just how things are. Insofar as philosophers have any competitive advantage in contributing to the direct policy process it is through the time and care they have spent informing themselves about the analysis of values and how to approach dilemmas, and how this has been done throughout the history of philosophy. We are stocked with an understanding of values, theories, and principles of inference. We are used to patterns and repertoires of arguments, making distinctions, and at least attempting to convey what we know clearly and simply. But if this is a difference to those in other specialisms or social roles, it is generally a difference of degree, not of kind.

Does this mean that the type of theory that is associated with the applied philosophy approach is useless? Not at all. I see at least three types of roles or functions for grand theory. First, and most obviously, these theories form part of the inherited intellectual stock of values and arguments. From the perspective of policy, the common mistake made by philosophers is to think they have the whole of the truth when they have just part of it. However, as Mill observed in relation to Bentham, intellectual progress probably needs 'one-eyed' philosophers who see one aspect in a level of detail and clarity that they would not have pursued if they thought it was only one consideration among many (Mill 1859).

A second role, however, is equally or even more critical. I have said that there is a type of status quo bias in policy that favours incremental change over large change. This may seem disappointing. But it also may seem simply untrue. Surprising, large changes do take place. Also, over a longer stretch of time we can end up in a place we would have never imagined earlier. Who would have predicted, even ten years ago, that same-sex marriage would be so widely accepted now? Going back two generations, the same thing may have been said about the decriminalisation of homosexuality, the abolition of the death penalty, the legalisation of abortion, and the end of capital punishment. All of these caused a significant rupture with the status quo.

I think this is an important challenge, but to answer it I would distinguish 'status quo policy' from 'status quo public opinion'. It may be that there is an opportunity for substantial change when public opinion is out of balance with public policy, at which point significant reform has a chance of taking hold if it aligns with public opinion, or at least the opinion of those who are in a position to object and protest. And here there is a highly significant role for the philosopher. It might, for example, be impossible to implement Peter Singer's proposals for animal liberation, but Singer has contributed to a greater sense of awareness of animal suffering, and has helped shift public opinion so it was ready for, even demanded, more stringent welfare standards for animals. Although Singer's ideas have not been implemented, arguably they have had an effect through absorption into public opinion, which then allows for more modest reform. In sum, while philosophers need to make concessions and compromises while directly contributing to the policy process, they need have no such compunction when trying to move public opinion in a direction that will welcome reform. Votes for women in the early twentieth century bear the hallmark of Wollstonecraft and Mill as does some of the liberal legislation of the 1960s.[3]

Philosophical contributions over the decades can slowly shift first journalistic and then public opinion. However, policy change can also lead opinion. Such policy leadership is most likely to happen when it involves the protection of third parties, as in smoking, or is relatively costless for the ordinary person, as in decriminalising homosexuality. In these cases it becomes harder to formulate and find a rationale for reasoned opposition.

I said there are three roles for grand theory. The first was to inform policy debate, and the second to influence public opinion over a longer term. The third is simply that political philosophy and moral philosophy are branches of philosophy, which is a valuable activity in its own right independent of its effects. If some philosophers can spend their lives contemplating the metaphysics of numbers, there seems no less reason why others should not consider the analysis of the concept of justice, for its own sake. Policy relevance does not exhaust the value of moral and political philosophy.[4]

Notes

1 I can remember seeing a 'to-do' note on my teacher Jerry Cohen's desk saying, 'SUS'. I was excited that he was going to bring his considerable intellectual power to criticise what was then known as the 'Sus Law', which gave police the power to stop and search 'suspicious' people, and was generally regarded as being used in a racially discriminatory fashion. But I soon realised that this note was a reminder for him to update his lectures on Engels's text *Socialism: Utopian and Scientific*.

2 For related discussion see Poama (2019) and Howard (2019).

3 Although Mill himself as an MP spoke in favour of capital punishment and his arguments were cited in the debates in Parliament in the 1950s (House of Commons 1956). Mill's speech is reprinted in Wolff (2018).

4 For immensely helpful comments on this chapter I would like to thank Andrei Poama, Annabelle Lever, and Sarah Richmond.

References

Anderson, Elizabeth. (2013). *The Imperative of Integration*. Princeton, NJ: Princeton University Press.

Anderson, Elizabeth. (2017). *Private Government*. Princeton, NJ: Princeton University Press.

Barnes, Elizabeth. (2016). *The Minority Body*. Oxford: Oxford University Press.

Carruthers, Peter. (1992). *The Animals Issue*. Cambridge: Cambridge University Press.

Carver, Terrell. (2017). *Marx*. Cambridge: Polity Press.

Chinn, Carl. (2004). *Better Betting with a Decent Feller*. London: Aurum.

Dworkin, Ronald. (1981). "What Is Equality? Part 2: Equality of Resources", *Philosophy and Public Affairs*, 10, pp. 283–345.

Dworkin, Ronald. (1993). *Life's Dominion*. London: Harper Collins.

Feinberg, Joel. (1984). *Harm to Others*. Oxford: Oxford University Press.

Feinberg, Joel. (1985). *Offence to Others*. Oxford: Oxford University Press.

Hare, R.M. (1972). *Applications of Moral Philosophy*. London: Palgrave Macmillan.

Hare, R.M. (1989). *Essays on Political Morality*. Oxford: Oxford University Press.

Hare, R.M. (1996). *Essays on Bioethics*. Oxford: Oxford University Press.

Hare R.M. (1998). *Essays on Religion and Education*. Oxford: Oxford University Press.

House of Commons. (1956). "Capital Punishment" http://hansard.millbanksystems.com/commons/1956/feb/16/capital-punishment. Viewed December 27th, 2017.

Howard, Jeffrey. (2019). "The Public Role of Ethics and Public Policy" (this volume).

Husak, Douglas. (1989). "Recreational Drugs and Paternalism", *Law and Philosophy*, 8, pp. 353–381.

Jaggar, Alison. (2000). "Feminism in Ethics: Moral Justification", in *The Cambridge Companion to Feminism in Philosophy* (pp. 225–244), edited by Miranda Fricker and Jennifer Hornsby. Cambridge: Cambridge University Press.

Kittay, Eva Feder. (1999). *Love's Labor*. New York: Routledge.

MacAskill, William. (2015). *Doing Good Better*. London: Guardian Faber.

MacIntyre, Alasdair. (1981). *After Virtue*. London: Palgrave Macmillan.

Mill, John Stuart. (1859). "Bentham", in *Dissertations and Discussions* (Vol. 1, pp. 330–392). London: Parker.

Mill, John Stuart. (1986 [1832]). "The Effects of Gambling", in *Newspaper Writings*, edited by A.P. Robson and J.P. Robson. Toronto: University of Toronto Press.

Mill, John Stuart. (2003 [1859]). "On Liberty", in *Utilitarianism and Other Writings* (2nd edition), edited by Mary Warnock. Glasgow: Harper Collins.

Murphy, Liam and Nagel, Thomas. (2002). *The Myth of Ownership*. New York: Oxford University Press.

Nozick, Robert. (1974). *Anarchy, State, and Utopia*. New York: Basic Books.

Pateman, Carol and Mills, Charles. (2007). *Contract and Domination*. Cambridge: Polity Press.

Poama, Andei. (2019). "Application or Construction? Two Types of Public Policy Ethics" (this volume).

Pogge, Thomas. (1989). *Realizing Rawls*. Ithaca, NY: Cornell University Press.

Rawls, John. (1999a [1971]). *A Theory of Justice*. Cambridge, MA: Harvard University Press.

Rawls, John. (1999b). "A Kantian Conception of Equality", in his *Collected Papers* (pp. 254–266). Cambridge, MA: Harvard University Press, First published 1975.

Rawls, John. (2001). *Justice as Fairness: A Restatement*. Cambridge, MA: Harvard University Press.

Riddell, Roger. (2007). *Does Foreign Aid Really Work?* Oxford: Oxford University Press.

Sandel, Michael. (1982). *Liberalism and the Limits of Justice*. Cambridge: Cambridge University Press.

Scruton, Roger. (ND). "Understanding Music: Rousseau" www.roger-scruton.com/about/music/understanding-music/179-rousseau. Viewed December 27th, 2017.

Seanor, Douglas and Fotion, Nicholas. (1988). *Hare and Critics*. Oxford: Oxford University Press.

Sen, Amartya. (1981). *Poverty and Famines*. Oxford: Oxford University Press.

Sen, Amartya. (1990). "More Than 100 Million Women Are Missing", *New York Review of Books*, 37, December 20th.

Shakespeare, Tom. (2000). *The Disability Reader: Social Science Perspectives*. London: Continuum.

Silvers, Anita, Wasserman, David and Mahowold, Mary. (1998). *Disability, Difference, Discrimination*. Lanham, MA: Rowman and Littlefield.

Singer, Peter. (1995). *Animal Liberation* (2nd edition). London: Pimlico.

Srinivasan, Amia. (2015). "Stop the Robot Apocalypse", *London Review of Books*, 37(19), pp. 3–6.

Walzer Michael. (1983). *Spheres of Justice*. New York: Basic Books.

Weinstock, Daniel. (2012). Paper delivered at "Ideals and Reality in Social Ethics" conference, Newport, Wales.

Wolff, Jonathan. (2011). *Ethics and Public Policy*. London: Routledge.

Wolff, Jonathan. (ed.). (2018). *Readings in Moral Philosophy*. New York: Norton.

Young, Iris Marion. (1990). *Justice and Politics of Difference*. Princeton, NJ: Princeton University Press.

2

THE PUBLIC ROLE OF ETHICS AND PUBLIC POLICY

Jeffrey Howard

Introduction

How should we undertake scholarly work about the kinds of policies that the state morally ought to enact? There is strikingly little attention to questions of methodology in books and courses that carry the familiar label of "ethics and public policy" (EPP). But there is enormous attention to questions of methodology in the discipline of which ethics and public policy is undoubtedly a central part: political philosophy. In recent years, political philosophers have lavished attention on the nature of "ideal" and "non-ideal" theory (Stemplowska 2008; Valentini 2009, 2012; Stemplowska and Swift 2012); on whether their theories should be "realistic", and if so, in what sense (Williams 2005; Geuss 2009; Leader Maynard and Worsnip 2018; Rossi and Sleat 2014); on whether the principles they design should be sensitive to facts about human psychology and society (Cohen 2003; Miller 2008); on the role of public opinion in political theory (Baderin 2016); and whether to think of political philosophy as simply contributing to the accumulated body of human knowledge – akin to theoretical mathematics – or whether to think of political philosophy's aim as practical, as aiming to help real people solve real problems that they have (Swift 2008).

Here I aim to bring some of these recent methodological debates in political philosophy to bear on the question of how to undertake work on EPP. My thesis is that we should regard EPP as a special subfield of political philosophy, marked by a particular methodological commitment: to assist citizens and policymakers in their actual deliberations about public policy. EPP can assist the task of public deliberation on public policy in many ways, but I will discuss two. First, it can help to craft the normative menu of various policy options, and the arguments that underlie them, from which both policymakers and ordinary citizens can choose. To design a menu of this kind, scholars of EPP must not simply defend the views that they take to be correct. Rather, they must see their task as one of mapping out the logical space in a given policy debate – identifying a variety of positions one might hold and the arguments for holding them, often by rationally reconstructing positions commonly defended by citizens in the public sphere. In this way, EPP aspires to increase the intelligence of public debate. Second, EPP can bolster public deliberation about public policy by helping citizens to bypass needless disagreements – namely, by revealing why those who hold different underlying commitments can nevertheless converge to find policy agreement. The task of this chapter is to elaborate this vision for EPP and defend its importance.

To suggest that EPP ought to have a certain methodological commitment is not to make a conceptual claim about the meaning of the phrase "ethics and public policy". Nor is it to make a sociological claim about what all scholars who do EPP necessarily take themselves to be doing. Rather, it is to make a normative claim about the value of having a subfield of political philosophy that has this particular task. Still, one reason why EPP is a suitable candidate to play this distinctive role is because of how it is largely already understood. It is an intriguing question why so many books and syllabi insist on using the label of "ethics and public policy", rather than, say, "applied political philosophy". The label is fashionable, I suspect, because of the intimation that, in reading or studying EPP, one is aspiring not merely to study ethics but also to *do* something with the ethical principles at which one arrives: help real people solve the policy challenges they face. I offer a proposed characterisation of this otherwise mysterious subfield that is faithful to its burgeoning identity – the identity that has led so many students and scholars alike to be attracted to classes and books bearing its label.

Why should EPP have a public role?

Why think that EPP should have some kind of public mission?[1] There are several arguments that would all arrive at this claim or one like it, and not all of them are successful. Consider, first, the argument that *all* of political philosophy ought to have some kind of practical role. This is sometimes discussed in the context of a debate about whether political philosophy is "epistemological" or instead "practical" (Rawls 1980, pp. 518–19; Swift 2008, pp. 366–68). To suppose that political philosophy is epistemological is simply to say that its task is to discover and document truths, akin to academic disciplines like theoretical mathematics but simply with different content. To suppose that political philosophy is practical, in contrast, is instead to suppose that its task is to help people make actual decisions.

It is tempting to resist the epistemological approach by way of terminological fiat, or what H.L.A. Hart would have called a 'definitional stop' (2008, p. 5). We can simply stipulate that political philosophy *just is* practical in its very nature, and so any account of it that *fails* to provide guidance for actors in the real world is accordingly defective. Thus when G.A. Cohen writes that justice might 'not [be] something that the state, or, indeed, any other agent, is in a position to deliver' (2004, p. 18) and that political philosophy often 'makes no practical difference' to what we ought to do in the real world (2003, p. 243), he is simply guilty of a considerable category mistake (cf. Swift 2008, p. 367). The epistemological conception, this rebuttal goes, simply isn't a conception of political philosophy at all, and thus would surely be an unsuitable interpretation of the point and purpose of EPP.

But this is not the route I counsel. For starters, there is reason to question the tenability of the distinction at hand. Suppose we take political philosophy to have the so-called epistemological task of discovering truths. Even so, the truths that political philosophers aim to discover are typically *normative* truths about what citizens and their officials ought to do (Swift 2008, pp. 367–68). They are truths about *practical reason*. So it is not clear what the distinction is supposed to be. Even if some work describes normative truths that are not immediately applicable to anyone – say, because they concern how people should act in conditions that may arise in the future but have not yet arisen – such work is still practical insofar as it identifies normative truths that bear on what agents in those conditions ought to do. The fact that we don't find ourselves in the circumstances to which the normative claims apply makes no difference to their status as normative claims. Consider normative principles about permissible conduct in warfare, as a matter of *jus in bello*. There is a sense in which such principles are not practical for me, since I do not find myself in conditions to which they apply (I am not presently engaged in wartime hostilities). But this makes them no less normative. And even if no one in the human race were in such a situation presently, because there were no current wars, it would be puzzling to think that this fact alone means that such claims would suddenly become reclassified as "epistemological" rather than "practical", and so (on the view we are entertaining) would no longer be part of political philosophy.

The real divide between those who urge a more "epistemological" orientation to the discipline and those who insist that political philosophy be "practical" is not conceptual or meta-ethical at all. As Adam Swift astutely notes, it is normative: it is about the kind of work that political theorists *should* spend their time on (2008, p. 368). Should theorists spend time addressing vexed moral choices that real people are actually confronting in the world today, or should they spend their time addressing different normative questions? One argument for the former might go as follows: perhaps political philosophers are *morally required* to pursue work that helps people solve the problems they face. This, then, is a second argument for why EPP should have a public role: because it is part of political philosophy, and all political philosophers have moral duties to do work that is practical.

But this argument, too, is limited. Even if we regard political philosophers as under a duty to help advance justice, they hold this duty *qua* citizens, not *qua* political philosophers. As citizens, there are a multitude of ways in which one can discharge one's moral duty to improve the justice of one's own society.[2] So long as political philosophers are discharging their duty in other ways, outside of the strict confines of their day-job, why should we insist that they undertake work of a particular character, even when they are not intellectually interested in it?

Even if political philosophers are not necessarily required to do work that helps real citizens advance justice, there would still be considerable value in such work. The value of such work just is the value of helping advance the cause of political morality (whatever its demands might be). Insofar as political philosophy with such an aim has value, there is, at the very least, moral reason to make room for it. Moreover, it seems clear that many political philosophers *do* choose to discharge their duties of justice through their work; they genuinely aspire to help improve the justice of their society through the theory that they do. And presumably many of them think this precisely because they accept the idea of a division of labour in the pursuit of greater justice (Swift and White 2008, p. 50), and believe that as political philosophers they are best suited to contribute to justice most successfully through their philosophical work.[3]

It is in this modest spirit that I aim to explore what the public role of EPP might be. Insofar as we have reason to think that *part* of political philosophy should be oriented to helping citizens solve the problems they face, we have reason to theorise this part of our discipline in greater detail. My suggestion is that EPP already serves this role as a part of the field that focuses explicitly on concrete policy problems and what the just solutions to them are. In saddling EPP with this special role, I stress that we need not be committed to the implausible claim that *all* of political philosophy ought to play this role. Instead I shall argue that, among the rightful plurality of things going on in contemporary political theory, there is considerable value in preserving a certain subfield with a certain distinctive methodological cast of the sort I will defend.

Civic usefulness

What, exactly, does it mean for work in political philosophy (and EPP in particular) to play a public role? What I have in mind is normative theory that exhibits a certain virtue, what I will call *usefulness*. Normative theory is *useful*, I submit, when consumers of the theory would be better positioned to reason about what they morally ought to do in virtue of having consumed it. Clearly different sorts of normative theory can be useful in all manner of ways. Work in interpersonal ethics on love or on promising, for example, may well be useful in helping one to navigate – or at least understand – one's personal relationships. The potential value of the subfield of EPP must be something more specific, what I will call *civic usefulness*. Theoretical work on ethics and public policy is useful in this sense, I submit, when citizens are better positioned to reason about the policy choices they face in virtue of having been exposed to that work. In other words, EPP is useful if and when it supports the activity of reasoned civic deliberation about public policy. In a slogan, the aim of EPP is *the deliberative empowerment of citizens* (including policymakers).

This proposal rests on the idea that there is enormous value in citizens' intelligent reflection about the ethics of public policy, alone and with others. Some of this value is intrinsic: by engaging in such reflection and deliberation, citizens develop their moral capacities, and they express respect for the status of others by taking their interests seriously. But the primary value is the instrumental value of enabling critical thinking about public policy, given that such thinking increases the likelihood that citizens will actually identify and be moved to enact just policies. It supports such activity by equipping citizens with concepts, distinctions, theories, and arguments. In so doing, it gives them a language through which to discuss politics.[4] Note that we can affirm such instrumental value even while leaving completely open what it is that justice requires. EPP is not valuable because it simply can help us realise some antecedently specified account of justice's demands; it is valuable precisely because of its role as an ongoing, critical inquiry into what those demands might be.

The defining methodological feature of EPP, I propose, is its aspiration to civic usefulness. Those who take themselves to be doing EPP should have in mind the conscientious civic consumer of their work. They should take themselves to help the consumer reason better about the policies they should oppose and support, and why. Note that while EPP has the aim of assisting citizens and policymakers with their deliberations, they will not necessarily succeed. The aim is reflective empowerment – that is, empowering people with arguments and distinctions with which to engage in reflection more successfully (cf. Swift and White 2008).[5] But the citizens who consume the theory are themselves autonomous moral agents, who are morally responsible for forming their own views on what justice requires on any number of policy concerns. While we may expose them to reflection that increases the likelihood that they will reflect conscientiously on public policy, it guarantees nothing. The benchmark for success is that we better position citizens to reason better about the ethics of public policy, not that they actually reason better.

How can EPP live up to the goal of assisting citizens' moral reflections on public policy? For starters, political philosophers who teach EPP should view themselves as engaged in a process of civic empowerment. The aim should not simply be to prepare students for the particular essays and exams they must complete; it should be to help make them reflective citizens (*pace* Fish 2008). Furthermore, insofar as political philosophers engage the public by writing op-eds, appearing on television or radio, and giving public talks, they ought to take their task not merely to be that of advancing the normative views they take to be correct (though they are certainly free to do so); it should be to help listeners or viewers think more reflectively about the topic under consideration, by supplying them with the relevant concepts, arguments, and distinctions to think about a given policy debate more deeply.

Of course, these *ad hoc* engagements are bound to be less impactful than engagement with students in the classroom, which remains political philosophers' most obvious site of influence. The most important reforms that political philosophers can help achieve are institutional, helping to create spaces for serious civic reflection.[6] It is a problem that the vast preponderance of students make it through secondary school and university without ever taking a class that forces them to engage in normative reflection about public life; until this is remedied, and some kind of political theory becomes a compulsory element of all citizens' democratic education, the influence of political philosophers on the public is bound to be minimal. What that democratic education ought to involve, of course, is another matter (see Gutmann 1987; Callan 1997; Levinson 1999; and Steiner in this volume).

Political philosophers spend the preponderance of their time writing articles and books, which have the least direct influence on the public of all that they do. Even if the greatest ideas developed in philosophical journals bubble up to influence the public consciousness over time, this is typically a long process, and most of us stand very little hope of ever having such a long-term influence. This poses a problem for those of us who believe that at least part of political philosophy should be dedicated to helping real citizens confront their real challenges. If we are to aspire to greater engagement, we need to take seriously the way in which books and articles are presently written. The fantasy, I think, is a world in which the non-fiction books that educated laypersons read, and that top the bestsellers' lists of major newspapers, are not simply concerned with history or politics or current events or pop science. We should aspire to a world in which ordinary people read and think about political philosophy, too. And the very first step in the long road towards creating that intellectual culture is to make our work *intelligible*.

Roughly, for work in EPP to be intelligible to a consumer of the work, *the consumer needs to be able to follow the argument and understand why the author takes it to make sense.* This is simultaneously demanding and modest. It is demanding because it requires the political philosopher to explain her terms in clear language with minimal jargon, and to outline the various positions in the debate to which her argument is a contribution. Where a piece of work contributes to an ongoing debate among scholars, the work must bring readers up to speed with the debate; articles on EPP, unlike some other areas of political philosophy, must not become a vehicle for a discussion group among some small number of scholars who simply have each other in mind when they write. To fulfil EPP's public charter, the work must be written such that an educated layperson who made a reasonable effort at understanding the work would understand it. At the same time, this approach is modest because it does not require that the reader endorse the author's position. The reader simply needs to be able to understand what the position is, so he can then make up his own mind about it.

The insistence that work in EPP be intelligible is distinct from the suggestion that work in EPP be dumbed down, or shorn of its sophistication. To be sure, it may well be objectionable, at least presumptively, to defend basic terms of cooperation or principles of justice that are highly sophisticated (Bertram 1997). But even if we endorse such a view, it could not plausibly apply to reasoning about specific public policies, which can often require a sophisticated combination of normative and empirical premises.[7] If the moral truth on some policy question turns out to be complicated – if our best understanding of the moral and empirical facts leads us to believe that a particular complex claim is true – the fact that it will take extraordinary care and effort to explain that truth properly (and that some people will need to rely on expert testimony to accept the relevant empirical premises) is simply our fate. Writing to an audience of fellow political philosophers is difficult. Writing to a general audience of citizens, or a specialised audience of policymakers without philosophical training, is even harder. Those who aspire to do EPP, on the view I am proposing, need to get better at it, myself included.

Intelligibility is a necessary condition of civic usefulness; a work of theory cannot be useful to citizens' deliberations about the policies they should support or oppose unless they can understand what the work is saying.[8] No doubt a fully worked-out account would offer a more complete specification of what the standard of the "educated layperson" actually involves. Such an account would be nothing less than a normative vision of the educated citizen. But what I have said here is enough to set the stage for the actual issue: how can work in EPP help citizens reason about the policies they should support or oppose? There are many ways; I'll canvass two of the most important.

Building the menu

One way in which EPP can support the task of reasoned public deliberation is by helping to craft the menu of policy options from which citizens can choose. Of course, any article or book in EPP is bound to include the author's own view of what position in a policy debate is most defensible. But we do a disservice to our readers if we simply cut to the chase and defend the view we take to be right. It is important that we map out the logical space of positions on a given debate, showing the diversity of options from which to choose, outlining the attractions of each view and identifying the objections that afflict each.

When scholars of EPP write on a particular policy debate, they need to decide which positions in the debate to include. How should this process proceed? The natural answer is that they should include the most important contenders in the debate. What are the important positions? For starters, they are the positions that what we can call *reasonable contenders* in the debate. Here we can appeal to a familiar philosophical idea: the idea of reasonable disagreement.

What is it for a disagreement to be reasonable? In his treatment of reasonable disagreement, Christopher McMahon writes, '[T]he position taken by a party to a disagreement is reasonable if and only if it is or could be the product of competent reasoning'. He continues: 'Reasoning is competent when it is carried out in awareness of all the relevant considerations, the cognitive capacities exercised in extracting conclusions from the relevant considerations are appropriate, and these capacities are functioning properly' (2009, p. 8).

On this view, reasonable disagreement obtains on an issue when there are good arguments on both (or many) sides. As Rawls notes in his discussion of the burdens of judgement, people who 'share a common human reason' and hold 'similar powers of thought and judgment' – who are all equipped to 'draw inferences, weigh evidence, and balance competing considerations' and have access to similar evidence – arrive at competing answers to the question they are asking (1993, p. 55).

How should one decide what the reasonable contenders in a debate are? Clearly it is a matter of normative judgement. There is no way to settle the matter in advance; we need to inspect each debate in question to ascertain what the reasonable contenders in that debate are. Consider, for just a moment, the debate on pornography. We might think that pornography ought to be banned because it subordinates women (MacKinnon 1987, 1995). We might also think that pornography ought to be banned because it increases the likelihood that those exposed to pornography will engage in criminal violence against women (Langton 1993; Scoccia 1996). Against positions like these is the familiar view that bans on pornography are simply incompatible with the right to freedom of expression (Dworkin 1985). I take it to be wholly obvious that these are reasonable views in the debate, worthy of being studied and argued about.

Reasonable contenders in a debate ought to be included, or at least recognised as important candidate views, in a work of EPP that engages that debate. But that does not mean they are the only views that ought to be included. For example, the argument that pornography should be banned because it encourages people to believe that sex outside of marriage is morally acceptable is not, I believe, a reasonable position in the debate. Nor do I view the argument that pornography should be banned because it is offensive, generating psychological distress in those who are irked by its existence, as a reasonable position in the debate (cf. Devlin 1959). Of course, these are my judgements, and others may well disagree about what the reasonable contenders in this debate are – that is fine. My point is simply that there are bound to be some views in a debate that a scholar of EPP does not regard as reasonable. Because they are unreasonable, it is tempting to suppose that they should not be taken especially seriously in work on EPP. However, that would be a mistake.

Because EPP aims to contribute to the actual moral reflection of real citizens, it must engage with citizens' current thinking on the debate in question. And the obvious truth of the matter is that many citizens hold views that we rightly find unreasonable. The two aforementioned views on pornography are among them. Because of their presence in the public culture, they are on the menu of policy positions that citizens are contemplating. For that reason, they need to be taken seriously: scholars of EPP have reason to say something about widely held views on the policy issue they're addressing, even if they take those views to be unreasonable. The mere fact that such views are taken seriously by a sufficient number of democratic citizens means that philosophers should take them seriously.[9]

Specifically, *scholars of EPP should address commonly held but unreasonable positions so as to empower citizens to think critically about them.* Political philosophers should explain what, exactly, the best arguments for these unreasonable positions are, outlining the most important objections to these arguments. Of course, political philosophers should convey their judgement that these positions are, in fact, not worthy of being advanced as reasonable contenders in the policy debate. The right response to the judgement that these views are unreasonable is not to ignore them but to engage them. To give another example: many people believe that retributivism is an unreasonable view in the debate over how to justify punishment, casting it as barbaric (Tadros 2011, p. 63). But given its prevalence in the public culture, we fail citizens who are retributivists, or who are tempted by the view, if we ignore that view. We ought to engage it and explain, exactly, why we take it to be wrong. The hope, of course, is that citizens in the grip of unreasonable views will abandon their position. They may also come to reflect on what grievances motivated them to embrace unreasonable positions in the first place, and determine what policies might redress those grievances in a just manner.[10] (These considerations, it seems to me, also support the engagement of unreasonable positions in debates on university campuses, rather than purging campus discourse so that only reasonable views are permitted to be advanced and discussed.)

Consider an objection to this position. There is a risk in setting out the best possible argument for an unreasonable position: namely, that it will give intellectual ammunition to unreasonable persons in political life who seek to trumpet that view. Indeed, some political philosophers have even gone so far as to suggest that political philosophers ought sometimes to lie – to affirm simple falsehoods deliberately – rather than, by communicating a difficult and nuanced view, risk misleading citizens into forming mistaken beliefs about the demands of justice (cf. Jubb and Kurtulmus 2012). (Think, for example, of debates about torture.) However, it is simply an unavoidable risk that some people will misunderstand philosophical arguments. All we can do is to try to make them as clearly as possible. Barring exceptional circumstances, political philosophers should not fancy themselves politicians, strategising about whether to refrain from making a certain argument, or whether to make a disingenuous argument, on the basis of a calculation that justice will somehow be advanced by doing so. They are not principally in the business of manipulating public opinion. They are not rhetoricians (cf. Sandel 2014, 225ff). Such thinking compromises the value of political philosophy, and misconceives the proper role of political philosophy in helping to bring about a just society. The distinctive value of EPP lies not in directly advancing just policies but in equipping ordinary citizens and policymakers with the concepts, distinctions, and arguments so that they can reason about what just policies are.

Bypassing disagreement

Mapping out the space of possible positions on an issue is one important way in which EPP can contribute to citizens' moral reflection on what to think. But figuring out what to think is only one stage of public deliberation about public policy. The next step involves the active deliberation among citizens, endeavouring to understand and evaluate each other's initial positions, change each other's minds, and ultimately find some mutually acceptable solution, even in the face of continuing disagreement. EPP has an indispensable role at this stage in *facilitating agreement* on questions of public policy.

How might it do this? Much work in political philosophy suggests the following path: begin by stipulating the correct overarching theory moral and political philosophy, such as utilitarianism or political liberalism or luck egalitarianism, and then show how some particular policy position follows from it. But notice that such a work of EPP will facilitate agreement on that policy position only among those who already endorse the overarching theory from which it begins. It is unlikely to succeed in facilitating any agreement beyond the strict confines of that audience.

A more promising way in which EPP can facilitate agreement on questions of public policy disavows the aim of justifying public policies on the basis of a single, overarching view of moral and political philosophy. Scholars of EPP can instead argue for particular policies without presupposing the truth of any particular underlying theory. Just as Rawls argues that different comprehensive doctrines can nevertheless arrive at an overlapping consensus on fundamental liberal values (1993, pp. 133ff), scholars of EPP can show how citizens can together endorse particular policies despite disagreeing about why, exactly, those policies are justified.

Cass Sunstein refers to this mode of reasoning as 'incompletely theorized agreement' (1995). Incompletely theorised agreements (ITAs) can, he notes, come in many forms. We might agree on an abstract normative theory, but disagree about the mid-level principles to which the theory leads and thus its implications for particular cases. Or we might agree on mid-level principles, but disagree on both the abstract theory and the implications for particular cases. Sunstein defends a third sort of ITA, which obtains when we disagree about the abstract theory and even the mid-level principles, agreeing instead only on the outcome.

Sunstein notes this version of ITA is

> especially well suited to the institutional limits of the judiciary, which is composed in significant part of multimember bodies, consisting in turn of highly diverse people who must render many decisions, live together, avoid error to the extent possible, and show each other mutual respect.
>
> *(Sunstein 1995, p. 1738)*

But these features do not merely characterise judicial bodies, the focus of Sunstein's discussion, which mainly concerns the decisions that judges reach in court cases. They characterise democratic legislatures, and indeed the public of citizens.

EPP can play the vital role of helping citizens uncover agreement despite holding radically different conceptions of justice. Just as Sunstein argues that judges can reach the same result in a legal case despite holding different philosophies of legal interpretation, citizens can reach the same result in a debate about public policy despite holding different views about the properties in virtue of which policies are just.

While this methodological strategy is seldom explicitly defended,[11] it is reasonably common in our discipline. Consider some examples. In his classic paper 'Aliens and Citizens' (1987), Joseph Carens defends open borders as the immigration policy entailed by egalitarianism, libertarianism, and utilitarianism. Which conception of justice is correct is immaterial: so long as the consumer of the argument is committed to one of the three, she ought to be committed to open borders. This is precisely the kind of incompletely theorised agreement that EPP has the potential to facilitate. Focusing too much on foundational questions of political philosophy can distract us from identifying potential points of convergence.

Immigration policy is by no means the only area of EPP in which this model has succeeded. Consider the debate on the ethics of capital punishment. In his sweeping analysis of the subject, Matthew Kramer canvasses several different arguments for punishment – retribution, deterrence, communication, and so forth – and argues that capital punishment cannot be justified on any of these views (2011). Thus we need not settle the vexed debate about which theory of punishment is correct before finding common ground on this particular policy dispute.

Of course, ITA has its limitations. Even if adherents to two rival conceptions of justice could agree on the rough thrust of a policy position, the precise contours of the positions favoured by each would surely differ. Consider the argument, advanced by Matthias Risse and Richard Zeckhauser, contending that both consequentialists and deontologists should endorse racial profiling under certain conditions (2004; cf. Lever 2005). Plainly the exact conditions are bound to be different between consequentialists and deontologists, given the starkly different underlying views. Still, there is merit even in this limited form of ITA. Even if consequentialists and deontologists cannot agree on the precise details of a particular policy, there will be enough agreement that the ordinary democratic processes of bargaining and compromise can kick in.[12] Even if all EPP can do in some cases is help to narrow the terrain of disagreement, this would itself be of considerable civic usefulness.

Some might question why EPP scholars should bother spending their time searching for possible bases of agreement among citizens. Why not simply identify the overarching conception of justice one actually believes, and then defend its policy implications? To be sure, this more traditional form of normative political theory would also have value, by helping those citizens who agree with the philosopher's preferred conception of justice explore the implications of that conception. But EPP rightly has greater ambitions than that. The aim of public deliberation about public policy among citizens is not merely to enable *each individual*, one by one, to each arrive at her own view of what the perfectly just state's policies would be. It is to enable them to *reason together* to deliberate about what they ought to do in the face of their deeper disagreements. One citizen who aims to abolish the death penalty may think this is morally required because of her own retributive convictions, which deem the death penalty a disproportionately harsh penalty, whereas another contends that execution is simply an ineffective deterrent and so cannot be justified, whereas yet another views execution as incompatible with the dictates of the communicative theory of punishment. But insofar as they all care about the realisation of justice, they all accordingly care about the abolition of the death penalty. If EPP can enable the formation of justice-minded coalitions, this is of significant value in a democracy.[13]

The task of finding common ground on policies despite disagreement on more foundational questions has especial significance in far-from-just societies, in which the project of replacing unjust policies with just ones is urgent. Gopal Sreenivasan engages in a form of ITA when arguing that all plausible conceptions of ideal justice should mandate a 1 per cent transfer of wealth from the richest countries in the world to the poorest countries (2007, 2012, p. 246). Sreenivasan's novel point is that we need not have agreement on perfect justice in order for us to agree that some change in policy is required in the non-ideal here and now (cf. Sen 2009). However, this insight is not simply restricted to non-ideal theory. Even in a reasonably just society, we need not have agreement on what the right conception of justice is in order to find common ground.

Conclusion

I have argued that we should respond to the anxiety about what, exactly, EPP is by insisting upon a certain identity for it that has a particular methodological commitment: to support public deliberation. Yet the idea that university lecturers and intellectuals ought to see their work as practically connected to the real world in this way has some substantial critics. I want to address those critics here.

In his book *Save the World on Your Own Time*, Stanley Fish excoriates the image of the professor-*cum*-activist, shaping students and readers into virtuous democratic citizens. He writes that '[t]he judgment of whether a policy is the right one for the country is not appropriate in the classroom' (2008, p. 26). And later he notes,

> The [ideal] exam question is not, "If you were to find yourself in such and such a situation, what should you do?" The [ideal] exam question is, "If you were to find yourself in such and such a situation, what would Plato, Hobbes, Rawls, and Kant tell you to do and what are the different assumptions and investments that would generate their different recommendations?"
>
> *(p. 103)*

He thus concludes: 'Analyzing ethical issues is one thing; deciding them is another, and only the first is an appropriate academic activity' (pp. 26–27).

For starters, Fish relies on a false dichotomy between analysing others' arguments for and against certain courses of action and making up one's mind on what arguments are best. Surely the analysis *just ought to be* the assessment of what view on a topic, if any, one ought to endorse as correct. And if the view is *normative*, it more or less follows automatically that you should take it to be worthy of acting on in your decisions (though of course you may not). So Fish's distinction is unpersuasive. Likewise, surely a good answer to the exam question, "What would you do in such and such a situation?" would precisely *be* to work through what Rawls or Nozick would say in response and independently evaluate who is right.

Now perhaps Fish's point is simply that university faculty shouldn't be trying to mould their students, or readers of political philosophy generally, into blindly endorsing one particular view of politics. Daniel McDermott raises a variation of this worry outside the pedagogical context, when he writes that

> [t]he political philosopher who sees himself as a man or the left or the right, and his challenge to be one of providing intellectual ammunition for his side, is no different from a creationist who sets out to get a PhD in biology in order to better equip himself to defend the Bible against assaults by evolutionists.
>
> *(2008, p. 25)*

But it is important to see that the argument I have offered is not vulnerable to these criticisms. The kind of EPP I am defending does not aim to dupe people into dogmatically endorsing some sectarian view. It aims to be philosophy, not propaganda or ideology, and accordingly it strives to help students and readers see what's plausible and what's implausible about the different arguments on each side of a question, and to present the author's own provisional judgement about what is most plausible as a candidate position, so that the reader can then decide for herself. There is an important place in political philosophy for work that actually tries to help real people solve the actual normative challenges they face. The only question that remains about such work is whether our profession is up to the task.

Notes

1 After preparing this section, I discovered the instructive analysis of Swift (2008). Many of the points I make here align with his own earlier intervention; I indicate those points accordingly.
2 I take it that the duty to help improve the justice of one's own society is entailed by the natural duty of justice.
3 It seems plausible that if no one were undertaking political philosophy with a practical aim, it would not be so easy for political philosophers to let themselves off the hook. We might say that political philosophers are collectively under a duty to ensure that this vital public good is provided. So long as enough political theorists are providing it, others are free to do otherwise.
4 For the idea of political philosophy giving citizens a language through which to deliberate about policy, see Pettit 1999, p. 130.
5 I view this idea as similar to the notion of a "democratic underlabourer" discussed and endorsed in Swift's and White's analysis (2008) of the relationship between political theory and real politics.
6 I thank Andrei Poama for stressing the significance of institutions here.
7 Note that Bertram (2007) fully accepts this.
8 See the related claim by Swift and White (2008, p. 69), that 'at least some of us engage in the project of translation'.
9 See Badano and Nuti (2018) on the possibility of engaging those who hold unreasonable views.
10 I thank Andrei Poama for raising this possibility.
11 One instructive exception is the excellent article by Swift and White (2008, p. 53).
12 For a normative defence of compromise, see Gutmann and Thompson (2012).
13 There seems to be considerable potential in the area of criminal justice. For the argument that no plausible penal theory could justify punishing "crimes of misery", see Mitchell (2012). For the argument that harsher punishment for hate crimes can be justified according to each of the main penal theories, see Wellman (2006).

References

Badano, Gabriele and Alasia Nuti. 2018. "Under Pressure: Political Liberalism, the Rise of Unreasonableness, and the Complexity of Containment." *Journal of Political Philosophy* 26, 145–168.
Baderin, Alice. 2016. "Political Theory and Public Opinion: Against Democratic Restraint." *Philosophy, Politics & Economics* 15, 209–233.
Bertram, Christopher. 1997. "Political Justification, Theoretical Complexity, and Democratic Community." *Ethics* 107, 563–583.
Callan, Eamonn. 1997. *Creating Citizens*. Oxford: Oxford University Press.
Carens, Joseph. 1987. "Aliens and Citizens: The Case for Open Borders." *The Review of Politics* 49, 251–273.
Cohen, G.A. 2003. "Facts and Principles." *Philosophy & Public Affairs* 31, 211–245.
Cohen, G.A. 2004. "Expensive Taste Rides Again." In *Dworkin and His Critics*, ed. J. Burley. Oxford: Blackwell, 3–29.
Devlin, Patrick. 1959. *The Enforcement of Morals*. Oxford: Oxford University Press.
Dworkin, Ronald. 1985. "Do We Have a Right to Pornography?" In *A Matter of Principle*, Cambridge, MA: Harvard University Press, ch. 17.
Fish, Stanley. 2008. *Save the World on Your Own Time*. Oxford: Oxford University Press.
Geuss, Raymond. 2008. *Philosophy and Real Politics*. Princeton: Princeton University Press.
Gutmann, Amy. 1987. *Democratic Education*. Princeton, NJ: Princeton University Press.

Gutmann, Amy and Dennis Thompson. 2012. *The Spirit of Compromise*. Princeton, NJ: Princeton University Press.

Hart, H.L.A. 2008. *Punishment and Responsibility*, second edition. Oxford: Oxford University Press.

Jubb, Robert and A. Faik Kurtulmus. 2012. "No Country for Honest Men: Political Philosophers and Real Politics." *Political Studies* 60, 539–556.

Kramer, Matthew. 2011. *The Ethics of Capital Punishment*. Oxford: Oxford University Press.

Langton, Rae. 1993. "Speech Acts and Unspeakable Acts." *Philosophy & Public Affairs* 22, 293–330.

Leader Maynard, Jonathan and Alex Worsnip, 2018. "Is There a Distinctively Political Normativity?." *Ethics* 128, 4, 756–787.

Lever, Annabelle. 2005. "Why Racial Profiling Is Hard to Justify: A Response to Risse and Zeckhauser." *Philosophy & Public Affairs* 33, 94–110.

Levinson, Meira. 1999. *The Demands of Liberal Education*. Oxford: Oxford University Press.

MacKinnon, Catherine. 1987. "'Not a Moral Issue' and Francis Biddle's Sister: Pornography, Civil Rights and Speech." In *Feminism Unmodified*. Cambridge, MA: Harvard University Press, 146–162, 163–197.

MacKinnon, Catherine. 1995. *Only Words*. London: Harper Collins.

McDermott, Daniel. 2008. "Analytical Political Philosophy." In *Political Theory: Methods and Approaches*, eds. David Leopold and Marc Stears. Oxford: Oxford University Press, 11–28.

McMahon, Christopher. 2009. *Reasonable Disagreement: A Theory of Political Morality*. Cambridge: Cambridge University Press.

Miller, David. 2008. "Political Philosophy for Earthlings." In *Political Theory: Methods and Approaches*, eds. David Leopold and Marc Stears. Oxford: Oxford University Press, 29–48.

Mitchell, John B. 2012. "Crimes of Misery and Theories of Punishment." *New Criminal Law Review* 15, 465–510.

Pettit, Philip. 1999. *Republicanism: A Theory of Government and Freedom*. Oxford: Oxford University Press.

Rawls, John. 1980. "Kantian Constructivism in Moral Theory." *The Journal of Philosophy* 77, 515–572.

Rawls, John. 1993. *Political Liberalism*. New York: Columbia University Press.

Risse, Matthias and Richard Zeckhauser. 2004. "Racial Profiling." *Philosophy & Public Affairs* 31, 131–170.

Rossi, Enzo and Matt Sleat. 2014. "Realism in Normative Political Theory." *Philosophy Compass* 9, 689–701.

Sandel, Adam Adatto. 2014. *The Place of Prejudice*. Cambridge, MA: Harvard University Press.

Scoccia, Danny. 1996. "Can Liberals Support a Ban on Violent Pornography?" 106, 776–799.

Sen, Amartya. 2009. *The Idea of Justice*. London: Allen Lane.

Sreenivasan, Gopal. 2012. "What Is Non-Ideal Theory?" In *Transitional Justice NOMOS LI*, eds. Williams and J. Elster. New York: New York University Press, 233–256.

Sreenivasan, Gopal. 2007. "Health and Justice in Our Non-Ideal World." *Politics, Philosophy & Economics* 6, 218–236.

Stemplowska, Zofia. 2008. "What's Ideal About Ideal Theory?" *Social Theory and Practice* 34, 319–340.

Stemplowska, Zofia and Adam Swift. 2012. "Ideal and Nonideal Theory." In *Oxford Handbook of Political Philosophy*. Oxford: Oxford University Press.

Sunstein, Cass. 1995. "Incompletely Theorized Agreements." *Harvard Law Review* 108, 1733–1772.

Swift, Adam. 2008. "The Value of Philosophy in Nonideal Circumstances." *Social Theory and Practice* 34, 363–387.

Swift, Adam and Stuart White. 2008. "Political Theory, Social Science, and Real Politics." In *Political Theory: Methods and Approaches*, eds. David Leopold and Marc Stears. Oxford: Oxford University Press.

Tadros, Victor. 2011. *The Ends of Harm*. Oxford: Oxford University Press.

Valentini, Laura. 2009. "On the Apparent Paradox of Ideal Theory." *Journal of Political Philosophy* 17, 332–355.

Valentini, Laura, 2012. "Ideal vs. Non-Ideal Theory: A Conceptual Map." *Philosophy Compass* 7, 654–664.

Vallier, Kevin and Fred D'Agostino. 2014. "Public Justification." In *The Stanford Encyclopedia of Philosophy*, ed. Edward N. Zalta, available at https://plato.stanford.edu/archives/spr2014/entries/justification-public.

Wellman, Christopher Heath. 2006. "A Defense of Stiffer Penalties for Hate Crimes." *Hypatia* 21, 62–80.

Williams, Bernard. 2005. *In the Beginning Was the Deed: Realism and Moralism in Political Argument*. Princeton, NJ: Princeton University Press.

3

APPLICATION OR CONSTRUCTION?

Two types of public policy ethics

Andrei Poama

This chapter offers a conceptual map of the field of public policy ethics as currently practised. I argue that most prominent accounts of public policy ethics (EPP) fall under two general types or styles of theorising. These two types differ in the way they deal with the phenomenon of moral disagreement that punctuates or permeates public policy questions. In the attempt to decide what to make of morally controversial policies one can expect to come across ethical theories that belong to either two of the following salient types. According to the first type, one's moral stance on morally controversial policies needs to be ultimately derived from or constrained by a foundational ethical theory that solves the problem of moral disagreement. According to the second type, one's moral position on policy matters can (and sometimes ought to) be formed independently of the recommendations given by any one particular foundational theory. I call the first type *applied* EPP and the second one *constructive* EPP.[1]

Mapping EPP in terms of these two different types is meant both as a practical tool for the lay public and policy-makers who want to gain a bird's eye view of EPP *and* as an exploration of the theoretical upshots of this difference. I will argue that the two types of EPP are better understood as friends rather than foes. This is to say that, though representatives of the two types of EPP often engage in mutual criticism, EPP *as a whole* is better off if both types of theorising thrive in their own terms and indirectly contribute to each other's research programs.[2]

The chapter proceeds as follows. In the first section, I offer a working definition of EPP and place it in the domain of ethical theorising. I then move on in the second section to specifying the difference between applied and constructive EPP. As stated, the central difference between the two is that applied EPP relies on the premise that the phenomenon of foundational moral disagreement should be approached by formulating a foundational ethical theory *and* further holds that EPP is dependent on that theory, while constructive EPP takes foundational disagreement as an irreducible dimension of ethical thinking and tries to regulate rather than resolve it. On the applied ethics model, one cannot go about doing EPP in the absence of a solution to the problem of moral disagreement. On the constructive ethics model, no such prior solution is required. Finally, I conclude with some thoughts about the relationship between applied and constructive EPP. In particular, I argue that the two types should not be seen as zero-sum competitors, but as potential cooperative partners. Such a conciliatory move is important for defusing two of the objections against EPP – namely, the practical guidance and the under-theorisation objection.

The 'ethics' in 'public policy ethics'

What is EPP, as compared to other ways of ethical theorising? In answering this question, I will assume that EPP is a branch of practical ethics – namely, the branch whose subject matter is *policy* practice.[3] My attempt to delineate the theoretical *locus* of EPP in the space of different kinds of ethical theories is by no means definitive, and has mostly clarificatory purposes.

I will start by noting that the term *ethics* is not always used with the same meaning. A useful strategy for making sense of these different meanings is to rely on a plausible working definition of ethics itself and then distinguish between different kinds of ethics. One such definition is that of ethics as *theorised discourse about the moral domain*. This means that while the moral domain refers to the actual entities considered to be moral (or not) – for instance, actions, decisions, attitudes, dispositions, or entire practices and institutions – ethics refers to our thinking about these entities and how they come (or fail) to be moral. The relevant distinction here is that between ethics as theorising activity and morality as theorised subject matter. Though the terms *ethical* and *moral* are sometimes used loosely in common (or even academic) conversation – for example, when we talk about *ethical conduct* or *moral theory* – a more careful usage will employ the former as a predicate for theory and the latter for that which is being theorised.[4]

A first division of ethics thus construed (i.e., as theorising activity) usually splits it into meta- and normative ethics. Nuances aside, the most widely shared account of the distinction between the two disciplines is that meta-ethics covers theories about the kind of reality morality is and the status of moral judgements, while normative ethics is about theories that answer the normative question of the morally right thing to do. The former inquires into the nature of morality (*what is morality?*), while the latter ponders its normative content (*what should one do in order to be moral?*).

When it comes to meta-ethics, a non-exhaustive list of commonly discussed conceptions are realism, irrealism, and, more recently, constructivism.[5] Roughly formulated, realism argues that morality is made of moral facts and that, as a consequence, moral judgements are beliefs that report a matter of moral fact. Different versions of irrealism, on the other hand, hold that morality is about expressing pro and con attitudes (like in meta-ethical expressivism) or that it consists in imperatives and prescriptions (like in meta-ethical prescriptivism).[6] Finally, constructivism defines morality as part of the domain of practical problems individuals have to solve and construes moral judgements as tentative solutions to those problems.[7]

Unlike meta-ethical theories, normative ethics theories try to answer what I called the *normative question*, which is: *what is the morally right thing to do?* As I read it, the normative question can be either asked in the abstract – that is, *what is the morally right thing to do in general?* – or formulated more concretely, as in *what is the morally right thing to do in this particular case (or set of cases)?* The difference between the abstract and the concrete versions of the question matters, because it further subdivides the field of normative ethics. I will use the term *foundational normative ethics* to refer to those theories that take themselves to offer a fully theorised answer to the abstract version of the normative question and, somewhat unusually, introduce the term *practical normative ethics* to refer to those theories that concentrate on a specific set of practical cases (and not morality as such) as their subject matter.

The domain of foundational normative ethics (or *normative ethics* for short) is usually, if imprecisely, carved up into three contending theories – namely, consequentialism (with utilitarianism being the most prominent version thereof), deontologism (within which Kantian ethics occupies a central position), and virtue ethics (which tends to be specified either in the register of neo-Aristotelian ethics or in terms of feminist or care ethics).[8] These theories offer irreconcilable answers to the abstract normative question. Consequentialism often takes the ultimate principle of right action to reside in the maximisation of aggregate social utility (which can, for example, be understood in terms of pleasure, preference, or interest satisfaction). Deon-tologism takes morally right action to be the action whose motives derive from a sense of duty or the respect of individual rights. Finally, virtue ethics holds that an action is right if it con-tributes to an agent's relevant virtue (say, courage or justice) and, more critically, if it partakes in the agent's ultimate virtue (which can be understood either in terms of moral flourishing on the neo-Aristotelian account or as care on some other conceptions).

The domain of practical normative ethics (or *practical ethics*, for short) is not naturally ordered along the fault lines of foundational normative principles. Rather, it tends to track differences between practices that invite ethical reasoning. In its current state, practical normative ethics lists a series of scattered sub-disciplines, like health care ethics, business ethics, media ethics, criminal justice ethics, drug policy ethics, traffic ethics, engineering ethics, and so on.[9] Going beyond this untidy list would arguably require a systematic account of different practice types that we could then use to structure the domain of practical ethics. This is outside the scope of this chapter. Even so, it will be useful to think about the branches of practical ethics in terms of the kinds of practical interests that they characteristically take to constitute their subject matter. Doing this would present us with a rough distinction between three branches of practical ethics: *personal ethics* (relevant for persons' practical interests), *professional ethics* (pertaining to profes-sional interests), and *public policy ethics* (concerned with the public's interests). This distinction is hardly definitive, but it should be sufficient when it comes to placing EPP on the map of different types of practical ethics.

The field of EPP, as I read it, can be further parsed by looking at how it relates to the domain of foundational normative ethics. Doing this allows us to distinguish between different accounts of EPP on the basis of their commitment to or, conversely, independence from any one par-ticular foundational theory of normative ethics. Thus, there are theories that will be defined in terms of distinct normative conceptions. Take, for instance, Peter Singer's (1975/2002) or Tom Regan's (1983) accounts of the impermissibility of ongoing government policies that enable the eating of non-human animals. Though substantively distinct, both accounts anchor their critique of animal eating in foundational theories of normative ethics, with Singer defending a utilitarian principle that calls for the minimisation of aggregate suffering and Regan arguing for a deontological grounding of animals' individual moral rights.

Conversely, there are theories that rescind any affiliation with specific theories of norma-tive ethics. Take, for example, Mylan Engel's (2012) argument that one should ground the impermissibility of eating (and, therefore, of enabling the eating of) animals without relying on any 'theory that explains what it is about right actions that makes them right and what it is about wrong actions that makes them wrong' (52). Engel thinks that this is possible by assessing impermissibility beliefs according to whether they coherently fit with most of our other moral beliefs – say, beliefs about the moral badness of suffering – instead of tracking them back to foundational principles, like utilitarians or deontologists do. To assess coherence, all we need is an epistemic theory of coherence, not a deep ethical theory. Or so Engel argues.

For the purpose of this chapter, it does not matter whether Singer's, Regan's, or Engel's the-ories are substantively correct. What matters is clarifying the structure of the relation between EPP and the domain of foundational normative ethics. When the relation is organised such that EPP theories are taken to basically apply the content of any one foundational theory to policy practice, it is apt to talk of applied ethics and, more specifically, of utilitarian, deontological, virtue ethics EPP, and so on. When the relation is structured such that the content of EPP is defined in terms of the practical solutions for arbitrating among contending moral views on policy matters, it is apt to talk of constructive EPP.

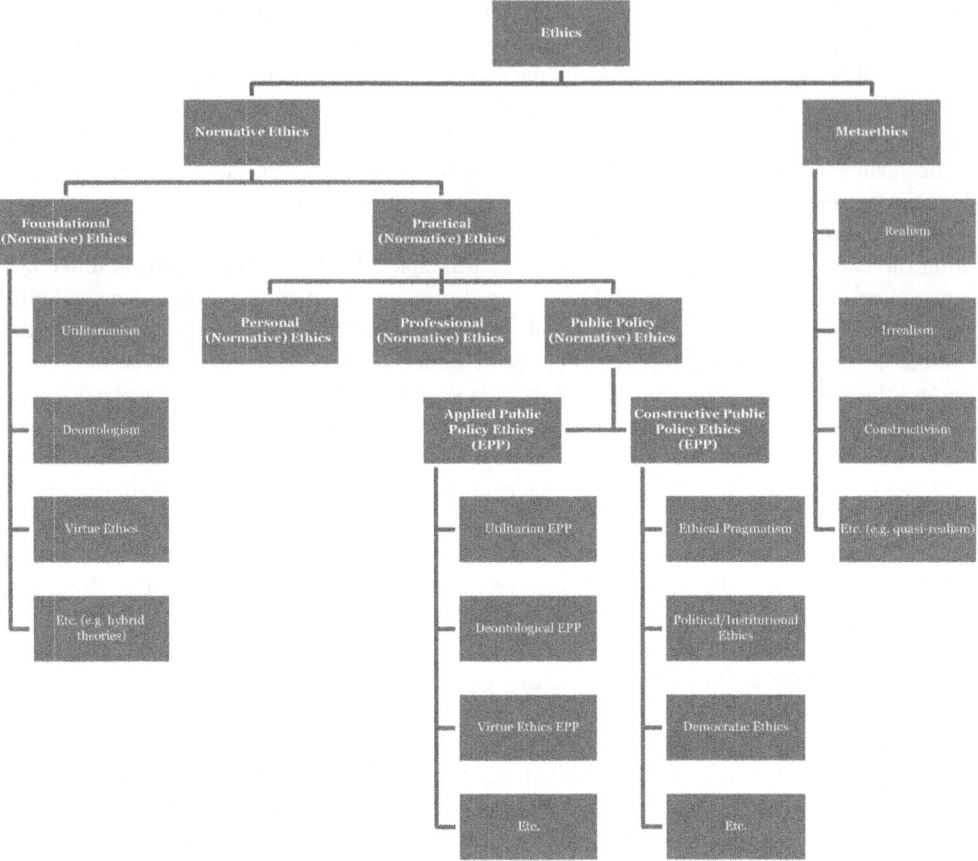

Figure 3.1 Classification of types of ethics

Furthermore, because constructive EPP is not predicated on any specific foundational theory, its underlying varieties will be more adequately referred to in terms of the procedures for managing instances of moral disagreement. Thus, for theories that set an accent on the importance of politics for dealing with morally controversial policies, one can speak of *institutional* or *political ethics*, or, more specifically, of *democratic ethics*. When the emphasis is on moral experiments and the relevance of social inquiry for ethical justification, it will make more sense to talk of *ethical pragmatism*.[10]

My attempt to place EPP within the broad landscape of ethical theorising can be summarised by means of Figure 3.1.

Before addressing the distinction between applied and constructive EPP, I want to highlight some features of this classificatory figure. First, as stated, the classification is not meant as a definitive ordering of ethical theories. Nor is it meant as an exhaustive one, since it excludes disciplines like descriptive ethics or doctrines like ethical relativism. Second, the classification is not a smooth one, in that the classificatory steps are not guided by the same conceptual criterion across the board. For instance, in distinguishing between meta- and normative ethics, the differentiating criterion is whether one asks what morality is (meta-ethics) or what morality should be about (normative ethics). Next, the distinction between different branches of practical ethics is based on the nature of their corresponding practices (personal, professional, or public), while the distinction between applied and constructive EPP is, as we will see in more detail, based on their underlying position towards the problem of fundamental moral disagreement. Third, and finally, the classification allows for further sub- or parallel orderings of additional ethical theories and does not say anything about the merits of the classified theories.

Application or construction? Two types of public policy ethics

The aim of this section is to specify the distinction between applied and constructive EPP. As already indicated, the distinction I defend is one between two standards of success in EPP. One such standard posits that morally justified policies are those that enact moral principles as articulated by the best available theory of (foundational) normative ethics. This is applied EPP. Another standard of success holds that, since there is extensive disagreement about whether such a theory is actually available, justified policies should instead draw on any theory that promises to push public policy towards moral improvements at the margin.[11] This is constructive EPP.

Disagreeing about moral disagreement

Supporters of applied and constructive EPP concur on the idea that morality matters for public policy. However, given that most people, and especially philosophers, disagree on what morality ultimately requires of us, there is ongoing divergence on how morality should be brought to bear on policy issues. Disagreement about what the right moral requirements are occurs both at the practical level – for instance, when we are confronted with morally controversial policy initiatives, like sanctioning hate speech or institutionalising euthanasia – and at the theoretical level, as when we are called to consider which foundational theory in normative ethics – say, utilitarianism, contractualism, or care ethics – should ultimately inform our practices.

Faced with the problem of fundamental moral disagreement, supporters of applied EPP argue that ethical theorising should start by formulating – or, more modestly, identifying – a foundational theory that solves that disagreement. This is typically done by first identifying the criteria that make an action eligible for moral consideration – for example, universality, equality, or stringency – and then showing that there is at least one ethical theory – say, utilitarianism, contractualism, or care ethics – that is well placed to satisfy those criteria. In so doing, supporters of applied EPP aim to show that there is one correct answer to what I called the abstract normative question – namely, *what is the right thing to do in general?* They then proceed to show why the answer given by contending theories to this same question is wrong – thus explaining fundamental moral disagreement away – and conclude with a discussion of the relevant policy implications of their thus putatively vindicated theory.

Unlike their applied counterparts, defenders of constructive EPP hold that the problem of fundamental moral disagreement is far from being settled and that, as a consequence, we are not entitled to hang our minds onto the hook of any one foundational theory. Constructive EPP thus takes disagreement to be a feature, not a bug of ethical thinking. It contends that, given our disagreement about whether morality is a matter of consequences, contracts, care, or some other core value, we should simply shun any presumption in favour of one of the foundational theories. In so doing, constructive EPP holds that there is (or might be) more than one good answer to the abstract normative question and that the real work in EPP will consist mostly in tackling different concrete versions of that question. Constructive EPP thus aims to show that there is no straightforward inference from one's account of normative ethics to one's EPP. To put it in terms of the classificatory figure earlier (Figure 3.1), constructive EPP is premised on the thesis that there is no direct connection between any one distinct conception of foundational normative ethics and any one distinct conception of practical normative ethics.

Note that my distinction between applied and constructive EPP is at least partly a *substantive* one and, as such, differs from the methodological distinction between top-down and bottom-up theorising, where the former consists in inferring ethical conclusions about policy from overarching moral principles in a syllogistic manner, while the latter derives principles from practice (Beauchamp 2003). I take the methodological distinction to be often overplayed, since most plausible EPP theories rely on both top-down and bottom-up reasoning. This is to say that, despite differences in *privileged* methods, there are no purely top-down or bottom-up theories of EPP. Most theories are mixes of the two (and, sometimes, other) methodologies.[12]

Note also that my distinction between the two versions of EPP is orthogonal to the distinction between monistic and pluralistic ethical theories, where the former reduce morality to one single foundational principle, while the latter parse the moral landscape into a plurality of such principles. On my reading, the fact of entertaining a pluralistic account of normative ethics does not necessarily dictate one's approach to EPP. This is because it is possible to imagine pluralistic foundational theories – for example, those developed by W.D. Ross (1930/2002) or McCloskey (1969) – that are then used as fixed frameworks for applied EPP. Thus, one can be a pluralist about foundational normative ethics and advocate applied EPP.

Who's who? The theory and practice of public policy ethics

In the rest of this section, I will try to flesh out the distinction between applied and constructive EPP. I will do this by listing some of the authors that I include in either of the two types, and by pointing to some salient family resemblances that better draw the profile of each type. For reasons of space, the distinction is bound to be broad-brush, and will need to be further nuanced on a later occasion.

The most salient examples of authors who share the applied ethics standpoint are Peter Singer (2011), Robert Goodin (1995), Richard Hare (1989), Bernard Gert (1984), Alan Donagan (1994), and, to some extent, Frances Kamm (2007) and Philip Pettit (Pettit & Marti 2010).[13] Other (numerous) examples of the applied ethics model are those EPP theories that extend a ready-made normative theory – quite often, Rawls's theory of justice – to one or several policy areas, such as anti-discrimination (Carcieri 2015) or criminal justice (Dolovich 2004).[14] What brings these authors under the same banner is their stable normative commitment to *one* normative theory, be that theory utilitarianism (Singer, Goodin, Hare), deontologism (Gert, Kamm), consequentialist republicanism (Pettit), or justice as fairness (some Rawlsians).

Some of the main authors who fit the constructive EPP category are Tom Beauchamp and James Childress (2013/1979), Dennis Thompson (1987), Albert Jonsen and Stephen Toulmin (1989), Jonathan Wolff (2011), John Uhr (2010), Eric Thomas Weber (2011), Andrew Cohen (2015), Annabelle Lever (2017), and most (if not all) the contributors to this volume. These authors will typically acknowledge that plausible EPP accounts are normatively non-committal, in the sense that they do not recognise a presumption in favour of any *one* normative theory at the foundational level. As Wolff (2011) notes, there is 'little prospect of demonstrating that any view is true or correct' (5) in the realm of normative ethics. Similarly, Uhr (2010) contends that 'our task is not to arrive at a consensus about agreed moral belief-systems' (89), and Cohen

(2015) argues that fundamental moral disagreement is not fatal, because 'addressing policy controversies (. . .) might not require resolving theoretical differences' (11).

Though there are various controversies within constructive EPP itself – for instance, about whether we should construe morality in terms of principles or about the degree to which ethics should diverge from the policy *status quo* – what holds the members of this broad philosophical family together is their agreeing that fundamental moral disagreement is here to stay *and* that this does not necessarily pose an obstacle (and might sometimes turn out to be an opportunity) for EPP. Constructive EPP holds that we do not need to wait for foundational convergence on one true (or otherwise best) conception of normative ethics to do EPP. Put differently, constructive EPP champions a non-convergentist position on issues of theoretical normative ethics, while applied EPP is convergentist in the sense that it presumes a normatively correct theory such that EPP can ultimately be referred back to it.[15]

This split between convergentist and non-convergentist attitudes towards the problem of fundamental moral disagreement has significant consequences for both the theory and the practice of EPP. For reasons of space, I will concentrate on only two of the differences in the theory and practice of EPP, as instantiated by the applied and constructive approaches. The first difference concerns the practical aim that ethics should play in relation to public policy. The second difference pertains to the theoretical priorities within each strand of EPP. The rest of this section is dedicated to outlining these two central differences.

On the question of the practical aims of EPP, applied EPP often tracks what I call an *ethos of overall approximation*, whereas constructive EPP usually pursues an *ethos of marginal improvement*. The ethos of approximation holds that EPP's main practical task consists in pulling public policy in the direction of an institutional set-up that best approximates one's normative theory. For example, Robert Goodin (1995) dedicates an entire book to showing that his favoured version of welfare-utilitarianism – which is roughly the idea that morality is about maximising people's overall welfare – is the ultimate target policy-makers and practitioners should be aiming at. Goodin thinks welfare-utilitarianism offers 'a complete normative guide for the conduct of public affairs' (4) and, furthermore, contends that 'it is almost indecent to apply any other [normative conception]' (4) to public policy.

Another example of the ethos of approximation is given by the application of Philip Pettit's republican theory of freedom to José L.R. Zapatero's political program (Pettit & Marti 2010). Pettit's republicanism defends the idea that government action should be geared towards making sure nobody is arbitrarily subjected to another individual or collective agent's will. In the political campaign running before the 2004 elections, Zapatero publicly adopted Pettit's version of republicanism as his governing strategy, and invited Pettit himself to evaluate his government's results at the end of his first mandate in 2008. After assessing Zapatero's policies in various domains – such as education, health care, or the regulation of state agencies – Pettit concluded that it was worth a 9 out of 10 on the normative scale drawn by his conception of republican freedom. This suggests that, on the applied ethics view, the typical practical task of ethical theorising is to provide a measure of the degree to which any given policy arrangement approximates (or diverges from) one's professed normative ideal.

The ethos of marginal improvement is not about practical pull. Rather, it is about practical push. By this, I mean that proponents of constructive EPP care less about pulling policy towards the pre-set destination of any given normative theory. Instead, they are more concerned with the ways in which it is possible to push policy away from practices that are obviously morally problematic. This is, I think, Jonathan Wolff's (2011) point in contending that 'the policy debate is not about ideals', but 'about change' (78). Similarly, Eric Thomas Weber (2011) insists that 'the fundamental problem in ethics (. . .) is that actions, decisions, policies (. . .) are worse than they could be and we need to figure out how to make them better' (68). Given this, the main practical task is to imagine rules and principles that push policy arrangements away from a morally undesirable *status quo*. It is not that of moving them closer to a normative ideal.

An example of marginal improvement is given by Wolff's principle of 'pragmatic equality' that he proposes for the reform of disability policies. The principle states that 'justice for people with disabilities requires that disability does not add to the other injustices in the world' (2011: 154). The principle does not make things perfect, but it promises to make them better. Moreover, Wolff's principle works even in a world where we are not clear about the overall direction that the government's (disability) programs should pursue, in that it shows how, irrespective of the normative ideal you endorse, it's possible to push for an ethically informed reform of the policy *status quo*.[16] From an applied EPP perspective, vindicating a principle like pragmatic equality looks like a bad compromise or business half-done. Seen from a constructive EPP standpoint, this is precisely the practical contribution ethics can realistically hope to bring to policy reform.

Applied and constructive EPP do not diverge only in their understanding of the practical relation between policy and ethics. They also differ in the way they organise their theoretical priorities. On the applied side, most theorising ultimately consists in fully working out one's first-order account of foundational normative ethics. Even when it considers specific policy examples – like the legalisation of euthanasia clinics or the permissibility of canteen nudging – different theories of applied EPP will give priority to figuring whether their underlying foundational theory offers a sound basis for allowing, requiring, or rejecting the policy.

When the implications of the theory look morally objectionable – as when they conflict with our reflective judgements about the policy issue at hand – applied EPP often either attempts to show that the objection is mistaken or, alternatively, draws on the objection in an effort to revise its underlying theory so that its primacy is preserved at the foundational level. The intellectual history of utilitarianism – moving from hedonic utilitarianism (Bentham and Mill) to preference- or welfare-utilitarianism (Singer and Goodin) – can be seen as series of responses to particularly powerful (and often policy-borne) objections, with the end-goal of articulating the correct foundational account of normative ethics. Applied EPP, then, looks like normative ethics by other means.

Unlike its applied counterpart, constructive EPP does not prioritise first-order reasoning about the correct account of foundational normative ethics. To come back to the terminology I introduced in the previous section, constructive EPP does not try to answer the abstract normative question. With fundamental moral disagreement taken as a potentially unsolvable problem, it focuses more on building theories of EPP that are compelling when (and insofar as) we abstain from foundational normative debates. Put differently, constructive EPP prioritises second-order ethical theorising about EPP. Second-order theorising, in this case, refers to EPP accounts that refrain from first-order theorising about the right thing to do *in general* and focus on the policies we have good second-order ethical reasons to pursue *given* our persistent disagreement in the domain of first-order normative theorising.[17] The proposal, then, is that we can rely on second-order ethical accounts of particular policy issues even if we espouse otherwise irreconcilable first-order views at the foundational level. Second-order ethical theories, in short, are those theories we want to have in light of the divergence between our first-order normative theories.

This restraint from first-order normative debates is often visible in the fact that work done in constructive EPP claims no special substantive affiliation with any of the contending conceptions of normative ethics. There is no theory such that it can be coherently characterised in terms of a foundational normative position – say, utilitarian or deontological – *and* constructive in the way I define the latter concept here. A good example of such restraint is Beauchamp and Childress's (1979) formulation of their four principles for health care policy – namely, autonomy, beneficence, non-maleficence, and justice – in a way that sidesteps their disagreeing on whether deontology or utilitarianism is the right foundational account of normative ethics. According to Beauchamp and Childress, deontologists and utilitarians ought to track the four principles at a second-order level of theorising, even if they are otherwise opposed in the way they model morality at the first-order level.

As I see it, there are at least three strands of second-order theorising that are being currently (and fruitfully) pursued within the constructive EPP approach. The first one includes attempts to formulate lower-level (i.e., non-foundational) principles – similar to the one articulated by Beauchamp and Childress – that can be reasonably supported irrespective of one's stand on foundational matters. These principles are often called mid-level, because they occupy an intermediate level of generality between first-order foundational principles – like welfare-maximisation as defended by utilitarians or happiness as developed by neo-Aristotelians – and particular moral judgements. The concept of mid-level principles was articulated by Michael D. Bayles (1986), and mid-principlism has since then fed into various public policy areas, such as the organisation of elections and political campaigns (Thompson 2004), the regulation of intellectual property (Merges 2011), and animal welfare policies (Fraser 2012).

Mid-level principles are usually advocated as mechanisms for bypassing foundational disagreement and securing an adequate, if narrower, basis for ethically informed policies. For Bayles as for others, the point of mid-level principles is that they enable agreement on moral considerations that have an intermediate level of generality – for instance, the principle of proportionality in assigning intellectual property rights or the principle of fairness in the allocation of financial resources between political candidates – even if the agreeing parties otherwise continue to diverge on moral fundamentals. To put it in Bayles's (1986) terms, 'if a particular judgment or rule can be shown to follow from mutually accepted principles, then it is practically justified, even if the disputants disagree about the norms that support or justify the principles' (62). The claim here is that policies can get all the justification they need from mid-level principles without resorting to foundational principles *and* that local agreement about specific mid-level principles is more likely to emerge than agreement on moral fundamentals.[18]

The second strand of constructive EPP is not directly invested in building principles that are more likely to secure ethical agreement. Instead, it focuses on formulating meta-principles for regulating ethical debates about public policy. A topical example here is Gutmann and Thompson's (1990) account of 'principles of preclusion' and 'principles of accommodation'. Principles of preclusion are meant to filter out morally invalid considerations – for instance, by testing whether they are internally coherent – while principles of accommodation regulate the ways in which putatively valid moral considerations are incorporated in policy decisions. Both kinds of principles require that suitable procedures be instituted for regulating policy debates – for instance, a requirement of public justification or a practice of periodic revision of 'important moral decisions' (85). Thus, meta-principles inform the way in which EPP is practically designed.

A third strand of constructive EPP focuses directly on the design of collective decision-making procedures for tackling moral disagreement. Here, there is an increasing amount of reflection that brings democratic theory to bear on EPP. For example, Annabelle Lever (2017) argues that we should use the values we agree on as citizens living in democracies – say, equality or the accountable exercise of power – to assist us in finding answers to otherwise intractable normative questions. In deciding whether a particular policy is justified, the proposal is to

> start from uncontroversial assumptions about democratic rights, duties, institutions and values, which can be treated as provisional fixed points for ethical reflection, and see what follows from them for philosophical controversies (. . .) or the relative merits of competing ethical approaches and values.
>
> *(6)*

The idea here is to rely on a set of democratically recognised propositions to seep through those normative propositions we might disagree on because of our commitment to foundationally contending theories.

Adding to Lever's (2017) 'democracy-centred approach to ethics', there is current work on designing decision procedures for dealing with moral disagreement that might turn out to be highly relevant for EPP. For instance, William MacAskill (2016) argues that, given our fundamental disagreement on the right thing to do in general, we could resort to different electoral methods to decide on the option that is most warranted in particular.[19] MacAskill argues that we can use a modified version of the Borda count – a method that favours broadly endorsed candidates and avoids the narrow majorities sometimes allowed by first-past-the-post voting systems – to decide which option is most supported by otherwise opposed foundational theories. Drawing on MacAskill, we can imagine a framework for EPP where different foundational theories are treated as voters, their rankings of policy options are counted as individual votes (whose weight might vary depending on the credence and relevance of each theory for the policy in question), and specific electoral methods (like the Borda count) are used to compute those votes into ethically justified policy outcomes.

Similarly, Searing and Searing (2016: 105–120) explore three methods for deciding whether a policy is morally justified when different foundational ethical theories value it differently.[20] The first method is simple aggregation: the policy outcome is computed as a *+1* if it is justified on a given theory and as a *−1* if it is not. A policy is conclusively justified if the sum of the scores given by each theory is itself positive. The second method is more fine-grained, in that it introduces a weighting scheme, whereby different theories are given different weights according to their relevance for the policy in question. For example, if the policy is most relevant for people's rights, rights-based ethical theories will have more weight in calculating the final score than, say, utilitarian theories. Third, and finally, Searing and Searing point out that there are policies where, because a categorical yes/no answer makes little sense, the line-drawing method used by casuists might be more adequate. The idea here is that, for each theory, there is a continuum running from 'permissible' to 'not permissible' such that a policy will be positioned towards one of the two ends for each of the continua corresponding to a given ethical theory. The permissibility of any given policy will depend on whether the chart that is constituted by the different permissibility points for each of the continua leans in the general direction of permissibility.

To sum up, most theorising within the constructive EPP framework goes into regulating foundational moral disagreement in a way that generates ethically informed policies. Constructive EPP avoids taking a position in favour of any given foundational theory of normative ethics. It does this most notably by focusing on principles that are indifferent between foundationally opposed normative theories or by devising decision-making procedures that give a fair weight to all of the relevant foundational theories.

As Figure 3.1 shows, most authors included in the constructive EPP category do not tie their theoretical positions to any of the foundational theories I mentioned in the previous section. Rather, in referring to their work, they use expressions that are normatively non-committal, like 'experimental ethics' or ethical pragmatism (Weber), 'democratic ethics' (Weber, Lever), or 'political ethics' (Thompson). This testifies to the fact that EPP is possible without taking a foundational position on questions of normative ethics.

Conclusion: better friends than foes

This chapter defended a distinction between two modes of ethical theorising. I have argued that, as currently practised, EPP is split between an applied and a constructive approach. On the applied approach, the focus is on bringing policy practice closer to theory and on refining theory in a way that prevents or solves the objections coming from practice. On the constructive approach, the emphasis is set on working out ethically justified policies in a way that does not presume that a solution to deep normative questions has been found.

A few remarks are required by way of conclusion. First, it bears repeating that my typology of EPP should not be read as a substantive argument favouring a specific ethical theory over others. Distinguishing between applied and constructive EPP is neither an endorsement nor a repudiation of one of the two approaches. Rather, my position is that each of the two approaches comes with its own set of theoretical and normative problems. For instance, the applied model problematically presumes that there is a correct answer to the abstract normative question, and does this despite historically enduring disputes about what the correct answer is. The constructive model, on the other hand, seems ill-placed in formulating the criteria for determining why a particular consideration counts as a moral one. This is because defending any such particular criterion seems to entail a commitment to a view of normative ethics that the constructive approach is meant to resist.

Second, the typology does not imply that the ongoing background project of articulating a conception of normative ethics is a degenerative one. Figuring out whether the most adequate way to think about morality should track a utilitarian, deontologist, neo-intuitionist, or mixed account remains an important task with potentially desirable practical effects.[21] Rather, the typology is meant to show that the there are other theoretical frameworks beyond the applied ethics one for approaching the morality of public policy.

Third, the typology creates the conceptual space for a more discerning view of varieties of practical ethics that are not structurally amenable to the applied approach. For instance, accounts of virtue ethics that model particular virtues in terms of their specific target-function within a practical domain – say, courage in warfare – without directly grounding them in any one overarching virtue – such as, most prominently, *eudaimonia* – are no longer necessarily criticisable for failing to spell out their normative foundations (Swanton 2003). Extending the distinction between applied and constructive ethics beyond EPP to the general field of practical ethics thus helps us identify relevant differences between theories that might otherwise be lumped together because they rely on confusingly identical terminology.

Fourth, it should be emphasised that the distinction between the two types of EPP is not a dichotomy. Though most authors who reflect on EPP tend to espouse either of these two approaches and to criticise others for not doing so, there is no knockdown *theoretical* ground for favouring one approach over the other *or* for saying that the two cannot benefit from each other. As I see it, each side should encourage more rather than less theorising on the other side. To wit, applied EPP could benefit from the constructive reflection on mid-level principles and decision-making procedures when it comes to rendering its otherwise abstract ethical principles more cogent for policy practice. Conversely, constructive EPP could use the advances in normative ethics – for instance, the formulation of unified foundational theories like Parfit's – to better define the range of considerations that matter for deciding whether a particular policy is justified. Thus, for all their differences, applied and constructive EPP are better thought of as friends rather than foes.

If I am right about the way in which applied and constructive EPP connect to the domain of foundational normative ethics, the two can be deployed in parallel rather than in alternative to each other. This is because they function at different levels of theorising and, as such, cannot come in direct theoretical conflict. Applied EPP is caught in first-order normative theorising – that is, in finding a solution to foundational moral disagreement – while constructive EPP engages mostly in second-order theorising – that is, in theorising those principles or principled practices that we all have moral reasons to follow given our disagreement on moral fundamentals.

Endorsing both modes of theorising might prove beneficial to EPP overall. In particular, it might provide EPP with the resources for answering two (jointly inconsistent) objections that are often raised against it. The first objection is that, in delving into policy questions, ethics risks losing sight of the normative issues that matter philosophically rather than practically. In lowering itself to the level of concrete policy questions, ethics forgoes one of its essential objectives, which is that of formulating the true theory of morality (Gaus 2005). The second objection is that, in prioritising research on moral fundamentals, philosophers neglect reflecting on the more concrete ways in which morality can be brought to bear on practical policy decisions. The first objection is one about under-theorisation in EPP, while the second one is about the deficient action-guidance of ethical theories.

My analysis of applied and constructive EPP helps defuse these two objections. It does so by showing that neither of the two objections tracks EPP as a whole. A lot of the work in *applied* EPP focuses on formulating the correct theoretical account of morality, and is thus relatively immune to the under-theorisation objection. Conversely, a lot of the work in *constructive* EPP deals with bringing ethics to bear on practice, and therefore fares well by the action-guidance objection. If this is correct, then the two objections have less of a bite on EPP overall.

My distinction between applied and constructive EPP thus makes a case for both the theoretical and practical relevance of ethics for public policy. Moreover, it suggests that there are good all-considered reasons for favouring both modes of theorising. Consequently, to the question *application or construction in EPP?*, my answer will tend to be *both, but never combined*.[22]

Acknowledgements

I would like to thank Annabelle Lever, Jonathan Wolff, and the members of my departmental reading group at Leiden University for their useful comments on earlier drafts of this chapter.

Notes

1 Given its ambiguous use in the literature, I define applied ethics somewhat stipulatively. Even so, those who refer to their work as applied ethics most often fit my characterization and the authors I associate with the constructive ethics model rarely characterise their work as applied ethics. The term *constructive EPP* should not be directly associated with the constructivist position in normative ethics, as represented by John Rawls, Onora O'Neill, or Christine Korsgaard. As it will become clear in the following sections, applied and constructive EPP are accounts of practical ethics, not distinct conceptions of normative ethics.

2 Wolff defends a partly similar argument in this section.
3 Practical ethics as a distinctive discipline goes back at least to the end of the 1960s and the beginning of the 1970s, when (especially British and US) moral philosophers start reflecting about some specific policy questions, such as nuclear deterrence, anti-discrimination programs, and abortion.
4 The distinction here is a strictly pragmatic one meant to clarify whether one is referring to theories or actions and practices that are being theorised.
5 For a more detailed picture of meta-ethics, see Copp (2006).
6 These two examples are by no means exhaustive of irrealism.
7 Bagnoli (2013).
8 See Baron, Pettit, and Slote (1997). For a unified view of normative ethics, see Parfit (2011).
9 For a survey of these different domain-specific sub-disciplines, see Hansson (2011).
10 These examples of constructive accounts of EPP are by no means exhaustive.
11 This is not to say that constructive EPP is necessarily bound to seek marginal improvements over profound policy reforms. Note also that marginal is not the same as minor and that, consequently, marginal improvements can sometimes be substantial.
12 Paulo (2016).
13 Including Pettit in this list is premised on the idea that his republicanism is a non-utilitarian version of consequentialism – namely, a consequentialism of freedom applied to politics and public policy. Thus construed, Pettit's republicanism counts as applied ethics.
14 For an inventory of different application of Rawls, see Doorn (2009).
15 For a critique of convergentism in meta-ethics, see Blackburn (1998).
16 For a view that partly overlaps with Wolff's, see Putnam in this volume.
17 I use the concept of second-order theorising in a way that draws on Joseph Raz's (1990) concept of second-order reasons.
18 The claim about a higher probability of agreement on mid-level (as opposed to foundational) principles relies on an implicit proposition, which is that the probability of X is higher than the probability of X and Y. Because of their narrower practical scope, mid-level principles cover shorter conjunctive chains of ethical propositions about practical cases than foundational ones, thus gaining a higher probability for ethical agreement. Bayles's claim about the probability of mid-level agreement is, then, a conceptual and not a normative one.
19 MacAskill articulates his proposal at the individual level, but there is no principled reason for not extending it to the inter-individual/public policy level.
20 This should not be confused with the policy analysis methods used for designing and selecting policies all things considered (where only some reasons are moral ones).
21 One such effect is given by the (policy) debates initiated by Singer's (1975/2002) critique of the animal meat industry.
22 This is because one cannot non-contradictorily both commit and not commit to a given theory of normative ethics.

References

Bagnoli, C. (ed.) (2013). *Constructivism in Ethics*. Cambridge: Cambridge University Press.
Baron, M., Pettit, P., Slote, M.A. (1997). *Three Methods of Ethics*. Oxford: Blackwell.
Bayles, M. (1986). Mid-Level Principles and Justification. Pennock, R.J., Chapman, J.W. (eds.). *Justification*. New York: New York University Press, 49–67.
Beauchamp, T.L. (2003). The Nature of Applied Ethics. Frey, R.G., Wellman, C.H. (eds.). *A Companion to Applied Ethics*. Malden, MA: Blackwell.
Beauchamp, T.L., Childress, J.F. (2013/1979). *Principles of Biomedical Ethics*. New York: Oxford University Press.
Blackburn, S. (1998). *Ruling Passions: A Theory of Practical Reasoning*. Oxford: Oxford University Press.
Carcieri, M. (2015). *Applying Rawls to the Twenty-First Century. Race, Gender, the Drug War, and the Right to Die*. Dordrecht: Springer.
Cohen, A. (2015). *Philosophy, Ethics, and Public Policy. An Introduction*. New York: Routledge.
Copp, D. (ed.) (2006). *The Oxford Handbook of Ethical Theory*. Oxford: Oxford University Press.
Dolovich, S. (2004). Legitimate Punishment in Liberal Democracy. *Buffalo Criminal Law Review*, 7(2): 307–442.

Donagan, A. (1994). *The Philosophical Papers of Alan Donagan*. Chicago: University of Chicago Press.

Doorn, N. (2009). Applying Rawlsian Approaches to Resolving Ethical Issues: Inventory and Setting of a Research Agenda. *Journal of Business Ethics*, 91: 127–143.

Engel Jr., M. (2012). Coherentism and the Epistemic Justification of Ethical Beliefs: A Case Study in How to Do Practical Ethics Without Appeal to a Moral Theory. *The Southern Journal of Philosophy*, 50(1): 50–74.

Fraser, D. (2012). A "Practical" Ethics for Animals. *Journal of Agricultural and Environmental Ethics*, 25(5): 721–746.

Gaus, G. (2005). Should Philosophers Apply Ethics? *Think*, 3(9): 63–68.

Gert, B. (1984). Moral Theory and Applied Ethics. *The Monist*, 67(4): 532–548.

Goodin, R.E. (1995). *Utilitarianism as a Public Philosophy*. Cambridge: Cambridge University Press.

Gutmann, A., Thompson, D. (1990). Moral Conflict and Political Consensus. *Ethics*, 101(1): 64–88.

Hansson, S.O. (2011). The Topics of Applied Ethics. *Theoria*, 77: 195–197.

Hare, R. (1989). *Essays on Political Morality*. Oxford: Clarendon Press.

Jonsen, A., Toulmin, S. (1989). *The Abuse of Casuistry: A History of Moral Reasoning*. Berkeley: University of California Press.

Kamm, F. (2007). *Intricate Ethics: Rights, Responsibilities, and Permissible Harm*. Oxford: Oxford University Press.

Lever, A. (2017). Towards a democracy-centred ethics. *Critical Review of International Social and Political Philosophy*. (online first).

MacAskill, W. (2016). Normative Uncertainty as a Voting Problem. *Mind*, 125: 967–1004.

Mccloskey, H.J. (1969). *Meta-Ethics and Normative Ethics*. Dordrecht: Springer.

Merges, R.P. (2011). *Justifying Intellectual Property*. Cambridge, MA: Harvard University Press.

Parfit, D. (2011). *On What Matters*, vols. 1 & 2. Oxford: Oxford University Press.

Paulo, N. (2016). *The Confluence of Philosophy and Law in Applied Ethics*. London: Palgrave Macmillan.

Pettit, P., Marti, J.L. (2010). *A Political Philosophy in Public Life: Civic Republicanism in Zapatero's Spain*. Princeton, NJ: Princeton University Press.

Raz, J. (1990). *Practical Reasons and Norms*. Princeton, NJ: Princeton University Press.

Regan, T. (1983). *The Case for Animal Rights*. Berkeley: University of California Press.

Ross, W.D. (1930/2002). *The Right and the Good*. Oxford: Oxford University Press.

Searing, E.A.M., Searing, D.R. (2016). Ethical Decision-Making. Searing, E.A.M., Searing, D.R. (eds.). *Practicing Professional Ethics in Economics and Public Policy*. Dordrecht: Springer.

Singer, P. (1975/2002). *Animal Liberation*. New York: Harper Collins.

Singer, P. (2011). *Practical Ethics*, 2nd edition. New York: Cambridge University Press.

Swanton, C. (2003). *Virtue Ethics: A Pluralistic View*. Oxford: Oxford University Press.

Thompson, D. (1987). *Political Ethics and Public Office*. Cambridge, MA: Harvard University Press.

Thompson, D. (2004). *Just Elections: Creating a Fair Electoral Process in the United States*. Chicago: University of Chicago Press.

Uhr, J. (2010). Be Careful What You Wish for. Boston, J., Bradstock, An., Eng, D. (eds.). *Public Policy: Why Ethics Matters*. Canberra: Australian National University Press.

Weber, E.T. (2011). *Morality, Leadership, and Public Policy: On Experimentalism in Ethics*. London, New York: Continuum.

Wolff, J. (2011). *Ethics and Public Policy: A Philosophical Inquiry*. New York: Routledge.

4

PUBLIC POLICY AND NORMATIVE METHODS

Albert Weale

Introduction

A legislature permits physician-assisted suicide. A government forbids human stem-cell research. Countries agree an international treaty to stop human trafficking. A consumer movement boycotts goods produced by exploited child labour. A referendum endorses same-sex marriage. A constitution protects family life. Such examples illustrate how public policy issues can have a clear ethical character. In such cases, ethical concepts – concepts like professional duties, respect for persons, or the sanctity of human life – play a decisive role in coming to a judgement, individually and collectively, on what is the right policy or constitutional principle.

Such issues are clearly ethical, but they are not the only public policy issues prompting ethical reflection. Indeed, few, if any, issues of public policy are exempt from potential ethical appraisal. Seemingly technical sectors of policy, like banking or commercial regulation, involve questions of social responsibility or the legitimate exercise of corporate power. For example, the law may restrict the types of contracts that finance companies may enter into with their customers, limiting chargeable interest rates, in order to prevent exploitation of the poor. Commercial advertising may be regulated to preserve truthfulness and prevent public offence. High salaries of chief executives may be controlled to reduce unjust enrichment. Since any human activity is potentially subject to ethical appraisal, normative reasoning is not the preserve of specific sectors of public policy labelled 'ethical'. Ethical considerations are always latent in any public policy.

Normative reasoning in policy

It is common to make a sharp distinction between the empirical study of how public policies are made and the normative study of how those policies may be justified and evaluated. Explaining why a policy was adopted is logically distinct from justifying or evaluating that policy. What is and what ought to be are separate. Sometimes governments do what they ought not to do, or do not do what they ought to do. The wrong policies can be adopted or the right policies rejected as a result of vested interests or prejudice. Without contrasting the empirical and normative, it would be impossible to make these elementary distinctions. However, a rigid distinction between the empirical and the normative disguises the extent to which policymaking is a matter of 'evidence, argument and persuasion in the policy process' (Majone, 1989).

Understanding how policies are made requires essential reference to the arguments used by policy actors, and such arguments can themselves be evaluated and their merits assessed.

In the making of policy actors advocate policy positions in coalition with others who share a similar policy position, and they face competing coalitions advocating opposing arguments and policy choices. Often the competition of ideas relates solely to the comparative efficiency of different policy instruments – for example, the relative merits of pollution charges and administrative regulation for environmental protection or the comparative efficacy of tax cuts versus interest rate reductions in stimulating the economy. Where goals are agreed, policy arguments over instruments and their settings can still be pervasive. However, on many occasions, policy advocacy engages the 'deep normative core' (Sabatier, 1987: 667; Jenkins-Smith, Nohstedt, Weible and Ingold, 2018: 140) of the positions that different actors hold, invoking such ideas as the legitimate role of the state or the boundaries of personal responsibility. For example, some environmental policy advocates resist the use of pollution charges as instruments of policy because they have an ethical concern about the extent to which adopting such a device implies putting a monetary price on nature. In tax policy some advocate the principle of neutrality between individuals of different marital status, holding that the state should be impartial between different conceptions of marriage and sexual partnership, whereas others believe that the tax system has a role in supporting the institution of traditional marriage. In education policy, many think the value of parental choice makes a difference to judgements about the justice of private education or the provision of religious education in schools. In urban renewal policies, questions arise about fair access for the poor to open spaces and public transport. Located at the core of policy arguments, normative considerations can be crucial in shaping choices between policy alternatives.

Questions about the appropriate balance between markets and administrative regulation draw upon ideas of personal freedom and responsibility, just as issues about educational provision or sub-national government draw upon ideas about cultural diversity or the value of the wide sharing of power in democracy. Ethical principles, like that of personal responsibility, or views about the legitimate role of the state do not float free and independent in policy debate. Instead they hang together in characteristic and relatively enduring ways defining distinctive policy positions over time. For example, those who advocate the use of market-mimicking instruments in environmental or health policies – favouring pollution charges over administrative regulation in environmental policy or personal budgets for patients to buy health and social care services – typically hold not only that such instruments are economically more efficient than conventional regulation but also that their use decentralises decision making in ways that are intrinsically valuable. Public policy advocacy is a form of a contest among ideas joined together in webs of belief linking goals, instruments, and conceptions of social and political order.

Policy choice also involves partisan contest by political parties and social movements who define their distinctive identity as being liberal, libertarian, conservative, social democrat, environmental, feminist, socialist, and so on. In other words, both policy advocacy and paradigms are linked in political contest to competing ideologies, ideologies being understood as systems of political thinking through which individuals and groups construct an understanding of the political and policy world combined with claims about how to act given that understanding (compare Freeden, 1996: 3). Ideologies thus link value commitments to empirical claims, the union of these forming a general conception of society and social relations. Consider employment policy as an example. Should full employment be taken to be a goal of public policy or not? Answers to this question involve disputes in economic theory about the conditions under which slumps in activity in the economy can be overcome by public spending. Differences also turn on the question of what institutional arrangements are in place for the conduct of economic policy – for example, the mandate given to central banks. However, an important source of dispute is about how governments acquire a democratic mandate for policy action and whether the freedom to work is primarily a matter of the lifting of constraints on the right to compete in the labour market or the positive creation of opportunities to be employed. How the freedom to work is defined relates to broader ideological differences about the role of government in the economy and the decentralisation of decision making in society.

As well as ideological traditions, policy paradigms also draw upon or implicitly make use of certain philosophical assumptions, whether those assumptions be utilitarian, rights-based, or pluralistic. In many countries the philosophical tradition of utilitarianism in particular has been important in shaping policy and political cultures, reflecting the intellectual origins of welfare economics in utilitarian thought and the standing of economics as a discipline in the policy process. For example, over many years, UK pollution control policy was implicitly utilitarian, based on the principle that the benefits of pollution control should be balanced against their costs, with the task of the pollution regulator being to promote the overall well-being of society. Precepts from the utilitarian philosophical tradition were thereby embedded in practical decision processes until they came under the challenge of principles that stressed precaution and the protection of citizens from the hazards of a risk society (Owens, 2015).

Empirical policy studies thus underscore the view that the policy process is a contest of ideas, arguments, and principles. The making of public policy is not simply a matter of the pulling and hauling of mechanical forces; it is also a matter of advocacy and persuasion, as proponents of different points of view engage in argument and counter-argument over the right course of public action. So, public policy-making is a matter of practical public reasoning. It is practical, because it concerns the right course of action. It is public, because it concerns the use of public authority and because in a democracy policy arguments are conducted openly in the public forum as well as privately within the corridors of power. And it is reasoning, because competing policy advocates seek to connect the premises of policy arguments to social values, policy principles, empirical evidence, and ideological positions into a persuasive set of considerations 'capable of determining the intellect' (Mill, 1861: 135).

From this characterisation of the policy process, one important methodological implication follows. If the policy process is the site of practical reasoning, then the techniques and methods used to understand policy arguments from a normative point of view are also required to understand policy arguments from an empirical point of view. The normative analysis involves the identification of policy arguments as those arguments are advanced in the making of policy. Such arguments are usually recorded in party programmes, major speeches by politicians, government reports and reviews, hearings of parliamentary committees, coalition government agreements, reports from think tanks and academics, journalistic commentary, and so on. These sources form the texts of public policy, collections of sentences, both written and spoken, containing policy arguments. Understanding such texts requires interpretation to determine the role normative values play in policy arguments, both in relation to the empirical task of understanding what values and principles were influential in forming policy and for the normative task of evaluating the justification of a policy choice that was made in the light of those values and principles.

An important skill in this context is that of logical reconstruction. Within the decision-making process, policy arguments are typically stated in a piecemeal way, often making many taken-for-granted assumptions rather than stating fully articulated chains of reasoning. Logically speaking, the policy texts are usually made up of enthymemes: incomplete fragments of argument rather than a fully articulated chain of reasoning linking premises to conclusion. The theoretical task is to recover and reconstruct the full chains of reasoning suggested by those enthymemes. The relevant methods involve the identification of key principles and values and the delineation of the logical patterns by which key ideas related to one another. For example, in the UK blood transfusion system, blood donors are required not only to consent to have their blood tested for infectious diseases but also to consent to be told the results of those tests. Why not opt for a policy of testing and then discarding contaminated blood in those few cases where donors have been found not to know their infected status? The answer is that the service values the integrity of the relationship that it has with its donors, and does not want to stand in a false position with respect to those donors. Such a value commitment is typically implicit rather than explicit, but it would be an essential element in any chain of reasoning that sought to reconstruct the rationale of the policy requiring consent to being told the test results.

It is one thing to reconstruct a pattern of policy reasoning; it is another to evaluate a pattern of reasoning assessing how far it is justified. Beyond the analysis of texts to reconstruct chains of policy argument, there is the evaluation of principles and values found in those arguments. It is at this point that a difference of perspective opens up between empirical and normative approaches. When studying policy-making, empirical political scientists typically take up a third-person perspective. They are concerned to identify which principles and ways of thinking influence policy developments over time or which body of ideas shapes cross-national variations in policy preferences and choices. In this respect, they adopt the role of observers rather than actors. By contrast, normative political theorists typically adopt a first-person plural perspective. They ask not '*what did influential agents think* were the principles and values relevant to a policy problem?' but '*which principles and values should we adopt* in relation to a policy problem?' In this regard, they take the same viewpoint as policy-makers themselves. The stance of policy-makers is concerned with practical reasoning from the first-person point of view rather than the observational reasoning of political scientists from the third-person point of view. Normative theorists, like policy-makers, look to connect the understanding of principles and action in a chain of practical reasoning justifying or at least suggesting the eligibility of a course of public action.

Yet, while normative theorists and policy-makers share this first-person point of view, they characteristically differ from one another in the way in which they relate decision premises to conclusions. From a policy-maker's point of view, political and policy agreement often requires those holding different and incompatible premises to share a common policy conclusion. If conservatives, socialists, and greens can agree on measures for environmental protection, it is relatively insignificant from the practical policy point of view that they do it for different reasons. If conservatives wish to preserve national heritage, socialists wish to bring about the modernisation of production methods, and greens wish to respect the intrinsic value of the natural world, all may concur on policies of environmental regulation.

Normative political theorists take the opposite point of view. Because their focus is on the premises of practice policy reasoning, they distinguish among the different types of reasons that will lead to the same conclusion. An argument for environmental protection that appeals to the value of national heritage has a different character from an argument that appeals to the importance of internalising externalities to achieve an economically efficient allocation of resources, which in turn will have a different character from an argument based on the intrinsic value of nature. Differences in the assumptions that policy advocates adopt are what matters to normative theorists. Policy-makers welcome consensus on action despite differences of premises, principles, and values; political theorists seek to distinguish premises, principles, and values despite consensus on action.

Moreover, normative theorists have an interest in ideas in themselves by contrast with policy-makers, for most of whom the sole interest lies in assessing the implications of ideas for policy choices. For political theorists, the deep normative core of policy choices is the focus of their subject of study. Since normative ideas are always latent in policy processes and may become manifest in decision, there are at least three tasks that normative analysis can perform in relation to those ideas:

1 It can identify and formulate in relatively rigorous terms key concepts that form the principles and values of policy reasoning.
2 It can identify the patterns of argument used in policy processes, linking those patterns to well-established philosophical accounts of normative reasoning.
3 It can assess the extent to which those patterns of argument do or do not justify the policy arguments and the conclusions drawn from those arguments.

Conceptual analysis

Within the deep normative core of policy discussion and advocacy, concepts like freedom, rights, equality, and democracy are frequently used. A public works programme may be introduced to give people the freedom to work. A data sharing policy may fall foul of the right to personal privacy. A wealth tax may be imposed to promote greater economic equality. Such policy positions are unintelligible unless reference is made to the relevant value concepts. However, the way in practice in which core values are introduced into policy discussions is often ambiguous. An important analytical task is to remove this ambiguity, because the practical import of policy principles depends upon the meaning of those. Moreover, within a democracy, removing ambiguity is important in itself, since negative or low-quality campaigning and poor policy advocacy often rest on the systematically ambiguous use of words or on slogans (like 'Make America great again') that mean nothing at all, the latter being, to use Frankfurt's (2005) term, bullshit.

When claims are ambiguous, rather than just meaningless, a useful technique is to distinguish between *concepts* on the one hand and *conceptions* on the other. A concept is the core idea that gives a basic meaning to a term, whereas a conception is one of the different forms that the core idea can take. In a well-known analysis, Gerald MacCallum (1967) suggested that freedom as a concept should be understood as a three-place relation, holding between persons, the actions that those persons could perform, and the constraints to which they might be subject. When we talk about freedom we are always – implicitly if not explicitly – talking about persons or agents, who may or may not be subject to constraints in relation to some activity or process of becoming to which they aspire. Differences in definitions of freedom correspond to the different ways in which we can think about these three elements.

As an example consider how this technique might be used to understand the idea of the 'freedom to work'. Some understand the freedom to work as a right to compete for work in the labour market unconstrained by legal burdens. Thus, the removal of feudal restrictions on freedom of movement or the abolition of internal passport controls on the movement of people is sufficient to secure the freedom to work. By contrast, others see the freedom to work as a right of individuals to be secured work if the labour market fails. On this second understanding, the freedom to work is not achieved solely by absence of legal restrictions, but also requires consideration of the aggregate effects of labour supply during economic slumps. These contrasting definitions are related to broader differences of opinion about how labour markets function, or whether economic slumps can be counteracted by government spending. Between policy advocates who think of the freedom to work merely as absence of legal restrictions and policy advocates who propose securing the freedom to work through positive social programmes there is a difference of view about what counts as a constraint. For the former, the relevant constraint is the legal system; for the latter it is the state of the labour market. Both agree on the core concept: the freedom to work is the ability to undertake productive activity for reward; they disagree about the conditions under which this freedom is present or absent and in that sense they hold different conceptions of that freedom.

Competing conceptions of key policy-related ideas thus define competing ideological positions in policy debates. If we interpret the freedom to work as the ability to seek work in a labour market, unconstrained by feudal obligations, but without any guarantee of finding suitable employment, then we have one element of the liberal individualist theory of freedom of contract associated with the rise of laissez-faire. By contrast, if the freedom to work is held to be constrained by deficiencies in the labour market brought about through a slump caused by lack of aggregate demand in the economy, then we have a conception of the freedom of work associated with collectivist attempts to go beyond laissez-faire. The ideological contrast between collectivism and individualism in part rests on these different conceptions of the same concept. Because ideologies are schemes of thought that define political concepts in particular ways, they decontest those concepts into particular conceptions (Freeden, 1996: 76).

Conceptual clarification is sometimes thought to be a minor task, confining the political theorist to the role of under-labourer. However, this charge neglects the importance of conceptual analysis as the inevitable preliminary to further work. As the example of the freedom to work goes to show, understanding the logical structure of a concept and specifying the different conceptions associated with that logical structure connect to differences in broader orientations in policy advocacy. Even when more is needed than conceptual analysis, an important function of such analysis is to diagnose situations in which partisan advocates talk past one another in public policy debates. When partisans are using different conceptions of key ideas, the crucial debate is not conceptual (what 'the freedom to work' *really* means) but substantive: under what conditions does productive activity take place and what are the implications of having one set of conditions in place rather than another set. Policy rhetoric is replaced by careful policy analysis (compare Carter, 2015).

Policy argument and practical reasoning

Normative concepts are the elementary particles of practical public reasoning, identifying and distinguishing the different positions that policy advocates take. However, normative analysis is also needed to understand the different ways in which these elementary particles are bound together, and linked to broader assumptions about the role of government in society. Key normative concepts in policy advocacy are embedded within broader patterns of argument. These patterns of argument replicate forms of argument found in different normative theories, such as utilitarianism, intuitionism, and rights theory.

Consider the pattern of policy argument that derives from welfare economics and so ultimately from utilitarianism. In this pattern the key normative concepts define policy goals (e.g., prosperity, scientific innovation, population health, national security), and the structure of practical reasoning enjoins the policy-maker to maximise the achievement of these goals, subject to budgetary or other constraints. In this maximising pattern of argumentation, governments and policy-makers are assumed to be taking decisions for the whole of society; their goals are supposed to promote the interest of society as a whole or some relevant portion it – for example, the sick.

A good example of this approach is provided by the principles of priority setting for health care resources used in the UK by the National Institute for Health and Care Excellence (NICE) (see NICE, 2008, for a statement). The approach aims at the greatest possible improvement in health status for the population at any given level of expenditure. The goal is to maximise health gain, treating all individuals equally as potential beneficiaries. To achieve this goal, NICE's decision procedure evaluates interventions – pharmaceuticals, surgery, or preventive measures – by their incremental cost-effectiveness ratio, defined as the added value a new intervention offers for the extra cost it involves per patient. The procedure is like taking books down from a shelf in which the tallest books (representing interventions with greatest effect per unit of expenditure) are removed first until the budget can afford no more books (Culyer, 2016). Applied over time and assuming that relatively cost-ineffective treatments are withdrawn, the NICE decision process should mean that every intervention funded is more cost-effective than any intervention not funded. In consequence, there will be maximum health gain for any given level of expenditure. Of course, many questions arise as to how the approach can be operationalised, but the most distinctive feature of this pattern of public reasoning is its maximising form. It assumes the good of health gain as a goal and judges courses of action right or wrong by reference to the extent to which that goal is advanced. In a broad sense it is utilitarian.

A maximising paradigm requires commensurability of competing goals. However, commensurability is sometimes unobtainable. Where we find a plurality of goals not comparable with one another by a common measure, then we find forms of policy argument requiring a judgement among incommensurable considerations. Consider the balancing of increased security in a time of terrorist threats against the demands of personal freedom. An increase in terrorist threats will typically lead governments to reduce personal liberties. The police may be given wider powers to detain suspects and question them, intelligence services are permitted to track emails and other communication, spokespersons for particular organisations may be prevented from speaking in public, security procedures are tightened at airports, and general street surveillance may be increased. All of these measures will reduce individual liberty. However, insofar as they are effective, they will also increase personal security. Yet, there is no obvious way of bringing these two sets of consequences together in a common measure. A utilitarian might say that one should measure the loss in personal freedom against the gain in the value of personal security, reducing personal freedom to the point where the value of the marginal loss is equal to the value of the marginal gain. But by what measuring rod are these gains and losses to be compared? The decision-maker has to make a value judgement. The philosophical theory that parallels such a pattern of policy argumentation is intuitionism as formulated by Ross (1930) and discussed by Rawls (1999: 30–6). According to the intuitionist, normative reasoning consists of an irreducible plurality of principles or values without there being any higher-order theoretical structure, like utilitarian maximisation, to guide the process of balancing (compare Barry, 1965: 3–8).

A third distinct pattern of reasoning is rights-based. Consider, for example, the First Amendment to the US Constitution, which says that Congress shall make no laws abridging freedom of speech, or Article 12(2) of the German Basic law, which says that no person may be required to perform work except within the framework of a traditional duty of community service applying generally and equally to all. These formulations do not establish goals that it is the task of government to maximise. Rather they create constraints on the pursuit of any goals that governments might pursue. The First Amendment right to freedom of speech does not provide a basis for the US government actively to promote freedom of speech – for example, by establishing a system of public broadcasting. Rather, the principles are constraints on the powers that government can exercise. The pursuit of goals may be restricted by respect for rights.

In these three examples, different forms of policy reasoning correspond to the ethical theories of utilitarianism, intuitionism, and rights theory. The analysis of policy reasoning thus recapitulates the philosophical understanding of three of the principal methods of ethics. For convinced proponents of any one of these methods of ethics, this parallel suggests that disputes in public policy can be resolved by the adoption of the correct method of ethics. However, at this point there is a clear danger of logical circularity. If a correct method of ethics can be assumed, then patterns of practical policy reasoning should conform to that pattern. However, it is begging the question to assume that there is an identifiable correct method of ethics. Practical public reasoning is not simply a matter of choosing a philosophical method and applying it mechanically (compare Wolff, 2011: 9). It is a process of determining the inter-relationship between particular judgements on the one hand and patterns of normative reasoning on the other. In short, it is a matter of whether practical public reasoning is susceptible to evaluation through higher-order techniques of analysis.[1]

Evaluation and accountability

One of the central methods in normative analysis is the use of reflective equilibrium in the Rawlsian mode (Rawls, 1999: 18–19, 42–5). Reflective equilibrium tests ethical theories by the extent to which their application yields conclusions consistent with 'our considered judgments' (Rawls 1999: 19). For example, to use the example familiar from Rawls, if a purported theory of justice carried the implication that under certain conditions slavery would be justified, then that theory would be deficient by the test of reflective equilibrium. Similarly, when we understand particular policy positions as implications of policy paradigms, we can test how much intellectual credibility can be given to that paradigm by seeing whether its practical implications are consistent with our considered judgements. For example, if a liberal paradigm stressing personal responsibility led to the conclusion that it was an acceptable public policy to allow individuals to starve if they had brought their misfortune on themselves, for many people that would be a decisive count against that paradigm.

Some ethical theorists reject the method of reflective equilibrium, arguing that if we start with justifiable premises and reason soundly, then we should be willing to accept the implications of our principles come what may. Gauthier (1986: 269) argues for this position. While he acknowledges that his theory of justice entails, counter-intuitively, that the able-bodied have no obligations of justice to the disabled, he takes this to be a regrettable implication of an otherwise sound theory rather than a decisive rejection. Yet, there are at least two problems with rejecting reflective equilibrium. Firstly, without reflective equilibrium, one cannot tell the difference between a strikingly counter-intuitive, but valid, implication of an ethical theory on the one hand and a *reductio ad absurdum* on the other. A *reductio ad absurdum* works by drawing out the untoward conclusions of a set of premises showing those premises to lead to absurd conclusions. Such arguments are well known and understood within patterns of normative argument. Secondly, public policy recommendations have to meet a test of political legitimacy and general acceptability. If the members of a society know that they will not be able to allow their fellow citizens to starve even as a result of those citizens' lack of personal responsibility, then a policy position that advocated such an outcome would simply lack practical relevance. Indeed, even libertarian writers like Hayek (1960: 285–6) have argued for some basic redistribution on the grounds that in the absence of a scheme guaranteeing protection from poverty, citizens would be subject to moral blackmail by those who were destitute as a result of their own irresponsibility.

However, as the examples of slavery or destitution show, the method of reflective equilibrium presupposes that there is a general social consensus about matters of value or principle that can provide the touchstone by which implied judgements can be assessed. Slavery or preventing starvation, at least in societies where there is an ethos of basic human decency (Barry, 1989: 352), are examples where a general social consensus forbids their occurrence. However, beyond such core examples, even in decent societies, there may not be the social consensus required for the method of reflective equilibrium to persuade. Consider, again, the broadly utilitarian paradigm exemplified by the NICE principles of priority setting in health care. Normative theorists have raised many questions about the plausibility of NICE's approach, criticising its reasoning's simple maximising structure. A policy of maximising total health gain can lead to a preference for treating a large number of people with a relatively minor condition as against treating a small number of people each of whom has a serious condition. The approach equates medical need with the ability to benefit from an intervention, although some think that those in greatest need should be given priority, even when their chance of gaining health is relatively low. The approach pays no attention to special circumstances – for instance, patients at the end of their lives, where there might be a case for priority over and above considerations of cost-effectiveness. It ignores considerations of personal responsibility in bringing about the condition that is being treated. These critiques of the policy paradigm are echoes of the familiar philosophical critiques of utilitarianism, at least in its simple maximising form.

However, it is not easy to establish how decisive these objections are in undermining the legitimacy and justification of the NICE paradigm. Paradigms of practical reasoning do not function mechanistically. In the process of their application they are developed through modifications and amendments, some of them *ad hoc* and others more fundamental. The question of whether to abandon a paradigm of reasoning is not settled by identifying counter-intuitive implications, since those implications may be dealt with through modification as NICE has done in respect of end-of-life situations (Rumbold et al., 2017). Within Rawls's own theory the method of reflective equilibrium does not have this indeterminacy, since Rawls relies upon the assumption that his principles of justice apply in a well-ordered society in which, by definition, everyone shares a certain conception of justice and knows that everyone else shares that conception. However, when there is not underlying social agreement on a conception of justice, policy disagreements cannot easily be resolved by an assessment of how far a paradigm is in reflective equilibrium with social and political principles.

Does this mean that policy principles can be in reflective equilibrium only given a set of ideological and philosophical presuppositions? If so, we should have to say that in order to evaluate different policy positions, we should have to take as given certain ideological assumptions. These assumptions may be widely shared and in the case of some societies they could form the broadly accepted principles of a constitutional democracy. On the other hand, in societies that were deeply divided ideologically, a principle or policy that was in reflective equilibrium given one set of ideological presuppositions would not be in equilibrium with the other set. For example, within some ways of thinking, prioritising health care by age and denying expensive treatments to those at the end of life would be acceptable, whereas from other points of view they would not. Given an acceptance of a broadly utilitarian approach, rationing by age may be in reflective equilibrium; from a rights perspective it may be out of reflective equilibrium. We cannot judge the particular without making commitments to a wider set of views, but those wider commitments may not be easy to evaluate with respect to one another.

Practical public reasoning requires assumptions, including assumptions as to how best to reason in practical terms, but those assumptions are neither self-evident nor universally shared. The implication is that reasoning will take us only so far in making policy decisions. Partisans reason (White and Ypi, 2010, 2011), but they reason from premises that they share with other partisans of a similar persuasion, not shared with citizens at large. From one point of view, this simply shows how in politics individuals and groups are bound together affectively rather than intellectually. Practical public reasoning will take us only so far. In evaluating public policy proposals, beauty, it might be thought, will always be evaluated by the eye of the partisan beholder.

However, such a conclusion is premature. Even if practical public reasoning is inherently incomplete, there may be ways of reducing gaps in understanding between advocates of competing policy principles in ways that contribute to the quality of public deliberation and decision. A useful idea to that end is that of accountability for reasonableness (Daniels and Sabin, 2008). Accountability is the principle that those who exercise or seek to influence public policy should be able to explain and justify the positions that they take in practical public reasoning. Sometimes accountability implies sanctions, as with political parties in office whose record and promise are judged regularly through elections. However, the idea of sanctions is not essential to the idea of accountability. Many non-elected public bodies – for example, regulatory agencies – regard themselves as accountable through their reporting requirements, their duty to consult on changes in policy, their obligation to appear before legislative committees, and so on. In these different forums they explain the principles upon which their decisions are based, point to the evidence that they believe justifies their policy choices, and provide an opportunity for scrutiny and criticism.

To be accountable in these ways is not to secure consensus. The principal element of accountability is to set out a chain of reasoning in such a way that the policy conclusions can be seen to follow from the premises of the reasoning. For example, if it is thought that end-of-life situations do not imply a claim for extra health care resources, then an agency would still be accountable for a paradigm in which there was no modification on these grounds, even if there were many citizens in society who thought that end-of-life situations were special. Someone who disagreed with the premises of the reasoning could still understand the justification of the policy choice, provided they could understand that there was a chain of reasoning leading from premises to conclusion.

For Daniels and Sabin the requirements of reasonableness are procedural rather than substantive. Reasonableness is exhibited in such requirements as publicity in policy justification, revisability in the judgements that are made, the relevance of the reasons offered for the policy, and the assurance that the conditions being presupposed are actually being met. How far one can go beyond these procedural requirements in any practical policy situation will depend upon the actual degree of consensus that obtains in a political system. However, even a formal requirement of accountability is likely in practice to issue in substantive conclusions, since those discharging the responsibility of accountability will have to present their policy position in a way that it is seen to serve the common good. For example, since the ageing process is something that everyone goes through, a proposal for rationing by age in health care is likely to meet the procedural requirements, whereas a proposal to limit care by ethnic group would not meet the relevance test and so lead to substantive rejection.

Conclusions

Evaluating any particular piece of policy reasoning is a complex task, requiring an understanding of relevant principles, and the different ways in which those principles may be defined, as well as an appreciation of the patterns of reasoning within which those principles feature. Because policy arguments are always normative, involving the first-person plural point of view, their structure resembles the structures of ethical argument that philosophers have identified, including utilitarian, intuitionist, and deontological forms of argument. Hence the philosophical methods that are characteristically used to evaluate ethical theories, most obviously the test of reflective equilibrium, can also be used to evaluate competing policy positions. Unlike the philosophical appraisal of ethical theories, however, the evaluation of policy arguments is subject to the constraint that public decisions have to be made, not least because delaying a decision is itself a form of decision. Evaluating policy principles and policy arguments is a task that is never fully completed.

Note

1 On this question, see also Poama in this volume.

References

Barry, Brian (1965). *Political Argument*. London: Routledge and Kegan Paul.

Barry, Brian (1989). *Theories of Justice*. London: Harvester-Wheatsheaf.

Carter, Ian (2015). 'Value-Freeness and Value-Neutrality in the Analysis of Political Concepts', in David Sobel, Peter Vallentyne and Steven Wall (eds), *Oxford Studies in Political Philosophy, Volume 1*. Oxford: Oxford University Press, pp. 279–306.

Culyer, Anthony J. (2016). 'Cost-Effectiveness Thresholds in Health Care: A Bookshelf Guide to Their Meaning and Use', *Health Economics Policy and Law*, 11, pp. 415–32.

Daniels, N. & Sabin, J.E. (2008). *Setting Limits Fairly: Learning to Share Resources for Health*, second edition. Oxford: Oxford University Press.

Frankfurt, Harry G. (2005). *On Bullshit*. Princeton and Oxford: Princeton University Press.

Freeden, M. (1996). *Ideologies and Political Theory*. Oxford: Clarendon Press.

Gauthier, David (1986). *Morals by Agreement*. Oxford: Clarendon Press.

Hayek, F.A. (1960). *The Constitution of Liberty*. London and Henley: Routledge & Kegan Paul.

Jenkins-Smith, Hank C., Nohrstedt, Daniel, Weible, Christopher M. and Ingold, Karin (2018). 'The Advocacy Coalition Framework: An Overview of the Research Programme', in Christopher M. Weible and Paul A. Sabatier (eds), *Theories of the Policy Process*, fourth edition. New York: Westview Press, pp. 135–71.

MacCallum Jr., Gerald C. (1967). 'Negative and Positive Freedom', *Philosophical Review*, 76, pp. 312–34.

Majone, Giandomenico (1989). *Evidence, Argument and Persuasion in the Policy Process*. New Haven and London: Yale University Press.

Mill, John Stuart (1861). 'Utilitarianism', in John Gray (ed. with an Introduction), *On Liberty and Other Essays*. Oxford: Oxford University Press, pp. 129–201.

NICE (2008). *Social Value Judgements*, available at: www.nice.org.uk/Media/Default/About/what-we-do/Research-and-development/Social-Value-Judgements-principles-for-the-development-of-NICE-guidance.pdf. (Accessed 23/1/2018).

Owens, Susan (2015). *Knowledge, Policy, and Expertise: The UK Royal Commission on Environmental Pollution 1970–2011*. Oxford: Oxford University Press.

Rawls, John (1999). *A Theory of Justice*, revised edition. Oxford: Oxford University Press.

Ross, W.D. (1930). *The Right and the Good*. Indianapolis and Cambridge: Hackett Publishing Company.

Rumbold, Benedict, Weale, Albert, Rid, Annette, Wilson, James and Littlejohns, Peter (2017). 'Public Reasoning and Health Care Priority Setting: The Case of NICE', *Kennedy Institute of Ethics Journal*, 27: 1, pp. 107–34.

Sabatier, Paul A. (1987). 'Knowledge, Policy-Oriented Learning and Policy Change: An Advocacy Coalition Framework', *Knowledge: Creation, Diffusion, Utilization*, 8: 4, pp. 64–92.

White, Jonathan and Ypi, Lea (2010). 'Rethinking the Modern Prince: Partisanship and the Democratic Ethos', *Political Studies*, 58: 4, pp. 809–28.

White, Jonathan and Ypi, Lea (2011). 'On Partisan Political Justification', *American Political Science Review*, 105: 2, pp. 381–96.

Wolff, Jonathan (2011). *Ethics and Public Policy*. London and New York: Routledge.

5

MODELS, MECHANISMS, METRICS

The entanglement of methods of policy inquiry with democratic possibilities

Susan Orr and James Johnson

Introduction

Policy-makers operate within a broader framework of political-economic institutions. We understand institutions as consisting of sets of rules and roles that define who can do what to whom, when, and for what purposes, as well as what happens when the rules are breached. Institutions are tools for coordinating our ongoing social, political, and economic relations. That much, of course, is a truism. The sorts of policy-makers that we are concerned with work in the context of *democratic* institutions. That too is a truism. Here we think of democracy as a set of institutional arrangements that involve the active participation of ordinary citizens, sometimes directly in making policy, but more often in holding accountable officials and representatives who are more proximately involved in policy-making. We will not elaborate this conception of democracy here other than to make two points. First, democracy involves two central mechanisms. On the one hand democracy involves argument, discussion, debate. On the other hand, it relies on voting or some other means of aggregation. In order to be democratic, argument and aggregation presuppose conditions of freedom and equality. And, second, while citizens might want to rely on non-democratic institutional arrangements to coordinate their ongoing activities in some domain, any such determination is itself subject to democratic decision-making. Such determinations are themselves experiments subject to reconsideration, revision, and refinement in the course of democratic politics. In what follows we speak repeatedly of democracy. We do so against this background (Dewey 1927, 1939; Knight and Johnson 2007, 2011; Unger 2009).

Policy-makers often find democratic politics frustrating. They regularly lay responsibility for what they see as the persistent ills of democratic politics (e.g., uninformed citizenry, conflict driven by myopia and self-interest, etc.) less at the feet of elites than at those of popular constituencies. This is true not just of conservatives but also of liberals. Peter Orszag is one recent proponent of this diagnosis. As he departed his post as director of the Office of Management and Budget in the Obama administration, Orszag notoriously recommended insulating an expansive domain of economic policy decision-making from the demands of democratic politics and specifically from the influence of popular constituencies. In particular, he suggested we could improve the policy-making process by 'relying more on automatic policies and depoliticized commissions' staffed by apolitical experts, thereby improving 'our political institutions by making them a bit less democratic' (Orszag 2011, 11–12). The task, as he depicted it, was to protect decision-makers from democratic politics so that they can formulate policies based on the conclusions of political-economic inquiry.

We reject the technocratic impulse to which Orszag gives voice. One obvious ground for doing so would be to reiterate a point articulated long ago by Dewey (1927), who replied to an earlier generation of technocrats by pointing out that, whatever specialised knowledge they might have, putatively disinterested experts have neither special insight into nor aptitude for framing the public interest. Further, once insulated from democratic politics, technocrats lack any sound basis for gleaning information for either purpose. And just there the technocrat risks running aground: 'A class of experts is inevitably so removed from common interests as to become a class with private interests and private knowledge, which in social matters is not knowledge at all' (Dewey 1927, 154). In short, for officials concerned with advancing the public good, it is not obvious that *democratic* influences pose the greatest risk to the public or its interests. Ironically, Orszag's own career path from Washington to Wall Street seemingly confirms Dewey's suspicions. He hardly is alone in this regard, of course. Rather, he serves here to exemplify how susceptible the technocratic impulse is to Dewey's suspicions.

We in no way wish to deny that the experts who occupy centre stage in the technocratic vision might well, in Dewey's words, become 'the willing tools of big economic interests' (Dewey 1927, 153). That, however, is a contingent claim, one that, in practice, will often come down to assessing the behaviour – ethical, legal, or otherwise – of particular individuals. We hope instead to press another, more general criticism – namely, that the technocratic vision suffers from a rather anaemic understanding of inquiry, of how our knowledge of social, political, and economic matters is generated and disseminated. This is damning insofar as it is precisely on his ready grasp of the conclusions of inquiry that the technocrat recommends that experts like himself should be afforded privileged, insulated status in decision-making processes.

In recent years a strain of argument regarding the relationship of inquiry and democracy in policymaking has emerged as a counter to technocratic impulses. These arguments take as a point of departure questions concerning the nature of inquiry arising as much from what might broadly be considered philosophy of science as from ethics or political philosophy (Anderson 2006, 2011; Cartwright 2006; Cartwright and Hardie 2012; Kitcher 2006, 2011; Putnam 2002). It is, we believe, no coincidence that those engaged in this enterprise, despite whatever differences exist among them, have engaged the intellectual tradition of American pragmatism of which Dewey is the greatest proponent. Our argument is situated within this ongoing tradition. Our concern, though, is broadly methodological. We focus on models, mechanisms, and metrics in order to underscore how the task of formulating political-economic policy requires not just an "evidence-based" approach but also a broader appreciation of how evidence itself is generated and assessed and how it enters into political processes.

That said, we do not seek here either to explore particular techniques of inquiry or legislate methodological rules. Instead we will illustrate, using the work of Nobel laureates Thomas Schelling, Elinor Ostrom, and Amartya Sen, how the methodological matters we take as our focus already are much in evidence in policy-oriented political-economic inquiry. In different ways, each of these thinkers reveals how normative, analytical, and explanatory concerns are, to borrow Putnam's (2002) characterisation, thoroughly "entangled" in political-economic inquiry (Knight and Johnson 2015). Their work also suggests that grappling with such entanglement compels us to rely *more* rather than *less* systematically on democratic politics.

Models and mechanisms as tools for communicating:
Thomas Schelling

It commonly is thought that political economists can justify the use of formal models in one of two ways. One can be a "realist" and thereby preoccupied with the truthfulness of the assumptions that enter into the model. Or one can be an "instrumentalist" and thereby concerned primarily with the model's usefulness at generating empirically testable predictions. Thomas Schelling departs from both of these canonical views in an instructive way. He insists that a 'model is a tool' and that, as such, it provides 'help in communicating' (Schelling 1978, 90). In other words, he is an instrumentalist of an uncommon stripe. He emphasises the communicative utility of models in contrast to those who reduce usefulness to the making of testable predictions. In this way, Schelling calls into question the basic premise of both realist and instrumentalist justifications as conventionally understood – namely, that we should assess formal models in empirical terms. Schelling relies on models for conceptual purposes. He uses them to explore how (typically unobservable) mechanisms operate and the conditions under which they do so. He also invites us to consider the uses of models in making normative arguments or, more generally, as instruments of practical reasoning (Johnson 2014, 2017).

Consider Schelling's famous checkerboard model of residential segregation. In this model, he does not aim to make testable empirical claims of any sort. Indeed, the model generates no predictions whatsoever. He instead is exploring one among several possible 'mechanisms of segregation' (Schelling 1978, 139). Specifically, he is concerned to explore the conditions under which dramatic patterns of residential segregation by race can arise even where, improbably, they are not driven by such familiar mechanisms as intentional public policy (e.g., Massey and Denton 1998) or unintended consequences of market decisions (e.g., Wilson 1997). Schelling focuses instead on the 'discriminatory behavior' of individuals motivated not by racial animus towards those *unlike* themselves but by more innocuous preference to reside among those *like* themselves (Schelling 1978, 138). His model explores the conditions under which this mechanism rapidly produces dramatic aggregate patterns of segregation that individual residents neither intend nor desire.

Schelling's approach, of course, raises a set of important theoretical matters that we will not pursue here (e.g., Aydinonat 2007; Aydinonat and Ylikoski 2014; Muldoon et al. 2012). What is important for present purposes is that what Schelling's model affords is 'help in communicating' about a class of causal mechanisms – namely, the *reasons* (beliefs and preferences) of individual agents that are themselves unobservable, and how those mechanisms might combine to generate aggregate consequences unintended and unwanted by those individuals. The lesson he conveys is *not* that competing explanations are false – segregation may, in fact, result from factors far less innocuous and generate consequences more dire than those captured in his models (Anderson 2010). Instead, he encourages us to entertain possibilities and, thereby, warns us to resist inferring from some observed pattern of macrobehavior to claims about micromotives or, as he puts it, to what is in the 'hearts and minds' of individual agents (Schelling 1978, 140–1, 146). In the case at hand, it is important to not too readily conclude on the basis of stark racial segregation at the macro level that members of the relevant population are motivated by racial animus. This, Schelling suggests, sounds 'a note of hope' for those critical of residential segregation (Schelling 1978, 154). If many of those caught in segregated residential patterns do not themselves either intend or want such configurations, it might be possible to forge broad multiracial constituencies in support of policies that could mitigate segregation and its consequences. This possibility survives even if the actual causes of residential segregation lie in the workings of broader political-economic forces. But it could be actualised, of course, only through the workings of democratic politics.

In his checkerboard model, then, Schelling, on our account, is engaged in conceptual exploration where "positive" and "normative" considerations are thoroughly entangled. And, as we suggest, he invites us to consider democratic possibilities as we navigate the complexities involved. He emphasises elsewhere how his methodological preoccupations with models and with mechanisms systematically intersect (Schelling 1998). In that sense, the checkerboard model is representative of his general approach to political-economic inquiry.

Schelling elaborates an approach to modelling that is avowedly low-tech. Thus, in one interview he suggests 'game theory is intellectually useful . . . but only at the most elementary level' (Swedberg 1990, 190). And, in a subsequent lecture, he insists that the 2x2 matrix is the most valuable contribution of game theory to social science. Such matrices afforded him, he says, a formal structure for exploring and clarifying the concept of commitment and how it operates via threats agents might issue or promises they might make (Schelling 2010, 28–9). Two comments are germane here. First, Schelling sees game theoretic models as affording us a language for talking about complex processes that are not readily observable. He hardly is alone in seeing this as perhaps the primary use of such models (Kreps 1990, 6, 41; Rubinstein 1991, 2012). Second, it is important to see that for Schelling a model seems useful not simply in communicating about unobserved mechanisms that it explicitly incorporates. In the case of conventional game theory these mechanisms include the beliefs and preferences of individual players and how they interact in complex ways to generate unchosen and often unforeseen aggregate outcomes (Hausman 2000). Schelling sees the value of game theoretic models as residing equally in their usefulness for drawing attention to and discussing a range of mechanisms that are external to the mathematical structure of the model itself. The latter are part of the "incidental detail" we cast aside when constructing a model, but whose operation analysis of the model compels us to consider. But they are hardly incidental to the actual workings of argument and debate at the core of democratic politics.

The most important of these mechanisms is the 'salience' embodied in 'focal points' and deployed in the 'creation of traditions' that structure expectations of agents facing coordination problems (Schelling 1960, 106–118). Schelling's discussion of salience has had enduring intellectual impact, not just as what many might deem an 'ad hoc' way of addressing the indeterminacy that plagues the game theoretic enterprise but as a spur to technical advances in the field (Myerson 2009; Sugden and Zamarrón 2006; Kreps 1990). That example is not unique. Indeed, Schelling insisted that while abstract game theoretic models are useful for analysing the underlying strategic structure of political-economic interactions, they perform relatively poorly when it comes to identifying solutions to the problems such structures generate. The latter task requires that we explore mechanisms – 'culture, institutions, precedents, reputations, identifications, even signaling or conversation', for instance – that, while very rarely explored in formal game theoretic models, are crucial to the resolution of strategic problems in practice (Schelling 2010, 35, 32).

Schelling nonetheless grasps the limits of 2x2 matrices. This led him to develop what are known as "Schelling diagrams" for analysing binary choice in various multi-person interactions. He used these especially for understanding the mechanisms that might prompt and sustain cooperation in diverse settings where individual actions threaten to generate sub-optimal or inefficient collective outcomes. He aimed to illuminate various other possibilities available to actors in such circumstances (Schelling 1978, 213–43). And, as with his checkerboard model, his models of the dynamics of binary choice are neither directly empirical nor properly explanatory. They are explorations of possibility. They are aimed at expanding the range of causal factors to which we might attribute a given collective action problem and, thereby, at sharpening both our diagnosis and the range of interventions we might adopt to remedy it. Here

Schelling's concerns intersect with those of Elinor Ostrom, who also is engaged in deflating the inference of necessity and impossibility social scientists and policy analysts too frequently draw from formal models. Ostrom both amplifies Schelling's approach to thinking about models and mechanisms and more explicitly considers the audiences with whom we might communicate the expanded possibilities such an approach reveals.

Models and mechanisms as vehicles of imagination: Elinor Ostrom

Elinor Ostrom insists that her inquiries into collective action, institutions, and their vicissitudes disclose 'a world of *possibility* rather than of *necessity*' (Ostrom 1998, 16). She details the quite various products of what Unger (2009, xi) calls our 'institutional imagination' and thereby reveals underappreciated political-economic possibilities. In this sense, she assumes that the domain of political economy is in crucial ways less determinate and more plastic than we often suppose.

Ostrom is concerned with the persistence and success (or otherwise) of institutional arrangements and specifically with 'understanding . . . the factors that enhance or detract from the capabilities of individuals to organize collective action related to providing local public goods'. In perhaps more telling language, she sees herself addressing a particular quandary: 'How a group of principals – *a community of citizens* – can organize themselves to solve problems of institutional supply, commitment and monitoring' (Ostrom 1990, 27, 29, emphasis added). A former student captures this theme tellingly, depicting the various accolades bestowed on Ostrom as signalling 'the triumph of an idea: democratic self-governance' (Allen 2014, 242).

As is well known, Ostrom focuses on problems posed by the need to govern what she calls 'common pool resources', which she defines as 'a natural or man-made resource system sufficiently large to make it costly (but not impossible) to exclude beneficiaries from obtaining benefits from its use' (Ostrom 1990, 30). In the face of such problems, she articulates a robust commitment to institutional pluralism. She articulates that commitment in a negative slogan. There are, she insists, 'no panaceas' for the sorts of collective action problems we face (Ostrom et al., 2007). Put otherwise, there is no single best way to coordinate our ongoing activities when confronting problems posed by common pool resources or local public goods. Specifically, Ostrom insists that we should not presume that addressing such problems *requires* any of the institutional mechanisms – neither centralised state provision *nor* market incentives *nor* a regime of private property – that policy analysts of different ideological predilections insist are necessary to the task.

Technocrats frustrated with what they take to be the persistent barriers that democratic politics pose to sound policy-making might welcome the anti-ideological thrust of Ostrom's brand of institutional pluralism. Such an inference, however, is superficial. A more plausible one might be that steadfast commitment to institutional pluralism of the sort Ostrom articulates actually recommends the priority of democracy as a uniquely useful way for communities to address the perplexities and problems of coordinating ourselves across domains of social, political, and economic interaction (Knight and Johnson 2007, 2011). We pursue this point in the conclusion. Here we focus on how Ostrom herself appreciates the democratic implications of her work and, in turn, how that reflects her methodological commitments.

Ostrom (1990, 1) quite literally starts from the observation that 'communities of individuals have relied on institutions resembling neither the state nor the market to govern some resource systems with reasonable degrees of success over long periods of time'. She identifies a set of 'principles' that characterise successful institutions for governing common pool resources. These cover such matters as membership, appropriation rights, collective decision-making, monitoring of performance, and dispute resolution that, she argues, explain the persistence of institutions that facilitate self-governance (Ostrom 1990, 90f). Empirically she finds that decentralised institutions of collective action that persist over time do so because they sustain a close proximity between these principles and the ordinary women and men who implement them. It therefore is unsurprising that her principles place a premium on participation and accountability. They reflect the ways successful institutions for collective action elicit and encourage the active participation of the individuals who populate them.

Policy analysts often depict the intellectual terrain over which Ostrom ranges as strewn with inescapable dilemmas, logics, and tragedies and infer that these conspire to thwart the efforts of agents to coordinate themselves for common purposes. They do so, she believes, because they interpret their models as capturing ineluctable constraints. Ostrom, by contrast, resists such dire prognoses, declaring that she 'would rather address the question of how to enhance the capabilities of those involved to change the constraining rules of the game to lead to outcomes other than remorseless tragedies' (Ostrom 1990, 27, 7). She shares this preoccupation with Schelling (1960), who argued that both the coordination aspect of strategic interactions and the ability of agents to undertake 'strategic moves' that alter the terms of those interactions reflect and contribute to the open-ended character of our political-economic world.

Ostrom insists that each of the 'design principles' she identifies is 'an essential element or condition that helps to account' for the 'institutional robustness' of arrangements that, in turn, govern some common pool resource sustainably. She suggests that together they afford 'a credible explanation' for such success when it occurs (Ostrom 1990, 90–1). Several observations are in order here. First, Ostrom's findings constitute something of an existence result. She admits that her inquiries do not say much about the emergence of such institutions (Ostrom 1990, 103). She instead aims to expand the constricted range of possibilities available to us by investigating institutional arrangements that we neglect when blinded by the conventional dichotomies of state and market, public and private. And, on that terrain, she details characteristics that differentiate successful from less successful or unsuccessful governance arrangements. Second, like Schelling's discussion of various mechanisms of commitment, Ostrom discovers her "principles" precisely because formal models prompt her to look beyond their own narrow confines. Her principles are practical tools that generate conceptual resources that help citizens evade the dire predicaments the models depict as inexorable tragedies. Third, to sound a recurring theme, Ostrom's analyses exemplify the entanglement of positive and normative concerns in political economy (Putnam 2004). She clearly presents her principles as explanatory mechanisms. She *simultaneously* proffers them as 'design principles', recommendations addressed to this or that 'community of citizens' seeking to create self-governing institutions of collective action (Ostrom 1990, 29, 90). Finally, Ostrom clearly considers herself to be an advocate for efforts at *self*-governance in the face of the overriding presumption among policy analysts that they surely can identify some panacea and recommend it to government officials, who, in turn, can impose it on passive constituencies. Her audience consists less of government agencies or politicians, let alone technocrats, than of those whom they would banish from policy debate.

The matter of metrics: Amartya Sen

Amartya Sen too addresses a public audience, claiming that his commitment to democratic processes largely precludes 'giving advice to the authorities', leading him to advocate instead 'public discussion as a vehicle of social change and economic progress' (Sen 1998, xiii–xiv). As a practical concern, then, Sen picks up in close proximity to where Ostrom just deposited us. In political terms, at least, their arguments are more complementary than overlapping.

Where Sen's work occupies a familiar tradition that sees 'democracy as public reasoning and representative government by discussion', Ostrom exemplifies 'the tradition of democracy as non-violent cooperative self-government: of the people exercising the capabilities of self-government together in their social and economic activities on the commons' (Tully 2013, 223). Yet while the two theorists face in different directions, it is crucial to see that their democratic convergence is not coincidental.

Ostrom considers the development of the capabilities integral to self-governance as central to political-economic development. Yet while she speaks of capabilities, there is no indication that she understands the term in anything but a colloquial sense. She lacks the language with which to articulate – let alone measure – that importance. Here the substantive convergence between the aspiration that animates her inquiries and how Sen articulates the "capabilities approach" to political-economic development emerges clearly.

As used here *capability* has a particular meaning. It refers to the substantive freedoms available to individuals, to the opportunities available to them to do or be things they themselves aspire to do or be (Sen 1998, 2009; Nussbaum 2011). Several aspects of this conception are important. First, capabilities operate at the individual level (Sen 2009, 244–5; Nussbaum 2011, 35). They can be attributed to collectivities (associations or communities) only correlatively. Thus, capabilities talk does not introduce anything especially mysterious or unfamiliar into policy discussions. Second, the capabilities approach nevertheless complicates such discussions. Capabilities are 'irreducibly diverse' (Sen 2009, 239–41). They therefore differ from familiar measures of well-being – utility or resources or primary goods – which presume it is possible to first specify some metric that homogenises what individuals have reason to value and then focus on the means necessary to freedom. Capabilities direct attention to the ways individuals exercise freedoms (Sen 1998, 54–86; Nussbaum 2011, 46–68). Finally, capability refers to the opportunities available to individuals, not directly to what they choose to do. Advocates of the approach talk about the way individuals realise opportunities in terms of the related concept of "functionings". The latter refers to what, given a range of opportunities, individuals actually choose to achieve (Sen 2009, 235–8; Nussbaum 2011, 24–7). The distinction between capabilities and functionings underscores the importance of what Sen calls "substantive freedoms" and "agency" in this approach. It also underscores, as Sen himself notes, one important sense in which his analyses traffic in possibilities. And just here his work intersects most importantly with that of Schelling and Ostrom.

From a narrow methodological perspective, all this raises important theoretical and technical issues of conceptualisation and measurement (e.g., Anand et al. 2009; Brighouse and Robeyns 2010; Comim et al. 2008; Wolff and De-Shalit 2007). We set these aside, for, as important as they are, engaging these technical matters risks diverting attention from the democratic impulse that informs the use of capabilities as a metric.

Advocates of a capabilities approach agree on the positions we just sketched. A sharp disagreement nonetheless persists about how to identify and weight capabilities. Nussbaum (2011, 17) proposes a list of 'central capabilities' that are more or less invariant across locales. Sen, however, rightly insists that any list of capabilities and the ordering and weighting of constituent items on that list should be derived democratically with the active participation of relevant constituencies. We do not attempt to adjudicate this disagreement. We do, however, take sides in order to highlight how, once again, concern for a narrow methodological matter – specifying a metric by which to assess political-economic development – recommends not that we restrict or displace democracy but that we instead incorporate a more robust place for democratic participation in political-economic policy-making.

Sen (1998, 78–9) presents the democratic commitment expressed in his understanding of the capabilities approach as a repudiation of technocratic impulses. It is important to see that this stance is neither contingent nor simply the statement of abstract principle. It reflects the basic terms of Sen's consequentialism and how that commitment, in turn, demands embodiment in political-economic institutions. This might seem to represent something of a tension given Sen's criticism of what he calls 'transcendental institutionalism' among political theorists (Sen 2009, 4–10). Yet his constructive position is a complex brand of consequentialism in which agents are thought to be concerned not just with *culmination* outcomes but with more encompassing *comprehensive* ones, where what is important to an individual or group is not just attaining certain sought after results or outcomes but attaining them in a particular manner (Sen 2009, 22–3, 217–8). Against that background, the capabilities perspective demands that we attend to institutional arrangements, rules, and procedures that structure how assessments of relative advantage and disadvantage can be determined through reflexive practices of public reasoning wherein such individuals and groups themselves articulate and weigh the irreducible plurality of capabilities. In other words, the assessment of capabilities presupposes some institutional scaffolding, where that is understood to consist in procedures, rules, and so forth that structure how capabilities are debated, promoted, inhibited, sustained, and so forth (Sen 2009, 296–7). As a metric of individual well-being, "capability" necessarily is entangled with an institutional arrangement of *some* sort.

Here we encounter the converse of the observation from which we proceeded in this section. At the outset we noted that, in order to elaborate her democratic commitments, and persuasively articulate what it means for institutions to promote the capacity of individuals for self-governance, Ostrom needs Sen (or someone quite like him). Here we see that in order to ground his own democratic commitments, and suggest how capabilities can be democratically identified and weighed in various local contexts, Sen needs Ostrom (or someone like her). While Sen recognises the crucial role institutional arrangements play in political-economic development and our assessments of it, he spends little time on the matter. What attention he does devote to institutions remains at a high level of abstraction as he refers to 'public reason' and 'social choice' (Sen 2009, 321–39). The principles that, on Ostrom's account, animate successful self-governing institutions offer the sort of ballast Sen's democratic version of the capabilities approach seems to require.

Technocrats strike back? Libertarian paternalists

This democratic impulse we ascribe to Schelling, Ostrom, and Sen stands in stark contrast to what is perhaps the most noteworthy recent approach in the technocrat's arsenal. Here we refer to "libertarian paternalism" (Thaler and Sunstein 2009; Sunstein 2015). This approach, which extends the experimental results of behavioural economics into the policy arena, focuses on the "choice architecture" within which people make decisions and on how well-designed policy might alter that context in ways that "nudge" people to make better decisions. It is remarkably influential in practical terms. In the United Kingdom this approach to regulatory policy was institutionalised by Prime Minister Cameron in the Behavioral Insights Team or "Nudge Unit" within the Cabinet office (Halpern 2016). In the United States it was, during the Obama administration, ensconced in the White House Office of Information and Regulatory Affairs (Sunstein 2013). Governments in many other countries have embraced "nudging" as an integral instrument of policy-making (Whitehead et al. 2014).

We do not offer a detailed assessment of libertarian paternalism as a broad approach to policy-making. But the difference between it and the approach we distil from Schelling-Ostrom-Sen hopefully is obvious. The former, after all, is avowedly paternalist, representing an 'attempt to substitute the policy-maker's judgment of what is good for the agent for that of the agent' (Hausman and Welch 2010, 129). By contrast, the work we have canvassed places a premium on enhancing the agency of individual citizens, seeking thereby to empower the communities of which they are members. This need not count against the libertarian paternalists insofar as they recommend a range of strategies to influence the choice architecture of individuals. Some of the strategies they endorse, for instance, involve simply supplying information in ways that might influence individual decision-making. In that sense, they provide people with reasons to act one or another way. Yet some, at least, of the strategies they recommend are quite unabashedly manipulative – meaning policy is designed to operate behind the backs of those to whom it is applied (Hausman and Welch 2010; Waldron 2014). And there is a further worry about the dynamic consequences of paternalist policies. They might, over time, impair the capacity of individuals to make reasoned choices or engage in reasoned discussion (Hausman and Welch 2010, 135).

It hardly suffices to assert in defence of any of the strategies libertarian paternalists recommend that 'What matters is whether they work' (Sunstein 2013, 9). Likewise, it is implausible to suggest that a strategy for implementing policy is unobjectionable so long as it avoids outright coercion. Libertarian paternalists, of course, acknowledge as much and seek to navigate such normative concerns (Sunstein 2016). We will not assess their arguments other than to point out that they hew closely to the sort of constrained consequentialism that insists not just on attaining some outcome but on doing so in justifiable ways (Sen 2009). And from there it is but a short step to conceding the priority of democracy not just to technocratic views in particular but also to libertarian attachments to markets or market-mimicking mechanisms more generally (Knight and Johnson 2007, 2011). Justification for various sorts of "nudge" as policy instruments would need to be public and transparent, involve mechanisms of accountability, and so forth. In short, they would need to survive the very democratic processes that technocrats eschew. It is an open question whether, once subjected to such public examination, nudges of this or that type would actually continue to "work".

Those with technocratic inclinations might complain at this juncture that by grounding our argument in exemplars – Schelling, Ostrom, and Sen – we risk skewing the discussion in misleading ways. They might complain that our exemplars are preoccupied with substantive matters at a considerable remove from the policy concerns that, for instance, prompted Orszag's frustration with democratic politics. Or they might complain that our exemplars articulate idiosyncratic views regarding methodological matters in political-economic inquiry. We think such objections are misguided for a quite simple reason. The broad democratic implications we sketch connect with the views of political economists other than Schelling, Ostrom, and Sen who likewise articulate democratic views on the basis of similar methodological stances.

We lack space to explore these connections in detail and so rest content with identifying prominent examples. Most obviously, the capabilities approach articulated by Sen had a considerable impact on a quite visible public inquiry, initiated in 2008 by former French president Nicolas Sarkozy and conducted by a panel of eminent economists, exploring alternatives to more familiar metrics for assessing political-economic performance (Stiglitz et al. 2010). Similarly, Rodrik (2015) articulates a view of models and their uses that converges with the approach we attribute to Schelling and Ostrom. For our purposes, it is important to note three things. First, in his substantive analyses of economic development, growth, inequality, and so on, Rodrik underscores precisely the sorts of institutional pluralism, experimentalism, and role of democratic participation in selecting and designing political-economic arrangements that we sketch here. Second, he does so in the course of an extended argument against the possibility of discovering blueprints or panaceas for addressing pressing political-economic problems (Rodrik 2007, 2011). Finally, like our three exemplars, he stresses the importance in policy processes of 'pragmatism, experimentation and local knowledge' (Rodrik 2007, 6) and, by extension, why it is crucial to enhance the agency of those who confront insurmountable political-economic predicaments. He, like Schelling, Ostrom, and Sen, thus stands at considerable distance from the libertarian paternalists for whom matters of agency appear primarily as a side constraint.

Conclusion

Our discussion of models, mechanisms, and metrics starts from *methodological* concerns. How, and for what purposes, do we rely on models, especially those that capture strategic interactions and the aggregate outcomes they can produce (Johnson 2010, 2014, 2017)? How do we examine the unobservable mechanisms that constitute causal relations (Johnson 2006)? How do we conceptualise and measure the outcomes of policy initiatives specifically and political-economic processes more generally (e.g., Orr and Johnson 2017)? It seems clear that the ways Schelling, Ostrom, and Sen each approach the methodology of political-economic inquiry and the ways their discussions of models, mechanisms, and metrics intersect push in democratic rather than technocratic directions. Put otherwise, we hope it is clear that each of these thinkers pushes us to expand the boundaries of "we" in each of the preceding sentences so that it includes not just government officials and policy-makers but also ordinary citizens.

In closing we anticipate two reactions to and address one implication of the democratic impulse we trace. First, nothing we say entails a naïve view of science and how it operates. Our argument emerges against a background provided by conceptions of 'well-ordered science' and of how practices of inquiry depart from it (see Cartwright 2006; Kitcher 2006, 2011). This approach requires neither that we surrender commitment to a plausible division of cognitive labour nor that we harbour any illusions about the obstacles to generating, certifying, and disseminating scientific knowledge. It does, however, focus on a small handful of characteristics of public knowledge. Most importantly, it focuses on the *significance* of the knowledge generated by inquiry, where significance doesn't just reflect the opinions of ordinary citizens but elicits their active engagement (Kitcher 2006, 1208, 1217).

Although examples of such participation are relatively uncommon, they hardly are either non-existent or inconsequential. Often instances of such participation emerge in response to crisis. For instance, in the United States groups such as ACT-UP (AIDS Coalition to Unleash Power) responded to the AIDS crisis by, among other things, successfully demanding inclusion of activists on panels at the National Institutes of Health and the Centers for Disease Control that conducted and monitored drug trials. These activists were instrumental in arguing for revisions and exceptions to experimental protocols and hastened approval of drugs for use in treating HIV. They were instrumental in disseminating the results of biomedical research both to communities threatened by the epidemic and to the public at large (Epstein 2000). Similarly, following the recent financial crisis, the Occupy movement in the United States spawned a group called Occupy the SEC (www.occupythesec.org). It consists of citizens who have worked in the finance sector, and it intervenes regularly and with some modest successes in the rule-making process at the Securities and Exchange Commission and other regulatory agencies as well as in the courts and the legislative processes in Congress. Between 2012 and the fall of 2017 Occupy the SEC drafted and filed in official procedures over 30 comments, briefs, and letters on various technical aspects of financial regulation. The group also offered a steady stream of reports to the popular press.

These sorts of direct engagement in policy processes aimed to establish priorities and assert what is significant in politically charged circumstances. They need not be driven by episodic crises. Nor, as the ongoing activity of Occupy the SEC suggests, need they be fleeting. There are good reasons to suppose that participation in the conduct and dissemination of inquiry in democratic politics might be regularised (Fung 2006, 2015). There are good reasons too to suppose that citizens generally are in fact (or can be encouraged to be) capable of such participation (Anderson 2006, 2011). There is, of course, much to be spelled out in all this. The primary point is that this view recapitulates the pragmatist quest to see inquiry thoroughly 'absorbed and distributed' such that it might serve as the 'instrumentality of that common understanding and thorough communication which is the precondition of the existence of a genuine public'. In short, it underwrites a vision of political-economic inquiry as informing, or entering "in" to democratic politics rather than being applied "to" it by putatively disinterested experts (Dewey 1927, 136).

Second, nothing in our argument entails a naïve view of democracy or how it operates. Our argument, as we noted at the outset, assumes a background understanding of democracy, the institutional mechanisms by which it operates, and the conditions that sustain those mechanisms. Clearly, the convergence we identify between Ostrom and Sen suggests a considerable expansion of the *scope* of democratic participation (Dewey 1927; Tully 2013; Orr and Johnson 2018). Likewise, recognition of institutional diversity suggests a crucial role for democratic decision-making. Since no "blueprint" exists for elaborating institutional arrangements, it is plausible to accord a second-order priority to democracy in deciding which mechanism or combination of mechanisms we might rely on to coordinate ongoing interactions in any given domain (Knight and Johnson 2007, 2011). 'Indeed, it is helpful to think of participatory political institutions as *metainstitutions* that elicit and aggregate local knowledge and thereby help to build better institutions' (Rodrik 2007, 166). There is much here too that requires elaboration and defence. The basic point? In the domain of political-economic policy, methodological concern for models, mechanisms, and metrics is deeply entangled with commitment to democratic possibilities.

With this, finally, we confront the matter of ethics. Due to the methodological commitments that inform their inquiries (and, we think, policy-making more generally) Schelling, Ostrom, and Sen show how social, political, and economic arrangements are more open-ended, indeterminate, and malleable than is commonly supposed. In other words, they disclose possibilities. These are the arrangements with which policy-makers are concerned. But this understanding implies it is unlikely we can usefully think of ethics as a system of principles (e.g., blueprint, panacea) as do Kantians or utilitarians. It invites us instead to see ethics not just as 'a motley', but as an especially unkempt, boisterous one at that (Putnam 2004, 22–3, 72–3).

Putnam articulates this broadly pragmatist approach constructively: 'ethics [is] concerned with the solution of practical problems, guided by many mutually supporting but not fully reconcilable concerns'. Or, as he says more allusively, it is 'a table with many legs, which wobbles a lot, but is very hard to turn over' (Putnam 2004, 32, 28). On this pragmatist view, progress consists more in the resolution or even setting aside of problems than in approximating some ideal. Any such resolution or setting aside is of course treated as fallible and revisable. Pragmatists hence endorse a tempered consequentialism that, like Sen's concern for comprehensive rather than culmination outcomes, recognises that any focus on consequences is entangled with procedural concerns like fairness and reflexivity (Knight and Johnson 2007, 2011). Likewise, pragmatists also evince a 'faith in the capacity of human beings for intelligent judgement and action if proper conditions are supplied' (Dewey 1939, 342).

Indeed, this faith animates their commitment to democracy more generally. Ordinary citizens, on this view, are capable of actively participating in democratic politics and policy-making. Their agency depends as Sen suggests not on innate ability but on the distribution opportunities. And, as Schelling and Ostrom both observe, it underwrites possibilities, openings that allow individuals to coordinate to transform or evade seemingly inevitable tragedies, logics, and dilemmas.

A pragmatist conception of ethics then, one consonant with the variety of inquiry that Schelling, Ostrom, and Sen simultaneously exemplify and press upon policy-makers, is indeed a table with many legs. In just the last sentence we note concern for consequences, fairness, reflexivity, and agency as well as faith in human capacities and creativity and awareness that their full exercise rests on an array of material and institutional conditions. While, from a pragmatist perspective, all of this gestures towards an ethics of possibility, it is unclear as Putnam suggests, whether these various concerns are entirely compatible. In that sense there is much here, once again, that requires exploration and elaboration. For a pragmatist that is a problem better addressed by citizens engaged in democratic politics than by philosophers or policy analysts.

References

Allen, Barbara. 2014. "A Role for Cooperatives in Governance of Common Pool Resources and Common Property Systems." In *Co-operatives in a Post-Growth Era: Creating Co-Operative Economics*. Edited by Sonja Novkovic and Tom Webb. London: Zed Books.

Anand, Paul, *et al.* 2009. "The Development of Capability Indicators," *Journal of Human Development and Capabilities* 10:125–52.

Anderson, Elizabeth. 2006. "The Epistemology of Democracy," *Episteme* 3:8–22.

Anderson, Elizabeth. 2011. "Democracy, Public Policy & Lay Assessments of Scientific Testimony," *Episteme* 8:144–64.

Anderson, Elizabeth. 2010. *The Imperative of Integration*. Princeton: Princeton University Press.

Aydinonat, N. Emrah. 2007. "Models, Conjectures and Exploration: An Analysis of Schelling's Checkerboard Model of Residential Segregation," *Journal of Economic Methodology* 14:429–54.

Aydinonat, N. Emrah and Petri Ylikoski. 2014. "Understanding with Theoretical Models," *Journal of Economic Methodology* 21:19–36.

Brighouse, Harry and Ingrid Robeyns, eds. 2010. *Measuring Justice: Primary Goods and Capabilities*. Cambridge: Cambridge University Press.

Cartwright, Nancy. 2006. "Well-Ordered Science: Evidence for Use," *Philosophy of Science* 73: 981–90.

Cartwright, Nancy and Jeremy Hardie. 2012. *Evidence Based Policy: A Practical Guide to Doing It Better*. Oxford: Oxford University Press.

Comim, Flavio, Mozaffar Qizilbash and Sabina Alkire, eds. 2008. *The Capability Approach: Concepts, Measures and Applications*. Oxford: Oxford University Press.

Dewey, John. 1927 [2012]. *The Public & Its Problems: An Essay in Political Inquiry*. Edited by Melvin Rogers. University Park, PA: Penn State University Press.

Dewey, John. 1939 [1998]. "Creative Democracy: The Task Before Us." In *The Essential Dewey: Volume One – Pragmatism. Education, Democracy*. Edited by Larry Hickman and Thomas Alexander. Bloomington, IN: Indiana University Press.

Epstein, Steven. 2000. "Democracy, Expertise and AIDS Treatment Activism." In *Science, Technology & Democracy*. Edited by Daniel Lee Kleinman. Albany, NY: SUNY Press.

Fung, Archon. 2006. "Varieties of Participation in Complex Governance," *Public Administration Review* 66:66–75.

Fung, Archon. 2015. "Putting the Public Back into Governance: The Challenges of Citizen Participation and Its Future," *Public Administration Review* 75:513–22.

Halpern, David. 2016. *Inside the Nudge Unit: How Small Changes Can Make a Big Difference*. London: Ebury Press.

Hausman, Daniel. 2000. "Revealed Preference, Belief, and Game Theory," *Economics and Philosophy* 16:99–115.

Hausman, Daniel and Brynn Welch. 2010. "To Nudge or Not to Nudge," *Journal of Political Philosophy* 18:123–36

Johnson, James. 2006. "Consequences of Positivism: A Pragmatist Assessment," *Comparative Political Studies* 39:224–52.

Johnson, James. 2010. "What Rationality Assumption? Why 'Positive Political Theory' Rests on a Mistake," *Political Studies* 58:282–99.

Johnson, James. 2014. "Models Among the Political Theorists," *American Journal of Political Science* 58:547–60.

Johnson, James. 2017. "Models as Fables." Unpublished Manuscript, University of Rochester.

Kitcher, Philip. 2006. "Public Knowledge and the Difficulties of Democracy," *Social Research* 73:1205–24.

Kitcher, Philip. 2011. *Science in a Democratic Society*. Buffalo, NY: Prometheus Books.Knight, Jack and James Johnson. 2007. "The Priority of Democracy: A Pragmatist Approach to Political-Economic Institutions and the Burden of Justification." *American Political Science Review* 101:47–61.

Knight, Jack and James Johnson. 2011. *The Priority of Democracy: Political Consequences of Pragmatism*. Princeton, NJ: Princeton University Press.

Knight, Jack and James Johnson. 2015. "On Attempts to Gerrymander 'Positive' and 'Normative' Political Theory: Six Theses," *The Good Society* 24:30–48.

Kreps, David. 1990. *Game Theory & Economic Modelling*. Oxford: Oxford University Press.

Massey, Douglas and Nancy Denton. 1998. *American Apartheid*. Cambridge, MA: Harvard University Press.

Muldoon, Ryan, Tony Smith and Michael Weisberg. 2012. "Segregation That No One Seeks," *Philosophy of Science* 79:38–62.

Myerson, Roger. 2009. "Learning from Schelling's *Strategy of Conflict*," *Journal of Economic Literature* 47:1109–25.

Nussbaum, Martha. 2011. *Creating Capabilities*. Cambridge, MA: Harvard University Press.

Orr, Susan and James Johnson. 2017. "Cooperative Democracy & Political-Economic Development: The Civic Potential of Worker Coops," *The Good Society* 26:234–54.

Orszag, Peter. 2011. "Too Much of a Good Thing," *The New Republic* (6 October) 11–12.

Ostrom, Elinor. 1990. *Governing the Commons*. Cambridge: Cambridge University Press.

Ostrom, Elinor. 1998. "A Behavioral Approach to the Rational Choice Theory of Collective Action," *American Political Science Review* 92:1–22.

Ostrom, Elinor, Marco A. Janssen and John M. Anderies. 2007. "Going Beyond Panaceas," *PNAS: Proceedings of the National Academy of Sciences* 104: 15176–15178.

Putnam, Hilary. 2002. *The Collapse of the Fact Value Dichotomy and Other Essays*. Cambridge, MA: Harvard University Press.

Putnam, Hilary. 2004. *Ethics Without Ontology*. Cambridge, MA: Harvard University Press.

Rodrik, Dani. 2007. *One Economics, Many Recipes: Globalization, Institutions and Economic Growth*. Princeton, NJ: Princeton University Press.

Rodrik, Dani. 2011. *The Globalization Paradox: Democracy & the Future of the World Economy*. New York: W.W. Norton.

Rodrik, Dani. 2015. *Economics Rules: The Rights and Wrongs of the Dismal Science*. New York: W.W. Norton.

Rubinstein, Ariel. 1991. "Comments on the Interpretation of Game Theory," *Econometrica* 59:909–24.

Rubinstein, Ariel. 2012. *Economic Fables*. Cambridge: Open Book Publishers.

Schelling, Thomas. 1960. *The Strategy of Conflict*. Cambridge, MA: Harvard University Press.

Schelling, Thomas. 1978 [2006]. *Micromotives & Macrobehavior*. New York: W.W. Norton.

Schelling, Thomas. 1998. "Social Mechanisms and Social Dynamics." In *Social Mechanisms*. Edited by Peter Hedström and Richard Swedberg. Cambridge: Cambridge University Press.

Schelling, Thomas. 2010. "Game Theory: A Practitioner's Approach," *Economics & Philosophy* 26:27–46.

Sen, Amartya. 1998. *Development as Freedom*. New York: Knopf.

Sen, Amartya. 2009. *The Idea of Justice*. Cambridge, MA: Harvard University Press.

Stiglitz, Joseph, Amartya Sen and Jean-Paul Fitoussi. 2010. *Mismeasuring Our Lives: Why GDP Doesn't Add Up*. New York: The New Press.

Sugden, Robert and Ignacio Zamarrón. 2006. "Finding the Key: The Riddle of Focal Points," *Journal of Economic Psychology* 27:609–21.

Sunstein, Cass. 2013. *Simpler: The Future of Government*. New York: Simon & Schuster.

Sunstein, Cass. 2015. *Why Nudge? The Politics of Libertarian Paternalism*. New Haven, CT: Yale University Press.

Sunstein, Cass. 2016. *The Ethics of Influence: Government in the Age of Behavioral Science*. Cambridge: Cambridge University Press.

Swedberg, Richard. 1990. "Interview with Thomas Schelling." In *Economics and Sociology*. Princeton, NJ: Princeton University Press.

Thaler, Richard and Cass Sunstein. 2009. *Nudge: Improving Decisions About Health, Wealth, and Happiness* (Revised & Expanded Edition). New York: Penguin.

Tully, James. 2013. "Two Ways of Realizing Justice and Democracy: Linking Amartya Sen and Elinor Ostrom," *Critical Review of International Social and Political Philosophy*. 16:220–32.

Unger, Roberto Mangabeira. 2009. *The Left Alternative*. London: Verso.

Waldron, Jeremy. 2014. "It Is All for Your Own Good," *New York Review of Books* (9 October) Volume 61, #15.

Whitehead, Mark, *et al.* 2014. *Nudging All Over the World*. Swindon, UK: Economic and Social Research Council.

Wilson, William Julius. 1997. *When Work Disappears: The World of the New Urban Poor*. New York: Vintage.

Wolff, Jonathan and Avner De-Shalit. 2007. *Disadvantage*. Oxford: Oxford University Press.

6

ETHICAL EXPERTISE AND PUBLIC POLICY

John Harris and David Lawrence

Introduction: ethical expertise and public affairs

Never before have ethical expertise and opinion on ethical issues (not the same thing at all!) been so sought after, the former so little regarded and the latter so highly featured in the media. A chain of recent legal cases, public scandals, and personal tragedies has featured and been discussed, as much for the ethical issues they raise or illustrate as for what is sometimes called their "human interest". In this chapter we first analyse the nature of ethical expertise, distinguish such expertise from the mere expression of opinions on matters of ethical significance (however sincerely or passionately held), and set out minimum tests that statements on ethical issues have to meet before they can either be seriously treated as constituting ethical judgements or count as the deployment of ethical expertise. Finally we use a contemporary case – a United Kingdom case which has literally caught the headlines worldwide to the extent that it has attracted interventions from both Pope Francis I and President Trump, to make clearer the engagement between ethical expertise and public policy.

Ethical expertise in theory: what it is

"Ethical expertise",[1] if and where it exists, must consist principally in the ability to create or assemble, analyse or present the combination of evidence and argument required to establish, defend, qualify, weaken, or demolish a proposition of ethical significance. Or, to reveal problems or ambiguities, contradictions or inconsistencies – in short strengths and weaknesses – in ethical positions, judgements, claims, or conclusions or indeed in any reasons or reasoning, adduced in discussion of ethical issues. While it is true that these are forensic, procedural, or even rhetorical skills (in Cicero's sense of rhetoric)[2] they are forms of expertise that when applied to moral issues allow the emergence of objective moral judgements, judgements that are almost universally accepted as right.[3] It is of course important that where the purported moral expertise is deployed – for example, in analysing or commenting upon a scientific medical or technological issue – that an adequate knowledge of the relevant science or technology is possessed and deployed by the moral expert.

Moving from process to content, a proposition or statement of ethical significance will be any claim that conduct, proposals, policies, or states of affairs are right or wrong, good or bad, wicked or virtuous in any or all of the ways that such 'things' can be so designated. In short, those things that cause benefit or harm to persons or to their rights or interests.

To give more flavour of what is meant by right or wrong when making considerations: 'things' may be bad because they cause unjustified pain, suffering, or distress to a sentient creature – that is, a creature capable of experiencing pain suffering or distress. Add to these features violations of rights or interests, injustice or unfair or discriminatory treatment of a person, and a fuller account emerges.

If that creature is a person in John Locke's forensic use of that term, and if moreover they are capable of autonomous choice, then anything done to them against their will or without their consent is a harm requiring justification.

John Locke's famous characterisation of the proper use of the term 'person' has stood the test of time:

> We must consider what person stands for; which I think is a thinking intelligent being, that has reason and reflection, and can consider itself the same thinking thing, in different times and places; which it does only by that consciousness which is inseparable from thinking and seems to me essential to it; it being impossible for anyone to perceive without perceiving that he does perceive.[4]

Finally, although we concentrate on human persons here, any sentient creature has interests which make moral claims, but exploring these – for example, as they apply to animals or as they may apply to 'persons' with artificial intelligence[5] – is a subject for another occasion.

Note that that this is not intended as an exhaustive list or catalogue. The ways that persons can be benefited and harmed are infinite, and when such benefits or harms occur or are in contemplation, ethics are engaged. These matters are not occult, obscure, or technical but commonplace, and as such require common sense and inclusive application. The identification of benefits or harms to persons does not require ethical expertise of any kind at all. We have not tried to indicate a determinate set of features but, on the contrary, to signal inclusiveness and an absence of pedantry about the sorts of issues that engage morality. But further qualification is also necessary.[6]

Tests of adequacy and authenticity

To count as a contribution to ethics – that is, to count as an ethical judgement by an agent – the putative "judgment" must, in addition to being about something of moral significance, meet certain tests of what we might call "adequacy or authenticity".

These tests do not need to be self-consciously articulated and "ticked off" by the agent, but she must have arrived at them for herself on the basis of considerations that establish the relevant proposition as her own by a process analogous to that required to arrive at *informed consent*[7] in medicine or research.

To be of ethical significance then, putative moral claims must, in addition to meeting the more forensic and procedural criteria mentioned earlier, meet certain tests of adequacy. Not "certain" in the sense of determinate and agreed, but certain simply in the sense of "sufficient" to establish the *bona fides* and authenticity of the individual advancing the proposition. This involves demonstrating that that person has understood it, and has adopted it as her own – for reasons that are adequate, not simply to their own purpose or purposes, but adequate in the sense of capable of being plausible, if not totally persuasive, to others of their honesty of purpose and good faith as well as evidencing their consideration of relevant information tending to strengthen or weaken the claim.

What such sufficiency consists in more precisely is necessarily uncertain but not indeterminate or vacuous, as we shall now see.

As John Harris argued in a recent book, *How to Be Good*[8] (142–3),

> [A] decision which makes a moral difference is not for that reason a moral decision, nor is a dilemma the resolution of which has moral consequences for that reason a moral dilemma.[9] As Ronald Dworkin[10] has convincingly shown, moral judgements command a special respect . . . due to them partly because they are taken to reflect the considered values of the individual making them, and partly because moral judgements have to meet certain minimum standards of evidence and argument which exclude a number of disqualifying features. Such disqualifying features include gut reactions, and instinctive or automatic responses. Moreover moral judgements are required to be distinguishable from prejudices, arbitrary preferences, personal tastes, arguments or conclusions based on manifest self interest or partiality, or arising from a personal emotional response "they make me sick!", "it is disgusting!" and the like. Finally someone claiming to act out of moral principle or on the basis of moral judgement must be able to explain just what is wrong with the conduct to which he objects or right about the decision she endorses.
>
> [E]xactly as not just any judgment about things in which science is interested is "scientific" so not just any judgement about things with which morality is concerned are [sic] moral judgements. There may of course be argument about just what more is required in each case. I have, following Dworkin,[11] suggested some minimal standards for morality; these severally, and perhaps even jointly, are certainly contestable. But that some such standards are required is not I suggest open to doubt. Something must distinguish morality from other normative systems or systems of belief more generally. And just as not all rules about things that interest the law are legal rules so not all judgements about things that interest morality are moral judgements and not all normative systems are either legal or moral (dress codes in the workplace or the "laws" of cricket). To be sure, the elements of any particular legal system, or code of conduct, may be contested jurisprudence; but uncertainty does not mean "anything goes", uncertainty almost always has parameters which are well understood, just as some uncertainty about linguistic meaning, "ambiguity", is not total uncertainty, but uncertainty within a range.[12]

Such expertise is not the prerogative of any discipline or field of study, but it can, to an extent, be learnt and even taught, and of course, because ethics is not uncontroversial, claims to such expertise or the propositions, evidence, or arguments flowing from its deployment are also likely to be contested, perhaps essentially so.[13]

Ethics is for bad guys

One thing which should of course be clear, but which bears repeating, is that ethical expertise is no guarantee of good conduct or moral rectitude in the ethical expert.[14] Just as medical doctors can lead unhealthy lives and set a bad example in wellness, so ethical experts can also act unethically (although they may lack some of the excuses that might be available to others). Indeed, again as argued in *How to Be Good*,[15] 'ethics is for bad guys'! This is because those who are naturally, dispositionally good or who might be engineered to be good by chemical or other means can, so it is sometimes claimed, do the right thing unreflectingly. We refer here to the claims made by advocates of so-called moral bioenhancement,[16] claims which we largely reject and trust to have been refuted by Harris in *How to Be Good*.[17] Those without natural or synthetic goodness, which is most of us, need to use reason to work through arguments for and against particular forms of conduct or decisions.

The principle of neutrality

When such expertise is applied to public policy this must happen in a way that does not violate a principle of ethical neutrality.[18] Such a principle does not imply, of course, that moral propositions or proposals are neutral from an ethical perspective, but rather that they are accessible to reason and not partisan in the sense that they are capable of appealing only to those who already share the faith, or the ideals or the prejudices of an individual, God, or prophet, even those of a Mount Olympus full of diverse Gods – or for that matter the moral code devised by a club, political party, group, society, or indeed a philosopher. In short, they must avoid appealing to any who accept ideas or propositions that are not accessible to reason, such as the tenets or beliefs of particular religions or which flow from cultural practices or beliefs not shared by other cultures.

This means that ethical tenets or propositions must be capable of appealing in principle, if not in fact, to all citizens of a society regardless of their religious beliefs, cultural practices, or personal preferences in a way that determines legislation or "binds" the decisions of the courts or other public bodies. It must in short preserve the expectation that such decisions will be fair, reasonable, and accessible to all regardless of what might be called "the usual suspects": race, religion, colour, gender, sexual orientation, and so forth. This of course rules out any suggestion that the fact (if it is one) that a course of action, policy, or position is either required or forbidden by any particular religion – or set of beliefs, or by membership of any society – means that it can be enforced for that reason alone. Any proposition that cannot be supported by a combination of evidence and argument independent of its being enjoined or forbidden by any of such organised bodies of faith or belief has no role to play in either morals or legislation, nor in the principles of morals and legislation.

The commandments or abominations of religion (e.g., of *Leviticus*)[19] can at best appeal only to the adherents of the religion or prophet issuing the commandments or abominating the abominations, or to people who already accept them for other reasons, perhaps because they reinforce prejudices which make the individual comfortable. Any democracy worthy of the name must be governed according to principles, laws, and institutional arrangements that are capable of appealing to and, most important, of being justified to and seen as fair or reasonable by all citizens, of any religion, philosophy, or ideology, or none.

Finally it is clear that anyone acting as a moral expert has a duty of honesty and openness. This involves more than merely setting out and analysing the issues but also making clear what judgements or conclusions flow from such an analysis, if any do. If there is no such thing as right or wrong there can be no ethics and no law, or at least no moral basis nor justification for either. Mistakes can be made; that is how moral (and scientific) progress is made.

All judgements, moral or scientific, are revisable in the light of new evidence and/or new and more plausible interpretations of old evidence. The story is told that Ludwig Wittgenstein accosted a student in Great Court Trinity College Cambridge and demanded, 'Tell me why did people think that the Sun went round the Earth rather than that the Earth was rotating?' The student replied, 'Well, I suppose it looked as though the Sun was moving round the Earth'. To which a triumphant Wittgenstein responded, 'Yes! But what would it have looked like if it had looked as though the Earth was rotating?'.[20]

The fact that we might be wrong does not entail that we cannot ever be right, nor that we are not right on any particular occasion. Doubt is built on certainty, not the other way round. As Wittgenstein also remarked, 'The child learns by believing the adult. Doubt comes after certainty', and 'The game of doubting itself presupposes certainty'.[21] 'A person can doubt only if he has learnt certain things; as he can miscalculate only if he has learnt to calculate'.[22] In this respect morality is the science of the good and ethics is the study of that science. Morality is a science in the way that biology, cosmology, and even history are, and it can be conducted well or badly, using well-established methodologies, the formulation of hypotheses, and the collection and application of relevant evidence. There are "truths" and "facts", but most of them may be revised in the light of new evidence and argument – in other words, by the empirical method. "Smoking causes lung cancer" is an important discovery of science, although not everyone who smokes contracts lung cancer and some who do have never smoked. Killing the innocent is wrong, but can be morally justified in particular instances, which brings us to the practical uses of moral expertise.

Ethical expertise in practice: guarding Charlie, a case study[23]

Over recent months the fate of Charlie Gard, an infant who could not see, nor hear, nor make a noise, nor move, has mesmerised the world, provoking countless discussions and even occasioning interventions from Donald Trump and the pope.[24] His parents, Chris Gard and Connie Yates, wanted Charlie to undergo an experimental therapy trial in the US and had raised around 1.3 million pounds by "crowdfunding" via the Internet to support this endeavour. His medical team, on the other hand, believed his case was hopeless, that he might be exposed to uncertain but probable continued pain, suffering, and distress without being able to indicate what was happening to him, trapped in an unresponsive body.

Charlie was an 11-month-old patient in intensive care at Great Ormond Street Hospital (GOSH) in London. He had been born on August 4, 2016, apparently healthy; but after about a month, Charlie rapidly deteriorated and his parents noticed that he was less able to lift his head and support himself than other babies of a similar age. Charlie suffers from an extremely rare inherited condition called infantile onset encephalomyopathic mitochondrial DNA depletion syndrome, referred to as "MDDS". The consensus of medical and legal opinion has been that this condition is incurable and irreversible and had already caused severe brain damage to Charlie.

A brief timeline of the case[25]

August 4, 2016: Charlie Gard was born.

September 2016: Charlie was taken ill and diagnosed with a rare genetic condition at Great Ormond Street Hospital (GOSH). The condition causes progressive muscle weakness and brain damage.

January 2017: Charlie's parents set up a "GoFundMe" page to pay for Charlie to travel to the US and receive an experimental nucleoside therapy. This "crowd funding" exercise is reported to have raised more than 1.3 million pounds so far.

March 3, 2017: GOSH asked Mr Justice Francis to rule that life-support treatment should stop. Evidence was presented to the court to the effect that Charlie cannot see, nor hear, nor make a noise, nor move, that he could breathe only through a ventilator and was fed through a tube. There was uncertainty as to whether Charlie was experiencing pain, distress, or discomfort, though it was seen as probable.

April 11: Mr Justice Francis said doctors could stop providing life-support treatment after analysing the case at a hearing in the Family Division of the High Court in London. He concluded that life-support treatment should end and said a move to a palliative care regime would be in Charlie's best interests.

May 3: Charlie's parents then asked Court of Appeal judges to consider the case.

May 23: After analysing the case, three Court of Appeal judges dismissed the couple's appeal two days later.

June 8: Charlie's parents then took their case to the Supreme Court. Charlie's mother broke down in tears and screamed as justices announced their decision. She was led from the court by lawyers.

June 20: Judges in the European Court of Human Rights started to analyse the case after lawyers representing Charlie's parents made written submissions. A European Court of Human Rights spokeswoman said that 'in light of the exceptional circumstances of this case, the court has already accorded it priority and will treat the application with the utmost urgency'.[26]

June 27: On Tuesday, European court judges refused to intervene. A Great Ormond Street spokeswoman said the European Court decision marked 'the end' of a 'difficult process'.[27] She said there would be 'no rush' to change Charlie's care and said there would be 'careful planning and discussion'.[28]

July 2: Pope Francis sent a message of support to Charlie's parents, saying that life support must not be turned off until Charlie dies of natural causes. The Vatican-owned *Bambino Gesù* paediatric hospital in Rome said it was willing to continue Charlie's end-of-life care and wrote to GOSH purporting to have new evidence in support of nucleoside treatment. The mistaken premises behind these statements are discussed ahead.

July 3: US president Donald Trump also sent a message of support to Charlie's parents.

July 10: Chris Gard and Connie Yates returned to the High Court to present fresh evidence about treatment they said could prolong 11-month-old Charlie's life. There were dramatic scenes in which both parents stormed from proceedings, including accusing the court of not being independent where remarks appeared critical of their case.

July 23: Death threats against medical staff become public.

July 24: Withdrawal of legal challenge by Charlie's parents. Statements are read by representatives of both parties and the hospital offering very different versions of events.

July 25: High Court asked by Connie Yates to allow Charlie to be taken home to die. GOSH argues that this is unfeasible as there would be no way to provide the necessary care staff or machinery required.

July 26: Charlie's parents ask for the right to keep Charlie alive in a hospice for a week for goodbyes. GOSH indicate that this will require 24/7 specialist care. Justice Francis rules that if no such team can be found, Charlie will be taken to a hospice approved by GOSH for a shorter period.

July 27: No agreement is reached and Charlie is transferred to a GOSH-approved hospice where life support will be withdrawn. Charlie's parents claim that they have been denied their final wish and make accusatory remarks to Justice Francis.

July 28: Death of Charlie Gard.

Over many of these months both present authors have been interviewed variously on radio and television, and by the press, local national and international, as so-called ethical experts to discuss the ethical issues involved in the case and to comment on various developments. In this second part of our discussion of ethical expertise we will set out in narrative form an amalgam of the various interviews given and comments made.[29] We are not sure that we have lived up to the "job specification" outlined earlier, and of course in the nature of media interviews, with very limited time to speak and "sound-bite" imperatives, the nature of ethical expertise is usually attenuated to say the least, not to say edited to suit the needs of broadcasters.

Of course the tragedy of Charlie Gard is heart-rending and one which must be every parents' worst fear. Also, as defenders of the autonomy of the individual, accepting the force of arguments derived from a libertarian, Millian tradition,[30] we were very much in sympathy with Charlie's parents and their desire to have the freedom to do everything possible for their child, but we soon found that while our sympathy for them did not wane, other considerations demanded equal and even greater attention. Many interviewers and protestors against the intervention of the courts wanted to know what right the law had to intervene between parents and their child.

What right do the courts have to intervene?

In English law the presumption is always that parents will act in the best interests of their child. And only when this seems no longer to be the case do the courts respond to their inescapable duty to intervene and decide for themselves what is objectively in the child's best interests in so far as this can be ascertained. In this case facing an impasse between what Charlie's medical team at GOSH felt was in Charlie's best interests and the very different approach of the parents, the courts had to adjudicate between what had become tragically opposed conceptions of the good for Charlie.

In Charlie's case, three successive different and independent English courts considered the evidence and, culminating in a decision of the Supreme Court, decided that the medical team at GOSH was right and that Charlie should not be subjected to further treatment and should be allowed, in his own interests, to "die with dignity". The basis of all these decisions was that Charlie had suffered irreversible brain damage, that there was no evidence that this could be reversed by any existing treatments, and that to subject Charlie to further treatment which was causing him uncertain but probable distress, suffering, and pain to no purpose (i.e., with no possibility of amelioration of his condition) was not in his interests, agreeing with his medical team at GOSH that regrettably it was time to permit Charlie to die with dignity.

Chris Gard and Connie Yates then took the case to the European Court of Human Rights (ECHR), which confirmed the judgement of the UK Supreme Court, remarking that the decision of the Supreme Court 'was meticulous'. The ECHR determined 'it was most likely Charlie was being exposed to continued pain, suffering and distress and that undergoing experimental treatment with no prospects of success would offer no benefit, and continue to cause him significant harm'.[31]

However, despite this legal certitude, but in the light of the risk of further litigation, GOSH itself decided to re-apply to the High Court to confirm the previous judgements and the legality and appropriateness of GOSH withdrawing life-sustaining treatment, following claims of fresh scientific evidence and misleading interventions by Pope Francis and Donald Trump.

Is the Gard case unprecedented?

Many of the questions coming from the press and other media have wanted to ask: will this case set a precedent? The answer seems a clear "no"; no ground-breaking new legal precedent has been set. The principles of English law under which the courts have operated are well established. The use by the courts of expert scientific, medical, and ethical opinion is also well established.

What the case may actually set a precedent for is, in a sense, more subtle and secondary than paving the way for legal reform, though no less important.

Mistaken premises and the vilification of expertise

Mistaken premises such as that presented by Pope Francis in his July 2 statement have fuelled a veritable circus of publicity and activism associated with this case, with noisy demonstrations outside the High Court, joined by a controversial pastor, Patrick Mahoney, flying in from Washington and declaring to anyone who would listen that 'God has already played a part by making Donald Trump and Pope Francis speak out for the sick 11-month-old'.[32] The reverend pastor appeared not to notice that a God who micro-manages the actions of individuals, such as the pontiff and the president, must surely also be credited with afflicting Charlie Gard with the malady in the first place, or at least deciding not to perform a miracle!

If anything, these sorts of interventions make the role of ethical expertise in such a case even more difficult. The high profile of these commentators – the US president and the head of the Catholic faith – lends airs of legitimacy to their statements. Pope Francis's claim that life support should be provided until Charlie should happen to die of natural causes is problematic because it ignores the fact that while Charlie remained on life support it was virtually impossible for him to die 'naturally', life support being of its nature unnatural and subject to human decision-making. If matters were put on hold awaiting such an event, then there might never be any resolution. Plainly the pope's comments were made with the best of intentions, but they serve to obscure the realities.

The same might be said of the leaked letter to GOSH from doctors at and affiliated with the Vatican children's hospital, purporting to present new information and evidence unconsidered by the court in favour of treatment. The existence of such a letter, signed by active scientists at respectable institutions, presents a certain image of scientifically endorsed hope to the public, when that image is perhaps not as sound when closely examined. Only one of the seven cited pieces of research in the letter is from 2017, and in a statement by lawyers for GOSH it became apparent that all had been available for consideration by the court in April.[33] Further evidence in the letter is admitted to being unpublished, and therefore uncorroborated, without independent evidence of reliability, and furthermore is a result of work only on mice. There is of course great and long established validity to using mouse models in medical research, including cognitive neuroscience, but the letter fails to make clear that the claims of improved function do not pertain to the reversal of structural brain damage, a feat it is presently agreed is highly unlikely (let alone the same in humans as in mice). In fact, the letter fails to suggest how this may pertain to Charlie's case whatsoever, because the argument presented – that deoxynucleosides may indeed cross the blood-brain barrier – is not truly the issue in hand. It remains unmentioned quite how, and to what extent, this would be of benefit to Charlie even if their evidence was new and accurate. It warrants noting that the original US doctor involved with the case at the very beginning admitted that '[Charlie] is so severely affected by encelopathy [sic] that any attempt at therapy would be futile. I agree that it is very unlikely that he will improve with that therapy. It is unlikely'.[34]

The vast majority of interventions – such as this letter from a group of scientists, the pledges of support from major figures, and indeed those so affected by the case that they chose to demonstrate to have their voices heard – are done with positive and honest intent. However, it remains true that they can in fact be harmful to the ethical debate by obfuscating the truth of the matter in the eyes of the public, and indeed in the thinking of an "ethical expert", who cannot be expected to also entirely understand the complex and advanced science involved at first glance. Such things lead to situations such as those seen in the return to the High Court, in which Mr Justice Francis was accused of being insufficiently independent by Mr Gard, because the judge remained unconvinced of the value of the new evidence.

A report in London's *Guardian* (July 23, 2017) notes,

> Mary MacLeod, chair of Great Ormond Street hospital, said: "In recent weeks the GOSH community has been subjected to a shocking and disgraceful tide of hostility and disturbance. Staff have received abuse both in the street and online.
>
> Thousands of abusive messages have been sent to doctors and nurses whose life's work is to care for sick children. Many of these messages are menacing, including death threats. Families have been harassed and discomforted while visiting their children and we have received complaints of unacceptable behaviour even within the hospital itself.
>
> Great Ormond Street hospital is in close contact with the Metropolitan police and we will do everything possible to hold to account anybody who is involved in this kind of deplorable behaviour."[35]

The deployment of ethical and scientific expertise in the public domain is then not without its risks both to the experts and to innocent "by-standers". There seems little doubt that much of the more visible protest surrounding this case has been organised by various extremist groups.

It does not require explaining that the staff of GOSH and indeed Justice Francis should not have had to suffer such abuse for performing their jobs. This circus itself, of course, does nothing to mitigate the heavy and heart-breaking decisions for the parents, for the medical team at GOSH, and for the courts and the sympathetic engagement of all the extraordinary and ordinary people throughout the world who have tried to think through the dilemmas of Charlie's case for themselves.[36]

The precedent that risks being set is therefore one of fear, and of the erasure of expertise in favour of emotive responses. It is nothing new for ethical commentators to be sent threats – our academic contact details, even office addresses, are matters of public record. Though we have received none on this particular issue, death threats regarding other controversial questions of bioethics have been a fact of life – if thankfully rare. The difference in this case, however, is the volume of public opposition to the word of the expert. Anecdotally, we know of several ethical experts who have admitted to turning down some of the invitations to speak publically on radio and television news around the case as the situation proved itself increasingly intemperate. It is of course the duty of academic experts to disseminate that expertise; however, particularly for less senior academics, there is a need to practice a degree of self-preservation. If one's expert opinion runs counter to the prevailing public feeling (or more pertinently to the most active sentiment as in this case), it often matters not whether that opinion is informed by understanding and contextual knowledge of ethics. The modern media rapid cycle does not lend itself to nuance or background explanation, nor to explorations of repercussion. Rather, it lends itself to soundbites, and few things make a worse sound bite than expounding on the nature of moral goods. Emotive language is rather punchier, and easier to sell.

This has been illustrated perfectly throughout the Gard case, and perhaps never better than if we compare the statements delivered by both Charlie's parents and by GOSH immediately after the legal challenge was withdrawn. The former contained phrases such as 'we are so sorry that we couldn't save you but we weren't allowed to'[37] and claims that Charlie would have lived a 'normal' life had treatment not been delayed by the courts. The latter[38] outlined the facts of the case once again, at some length, and provided factual evidence directly opposing these claims. It also highlighted some concerning issues regarding the basis of these claims; that Professor Hirano, the leading author of the letter discussed earlier, had neither seen Charlie nor his scans or records at the time he suggested to Charlie's parents that there was hope.[39] The GOSH statement saw very little coverage in the days after Charlie's parents withdrew, whereas their own was endlessly quoted and served to reinforce the mistaken sentiments behind much of the public opinion. A *Telegraph* editorial[40] we published immediately thereafter received numerous comments[41] condemning us for disregarding what the commenters saw as "fact" – that is, the claims in the parents' statement.

The vilification of expertise – a situation that has been building in the UK and elsewhere for some years[42] – carries with it many dangers. We are perhaps biased as authors who are, ostensibly, ethical experts; but this case has highlighted the growing difficulty for experts to work generally either for fear of being targeted or for fear of being ignored. We must hope that no precedent is indeed set as it will become ever more important for such commentary to retain its purity of purpose – to educate and illuminate – in order to try to quell situations such as this. The same of course applies across the gamut of the duties of all those who have relevant expertise; but here we will not comment further on, for example, exposure of holocaust denial, honesty and product liability (snake oil salesmen and worse), abuse of intellectual property protection, the "ever-greening" of patents, and so on.[43]

Charlie should have had every chance?

For those who have said that "it seems heartless" not to do everything possible for Charlie and that "Charlie should be given every chance", the agonising question, to which the answer is not, and could not be, completely clear, is "every chance of what"? On the one hand there is the chance of Charlie being exposed to probable continued pain, suffering, and distress, and on the other, the chance of restoration of almost certainly not a worthwhile life, but a somewhat extended life.

We all surely know that life is not always an unmitigated blessing and that there are many circumstances which rational and autonomous individuals choose to avoid if they can, even by death. This is why English law permits "advance decisions" which competent adults can sign, refusing life-prolonging medical interventions in specified circumstances. But competent individuals do not even need a good reason to refuse medical treatment; they can refuse it by a simple indication of refusal, whether verbal or not, and whether the refusal is objectively in their best interests or not. Indeed the English courts grant those, like Tony Bland,[44] who are permanently unconscious, a death they neither seek nor fear.

We should be clear that the United Kingdom has not, as yet, permitted assisted dying or voluntary euthanasia. The Common Law tradition of English law has drawn a distinction between withholding and withdrawing treatment on the one hand and assisted dying on the other, a distinction which mirrors the so-called acts and omissions distinction. The suspect nature of this distinction is not a matter that can fruitfully be further developed here.[45]

Equally, none of us are strangers to legitimate legal constraints on the choices parents can make for their children when such choices may prejudice the child's best interests. These range from legislation requiring parents to ensure that their children receive adequate education and nutrition, to the wearing of seat-belts or other restraints in motor vehicles, to being protected from literally everything, from cigarette smoke to unsuitable material on the Internet. Of course Charlie's parents sincerely believe they are indeed protecting their child; but deeper examination by legal and medical experts has cast severe doubt on the soundness of this belief.

Those who think that child welfare is not the laws' business but that of the parents or guardians have to reflect on the many cases of child abandonment, child neglect, and child cruelty. Then there are cases like perhaps the Charlie Gard case, where it is not entirely or immediately clear, scientifically or factually, which course of action is more in Charlie's interests, bearing in mind that continued life can be against the interests of a sentient being. Where there is doubt of course in a case like that of Charlie, the child affected should receive the benefit of that doubt. But in which direction does benefit lie here? The issue which ethical expertise may or may not help to resolve is a factual one and one in which no one has access to the most relevant facts – namely, what exactly was Charlie currently able to experience and what did the future hold? Given the unavoidability of a decision one way or the other, all must try to consider what, on balance of probability, was in Charlie's best interests? The overwhelming balance of medical and judicial opinion has been that the future held no prospects of recovery from the damage to Charlie's brain and that he was highly probably suffering pain, discomfort, and distress and would also have probably continued to be unable to see, nor hear, nor make a noise, nor move. Many would not welcome being kept alive in such a condition.

Now that Charlie Gard's interests have been meticulously considered by national and international courts, it has become as clear as any such things can be that he would never have had, nor experienced, "a life", as most people understand that idea, never have formed hopes nor wishes of any kind, nor been able to make choices. Regardless of their reasoning, Charlie's parents have made many unthinkably hard decisions and accepted his best interests, and should be praised for doing so. It might have been thought that this was an appropriate moment for Charlie to be able to rest in peace.

Notes

1 We are indebted to many helpful conversations with and suggestions from Giulia Cavaliere.
2 Cicero. (1942). *De Oratorio III. Cicero, on the Orator*, trans. H. Rackham. London: Harvard University Press, p. 221.
3 This idea is expanded in Chapter 2 of Harris, J. (2016). *How to Be Good*. Oxford: Oxford University Press.
4 Locke, J. and Pringle-Pattison, A. Ed. (1964). *An Essay Concerning Human Understanding*. Oxford: Clarendon Press. Book II. Chapter 27. Locke formulated this definition in the middle of the seventeenth century. Harris elaborates on this use of Locke's account of "personhood" in Harris, Op cit 3. Chapter 2.
5 Harris, J. (2018). The Chimes of Freedom: Bob Dylan, Epigrammatic Validity & Alternative Facts. *The Cambridge Quarterly of Health Care Ethics*, 27(1).
6 See Harris, Op cit 3. Chapter 2.
7 Accounts of "informed consent" in "the literature" are so many and various that they defy catalogue and certainly make citation superfluous. For Harris's own "take" on this see Harris, J. (1985). *The Value of Life*. London: Routledge. Chapters 10 and 11.
8 Early in Chapter 9, from which we quote here, the author made an embarrassing mistake pointed out to him recently by a dear friend, the poet Bill Dodd. Somehow the poet Wilfred Owen was substituted for Edward Thomas as the friend of Robert Frost when referencing his poem "The Road Not Taken". This is his first opportunity to acknowledge this mistake in print.
9 Harris, J. (2001). Introduction: The Scope and Importance of Bioethics. In: J. Harris, ed., *Bioethics: Oxford Readings in Philosophy*. Oxford: Oxford University Press.
10 Dworkin, R. (1977). *Taking Rights Seriously*. London: Duckworth. Chapter 9.
11 Op cit. 3. Chapters 1, 2, and 3.
12 Empson, W. (1970). *Seven Types of Ambiguity, a Study of its Effects in the English Verse*. 3rd ed. London: Chatto and Windus. The range in question may be indefinite but it is not infinite.
13 Gallie, W. (1956). Essentially Contested Concepts. *Proceedings of the Aristotelian Society*, 56(1), pp. 167–198.
14 And indeed moral philosophers might be the worst, despite Plato's oft repeated claim that 'to know the Good is to do the good'. Abrahams, M. (2010). Why Are Books on Ethics so Likely to Be Stolen? *The Guardian*. [online]. Available at: www.theguardian.com/education/2010/dec/13/ethics-study-steal-books-moral [Accessed 9 Aug. 2017].
15 Harris, Op cit. 3 Chapter 7.

16 Persson, I. and Savulescu, J. (2008). The Perils of Cognitive Enhancement and the Urgent Impera-tive to Enhance the Moral Character of Humanity. *Journal of Applied Philosophy*, 25(3), pp. 162–177. Douglas, T. (2008). Moral Enhancement. *Journal of Applied Philosophy*, 25(3), pp. 228–245.
    See also Faust, H. (2008). Should We Select for Genetic Moral Enhancement? A Thought Experi-ment Using the MoralKinder (MK+) Haplotype. *Theoretical Medicine and Bioethics*, 29(6), pp. 397–416.
17 Harris, Op cit. 3 Chapters 1–7.
18 Harris discusses the concept of neutrality in his 1980 book *Violence and Responsibility*. London: Rout-ledge and Kegan Paul. Chapter 8.
19 Christianity.com. (2017). Leviticus Bible Book Chapter List. *King James Version*. [online]. Available at: www.christianity.com/bible/bible.php?book=3. [Accessed 9 Aug. 2017].
    See also Douglas, M. (1970). *Purity and Danger*. London: Routledge & Kegan Paul.
20 Anscome, Elizabeth. (1959). *An Introduction to Wittgenstein's Tractatus*. London: Hutchinson University Library, p. 151.
21 Wittgenstein, L. (1969). *On Certainty*. Eds. Anscombe, G.E.M. and Von Wright, G.H. Oxford: Basil Blackwell, Para 160 and Para 115.
22 Wittgenstein, L. (1967). *Zettel*. Eds. Anscombe, G.E.M. and Von Wright, G.H. Oxford: Basil Black-well, Para 410.
23 Quite literally "a case" since it is also a legal case that has been taken to the highest English courts and to the European Court of Human Rights.
24 Sheldon, T. (2017). Why We Need Scientists on Charlie Gard. *Sciencemediacentre.org*. [online]. Avail-able at: www.sciencemediacentre.org/charlie-gard/ [Accessed 9 Aug. 2017].
25 For this timeline we have consulted reports in: The Telegraph. (2017). Who Is Charlie Gard, What Is the Disease He Suffered from and What Happened in the Court Case? [online]. Available at: www.telegraph.co.uk/news/0/charlie-gard-mitochondrial-disease-suffers-legal-battle/ [Accessed 9 Aug. 2017].
    Sky News. (2017). Timeline: Parents' Battle to Save Charlie Gard. [online]. Available at: http://news.sky.com/story/timeline-parents-battle-to-save-charlie-gard-10914755 [Accessed 9 Aug. 2017].
    And the BBC News. (2017). Charlie Gard Parents Lose European Court Appeal. *BBC News*. [online]. Available at: www.bbc.co.uk/news/uk-england-40423371 [Accessed 9 Aug. 2017].
    We have also relied to some extent on our personal knowledge of these events.
26 *The Telegraph*. (2017). Charlie Gard: Doctors Must Continue to Provide Treatment to Allow European Court Scrutiny. *Telegraph*. [online]. Available at: https://www.telegraph.co.uk/news/2017/06/19/charlie-gard-doctors-must-continue-provide-treatment-allow-european/ [Accessed 19 Aug. 2018].
27 BBC News. (2017). Charlie Gard Parents Lose European Court Appeal. *BBC News*. [online]. Avail-able at: https://www.bbc.co.uk/news/uk-england-40423371 [Accessed 19 Aug. 2018].
28 Ibid.
29 In the main by Harris.
30 Mill, John Stuart. (1971). On Liberty. In: John Stuart Mill, ed., *Three Essays*. London: Oxford University Press.
31 Bowcott, O. (2017). Charlie Gard: European Court Rejects Plea to Intervene in Life-Support Fight. *The Guardian*. [online]. Available at: https://www.theguardian.com/law/2017/jun/27/charlie-gard-european-court-rejects-plea-to-intervene-in-life-support-fight [Accessed 19 Aug. 2018].
32 Greenhill S. (2017). Charlie Gard Judge Dismisses Interventions by Pope Francis. *Daily Mail*. [online]. Available at: https://www.google.com/url?sa=t&rct=j&q=&esrc=s&source=web&cd=2&cad=rja&uact=8&ved=2ahUKEwiPi8bzyvncAhUDC-wKHZW5BooQFjABegQICRAB&url=http%3A%2F%2Fwww.dailymail.co.uk%2Fnews%2Farticle-4679334%2FAmerican-pastor-travelled-UK-pray-Charlie-Gard.html&usg=AOvVaw3s3VVE6kZ2u4d3N6XUB8t2 [Accessed 19 Aug. 2018].
33 BBC News. (2017). Charlie Gard Evidence Not New, Hospital Claims. *BBC News*. [online]. Avail-able at: www.bbc.co.uk/news/uk-england-london-40552026 [Accessed 9 Aug. 2017].
34 Judiciary of England and Wales. (2017). Decision and Short Reasons to Be Released to the Media in the Case of Charlie Gard, p. 5. [online]. Available at: www.judiciary.gov.uk/wp-content/uploads/2017/04/gard-press-summary-20170411.pdf [Accessed 9 Aug. 2017].
35 Connett, D. (2017). Great Ormond Street Staff 'get death threats' over Charlie Gard. *The Guard-ian*. [online]. Available at: www.theguardian.com/uk-news/2017/jul/22/great-ormond-street-staff-receive-death-threats-over-charlie-gard [Accessed 9 Aug. 2017].
36 Just Google "Charlie Gard" and take your pick of the accounts.

37 Siddique, H. and Boseley, S. (2017). Charlie Gard's Parents End Legal Battle as Time Runs Out for Critically Ill Baby. *The Guardian*. [online] Available at: www.theguardian.com/uk-news/2017/jul/24/charlie-gard-parents-end-legal-fight-over-critically-ill-baby [Accessed 9 Aug. 2017].
38 Great Ormond Street Hospital Press Office. (2017). GOSH Position Statement 25 July 2017. [online]. Available at: www.gosh.nhs.uk/news/latest-press-releases/gosh-position-statement-issued-high-court-24-july-2017 [Accessed 9 Aug. 2017].
39 To say nothing of his financial interest in the technologies of the proposed treatment.
40 Harris, J. and Lawrence, D. (2017). A Civilised Society Doesn't Let Parents Do What They Like with Their Children – However Much They Love Them. *The Telegraph*. [online]. Available at: www.telegraph.co.uk/news/2017/07/25/charlie-gard-case-civilised-society-doesnt-let-parents-do-like/ [Accessed 9 Aug. 2017].
41 As they say, one should "never read the comments"; but it does illustrate a point!
42 As famously encapsulated by Michael Gove Ft.com. (2016). Britain Has Had Enough of Experts, says Gove. [online]. Available at: www.ft.com/content/3be49734-29cb-11e6-83e4-abc22d5d108c [Accessed 9 Aug. 2017].
43 The University of Manchester Institute for Science Ethics and Innovation. (2009). Who Owns Science? The Manchester Manifesto. Available at: www.isei.manchester.ac.uk/TheManchesterManifesto.pdf [Accessed 9 Aug. 2017].
44 Airedale N.H.S. Trust v Bland [1993] A.C. 789 House of Lords.
45 Harris discusses this distinction at length in his books *Violence and Responsibility*. London: Routledge and Kegan Paul, 1980. And *The Value of Life*. London: Routledge, 1985.

PART II

Public policy and the basics of government

7

SECURITY AND POLICE ETHICS

John Kleinig

Introduction

Of recent times there has been a preoccupation with national security. Cold War concerns have been largely replaced by concerns about international terrorism. It was not always so. The architects of liberal democratic theory placed equal if not greater weight on individual security – especially the security of individuals in the exercise of their fundamental rights – "lives, liberties and estates" to use John Locke's triad.[1] They considered the provision of individual (and domestic) security no less a fundamental governmental task than the security of borders.[2] Yet there were (and are) important differences. The security of borders was (and is) seen as a license to kill those who threaten to invade, and there were (and are) thought to be fewer constraints on harms to innocent foreign non-combatants. The police task has not been to eliminate threats but to minimise and contain them and to ensure that those posing a threat are brought before an adjudicatory body (a court). Those who were authorised to protect the rights of citizens[3] are therefore under greater moral constraint with respect to how they go about their job and the risks they can impose on innocent others. Even though the challenge of domestic terrorism and of terrorism by infiltrators has blurred some of the traditional lines between soldiering and policing, there is still believed to be a significant difference in the moral constraints placed on the two roles.[4]

Although life and bodily integrity are central to the idea of individual security, such security has almost always been construed more broadly. Securing the rights to life, liberty, and possessions, though sometimes interpreted narrowly, usually encompasses the protection of social and psychological aspects of well-being and more broadly the protection of a way of life. It encompasses a social order that is both stable and opportunity-laden. Where we stand on the spectrum of narrow versus more extensive accounts of such security is likely to reflect much larger political perspectives, including the role of government in mediating social life. One of the great challenges for early theorists was to articulate a case for individual and domestic security – and hence for policing activity – in a way that ensured individual and communal safekeeping but avoided overbearing governmental intrusiveness.[5] It presumed – or at least was thought to presume – an Enlightenment conception of the essential dignity of individuals – and, ancillary to that, a series of ethical constraints on governmental action. The purpose of this essay is to articulate this challenge as a foundation for ethical policing.

This is not the place to develop and defend a theory of political legitimacy.[6] Many Enlightenment theorists view legitimate political authority as a prudential and/or moral requirement of human flourishing, where that flourishing includes the recognition of certain basic rights as the requisites for human dignity.[7] Here, however, I shall track one cluster of variants in this tradition – the theoretical conceit of a social contract – the idea that civil society is a consensualised institution in which its participants agree (or could be expected to agree) to an authoritative civil order in return for certain benefits. Despite its acknowledged problems, especially with regard to consent, it avoids appeals to monolithic moral theorising and sits comfortably with the dignitarian presumptions of democratic moral and social theory. The idea of "policing by consent" is well established in British policing, where it acknowledges that policing authority comes from below rather than above, and is responsive to a particular conception of human personhood and well-being.[8]

On contractualist accounts, legitimate governmental authority can be deemed an expression rather than an infringement of human dignity. Although this approach might easily be sourced in the writings of Thomas Hobbes, the more familiar Lockeian account provides a better entrée. On Locke's version, mature human beings – those no longer subject to parental nurture and discipline – are the possessors of certain fundamental rights. Admittedly, as I suggested earlier, how these rights are characterised and interpreted is a matter of ongoing discussion and clearly of some importance in debates about the appropriate reach of governmental authority. But I shall take the view here – controversially, but not too controversially – that these rights will include the means of subsistence, freedom, life, some access to the wherewithal needed to make something constructive of one's life, and, in the event of threats to or violations of these rights, a liberty to defend and proportionately retaliate/punish.[9]

The way in which policing gets into this picture is similar to the way in which governmental authority is legitimated. Locke sees three critical problems with a state of nature – that is, a social order in which our capacity for moral judgement functions independently of a framework of civil institutions.[10] *As we find them*, human beings cannot mediate their social relations adequately without having some collective understanding about the social rules that should order their public interactions. There needs, he suggests, to be a consensualised process for formulating social rules. What he has in mind are the workings of what we would characterise as a legislature, in which jurisdictionally agreed-upon rules are promulgated. That is not enough, however, absent some adjudicatory process for interpreting and applying such rules – what we can broadly understand as a judicial process to which those who appear to breach the agreed-upon social rules are subject. Even that, however, is not sufficient for humans as we find them. There must also be some form of executive institution or institutions to ensure that the legislative rules and judicial determinations are effectuated. It is into the latter social need that what we see as policing and correctional functions are slotted. It is the role of police to help effect the requisites of a social order as they are embodied in the legislative understanding and to ensure that those who are reasonably considered to breach such requirements are brought before the courts for the adjudication of their acts.[11]

Of course, this is a considerable simplification of the social processes that we actually find and takes little account of the variations that liberal democratic societies may embody.[12] But it is a tolerable representation of the broad kind of social order that is needed if those acknowledged as right-holders or possessors of dignity are to engage securely with each other. It also helps us to understand the broad constraints on governmental authority – agents of government have a fiduciary responsibility to do for citizens what citizens are not able to legitimately and effectively accomplish for themselves.[13] Only powers available to individuals in a state of nature are vested in those who have the task of guarding rights within civil society.

Locke recognised that any kind of imposed social order constituted a challenge to those with fundamental rights to life, liberty, and possessions (however we choose to represent them) and so the argumentative conceit of a social contract, understood as a consensualised understanding – what rational rights-possessors would recognise as essential to security in exercising their rights – also becomes central to the legitimate exercise of police powers. Police are given powers that would individually be ours as right-holders in a state of nature. Because of the powers vested in them, police are, of all social agents, in a particularly advantageous position to infringe the rights or freedoms of others, and so their activities must be accommodated within the larger understanding of political obligation.

Construed in terms of basic social and political theory, we accord police an authority to act on our behalf so that we might effectively secure the exercise of our fundamental rights – rights articulated by law and adjudicated by the courts. To enable police to carry out their executive role, we vest in them a number of coercive, investigative, and decisional powers that are now limited in the case of other citizens. These are powers for which we would be eligible in a state of nature but which (for the most part) we restrict to those who accept policing roles in civil society. We restrict them, because, were we not to, their use would be haphazard and corrupted by circumstance.[14]

Use of force

Most importantly and intrusively, we permit police to use forcible means to maintain or restore social order and act as first responders to breaches of the legislated rules as interpreted by the courts. They may be armed and/or otherwise provided with means for coercing the compliance of others. Because police, unlike soldiers, are not primarily in the business of defending borders by killing or repelling attackers, their powers are constrained. They operate under the law to bring allegedly or probably errant fellow citizens before the courts for adjudication. Given that those they police may not be cooperative, they have powers to coerce and arrest apparent lawbreakers. The extent to which police, individually and collectively, have access to particular means of exercising coercive force (batons, pepper spray, tasers, handcuffs, and firearms) will probably reflect social conditions.[15] In the case of police, use of deadly force, central to the role of soldiers, is limited to the protection of themselves and/or others only in response to grave harms, threatened or inflicted. Otherwise it subverts the process whereby those allegedly involved in criminal violations are delivered to the court for adjudication and – if so determined – punishment.

Broadly speaking, police use of force is limited by the following considerations:[16]

1   Coercive police authority is to be exercised in a manner that respects our status as moral agents. It is by virtue of that status that we have the dignity of personhood, and the authority we vest in police is not intended to be such as would undermine that status. In other words, the ends of policing do not authorise the use of whatever means might appear to secure them. Those ends must be pursued in the context of a particular understanding of their beneficiaries. Such understandings are often enshrined in constitutional protections, such as the Bill of Rights that operates in the United States. The use of force needs to be "reasonable" and nondiscriminatory. True, the interpretation and scope of our rights are contestable and will remain so, but that does not gainsay their relevance and importance. The social order that is to be maintained or restored is an order characterisable in ways that is responsive to our status.

The requirement that police use force in manner that respects our dignitarian status rules out certain techniques of investigation, containment, and interrogation that police might otherwise be tempted to use. Torture and use of the third degree are ruled out, along with techniques that humiliate or invade legitimate privacy. Thus care must be taken that certain security measures, such as strip and body cavity searches, are conducted in ways that minimise the likelihood that humiliation will be experienced by those subjected to them.[17] Use of the "perp walk", in which arrestees are paraded for media purposes, might also be called into question. Arrest is no guarantee of guilt, and televised images of arrest, with the presumption of guilt that a perp walk tends to convey, may leave a social stain that subsequent acquittal or proof of innocence will not remove. Even though criminality is intended to reflect conviction for a particular crime, the social opprobrium associated with criminality generally reflects on character and dignitarian standing.[18]

2   The proportionality that contract theorists consider appropriate to punishment of rights violations should also be manifested in the processes that lead to it. There needs to be some match between the seriousness of the matter at hand and the coercive tactics that are used to deal with it. This is a simple matter of justice, but it can also be seen viewed in consequentialist terms. That is, using more force than is necessary is excessive.

Many police departments employ what is termed a use of force continuum that links the tactics that police may use in the apprehension of suspects with the level of threat involved.[19] Even though such continua tend to be coarse-grained and difficult to apply, they constitute some kind of proportionate curb on what is inclined to be an excessive use of force.[20] There are many temptations available to police to use their coercive force disproportionately. A simple but extremely common one is the overtightening of handcuffs.[21] Another is the excessive force that is often administered after a chase or high-speed pursuit. When caught, fleeing suspects are often beaten before (or after) they are handcuffed, as police officers react to the adrenaline rush produced by the pursuit. Police departments are inclined to turn a blind eye to such excess (unless, perhaps, it is videoed), even though there are strategies that police can adopt to deal less problematically with adrenaline rush.[22]

3   The "reasonableness" requirement may also be invoked to underpin a more restrictive principle, that of the least restrictive alternative. Even though proportionate force may be morally permissible, that permissibility is called into question when less force would have been sufficient to achieve the same legitimate purposes.

A disturbed person with a weapon may be unlikely to use it and unresponsive to demands to drop it – two of a variety of cases in which the use of deadly force represents coercive overkill. Police culture tends to be quite unforgiving of refusals to use less than proportionate permissible force, bewildered though the unresponsive person may be, and can even be unforgiving of police who refuse to use their weapons in such a situation.[23]

To some extent, the development of various intermediate force techniques, such as tasers and pepper sprays, is a response to the moral imperative to use as little force as necessary. Unfortunately, however, practices and even a culture often develop in which even these are used unnecessarily, simply because they represent an easy and effective (and, moreover, relatively non-accountable) means of bringing a situation under control.[24]

4   Uses of coercive force should be practicable – that is, likely to achieve their purpose. It is not enough to speculate that some coercive techniques are more likely to succeed in achieving the ends of justice and public order than others. There needs to be some empirical evidence for this. For example, does the presence of police in full riot gear tend to provoke rather than deter public confrontation?[25] Are tasers overused?[26]

Taken at face value, the use of deadly force circumvents the role of police to gain control of a situation so that courts may determine guilt or innocence. Although a serious threat to police officers or others takes precedence over that goal, it was not until 1985 that the US Supreme Court disallowed the use of deadly force simply to prevent a fleeing person from escaping.[27] Such action effectively circumvented the role that police have within the larger criminal justice system. Also, although there are powerful moral reasons for not using torture or certain other coercive techniques ("the third degree") on suspects, there has also been considerable debate about whether such techniques are as effective as they are claimed to be by their protagonists.[28] The use of Reid interrogational techniques by US police[29] has been known to result in cases in which innocent people have pleaded guilty to crimes – even serious ones – they have not committed. Groups such as the Innocence Project have uncovered well over 300 cases in which, inter alia, innocents convicted of serious felonies had (false) confessions extracted from them.[30]

5   Ethically speaking, there is a subjective motivational constraint on the use of force, lest otherwise reasonable coercive force be infused with morally unacceptable attitudes and intentions (say, racist or religious repugnance). Although the reasonableness requirement might well be interpreted to include a reference to motivational considerations, as it has developed in US law it is now interpreted objectively.[31]

In practice, it is not easy to know what motives are operative when police engage with the public. Occasionally, giveaway words are used that betray a particular bias, and statistics may suggest that particular groups are being singled out and treated more roughly for prejudicial reasons, but more often the sources of inappropriate motivation are likely to be found in a police culture that swaps racist emails or ethnic and sexist jokes. In such an environment, permissible discretion is more likely to be misused, even if those stopped or apprehended are legitimate targets of police activity.

In the real experience of police work, the foregoing five considerations are, unfortunately, too often ignored,[32] and, to the extent that they are, legitimate police authority is undermined. Police come to be seen as an invading force rather than as protectors of rights, leading sometimes to escalating and unwarranted confrontations. As a society we treat attacks on police much more seriously than others. There is a good reason for that, given the social role that police must fulfil. Yet one must wonder, sometimes, when an attack on police occurs, whether an unhealthy policing environment has contributed to such a situation. Although it is generally accepted that police have close to a monopoly on the use of coercive force within public life, they have a responsibility to ensure that its display is not provocative. The riots that erupted in Ferguson, Missouri, following the shooting of Michael Brown owed something to the effects of police militarisation.[33]

The forcible means that police are enabled to use when intervening in prohibited behaviour or apprehending those believed to have engaged in it are not the only special powers they are permitted to use. Although the 1829 origins of modern policing focused on the "prevention of crime" (an implicit nod to the idea of police as social peace keepers), initially leaving detective work to other agencies, a little more than a decade later police were also given investigative functions. In the early days these investigative functions sometimes countenanced the use of force ("the third degree") but, as policing matured and professionalised, alternative infringements were substituted – most importantly engagement in various deceptive practices and permissions to invade private spaces.

Police deception

Ordinarily, human relations work best when people are truthful with each other. To a significant degree, responsible agency requires that we can make decisions on the basis of relevant facts, and that we can – to some extent at least – trust our sources. Deception throws a moral spanner into this presumption. Not only does it make rational and responsible decision making more difficult, not only does it tend to undermine the human relationships that we value for their own sakes as well as for their ability to make our way in the world, but also it tends to be manipulative, reducing us to mere means in the purposes of others. Recourse to deception is a morally hazardous business.

The moral hazards involved in the recourse to deception are evident in the case of entrapment, which, in the United States, is a legal defence against governmental/police deception. Whether construed as an overreach of police powers or as the sowing of criminal offence in the mind of an otherwise innocent person, entrapment of the innocent person is a legally acknowledged form of illegitimated police deception. Other hazards, as we shall see, are also present.[34]

Nevertheless, not all deception is to be rejected. As with the use of coercive force, the moral complexity of our world may sometimes make it advisable, even meritorious, to employ deception. Deceptions will vary in the disrespect they show and in the magnitude of the harms they are likely to cause, and, in certain circumstances, deceptions may minimise or even avert harms. In the cause of justice, some deceptions will advance rather than undermine it.

Policing is one of the special cases in which some deception may be justifiable. Given that the larger contractualist role of police is to secure social peace through the protection of rights – the prevention and investigation of crime and responses to social crises and disorder – it may sometimes be the case that these ends are not merely more efficiently but also more acceptably achieved if some deception is used. Especially with regard to criminal activity, police may anticipate that those who engage in it will not wish to have their identity revealed or conduct punished. Police may have to employ deceptive stratagems – sting operations, unmarked cars, undercover work, and so forth – if they are to advance the causes of social peace and justice. This of course does not mean that police may deceive with impunity – all such deception will need to be justified in the broader context of social morality – but there will be role-related reasons why that option may be integral to their role.

The permissibility of deception on the part of police does not permit its untrammelled use. We have already instanced entrapment. One other important general reason for constraining police deception is that if police work comes to be too closely identified with deceptive practices, this is likely to interfere with police-community interactions. Citizens should expect that their relations with police will ordinarily be candid and able to be taken at face value. Deception should be the exception rather than the rule.[35]

Some part of the constraints that deception requires will involve regulatory curbs, but others will require wise discretionary decision making. Since certain kinds of deceptive practices will involve intrusions into matters ordinarily considered private, deception will need to be scrutinised lest enthusiasm for "information" improperly cross moral boundaries. So, for example, the use of phone tapping and bugging devices will ordinarily need the approval of an impartial judge. Other deceptions, such as sting operations, may require supervisory approval, and individual discretionary decisions will need to be defensible in the event that they come up for review.[36] Particularly egregious have been police sting operations in which guilty parties have been manipulated into indefensible deceptive behaviour.[37]

As is the case with uses of force and as should be the case also with invasions of privacy, the means that police use to secure their socially sanctioned ends should be able to respond satisfactorily to a range of overlapping questions: (a) whether the ends are really good or good enough; (b) whether there is some proportionality between the ends and the means; (c) whether the ends could be as well achieved by less costly means; (d) whether there is something intrinsically or otherwise problematic about the means used; (e) whether the means are likely to secure the ends sought; and (f) whether there are other contingent costs that might make the use of a particular means inappropriate. These are standard normative questions that all means–ends decisions have to confront. How they are embodied in policy is a more complex matter. In some cases, individuals charged with discretionary decision making will need to address them before acting. In other cases, when institutional policies are being developed, they will need to be addressed at an institutional level, and that may involve a confluence of several different social inputs – institutional leadership, legal decision making, and expressions of media and public concern. Obviously there will also be political pressures, though in a robust democratic environment, we can hope for correctives to over- or under-reaching.

Invasions of privacy

The third intrusion that we accommodate within the police role is infringement of privacy. Although some would see privacy simply as an element of liberty, there is an informational dimension to privacy that sets it apart. The bedroom voyeur may not directly intrude on our liberty but most certainly invades our privacy. He gets to know things about us that are not his to know (at least without our consent). As with other values that we sometimes permit to be compromised by the police role, privacy is closely related to our dignitarian status and our agency (though it is not reducible to the latter).[38] For the most part, privacy enables us to secure a morally relevant space around our lives and thus retain some control over the terms of our self-presentational engagement with the world. If I am having a conversation with a close friend on a park bench – even a public bench – and you sidle up to us and begin to listen in to our conversation, you are most likely to transform the terms of our conversation. We lose some control over what we say to each other and how we say it. Among the more oppressive aspects of *Nineteen Eighty Four* was the removal of privacy and the constricting effect that that had on personal agency. Similar, though for the moment less overwhelming, fears have been generated by the ubiquitousness of CCTV cameras in large cities, and the unconstitutional overreach of governmental monitoring that came to light with Edward Snowden's unauthorised release of classified NSA documents in 2013.[39]

Determinations of what is private and what is public are a matter of ongoing debate, and there are interesting cultural differences. European countries focus very heavily on treating personal information as private, whereas Americans tend to concentrate on private places (e.g., the home).[40] Perhaps the most general point to be made is that people wish to have some control over the terms by which they engage with their fellows, and if they lose control over that, their privacy is breached. What I reveal about myself to my doctor or financial advisor is generally of no relevance to my neighbours or the powers that be, unless I choose to reveal it or there is some compelling reason why they should know such things about me. Privacy is not absolute, but a case needs to be made why breaches of privacy should be permitted.

Privacy is not secrecy, though respect for privacy may sometimes involve keeping certain matters secret. Secrecy – intentionally keeping certain information from others – has a prudential value, whereas privacy is valued for its own sake (quite apart from the instrumental benefits it may have).[41] By creating an informational space over which we have control, privacy is a condition of our agency, and, whatever other harms may come from its loss, it is to be respected for its own sake.[42] We keep things secret mostly to minimise certain harms to ourselves and others. Criminals may wish to keep information about their activities secret, even though what they wish to keep secret is a matter of legitimate public concern. Although it is true that we may sometimes treat as private matters that really have no business being kept so – thus making it important that we draw appropriate boundaries around public and private information – this does not gainsay the importance of making the distinction and therefore of the kinds of moral constraints that should attach to police work.

Discretion

Associated with all such police permissions and modifying the restrictions that are placed on police enforcement and investigative practices will be an authority to use discretion. Police work is complex and often takes place in changing and uncertain social environments, and the special powers police are accorded and how they use them will often require an appeal to judgement – professional judgement – rather than rules. They are given considerable discretion. Lest police decision making become a substitution of the rule of man for the rule of law, the exercise of discretion is a bounded activity requiring the appeal to reasons of an appropriate kind. Thus, letting off a speeding motorist with a warning – a common exercise of police discretion – rather than a summons ought to take account of factors such as whether the driver was driving recklessly and whether the driver appeared contrite, and it should exclude factors such as the race of the driver or the offer of a bribe (the latter an aggravation rather than a reason for concession).[43]

How police discretion should be constrained and justified is a tricky issue that may require multiple approaches. In theory at least, one might expect those who have responsibility for the exercise of discretion to bring their professional judgement to bear on the matter of discretionary boundaries, whether as individual officers or perhaps as police departments (e.g., whether or when to make arrests in the matter of marijuana possession). But as we know individuals and organisations are often self-serving or tunnel-visioned, and it is sometimes necessary that a wider public or even the courts should have significant input into the ways in which discretion is exercised. Although there is some reason, given the powers we place in the police, to institutionalise processes for discretionary decision making, much actual discretionary policy is incident-driven. Nevertheless, insofar as policing authority is consensual and committed to liberal values, there is good reason for discretionary policies to be open to wider scrutiny.

Conclusion

Our security as individuals and communities, especially in a complex social environment of the kind we ordinarily experience in liberal democratic societies, requires that we have in place people who are willing and competent to provide that security for us. Most directly they will seek to ensure that our fundamental rights are maintained and that breaches are redressed, though the remit of police generally goes somewhat narrower to exclude punishment,[44] and broader to what I have called social peace keeping – doing what is necessary to ensure the smooth turning of our social wheels. Sometimes police have not lived up to our social hopes for them. Because they are themselves first and foremost members of the communities they police, they may be infected by some of the least desirable traits of their community (racism, sexism, xenophobia, homophobia – and, more subtly, the attitudes and stereotypes associated with implicit bias). And sometimes they may be so focused on aspects of their work – such as crime fighting – that the protections they provide are purchased at too high a social price (e.g., recent controversies about stop-question-frisk in New York). What are regular calls for more "community policing" can be read as calls for policing that fulfils its consensual remit as social peace keeping.

Notes

1 John Locke, *Second Treatise of Civil Government* (1689), §123, many editions, but available online at: www.earlymoderntexts.com/assets/pdfs/locke1689a.pdf. This Lockean phrasing is simply a shorthand for a variety of formulations that he provides in the course of his work.

2 See also Jeremy Waldron, "Safety and Security," *Nebraska Law Review*, 85 (2006): 454–507. Waldron focuses much of his attention on Thomas Hobbes.

3 I use this term broadly to include those who are geographically present within a jurisdiction.

4 The boundary problems have been further exacerbated by the peace keeping role that the modern military has often been given in troubled areas of the world.

5 Beyond the issue of individual rights there was also an issue of public order and concern that too great a focus on the latter would be achieved at an unjustifiable cost to some individuals (as sometimes in profiling and internment). Maximising concerns needed to be curbed by dignitarian ones.

6 A helpful overview of the issues can be found in Fabienne Peter, "Political Legitimacy," in *The Stanford Encyclopedia of Philosophy* (Summer 2016 Edition), Edward N. Zalta (ed.), available at <http://plato.stanford.edu/archives/sum2016/entries/legitimacy/>.

7 For an attempt to show their connections, see John Kleinig and Nicholas G. Evans, "Human Flourishing, Human Dignity, and Human Rights," *Law and Philosophy* 32, no. 5 (September 2013): 539–564.

8 See, for example, "Definition of Policing by Consent", available at: www.gov.uk/government/publications/policing-by-consent/definition-of-policing-by-consent. The phrase "policing by consent" is not as commonly invoked in the US, though the US is more overtly contractualist in its political theorising. Ironically, what are referred to as policing "consent decrees" in the US are generally imposed oversight agreements.

9 For the former, see Henry Shue, *Basic Rights: Subsistence, Affluence, and U.S. Foreign Policy*, second ed. (Princeton, NJ: Princeton University Press, 1996). With regard to the latter, see A. John Simmons, "Locke and the Right to Punish," *Philosophy & Public Affairs*, 20, no. 4 (Autumn 1991): 311–349.

10 They are summarised in ch. 9 of *Second Treatise of Civil Government*.

11 Correctional institutions and personnel might also be included as part of the executive function.

12 For a fuller representation of the US criminal justice system, see the commonly reproduced diagram, "What Is the Sequence of Events in the Criminal Justice System?" available at: https://en.wikipedia.org/wiki/Criminal_justice#/media/File:Cjsflowco.svg. For a typical UK representation, see: www.gmvictims.org.uk/_Media/Cache/1030x/1b941a69-9bf6-4f18-ab2d-1879a176a7bf.PNG.

13 Although libertarians often appeal to Locke as morally individualistic and supportive only of minimal government, his moral vision is much broader: "twould always be a Sin in any Man of Estate to let his Brother perish for want of affording him Relief out of his Plenty" (*First Treatise of Civil Government* (1689), §42, where this is developed at greater length). In civil society, governmental authority, expressed in part through taxation, is intended to give substance to this moral obligation. For an exposition, see Virginia Held, "John Locke on Robert Nozick," *Social Research* 43, no. 1 (1976): 169–195.

14 Vesting natural moral entitlements in police does not require that we relinquish them entirely. If we are attacked and there are no police around, or if social agencies collapse or become too perverted, we may be left in the position of reasserting our "natural" rights.

15 Traditionally police in the US have been more heavily armed than police in the UK, though that may be changing along with social circumstances.

16 I have dealt with these at greater length in "Legitimate and Illegitimate Uses of Police Force," *Criminal Justice Ethics* 33, no. 2 (2014): 83–103.

17 No doubt, as with gynaecological examinations, some people will feel profoundly embarrassed by a body-cavity search. One may, however, minimise the embarrassment that is felt. See, further, Daphne Ha, "Blanket Policies for Strip Searching Pretrial Detainees: An Interdisciplinary Argument for Reasonableness," *Fordham Law Review* 79 (2011): 2721–2760.

18 See, for example, Ernest F. Lidge, III, "Perp Walks and Prosecutorial Ethics," *Nevada Law Journal* 7 (2006): 55–72.

19 See, for example, William Terrill, *Police Coercion: Application of the Force Continuum* (El Paso, TX: LFB Publishing, 2001). Many different models can be accessed by googling "use of force continuum" images.

20 The danger of excess that Locke and other contract theorists discerned in the state of nature doesn't disappear with the formation of police organisations. Police are not "naturally" distinguished from others. Part of the drive for professional training in policing is precisely to curb the anarchical tendencies of the state of nature.

21 See Donald A. Stone and Robert Laureno, "Handcuff Neuropathies," *Neurology* 41, no. 1 (1991): 145. One might of course even question the use of handcuffs in some arrests. See François Quintard-Morénas, "The Widespread Handcuffing of Arrestees in the United States," http://works.bepress.com/cgi/viewcontent.cgi?article=1003&context=francois_quintard_morenas.

22 See Jonathan Walsh, "Police Dealing with the Adrenaline Rush," available at: www.wtol.com/story/10399746/police-dealing-with-the-adrenaline-rush. The recent case in which Michael Slager shot Walter Scott is a good example. See Jon Swaine, "Walter Scott Shooting: Officer Laughs About Adrenaline Rush in Recording," *The Guardian*, 4/13/2015, available at: www.theguardian.com/us-news/2015/apr/12/walter-scott-shooting-officer-michael-slager-audio-recording?CMP=share_btn_tw. Ironically, but not surprisingly, the first trial ended with a hung jury.

23 Female police officers are often more willing to talk a person into surrender before using their weapons. See Kenneth Winston, "Teaching with Cases," in *Teaching Criminal Justice Ethics: Strategic Issues*, John Kleinig and Margaret Leland Smith (eds.). (Cincinnati: Anderson, 1997), 145–165. In a recent case, a police officer was fired for his refusal to shoot an armed person whom he had good reason to believe was trying to commit "suicide by cop" – see Radley Balko, "West Virginia Cop Fired for Not Killing a Man with an Unloaded Gun," *Washington Post*, 9/12/2016, available at: www.washingtonpost.com/news/the-watch/wp/2016/09/12/west-virginia-cop-fired-for-not-killing-a-man-with-an-unloaded-gun/?postshare=3111473784401066&tid=ss_mail.

24 I have developed this further in *The Ethics of Policing* (Cambridge: Cambridge University Press, 1996), ch. 6.2.

25 See the references in D. Steven, "How Balt: Police Helped Spark the Rioting – The Psychology of Militarized Police & Crowds," *Daily Kos*, 4/28/2015, available at: www.dailykos.com/stories/2015/4/28/1380894/-How-Balt-Riot-Police-Helped-Spark-the-Rioting-The-Psychology-of-Militarized-Police-Crowds. For a challenging view, see P.A.J. Waddington, "Both Arms of the Law: Institutionalised Protest and the Policing of Public Order," *Proceedings, British Society of Criminology* (1995), available at: www.britsoccrim.org/volume1/008.pdf.

26 See, for example, Dan Hinkel and Jennifer Smith Richards, "Chicago Cops Get More Tasers, But Red Flags Remain," *Chicago Tribune*, 9/27/2017, available at: www.chicagotribune.com/news/local/breaking/ct-chicago-police-tasers-met-20170825-story.html; J. David Goodman, "Complaint Board Softened Report on Police Use of Tasers," *New York Times*, 26/12/2016, available at: www.nytimes.com/2016/12/26/nyregion/complaint-board-softened-report-on-police-use-of-tasers.html. More generally, see: John Kleinig, "Ethical Constraints on Taser Use by Police," *Policing* 1, no. 3 (2007): 284–292.

27 Tennessee v. Garner, 471 US 1 (1985).

28 See Ali Soufan and Daniel Freedman, *The Black Banners: The Inside Story of 9/11 and the War Against al-Qaeda* (New York: W.W. Norton, 2011); John W. Schiemann, *Does Torture Work?* (New York: Oxford University Press, 2015).

29 These techniques, originally developed by John E. Reid in the 1940s, now dominate the US interrogational process. An initial, and problematic, behavior analysis interview is used to trigger a nine-step process of interrogation in which the presumption is that the person interrogated is criminally involved and a confession or inculpatory information is extracted. For a review, see Saul M. Kassin, Sara C. Appleby and Jennifer Torkildson Perillo, "Interviewing Suspects: Practice, Science, and Future Directions," *Legal and Criminological Psychology*, 15, no. 1 (2010): 39–55.

30 The Innocence Project, www.innocenceproject.org.

31 Graham v. Connor et al., 109 S Ct 1865 (1989), superseding Johnson v. Glick 481 F 2d 1028 at 1033 (2d Cir) cert. denied, 414 US 1033 (1973).

32 See some of the references in Kleinig, "Legitimate and Illegitimate Uses of Police Force".

33 See the discussion in John Kleinig, "What's All the Fuss with Police Militarization?" *The Critique*, 3/17/2015, available at: www.thecritique.com/articles/whats-all-the-fuss-with-police-militarization/.

34 On entrapment, see John Kleinig, *The Ethics of Policing* (Cambridge: Cambridge University Press, 1996), ch. 8; Jeffrey W. Howard, "Moral Subversion and Structural Entrapment," *Journal of Political Philosophy* 24 (2016): 24–46.

35 Andrew Ashworth, "Should the Police Be Allowed to Use Deceptive Practices?" *Law Quarterly Review* 114 (January 1998): 108–140.

36 Perhaps that is putting it too weakly. Officers should be able to appreciate the legitimate reasons for their discretionary decisions before they take them, not merely be able to construct them after them after the event. Designing institutional mechanisms to hold discretionary decision making to account is a major challenge, and even the most careful procedures may be subverted.

37 For some egregious examples, see Sarah Stillman, "The Throwaways," *New Yorker*, 9/3/2012, available at: www.newyorker.com/magazine/2012/09/03/the-throwaways.

38 Leaving a naked corpse exposed to public view will not affect agency, though it violates dignity and privacy.

39 For the documents released by Snowden, see ACLU, "NSA Documents," available at: www.aclu.org/nsa-documents-search?f%5B0%5D=field_foia_document_date%3A2017.

40 See, for example, James Q Whitman, "Two Western Cultures of Privacy: Dignity versus Liberty," *Yale Law Journal* 113 (2004): 1151–1221, available at: http://digitalcommons.law.yale.edu/cgi/viewcontent.cgi?article=1647&context=fss_papers.

41 There are some critics of privacy who maintain that we would be better off were our lives more transparent than they are, and that we should – more or less – eschew privacy. We would not be (as) vulnerable to blackmail and fraud, there would be less hypocrisy and deceit, and greater candour. Some would maintain that we would be healthier psychologically had we fewer hang-ups over things we tend to treat as private (e.g., matters of sexual preference and potency, penis size, and religious commitment) – or that the desire for privacy is connected to shame – our having something to hide. No doubt privacy can function as a cloak for secrecy, but what often seems to be complained about is not privacy but secrecy.

42 For a useful defence, see Jeffrey H. Reiman, "Privacy, Intimacy, and Personhood," *Philosophy & Public Affairs* 6 (1976): 26–44.

43 Police training in professional responsibility ought in part to be directed to sensitising police to appropriate and inappropriate occasions and reasons for exercising discretion. Reviews of police decision making may discern problematic decision-making patterns.

44 See John Kleinig, "Punishment and the Ends of Policing," in *Liberal Criminal Theory: Essays for Andreas von Hirsched*, A.P. Simester and A. Du Bois-Pedain (eds.). (Oxford: Hart Publishing, 2014), 283–303.

8

MORE THAN PRIVACY

Thinking ethically about public area surveillance

Benjamin Goold

Over the last 40 years, there has been a staggering increase in the use of video surveillance technologies – such as closed-circuit television (CCTV) and body-worn cameras – by governments around the world. In cities throughout Asia, Europe, and North America, the sight of surveillance cameras attached to the sides of buildings or on top of lampposts is a common one. For people living in major urban centres like Beijing, London, and New York, it is now virtually impossible to move through public spaces without being captured on video by the police or some other state agency. In addition, as more and more police forces equip their officers with small body-worn cameras, the reach of the state's surveillance capacity has expanded well beyond public areas like streets and parks. Now, when a police officer enters a private property or residence, the surveillance power of the state goes with them, with the result that there are fewer and fewer spaces in which people can hope to be free from the state's gaze.[1]

Given the speed at which this technology has been developed and harnessed by law enforcement agencies around the world, it is not surprising that policy-makers and courts have struggled with the question of how best to regulate the use of public area surveillance. In part, this struggle reflects the fact that our political and legal processes are ill-equipped to deal with rapid technological change. These processes are, by their very nature, frequently slow and conservative, and those charged with making decisions – members of government, public officials, and judges – often lack the expertise required to understand the capabilities of new technologies, or to assess claims about their likely costs and benefits. But an additional problem lies with the fundamental question of what is at stake when we allow the police to turn streets, parks, and other public spaces into sites of state surveillance. What are the implications of public area CCTV for individual members of the public, communities, and society at large?

To date, in Canada, the United States, and many EU countries, the question of whether we should place limits on the use of public area surveillance technologies has been framed in terms of a fundamental tension between a commitment to protecting the privacy interests of individuals on the one hand and a desire on the part of the state to reduce crime, combat public disorder, and increase security on the other.[2] This framing has had significant implications for both sides of the debate. By focusing on privacy, those concerned about the potential dangers of mass public area surveillance have been faced with the unenviable challenge of convincing policy-makers, courts, and the public at large that it makes sense to even speak about privacy rights in public.[3] Aside from the fact that this is challenging rhetorically – the idea of "privacy in public" striking many, initially at least, as inherently contradictory – there is also the problem of delineating the scope of such a right. As many commentators have observed, defining privacy is notoriously difficult.[4] Even when talking about physical settings, personal circumstances, or specific forms of information that most would agree give rise to some sort of expectation of privacy, the reasons behind this agreement can vary dramatically. Privacy can be justified in terms of appeals to the need for secrecy, limited access to the self, arguments about choice and autonomy, and the importance of intimacy and identity formation.[5] Depending on the underlying justification – and the values that one is seeking to promote or protect – the precise scope of the privacy right will vary considerably. The situation is made all the more complex by the fact that privacy, in many of its forms, is regarded as deserving of protection not only because we regard it as inherently important but also because of the crucial role that privacy plays in the exercise of other rights. Freedom of expression, freedom of association, and freedom of religion are all rights that are extremely hard to exercise without some expectation of privacy.[6] As a result, discussions about privacy often become arguments about other rights, making the problem of definition and scope even more difficult.

On the other side of the debate, the desire to couch arguments in favour of public area surveillance in terms of safety and security has created its own set of problems. Despite the fact that advocates of CCTV are often quick to make expansive claims about its effectiveness at reducing crime and preventing acts of terrorism, clear empirical evidence to support such claims has been somewhat elusive.[7] Indeed, one of the most striking things about the use of public area surveillance is the lack of independent research on its effectiveness as a law enforcement tool. In part, this is because isolating the effects of CCTV on crime and disorder is methodologically challenging, and even where we might be confident that a reduction in crime is attributable to public area surveillance, measuring the potential displacement effects of such technology is difficult. Insofar as CCTV can be justified as an investigation tool, the picture is also unclear. While it is common for the police and other law enforcement agencies to highlight the important role played by public area video footage in apprehension of suspects after a major crime or terrorist incident, there is always the question of whether that person would still have been apprehended if the footage had not been available. Would other investigative and evidence-gathering techniques – which do not require subjecting the public to continuous, potentially intrusive video surveillance – have yielded similar results?

There is a great deal more that could be said about the impact of this framing of the issues and the role that disagreements over the relationship between privacy and security have had on policies governing the use of public area surveillance technologies like CCTV. Although these are important discussions, this chapter deliberately avoids reopening the "privacy-versus-security" debate and instead asks whether there are other ethical issues that should be considered when deciding whether (and under what circumstances) technology such as CCTV should be used in public spaces.

In particular, this chapter focuses on two key ethical questions. The first is whether decision-makers have an ethical obligation to consider alternatives to the use of public area surveillance, as well as an associated responsibility to provide clear, public justification for any decision to instal cameras. Here, the focus is not on deontological concerns about whether CCTV is acceptable in terms of its actual (or potential) impact on individual rights, but rather on the consequentialist concern with making the best use of available resources when seeking to promote the public good. The second question is focused on the relationship between public area surveillance and trust. It is often argued that maintaining high levels of trust in the key institutions of state power – such as the police – is vital to the health of any democratic system of government. If we accept that the use of CCTV has the potential to undermine that trust – by signalling to members of the public that they are the subjects of a generalised suspicion – then the question arises as to whether it is ethical for the state to engage in such activity. Put another way, if one of the potential consequences of mass public surveillance is a general loss of trust in the state, can it be ethical for the police and other law enforcement agencies to engage in such activities?

Before moving to a consideration of these arguments, it is important to note that the focus of this chapter is on the ethical implications of public area surveillance carried out by (or on behalf of) the state. While it remains the case that the majority of public area CCTV systems around the world are state-run, the use of surveillance technologies in semi-public spaces like airports, train stations, university campuses, and shopping malls is also increasingly common in countries like the United Kingdom and United States. As many commentators have noted, private-sector involvement in the surveillance of these semi-public spaces raises serious social and ethical questions, particularly because such surveillance often aims to identify "undesirable" individuals with a view to exclusion.[8] Although the managers of a shopping mall, for example, clearly have an interest in ensuring that this seemingly public space is free from crime, they also have an interest in excluding those who are not "consumers". As such, the involvement of private-sector actors in operation of CCTV in spaces that if not strictly public are treated as such by the community raises the danger of routine discrimination based on age, race, class, and socio-economic status.

As worrying as this is, it can be argued that public area surveillance by the state raises even more serious ethical concerns. In part, this is because the state typically has the resources and legal authority to instal camera systems that cover large areas and that are directly connected to other state-run surveillance systems. Moreover, unlike private-sector organisations, the police and other law enforcement agencies have a range of powers – including a monopoly on the legal use of force – that they can use in conjunction with the surveillance of public spaces to exercise a degree of control and to constrain rights in ways that are fundamentally different from any other group in society.[9] For the purposes of this chapter, the importance of focusing on the state also derives from the fact that actors like the police are in a unique position with respect to the public, in terms of both the impact their actions have on public trust in government and their clear obligation to serve the public good. Put another way, when the state uses technology like CCTV in public spaces, the ethical implications – not just for privacy but also for the way individuals understand and experience their relationship to the state – are fundamentally different.

Public area surveillance, consequentialism, and state obligations

As has already been noted, much of the discussion about the ethics of public area surveillance has focused on the potential impact of technologies like CCTV on individual privacy interests. Although we might disagree about why privacy is valuable – and as a result, we may be more or less convinced by the various justifications for CCTV – the fact remains that the discussion is essentially a deontological one. Because we start from the position that privacy is (for whatever reason) inherently valuable, it follows that activities that that infringe on privacy – like the use of CCTV in public spaces – are wrongful and require justification.

But what other types of ethical issues might be raised by the spread of public area surveillance? Are there reasons to be concerned about the use of CCTV that are not directly related to questions of privacy? Are there reasons to limit the state's use of surveillance technology in public spaces that are not based on deontological claims about the value of privacy and the wrongfulness of surveillance? Perhaps the most obvious alternative to the deontological approach is a consequentialist one. Rather than focusing on the rightness (or wrongness) of public area surveillance – measured in terms of the impact of CCTV on individual rights – a consequentialist approach is concerned with the rightness (or wrongness) of the consequences that flow from using such technologies. Importantly, however, in this context consequences must be understood as referring to more than effectiveness. Instead, a consequentialist approach asks us to consider the full range of costs (including forgone opportunities) associated with CCTV, and it requires us to be able to justify the use of cameras with reference to all reasonably available alternatives. The value of this approach is that it enables us to look past disagreements about privacy rights and ask: is public area surveillance the best solution to the particular problem the state is seeking to solve?

In addition to drawing attention to the costs of CCTV, a consequentialist approach also requires us to think about the distributional outcomes – in terms of the provision of crime prevention and security – that follow from the use of public area surveillance technologies. By devoting limited resources to the installation of CCTV cameras in city centres, for example, we risk privileging the safety and security of those who live and work in densely populated urban centres over those who live in suburban or rural communities. As with a consideration of opportunity costs of CCTV, arguments about what constitutes a fair distribution of safety and security need not engage with the question of whether individuals have an expectation of privacy in public spaces. Even those who flatly reject the idea of privacy rights in public spaces would be hard pressed to argue that questions of distribution do not matter when we talk about safety and security.

For the sake of argument, imagine a policy-maker who is convinced that privacy rights do not extend to public spaces and who as a result does not regard the use of public area surveillance technologies like CCTV as wrongful (in the sense that they infringe on individual privacy). Does this mean that policy-makers are free from ethical considerations when deciding on whether to instal cameras in their city? Can they simply put up as many CCTV cameras as they like, provided they are in clearly delineated public spaces? Is there anything for them to consider if they are unconcerned with rights?

To a large extent, the answer to this question will turn on whether we believe states can have positive moral obligations and, if so, what those obligations might look like. Although it is well beyond the scope of this chapter to survey the various arguments for (and against) treating states as moral actors, for the time being let us assume that a commitment to democracy and the rule of law imposes certain duties and constraints on the state. These duties and obligations could take many different forms, but one such duty might be to maximise the utility of citizens and to ensure that state resources are used as efficiently as possible. In such circumstances, public officials would be under a positive moral obligation to ensure that their decisions promote the public good (at the very least) and lead to an optimal use of state resources (at the very best). In the event that a decision does not lead to an increase in utility or results in an inefficient use of resources, citizens would be entitled to hold the officials in question – and the state – to account on the ground that the decision is unethical.

If we take this view of the state – and it is a view that closely mirrors the constitutional reality in many liberal democracies – then it follows that ethical arguments about public area surveillance must be about more than the protection of privacy rights. Going further, it will also not be enough for decision-makers to be confident that CCTV "works" – as a crime prevention tool, as an aid to police investigations, or for any other supposed purpose. Instead, they must be able to demonstrate that CCTV works *better* than any available alternatives, and that the resulting distribution of safety and security is fair. For example, the question 'Does CCTV reduce crime and make public spaces safer?' might become: 'Does CCTV reduce crime and make public spaces safer than increasing the number of uniformed police officers on the streets?' Further, there is the additional question: 'Is the redistribution of resources resulting from the installation of public area CCTV fair?' If the decision-makers are not able to answer these questions – with reference to evidence and some account of distributional justice as it relates to the provision of safety and security – then they leave themselves open to accusation that they have – in using scarce public resources less than optimally – behaved unethically.

This ethical requirement – to consider fully the opportunity costs and distributional implications of public area CCTV – is perhaps easier to see if we use an example unrelated to public area surveillance. Imagine that a government decides to spend all of the tax revenue collected in a given year on beautifying cities and towns across the country, leaving nothing for spending on health, education, or the other core functions of the state. Although we might not go so far as to say that spending money on parks, community gardens, and uplifting public art installations is inherently wrongful, we would no doubt say that the officials in question have acted unethically by failing to spend some of this money on things we regard as more important and essential to the proper functioning of the state. Further, we might also say that by spending all of the funds collected nationally on the beautification of cities and towns, the policy-makers have neglected the interests of those who live outside of these urban areas. Similarly, spending money on a vast array of CCTV cameras – when it can be shown that an increase in police patrols will do more to reduce crime and promote public safety – might also be described as unethical, irrespective of the impact that the cameras may have on individual rights.

When considering this argument, it is important to remember that government officials – acting on behalf of the state – are in a fundamentally different ethical position to that of private individuals. Although most deontological theories of ethics accept that individuals, when confronted with a range of permissible course of actions, are not required to choose the most ethical action, it can be argued that the same is not true when it comes to state actors. Although it would clearly be unrealistic to expect decision-makers to always make the best possible choice – particularly given that such choices are rarely made in isolation or with full information – it is reasonable to require that whatever choice they do make bears some rational relationship to relevant objectives, and that opportunity costs and distributional outcomes have been considered. Put another way, we can say that decision-makers have an ethical obligation to consider the consequences of any decision on the common good.

Although this obligation is sometimes framed in vague terms – for example, the argument that officials are required to spend public money "wisely" or to make sure that "taxpayers' money isn't wasted" – the underlying ethical claim is clear: public decisions must be directed towards furthering some substantive conception of the greater good. As such, when confronted with a range of ethically permissible courses of action, the decision-maker should choose the one that leads to the best possible outcome for as many people as possible.[10] While it may be ethically acceptable for an individual to choose any course of conduct that is not demonstrably wrongful – we expect such individuals to do the right thing, rather than the best thing – in contrast, an official is expected to make a choice that promotes the greater good.

What does this mean for the ethics of public area surveillance? For officials who wish to instal CCTV cameras in their towns or cities – rather than, for example, increase the number of patrols by uniformed police officers – they need to be able to justify their decision on several related grounds. First, they must be able to demonstrate not only that public area CCTV will reduce crime and improve safety but also that it is likely to be more effective at achieving these goals than any reasonably available alternative. Second, the officials must be able to justify any distributional consequences arising from the decision. Even though we might disagree as to what is required of the decision-makers in order to discharge these obligations – that is, what sorts of evidence of effectiveness are required, what kinds of distributional criteria are acceptable, and so forth – by focusing on the need for a consequentialist justification, we can avoid being mired in deontological disputes about the individual rights or interests – such as privacy – that might be harmed by the use of CCTV in public spaces.[11]

It is important to note that these arguments – at least as they are presented here – are not meant to be taken as legal or even political claims. The question of how public officials should exercise their discretion when choosing from a range of potential solutions to an identified problem is typically one which is subject to a host of legal principles and constraints. Instead, the aim of this section is to draw attention to the fact that an ethical examination of the implications of public area surveillance does not require us to consider both sides of the privacy-versus-security debate. Rather, it suggests that there is value in directing our focus to one side of the equation – the "security" side – and demanding that decision-makers examine the opportunity costs of CCTV and be able to explain why they have chosen public area surveillance over other crime-reduction or security-enhancing programs or technologies.

Public area surveillance and loss of trust

Assuming that it is possible to provide a convincing, consequentialist justification for the use of public area CCTV based on a consideration of opportunity costs, does it then follow that the use of such technology is ethically acceptable? Is the consequentialist calculus exhausted in such circumstances? If CCTV represents the best and most cost-effective way to combat crime and enhance security – when compared with a range of reasonable alternatives – does that make it ethical (absent arguments about the potential impact on privacy)? One way to approach this question is to consider the potential externalities of public area surveillance. Unlike the opportunity costs considered in the previous section, such externalities are not the product of a choice between CCTV and something else (e.g., an increase in uniformed police officers) but rather an unwelcome consequence of the use of such technology in public spaces.

There are many potential externalities associated with the use of public area CCTV. Empirical studies of the behaviour of camera operators suggests, for example, that women, the young, and visible minorities are far more likely to be targets of surveillance.[12] If this is the case, then any discussion about the ethics of public area surveillance should include a consideration of not only opportunity costs but also the dangers of discriminatory surveillance on the part of the state – such as racial profiling, the over-policing of minorities and already marginalised groups (e.g., the homeless), and the use of technology as a tool for segregation and exclusion.

But there are also other less obvious externalities that can arise from the use of public area surveillance. One of these is the loss of trust. Although the notion of trust is a complex one – particularly as it applies to both communities and the state – it can be argued that the widespread use of highly visible surveillance technologies like CCTV is a symbol of the breakdown of trust.[13] Contrary to the rhetoric that often accompanies the introduction of new CCTV systems – that their presence makes people feel safer – the installation of cameras can also be interpreted as a signal to the public that they have something to fear. More significantly, in spaces like schools, airports, and government buildings, the presence of CCTV can also be seen in more starkly oppositional terms. Put simply, cameras send the message that members of the public represent a threat to security and must be constantly watched by the state in order to maintain order, reduce crime, and – in the case of airports and public buildings – prevent some catastrophic terrorist event.

As Beck, Garland, and many others have noted, one of the key features of late-modern society is a growing obsession with risk and a demand for the state to provide safety and security.[14] But as states have erected increasingly sophisticated and intrusive systems of domestic surveillance, they have also contributed to the erosion of trust – between individuals within communities (who increasingly see each other as threats) and between individuals and the state itself (which now sees everyone as a potential criminal or terrorist). By its very nature, surveillance is about mistrust: we watch because we fear that someone may transgress against social or legal norms and cause harm to others or to the social order. When the surveillance is being undertaken on the part of government, the symbolic impact of this display of mistrust has the potential to seriously undermine the relationship between the state and the public.

If we begin to think about costs and benefits of CCTV in terms of trust – whether it creates trust or erodes it – ethical arguments about public area surveillance start to take on a very different character. Even if we accept that CCTV is effective – in terms of reducing crime, promoting order, or keeping us safe from terrorist attacks – and even if we are unconcerned about costs (either in terms of privacy or forgone crime prevention alternatives), we still need to think carefully about how the use of CCTV changes the relationship between the public and the state. The twentieth century is awash with examples of countries where there has been a complete breakdown of trust between the public and the state, and in many cases this breakdown was accompanied and fuelled by the growing use of state surveillance. Perhaps the most extreme example of this, at least in the European context, was in the former German Democratic Republic (GDR). By the time the Berlin Wall fell in 1989, the former East German state had completely destroyed the relationship of trust between itself and the public, in part through its relentless use of surveillance in both public and private spheres. While it is important to be cautious when drawing comparisons between countries and political regimes – especially across time – the experience of the GDR stands as a salutary reminder of what can happen when trust in the state collapses.[15]

At a more mundane level, there are other potential costs associated with trust that can arise from the use of public area surveillance technologies like CCTV. One of these is loss of trust in specific institutions, such as the police. In many democratic countries, the dominant model of law enforcement is "policing by consent". Under this model, the police are granted certain powers – such as the right to use force (the so-called monopoly on violence) – in exchange for providing protection to members of the public and enforcing the criminal law.[16] Although an institution of the state, the police exist to serve the public rather than the government of the day, and as such they are expected to act in the public interest and remain politically neutral. When this relationship is functioning well, and the police have the trust and support of the communities they are responsible for, they are able to rely on the voluntary cooperation of the public when carrying out their day-to-day activities. When trust and confidence in the police are high, members of the public are more likely to cooperate with the police, bring valuable information to them, and recognise their legal authority. As a consequence, the police do not have to resort to the exercise of their legal powers in their routine interactions with the public: they do not, for example, have to arrest people in order to compel them to identify themselves or answer general questions. The public willingly cooperate because they trust the police.

If the use of CCTV is interpreted by the general public – or even by specific groups within the wider community – as a sign that the police do not trust them, there is a danger that it will undermine the public's belief in policing by consent, and with it the fundamental relationship between the police and the policed. If this happens, then not only do many of the day-to-day activities of the police become more difficult and fraught but also in extreme cases they can become impossible. In the United States, there are many examples of what happens when the relationship of trust between the police and the community breaks down, and what this does to the ability of the police to carry out even basic law enforcement tasks. One only has to look to the problems that have beset the police in predominantly African American communities over the last 50 years to see a clear example of what happens when trust is eroded or collapses completely. More specifically, there is also evidence to suggest that when the police place specific communities under surveillance – using technologies like CCTV – trust can be significantly damaged.

This is a lesson that the UK police learnt in the aftermath of the "Project Champion" scandal in the early 2000s. Established in response to a series of terrorist events in 2007, Project Champion was a surveillance operation carried out by the West Midlands police, which involved setting up what amounted to a "CCTV net" of over 200 cameras around two semi-residential, predominantly Asian communities within the city of Birmingham. After members of the public noticed the cameras in 2010 – and made inquiries to their local representatives – it was eventually revealed that the system had been set up in the absence of public consultation or notification, and that aspects of the operation were clearly unlawful. The project was discontinued in response to the public outcry, and an independent inquiry was established for 'review of the commissioning, direction, control and oversight of Project Champion; including the information given to, and the involvement of, the community'.[17] In her forward to the inquiry's final report, then chief constable Sara Thornton noted,

> There is nothing more important to policing than its legitimacy in the eyes of the public. The concerns of the community need to be a central preoccupation of policing and transparency needs to be a constant consideration. In the course of this review I have met members of the community and have read the press reports and it is clear that many people feel that their civil liberties have been disregarded. As a consequence, the trust and confidence that they have in the police has been significantly undermined.[18]

Going further, later in the report Thornton also noted, '[T]he lack of transparency about the purpose of the project has resulted in significant community anger and loss of trust. As one community leader stated to the Review Team, "this has set relations back a decade" '.[19] This last point is particularly striking, and from reading news reports from the time, it is clear members of the public were deeply troubled by the fact that the police had surrounded their communities with "mystery" CCTV cameras.[20] Aside from the fact that CCTV is a very visible reminder of the surveillance power of the state, the presence of cameras such as those installed in Birmingham is hard to reconcile with the idea that the police are also members of the community, and that 'police are the public and the public are the police'.[21]

If trust in the police is a "good" in democratic societies, then it follows that any ethical analysis of the use of public area CCTV must include a consideration of the possible implications for that trust. Going further, decision-makers should also look to the potential implications for the relationship between the state and the public more generally. Although the existence of trust is something that many of us might take for granted in our relations with the state, we should not take its loss lightly. Not only does a state without the trust of the population at large find it hard to govern or maintain its legitimacy, but also it makes the job of those tasked with enforcing the law substantially more difficult and dangerous. For these reasons alone, any ethical consideration of public area CCTV should take the question of trust seriously.

Public area surveillance and the changing nature of the "public"

In this final section, I want to briefly explore another ethical question raised by the use of CCTV by the state: namely, what is this technology doing to our idea of the public? Although it has become increasingly common in academic circles to speak of the creeping privatisation and commodification of public spaces, there has been surprisingly little discussion of what we mean when we speak of public spaces and – more importantly perhaps – why it is that we regard such spaces as valuable and worth protecting. While privacy scholars, such as Pricilla Regan and Helen Nissembaum,[22] have drawn attention to the crucial role that public spaces can play in the exercise of free speech and freedom of association, the impact of surveillance on how we understand and use public space in early twenty-first-century urban communities remains under-examined. More crucially, even the most cursory examination of policy debates about the costs and benefits of CCTV reveals that the notion of the public – and what camera surveillance does to it – is rarely mentioned.

Although this chapter is not the place for a wide-ranging examination of the various ways in which we understand public space, there are a number of things that can be said. First, there is clearly a need for more discussion of the public aspect of public area surveillance. As noted earlier, discussions about privacy rights in public often get derailed by disagreements about the fundamental value of privacy. One of the unfortunate consequences of this is that such discussions rarely turn to the question of what exactly it is we mean when we speak of public spaces. Are urban streets that are lined with a mixture of residential and commercial buildings public? Are parks, often enclosed by such streets and accessible only by travel along them, public? To what extent is it meaningful to speak of public spaces when it is impossible to reach them without subjecting oneself to surveillance by other individuals, private organisations, or the state? Once we are in those spaces, does the presence of CCTV cameras diminish what makes them valuable to us, such as the ability to be anonymous or simply blend in with the crowd? Is there any point in even talking about public spaces in the twenty-first century?[23]

In previous works, I have discussed the importance of public spaces to the development of identity, and how the presence of state-run CCTV cameras can have a chilling effect on the choices we make in those spaces.[24] But the impact of cameras on individuals is only part of the story. We also need an account of the communal value of these spaces. Shared values emerge in part from the need to share space and being forced to interact with each other, and public spaces, such as streets and parks, have historically played a vital role in the development of community and collective identity. Although it is tempting to downplay the importance of physical spaces – particularly given that many of us spend more and more time living our social and political lives online – it is still the case that most of us spend large amounts of time moving through physical spaces, either on our way to work, while shopping, or while simply spending time outside of our homes. In order to develop an ethical approach to the use of CCTV cameras in public, we need to go beyond discussions of privacy and the effectiveness of cameras: we also need to be clearer about what it is we think public spaces are for.

The second, and final, point I wish to make here concerns the scope of the debate over public area CCTV. Although there has been an explosion in academic interest in surveillance over the last 30 years – as exemplified by the emergence of "surveillance studies" as a discipline in its own right – debates about CCTV continue to be dominated by sociologists, criminologists, urban geographers, and, to a lesser extent, legal academics. Philosophers and political theorists, however, have been noticeably absent. If we are to move beyond arguments about privacy and Foucault-inspired fears of a surveillance society – and towards a more comprehensive ethics of surveillance – we need to be willing to take a more holistic view of the challenges presented by technologies like CCTV. As someone deeply rooted in legal scholarship and the criminological theory, writing a chapter such as this one serves only to reinforce my belief that we need more philosophers writing about ethical dimensions of CCTV, and more political theorists worrying about what CCTV surveillance does to our relationship with the state and our experience of "the public".[25] Although this chapter seeks to draw attention to a number of arguments that have been neglected in debates about the use of CCTV, it is little more than a starting point. Hopefully others can take these questions forward.

Conclusion

As noted at the beginning of this chapter, it is sometimes difficult to move discussions about public area CCTV beyond disagreements about the nature of privacy and the effectiveness of camera surveillance. This is unfortunate, as the use of CCTV cameras in public spaces raises a whole host of questions that go beyond concerns about privacy and crime prevention. What are the ethical considerations that policy-makers should take into account when considering whether to instal cameras in public, and how should cameras be compared with other policing tools? Do state agents have specific ethical obligations when making choices about surveillance technologies like CCTV? What is the impact of state-sponsored CCTV on trust? How does the use of surveillance technologies in public spaces like streets and parks transform our understanding and experience of the "public"?

In raising these issues, this chapter has sought to move the debate about public area CCTV in a more "ethical" direction – that is, by suggesting that is a place for ethical arguments that go beyond the tension between privacy and security, and by focusing attention on the specific ethical implications of state-sponsored CCTV surveillance. There is, of course, much more that can be said about all of these issues. Hopefully, however, what is clear from even this brief discussion is that there is a role for ethical arguments in the debate over CCTV, and that not every argument for or against the use of this technology by the state needs to start with some claim about privacy. Although privacy is important, it is not the only thing at stake from the steady expansion in public area surveillance. Instead, we must also remember to place the public aspect of public area CCTV at the centre of any discussion, and to think carefully about how allowing the state to see into our public lives changes not only our relationship with the state but also how we experience those spaces and, ultimately, the value we find in them.

Notes

1 For an account of the development and spread of CCTV surveillance, see: Doyle, A., Lippert, R. and Lyon, D. (2013) (eds.) *Eyes Everywhere: The Global Growth of Camera Surveillance* New York: Routledge; Ball, K., Lyon, D., Murakami Wood, D., Norris, C. and Raab, C. (2006) *A Report on the Surveillance Society* London: Office of the Information Commissioner; Norris, C., McCahill, M. and Wood, D. (2004) "Editorial: The Growth of CCTV: A Global Perspective on the International Diffusion of Video Surveillance in Publicly Accessible Space" *Surveillance and Society* 2(2/3): 110–135; Goold, B. (2004) *CCTV and Policing: Public Area Surveillance and Police Practices in Britain* Oxford: Oxford University Press; and Norris, C. Moran, C. and Armstrong, G. (1998) (eds.) *Surveillance, Closed Circuit Television and Social Control* Aldershot: Ashgate.
2 For a discussion of the privacy issues that arise from CCTV in these jurisdictions, see: Lai, D. (2007) "Public Video Surveillance by the State: Policy, Privacy Legislation, and the Charter" *Alberta Law Review* 45: 43–77; Slobogin, C. (2002) "Public Privacy: Camera Surveillance of Public Places and the Right to Anonymity" *Mississippi Law Journal* 72: 214–285; and *Surveillance: Citizens and the State*, HL 18-I (report) and HL 18-II (evidence), House of Lords Constitution Committee, 6 February 2009.

3 This is a point I have raised elsewhere. See: Goold, B. (2006) "Open to All? Regulating Open Street CCTV and the Case for 'Symmetrical Surveillance'" *Criminal Justice Ethics* 25(1): 3–17: and Goold, B. (2004) "Privacy Rights and Public Spaces: CCTV and the Problem of the 'Unobservable Observer'" *Criminal Justice Ethics* 21(1): 21–27. See also: Lever, A. (2011) *On Privacy* London: Routledge, Chapters 3 and 4.

4 Solove, D.J. (2002) "Conceptualising Privacy" *California Law Review* 90(4): 1087. As Solove notes, 'The difficulty in articulating what privacy is and why it is important has often made privacy law ineffective and blind to the larger purposes for which it must serve . . . Judges, politicians, and scholars have often failed to adequately conceptualise the problems that privacy law is asked to redress. Privacy problems are often not well articulated, and as a result, we frequently do not have a compelling account of what is at stake when privacy is threatened and what precisely the law must do to solve these problems'.

5 For excellent accounts of the main theories of privacy, see: Solove, D.J. (2002) "Conceptualising Privacy" *California Law Review* 90(4): 1087–1155; and Nissenbaum, H. (2010) *Privacy in Context: Technology, Policy, and the Integrity of Social Life* Stanford: Stanford University Press. On the specific relationship between privacy and social identity, see: Schoeman, F. (1992) *Privacy and Social Freedom* Cambridge: Cambridge University Press; and Steeves, V. (2009) "Reclaiming the Social Value of Privacy" in Kerr, I., Steeves, V. and Lucock, C. (eds.) *Lessons from the Identity Trail: Anonymity, Privacy and Identity in a Networked Society* New York: Oxford University Press.

6 Goold, B. (2009) "Surveillance and the Political Value of Privacy" *Amsterdam Law Forum* 1(4): 3–6. See also: Regan, P. (1995) *Legislating Privacy: Technology, Social Values, and Public Policy* Chapel Hill: The University of North Carolina Press.

7 For a discussion of research on the effectiveness of CCTV, see the editors' introduction to Part I of Doyle, A., Lippert, R. and Lyon, D. (2013) (eds.) *Eyes Everywhere: The Global Growth of Camera Surveillance* New York: Routledge.

8 See: Lyon, D. (2002) (ed.) *Surveillance as Social Sorting: Privacy, Risk and Automated Discrimination* Abingdon: Routledge; Lomell, H.M. (2004) "Targeting the Unwanted: Video Surveillance and Categorical Exclusion in Oslo, Norway" *Surveillance & Society* 2(2): 346–360; and von Hirsch, A. and Shearing, C. (2000) "Exclusion from Public Space" in von Hirsch, S. Garland, D. and Wakefield, A. (eds.) *Ethical and Social Perspectives on Situational Crime Prevention* Oxford: Hart; and Hier, S. (2004) "Risky Spaces and Dangerous Faces: Urban Surveillance, Social Disorder and CCTV" *Social and Legal Studies* 13(4): 541–554.

9 Goold, B. (2008) "The Difference Between Lonely Old Ladies and CCTV Cameras: A Response to Jesper Ryberg" *Res Publica* 14(1): 43–47. See also Lever, A. (2008) "Mrs. Aremac and the Camera: A Response to Ryberg" *Res Publica: A Journal of Legal and Social Philosophy* 14(1): 35–42.

10 This statement, of course, raises the question of what constitutes the "best possible outcome" in a given set of circumstances. Although this chapter is not the place for a detailed discussion of the moral (and legal) obligations of public officials, the key here is to note that such officials are obliged to consider the interests and well-being of others when making their decisions. At the very least, such decisions must have a grounding in rationality and, at the very least, lead to outcomes that are "good enough".

11 In response to these points, it can be argued that the distinction being drawn here between deontological and consequentialist approaches is perhaps too sharp, and that the discussion of opportunity costs – and what constitutes an ethically defensible allocation of resources – is overly simplistic. To be clear, my purpose in raising these points is not to suggest that questions of distribution are the exclusive preserve of consequentialist theories. Instead, the aim is to move the discussion away from a narrow focus on the moral right to privacy, and to draw attention to some of the other costs of surveillance. For a fuller discussion of the distributional costs of surveillance, see: Lever, A. (2006) "Privacy Rights and Democracy: A Contradiction in Terms?" *Contemporary Political Theory* 5: 142–162.

12 See: Norris, C. and Armstrong, G. (1998) *The Maximum Surveillance Society* London: Bloomsbury Publishing; and Goold, B. (2004) *CCTV and Policing: Public Area Surveillance and Police Practices in Britain* Oxford: Oxford University Press.

13 For some of my earlier thinking on this issue, see: Goold, B. (2008) "Technologies of Surveillance and the Erosion of Institutional Trust" in Aas, K., Gundhus, H.O. and Lomell, H.M. (eds) *Technologies of Insecurity* Abingdon: Routledge: 207–218.

14 See: Garland, D. (2002) *The Culture of Control: Crime and Social Order in Contemporary Society* Chicago: University of Chicago Press; Beck, U. (1992) *Risk Society: Towards a New Modernity* London: Sage; and Ericson, R. and Haggerty, K. (1997) *Policing the Risk Society* Toronto: University of Toronto Press.

15 For an interesting discussion of the political value of trust, see: Mishler, W. and Rose, R. (2001) "What Are the Origins of Political Trust? Testing Institutional and Cultural Theories in Post-Communist Societies" *Comparative Political Studies* 34(1): 30–62.
16 According to the UK Home Office, 'policing by consent' is in part based on the idea that the police must 'maintain at all times a relationship with the public that gives reality to the historic tradition that the police are the public and that the public are the police, the police being only members of the public who are paid to give full-time attention to duties which are incumbent on every citizen in the interests of community welfare and existence'. See: www.gov.uk/government/publications/policing-by-consent (accessed 4 March 2018).
17 Thames Valley Police. (2010) *Project Champion Review*: 10.
18 Thames Valley Police. (2010) *Project Champion Review*: 1.
19 Thames Valley Police. (2010) *Project Champion Review*: 47. Earlier in the same section of the report (at page 46), it is noted that this lack of transparency regarding the purpose of the cameras 'caused significant damage to community relations, with many suggesting that the only solution is the removal of all the cameras'.
20 See: www.birminghammail.co.uk/news/local-news/mystery-cctv-lamp-posts-spark-123606; http://spyonbirmingham.blogspot.ca/; and www.theguardian.com/commentisfree/libertycentral/2010/jul/06/birmingham-cctv-unlawful-liberty (all accessed 3 March 2018).
21 According to Sir Robert Peel in his Principles of Law Enforcement (1879), 'The police at all times should maintain a relationship with the public that gives reality to the historic tradition that the police are the public and the public are the police; the police are the only members of the public who are paid to give full-time attention to duties which are incumbent on every citizen in the intent of the community welfare'. See: www.durham.police.uk/About-Us/Documents/Peels_Principles_Of_Law_Enforcement.pdf (accessed 3 March 2018): 1.
22 Regan, P. (1995) *Legislating Privacy: Technology, Social Values, and Public Policy* Chapel Hill: The University of North Carolina Press: 221; Nissenbaum, H. (2010) *Privacy in Context: Technology, Policy, and the Integrity of Social Life* Stanford: Stanford University Press: 86–87. See also: Boone, C. K. (1983), "Privacy and Community" *Social Theory and Practice* 9(1): 8.
23 For an example of the gradual erosion of the boundaries between public and private space, see: www.theguardian.com/cities/2017/jul/24/revealed-pseudo-public-space-pops-london-investigation-map?CMP=share_btn_link.
24 Goold, B. (2007) "Privacy, Identity and Security" in Goold, B. and Lazarus, L. (eds.), *Security and Human Rights* Oxford: Hart Publishing: 45–72.
25 A notable exception here is the co-editor of this collection. See in particular: Lever, A. (2006) "Privacy Rights and Democracy: A Contradiction in Terms?" *Contemporary Political Theory* 5: 142–162; Lever, A. (2011) *On Privacy* London: Routledge; Lever, A. (2013) "Privacy, Democracy and Surveillance" *The Philosophers Magazine*, Autumn; and Lever, A. (2015) "Privacy, Democracy, and Freedom of Expression" in Roessler, B. and Mokrosinska, D. (eds.) *Social Dimensions of Privacy: Interdisciplinary Perspectives* Cambridge: Cambridge University Press.

References

Ball, K., Lyon, D., Murakami Wood, D., Norris, C. and Raab, C. (2006) *A Report on the Surveillance Society* London: Office of the Information Commissioner.
Beck, U. (1992) *Risk Society: Towards a New Modernity* London: Sage.
Boone, C.K. (1983) "Privacy and Community" *Social Theory and Practice* 9(1): 8.
Doyle, A., Lippert, R. and Lyon, D. (2013) (eds.) *Eyes Everywhere: The Global Growth of Camera Surveillance* New York: Routledge.
Ericson, R. and Haggerty, K. (1997) *Policing the Risk Society* Toronto: University of Toronto Press.
Garland, D. (2002) *The Culture of Control: Crime and Social Order in Contemporary Society* Chicago: University of Chicago Press.
Goold, B. (2004a) *CCTV and Policing: Public Area Surveillance and Police Practices in Britain* Oxford: Oxford University Press.
Goold, B. (2004b) "Privacy Rights and Public Spaces: CCTV and the Problem of the 'Unobservable Observer'" *Criminal Justice Ethics* 21(1): 21–27.
Goold, B. (2006) "Open to All? Regulating Open Street CCTV and the Case for 'Symmetrical Surveillance'" *Criminal Justice Ethics* 25(1): 3–17.

Goold, B. (2007) "Privacy, Identity and Security" in Goold, B. and Lazarus, L. (eds), *Security and Human Rights* Oxford: Hart Publishing: 45–72.

Goold, B. (2008a) "The Difference between Lonely Old Ladies and CCTV Cameras: A Response to Jesper Ryberg" *Res Publica* 14(1): 43–47.

Goold, B. (2008b) "Technologies of Surveillance and the Erosion of Institutional Trust" in Aas, K., Gundhus, H.O. and Lomell, H.M. (eds), *Technologies of Insecurity* Abingdon: Routledge: 207–18.

Goold, B. (2009) "Surveillance and the Political Value of Privacy" *Amsterdam Law Forum* 1(4): 3–6.

Hier, S. (2004) "Risky Spaces and Dangerous Faces: Urban Surveillance, Social Disorder and CCTV" *Social and Legal Studies* 13(4): 541–554.

Lai, D. (2007) "Public Video Surveillance by the State: Policy, Privacy Legislation, and the Charter" *Alberta Law Review* 45: 43–77.

Lever, A. (2006) "Privacy Rights and Democracy: A Contradiction in Terms?" *Contemporary Political Theory* 5: 142–162.

Lever, A. (2008) "Mrs. Aremac and the Camera: A Response to Ryberg" *Res Publica: A Journal of Legal and Social Philosophy* 14(1): 35–42.

Lever, A. (2011) *On Privacy* London: Routledge.

Lever, A. (2013) "Privacy, Democracy and Surveillance" *The Philosophers Magazine*, Autumn.

Lever. A. (2015) "Privacy, Democracy, and Freedom of Expression" in Roessler, B. and Mokrosinska, D. (eds.), *Social Dimensions of Privacy: Interdisciplinary Perspectives* Cambridge: Cambridge University Press.

Lomell, H.M. (2004) "Targeting the Unwanted: Video Surveillance and Categorical Exclusion in Oslo, Norway" *Surveillance & Society* 2(2): 346–360.

Lyon, D. (2002) (ed.) *Surveillance as Social Sorting: Privacy, Risk and Automated Discrimination* Abingdon: Routledge.

Mishler, W. and Rose, R. (2001) "What Are the Origins of Political Trust? Testing Institutional and Cultural Theories in Post-Communist Societies" *Comparative Political Studies* 34(1): 30–62.

Nissenbaum, H. (2010) *Privacy in Context: Technology, Policy, and the Integrity of Social Life* Stanford: Stanford University Press.

Norris, C. and Armstrong, G. (1998) *The Maximum Surveillance Society* London: Bloomsbury Publishing.

Norris, C., McCahill, M. and Wood, D. (2004) "Editorial: The Growth of CCTV: A Global Perspective on the International Diffusion of Video Surveillance in Publicly Accessible Space" *Surveillance and Society* 2(2/3): 110–135.

Norris, C., Moran, C. and Armstrong, G. (1998) (eds.) *Surveillance, Closed Circuit Television and Social Control* Aldershot: Ashgate.

Regan, P. (1995) *Legislating Privacy: Technology, Social Values, and Public Policy* Chapel Hill: The University of North Carolina Press.

Schoeman, F. (1992) *Privacy and Social Freedom* Cambridge: Cambridge University Press.

Slobogin, C. (2002) "Public Privacy: Camera Surveillance of Public Places and the Right to Anonymity" *Mississippi Law Journal* 72: 214–285.

Solove, D.J. (2002) "Conceptualising Privacy" *California Law Review* 90(4): 1087.

Steeves, V. (2009) "Reclaiming the Social Value of Privacy" in Kerr, I., Steeves, V. and Lucock, C. (eds.) *Lessons from the Identity Trail: Anonymity, Privacy and Identity in a Networked Society* New York: Oxford University Press.

Surveillance: Citizens and the State, HL 18-I (report) and HL 18-II (evidence), House of Lords Constitution Committee, 6 February 2009.

Thames Valley Police. (2010) *Project Champion Review*.

von Hirsch, A. and Shearing, C. (2000) "Exclusion from Public Space" in von Hirsch, S. Garland, D. and Wakefield, A. (eds.) *Ethical and Social Perspectives on Situational Crime Prevention* Oxford: Hart Publishing.

9

ETHICS AND CRIMINAL JUSTICE POLICY

Matt Matravers

Introduction

Any attempt to write a chapter encompassing all the ethical questions in criminal justice policy faces at least three insuperable hurdles. First, criminal justice policy extends over a vast range of activities. Entire books have been written on the ethics of criminalisation; policing; prosecutorial decision-making; evidence, trial and conviction; sentencing; and sanctions, including the ethics of prison policy. Second, policy-making with respect to criminal justice takes place at many levels (in particular, but not only, in federal states). A neighbourhood may set up a neighbourhood watch scheme; local government or localised police authorities may implement rules specific to their area and determine their policing priorities with respect to those; prosecutors and judges may have discretion at critical stages of the process; and prisons may, or may not, be federal, state, local, or privately owned. Third, the decision-makers in each of these instances will be subject to a large number of political, economic, and other forces, many of them specific and local. So, a decision over prosecutorial priorities in Minnesota may reflect politics and economics in Minnesota that have no parallel in, say, New Mexico, just as a decision about policing in Greater Manchester may be driven by entirely different factors to a policing decision made in Devon and Somerset.

Thus, with respect to *what* decisions, *who* makes them, and *why* they are made, the landscape of criminal justice policy is vast and diverse. For these, and other, reasons this chapter focuses mainly on ethical questions as they arise for criminal justice policy as a whole with respect to what Hyman Gross has called 'a composite of convenience that might be called the Anglo-American legal system' (Gross 2012: 1).[1]

To do this, the chapter initially utilises the structure identified by Albert Weale in this volume. Weale argues that

> on many occasions, policy advocacy engages the 'deep normative core' (Sabatier and Jenkins-Smith, 1993; Weible and Sabatier, 2006) of the positions that different actors hold, invoking such ideas as the legitimate role of the state or the boundaries of personal responsibility.[2]

This deep normative core is connected to actual policy by policy paradigms that involve, as Weale puts it, 'webs of belief linking goals, instruments, and conceptions of social and political order'. In this way, policy paradigms link to competing ideologies, which are 'systems of political thinking through which individuals and groups construct an understanding of the political and policy world'.[3]

The first three parts of the chapter illustrate this interplay between deep normative commitments, policy paradigms, and policy, by offering a short (and, to an extent, stylised) history of criminal justice policy from the end of the Second World War to the present. The point of these sections is not primarily historical. Rather, first, criminal justice policy is often affected by a temporal myopia and it is good to remind ourselves that things that are today judged as unthinkable were common practice in living memory. Second, the sections illustrate the huge variation in practice and the range of policies from which contemporary policy has emerged. Third, the chapter goes on to argue that the normative connection between theory and practice has broken down, leading to an incoherent mishmash of policy paradigms and practices. Finally, it considers the contexts of democracy and inequality, which must frame any discussion of criminal justice.

Penal welfarism

> In the penal-welfare framework, the rehabilitative ideal was not just one element among others. Rather it was the hegemonic, organizing principle, the intellectual framework and value system that bound together the whole structure and made sense of it for practitioners. It provided an all-embracing conceptual net that could be cast over each and every activity in the penal field, allowing practitioners to render their world coherent and meaningful, and to give otherwise unpleasant, troublesome practices something of a benign, scientific gloss.
>
> *(Garland 2001: 35)*

For the first two-thirds of the twentieth century, criminal justice thinking was dominated by an optimistic rehabilitative outlook and by a rejection of 'the principles of retribution' as 'repugnant to modern sensitivities' (Mays 1963: 118). The deep normative core was consequentialist – that is, reflected the view that the morally correct policy was that which, of all available policies, was expected to realise the greatest net welfare – but few criminal law scholars and even fewer practitioners would have identified with this in the first instance. Rather, identification would have been with the (slightly) more specific issues mentioned by Weale with respect to the legitimate role of the state and personal responsibility.

With respect to the state and personal responsibility, the prevailing view revolved around social progress and the malleability of human nature. It seemed obvious that the state should seek to improve the outlook of its citizens in the future. Moreover, this confidence in what the state should do was matched, if not surpassed, by the certainty that there was no place for retributivism in the modern world: 'official social institutions should not be predicated on the destructive emotion of vengeance, which is not only the expression of an infantile way of solving a problem, but unjust and destructive of the purpose of protecting society' (Glueck 1928: 456–457). As Michael Tonry points out, in a standard reference published in 1940 – Michael and Wechsler's *Criminal Law and Its Administration* (Michael and Wechsler 1940) – 'anyone looking up "punishment" in the index would have found, "see Treatment"' (Tonry 2011c: 17).

The policies that resulted were oriented towards reform and rehabilitation administered by experts who would use the latest social scientific evidence to fine-tune the system. Incarceration, it was thought, in the right hands and of the right type, provided 'a marvelous opportunity to promote the welfare of the society along with the welfare of the offender. [It] could at once advance public safety and improve the lot of the offender' (Gaylin and Rothman 1976: xxx).

Three inter-related features of the policy environment that grew out of this paradigm are worth noting: first, the displacement of normative questions in favour of empirical ones (to be decided by experts). As Brian Barry has pointed out, this is a generic feature of consequential-ism since 'once the goal has been postulated. . ., everything else is a matter of arguing about the most efficacious means to that end' (Barry 1990: xxxv). Second, since judges are not experts in reform and rehabilitation, their role was to hand offenders over to those who were. The form this took was of 'indeterminate sentences'. In California and Washington, for example, con-victed offenders condemned to state prison were sentenced to between one year and the statu-tory maximum for the offence. How long the offender would serve would be for the Parole Board to decide; 'just as we did not tell doctors when to pronounce a patient cured, we were not, in the guise of fixed sentences, to tell wardens or parole boards when to release an inmate' (Gaylin and Rothman 1976: xxxi).[4] Third, the nature of the 'treatment', as well as its length, needed to relate to the 'clinical need', and thus sprung up a variety of correctional facilities, including some aimed specifically at young offenders, those with addictions, and so on.

That said, remnants of traditional punishment remained – not least the continued use of incarceration – and adherence to the rehabilitative/welfarist paradigm was not universal (Lewis 1949).[5] Moreover, the language of 'reform' and 'reformatories' – sometimes used interchange-ably with 'rehabilitation' – masked a history of belief that reform could be achieved (only) *through* punishment (rather than of thinking of rehabilitation as an alternative to punishment).

In short, and at the risk of flattening the landscape, the penal welfarism that dominated the first three-quarters of the twentieth century was consequentialist in its normative core, adopted rehabilitation as its paradigm, and so resulted in policies such as indeterminate sentencing aimed at rehabilitation under the guidance of experts who could determine 'the most efficacious means to the desired ends' (Barry 1990: xxxv).

The 'retributive turn'

In criminal justice, and in particular in punishment theory, there had been some early signs of dissatisfaction with consequentialism (Armstrong 1961; Charvet 1966; McCloskey 1968; Morris 1968), but the transformative decades followed from 1970 with the publication of the American Friends Service Committee report *Struggle for Justice* (1971) and Andrew von Hirsch's *Doing Justice: The Choice of Punishments* (1976).

These works were fundamentally critical of the existing system. Penal welfarism depended for its legitimating narrative on its being 'rational', 'scientific', 'efficacious', and so on. It rep-resented progress from the irrational and barbaric retributive theory that had preceded it. This, perhaps more than anything else, was its undoing.

As early as 1959, Francis Allen had expressed concern that 'the rehabilitative ideal' had been 'debased in practice', particularly with respect to identifying 'dangerous' offenders, disguising punishment as 'therapy', and increasing the length of penal sanctions (Allen 1959). Others argued that the deference to experts meant that there was no administrative oversight of, or appeal against, the decisions of parole boards and other actors who were thus free to exercise, and potentially abuse, their discretionary powers (Frankel 1973; Allen 1959; Davis 1969; Com-mittee 1971).

Perhaps most damning was the publication in 1974 of 'What Works? Questions and Answers About Prison Reform' by Robert Martinson. Martinson's research had been commissioned by the State of New York in 1968, but by the time it was ready 'the state planning agency [viewed] the study as a document whose disturbing conclusions posed a serious threat to the programs which, in the meantime, they had determined to carry forward' (Martinson 1974: 23). The most disturbing of those conclusions, sometimes glossed as 'nothing works', was that '*with few and isolated exceptions, the rehabilitative efforts that have been reported so far have had no appreciable effect on recidivism*' (Martinson 1974: 25, emphasis in the original). In short, the rehabilitative ideal that rested on notions of humanitarianism, science, and progress was unscientific, discriminatory, and, given that many offenders were kept in prison because of their skin colour or political beliefs, deeply reactionary (Blumstein et al. 1983a, 1983b).

This empirical undermining of the rehabilitative paradigm and policies of penal welfarism occurred just as its consequentialist deep normative core came under sustained attack that culminated in John Rawls's hugely influential *A Theory of Justice* (Rawls 1971). For Bernard Williams, writing in 1973, utilitarianism had exhausted itself. 'The day cannot be too far off', he concludes, 'in which we hear no more of it' (Williams 1973: 150).

The fundamentally critical nature of the rebellion against penal welfarism underpinned immediate developments, but the failure to articulate a positive alternative – to latch practice on to some deep normative core – would have serious consequences. In the short term, the policy paradigms revolved around proportionality – that is, the severity of an individual's punishment should be proportional to the seriousness of his offence – as a matter of fairness and respect for the individual. Rehabilitation was side-lined; sentencing guidelines established; and punishment as a response to individual culpability made more central.

However, although a number of retributive theories emerged in the period, none became dominant and the arguments that filled the firmament remained mainly focused on policy paradigms rather than the deep normative core (Matravers 2018). For the moment, the demands of fairness (understood both procedurally in terms of reducing discretion and substantively in terms of proportionality) were enough to motivate and to explain policies on the ground.

The fracturing of criminal justice theory and policy

The absence of an agreed or even implicit single normative core meant that various policy paradigms (re-)emerged, some of which gained momentum following the election of right-wing governments in both the US (in 1980 under President Reagan) and the UK (in 1979 under Margaret Thatcher). In short, punishment theory and practice fractured.

On the one hand, in part in response to the failure of prisons to reduce recidivism and evidence of the cost-effectiveness of drug and other treatment programmes, a strong current of rehabilitative theory and practice persisted in the form of restorative justice and therapeutic jurisprudence. Perhaps the most visible manifestation of this was (and remains) the expansion of 'drug courts' (Husak 2011: 216–218).

On the other, the emphasis on individual responsibility, 'traditional' values such as self-reliance, and other conservative tropes pushed in the direction of greater punitiveness, a phenomenon exacerbated by the first-past-the-post electoral systems in both countries that meant that the politicisation of criminal justice led to an 'arms race' between the two parties on who could be 'tougher' on crime (Lacey 2008). By 1993, John Major (Mrs Thatcher's successor as prime minister) was endorsing the idea that 'society needs to condemn a little more and understand a little less' (*Mail on Sunday*, 1993) just as his Labour opponent, Tony Blair, prepared to launch his flagship policy of being 'tough on crime, tough on the underlying causes of crime' (*New Statesman*, 1993).

The results – at least when it came to many of the headline-grabbing policies of the post–penal welfare era – had nothing to do with proportionality, but instead reflected various political considerations. The 'war on drugs', for example, resulted in mandatory minimum sentences for some non-violent offences far in excess of those handed down for some serious violent offences (and the number of people imprisoned for non-violent drug offences across the US increased from 50,000 in 1980 to over 400,000 by 1997).[6] Similarly, 'three-strikes' laws imposed enhanced sentences for third offences. The most notorious of these was passed in California in 1993 and, in its first manifestation, led to a life sentence for the theft of a pair of socks (Curtis Wilkerson) and a sentence of 25 years to life for that of three golf clubs (Gary Ewing), among many other disproportionate outcomes.[7] As Michael Tonry puts it, some policy entrepreneurs used retributive-sounding language – "Do the crime, do the time", but this simply meant,

> that offenders should receive whatever punishments policy makers specified, whether or not those sentences respected retributive principles or ideas about proportionality, and whether those policies were adopted for substantive reasons or to demonstrate that politicians were tough on crime.
>
> *(Tonry 2011a: vii)*

Much of the 'retributive-sounding' language and the policies related to that (e.g., 'three strikes') was concerned with 'risk'. As one of the most strident advocates of California's initial three-strikes initiative put it, those who would be targeted were 'little more than animals. They look like people, but they're not. And the unfortunate thing is they're preying on us. And we have to get them out so the rest of us can go on living our lives' (quoted in Beale 2011: 432).[8] More broadly, 'the risk society' (Beck 1992; for an application of the risk society to criminal justice, see Hudson 2003) meant an increase in preventive justice as the criminal justice system moved from proportional punishment to preventing future offending through the incarceration and control of dangerous offenders; or at least of offenders deemed dangerous. In practice this meant longer sentences, enhancements for perceived dangerousness (determined, e.g., by evidence as to 'treatability' or of gang membership). In addition, the preventive rationale extended beyond incarceration to risk-management in the form of sex-offender registers and other post-punishment restrictions. While clearly preventive in intent, most of these policies were 'cloaked' in the language of retribution, further muddying the waters of the relation between theory and punishment (Robinson 2001: 1429).

In short, contemporary criminal justice policy and practice are in a mess. There is no agreed normative core, and policies proliferate across a number of paradigms – retributive, rehabilitative, incapacitative – although often even this is obscured by the language in which they are presented. We do not, as Gary Watson put it in a review of the insanity defence, 'know what we are doing' (Watson 2010: 221).[9]

Ethics and the mess we're in

From the point of view of an ethical evaluation of public policy, the fact of competing, incompatible aims is important because it undermines any attempt to judge whether the policies we are pursuing are effective. If we do not know what we are trying to do, we cannot know how to evaluate our doing of it. Moreover, criminal justice policy – like all public policy – occurs in a certain context. In particular, it is subject to democratic decision making and, in the Anglo-American world, exists in circumstances of extreme social, economic, and political inequality. The remainder of the chapter considers the aims, some applicable ethical principles, and these elements of context.

Aims and examples

Taking stock of the foregoing history, we might think of the following as (among the) aims of the criminal justice system together with some exemplars of the policies that follow:

1   To impose punishment on properly convicted offenders where the severity of the punishment is scaled to the culpability of the offender (e.g., proportionality theory as espoused in Scandinavia, some US states, in part in the reasoning of the Sentencing Council of England and Wales, and so on);
2   To reduce the risk of future wrongdoing through:

   a   Positive general prevention (the argument that the existence of prohibitive laws that threaten sanctions for their violation has, in virtue of norm-reinforcement, the general effect of reducing violations of those laws);
   b   Individual deterrence (the threat of sanctions deters those who would otherwise commit crimes);[10]
   c   (Partial) incapacitation (e.g., 'three-strikes', mandatory minimum sentences, life sentences without the possibility of parole, 'sexual predator' and 'dangerous offender' laws, 'dangerousness enhancements' to sentences, sex-offender registers);
   d   Prevention through criminalisation (e.g., increasing the number and reach of strict liability and pre-inchoate crimes, such as possession and conspiracy offences);
   e   Rehabilitation (e.g., drug and other treatment courts, sex-offender programmes, therapeutic interventions, community work orders).

On the one hand, various attempts have been made to bring these differing aims – if not all the attendant policies – within a single theoretical framework. The most famous is H.L.A. Hart's so-called mixed theory, which proposed capturing consequentialist aims (the reduction of future wrongdoing) in addressing 'the general justification' of punishment and 'desert' aims (proportional punishment) in answering the question of 'distribution' (Hart 2008; see also Rawls 1955). Others have held the general justification to be answered by retributive proportionality and that such an account need not have anything specific to say in answer to the question of 'how much and what kind of punishment should the state mete out' (Markel and Flanders 2010: 949).

On the other hand, some theorists have insisted on their favoured retributive theory and simply denounced or ignored those policy initiatives that fell out with what could be justified by that theory. As Tonry puts it, 'philosophers and other theorists have paid mostly denunciatory attention to severe proportionality-defying punishments' (Tonry 2011b: 10).

None of these responses to current practice has been entirely satisfactory. The former fail to explain how to combine incompatible goals and the latter fail to attend to Nicola Lacey's warning that legal theory 'is engaged in theorising social phenomena which have a "real" existence, and to the contours of which the philosophical account is hence in some sense answerable' (Lacey 2007: 138).

The concern of this chapter, though, is not to offer a critique of current philosophical theories of criminal justice and punishment since even if the relative theoretical superiority of one could be demonstrated, the deep normative divide between those who favour some form of retributivism and those who believe that the aims of criminal justice must be forward-looking means that there is no prospect of it enjoying support of a kind that would allow it to form the basis for a general ethical appraisal of current criminal justice policy. That does not mean that ethical critique is impossible – only that we need to abstract to broader ethical principles to guide us (although, even then, matters are not simple). In other words, rather than ask whether criminal justice policy accords with this or that criminal justice theory, we can look to more abstract principles, such as effectiveness, equality, and fairness (in both its procedural and substantive forms), as providing a means to think through policy in this area. Some illustrative examples of how this might be done are given ahead.

Effectiveness and parsimony

Effectiveness is perhaps not usually thought of as a distinctly ethical virtue (indeed, it is some-times deployed by anti-consequentialists in contrast to genuinely ethical concerns), but there are (at least) two reasons to include it here. First, punishment inflicts significant harms on the punished (who will inevitably include some of the factually innocent). Second, it is expensive and there is an opportunity cost in spending public money on criminal justice, enforcement, and prisons rather than on, say, public education or public health. Criminal justice policy, then, needs to show 'value for money'. Of course, in the absence of agreed aims it is not possible to offer an account of what this means – a policy that delivers proportionate punishment but fails to deter, reform, or prevent might be thought by a proportionality theorist to meet the need to demonstrate value for money, but will not convince anyone else of the same – but insofar as policies are commended on the basis that they deliver certain results, they can and should be assessed against those results.

That said, effectiveness in public policy is not merely about whether something 'works' (about the outputs) but about efficiency – whether the same or better could be achieved with the same or fewer resources (inputs, broadly understood). In criminal justice generally, that means considering each policy proposal against what it purports to do, and in punishment spe-cifically it means adhering to a principle of parsimony that requires that we impose the mini-mum punishment consistent with the aim(s) to be achieved (Frase 2009).

Equality

Equality requires that things that are alike in relevant respects are treated alike (and things that are relevantly unlike one another are treated differently). Unfortunately, this formal definition does not help us very much with fundamental questions related to theories of punishment given the absence of agreed aims. After all, if one's overriding concern is rehabilitation, then the fact that one person will respond quickly to therapy and another slowly is a *relevant* difference between them and might underwrite one spending a great deal less time in prison than the other (and similarly for other aims of punishment).

However, a critical role for equality remains both in issues of criminalisation and in the operation of criminal justice. With respect to the former consider two examples from the so-called crack epidemic in the US. Crack use was concentrated in the African American commu-nity (white men tending to prefer powdered cocaine). When crack cocaine hit the headlines, the US authorities' reaction was punitive both in the sense that the policy paradigm invoked was that of punishment and in the sense that sentences for crack-related offences were increased significantly.

One result of this policy choice, which garnered some attention, was that federal penalties in relation to crack cocaine offences were roughly 100 times harsher than those for powdered cocaine offences, which in turn meant African Americans disproportionately sentenced to much lengthier terms in prison than their white comparators (this disparity was reduced to around 18 to 1 in 2010).[11]

Fast-forward 30 years, and America finds itself in the grip of an opioid epidemic involving large numbers of (predominantly white) (ab)users of prescription opioids and heroin. However, as Ekow Yankah has powerfully pointed out, in that case the policy paradigm adopted in response has been one of public health: 'White heroin addicts get overdose treatment, rehabilitation and reincorporation, a system that will be there for them . . . Black drug users got jail cells and "Just Say No"' (Yankah 2016).

The crack and opioid example is a particularly stark one, but the point applies across the board. What is not often noticed when the appeal goes up that 'something must be done' about some purported undesirable conduct is that we must ask not one but two questions: 'ought something to be done (ought the state to regulate *x*)?' and, if so, 'ought the state to regulate *x* through the *criminal law* or through some other form of intervention?'. In answering those questions, the value of equality has a critical role.

In the operation of criminal justice across jurisdictions and times, research consistently shows that members of minority communities suffer from discrimination from start to finish: they are more likely to be stopped, searched, arrested, prosecuted, convicted, and incarcerated than relevantly similar non-minority citizens. Here, equality plays an uncontroversial role in condemning these facts, although effective public policy remedies have proved elusive (Donziger 1996).

Finally, it might be thought that we can appeal to a deeper sense of equality – that is, the claim that all adult human beings (or perhaps for political theory purposes, all adult citizens) are of fundamental equal worth or enjoy a status of equal dignity (Vlastos 1962; Waldron 2017). Although the nature and origin of any such status are disputed (Charvet 2013), it has been deployed in a variety of ways as a 'trump' to resist consequentialist arguments, which are said to permit the 'sacrifice' of the few to further the general good of the many; severe punishments; corporal sanctions; and so on. More positively, Michael Tonry has urged that a concept of human dignity can act as the organising principle to bring together the various aims of punishment (Tonry 2018).

Unfortunately, although there is widespread agreement with respect to this sense of equality (at least in the sense that any argument that rested on the claim that, for example, women or Jewish people were 'less than human' would be treated as preposterous today), no consensus has emerged on what follows for how people ought to be treated whether with respect to distributive or retributive justice.[12] As a result, this deeper sense of equality tends to be used as a rhetorical device to reinforce existing conclusions rather than as a basis for those conclusions.

Fairness

Issues of substantive fairness overlap with those of equality; it is unfair to treat one community's addiction issues differently to those of a relevantly similar other community. But the value of fairness extends further than that. As H.L.A. Hart (and others) have emphasised, a liberal criminal law ought to provide predictability and in core cases ought to be such that those who fall within its purview do so because of their choices, not because of happenstance; they receive what Hart called a 'fair opportunity' to avoid criminal liability (Hart 2008: 23). For example, in evaluating whether to break the speed limit to get home at the end of a long day, I should know – or, at least be able to know – the relevant offence, the likely penalties attached, and that if I am apprehended these will be applied even-handedly.

Yet, as Douglas Husak and William Stuntz have pointed out, this Hartian picture is far from the reality in the US and UK (Husak 2008; Stuntz 2011). The scope of the criminal law is now so great that few, if any, citizens can know what it contains. Moreover, much of the recent expansion in the criminal law has been driven by crimes of, or containing elements of, strict liability (Ashworth 2000). So, in the unlikely event that I know what the relevant law is, it may not be a matter of my choice whether I break it. If I do, the police will often exercise discretion in responding to offences, prosecutors will choose whether to prosecute and, if so, for what, and my conviction and sentence may well be determined by some kind of plea bargain.

It is important to recognise both the degree and scope of arbitrariness that is possible. Husak gives as an example Rudolph Giuliani, who, when serving as a federal prosecutor in New York,

> sought to keep drug dealers "off balance" by instituting "federal day": one day each week chosen at random [and not disclosed] in which street-level drug dealers arrested by local police were prosecuted in federal rather than state court, where sentences are far more severe.

As Husak quips, 'no person would contend that the same criminal behavior becomes more serious and should be punished more harshly because it happens to be perpetrated on a Tuesday rather than on a Wednesday' (Husak 2008: 28).

As can be seen, although the meaning and implications of abstract principles such as the ones discussed earlier can be contested, they provide frameworks through which criminal justice policies can be examined. In some cases, they may reflect existing disagreements – for example, as to whether incarceration does, or does not, violate human dignity – but in others – for example, in the unequal treatment of like cases or factual claims about how 'prison works' – they can have real bite.

The context(s) of criminal justice: democracy and inequality

The chapter so far has tried to lay out the many and various purposes, aims, and justifications of criminal justice that have, and continue to, characterise theory and practice in this area. The final section briefly touches on two aspects of the context in which criminal justice policy operates: democracy and unjust distributive inequality (massively exacerbated in the US by matters of race).

Democracy is important both because criminal justice policy reflects decisions about the kind of society in which we (choose to) live and because it might be thought that it provides the appropriate means by which societies can choose among the competing normative positions and policy paradigms discussed earlier (Lever 2017). Inequality is important because we are discussing criminal *justice* and that cannot be done outside the context of justice more widely understood.

Democracy

The perception that public opinion is 'punitive', the history of popular votes such as that in California that initiated the three-strikes legislation discussed earlier, and the sense that the politicisation of criminal justice leads only to competition to be seen to be 'tougher on crime' than one's opponents have led some, perhaps the majority, of penal theorists to be sceptical of overtly democratic control of punishment policy. The result is a 'strong normative preference for what is called independence' and proposals for a 'deliberate' institutional design 'to mini-mize . . . responsiveness to popular preferences and to the legislative bodies created by rep-resentative democracy' (Zimring et al. 2001: 204, comparing the proposal with independent central banks; see also Lacey 2008 and Pettit 2002).

Yet, there is something deeply uncomfortable in the suggestion that we should insulate criminal justice policy from the people (Dzur 2012). The flip side of Winston Churchill's famous statement that 'the mood and temper of the public in regard to the treatment of crime and criminals is one of the most unfailing tests of the civilisation of any country' (Hansard 1910) is surely that criminal justice *is* properly an expression of the kind of society in which we wish collectively to live. Of course, that does not mean popular decision making with respect to individual punishments, but inevitably the 'mood and temper' of the public will make itself heard in the shape of the overall scheme (even if mediated through quasi-independent bodies, such as sentencing commissions).[13]

This is not necessarily a cause for despair. There is evidence that the cost and ineffectiveness of mass incarceration are causing people and legislatures to rethink penal policy and change is not impossible (Michelle and Devah 2015). Moreover, there are examples to follow, includ-ing the Netherlands and Finland, where 'deliberate, long-term, and systematic policy choices' (Lappi-Seppälä 2001: 122) have succeeded in reducing prison populations.[14]

Inequality

Writing in 1973, Jeffrie Murphy argued that it was impossible to achieve justice in punishment in a distributively unjust society (Murphy 1973; see also Alexander 2010 and Shelby 2016). Since then, inequality has risen rapidly across most developed societies, exacerbating the point Murphy made. Murphy's argument was based on a theory of punishment in which punishment restored the *status quo ante* in the distribution of benefits and burdens that had been unsettled by the crime (and, in short, since the initial distribution was unjust, punishment could not justifi-ably do this).

That account of punishment is now widely regarded as unsatisfactory (see Matravers 2000: 52–72), but the problem persists. Crime – or at least those crimes that do not require access to advantage, such as insider trading or large-scale fraud – is disproportionality committed by those who are relatively disadvantaged, and the same group makes up a disproportionate share of the victims of these crimes (Braithwaite 1989: 44–53). Moreover, most forms of punishment – including the most common forms of financial penalties and incarceration – are likely to make matters worse; to further impoverish the poor and their dependents (a situation further exacerbated if there are additional sanctions, such as loss of access to housing or welfare) (Alexander 2010; National Research Council 2014).

The enduring nature of the question of 'doing penal justice in an unjust society' owes some-thing to the structure of the problem. There is the danger of being patronising or of denying the agency of those who are disadvantaged – 'of course, they cannot help it' – but more than that there is the danger that allowing certain *explanations* of human behaviour to *excuse* will open the floodgates; after all, all of us have histories that, together with our genes, explain our actions (Morse 2000, 2015).

However, we might think of the problem differently and focus not on the offender and what he did but on the state and its 'standing' to hold the offender to account (Duff 2003). There is a great deal that is appealing and intuitive about this thought. In our ordinary lives, we appeal to the claim 'who are you to judge?' in response to one person, without denying that we might be answerable to another. However, appealing as it is in interpersonal morality, the theory fails when applied to state punishment (Matravers 2006; Holroyd 2010).

Perhaps the failure to find an adequate response to this problem points in a different direction, one on which it is appropriate to close. Although, as argued earlier, it is hard to say what exactly we are trying to achieve when we deploy the awesome power of the state in the field of criminal justice, and so hard to know what would count as success, any plausible policy to address the problems with which criminal justice is concerned – including the commission of offences that harm others – would not be one concerned *only* with criminal justice.

That is, when we consider the ethics of criminal justice policy, we should ask not only about those policies but also about their value in relation to policies in other areas. Criminal justice is a blunt tool that often imposes 'collateral damage' on the innocent (Lippke 2017) and criminalising, convicting, and punishing may, in some cases, be far less effective than other forms of regulation and/or addressing the context in which crimes occur. The ethics of criminal justice policy, then, cannot be detached from the ethics of public policy more broadly understood.[15]

Notes

1 Even this restriction is potentially misleading given the exceptional nature of the criminal justice system – or, more accurately, systems – in the US. In addition to having separate jurisdictions across 50 states and one federal system, the US is unique amongst Western 'developed' nations in having judges and prosecutors who are elected and, in many cases, overtly political.

2 Weale (this volume: 52).

3 Weale (this volume: 52).

4 As the influential criminologist Sheldon Glueck argued in 1928 (Glueck 1928: 475), 'the treatment (sentence-imposing) feature of the proceedings must be sharply differentiated from the guilt-finding phase' and 'the decision as to treatment must be made by a board or tribunal specially qualified in the interpretation and evaluation of psychiatric, psychological, and sociologic data'.

5 It is worth noting, though, that Lewis explained that his decision to send the paper to a relatively obscure Australian journal was because he could not get it published in England (Lewis 1949: 12).

6 (Husak 2008: 16). As Scott Petersen puts it (1993: 748), 'another casualty of the war' on drugs turned out to be 'the right to a punishment proportionate to the underlying crime'. Petersen's article is a discussion of the case of Ronald Harmelin, who was sentenced under Michigan law to mandatory life imprisonment without possibility of parole for (mere) possession of 673 grams of cocaine (Harmelin had no prior felony convictions). The US Supreme Court upheld the sentence as constitutional (as not violating the prohibition on cruel and unusual punishment). The mandatory life imprisonment requirement was later reversed by the Michigan State Supreme Court (as in violation of the State Constitution) and those sentenced under it (including Harmelin) declared eligible for parole after ten years.

7 In 2012, partly in response to appalling stories such as these, California overwhelmingly voted for a reform to the three-strikes system (Proposition 36), eliminating life sentences for non-serious, non-violent crimes. It also established a sentence review procedure for inmates sentenced to life in prison for such offences. Interestingly, the criteria for review relate not to desert or culpability but entirely to public safety.

8 Such a position – in which some persons are treated not as persons at all but as 'animals' to be controlled – is of course incompatible with any standard deontological defence of retributivism as giving responsible agents what they 'deserve'.

9 As mentioned at the outset, no sweeping statement of this kind does justice to the complexity of the situation even in the US and UK. Across democratic, liberal states, the situation is varied. Broadly, Scandinavia embraces proportionality theory, although with a cardinal scale of punishments far less severe than those found elsewhere. Across much of the rest of Europe, proportionality is 'first amongst equals' amongst a range of policy aims that include incapacitation, positive general prevention, deterrence, and rehabilitation (Tonry 2017).

10 For a standard account of positive general prevention, see Andenæs 1974; for discussion of the ways in which the criminal law may change behaviour other than through the threat of punishment, see Matravers 2011. For a critique of the claims of individual deterrence, see von Hirsch 1999.
11 www.drugpolicy.org/issues/race-and-drug-war. Accessed on 15/01/2018.
12 To give just a flavour of the arguments: in distributive justice, some have argued that equality requires (only) equal rights or an equal distribution of resources. Others, following Ronald Dworkin's distinction between 'equal treatment' and 'treatment as an equal' (Dworkin 1977: 370), allow inequalities in outcome, but disagree about whether the best interpretation of the latter is in terms of a distribution of resources or of welfare. Finally, it is worth noting that an argument that human dignity requires that each person's preferences (say) are counted equally can underpin a form of utilitarianism. For this reason, the invocation of 'dignity' is usually unhelpful.
13 I have argued elsewhere that proportionality theory alone does not have the resources to rebut the setting of overall punishment levels in accordance with popular opinion and that this has been instrumental in the increased punitiveness of the US and UK (Matravers 2014, 2018).
14 In 1950, Finland had an incarceration rate of 200/100,000 and its near 'Nordic' neighbours around 50/100,000. By 1990, Finland was in step with its neighbours (Lappi-Seppälä 2001). Of course, policy choices have to go hand-in-hand with (the management of) popular opinion. There is perhaps room for policy 'nudges' in changing the latter (see Lepenies and Małecka, this volume).
15 I am grateful to Jonathan Jacobs for discussing many of the ideas in this chapter and to the editors for comments on an earlier draft.

Bibliography

Alexander, M. (2010) *The New Jim Crow: Mass Incarceration in the Age of Colorblindness*, New York, New Press.
Allen, F. A. (1959) 'Criminal Justice, Legal Values and the Rehabilitative Ideal', *Journal of Criminal Law and Criminology*, 50: 226–232.
American Friends Service Committee. (1971) *Struggle for Justice: A Report on Crime and Punishment in America*, New York, Hill and Wang.
Andenæs, J. (1974) *Punishment and Deterrence*, Ann Arbor, University of Michigan Press.
Armstrong, K. G. (1961) 'The Retributivist Hits Back', *Mind*, 70: 471–490.
Ashworth, A. (2000) 'Is the Criminal Law a Lost Cause', *Law Quarterly Review*, 116: 225–256.
Barry, B. (1990) '*Political Argument* After Twenty-Five Years', in *Political Argument: A Reissue with a New Introduction*, Berkeley, University of California Press.
Beale, S. (2011) 'The Story of Ewing v. California: Three Strikes Laws and the Limits of the Eighth Amendment Proportionality Review', in D. Coker & R. Weisberg (eds.), *Criminal Law Stories*, New York, Thomson Reuters/Foundation Press.
Beck, U. (1992) *Risk Society: Towards a New Modernity*, London, Sage.
Blumstein, A., Cohen, J., Martin, S. E. & Tonry, M. (1983a) *Research on Sentencing: The Search for Reform, Volume I*, Washington, DC, The National Academies Press.
Blumstein, A., Cohen, J., Martin, S. E. & Tonry, M. (1983b) *Research on Sentencing: The Search for Reform, Volume II*, Washington, DC, The National Academies Press.
Braithwaite, J. (1989) *Crime, Shame, and Reintegration*, Cambridge, Cambridge University Press.
Charvet, J. (1966) 'Criticism and Punishment', *Mind*, 75: 573–579.
Charvet, J. (2013) *The Nature and Limits of Human Equality*, Basingstoke, Palgrave Macmillan.
Davis, K. C. (1969) *Discretionary Justice: A Preliminary Enquiry*, Baton Rouge, Louisiana State University Press.
Donziger, S. (1996) *The Real War on Crime: The Report of the National Criminal Justice Commission*, New York, Harper Perennial.
Duff, A. (2003) 'I Might Be Guilty, But You Can't Try Me: Estoppel and Other Bars to Trial', *Ohio State Journal of Criminal Law*, 1: 245.
Dworkin, R. (1977) *Taking Rights Seriously*, Cambridge, MA, Harvard University Press.
Dzur, A. W. (2012) *Punishment, Participatory Democracy, and the Jury*, New York, Oxford University Press.
Frankel, M. E. (1973) *Criminal Sentences: Law Without Order*, New York, Hill and Wang.
Frase, R. (2009) 'Limiting Excessive Prison Sentencing', *University of Pennsylvania Journal of Constitutional Law*, 11: 43–46.

Garland, D. (2001) *The Culture of Control: Crime and Social Order in Contemporary Society*, Oxford, Oxford University Press.

Gaylin, W. & Rothman, D. J. (1976) 'Introduction', in A. von Hirsch (ed.), *Doing Justice: The Choice of Punishments*, New York, Hill and Wang.

Glueck, S. 1928. 'Principles of a Rational Penal Code', *Harvard Law Review*, XLI: 453–482.

Gross, H. (2012) *Crime and Punishment: A Concise Moral Critique*, Oxford, Oxford University Press.

Hall, L. & Glueck, S. (1940) *Cases and Materials on Criminal Law*, St. Paul, MN, West Publishing Co.

Hansard (1910) House of Commons Debate, 20 July, 19: c1354 https://api.parliament.uk/historic-hansard/commons/1910/jul/20/class-iii#column_1354

Hart, H.L.A. (2008) 'Prolegomenon to the Principles of Punishment', in *Punishment and Responsibility: Essays in the Philosophy of Law*. 2nd ed., Oxford, Oxford University Press.

Holroyd, J. (2010) 'Punishment and Justice', *Social Theory and Practice*, 36: 78–111.

Hudson, B. (2003) *Justice in the Risk Society: Challenging and Re-Affirming Justice in Late Modernity*, London, Sage.

Husak, D. (2008) *Overcriminalization: The Limits of the Criminal Law*, Oxford, Oxford University Press.

Husak, D. (2011) 'Retributivism, Proportionality, and the Challenge of the Drug Court Movement', in M. Tonry, (ed.), *Retributivism Has a Past: Has It a Future?*. New York, Oxford University Press.

Lacey, N. (2007) 'Interview', in M. Nielsen (ed.), *Legal Philosophy: 5 Questions*, Copenhagen, Automatic Press/VIP.

Lacey, N. (2008) *The Prisoners' Dilemma: Political Economy and Punishment in Contemporary Democracies*, Cambridge, Cambridge University Press.

Lappi-Seppälä, T. (2001) 'Sentencing and Punishment in Finland: The Decline of the Repressive Ideal', in M. Tonry & R. Frase (eds.), *Sentencing and Sanctions in Western Countries*, New York, Oxford University Press.

Lever, A. (2017) 'Towards a Democracy-Centred Ethics', *Critical Review of International Social and Political Philosophy*. https://doi.org/10.1080/13698230.2017.1403120

Lewis, C. S. (1949) 'The Humanitarian Theory of Punishment', *20th Century: An Australian Quarterly Review*, 3: 5–12.

Lippke, R. (2017) 'Punishment Drift: The Spread of Penal Harm and What We Should Do About It', *Criminal Law and Philosophy*, 11: 645–659.

Mail on Sunday. (1993) 21 February. https://www.independent.co.uk/news/major-on-crime-condemn-more-understand-less-1474470.html

Markel, D. & Flanders, C. (2010) 'Bentham on Stilts: The Bare Relevance of Subjectivity to Retributive Justice', *California Law Review*, 98: 907–988.

Martinson, R. L. (1974) 'What Works? Questions and Answers About Prison Reform', *The Public Interest*, 35: 22–54.

Matravers, M. (2000) *Justice and Punishment: The Rationale of Coercion*, Oxford, Oxford University Press.

Matravers, M. (2006) '"Who's Still Standing?" A Comment on Antony Duff's Preconditions of Criminal Liability', *Journal of Moral Philosophy*, 3: 320–330.

Matravers, M. (2011) 'Reassurance, Reinforcement, and Legitimacy', in M. Tonry (ed.), *Handbook of Crime and Criminal Justice*, New York, Oxford University Press.

Matravers, M. (2014) 'Proportionality Theory and Popular Opinion' in J. Ryberg (ed.), *Popular Punishment: On the Normative Significance of Public Opinion for Penal Theory*, Oxford, Oxford University Press.

Matravers, M. (2018) 'Rootless Desert and Unanchored Censure', in A du Bois-Pedain & A. Bottoms (eds.), *Penal Censure: Engagements Within and Beyond Desert Theory*, Oxford, Hart Publishing/Bloomsbury.

Mays, J. B. (1963) *Crime and the Social Structure*, London, Faber & Faber.

McCloskey, H. (1968) 'A Non-Utilitarian Approach to Punishment', in M. Bayles (ed.), *Contemporary Utilitarianism*, New York, Doubleday.

Michael, J. & Wechsler, H. (1940) *Criminal Law and Its Administration: Cases, Statutes, and Commentaries*, Chicago, Foundation Press.

Michelle, S. P. & Devah, P. (2015) 'Inequality and Punishment: A Turning Point for Mass Incarceration? *The Annals of the American Academy of Political and Social Science*, 663: 185–203.

Morris, H. (1968) 'Persons and Punishment', *Monist*, 52: 475–501.

Morse, S. J. (2000) 'Deprivation and Desert', in W. C. Heffernan & J. Kleinig (eds.), *From Social Justice to Criminal Justice: Poverty and the Administration of Criminal Law*, New York, Oxford University Press: 114–160.

Morse, S. (2015) 'Neuroscience, Free Will, and Criminal Responsibility', in W. Glannon (ed.), *Free Will and the Brain*, Cambridge, Cambridge University Press.

Murphy, J. (1973) 'Marxism and Retribution', *Philosophy and Public Affairs*, 2: 217–243.

National Research Council. (2014) *The Growth of Incarceration in the United States: Exploring Causes and Consequences*, Washington, DC, The National Academies Press.

New Statesman. (1993) 29 January. https://www.newstatesman.com/2015/12/archive-tony-blair-tough-crime-tough-causes-crime

Petersen, S. K. (1993) 'The Punishment Need Not Fit the Crime: Harmelin v. Michigan and the Eigth Amendment', *Pepperdine Law Review*, 20: 747–794.

Pettit, P. (2002) 'Is Criminal Justice Politically Feasible?' *Buffalo Criminal Law Review*, 5: 427–450.

Rawls, J. (1955) 'Two Concepts of Rules', in J. Rawls & S. Freeman (eds.), *Collected Papers*. Cambridge, MA, Harvard University Press.

Rawls, J. (1971) *A Theory of Justice*, Cambridge, MA, Harvard University Press.

Robinson, P. (2001) 'Punishing Dangerousness: Cloaking Preventive Detention as Criminal Justice', *Harvard Law Review*, 114: 1428–1456.

Shelby, T. (2016) *Dark Ghettos: Injustice, Dissent, and Reform*, Cambridge, MA, Harvard University Press.

Stuntz, W. J. (2011) *The Collapse of American Criminal Justice*, Cambridge, MA, Harvard University Press.

Tonry, M. (2011a) 'Preface', in M. Tonry (ed.), *Retributivism Has a Past: Has It a Future?* New York, Oxford University Press.

Tonry, M. (2011b) 'Can Twenty-First Century Punishment Policies Be Justified in Principle?' in M. Tonry (ed.), *Retributivism Has a Past: Has It a Future?* New York, Oxford University Press.

Tonry, M. (2011c) 'Introduction: Thinking About Punishment', in M. Tonry (ed.), *Why Punish? How Much? A Reader on Punishment*, New York, Oxford University Press.

Tonry, M. (ed.) (2017) *Crime and Justice, Volume 45: Sentencing Policies and Practices in Western Countries: Comparative and Cross-National Perspectives*, Chicago, Chicago University Press.

Tonry, M. (2018) 'Punishment and Human Dignity: Sentencing Principles for Twenty-First Century America', *Crime and Justice – A Review of Research*, 47: 119–167.

Vlastos, G. (1962) 'Justice and Equality', in R. Brandt (ed.), *Social Justice*, Englewood Cliffs, Prentice Hall.

von Hirsch, A. (1976) *Doing Justice: The Choice of Punishments: Report of the Committee for the Study of Incarceration*, New York, Hill and Wang.

von Hirsch, A. (1999) *Criminal Deterrence and Sentence Severity: An Analysis of Recent Research*, Oxford/Portland, OR, Hart Publishing.

Waldron, J. (2017) *One Another's Equals: The Basis of Human Equality*, Cambridge, MA, Harvard University Press.

Watson, G. (2010) 'The Insanity Defense', in L. May & J. Brown (eds.), *Philosophy of Law: Classic and Contemporary Readings*, Oxford, Wiley-Blackwell.

Williams, B. (1973) 'A Critique of Utilitarianism', in J. J. C. Smart & B. Williams (eds.), *Utilitarianism: For and Against*, Cambridge, Cambridge University Press.

Yankah, E. (2016) 'When Addiction Has a White Face', *The New York Times*, 09/02/2016.

Zimring, F. E., Hawkins, G. & Kamin, S. (2001) *Punishment And Democracy: Three Strikes and You're Out in California*, Oxford, Oxford University Press.

10

TERRITORIALITY AND PERSONALITY

Concepts and normative considerations

Helder De Schutter

Introduction

To what extent do we live in a *territorial* political order? And is political territoriality something good or should we instead seek to reduce its relevance today? What is the alternative? These are the questions this chapter seeks to answer.

I first conceptualise political territoriality and its alternative, personality, as modes of jurisdictional authority, and argue that we live in a 'Mostly Territorial Order', a world based on territoriality but punctured by some instances of personality. In a second step, I present normative reasons for and against territoriality and personality, to resolve the question of whether we should allow for more personality than our Mostly Territorial Order currently does. I argue that the most important reasons for territoriality are the effective and efficient management of public policy. The most important reason for allowing personality is jurisdictional freedom. I argue indeed for more scope for personality than allowed for by the current Mostly Territorial Order: in my view, we should have territorial political communities, but at the same time it is desirable to decentralise many competences in the domain of what I call 'essentially personal matters' to non-territorial or personality-based jurisdictional units. This leads to a 'Mixed Order'.

Territoriality and personality: concepts

We live in territorial states. The modern connection between states and their territories is so intimate that many consider the notion of a territorial state a pleonasm: 'territory' is taken to be part of the very definition of statehood. For example, in Weber's classical definition, the state is 'the form of human community that (successfully) lays claim to the monopoly of legitimate physical violence within a particular territory' (Weber 2004: 33). This understanding of the state as a territorial entity is widely shared. Excepting the horizontal limit posed by the high seas (at which point *mare liberum* begins), a state simply ends horizontally where another state begins: territorial borders differentiate states. This territoriality also extends vertically, up till a certain point: airplanes need permission to enter a state's airspace, but the limit of states' vertical control is set by outer space.

So states have three-dimensional jurisdiction over land; they determine policies that apply to the entire territory that they control horizontally and vertically. For example, states can decide to dig up oil and thereby change the landscape, to give permissions to build skyscrapers or windmills, or to reduce the number of airplanes flying out at night. Yet, while states control three-dimensional territories, they also command individuals: they set out rules regulating the lives of individuals and the relationships between them – for example, they hold jurisdictional authority over whether an individual has a right to abortion, is to be punished for theft, is entitled to citizenship, or can get married to someone else.

In what follows, and based on terminology indebted to Karl Renner (1899), I will refer to these two features as instantiating a territoriality and a personality logic respectively. The state's territoriality logic entails that the state rules over a territory. The state's personality logic occasions that the state rules over individuals.

At first sight, one might think that the state's territoriality completely encapsulates its personality logic: the state's control of a territory entails control over all the people in that territory. For example, when the state engages in planning permission for buildings, those rules and permissions apply to the entire territory of the state: everyone who builds somewhere on the territory is subject to them. And while the state does claim authority over people by regulating their rights to abortion, it does so only for the individuals within the state's territory. When the state's citizens are outside of the state, they are subject to the territorial rules of another state.

However, this idea that the personality logic of the state is fully captured by the state's territoriality is misguided; the latter does not fully encapsulate the former. It is not the case that all the people on the territory of state A are subject *only* to the legal rules of A, and that all the citizens of A are subject to A's rules *only* when they are on A's territory. Some people in A are foreign nationals and A itself also has some citizens in other states. Citizenship does not end at the border: it follows the persons wherever they go. This implies that states have at least some jurisdictional authority[1] over their citizens even when citizens are abroad: a state could, for example, take a citizen's citizenship away while the citizen is abroad. Moreover, there are some rights and duties that foreign nationals retain when they are abroad. Under the Vienna Convention on Consular Relations, for example, consular officers of a detainee's nationality have the right to visit the detainee imprisoned in a foreign country and arrange for his legal representation. More generally, many states claim some jurisdiction over citizens living abroad, such as their subjection to the state's criminal law, including even the possibility for such citizens to be tried and punished in the home country, irrespective of the citizens' consent (Watson 1992: 67). States' extraterritorial jurisdiction also includes aspects of competition law, diplomatic missions, the command of military forces abroad, the imposition of taxation to citizens living abroad (as in the US), and the punishment of treason.

So the distinction between the territorial and the personal scope does not collapse: it is useful to think of the state as both setting out territorial rules *and* ruling over people; these logics overlap to a large extent, but they are not identical. As a territorial actor, the state decides territorial legal rules for its own territory, but this territorial jurisdiction is to some extent limited by the personality reach of another state, and it is supplemented by a state's own personality powers beyond its territory.

Yet, it would go too far to see the two logics as of equal size or importance today. While personality was crucial in the pre-modern feudal world, today the territorial logic is the far more dominant of the two logics. The laws and regulations that apply to foreign nationals are limited in number and scope. Moreover, the discussed extraterritorial personal powers could in principle be flat out denied by other states: states can choose to refuse extradition for instance, cancel consulatory presence, and choose not to have any dealings with other states. Territoriality rules in today's world, even if it is still important to realise that it is punctured at the margins by personality.

Apart from the discussed case of non-citizen residents retaining certain rights and obligations connected with the country of citizenship, it makes sense to point to three further examples of personality in the contemporary world. The second example is arbitration. Arbitration, especially popular for international commerce disputes, allows for private dispute resolution outside the courts between parties who agree to be bound by the judgement reached by a mutually agreed-upon third party. In most cases, the rules that apply (the *lex arbitri*) are those of the chosen seat of the arbitration. This seat does not have to be the place where the adjudication actually takes place: 'The seat constitutes a voluntary, juridical nexus between an arbitration and a given legal system; it is not a geographical notion' (Kaufmann-Kohler and Rigozzi 2015: 61). So by allowing for some choice of judges and legal systems, arbitration allows companies to effectively escape the state's territorial scope of jurisdiction when it comes to international commerce.

Thirdly, companies can often choose the jurisdiction within which their core activities are legally embedded, even if their real activities take place elsewhere. Within the US, for instance, '[i]n essence, companies can choose in which state they will have their legal seat' (Nordberg 2011: 77). A similar dynamic – the ability to legally incorporate a company in another country – combined with Ireland's particular policy of allowing companies to book income in subsidiaries outside Ireland that then remains untaxed by Ireland, helps explain why Ireland has been such a popular destination for multinational companies like Apple.

Fourthly, several states have internal non-territorial forms of minority protection (Coakley 1994). For example, a personality-based system of distributing political authority currently exists in Brussels, where two parliament-like institutions called "Community Commissions" exist – one catering to French speakers, the other to Dutch speakers – that issue laws and policies over competences such as culture and education. So, for example, there are French and Dutch schools on the territory of Brussels each administered by their own community. Other forms of non-territorial autonomy for ethnocultural groups in the domains of education and culture exist in northern Italy, Hungary, Estonia, Russia, Croatia, Slovenia, and Montenegro (see Osipov 2013: 9–12; Coakley 1994). These intra-state examples enable non-territorial autonomy in the sense that several ethnocultural or linguistic groups can provide services and forms of self-government to their members *wherever they are* within the state's (or part of the state's) territory.

These examples are good illustrations of personality but they are fairly peripheral. They don't affect the essential territoriality of states in the modern world. In general, where you live – your location – is what determines the legal rules that apply to you. The only way for you to change the legal rules to which you are subject is to move to another territory. We live in a territoriality-dominated system that is only tempered by marginal personality perforations.

Realising the presence of the perforations, however, allows us to reflect on whether we want more of them, or perhaps less of them. For example, we could extend the number of cases of non-territorial autonomy (i) or, more fundamentally, we could allow for personality in more domains everywhere, as a general rule (ii).

More cases

As far as increasing the number of cases is concerned, we can grant or stimulate requests for personality regimes in certain contexts where they are currently contemplated. Some small island countries, such as Tuvalu or Kiribati, risk becoming deprived of all their land due to rising sea levels. One future possibility would be for them to become non-territorial states, states without land. The state could still have a parliament and citizens could have the state's citizenship, with corresponding rights and obligations, without there still being (enough) land for them to live on

(Roberts 2007). Similarly, a non-territorial state has been imagined for the Roma in Europe (see Klímová-Alexander 2007), with, for example, the possibility for the Roma to be represented at EU level by their own EU commissioner representing the non-territorial people. Finally, the fact that no nation can claim territorial sovereignty over the high seas, the moon, and outer space allows us to imagine non-territorial ways of organising political power there. For outer space, for instance, there are only three solutions: (1) anarchism (no legal rules); (2) jurisdictional authority according to an extension of the territorial model whereby we either place the entire outer space under the jurisdiction of the International Court of Justice, or we delineate 'zones' (e.g., orbital slots where satellites can be placed, or particular planets and moons or parts of them) where the legal rules of a particular nation apply; or (3) we allow for non-territorial settings there. The latter might mean, for instance, that different rules (e.g., about blasphemy, anti-discrimination, marriage, euthanasia, abortion) apply to Russians and Americans in space, and any conflicts between members of different nations in space – for example, in the event of colliding space ships – would have to be resolved via treaties between nations.

More domains

While we could indeed in this way add some extra cases of non-territoriality (like Kiribati or the Roma) to the currently predominantly territorial system, doing so would leave the territorial system itself untouched: we would keep the territorial world order and, in addition, increase the number of 'exceptional' personality cases. Yet, a second, more fundamental approach would be to increase the number of personality domains everywhere. On this second approach, the relationship between territoriality and personality could fundamentally alter. To show this, we can conceive of the following five political systems, graded on a scale from pure territoriality to pure personality:

Order 1, the Purely Territorial Order, effaces all traces of personality. Political power applies to people entirely on the basis of where they are located. On the territory of state A, only A's rules apply, and A's rules do not apply beyond the territory of A. Once we leave the state, the state's power in no way still reaches us. Correspondingly, foreign nationals on the territory cannot claim foreign rights or duties. Moreover, we cancel all existing forms of non-territorial autonomy, as well as international commerce's possibilities of choosing arbitration places and legal seats.

Order 2, the Mostly Territorial Order, is the world in which we live. Most of our rights and duties depend on our territorial location, but some traces of the logic of personality remain, such as the four discussed earlier (extraterritorial reach over citizens abroad, arbitration, choice of territorial legal seat, and non-territorial autonomy for some minority nations). These traces occur at the fringes.

Order 3, the Mixed Order. Here the number of domains of personality is substantially increased, so that citizens live in two orders, one with territorial, and the other with personal jurisdiction. Both orders have significant impact on people's lives. In a Mixed Order, what is to be ruled territorially and what is to be ruled personally have to be decided, according to a principle of allocation of competences. Ahead I suggest one principle on the basis of which such decisions can be made. This is the model I will defend in the second half of the chapter.

Order 4, the Mostly Personal Order. This is the mirror position of Order 2: it is a non-territorial order where certain minimal competences are territorially exercised. This is just a weak version of Order 5.

Order 5, the Purely Personal Order. In the Purely Personal Order, no rights and duties depend on location. The citizens of a non-territorial polity are subject to the rules of the polity no matter where the citizens are: they could be on the territory of Russia, Brazil, or Antarctica, or in outer space, but they would still be subject to the legal rules of their polity based on personal jurisdiction. This implies that all interactions with people from other personal polities occur in a state of nature, unless the interaction is between people whose polities have made international treaties with each other: individuals are then subject to the legal rules of their own non-territorial states but their states have worked out rules about whose legal rules apply if disputes arise between their citizens. So, in case of conflict between a citizen of non-territorial state A with a citizen of non-territorial state B, A and B have worked out whose law applies or what to do. A and B could, for instance, rule that all conflicts have to be decided by B or even by a third state C, or it could rule that conflicts between a woman and a man of different nationalities have to be judged according to the legal rules of the state of the woman, or it could resort to any other principle as long as it is clear what the relevant laws are that are to judge the conflict. In the absence of treaties establishing such rules, anarchy applies. Note finally that in this Purely Personal Order, no territorial jurisdiction can exist: oil fields, gold mines, forests, or seas cannot fall under the jurisdiction of any particular nation, since that would bring back territorial rule. Of course, personal polities can make rules delineating what their own citizens can or cannot legitimately do (e.g., 'do not extract oil'), and they can make treaties with other personal polities over what the citizens of those polities can do, but no territory can uniquely fall under the territorial rule of any particular polity.

The current system is a type 2 order, as I argued earlier. Realising the contingency of our current order – that it is just one of several possible types – invites the normative question of whether this Mostly Territorial Order embodies the most desirable one, whether perhaps moving up or down the list would be better. It is to this question that I will now set myself. Before moving on to the next section, where I will weigh some of the advantages and disadvantages of allowing for more personality, or instead seeking to reduce the current instances of personality by moving to a type 1 order, two more things need to be added about the distinction between territorial and personal jurisdiction.

First, something must be said on what kinds of groups personal jurisdiction allows for. The essential difference between personality and territoriality lies in the fact that in the personality mode, jurisdictional authority is held over a subset of the population living within a particular territory. The subset could in principle be based on any group-distinguishing feature in so far as it is not territorial: it could be religion, age, familial affiliations, hobbies, nationality, political ideologies, or simply not be circumscribed in any other way than by a list of names. In the territorial mode, in contrast, jurisdictional authority is exercised over *all* the people within a certain territory. So what defines membership of the authority in the personality mode is membership of a non-territorially defined subset of the people within the territory. What defines membership of the authority in the territoriality mode is presence on the territory. Territoriality simply identifies the relevant people by targeting everyone who is on the territory.

Second, something must be said about how to combine territorial and personal jurisdiction in any regime that falls in between the two extremes of type 1 and type 5. Types 2, 3, and 4 combine in different measures both systems, so there must be a way of deciding which competences shall be ruled territorially, and which personally. Of course, there might not be a neat principle; these things might be decided ad hoc, through compromises or by balancing power. Still, the following division seems logical, which I take to be the ideal-typical principle for the

Mixed Order. Jurisdictional matters[2] can be divided into what I will call *essentially territorial matters* and *essentially personal matters*.

Essentially territorial matters concern governable entities that occupy physical space and that are immovable (or nearly immovable). Examples are rivers, mountains, lakes, buildings, oil fields, and landscapes. They are crucial in governmental domains such as environmental policies, natural resource management, and road maintenance. It is impossible to effectively rule over essentially territorial matters without ruling territorially: to govern them, a state must have territorial jurisdiction.

Essentially personal matters are all other governable matters. Examples are behaviour, knowledge, freedom of speech, languages, cars, and watches. They are crucial in governmental domains such as language management, education policy, anti-discrimination policy, and criminal law. Essentially personal matters are either intangible (as in language management) or tangible but easily movable (as with cars). One might object that human beings occupy physical space, and argue that all jurisdiction over people must therefore be territorial. Ruling them does imply the ability to act with authority on a given physical spot. But for that the territories don't need to be assigned to particular polities: in a system with personal jurisdiction, individual A1 from polity A might be coerced by A on the same territorial spot on which individual B1 from polity B was coerced the day before.

This distinction between essentially territorial matters and essentially personal matters suggests an evident principle for differentiating between powers to be handled by territorial and personal jurisdiction: the principle of jurisdictional dualism.

> *Principle of Jurisdictional Dualism*: essentially personal matters are to be governed by a personal polity, and essentially territorial matters are to be governed by a territorial polity.

This would imply that in a given territory, one territorial polity rules over essentially territorial matters, and multiple personal polities can rule over essentially personal matters. The territorial polity would rule over road maintenance or housing regulation for all the inhabitants of the land, whereas the personal polities would rule over issues like marriage law or language maintenance. In the next section, I will evaluate the jurisdictional dualism principle from a normative angle, and defend a version of it.

Taking stock, we have encountered two jurisdictional logics: personality and territoriality. In personal jurisdiction, rights and duties depend on *who* you are. In the territorial order, rights and duties depend on *where* you are. And we have also seen that today territoriality reigns but that the territorial world is punctured by several instances of personality. Theorising those punctures invites the question of whether we should seek to remove those cracks, or perhaps move towards more personality (or keep the status quo), to which I now turn.

Combining personality and territoriality: normative considerations

Perhaps surprisingly, not much engagement exists in normative political theory over reasons for and against territoriality and personality.[3] In what follows, my central question is whether the current Mostly Territorial Order (type 2 from my list earlier) is the most desirable option, or whether we have good reasons to move up or down the list of six orders. To answer this question, I articulate three arguments that impact on the personality/territoriality debate: the argument from jurisdictional freedom, the argument from efficient and effective governance, and an argument about the race-to-the-bottom mechanism. As I will argue, the first ends up favouring personality where possible. The second is a strong argument in favour of at least partial territoriality. And the third argument poses limits to personality. Taking these arguments together leads in my view to the desirability of a Mixed Order (the third order in the foregoing list), instantiating a version of the principle of jurisdictional dualism. I should add that I am writing with contemporary liberal democratic states in mind: here I will not deal with the question of to which extent my favoured version of jurisdictional dualism is applicable in non-democratic and non-liberal contexts.

Jurisdictional freedom

The most important argument for territorial autonomy is that it allows for jurisdictional freedom. By jurisdictional freedom I mean the freedom to choose the legal rules one is to obey. Jurisdictional freedom is to be distinguished from legal freedom. Legal freedom is the freedom to exercise choice in all areas allowed for by the law. I can, for example, make use of my legal freedom to smoke (where the law allows me to smoke) or not to smoke, to have children or not, to get married, to enjoy art, to collect stamps, to have a hobby, to build friendships with particular people, to join clubs or churches or networks. My legal freedom ends where transgression of the law begins: I don't have legal freedom to murder. I have legal freedom to do whatever is lawful.

It is evident that legal freedom is of paramount importance; I will here not explore the moral justification of our interest in legal freedom but simply presuppose it is a fundamental interest that should not easily be overridden. We legitimately desire freedom of choice in our lives, provided that what we do is legal. But our freedom is of course influenced by what the legal rules stipulate: the laws under which I live shape and limit my freedom. Imagine now that I could not just choose how to live my life under the laws – how to exercise legal freedom – but that I could also choose my laws, that I had the freedom to choose a context of legal freedom. I would then have jurisdictional freedom: the freedom to choose a context of legal freedom. If legal freedom matters, then jurisdictional freedom must matter as well, since jurisdictional freedom is a means of choosing the scope of legal freedom.

Jurisdictional freedom can and does exist under a system of territorial jurisdiction, both inside states and between states. Inside states, one can move from one municipality or province of the country to another, to be subject to the policies and legal rules of the new location. Almost all states allow for internal freedom of movement. Such 'foot voting' is an often-discussed dimension of federalism.[4] In a federal system, the citizens can move from one partially self-governing unit, such as Texas, to another, such as California. Imagine, for example, a federal system where state 1 accepts gay marriage and another, state 2, does not:

> [S]tate 1's acceptance of same-sex marriage is a signal that it is a gay-friendly jurisdiction. One might assume that at least some state 2 residents who are gay or who do not want to live in a gay-negative place would relocate to state 1. Correlatively, state 2's stance signals to state 1 citizens who would be miserable living under same-sex marriage that they could relocate there. Although the numbers of people "voting with their feet" would be modest, the democratic payoff is impressive.
>
> *(Eskridge and Spedale 2006: 248)*

Jurisdictional freedom is also possible between states, at least where it is allowed: where migration is possible, jurisdictional freedom exists. Freedom of movement within the current European Union, for instance, effectively allows someone living in Lithuania to move to Denmark.

So within the current territorial system, individuals can exercise far-reaching forms of jurisdictional freedom – the freedom to choose a context of legal freedom – through forms of intrastate or interstate foot-voting. There is, however, a significant obstacle to foot-voting: moving costs. It takes time, money, and energy to relocate. On top of that, it has psychological and social costs in terms of losing vicinity to one's family, friends, schools, living environment, and other local networks.

This is where the alternative of personality comes in. Under a system of personal jurisdiction, the rights and duties that fall upon citizens do not depend on their location. This means that the moving costs virtually disappear. If an individual wants to change her membership of a polity with personal jurisdiction, she would not have to move. Take the same gay marriage issue discussed earlier in the discussion over foot-voting. To become subject to the territorial jurisdiction of a gay-friendly state, one would have to move. But to be subject to the personal jurisdiction of a polity that recognises gay marriage, no physical moving is required. It suffices to leave one's current personal polity and to be allowed by the desired personal polity. On the same territorial unit, an in principle unlimited number of personal polities could exist. The personality system thus virtually removes moving costs. There surely could still be administrative hurdles taking up some time and energy involved in changing one's membership: exiting a previous polity and registering with a new one. But in terms of the cost obstacle to exercising jurisdictional freedom, personality outrivals territoriality.

To this one might reply that moving between non-territorial jurisdictions might be made illegal or impossible, thereby disabling jurisdictional freedom. This is certainly possible. But it would be incorrect to see this as an argument against non-territoriality, since it is also perfectly possible for a territorial state to try to prevent immigrants from entering, as we all know well today. Foot-voting is possible only if migration is allowed. It is therefore unfair to hold unwillingness to take on (certain) new members as an argument against personality, since such unwillingness equally exists as an option in the territorial system.

Efficient and effective government

The manner in which legal rules are exercised must allow for efficient and effective management. To do something *efficiently* is to do it with little waste of time. To do something *effectively* is to be able to get it done. A solution is efficient when it is done fast and it is effective when the objective is reached. For example, fishing with a net is typically more efficient than with hands, since more fish can be hauled in less time. Yet, fishing with a net with holes too big for the fish to remain inside is not an effective way of fishing; fishing with smaller net holes is effective.

The fact that changing personal jurisdiction – for example, through individual declaration – requires less time and effort than moving between territorial locations makes personality more *efficient* than territoriality. That fact that monetary, social, and psychological moving costs are often so hefty that moving one's territorial location is not a realistic option also speaks to personality's advantage in terms of *effectiveness*. So both efficiency and effectiveness of jurisdictional freedom are served by personality.

However, jurisdictional freedom is of course not the only thing we want to do efficiently and effectively. We want efficiency and effectiveness overall, with respect to all functions that we ordinarily believe government should exercise. It is here that an argument for territoriality begins to appear. Recall the distinction earlier between essentially personal matters like marriage and inheritance, and essentially territorial matters like rivers and forests. Personality can surely be an efficient and effective way of governing essentially personal matters. But it is not an efficient and effective way of implementing policies for essentially territorial matters. Such matters are stuck to the territory and if they are to be governed, they will require territorial jurisdiction. To see this, consider the following two examples: environmental policy and dispute resolution.

1   Protecting the environment efficiently and effectively. Take the efficient and effective management of an environmental issue such as a forest: imagine that the quantity of waste left behind from picnicking by visitors of the forest makes the forest unattractive. Keeping this forest clean is more efficiently done through territoriality than through personality. The reason is that a polity operating with personal jurisdiction can coerce only the individuals belonging to its own jurisdiction. A polity with territorial jurisdiction claims authority over all the individuals in the polity. It could, for instance, place fences around the forest, to prevent anyone in the territory from accessing it. It could do so because it claims authority over everyone; a personality polity could place only fences that stop its own citizens. The territorial polity could also have the police patrol the forest and fine any waste-dumpers or take them into custody without first having to check whether the offenders belong to the right jurisdiction, since everyone in the territorial unit belongs to the same jurisdiction. The personality-based polity could prevent its own people from entering, but no others. There is one solution to this: the personality-based polities could all come together, and make treaties with other non-territorial policies to together solve the local territorial problem. But this would involve significant complexities, which make the territorial solution more *efficient*, since it is faster and requires less effort. Territoriality is also more *effective* for such matters since efficiency spills over here into effectiveness: to reach the objective – forest maintenance – fast action is a prerequisite: the objective cannot be reached without the ability to act quickly, especially when new and sudden developments occur (e.g., a forest fire, or the arrival of a large camping group).[5]

2   The efficient and effective resolution of conflicts. Take law enforcement to prevent or end unlawful behaviour. In a simple model of a Pure Personality Order, different police forces would patrol the state, each controlling their own population. Imagine person A attempts to kill person B by shooting. In a Pure Personality Order (with personality for all matters, territorial and personal), each police unit would in each case of a seeming offence have to check (1) whether the perpetrator belongs to their citizenry, (2) whether the victim does, and (3) what the rules are in case perpetrator and victim belong to different polities. Of course, the polities could make treaties about what happens in the case of 3, just like territorial nations today can make international treaties about repatriation or other international conflicts between individuals. In a perhaps more sensible model, there would be a joint police force, resulting from cooperation between the polities. Still, this united police force would, in order to know what to do upon seeing what looks like an offence, still have to perform the same three checks. It might even be the case that different polities have different rules about when shooting is allowed: polity A may stipulate it is allowed as an act of self-defence against robbery, whereas polity B may have rules outlawing shooting in such a case. Polity B may even have outlawed carrying weapons. So even such evident actions as taking the gunner into custody and preventing him from inflicting more violence require complex steps, which make territoriality superior in terms of efficiency. In many cases, law enforcement can also not be effective; the very functions of law enforcement – such as realising safety and corrective justice – come into peril because of the complex steps involved: effective law enforcement often requires immediate intervention in the crime scene. Here too efficiency spills over into effectiveness; effective government

implies efficient government. Only if everyone on the territory is subject to the exact same legal rules for essentially territorial matters, and the identical corresponding legal freedom, can law enforcers effectively prevent crimes.[6]

What is the upshot of these problems for personality as a mode of jurisdictional authority? My analysis suggests that personality is neither efficient nor effective for a significant number of fundamental governmental functions, such as environmental protection or immediate conflict resolution. We should therefore restrict the scope of personality. This does not imply that we should entirely give up on personality and make (or continue to make) all rule territorial, given the benefits of jurisdictional freedom that personality brings. Personality can be an efficient and effective way of exercising (fundamental) governmental functions like educational and cultural affairs, and it brings the added benefit of great jurisdictional freedom. But it is not efficient and effective for essentially territorial matters, such as the maintenance of forests (example 1 earlier), and not for certain other matters that are not essentially territorial matters but that are governed more efficiently and effectively by territorial rule, such as law enforcement for purposes of immediate safety (example 2 earlier).

This points to the following possible principle for combining territorial and personal jurisdiction: personal jurisdiction for the essentially personal matters minus those fundamental governmental functions of which the efficient and effective management requires territoriality (e.g., the immediate resolution of violence between citizens), coupled with territorial jurisdiction for all other matters – that is, essentially territorial matters plus those fundamental governmental functions that require territoriality for efficient and effective management. Note that this principle adds a qualification to the earlier-discussed Principle of Jurisdictional Dualism, which claimed that essentially personal matters are to be governed by a personal polity, whereas essentially territorial matters are to be governed by a territorial polity. The qualification it adds is the following: personal matters are *also* to be ruled territorially if they concern essentially personal matters of which the effective and efficient management requires territoriality. So the qualification narrows the Principle of Jurisdictional Dualism down, to

> *The Qualified Principle of Jurisdictional Dualism*: to be governed by territorial jurisdictions are (1) all essentially territorial matters *and* (2) those essentially personal matters that require territoriality for their efficient and effective management. All other matters are to be governed by personal jurisdictions.

This then embodies an instantiation of the Mixed Order: it is possible to have certain competences placed under territorial jurisdiction, whereas others are directed by personal jurisdiction.[7] It poses certain limits to personality: some things are to be done territorially. But there is still much scope left for personal jurisdiction.

Social justice

My third normative consideration is based on social justice. Social justice requires a form of redistribution from the well-off to those who are less well-off. Redistribution clearly is not an essentially territorial matter: taxes could flow to less-advantaged compatriots at the other side of the planet just as much as to co-territorial citizens sharing the same locality, especially with today's fast and online ways of communicating and transferring money. Social justice is therefore a candidate to be ruled by personal jurisdiction. Is it, however, a matter of which the efficient and effective resolution requires territorial jurisdiction? If so, territorialising it would be in order, under the just-defended Qualified Principle of Jurisdictional Dualism.

This question becomes acute due to the 'race to the bottom' problem. The problem refers to a possible chain of events whereby states seek to lower their taxes and other regulations in order to attract the rich. As soon as state 1 lowers its taxes, state 2 feels compelled to follow suit so as not to lose its wealthy citizens and businesses, after which state 1 may lower again, and so on. The net result is a reduction of solidarity from rich to poor, as in this system the states evolve towards minimal states with little distribution, or at least less redistribution than before (Rudra 2008). It is also thought to lead to reduced environmental protection and other safety nets.

In the context of the discussion over personality, the race-to-the-bottom fear could be presented as follows: if non-territorial polities have social competences, and if anyone can change their non-territorial memberships, then each non-territorial polity has an incentive to lower its taxes and social protection in order to attract wealthy non-territorial 'migrants'. Citizens with high incomes or investors may flock to the polities with the least taxation, thereby pressuring other polities to lower their taxes as well. The end result may be non-territorial polities with very little redistribution from rich to poor. Is this a concern that may prompt us to keep all fiscal and social policies territorial?

Before answering this question, it is important to realise that territorial jurisdictions are not thought to be exempt from races to the bottom. On the contrary, it is in territorial contexts that they are normally observed. Yet the race to the bottom may be thought to play up more significantly in personality settings, because of the ease of changing jurisdictions. The presence of lower moving costs is what makes the personality model outrival territoriality in terms of jurisdictional freedom. But that same feature makes the race-to-the-bottom mechanism more pernicious: the easier it is for the rich to leave, the quicker social policies can level down, or at least that is what armchair speculation suggests, as there are almost no real cases where social justice is pursued by non-territorial polities, and hence no studies.

A few reassurances are in order, though. Firstly, we can expect some levelling among living conditions – and thus some partial off-setting of the inequality effects from a race to the bottom – to occur as a result of sharing the same climate, or streets, and especially stores and businesses: if indeed some polities have richer citizens than others, the richer citizens will still buy from the stores where less-advantaged employees work, or the salaries of less-advantaged employees can be expected to be higher than in territorially administered territorial zones where only less-advantaged people live.

Secondly, many of the traditional worries associated with the race-to-the-bottom argument would not occur in the Mixed Order realisation that follows the rule outlined earlier, simply because essentially territorially bound policies would be exercised in this type 3 order by the territorial polity. Environmental regulation, a prime example of a context where the race-to-the-bottom argument plays out, is an essentially territorial matter that would not come under personal authority. The same goes for other territorial competences with social justice implications, such as housing regulations or taxation for territorial matters.

And thirdly, just like in the case of territoriality, there are ways to respond to this phenomenon. One way to respond would be to coordinate between various non-territorial polities to together uphold a high enough social minimum or not to lower taxes beyond a certain point, much like in the European Union interventions have in some way reduced the Irish tax benefits granted to multinational companies. Another response is simply to make changing jurisdictions more cumbersome. This could be done by implementing a waiting period, by installing an exit tax, or even by reducing the number of permitted changes between personal polities within an individual's lifetime (to, e.g., 'one change only'). This would reinstall some non-territorial analogues to 'moving' costs. And finally, there is always the option of relegating the competence back to the territorial zone of jurisdiction, which in the Mixed Order regime always still exists.

So a non-territorial race to the bottom may occur and may in some cases be more significant than it would be in the territorial case. Yet shared living conditions, a Mixed Order–type realisation, inter-polity coordination, and the implementation of a certain cumbersomeness in changing jurisdictions may attenuate it, and where these measures do not offset the pernicious effects for social justice, we can still intervene by relegating the particular social policy to territorial jurisdiction or never assigning it to personality in the first place.

Conclusion

Today, we live in a Mostly Territorial order that is punctured by some personality features. Focusing on these punctures allows us to imagine more radically personal orders. Should we indeed allow for more personality and move to a Mostly Personal Order or a Purely Personal Order? My answer in this chapter has been: yes, we should allow for more personality, but we should not aim for a Mostly or Purely Personal Order. In my view, the Mixed Order is the normatively preferred option. This conclusion was reached through the following reasoning. The important value of jurisdictional freedom justifies moving towards more personality, because personality can virtually remove all moving costs. This is particularly appropriate in the case of national minorities who desire forms of self-government but for whom territorial self-government is impossible due the presence of other nations on the same territory. However, the efficient and effective exercise of certain essentially territorial matters (e.g., environmental protection) and certain essentially personal matters of which the effective and efficient government requires territorial rule (e.g., the prevention of violence) speaks for at least keeping a significant number of competences territorially managed. In some cases, doing so may also help prevent a pernicious race to the bottom in terms of social justice. Therefore, it would be desirable to move from our current Mostly Territorial Order to a Mixed Order.

Acknowledgements

Versions of this chapter were presented in the workshop *Sovereignty in Contested Spaces* at Princeton University on September 29–30, 2016, and in a political theory seminar of the *Centro de Investigaciones Jurídicas y Sociales* of the Universidad Nacional de Córdoba (Argentina) on November 1, 2017. I thank the audiences of both workshops, and in particular Ercilia Adén, Adam Clulow, Cristián Fatauros, and Anna Stilz for intense conversations on personality. I am very grateful to Andrei Poama and Annabelle Lever for their detailed engagement with the chapter for this volume.

Notes

1 Following Allen Buchanan, I understand jurisdictional authority as 'the right to make, adjudicate, and enforce legal rules' (Buchanan 2003: 233). In this chapter I avoid the notion 'sovereignty', because it is not necessary for an agent to have sovereignty (understood as supreme control) to have jurisdictional authority – there could be two or more agents exercising jurisdiction (whether territorial or personal in kind) irrespective of which of them (if any) has sovereignty over the land or the people.
2 By jurisdictional matters, I mean all matters subject to public policies – that is, all matters that are governed by a jurisdictional unit, such as marriage law and road maintenance.

3 There is a small group of normative political theorists who have explicitly written on personal jurisdiction. A few have expressed enthusiasm for this idea, either from libertarian premises (Tucker 2015) or from the prospects of non-territorial autonomy for sub-state nations (Nimni 2005). Yet, particularly with respect to the latter, most remain sceptical of the very idea of non-territorial autonomy, and prefer territorial jurisdiction for national minorities (Bauböck 2005; Keating 2005; Kymlicka 2005). I have replied at length to these critics in De Schutter (2015).

4 See Somin (2014) for an excellent treatment of this issue of foot-voting in territorial federal systems.

5 What does this imply for jurisdictional freedom? Jurisdictional freedom can still be personally organised for the essentially personal matters. But for essentially territorial matters, jurisdictional freedom can be effectively realised only through moving or through raising your democratic voice in the hope of influencing the people around you to change their mind or to vote in favour of your preferred territorial management.

6 Repeated discussions of this point with Anna Stilz significantly contributed to my current understanding of this important advantage of territoriality.

7 That is the reason why, from the point of view of the national minorities, territorial jurisdiction will still be seen as the best possible prize. If they get territorial autonomy, they can exercise self-government over both essentially territorial and essentially personal matters. If they get only personal autonomy, they can exercise it only for essentially personal matters. Yet, in some heterogeneous cases where two groups desire the same land, there are no better solutions than finding a form of joint, binational territorial management for the territorial matters. From the point of view of the national groups, the situation simply is not ideal and they have to settle with steering the territorial matters together with the other group(s) while decentralising other competences to personal polities.

References

Bauböck, R. (2005). Political Autonomy or Cultural Minority Rights? A Conceptual Critique of Renner's Model. In: E. Nimni (ed.), *National Cultural Autonomy and Its Contemporary Critics*. London: Routledge, pp. 97–211.

Buchanan, A. (2003). The Making and Unmaking of Boundaries: What Liberalism Has to Say. In: A. Buchanan and M. Moore (eds.), *Nations, States, and Borders: The Ethics of Making Boundaries*. Cambridge: Cambridge University Press, pp. 231–261.

Coakley, J. (1994). Approaches to the Resolution of Ethnic Conflict: The Strategy of Non-Territorial Autonomy. *International Political Science Review* 15, pp. 297–314.

De Schutter, H. (2015). Non-Territorial Jurisdictional Authority: A Radical Possibility in Need of a Critique. In: J. F. Grégoire and M. Jewkes (eds.), *Recognition and Redistribution in Multinational Federalism*. Leuven: Leuven University Press, pp. 35–56.

Eskridge, William N. and Spedale, Darren R. (2006). *Gay Marriage: For Better or for Worse? What We've Learned from the Evidence*. Oxford: Oxford University Press.

Kaufmann-Kohler, G. and Rigozzi, A. (2015). *International Arbitration: Law and Practice in Switzerland*. Oxford: Oxford University Press.

Keating, M. (2005). Territory, State and Nation in the European Union: How Relevant Is Renner? In: E. Nimni (ed.), *National Cultural Autonomy and Its Contemporary Critics*. London: Routledge, pp. 181–190.

Klímová-Alexander, I. (2007). Transnational Romani and Indigenous Non-Territorial Self-Determination Claims. *Ethnopolitics* 6 (3), pp. 305–416.

Kymlicka, W. (2005). National Cultural Autonomy and International Minority Rights Norms. In: D. Smith and K. Cordell (eds.), *Cultural Autonomy in Contemporary Europe*. New York: Routledge, pp. 43–57.

Nimni, E. (2005). Introduction: The National Cultural Autonomy Model Revisited. In: E. Nimni (ed.), *National Cultural Autonomy and Its Contemporary Critics*. London: Routledge, pp. 1–14.

Nordberg, D. (2011). *Corporate Governance: Principles and Issues*. London: Sage.

Osipov, A. (2013). Non-Territorial Autonomy During and After Communism: In the Wrong or the Right Place? *Journal on Ethnopolitics and Minority Issues in Europe* 12 (1), pp. 7–26.

Renner, K. (2005 [1899]). State and Nation. In: E. Nimni (ed.), *National Cultural Autonomy and Its Contemporary Critics*. London: Routledge, pp. 64–82.

Roberts, A. (2007). Islanders Without an Island: What Will Become of Tuvalu's Climate Refugees? *Der Spiegel*, International Edition, 14 Sept.

Rudra, N. (2008). *Globalization and the Race to the Bottom in Developing Countries: Who Really Gets Hurt?* Cambridge: Cambridge University Press.

Somin, I. (2014). Foot Voting, Federalism, and Political Freedom. In: J. Fleming and J. Levy (eds.), *Nomos LV: Federalism and Subsidiarity*. New York and London: New York University Press, pp. 83–119.

Tucker, A. (2015). The Best States: Panarchy as an Anti-Utopia. In: A. Tucker and G. P. de Bellis (eds.), *Panarchy: Political Theories of Non-Territorial States*. London: Routledge, pp. 140–165.

Watson, G. R. (1992). Offenders Abroad: The Case for Nationality-Based Criminal Jurisdiction. *Yale Journal of International Law* 17 (41), pp. 41–84.

Weber, M. (2004). *The Vocation Lectures*. D. Owen and T. B. Strong (eds.), R. Livingstone (tr.). Indianapolis: Hackett Publishing Company.

11

WHAT IS PUBLIC SPACE FOR? POLITICAL IMAGINARIES AND POLICY IMPLICATIONS

Bernardo Zacka

One autumn morning in the late 2000s, three public benches in Harvard Square in Cambridge, Massachusetts, were lifted by crane, flipped around, and bolted back to the ground on the very same spot.[1] It was only after the rotation that I noticed how peculiar their original placement, along the outer edge of the sidewalk, had been. Instead of facing inward, towards the shops and the main flow of pedestrians, they gave onto the road, their views of the university almost always obstructed by a stationary line of taxi cabs.

Now that they had been rotated, I found the benches more inviting. But others seemed to have liked them just fine before. Shielded from pedestrian traffic by their proximity to cars, their back turned to the "active frontage" of nearby buildings, they provided a semi-secluded space in an area otherwise teeming with movement. This made them popular with the homeless who, slouched awkwardly against the middle armrest designed to prevent them from being more comfortable, could nevertheless find there a modicum of tranquillity and rest. With the benches now fully exposed to public view, drawing students and tourists alike, that appeal had gone and with it, the original users.

The replacement of one public by another had required no change in zoning, no additional policing, no modification to rules of access, not even the introduction of new street furniture. All it took was a change in angle. Interestingly, it was us, the passers-by, who, through our fleeting gaze and the temptation to sit, had become unknowingly enlisted as the agents of this transformation.

The rotation of the benches was part of a broader effort by the City of Cambridge to revitalise open public space in Harvard Square. Also targeted was "the pit", a sunken quasi-circular area by the main subway exit that had for decades served as a meeting point for the homeless as well as for skaters, goths, and punks of all stripes. The City did not raze or redesign the pit; it proceeded, rather, to eliminate its enclosed, arena-like feel, by filling it with tables and chairs placed to attract tourists and visitors. Once again, the intervention was punctual, cost-effective, and non-coercive. As William Whyte, an urbanologist famous for his detailed observations of street life, put it, 'the best way to handle the problem of undesirables is to make a place attractive to everyone else' (2001, p. 63).

The plan to revitalise Harvard Square was not imposed unilaterally by City Hall, nor was it was forced upon local authorities by business interests run amok. It germinated, as has become *de rigueur* these days, through inclusive community discussions, lengthy subcommittee meetings, and workshops open to all concerned parties. One round was conducted by the city in 2005–2006, as the *Healthy Harvard Square Initiative*. Another took place in 2013 and 2014, in partnership with Harvard University and the Harvard Square Business Association.[2] It involved a series of workshops led by the Project for Public Spaces, a non-profit inspired by the work of Whyte and dedicated to disseminating his insights on how to make urban spaces come to life.

To someone from the 1960s, this partnership might have looked incongruous. The very voices that were then, along with Whyte and his contemporary Jane Jacobs, decrying the disappearance of public space at the hands of the automobile and modernist architecture and clamouring for a community-based approach to urban planning had, five decades later, become powerful forces in their own right, dotting cityscapes with movable furniture, sun shades, street pianos, food kiosks, and potted plants. One could be forgiven for finding the outcome ironic. At Harvard Square, it was in the name of broadening access to public space that the homeless had been displaced from the benches they used to occupy, and in the name of place-making that one of the most distinctive places in the city had been altered beyond recognition.

What should we make of these transformations to public space? And how should we understand the fact that both their proponents and detractors present themselves as defenders of public space? I propose to shed light on these questions by examining a range of competing visions of public space that co-exist, somewhat uneasily, in our democratic political culture. These imaginaries, as I will call them, emanate from four families of normative political views – liberal, egalitarian, civic republican, and democratic – that have played a significant part in shaping our political practices and self-understanding, and that are all, in that sense, *ours*. Each of these views provides us with a different account of what it is that makes public space valuable. Each brings into focus a distinctive type of threat to public space, and each charts, finally, a different course of action for public policy and urban design.

While these four families of views derive from different traditions of political thought, I do not attempt to trace their lineage, nor do I claim that they are mutually exclusive. Most contemporary theorists – be they liberal egalitarians, neo-republicans, or radical democrats – are in fact committed to a hybrid mixture of all four. Still, I believe that each of these strands exhibits a certain loose coherence, and that there is value in comparing and contrasting the imaginaries of public space they contain, if only to show where and why they diverge.

Rather than speak of imaginaries, political philosophers may prefer the language of values – referring to arguments from liberty, from equality, from civic community, and from democratic pluralism. Much of what I say in the following pages could indeed be captured under such rubrics. I have chosen the term "imaginary", however, because several of the arguments we will encounter are couched in evocative descriptions of what public space ought to look and feel like. These descriptions conjure up aesthetic and sensory experiences that exceed the bounds of principled argumentation.

In what follows, I hope to show that these imaginaries can provide a useful way to navigate the somewhat disjointed scholarly literature on public space, a literature scattered across various fields – urban planning, geography, political theory, and sociology – that often talk past one another. If I am successful, we will emerge with a diverse range of theoretical resources to explain why we care about public space, and with a better sense of why it is that proponents of public space often disagree so vehemently.

I begin with a short conceptual discussion of what public space is, then proceed to examine, in turn, liberal, egalitarian, civic republican, and democratic imaginaries of public space.

What is public space?

Before we begin to examine what public space is *for*, we first need a better understanding of what it *is*. Political theorists often use the term figuratively, to refer to the shared world of artefacts and institutions that relate us to one another (Arendt's "common world", 1958), or to designate the discursive spaces – such as salons, newspapers, and online platforms – in which people come together to discuss matters of common concern (Habermas's "public sphere", 1991). I here use the term more narrowly, to refer to *physical* public space, and I focus primarily on urban environments. Expanding on the work of Margaret Kohn (2004), I propose to think of public space along four dimensions – ownership, accessibility, sociability, and commonality.

One may be tempted to define public space by reference to public ownership. In our current property regime, ownership is a good, albeit imperfect, proxy for the power to set rules of access to a space and rules of behaviour in that space. Public space, then, would designate a territory over which we, *the people*, have control, as opposed to private space, where that power belongs to a particular individual or corporation.

Public ownership, however, sometimes fails to track another, equally important aspect of public space: accessibility. In common parlance, we use the term "public space" to refer to spaces that are open to all. Paradigmatic public spaces, like parks, are both publicly owned and openly accessible. But publicly owned spaces can be closed to the public at large (e.g., military facilities), and privately owned spaces may, in turn, be open to all (e.g., malls). Since ownership and accessibility are not reducible to one another, it is helpful to think of them as two separate dimensions along which we can assess the "publicness" of a space.

Each of these dimensions – ownership (understood as a proxy for control) and accessibility – admits further gradation. Somewhere on the continuum between publicly and privately controlled spaces are privately owned public spaces, better known under the acronym POPS. These spaces arise from incentive zoning, with developers permitted to build more than they otherwise would in exchange for incorporating open, but privately managed and policed, spaces into their designs. Like ownership, accessibility is also a matter of degree. Some spaces are open to all (e.g., sidewalks); others can be accessed by anyone who pays a fee (e.g., coffee shops); others still are restricted to members (e.g., gated communities).

There is more to public space, however, than ownership and accessibility. It also matters who else is there. Public space is a setting for enlarged sociability – it is space we share with *strangers*, people who are not part of our proximate circle of family, friends, and acquaintances (Walzer, 1986, p. 470). Not all publicly owned and openly accessible spaces are like that. Jane Jacobs describes, for instance, a small park in Baltimore surrounded by houses, isolated from stores and sidewalk traffic, and used almost exclusively by residents of nearby blocks, as a setting for the 'suburbanlike sharing of private lives' (1961, p. 63). Despite being publicly owned and accessible, the park effectively serves as a quasi-private space for the immediate community.

Besides the presence of strangers, public space also involves a certain kind of commonality of experience. It is space we do not merely *occupy* with others but *share* with them. The experience of walking on a sidewalk, sitting on a bench in a busy plaza, or taking a stroll in a park in the company of strangers is different in kind from that of driving our car alongside theirs on the freeway.

Michael Walzer (1986) tries to capture the difference between these two types of experiences by distinguishing between spaces that stimulate different qualities of attention: single-minded spaces, which we enter in a hurry, with one thing in mind; and open-minded spaces, designed for a variety of uses, which we enter prepared to loiter. While useful in theory, I believe that this distinction often flounders in practice. It forces us to differentiate too sharply between phenomena that are closely intermingled: many of the spaces that we consider public involve a mixture of single-minded purposiveness and open-minded loitering. The suburban mall, for instance, which Walzer characterises as the epitome of single-mindedness, strikes me rather as a hybrid. We venture into a mall not only to purchase specific goods but also to spend time socialising and window-shopping alongside others.

Margaret Kohn (2004, pp. 10–11) proposes to capture the kind of togetherness involved in public space by distinguishing between spaces that foster collective isolation, focusing everyone on a single object of attention (e.g., movie theatres, stadiums), and spaces that facilitate interaction among people, positioning them as co-creators of a common world. This distinction, which harks back to the situationists, is useful as a tool for social critique. But as a definition of public space, I think it sets the bar too high. Most of the public spaces we inhabit with others do not provide *interaction* in any meaningful sense. Being addressed by a stranger, or approached to sign a petition, is a rare occurrence. It is also worth noting that many public spaces, like the sloping plot in front of the Georges Pompidou Centre in Paris or the meandering alleys of Central Park, are designed to direct the attention of people towards an external object – the striking façade of the building, or the natural beauty of the park. This, however, does not seem to detract from the sociability that such spaces foster.

I propose to capture the kind of commonality involved in public space in a more modest and expansive way than Walzer or Kohn. A space is public, or so I suggest, when people are in one another's immediate presence, forming what Erving Goffman (1963, pp. 15–18) calls a "gathering". By this, I mean that people can perceive others through their naked senses and in turn be perceived by them, including in their perception (of others) and in their sensing of being perceived (by others). When people are together in this way, Goffman (1963, p. 16) writes,

> at least some of their world is made up out of the fact [. . .] that an adaptive line of action attempted by one will be either insightfully facilitated by the other or insightfully countered, or both, and that such a line of action must always be pursued in this intelligently helpful and hindering world.

This is one way of saying that a special mutuality or form of interdependence obtains. People are aware of one another's presence and must take each other into account. It is in this sense that the presence of others is a constitutive and shared component of the experience of being in public space.

To recapitulate, then: paradigmatic public spaces are publicly owned and open to all; they involve contact with strangers and a commonality of experience. Instead of thinking of these four attributes (ownership, accessibility, enlarged sociability, and commonality) as necessary and sufficient conditions for a space to be called "public", I believe we should think of them as four dimensions along which we can assess the "publicness" of a space. Some spaces may score well on one dimension and less well on others.

The liberal imaginary

One way to reflect upon the significance of public space is to consider what it means to those who are most dependent on it. This is the kind of exercise that Jeremy Waldron (1991) invites us to perform in relation to homelessness. Working from within the liberal tradition, Waldron observes that public space is the only place where the homeless are free to be without being dependent on the permission of private property owners. In a fully privatised society, the homeless would be comprehensively unfree: they would be legally liable to being removed from wherever they happened to be (Waldron, 1991, p. 302). This is already a powerful liberal argument in favour of having public space, at least in a society that does not provide all of its members with private property.

But Waldron goes further and takes aim at restrictions placed on behaviour in public space, such as prohibitions on sleeping and urinating in public. He argues that while such prohibitions might appear sensible to those who have access to other places where they can satisfy their basic needs, that option is typically not available to the homeless. Denying them the right to pee or sleep in public space is tantamount to denying them the right to pee or sleep altogether. So far as the homeless are concerned, Waldron argues, 'a rule against performing an act in a public place amounts *in effect* to a *comprehensive* ban on that action' (1991, p. 318). With that argument, Waldron brings into focus a distinctive type of threat to public space – sanitisation. He shows that if we are not sufficiently vigilant, attempts to tailor public space to the sensibilities of the majority can have inacceptable consequences for other segments of society.

I have chosen to begin with Waldron's essay because it presents us with a rather minimal vision of public space, as a kind of sanctuary in an otherwise unjust polity, where some of the most vulnerable members of society are permitted to exercise their basic freedoms. To be sure, this is not all that Waldron thinks a liberal society owes the homeless. His own version of liberalism is far more capacious. It involves a concern not just for securing liberties but also for creating the conditions under which it is possible to enjoy and exercise such liberties (Waldron, 1993, p. 7). This includes a commitment to welfare provision that would go a long way towards addressing the root causes of homelessness. But in the essay I have been discussing, Waldron does not appeal to this thicker conception of "liberal egalitarianism". He builds his argument on weaker premises, drawing solely on a concern for protecting basic negative liberties.

The very minimalism of Waldron's argument, however, seems to invite solutions that may strike us as problematic in their own right. One could grant that we have an obligation to provide the homeless with *some place* to exercise their basic freedoms. But consider Robert Ellickson's (1996) suggestion to institute a system of zoning within cities that would effectively confine the homeless and the "nuisance" they pose to a specific district. Ellickson worries that in the absence of strict controls on acceptable behaviour, city dwellers will desert public space even further, and retreat to the security and orderliness of gated communities and suburban malls. He proposes a pattern of zoning – with small permissive areas where the homeless would be permitted to satisfy their needs, and other, larger ones, where behaviour in public would be more strictly regulated – as a way to reclaim public space and save it from a downward spiral of degeneration.

This proposal, which is in fact a rehabilitation of the Skid Row model, might strike some of us as troubling. It would be easy, of course, to articulate our reservations by relying on Waldron's liberal egalitarianism, for surely Skid Row flies in the face of equality. Yet some scholars have expressed scepticism as to whether we can do so by relying on the more minimal liberalism that Waldron mobilises in his essay on homelessness (see Kohn, 2004, pp. 130–146). I believe that Waldron does, in fact, have a powerful rejoinder even on these terms. The problem with the zoning measures that Ellickson proposes is that while they are couched as general prohibitions they do in fact single out a specific subgroup of the population – the homeless. As such, they fly in the face of the liberal commitment to impartiality. These measures target actions that almost no one would perform in public if they had somewhere else to go (urinating); they prohibit behaviour that would not be a cause for concern if performed by people who were not homeless (sleeping in public); they stem from a conception of what is proper to do in public space that is formulated by people who are not themselves dependent on public space; and finally, they involve regulations that would most likely be altered if they had unwelcome effects on people who were not homeless (Waldron, 1991, p. 314).

While Waldron mobilises the traditional apparatus of liberal political thought, Nancy Rosenblum (1987) invites us to consider the question of public space from the standpoint of another kind of liberalism. For much of her career, Rosenblum has been concerned with how liberalism – a body of political thought often derided by its critics as formalistic, cold, and uninspired – can engage, attach, and bind people. The answer, she suggests, is in part aesthetic. The individual freedom accorded by liberalism is an invitation to self-affirmation. We can become enthralled by liberalism by witnessing what people make of themselves with such freedom, by looking at the dazzling array of personalities and identities that surround us.

While Rosenblum does not consign this 'spectacle of diversity' (1987, p. 118) to a single location, her references suggest that there may be no better place to observe it than on the streets and plazas of a vibrant city. She finds herself drawn, like early sociologists of the city, to Walt Whitman's poetry and the language of the sublime to describe the chaotic plenitude of city life, the spontaneous encounters it fosters with a diverse set of others, each of them unique in his or her own way.

On Rosenblum's vision, public space matters not just because it helps protect basic freedoms from encroachment by privatisation or regulation but also because it serves as a stage on which the fruits of individual freedom can be expressed and viewed by all. Teeming with activity and diversity, it offers an enticing spectacle that serves to reinforce our attachment to the value of individual freedom and to stimulate our own self-development by exposing us to a rich array of life possibilities. Like Waldron's, this more romantic conception of public space provides us with reasons to be suspicious of regulations on behaviour, but the threat it brings into focus is not so much sanitisation as uniformity. The worry is that a tightening of social rules might stifle spontaneity and exuberance, and leave us with an undifferentiated display of social conformism.

The egalitarian imaginary

As Rosenblum (1987, p. 124) herself acknowledges, however, there is something lost in aesthetic approaches to public space. Delighting in one another's presence is not the same as dealing fairly or respectfully with one another. One way to bring concerns of fairness to the fore is to think about public space as a material good that is essential for the welfare of all city dwellers and that must, as such, be distributed equitably.

Public space is used for recreation, exercise, and health; it allows people to commune with nature and to enjoy themselves in the company of others. One of the main purposes of Central Park according to one of its designers, Frederick Law Olmsted, was to make natural beauty available to those who could not afford to leave the city for vacation. 'To supply', in his words,

> to the hundreds of thousands of tired workers, who have no opportunity to spend their summers in the country, a specimen of God's handiwork that shall be to them, inexpensively, what a month or two in the White Mountains or the Adirondacks is, at great cost, to those in easier circumstances.
>
> *(Rybczynski, 2000, p. 177)*

This vision of public space, as a good that must be distributed fairly, alerts us to the importance of public policy decisions regarding its location and accessibility within the city. It also directs our attention to the various design strategies used to screen certain groups of people from spaces that are, in principle, accessible to all. Consider the well-known, though perhaps apocryphal, example of the overpasses that Robert Moses had built on Long Island's parkways. These were allegedly designed to be low enough to prevent the circulation of buses, thereby discouraging those relying on public transit – mostly poor and black – from accessing one of New York's most desirable public beaches (Winner, 1980; but see Joerges, 1999). One could also point to the ever-more-inventive use of "defensive architecture" or "deterrent design", such as surface studs, "pig ears", uncomfortable benches, and sprinkler systems that go off at random times. Such design interventions typically target specific publics. They are troubling in part on account of their inconspicuousness to everyone else. They give the illusion of a space open to all while concealing patterns of exclusion.

It is important to note, however, that while critics of defensive architecture fault it for unevenly restricting access to public space, some of its proponents justify it precisely on the grounds that it contributes to a more even playing field. They worry, for example, that the presence of youths performing acrobatics on skateboards might make a park less welcoming to senior citizens afraid of potential collisions. As John Parkinson (2012) reminds us, conflicts such as these are sometimes integral to the democratic adjudication of competing interests, although concerned parties often depict each other as undermining the very idea of public space.

I have focused so far on policy measures and design interventions that might prevent people from enjoying public space on equal terms. But egalitarian concerns about public space are not merely distributive. They also encompass the *expressive* qualities of public space. This dimension is important because public space is highly symbolic: it is there that we honour and immortalise certain aspects of our collective memory. In a society committed to equality, it matters *whose* history is represented and celebrated in public parks, squares, and monuments, and whose history is passed in silence.

The design of public space also conveys something to potential users about how they are regarded by their own political authorities. Public architecture can both elevate and demean. In *City of Quartz* (1998), Mike Davis discusses Frank Gehry's design for the Goldwyn Public Library in Hollywood. Davis describes the building, which replaced a library that had been destroyed by arson, as the 'most menacing library ever built', with 'its fifteen-foot security walls of stucco-covered concrete block, its anti-graffiti barricades covered in ceramic tile, its sunken entrance protected by ten-foot steel stacks, and its stylized sentry boxes perched precariously on each side' (Davis, 1998, p. 239). Unlike other buildings, which typically camouflage their defences by disguising them through landscape architecture, Davis notes, tongue in cheek, that Gehry's library has the merit of declaring openly what it expects from its neighbourhood. The symbolism of buildings is of course contestable. But if Davis's impressions were actually shared by city residents, this could be an example of architecture that stigmatises – especially if one were to compare the building to the more welcoming postures of libraries in other parts of the city.

While social critics with an egalitarian bent are typically keen on expanding access to public space, David Harvey (2006) reminds us not be too quick to equate more public space with a more just city. In a series of influential studies on the transformation of Paris under Haussmann, Harvey showed that the opening of new boulevards lined up with wide sidewalks not only was a strategy of state control (facilitating the movement of troops and preventing the erection of barricades) but also inaugurated a symbiotic relationship between open public space and commercial interests (turning sidewalks into spaces where the seductive spectacle of commodity could be displayed). Haussmann's reforms resulted in a city segregated along class lines, with a well-to-do west traversed by airy boulevards and a neglected east. Interestingly, public space in the poorer parts of the city took a different form than it did in the west. The foci of activity were not the boulevards with their cafés and boutiques but a myriad of smaller, dingier eating and drinking establishments, cabarets, and dance halls, which served as a breeding ground for a vibrant counterpublic.

There are two important points to take away from Harvey's work. The first is that public space takes different forms, and that these may be differentially suited to various political actors at different moments in time. In certain conditions, open public space may be an impediment to political mobilisation and relative obscurity, an asset. The other, methodological point is that we cannot understand the political valence of public space by looking at it in isolation. It is only when we consider the relationship between public space, housing, and commercial interests that we can begin to comprehend whose interests a program of re-development actually serves.

The civic republican imaginary

While thinking about public space as a good or service that must be distributed brings into focus concerns of fairness, it also raises a host of subsidiary questions. If public space is a service like any other, why should it be produced and allocated by public authorities rather than by the market? Wouldn't it be preferable to let people choose how much "public space" they want by charging them for use (e.g., at the entrance of a park or a beach)? A pay-per-use model might also allow for more customised offerings, with some spaces specialising in quiet recreation, others devoted to skateboarding, basketball, roller-skating, and so on. This would allow everyone to enjoy the activity they like without having to be in the same physical space at once.

To someone steeped in the civic humanist interpretation of the classical republican tradition, such suggestions would appear particularly unsavoury. In the civic republican imaginary, public space is not merely a good among others but one that plays a central part in constituting the civic community and imparting its members with civic virtue. Far from being a commodity that can be traded for others, it is a vital political institution – one whose production and distribution could not possibly be left to the vagaries of the market. Public space matters because it allows us to experience what it is like to be related to others as members of a civic community. When successful, it involves a form of interpersonal relationship premised on civic equality and commonality of purpose that differs in kind from the instrumental exchanges of the market.

Both Olmsted and Rousseau offer vivid depictions of such a vision of public space. For Olmsted, urban parks are valuable in part for their restorative influence on human character. They play an important civic role by replenishing a psyche drained by the toils of labour, and enervated by the demands of everyday life in a crowded and adversarial metropolis. While he describes the streets of the city as a breeding ground for a 'peculiarly hard sort of selfishness', Olmsted argues that the carefully crafted spectacle of natural beauty can in itself have a 'harmonizing and refining influence . . . favorable to courtesy, self-control, and temperance' (Hall cited in Roulier, 2010, p. 326). He claims, moreover, that by placing people in an open and convivial mindset, parks can inaugurate a distinctive form of togetherness fit for democratic society (see Cohen, 2017). He writes,

> Consider that the New York and Brooklyn Park are the only places in those associated cities where [. . .] you will find [. . .] with an evident glee in the prospect of coming together, all classes largely represented, with a common purpose, not at all intellectual, competitive with none, disposing to jealousy and spiritual or intellectual pride toward none, each individual adding by his mere presence to the pleasure of all others, all helping to the greater happiness of each.
>
> *(Olmsted, 1997, p. 186)*

When they live up to such a description, urban parks provide what Scott Roulier (2010, p. 330) calls a 'visual articulation' of civic equality. In such spaces, social hierarchies are temporarily suspended. A distinctive type of sociability is also fostered, one in which people are not in competition with one another, but in which they contribute by their very presence to *enhancing* the experience of others. In this way, parks do not only represent but also instantiate a form of being together in which others are not adversaries but partners in a cooperative enterprise. They help foster a sense of civic community and prefigure what relations between citizens ought to be like.

Rousseau (2003) strikes a similar, if somewhat more effusive, tone in his *Letter to D'Alembert*. Reacting to the latter's proposal to reintroduce the theatre to Geneva, Rousseau insists that republics call for another type of spectacle. In contrast to the theatre – performed in a closed room for an exclusive public, with spectators kept passive and isolated, their desires inflamed through the imagination – Rousseau vaunts the merits of public festivals. These take place outside and are open to all, with people moved to interact with one another in a spirit of collective euphoria. Rousseau insists on the simplicity and immediacy of such festivals, and on how they turn spectators into actors who then become the centrepiece of the event (see 2003, p. 182).

For Rousseau, like Olmsted, public festivals are not merely occasions where civic equality is on display; they are occasions where a genuine form of fellow-feeling arises. He recounts the memory, still vivid, of one such spectacle he witnessed in his youth – that of a military regiment dancing to music around a fountain in a public square, drawing nearby residents in a spontaneous, joyful, and innocent celebration. Rousseau describes the scene as one of collective exhilaration, a kind of communal trance that gripped participants at a visceral level and awakened feelings of fraternity and patriotism (Rousseau, 2003, p. 193). Unlike the liberal spectacle of diversity, the experience that Rousseau describes is not a form of revelling at the individuality of particular others but rather a kind of transcendence of individual differences that points beyond ourselves, towards a more encompassing community.

In its Rousseauian and Olmstedian variants, the ideal public space stands removed from the corrupting influence of other social forces, allowing us to experience a distinctive kind of social bond, one premised on equality and commonality, regardless of *whatever else* sets us apart. Aesthetically, this translates into a vision of public space as simple, natural, and devoid of pomp (even though the appearance of simplicity may, as in the case of Olmsted's parks, be achieved at the cost of great effort and artifice).

The civic republican imaginary of public space must contend with two corrosive forces: commercialisation and fragmentation. Commercialisation threatens to erase the distinctiveness of public space. It does so by introducing motives of private interest, by making way for social hierarchy between those who can pay and those who cannot, as well as by appealing, as commerce often does, to our "amour-propre" – a concern for how we compare to others that is at odds with the spirit of civic equality.

Civic republicans should also be concerned with the fragmentation of public space – its disaggregation into different services provided to different groups of people in separate locations. Such fragmentation may result from privatisation, with homogenous social groups retreating behind gated communities with their own communal space. But fragmentation could also be a consequence of urban sprawl and the reliance on the automobile, which disperses functions that would once have been performed in a single location (e.g., town square) to various spots remote from one another and catering to diverse publics. If public space were to be fragmented as such, it would lose its capacity to foster an inclusive sense of civic community.

The democratic imaginary

While the civic republican vision of public space, with its emphasis on civic community, has proved popular with some urban planners (Congress for the New Urbanism, 2013), it has met with considerable scepticism on the part of many democratic theorists (see Hayward, 2007). The democratic vision of public space, we will see shortly, is more sober and pluralistic than its republican counterpart. It deems public space valuable both because it contributes to broadening our awareness of the people with whom we share a polity and because it serves as a stage for forms of political activity that are essential to the proper functioning of democracy.

Democratic theorists have two reasons to be sceptical of the republican appeal to civic community. The first is empirical. If we reflect on our own experience in public space, it is not clear that contact with others does in fact incline us positively towards them, at least in any reliable way. While contact does sometimes foster a sense of community and mutual recognition, it can also engender tension and conflict (Hayward, 2007, pp. 195–197).

The second reason for scepticism cuts deeper. Democratic theorists worry that the republican fixation on a unitary conception of civic community can serve to conceal important differences between the plurality of groups that make up a polity. They are concerned that appeals to a transcendent community may in fact be no more than a cover-up for the interests of some, and a way to silence the perspectives of others (see Young, 1990).

Instead of stressing the importance of civic community, democratic theorists tend to celebrate the diversity of publics that make up a city. They understand public space as a space of encounter with *strangers* – people who are unlike us, and with whom we do not have, and do not care to have, an intimate rapport. Their vision of public space is one of sociability without community. Encountering strangers on sidewalks, parks, and plazas does not necessarily give rise to positive feelings but it expands citizens' awareness of the different perspectives they must take into account when making political choices that will affect everyone (Bickford, 2000, p. 370).

It is important to note that such mutual awareness can be generated even if our encounters with others are transactional, transitory, and occasionally conflictual. Unlike its civic republican counterpart, democratic public space is unabashedly chaotic, discordant, and less concerned with preserving its putative purity (see Sennett, 1970). The threat it finds most alarming is not commercialisation or fragmentation but segregation: the possibility that others with whom we share a polity might become – because of design, access, rules of behaviour, or pricing – invisible to us.

Democratic theorists also value public space because it plays an important part in the political life of democratic societies. According to John Parkinson (2012), public space is necessary for the fulfilment of democratic roles. On his view, the housing of public institutions in monumental buildings, located centrally and giving onto open public squares, signals to citizens that they should take what happens there seriously. It also provides citizens with a highly visible and symbolically charged focal point for protest. Parkinson invites us to remain vigilant about the securitisation of public space around government buildings and its cooptation by the tourism industry, both of which contribute to deflating the political potential of such space.

Drawing on the work of Michael Chwe, Josiah Ober (2008) provides another account of how public space matters for democratic politics. Ober argues that public architecture and rituals can contribute to resolving a central problem of democratic governance: how to achieve coordination in the absence of a centralised hierarchy. The key is to generate a repertoire of common knowledge on which citizens can draw to independently coordinate their actions. Inward-facing public spaces are particularly useful in that regard because they allow for interpresence and intervisibility. 'Each participant can personally observe not only *that* others know some piece of information in common, but *how others respond to* that information' (Ober, 2008, p. 192). Possessing such common knowledge is a prerequisite for being able to act effectively together.

While Ober makes this point in the context of participatory democracy, the insight holds in autocratic regimes too, where citizens are often afraid to share their views with one another. Being in public with others, sensing their dissatisfaction, seeing that they also find the regime's rhetoric empty, can be a spur to collective action. It is in part for this reason that mosques played a vital role in galvanising protesters throughout the Arab Spring, translating co-presence in physical space into a powerful asset for political mobilisation.

Margaret Kohn has argued, finally, that public sidewalks and streets are a vital platform for 'unscripted political activity' (2004, p. 3), with people gathering signatures, voicing grievances, distributing pamphlets, and haranguing passers-by. These face-to-face encounters allow people to engage one another in a direct and emotionally charged way, and have low barriers to entry, thereby providing valuable fora for marginal views. Kohn worries that the privatisation of public space would reduce the incidence of such political activity since private spaces, like malls, can place restrictions on free speech and political expression on their premises.

Conclusion

Our first reactions to public space may appear impulsive, but they are often guided by deeper commitments. When we are troubled by the rotation of a bench or pleased by the sudden appearance of a café, when we wish for more spontaneity or prize the feeling of safety brought about by its regulation, we betray a certain imaginary of what public space ought to look and feel like. I have tried to reconstruct some of these imaginaries and to trace them to four families of normative political views – liberal, egalitarian, civic republican, and democratic. These views all inform our liberal democratic political culture. Yet each of them gives us different reasons to value public space, and each casts a different set of threats to public space: sanitisation, normalisation, exclusion, stigmatisation, commercialisation, fragmentation, segregation, securitisation, and privatisation.

Some of our disagreements about public space are internal to these imaginaries. We may agree that public space is a good to be distributed fairly, but disagree as to whom precisely has been excluded from it. But some of our disagreements pit these various imaginaries against each other. At that level, our allegiances are perhaps less responsive to reasoned argumentation than to the seductive power of prose. Whitman, Olmsted, Rousseau, Davis, Jacobs, Sennett: if these authors have anything in common, it is their capacity to capture our imagination by distilling vivid facets of our experience in public space, and getting us to see what it is that we do, or what it is that we should, cherish about such places.

When we disagree about public space within or across these various imaginaries, any appeal to "democracy" to settle our disputes and resolve questions of policy will likely be hollow. These are disagreements that we need to address within the framework and institutions provided by democracy, not ones that it can resolve for us. For all the inflamed rhetoric that surrounds discussions of public space, policy-makers rarely find themselves having to choose between the security state, vapid consumerism, and rampant vandalism on the one hand and democratic openness on the other. They find themselves forced, rather, to strike a sensible balance between various ingredients that are all necessary for the success of democratic public space.

Commerce, incentive zoning, restrictions on access and regulations on behaviour are not unmitigated evils. They can serve to expand the availability of public space, to enliven it, and to make it more inclusive. Left unchecked, however, they can also erode its distinctiveness, stifle its spontaneity, and reinforce its exclusiveness. In striving for the right balance, I have tried to show that public policy-makers and city officials have access to a spectrum of instruments, some blunt, others more surgical. These range from decisions about zoning and about the location of new public space to decisions about rules of access and behaviour. And as for Harvard Square, these also include choices that affect the character of public space – choices that pertain, for instance, to the shape, colour, material, and positioning of urban furniture, all the way down to its orientation.

Notes

1 I am grateful to Julie Kleinman who first made me aware of this change, as well as to Valentina Pugliano and the participants in the Stanford Center for Ethics Postdoctoral Workshop for comments on an earlier version of this chapter in the spring of 2017.
2 www.cambridgema.gov/CDD/Projects/Parks/hsquarepublicspace, accessed on October 31, 2017.

References

Arendt, H. (1958). *The Human Condition*, Chicago, IL, The University of Chicago Press.
Bickford, S. (2000). Constructing Inequality: City Spaces and the Architecture of Citizenship. *Political Theory*, 28, 355–376.
Cohen, J. (2017). A Beautiful Public Good. *Boston Review*, Forum III.
Congress for the New Urbanism. (2013). *Charter of the New Urbanism: Congress for the New Urbanism*, New York, NY, McGraw-Hill.
Davis, M. (1998). *City of Quartz: Excavating the Future in Los Angeles*, London, Pimlico.
Ellickson, R. C. (1996). Controlling Chronic Misconduct in City Spaces: Of Panhandlers, Skid Rows, and Public-Space Zoning. *The Yale Law Journal*, 105.
Goffman, E. (1963). *Behavior in Public Places: Notes on the Social Organization of Gatherings*, New York, NY, The Free Press.
Habermas, J. (1991). *The Structural Transformation of the Public Sphere: An Inquiry into a Category of Bourgeois Society*, Cambridge, MA, MIT Press.
Harvey, D. (2006). The Political Economy of Public Space. *In:* Low, S. M. & Smith, N. (eds.) *The Politics of Public Space*, New York, NY, Routledge.
Hayward, C. R. (2007). Binding Problems, Boundary Problems: The Trouble with "Democratic Citizenship". *In:* Benhabib, S., Shapiro, I. & Petranovich, D. (eds.) *Identities, Affiliations, and Allegiances*, Cambridge, Cambridge University Press.
Jacobs, J. (1961). *The Death and Life of Great American Cities*, New York, Random House.
Joerges, B. (1999). Do Politics Have Artifacts? *Social Studies of Science*, 29, 411–431.
Kohn, M. (2004). *Brave New Neighborhoods: The Privatization of Public Space*, New York, Routledge.
Ober, J. (2008). *Democracy and Knowledge: Innovation and Learning in Classical Athens*, Princeton, NJ, Princeton University Press.
Olmsted, F. L. (1997). *Writings on Public Parks, Parkways, and Park Systems*, Baltimore, Johns Hopkins University Press.
Parkinson, J. R. (2012). *Democracy and Public Space: The Physical Sites of Democratic Performance*, Oxford, Oxford University Press.
Rosenblum, N. L. (1987). *Another Liberalism: Romanticism and the Reconstruction of Liberal Thought*, Cambridge, MA, Harvard University Press.
Roulier, S. (2010). Frederick Law Olmsted: Democracy by Design. *New England Journal of Political Science*, 4, 311–343.
Rousseau, J-J. (2003). *Lettre à d'Alembert*, Paris, GF Flammarion.
Rybczynski, W. (2000). *A Clearing in the Distance: Frederick Law Olmsted and America in the 19th Century*, New York, NY, Touchstone.
Sennett, R. (1970). *The Uses of Disorder: Personal Identity and City Life*, New York, Vintage Books.
Waldron, J. (1991). Homelessness and the Issue of Freedom. *UCLA Law Review*, 39, 295–324.

Waldron, J. (1993). *Liberal Rights: Collected Papers 1981–1991*, Cambridge, Cambridge University Press.

Walzer, M. (1986). Pleasure & Costs of Urbanity. *Dissent.*

Whyte, W. H. (2001). *The Social Life of Small Urban Spaces*, New York, Project for Public Spaces.

Winner, L. (1980). Do Artifacts Have Politics? *Daedalus*, 109, 121–136.

Young, I. M. (1990). City Life and Difference. *In: Justice and the Politics of Difference*, Princeton, NJ, Princeton University Press.

12

THE ETHICS OF EDUCATION POLICIES

David Steiner

I know no safe depository of the ultimate powers of the society but the people themselves. (A)nd if we think them not enlightened enough to exercise their control with a wholesome discretion, the remedy is not to take it from them, but to inform their discretion by education. This is the true corrective of abuses of constitutional power.

—*Thomas Jefferson in a letter to William Charles Jarvis, September 28, 1820*

A society perpetuates itself in part through its chosen forms of education: Plato and Aristotle make the choice of education structures and content an abiding focus of their work. As Aristotle argues in chapter 2, book VII of his *Politics*, the constitution of a state, its core values and aspiration, cannot be separated from its form of education (Aristotle 1982). Today, educational controversies on both sides of the Atlantic attest to the symbiotic relationship between citizens' fundamental values and their educational commitments. In France, the findings of the Stasi Commission on *laïcité* in December 2003 and subsequent new law forbidding the wearing of religious symbols in French public schools caused widespread debate (Asad 2006). In Spain between 2007 and 2009, the imposition of a secular framework for citizenship by the socialist government led to large demonstrations across the country. Courts ruled in favour of the state, but the next ministry of education reversed the policy (Glenn 2009). In the United States, where the Supreme Court has frequently had to rule on issues of schools and religion, publicly funded vouchers to enable parents to send children to private schools, and free speech in schools, the public frequently lists education just after economics and health care on the list of the political issues about which it cares the most (Rasmussen Reports 2014).

In the following chapter, I am going to use the United States as a case study (while referencing France also) to unpack a fundamental fissure in education policy – one with, or so I shall argue, major educational-ethical dimensions. This is the divide between those who would put the centre of education authority in the hands of parents and those who see an abiding and central role for the state in ensuring that future generations can think and act "independently" once they grow to adulthood. I will be arguing that the principal casualty in this debate has been education itself.

Contemporary American political theorists have largely accepted some version of Amy Gutmann's thesis, advanced almost 30 years ago, that students in a democracy must be provided an education adequate to participating in democratic politics, to choosing among (a limited range of) good lives, and to sharing in various sub-communities, such as families (Gutmann 1987, 47). The fact that future citizens are owed *some minimal level of education* is not controversial. Gutmann's interpretation of this minimum – summarised as enabling students to consciously shape the future of their society – and her inferences for what they require of policy, however, have been heavily contested.

To ensure students' future capacity to consciously shape their society, Gutmann (1987) infers the principles of "nonrepression" and "nondiscrimination" as foundational to the education of children. Nonrepression is a standard that would not allow for any group to curtail the 'rational deliberation of competing conceptions of the good life and the good society' (44). Nondiscrimination is the 'concept that . . . all educable children must be educated. No child or person, therefore, can be excluded from an education that will teach him or her tools for participating in democracy' (45). Together, these principles generate considerable power for the state, which can, for example, charge parents through taxation for public schooling even if the parents decide to privately educate their children and receive no public financial assistance to do so. It also gives the state the right to rule out the public funding of schools that fail Gutmann's "rational deliberation" test – religious schools being the foremost case.

Scholars such as Michael McConnell have pushed back at these inferences, arguing that a state monopoly on publicly funded schooling is 'wrong as a matter of liberal principle'. He argues that the ends of democratic values are better served by enabling 'families . . . to choose among a range of educational options', with public funding to support their choices (McConnell 2002, 87). He argues that there is no 'set of agreed-upon values for democratic citizens' that is sufficiently consensual in a modern pluralistic liberal state. If the values are defined minimally, he suggests, then the state can legitimately fund a wide set of schools so long as they teach 'the scant essentials' (103). This is the approach adopted in most European countries, where so long as schools follow some state curriculum guidelines and agree to have their students assessed on public exams, they can teach as they wish and receive public funds (Berner 2017a). Perhaps the strongest account of the pluralism that McConnell defends comes from William Galston's argument that the liberal values of social diversity and tolerance trump all others. In particular, 'As a logical matter . . . If there are no overriding values, then democracy cannot be such a value' (Galston 2002, 81). Galston, accordingly, defends the right of parents to raise children in ways consistent with their deepest commitments.

> Galston's liberals must learn to tolerate parents who treat their children in ways that neither expose their children to alternative ways of life nor encourage them to be critical of their own, so long as those parents neither brainwash their children nor teach them to disrespect the law and the general principles of democratic rule. A tolerant democrat is not required to understand, much less to respect, citizens who pursue a different vision of the good life – all that is required is that he or she forego use of state power to make that pursuit more difficult.
>
> *(Schrag 1998, 30)*

A decade after the first edition of *Democratic Education*, Gutmann wrote a new preface and epilogue, acknowledging that her argument for democratic education was more normative than foundational. That is, she argues that she had been advancing an argument about what democracy *should embody* by way of education rather than deriving that embodiment from first principles. In the new preface, the capacity for "deliberate decision making" becomes the activating assumption. Placing the justification for her educational theory in these terms thickens the content and skills demanded of a democratic model of education:

> Deliberation is not a single skill or virtue. It calls upon skills of numeracy, literacy, and critical thinking, as well as contextual knowledge, understanding, and appreciation of other people's perspective. The virtues that deliberation encompasses include veracity, nonviolence, practical judgment, civic integrity and magnanimity.
>
> *(Gutmann 1999, xiii)*

Gutmann understands that pressing this argument involves a potential contradiction: the possibility that adults in a democratic society would collectively decide to give themselves more authority over education, and thus choose schooling for their children that failed to meet this "thick" criteria that she believes is required by democratic values. Gutmann resists her earlier line of reasoning – namely, the argument that such a decision would embody a form of cross-generational performative contradiction (children not educated to deliberate would not have the capacity to make a well-informed choice about their own children's education). Gutmann now acknowledges that such a decision by adults would be ill-advised but couldn't be ruled out as illegitimate. Her foundational condition for any chosen education system falls far short of her normative wish list: all that can be said is that such a system does 'not . . . infringe upon the basic liberty or opportunity for their children as free and equal citizens' (xiv). What that means remains unexplained, but it sounds very close to McConnell's "scant essentials".

In short, Gutmann's re-stated thesis no longer attempts to derive, in Aristotelian fashion, the necessary political structure for, nor the telos of, a democratically acceptable education from the constitution, the enabling conditions, of democracy itself. Rather, she offers a normative portrait of a liberal democracy, populated by the kind of rationally deliberating citizens whose education she then outlines, and offers it for our consideration, approval, or rejection. Politically speaking, in the United States of 2017, her arguments are not in the ascendency.

McConnell's argument is fundamentally about the consequences of empowering a sector of the adult population – parents – to take the responsibility of choice over their children's education. While McConnell grounds his argument in the theoretical claim that there is no conception of the public good that is "thick enough" to constrain such choices beyond a minimal essential, what most distinguishes his thesis from Gutmann's (at least in her more recent version) is the temporal weight of the argument. McConnell takes adults as he finds them: no matter their own education or their capacity for "rational deliberation", their rights as citizens encompass their authority to make educational choices for their children. As defenders of pluralistic models contend, there *may* be positive consequences to exercising such choices: higher levels of commitment to the schools they choose for their children, a greater coherence to their family narratives and values, and a sense of continuity of their sense of the good with that of their children – a continuity that could support family cohesiveness. Education researchers offer some empirical support for McConnell's argument: they have found that, overall, the results of parental choice models do not *per se* produce citizens antithetical to civic participation or more prone to anti-liberal views (Campbell 2008; Pennings 2011, 2014). But none of this needs to follow for McConnell's argument: above all else, McConnell is defending a model that grants *a priori* political and pedagogical power to the views of whoever the current generation of parents may happen to be.

By contrast, Gutmann's normative theory is atemporal so long as the society she is describing is a liberal democratic one. The values of deliberative citizenship and the model of a just society that underpins those values – as she sees them – transcend the lived preferences of any generation, and thereby limit those preferences. While the appeal is to today's citizens, it is an appeal for self-restraint: it asks them to endorse the vision of democracy that Gutmann offers to them. Depending on their views, the theory may require adults to engage in a form of self-abrogation – to knowingly and willingly limit the temporal reach of their own particularistic vision of the good so as not to impose it on their children, who may thus strive to gain those skills of "rational deliberation" afforded by an appropriate publicly imposed education. The timeless political goods of the liberal democracy Gutmann defends, with its particular forms of procedural justice and publicly exercised magnanimity, are the *telos* that should, always already, constrain more particularistic inclinations of parents.

While Gutmann and McConnell weigh adult freedoms and liberal democratic values differently, both of their arguments are strikingly modern and stand in stark contrast to the classical tradition. Both McConnell and Gutmann agree that little can be derived from first principles. Gutmann's final appeal to "basic liberty and opportunity" is essentially indistinguishable from McConnell's "scant essentials".

What unites is the reduction of education to the purely instrumental and political: in Gutmann's case, to cultivate a set of democratically demanded skills; in McConnell's, to advance democratic rights through the act of choosing. As Schrag (1998) puts it, Gutmann values first and foremost the democratic capacity of understanding and respecting the panoply of world-views that co-exist in a democratic nation: 'Such mutual respect requires exposing future citizens to different versions of the good life and nurturing their ability to step back from their own vision of the good long and dispassionately enough to contemplate another's' (Schrag 1998, 29).

Gutmann notes that the stepping-back ability requires not only values but also skills, such as literacy and contextual knowledge: this is a strong argument, for it seems implausible to argue that a citizen who is unable to read well and place current issues into a wider context can make informed judgements as a fully participating adult citizen. At the same time, however, the overriding force of Gutmann's argument is that no *substantive* vision of the good can be over-emphasised lest it produce a commitment that could undermine that "stepping back" into a space of wise (one could say "neutral") judgement. And it is this commitment to a perspective that I would call "nowhere in particular" that has resonated most powerfully with the long commitment of American public education to values of neutrality – not only in legal and political terms but also in terms of the content of education itself – a key point to which we will return.

McConnell, too, is loathe to recommend, much less prescribe, the content of education – even in a general sense. No public authority has a right, in his understanding, to substitute its judgement for those of parents. As parents exercise choice over educational offerings, so they will shape a plethora of educational values, embodied in widely varied pedagogical approaches and curricula content. That act is "thick" – it brings its own virtues, strengthening the sense of citizenship by granting it the fundamental determination of the shaping of the next generation. By contrast, what *must* happen in the school is "scant" and, even here, subject to the market pressures of consumer choice.

One might suspect, therefore, that McConnell's theorising is less intrusive on education as a sphere of activity than Gutmann's. In fact, the impact of his thick parental rights argument is that the activity of education is held hostage to consumer preference. McConnell gestures at an argument that that the goods of democratic deliberation can be enjoined from a variety of perspectives (including the religious one) and that institutions that are not themselves democratic (i.e., the family and a non-public school) can support and encourage democratic participation.

But, in the end, his view is choice-driven: irrespective of any other quality (or lack thereof), if the educational content fails to attract parents, then the school will fail for want of students.

I draw two conclusions from the Gutmann-McConnell debate. First, in both cases, they position education as primarily a tool, an instrument used either to facilitate carefully circumscribed democratic ends or to protect a sphere of adult choice. Both theorists see governance issues as central to education: what matters is either the properly enlightened and activist state or parental preferences. The key issue is control: by privileging the question of the levels of control, be that of the state, the family, the teacher, or the market, and trying to derive the boundaries appropriate to one or more of those actors, both theorists end up occluding the space for education itself as a human intellectual activity with its own internal criteria and claims.

Second, for the different reasons unpacked earlier, both Gutmann and McConnell end up being largely and necessarily agnostic about educational content. In Gutmann's case, despite gestures towards "contextual knowledge", her insistence that education not privilege any conception of the good means that the educational engagement with different visions of the good life must never be more than an inch deep. The child's ability to disengage, to step back from any over-identification with any vision in particular, is crucial for the required deliberation across distance. In McConnell's case, there is no political authority that could claim the right to veto parents' choice for their child's educational content. Of course parents may choose a radical, or classical, or progressive school, and there will be nothing neutral about the content of the resulting education. But no public interest can correct a private choice: indeed, the very idea of a corrective has no place.

The remainder of this chapter will be devoted to the argument that the apparently opposed theoretical perspectives of Gutmann and McConnell – treating them as strong voices for larger groups of scholars, such as Nancy Rosenblum, Steve Macedo, and Peter de Marneffe – have together both embodied and contributed to a limited and even damaging way of thinking about education. I am not drawing a direct casual link between theory and practice. Theory moves through multiple channels of influence: in law, in the court of public opinion, in a simplified thought-world from which political actors draw many of their stock notions. My claim, rather, is that the instrumental and political approach to education articulated by Gutmann and McConnell has damaged American education policy and the polity as a whole.

My primary evidence for this thesis is the substance of education reform in the United States over the last quarter century, which has been procedural and structural rather than intellectual. Federal policy has been characterised by an attempt to press states into enhanced accountability protocols with respect to teachers, students, and schools. This stance has been driven by data that showed how deeply unequal were the outcomes from (largely minority-student-attended) inner-city schools and rural schools with their largely middle-class, suburban peers. Policies aimed at remedying these outcomes have included statutes such as the federal No Child Left Behind Act (2001); federal incentive and spending programs tied to states accepting prescribed policy interventions, such as the Common Core State Standards or the expansion of charter schools – the $4.3 billion "Race to the Top" competitive grant falls in this category; or the $7 billion federal School Improvement Grant program, which requires recipient states and districts to accept a federally defined set of improvement-actions through which to try to turn around low-performing schools. Such policies have been supported by the Republicans' business wing and the Democrats' reformist sectors and are loosely allied with Gutmann's educational theory.

On the other hand, we find the pressure for the decentralisation of funding and policy. Supported by the teachers' unions and their allies in the Democratic Party, and the libertarian sectors within the Republican Party, this coalition successfully pressed for ESSA, the 'Every

Student Succeeds Act (2015)', which rolled back the federal role in education. ESSA forbids the very kinds of dollars-in-return-for-policy conformity that had characterised the education reform initiatives during the first decade of the twenty-first century. Such policies map onto McConnell's frame, insofar as they cede power to the states with the full recognition that the states are, themselves, pluralising education through increased choice mechanisms.

Betwixt and between in this educational political football game were and are the charter schools: publicly funded, but largely free of control from local education authority and from the required unionisation of participating teachers. For the unions, the non-unionised charter school is an anathema. Democrats are split: those who support charter schools encourage strong accountability, so that poorly performing schools are rapidly closed. An increasing majority of Republicans seek the maximum degree of freedom for not only charter schools but also publicly funded private schools – a view endorsed explicitly by President Trump and his secretary of education, Betsy DeVos (Green 2017).

Lost in all of these initiatives and the political battles behind them has been the content of education. For all of the federally mandated reforms around evaluating teachers, increasing the number of charter schools, and imposing "college and career-ready" learning standards, we find a complete refusal to require access to specific domains of knowledge, still less specific books. The Common Core State Standards, beyond a gesture to "ancient mythology" and a few seminal documents in American history, are completely silent about academic content. The efforts to improve education through the No Child Left Behind Act and the Race to the Top grant focused on holding teachers and administrators to account for students' results, without in any way articulating the knowledge content that should be experienced in the classroom. The School Improvement Grants, for instance, assumed that if one approach to a school weren't working, the solutions were either to change the leadership or to close the school – hardly a substantive approach to improving the quality of education.

Throughout this period, we also find unceasing and successful efforts to ensure that textbooks and public assessments include no content that could possibly offend any reader. As with the accountability structures themselves, the focus has been upon skills against content, a high value assigned to "critical thinking" (as an end in itself as opposed to critical thinking *about something in particular*) and other "metacognitive skills" rather than to exploring particular domains of knowledge.[1]

What have been the real-world impacts of this confluence of neutrality-governed beliefs and policies on the actual academic outcomes of American education? In a word – zero. Results in the two academic skills that Gutmann highlights as essential to the effective exercise of democratic citizenship – literacy and numeracy – are at or below where they were in 1995 (National Center for Education Statistics 2015), while America's comparative educational performance has declined relative to other countries and is now middling or worse (Wiggins 2015).

What of the educational legacy of McConnell? For a period, the pressure to pluralise American education by giving greater political power to parental choice found a compromise position in the endorsement of charter schools. The idea was that, freed from much red tape and union control but held accountable by public authority for academic results, these schools, chosen by parents for their children to attend, would combine the best of public oversight and private engagement. While researchers have found the overall academic performance of these schools has been rather mediocre, results for economically disadvantaged urban students – especially African Americans – have indeed been stronger than those in traditional public schools (CREDO 2013, 2015).

But the train of empowering parental choice has not stopped with a regime of charter schools held tightly accountable for results. Choice mechanisms, especially in the forms of education tax credits and vouchers that enable low-income students to attend private schools, are multiplying and currently have the endorsement of the executive and legislative branches of government at the federal level and in many states.

What is the real-world impact of this, the counter-Gutmann movement in American education? Once again, in a word – zero. The research on the impact of these measures, read generously, shows only a modest educational advantage (Berner 2017b). Where advantages are found, they are just as likely to be due to the correlation of private schools with higher-calibre academic content rather than to their being a consequence of choice per se.

Defenders of each approach – let's call them the democratic and the pluralist – make multiple arguments to explain away the results: in the former case, they point, for example, to funding discrepancies that punish, rather than support, schools serving underprivileged students. In the latter, advocates can argue that the dollar value of the scholarships and vouchers is insufficient to give parents access to a quality private education. These arguments in turn generate counter-arguments, such as the notoriously weak correlation between funding and education performance,[2] or that it is unlikely that very strong private schools will ever – *en masse* – wish to reduce their fees sufficiently for low-income students to attend.

But ultimately, I would suggest, these endless arguments miss the point. Education is not, in the end, about political control – it is about education. And education, seen as it should be as an end in itself, is about what we teach and how well we teach it. In his seminal work *Spheres of Justice* (1983), Michael Walzer defends the view that we should approach claims about specific domains such as education by asking if the goods that sustain it are 'being distributed in accordance with its own meaning and the principles that flow from that meaning' (Dworkin and Walzer 1983). This strikes me as a promising way forward that has somehow been lost in the debates between education theory and education policy. And while in *Spheres of Justice* Walzer is certainly concerned with such policy issues as segregation, he focuses also on the intrinsic aspects of the practice of education in a particular culture, and what can be inferred from those aspects in terms of policy prescriptions.[3]

So what is education, understood in its own terms? Half a century ago, the political philosopher Hannah Arendt (1954/2006) argued that the act of teaching is an act of responsibility – the responsibility for choosing which narrative about the world will be taught to the next generation. Education, in this sense, is a choice about the cultural, social, and historical framing within which and from which future citizens will begin to understand, interpret, and explore their worlds.

Education is not only about the choice of narrative. If that choice is to be intentional, it incorporates an act of judgement. Indeed, it is the performance of judgement that defines the act of teaching, and it is the quality and degrees of transfer of the capacity to make discerning judgements on behalf of the next generation that are the yardstick of future educational achievement.

Put differently, education in any formal sense is censorship – understood in the sense of keeping out material that is regarded as of low educational value. Certainly, the United States has seen its share of direct censorship in education – the explicit elimination of materials from textbooks and assessments due to pressure from the left and the right (Ravitch 2004). But here, I am using censorship to mean a necessary act of choosing what to occlude. That is to say, those who design an education must censor an almost unimaginably vast and ineluctably chaotic mass of material so as to enable the student to focus on something in particular and to chart a path of discovery, memorisation, experimentation, practice, and knowledge acquisition. The educator's imposition of censorship in order to select a finite narrative – in the classroom presentation and through the materials placed before the child – is an act that can be abrogated – to the opinions of their parents, the algorithms of software, the vicissitudes of experience, the pulsations of social media, the pressure of peer behaviour – but then what takes place is interest-laden and, or so I would argue, no longer an education but an instruction informed by non-educational values.

If we had no evidence that such abrogation was harmful, then the difficult art of educating could be retired, consigned to a primitive period. But it turns out that this country pays a vast price – politically, socially, culturally, and economically – for the undermining of pedagogic judgement.

Our occlusion of judgement results in the infantilism of the act of educating. The flight from judgement, motivated by the fear of offence and by distrust in any canon, results in the sanitation of the classroom, the vacuous championing of skills – of critical thinking and metacognition – in the absence of knowledge, and the obsequious deference to immediate geographical or political fashion.

Most fundamentally, the inevitable result is the diminishment of our collective respect for the profession of teaching. Colloquial usage is brutal but precise: we are told that contemporary education theory has replaced the "sage on the stage" with the "peer in the rear" without realising that in doing so, we have all but demolished the profession of teaching itself.

No doubt, these statements are overly categorical. It would be obtuse to deny that good software can impart some writing and mathematical skills and create virtual scientific experiments or that the Internet can provide insights and immediacies of information that are unimaginably vaster in scope than those available in a textbook or within the knowledge belonging to a single teacher.

But the fact remains that education means an act of selection first, and teaching second, and that the quality of what is selected matters. Weak actors can try to perform great plays, and strong actors can certainly be given weak roles; powerful theatre happens when great actors are given great scripts. It is no different with teachers.

Fixated on the politics of educational control and the retreat from educational judgement, America has tried to run rough-shod over Arendt's insight. Rather than teach a specific narrative about virtue, a particular canon of literature, or a story about the country and its place in the world, the United States retreats. It has settled on the teaching of skills: not history, but historical analysis; not languages, but coding; not literature, but textual decoding. Learning how to learn has replaced learning, with the assumption that this new set of skills is sensitive to a transient world where facts are as fluid as professions. And the United States is not alone: in 1989, under the *loi Jospin*, the delineation of a set, content-rich curriculum for the schools of France was dealt a major blow. As Jospin himself explained, districts and schools would be free to select their own materials. All that would be left would be common standards, not content (Hirsch 2016). In England, "Ordinary" and "Advanced" Level examinations in English literature were explicitly based on identified texts until the introduction of the "Key Stages" approach to the national curriculum, which explicitly moved away from any identification of specific texts (Department for Education and Employment 1999).

In each of these three cases, educational decisions were driven primarily by the winds of political expediency. In the nineteenth century, by far the most used curricular material in the United States was the McGuffey readers, with their recommended texts that drew, self-consciously, on the British canonical tradition (McGuffey 2005). The shift to an anodyne, skills-based curriculum followed from the country's inability to negotiate a substantive replacement for this literary tradition. As Diane Ravitch notes, savage disputes over such matters as the New York City curriculum led the way to the contemporary reliance on teaching value-free skills (Ravitch 2000). As E.D. Hirsch (2016) makes clear, Jospin's damaging innovation in France was the direct consequence of the Left's decision that French canonical literature embodied a "privileged", hierarchical imposition on an increasingly multicultural France.

For this policy of politicising the curriculum, the least privileged children on both sides of the Atlantic pay the highest price.[4] It turns out that those who grow up in material comfort are far more likely to enjoy intellectual richness – the careful framing, the telling of tales, the reading of timeless texts, exposure to domains of history – than are their less fortunate peers. Finding the main idea in a text turns out to be no skill at all if you already know what the text is about. If you do not know, no mere skill can aid your quest.

And in the end, there may also be hypocrisy. As John Stuart Mill once argued, who among us would give up the jewels of our own education – the books we got lost in, the music, the art, the history? That much was chosen on our behalf does not diminish the benefits of such a choice. Yet in the name of neutrality, we will not give that gift to the next generation.

Notes

1 For a specific discussion of how these commitments have impacted education standards and assessments in America, see my piece in the *Huffington Post* (Steiner 2014).
2 See Hanushek (1981).
3 See, for example, his discussion of Japanese education, in *Spheres of Justice*, pp. 204–205.
4 For the French data, see Hirsch (2016, 145). For the current PISA rankings of the United States, France, and the United Kingdom, see Jackson and Kiersz (2016). This is in contrast to other, high-performing nations. As the Johns Hopkins Institute for Education Policy relays in a recent research report, "A comprehensive, content-rich curriculum [i]s the salient feature in nine of the world's highest-performing school systems as measured by the Programme for International Student Assessment. Despite the vast cultural, demographic, political, and geographic diversity of Finland, Hong Kong, South Korea, Canada, Japan, New Zealand, Australia, the Netherlands, and Switzerland, their educational systems all emphasize content-rich curriculum and commensurate standards and assessments" (Steiner 2017).

References

Aristotle. 1982. *Aristotle: The Politics.* Translated by Ernest Barker. Oxford: Oxford University Press.
Arendt, Hannah. 1954/2006. "Crisis in Education." in Arendt, H. *Between Past and Future.* New York: Penguin Books.
Asad, Talal. 2006. "French Secularism and the Islamic Veil Affair." *The Hedgehog Review* 8(1–2):93–106. www.iasc-culture.org/THR/archives/AfterSecularization/8.12IAsad.pdf.
Berner, Ashley. 2017a. *Pluralism and American Education: No One Way to School.* New York, NY: Palgrave Macmillan. www.palgrave.com/us/book/9781137502230.
———. 2017b. "Expanding Access to Non-Public Schools: A Research and Policy Review." *Johns Hopkins Institute for Education Policy* (blog). April 5, 2017. http://edpolicy.education.jhu.edu/wordpress/?p=1403.
Campbell, David. 2008. "The Civic Side of School Choice: An Empirical Analysis of Civic Education in Public and Private Schools." *Brigham Young University Law Review* 2:487–524. http://heinonline.org/HOL/LandingPage?handle=hein.journals/byulr2008&div=25&id=&page=.
CREDO. 2013. *National Charter School Study 2013.* Stanford, CA: Center for Research on Education Outcomes.
———. 2015. *Urban Charter School Study: Report on 41 Regions.* Stanford, CA: Center for Research on Education Outcomes. http://urbancharters.stanford.edu/download/Urban%20Charter%20School%20Study%20Report%20on%2041%20Regions.pdf.
Department for Education and Employment. 1999. *The National Curriculum: Handbook for Primary Teachers in England.* London, UK: Department for Education and Employment. www.educationengland.org.uk/documents/pdfs/1999-nc-primary-handbook.pdf.
Dworkin, Ronald, and Michael Walzer. 1983. "'Spheres of Justice': An Exchange." *The New York Review of Books.* June 21, 1983. www.nybooks.com/articles/1983/07/21/spheres-of-justice-an-exchange/.

"From Thomas Jefferson to William Charles Jarvis, 28 September 1820," *Founders Online*, National Archives. Last modified June 13, 2018, http://founders.archives.gov/documents/Jefferson/98-01-02-1540

Galston, William A. 2002. *Liberal Pluralism: The Implications of Value Pluralism for Political Theory and Practice*. Cambridge; New York: Cambridge University Press. http://dx.doi.org/10.1017/CBO9780511613579.

Glenn, Charles. 2009. "Are Educational Freedom and Social Integration Enemies." *International Journal for Education Law and Policy* 5:24–36.

Green, Beth. 2017. "Advice for Betsy DeVos from Canada – Education Week." *Education Week*. February 7, 2017. www.edweek.org/ew/articles/2017/02/08/advice-for-betsy-devos-from-canada.html.

Gutmann, Amy. 1987. *Democratic Education*. Princeton, NJ: Princeton University Press.

———. 1999. *Democratic Education: With a New Preface and Epilogue*. 1. print. of the rev. pbk. ed. Princeton, NJ; Chichester: Princeton University Press.

Hanushek, Eric. 1981. "Throwing Money at Schools." *Journal of Policy Analysis and Management* 1(1):19–41. http://hanushek.stanford.edu/sites/default/files/publications/Hanushek%201981%20JPAM%201%281%29.pdf.

Hirsch, E.D. 2016. *Why Knowledge Matters: Rescuing Our Children from Failed Educational Theories*. Cambridge, MA: Harvard Education Press. www.barnesandnoble.com/w/why-knowledge-matters-e-d-hirsch-jr/1123826690?ean=9781612509525.

Jackson, Abby, and Andy Kiersz. 2016. "The Latest Ranking of Top Countries in Math, Reading, and Science Is Out – and the US Didn't Crack the Top 10." *Business Insider*. December 6, 2016. www.businessinsider.com/pisa-worldwide-ranking-of-math-science-reading-skills-2016-12.

McConnell, Michael W. 2002. "Education Disestablishment: Why Democratic Values Are Ill-Served by Democratic Control of Schooling." *Nomos* 43:87–146. www.jstor.org/stable/24219996.

McGuffey, William Holmes. 2005. *McGuffey's Readers Sixth Eclectic Reader*. New York: Kessinger Publishing.

National Center for Education Statistics. 2015. "NAEP 2015 Mathematics & Reading Assessments on State Level Achievement in 12th Grade." *The Nation's Report Card*. 2015. www.nationsreportcard.gov/reading_math_g12_2015/#.

Pennings, Ray. 2011. *Cardus Education Survey*. Hamilton, ON: Cardus.

———. 2014. *Cardus Education Survey 2014*. Hamilton, ON: Cardus. www.cardus.ca/store/4291/.

Rasmussen Reports. 2014. "2014 Issues of Importance." *Rasmussen Reports*. 2014. www.rasmussenreports.com/public_content/politics/mood_of_america/importance_of_issues.

Ravitch, Diane. 2000. *The Great School Wars: A History of the New York City Public Schools*. Johns Hopkins University Paperbacks ed edition. Baltimore, MD: Johns Hopkins University Press.

———. 2004. *The Language Police: How Pressure Groups Restrict What Students Learn*. New York, NY: Random House. www.penguinrandomhouse.com/books/139366/the-language-police-by-diane-ravitch/9781400030644.

Schrag, Francis. 1998. "Diversity, Schooling, and the Liberal State." *Studies in Philosophy and Education* 17(1):29–46. https://doi.org/10.1023/A: 1005020602073.

Steiner, David. 2014. "The New Common Core Assessments: How They Could Stop Patronizing Our Students." *The Huffington Post*. February 21, 2014. www.huffingtonpost.com/david-m-steiner/the-new-common-core-asses_b_4809973.html.

———. 2017. "Curriculum Research: What We Know and Where We Need to Go." *StandardsWork*. https://standardswork.org/wp-content/uploads/2017/03/sw-curriculum-research-report-fnl.pdf.

Wiggins, Grant. 2015. "Some Excerpts from PISA Math Results – 15 Year Olds." *Granted, and . . .* (blog). May 11, 2015. https://grantwiggins.wordpress.com/2015/05/11/some-excerpts-from-pisa-math-results-15-year-olds/.

13

THE ETHICS OF TAX POLICY

Ira K. Lindsay

Nobody likes paying taxes, but almost everybody prefers to live in a society with taxation than in one without. Agreement about tax policy usually goes no further. This is not surprising since tax policy implicates fundamental and hotly contested questions of distributive justice. Given that developed nations typically collect at least a quarter of their GDP in taxes, the stakes are very high (OECD, 2016). Moreover, taxation is used for such a wide range of purposes that almost every area of public policy has at least some connection with taxation. Tax policy raises extremely complex ethical questions, including both large-scale questions of distributive justice, such as the extent to which the tax system should be used to redistribute income, and narrower questions, such as how tax rates should be set for different types of households.

This chapter provides an overview of some of the many debates in tax policy that have significant ethical dimensions, with a particular accent on the relationship between taxation and democratic government. It begins by outlining the function of taxation and the ways in which it interacts with ethical concerns. The bulk of the chapter is devoted to ethical questions raised by tax policy, including what should be taxed, how we should individuate taxpayers, and how we should allocate tax obligations between taxpayers. It examines theories of tax fairness based on ability to pay and on the benefits received from government spending. The latter part of the chapter discusses the tax base, the taxation of families, and the taxation of multinational corporations and concludes by exploring a few of the implications of this analysis for taxation in democratic theory.

The purpose of taxation

Taxation is the life blood of the modern fiscal system. The most basic function of taxation is to provide revenue for the state. The decision to devote a given fraction of income to tax puts the choice of how to use it in the hands of the government rather than private parties. In a democratic society, this means making consumption choices collectively, usually through elected representatives. Tax rates therefore establish the balance between private and public choices regarding consumption. Less obviously, tax policy may be used to influence choices about consumption and investment made by the private sector by making some options more expensive than others. Second, taxation is often used to pursue distributive aims. This is most obviously true of inheritance taxes, progressive tax rates, and the exemption of necessities from consumption taxes. A third important function of taxation is as a form of regulation that encourages or discourages certain activities. Taxes on pollution, for example, can force polluters to pay the social cost of their activities without outright prohibition. Taxation is thus a potential alternative to prescriptive regulation that allows the state to influence rather than prescribe individual choices.

Although the substance of tax policy is a source of perennial conflict, taxation itself is an important form of social cooperation. Any group of people that cannot muster resources for collective projects will not be able to act efficaciously as a group and any state that cannot successfully raise revenue will not long survive. Taxation might be viewed as a stress test for state efficacy. A state unable to collect taxes is probably feeble regardless of its formal powers, and a state that does not need to levy taxes (e.g., one that receives a great deal of money from state-owned natural resources) is in danger of atrophy since its rulers have less need to be concerned with the quality of public administration.

Tax collection is extremely expensive without some degree of willing cooperation between government officials and citizens. In pre-modern times, collection of direct taxes on income or wealth was administratively challenging and states often made do with other forms of public finance, such as feudal dues, tariffs, or state monopolies. States in the developed world now collect what is, from a historical perspective, a remarkable amount of revenue remarkably harmoniously. Public cooperation with the tax authorities, sometimes called "tax morale", depends in part on public perceptions of the legitimacy of the state and the fairness of the tax system (Kirchler 2007). Tax morale also depends on expectations about the behaviour of others. People often are willing to make sacrifices for the public good only if they think others will as well (Bicchieri 2006). High tax morale can thus lead to a virtuous cycle of high tax collection and high tax compliance, whereas low tax morale may lead to a vicious cycle in which most people attempt to evade taxes when possible, anticipating that most of their fellow citizens do the same. The importance of tax morale is a reason to avoid policies that are opaque or diverge too greatly from common moral intuitions even if they are desirable on other grounds. It is also a potential source of advantage for democratic government since citizens may be more likely to cooperate with tax authorities if they feel that they have influence over fiscal policy (Casal et al. 2016).

The allocation of tax burdens

Any system of taxation must address three questions: what is taxed, who is a taxpayer, and how tax burdens are allocated among taxpayers. The third of these questions raises the most fundamental normative questions. Traditional approaches to tax fairness include 'ability to pay' theories that apportion tax burdens on the basis of taxpayers' resources and 'benefits' theories that apportion taxes in proportion to benefits received from the state. Whereas ability-to-pay principles consider taxation apart from the rest of fiscal policy, benefits theories explicitly link taxes with spending by considering the fairness of tax burdens in light of the benefits received by the taxpayer from the state. As ability-to-pay theories are somewhat more straightforward, it makes sense to consider them first.

'Ability to pay' theories of tax fairness

'Ability to pay' theories evaluate the fairness of tax burdens in light of a taxpayer's income, wealth, or some other measure of ability to bear tax burdens. The underlying idea is that fair tax schemes allocate burdens between taxpayers impartially. John Stuart Mill (1848: 348) argued that 'equality of taxation . . . means equality of sacrifice', which means that every taxpayer should feel 'no more and no less inconvenience from his payments than every other person experiences from his'. It is quite difficult to specify what constitutes equality of sacrifice. Ability-to-pay theories therefore encompass a wide range of possibilities, including proportional taxation schemes in which all taxpayers pay the same tax rate for every increment of income and progressive schemes in which the marginal tax rate is higher for those with more income or wealth. Proponents of both views might agree on a more basic principle, horizontal equity. This is the principle that taxpayers with equal incomes should pay equal amounts of income tax (Musgrave 1959). Although horizontal equity sounds straightforward, applying it proves to be difficult. Much seems to depend on how income is defined. Two taxpayers might have equal incomes under one definition and quite different incomes under another. Although economic analysis might put some constraints on plausible definitions of income, there are numerous cases in which it is unclear whether a given item reflects true ability to pay. Many deductions from taxable income might seem fair on the grounds that they capture something important about the taxpayer's ability to pay, regardless of whether the deduction tracks income in a purely economic sense. For example, allowing taxpayers to deduct health care expenses might seem fair in that money spent on health care reduces disposable income without putting the taxpayer in a better position than healthy taxpayers with equivalent income. Horizontal equity might therefore be thought to merely shift the question of what taxes are fair to the question of what should count as taxable income. Even if horizontal equity is responsive to the requirement that the state treat citizens as equals, there are such a large number of candidates for what might constitute equal treatment that it is difficult to see how one can be selected without resort to some further theory of distributive justice.

This problem also infects the debate between proponents of proportionate and progressive income taxation, with each appealing to different conceptions of equality. The notion that taxes should be proportionate to income can be traced back at least to Adam Smith (1776). John Stuart Mill defended this principle as best approximating 'equal sacrifice' from every taxpayer (Mill 1848: 350–56). The grounds of the view are, however, a bit mysterious on closer inspection (Fried 1999). It is not clear that a rich person who pays £100,000 in tax on a £1,000,000 annual income is making an equal sacrifice to that of a poor person who pays £1,000 out of a £10,000 annual income. The former may go about life no differently as a result of the tax and merely be left with a smaller bank account at the end of the year, whereas £1,000 may make a sizable difference to the quality of life of a poor person. Extreme results of this sort can be mitigated by exempting income sufficient to cover the necessities of life from income tax and imposing a flat rate of tax upon the rest. But the objection does not depend on a poor person's ability to afford adequate food or shelter. The ability to go away on a relaxing vacation might make a real difference in the life of a taxpayer just above the tax exemption threshold. Alternatively, proportionate taxation might alternatively be defended in terms of the equal treatment of taxpayers. It seems quite plausible that every taxpayer should face the same tax rate at the given level of income. But why equal *marginal tax rates* at different levels of income should be required as a matter of treating citizens equally is rather mysterious. Perhaps the best defence of proportionate taxation is that it provides a simple, clear, and impartial rule for allocating tax burdens that diminishes the extent to which one group of citizens may unfairly shift the tax burden onto another. If proportionate taxation is not the best policy, at least it prevents worse. This is roughly the conclusion that Henry Sidgwick (1887) came to despite his acknowledgement that progressive rates of taxation could, in theory, have salutatory distributive effects.

In any case, proponents of progressive taxation have had their way in most developed countries since the early twentieth century. They advance a range of arguments for progressive taxation. First, one might argue that progressive taxation is required by some egalitarian theory of distributive justice. A second argument is that because marginal utility of income diminishes with income, progressive marginal tax rates maximise aggregate welfare. In other words, a 1 per cent tax will diminish the welfare of a poor taxpayer more than the welfare of a wealthy taxpayer. For this reason, one might think that ability to pay in the normatively relevant sense increases more with income for the wealthy than for middle-income taxpayers. Third, progressive taxation serves as insurance against bad outcomes for citizens who are uncertain about their future prospects. It may be worthwhile to accept the prospect of higher taxes in the case of economic good fortune in exchange for lower taxes in the case of ill-fortune. One need not be a utilitarian to see risk spreading as an important function of the social welfare state (Heath 2006). A final consideration is that material inequality may diminish social solidarity and make it more difficult to devise policies that serve the needs of both rich and poor. Designing effective public policy is easier when most citizens have income levels near the mean, since they are likely to have similar interests to each other. By contrast, the very rich and very poor have little in common with each other or with the middle class. Furthermore, inequality may tend to undercut loyalty to the nation or willingness to sacrifice for it if people perceive that the benefits from collective efforts accrue to only a few at the very top of society. And greatly unequal societies may find it difficult to prevent the ultra-wealthy from corrupting the political process or undermining democratic control of government altogether.

Opponents of progressive taxation, such as Mill and Sidgwick, worry that allowing higher rates for a small minority of taxpayers will encourage confiscatory tax rates or wasteful spending since only the very wealthy will bear this burden. Once progressivity is introduced to the tax code, it is difficult to find a principled limit. One might suspect, therefore, that there is a tendency for tax rates to rise to dysfunctional, confiscatory levels. Lower- and middle-income voters might readily vote for higher taxes on the wealthy without much regard for whether the revenue is well spent. Subsequent history should provide some reassurance on this point. Although marginal tax rates on the wealthy reached extremely high levels in the US and various western European counties during the mid-twentieth century, these rates have fallen very substantially since then. At the same time, the tax burden on middle- and lower-income citizens in many counties has increased substantially. It does not appear, therefore, that progressive taxation inevitably creates a one-way ratchet effect in countries with universal suffrage (Scheve & Stasavage 2016).

Opponents of progressive taxation also worry that excessively high tax rates discourage work by highly skilled workers, savings and investment by the affluent, or both. High marginal tax rates also encourage higher earners to devote their energies to tax avoidance rather than to socially productive activity. There is a vast economics literature on the incentive effects of high taxes on the rich. Many studies suggest that top tax rates in most developed countries are not enough to be seriously deleterious (Diamond & Saez 2011). This is not, however, a universal view and there is heated disagreement among experts (Feldstein 1995). As will be discussed presently, there are ways to mitigate the incentive effects of progressive taxation, although these strategies may also have undesirable distributive consequences.

'Benefits' theories of tax fairness

'Benefits' theories of tax fairness are a rival to both proportionate and progressive ability to pay theories. Benefits theories evaluate the fairness of tax burdens in light of benefits received from the state. The underlying idea is that of reciprocity: a tax is fair if benefits received from the state at least roughly compensate for the burdens of taxation. If one assumes, as Adam Smith (1776) did, that benefits received by the state vary in proportion to income, the normative upshot of the benefits theory might not differ greatly from ability-to-pay approaches. There is no reason, however, to believe that this is always the case. In any case, the normative foundations of the two approaches are very different. An important objection to benefits theories is that it is extremely difficult to value the benefit that each person receives from public goods such as national defence, a well-functioning legal system, environmental protection, or a high-quality system of education (Mill 1848). What is needed is some way to measure the benefits received by individual taxpayers. One strategy is to require unanimous consent for the imposition of new taxes (Wicksell 1958). Since taxpayers will not consent to a tax that does not produce sufficient benefits to leave them better off, all taxes under such a scheme should benefit every taxpayer. The unanimity rule thus forces taxpayers to reveal their private valuation of public spending. Furthermore, citizens that value a prospective spending project especially highly should be willing to assume the costs even if other citizens decline to raise their own taxes. In practice, of course, the problems of opportunistic holdouts and of irrationality make it prudent to relax the unanimity requirement to a large supermajority (Buchanan 1975). In principle, constitutional mechanisms could be designed to approximate a scheme of taxation based on the relative benefits enjoyed by different taxpayers. Such a system might turn out to have troubling distributive consequences, but its possibility shows that benefits theory proponents have more resources at their disposal than was recognised in Mill's time.

A second way to determine how different taxpayers value various government services is 'Tieboutian' competition, which involves citizens sorting themselves into groups for purchasing local public goods (Tiebout 1956). Decentralising some aspects of fiscal policy so that local governments can pursue different policies gives prospective residents a choice between different packages of taxes and government services offered in different jurisdictions. For example, parks and libraries might be funded out of local property taxes. Some citizens might select jurisdictions with higher taxes and more expensive services, while others might opt for the reverse, thus satisfying the mutually inconsistent preferences of both groups. The benefits of public goods are also more closely linked to the burdens of taxation since the value of high-quality public services tends to be capitalised into real estate prices. However, Tieboutian competition relies on a relatively high geographical mobility combined with fiscal decentralisation and so may have somewhat limited application outside of countries with a suitable tradition of local government. Local residents may be best positioned to monitor the quality of local public goods, but this matters only if political authorities are sensitive to local sentiments. Tieboutian competition also threatens to exacerbate inequalities if wealthier citizens are able to cluster together to purchase local public goods while withdrawing support for public goods at the national level.

A third strategy is to rely on special purpose taxes that raise funds for particular purposes from those who benefit. For example, funding road repairs from petrol taxes and tolls has the effect of collecting revenue from people in very rough proportion to the extent to which they benefit from their use. Creating an explicit link between taxation and spending that benefits the taxpayer may be useful in building political support. This seems to be the case for state pension and social insurance programs. Although there is no principled reason why they should not be funded out of general tax revenue, it is often the case that pension and disability insurance programs are supported by special payroll taxes, as in the US, the UK, France, Germany, and many other nations. Workers may be more likely to accept this tax as fair because social insurance payments during retirement are conditioned on prior tax contributions. This advantage must be weighed against the inefficiency of maintaining separate systems of payroll and income taxation.

Benefits theories have traditionally been associated with classical liberalism since they seem to provide a principled way to limit the potential obligations of taxpayers, especially wealthier ones. As a historical matter, however, benefits theories were often used to argue in favour of more rather than less progressive taxation. Until at least the nineteenth century, income and property taxation was not the primary source of government revenue. Tariff revenue and various consumption taxes likely were regressive compared to proportionate income taxation since the wealthy, who need not consume all of their income, would bear a relatively small proportion of the tax. Adam Smith's appeal for proportionate income taxation likely would have represented an increase in the progressivity of the tax system of his time. Likewise, Knut Wicksell (1958) saw his unanimity rule as a way to prevent the wealthy and powerful from shifting the tax burden to the poor and powerless.

Whether the benefits principle is inconsistent with progressive taxation depends on how one measures benefits. If benefits are measured in terms of cost to the state, the benefits theories will tend to suggest that taxes on the wealthy must be rather modest. But if benefits are measured, as contemplated by Wicksell, in terms of willingness to pay, the benefits received by wealthy taxpayers might be quite sizable since willingness to pay tends to increase with income for most good and services. This interpretation of the benefits principle provides a rule that limits oppressive taxation while being neutral between tax policies that benefit all taxpayers. A progressive interpretation of the benefits principle would suggest that wealthier taxpayers should pay higher tax rates because they derive the greatest benefit from the existing political order. Low-wage workers derive less benefit from the persistence of the present government because they have little property to protect and could continue to earn subsistence wages under a different political regime. The principle that taxpayers should not be forced to pay more in taxes than the benefits they receive in return therefore seems consistent with funding national defence, the legal system, and other public goods that protect property rights entirely out of taxes on the better off.

Egalitarianism and utilitarianism

In contrast to the tax-specific principles of fairness considered thus far, one might instead analyse tax policy in light of some egalitarian theory of distributive justice, such as Rawls's difference principle. Such principles of distributive justice are used to evaluate government policy as a whole rather than applying to tax policy in isolation. Taxes are simply a tool, albeit a very important tool, to be used alongside transfer payments and other government spending programs to achieve just distributive results. Liam Murphy and Thomas Nagel (2002) argue that since just post-tax distributions are all that matters, taxes should not be evaluated by comparison with pre-tax income or with the benefits received from public spending. Tax-specific principles of fairness that take the existing distribution of property rights and pre-tax income as a normative baseline are confused because the normative status of property rights depends on the resulting distribution of post-tax income and thus cannot provide any independent basis for evaluating the fairness of tax burdens. In other words, the property entitlements that produce taxable income are just only insofar as the entire system of property rights, tax obligations, transfer payments, and government spending is just. Measuring ability to pay in light of an unjust distribution of property rights will not yield a fair scheme of taxation. Nor will evaluating taxes in relation to the benefits of an unjust fiscal system.

Much of the reception of Murphy and Nagel's argument focused on the question of whether people have any pre-institutional claim to income from property or labour. If they do, then Murphy and Nagel's attack on principles of tax fairness that compare tax obligations to pre-tax income fails. Both this debate and the debate over the correct principles of distributive justice are far beyond the scope of what can be considered in this chapter. In any case, there are reasons to be sceptical of Murphy and Nagel's approach even if one sets aside objections grounded in natural rights. Although one might reasonably argue that people with special talents, wealthy parents, or good luck do not intrinsically deserve higher incomes than others, it does not follow that the state should be free to redistribute revenue from such assets as it sees fit. Whatever the theoretical virtues of Nagel and Murphy's approach, it has the disadvantage of seeming to reduce questions of tax policy to the most controversial questions of distributive justice. If the fairness of tax rules depends largely on broad questions about the fairness of the existing distribution of property rights, it is hard to see how one can achieve agreement between members of the public with differing ideological commitments. In a polity with deep disagreements about distributive justice, taxing power unconstrained by pre-institutional entitlements may seem less attractive. In the interest of minimising negative-sum political conflict, it may be reasonable to treat existing property entitlements as having some normative weight and patterns of pre-tax income as providing some constraints on the permissible degree of redistribution (Lindsay 2016). Ability to pay and benefits theories of taxation have the virtue of approaching questions of tax fairness in a way that may allow people with different views on broader distributive questions to find common ground.

Utilitarians may agree with Nagel and Murphy that there are no tax-specific principles of justice and argue that just tax policies are those that maximise aggregate utility (Kaplow 2008). In general, a utilitarian approach to tax policy will be concerned both to allocate the tax burden to those able to pay with the least loss in welfare and to impose taxes in a manner that distorts the behaviour of taxpayers as little as possible. However, these considerations are often at cross-purposes. Taxes that minimise economic distortions, such as lump-sum taxes that collect a fixed sum from every taxpayer regardless of income, tend to be regressive. Taxes that minimise the welfare loss of the taxpayer, however, tend to be progressive to the extent that the marginal utility of income declines as taxpayers become richer (Edgeworth 1897). Utilitarians more concerned with the first consideration will tend to favour relatively less progressive tax policies, while those concerned with the second consideration will tend to favour relatively more progressive tax policies. Agreement on ethical principles does not, therefore, assure agreement on tax policy, especially for those, such as utilitarians, who are committed to highly abstract ethical principles.

Utilitarian analysis of taxation sometimes reaches conclusions that seem peculiar from the perspective of competing theories and fly in the face of popular sentiment. On plausible assumptions about the effect of tax rates on work, marginal tax rates should decline over a certain level of income (Mirrlees 1971). The reason for this is that taxpayers with high earning capacity may be tempted to use their high income to cut back on labour effort and are especially likely to do so if facing a high marginal tax rate. This policy has the counter-intuitive result that extremely high earners actually pay lower marginal tax rates on their last dollar of income than those with much lower incomes. Similarly, it might be better to avoid direct taxes on labour entirely and instead tax some fixed attribute that is a proxy for capacity to earn so as to avoid disincentives for earning income.

Consumption taxation provides another illustration of the tension between economic efficiency and distributive concerns. As Frank Ramsey (1927) argued, consumption taxes are more efficient when applied to items for which demand is relatively inelastic – in other words for which consumers are unlikely to change their behaviour in response to higher taxes. This has the implication that sales tax rates should be set differently on different items, potentially with higher taxes on staples that are relatively price-insensitive.

That utilitarian reasoning sometimes yields results at odds with common intuitions about tax fairness should not be surprising. Hardline utilitarians will not find it disconcerting. Yet there is reason for utilitarians as well as for egalitarians such as Nagel and Murphy to be attentive to popular sentiments when designing tax policy. If, as was argued earlier, public perceptions of tax fairness are important in securing voluntary compliance with the tax system as well as political support, divergence between philosophical theories and "folk theories" of tax fairness may diminish cooperation with the tax authorities even if one believes that the folk are mistaken.

What to tax

Establishing principles for the allocation of tax burdens among taxpayers is only one task faced by policy-makers. Two other questions are perhaps even more fundamental: the question of what is to be taxed and the question of how to individuate taxpayers. The first of these questions concerns the nature of the tax base. Candidates include income, consumption, property, socially undesirable activities (e.g., pollution, smoking, drinking), and foreign trade. The choice of a tax base is of fundamental importance because it shapes the options available to every citizen. In addition, governments often exempt certain goods from taxation, which has the effect of making decisions about what constitutes taxable economic activity an important expression of public values and a significant component of social welfare policy. Caution must be exercised when approaching this issue because the person who pays a tax does not necessarily bear its economic cost. It is sometimes very different to determine tax incidence. For example, the incidence of sales tax depends on the responses of sellers and buyers to the imposition of the tax. Depending on these responses, the burden of the tax might fall predominantly on either party.

One long-running debate concerns the relative merits of income and consumption taxes. The main difference is that an income tax applies to income regardless of whether it is saved or consumed, whereas a consumption tax applies only to what is consumed. Thus, in a consumption tax system, a person who saves her income may postpone her tax liability until she chooses to consume her savings. One common argument for consumption taxes is that it is unfair to tax a person once when he earns income and then a second time on income from what he saves when a person who chooses to spend all of his earnings immediately is taxed only once (Mill 1848). Taxation of income likewise seems a socially undesirable disincentive to save and invest. Many experts favour a consumption tax on these grounds. Like income taxes, consumption taxes may be made progressive by imposing higher rates of taxation on those who spend more. Alternatively, a flat consumption tax, such as a value added tax, might be combined with an income tax that applies only to those with high incomes. The logic of this position is quite strong with respect to taxpayers with modest incomes and, in fact, many income tax systems provide ways to shield some amount of savings from taxation – for example, through pension plans or retirement accounts. On the other hand, a pure consumption tax system may allow great stocks of wealth to escape taxation altogether since taxation can be postponed indefinitely. This seems quite inequitable in the case of inherited wealth. In theory a vigorous inheritance tax regime should prevent wealthy heirs from escaping taxation, but in practice it is difficult for estate taxes to encompass all intergenerational wealth transmissions. A poorly designed inheritance tax system may serve as a trap for the unwary while allowing those with the benefit of the best advisors to avoid much of the tax. For these reasons, a progressive income or wealth tax may provide a useful backstop even in tax systems built primarily around consumption taxes.

An even more extreme proposal motivated by efficiency considerations is the so-called endowment tax, which taxes capacity to earn rather than actual income. By taxing people based on their potential earnings rather than the actual earnings, one could avoid the deleterious effect of discouraging highly compensated work and encouraging leisure. Income taxes are also arguably unfair to high earners who prefer consuming material goods to consuming leisure since those who prefer leisure enjoy their preferred good tax-free. Earning ability is not directly observable, so one would need to tax some proxy for it. Despite the economic case for such an approach, it is often felt that endowment taxes would be oppressive because they could force people to work at their highest paid occupation on pain of accepting a very low standard of living. For example, a talented investor who owes taxes based on the highest wage that she could receive in the market might have such a high tax liability that she could not afford not to work in finance. Opponents of endowment taxation bear the burden of explaining why this effect is less objectionable than income taxation compelling taxpayers to work longer to achieve a given post-tax income (Olson 2010).

An alternative to general taxes on income, earning ability, consumption, or wealth is to levy taxes on socially undesirable activities. So-called Pigouvian taxes seek to discourage externalities, such as pollution, by imposing a tax that is equal to the social harm caused by the externality. For example, one might impose a tax on carbon emissions designed to reflect the social harm of their contribution to global climate change. This has the fortuitous consequence of raising revenue by discouraging something socially undesirable, such as pollution, rather than something socially desirable, such as working or investing. Extensive use of Pigouvian taxes, however, risks imposing inequitable tax burdens since tax incidence will depend on factors only loosely related to ability to pay or the benefits received from public spending. It is better, therefore, to regard Pigouvian taxes as being primarily justified as a form of regulation rather than as a way to raise revenue.

How to define the taxpayer

In order to apportion tax burdens between taxpayers, one must first decide who counts as a taxpayer. Taxes may be assessed at the level of households or individuals. For example, some countries encourage spouses to file joint tax returns, whereas others tax each adult as an individual regardless of his or her marital status. Under a system of progressive taxation, these choices can have quite significant implications because married people with different incomes will face different tax rates depending on whether they are taxed individually or jointly. If, as in the US, a couple is taxed jointly under progressive tax rates, lower-earning spouses may face a much higher marginal income tax rate than they would as single persons. This is a substantial incentive for those with a high-earning spouse to drop out of the labour force. By contrast, there is no such incentive where, as in the UK, each adult is taxed separately. However, under the UK system, two households with the same income may owe very different amounts of income tax and single-income households may face a high marginal tax rates at a relatively modest household income. The US approach has the virtue of respecting horizontal equity between households and might be more supportive of middle-income families with children. The UK system avoids providing an incentive for second earners to drop out of the labour force or cut back on hours worked. Under progressive tax rates the trade-off between equal tax obligations for households with equal incomes and equal marginal tax rates for workers with equal incomes is unavoidable: one cannot have both at the same time.

The tax treatment of households with children likewise raises thorny questions. Income tax systems differ greatly in their treatment of children. Some countries, such as France, tax families in proportion to the number of members, thus substantially lowering the effective tax rate for families with children, especially for those with many children (Loutzenhiser 2016). At the other extreme, the UK does not consider family structure at all in taxation of income from labour and instead offers a "child benefit" outside of the tax code that is phased out at higher levels of income (Loutzenhiser 2016). Tax benefits for lower-income families with children might be justified as an anti-poverty measure. Tax policy regarding middle-class families with children depends crucially on whether it is fair for the state (and implicitly childless taxpayers) to defray the costs of raising children or whether costs should fall on parents. If the decision to have children is treated like a private consumption decision and does not trigger tax benefits, then child-rearing expenses will consume a large portion of the post-tax income of middle-income households with children. If, on the other hand, households with children are given extra tax exemptions, parents will owe substantially lower taxes than non-parents with equivalent income. This question is less urgent in societies where the majority of taxpayers will fall in each category over the course of their lifetimes. In places where a large fraction of taxpayers never have children, the stakes are much higher.

A final question is how to tax business enterprises. Most countries impose income taxes on large corporations directly. In part this is done for administrative convenience since it may be easier to collect taxes from one corporate entity than from its thousands of investors. To the extent that corporate taxes are not counted against the tax liability of investors, the justification for taxing corporations is unclear. Economists are uncertain whether the burden of taxes on corporate income falls on investors, employees, or consumers (Shaviro 2009). The answer may be different in different contexts. If it is consumers or employees rather than investors who ultimately pay, corporate taxes do not necessarily contribute much to the progressivity of an income tax system. The only clear justification for corporate taxation is that it prevents wealthy individuals from using corporate entities to shelter their income from tax.

In any case, increasing international capital mobility and the growth of cross-border transactions are undermining the ability of national governments to tax multinational corporations and capital income more generally (Kleinbard 2011). Multinational corporations increasingly organise transactions so as to realise income in low-tax jurisdictions even when mainly doing business in higher-tax jurisdictions. In one notorious case, the US coffee chain Starbucks managed to operate a large, fast-growing, and apparently profitable chain of coffee shops in the UK while recognising virtually no income for tax purposes in the UK by, for example, making payments to a Dutch subsidiary for use of Starbucks's "intellectual property", including its brand and its business plan (Kleinbard 2013). Shifting income to low-tax jurisdictions is even easier for multinationals that are genuinely dependent on ownership of intellectual property, such as Google or Apple (Kleinbard 2011). This tax avoidance behaviour is often openly abetted by countries that seek to attract investment by offering the promise of little taxation and no transparency to foreign tax authorities. Tax treaties have traditionally aimed to alleviate double taxation of income in which the same revenue is taxed concurrently in two jurisdictions. Today, the OECD and the G20 are grappling with how to avoid double non-taxation of income through the Base Erosion and Profit Shifting (BEPS) project. International cooperation on this front will require agreement on how to allocate income between jurisdictions. In light of these developments, tax theory cannot focus exclusively on the nation-state, but must consider the international dimensions of distributive questions. What is good policy from the perspective of citizens of one state may have adverse effects on foreign nationals.

Tax competition between nations is part of the reason for the recent trend away from reliance on taxation of capital and towards higher payroll and consumption taxes. Whatever the policy merits of this trend (itself a hotly contested question), one might worry that democratic governments, especially in smaller economies, have less policy flexibility and are therefore less responsive to the views of their own citizens. In this case, democratic control might require international agreements that carve out a space for tax policy on the national level that is protected from tax competition.

Taxation and democracy

The relationship between tax fairness and democracy is complex. Benefits theories of tax fairness might be thought to be in tension with democratic considerations because they tend to represent taxation as an exchange with the state and taxpayers as consumers of government services rather than regarding the taxpayer as one of many citizens who govern collectively (Mill 1848). Ability-to-pay theories, by contrast, regard taxation as a collective obligation shared by citizens. Mill's equal sacrifice principle establishes a link between tax fairness and the obligation of a state to treat citizens as equals that seems especially apt for democracies. This leaves much scope for disagreement about what equality requires. It may be argued that equality requires that tax policy mitigate economic inequalities between taxpayers or that equality requires only that that all make reasonable contributions to public goods in light of their means. Alternatively, Elizabeth Anderson's (1999) theory of democratic equality suggests that our focus should be on policies that allow all citizens to be able to relate to each other as equals. This might counsel in favour of income and inheritance taxes to dissipate fortunes that threaten to undermine social equality but allow for some degree of economic inequality so long as higher- and lower-income citizens are able to interact as equals. Anderson's theory might also imply that tax and transfer policies should be arranged such that low-income citizens pay at least a nominal amount of tax so that all citizens are seen as contributors to the public fisc.

Although ability-to-pay theories may appear more democratic in spirit, setting taxes according to benefits received may have advantages for polities deeply divided on questions of fiscal policy. Doing so allows governments to simultaneously satisfy the preferences of citizens who prefer high taxes and lavish public services and those of citizens who prefer low taxes and stingy public services. This might be accomplished by fiscal decentralisation that allows citizens to select jurisdictions that match their preferred levels of taxation and public spending or by funding services out of taxes that are targeted at users, such as fuel taxes that are earmarked to fund road repairs. Agreeing to disagree is one possible result of democratic deliberation. An alternative approach is to require universal consent to new taxation and government spending. This might both appeal to ideals of collective self-government and safeguard citizens against oppressive levels of taxation.

The best policy-making will combine rigorous thinking about the ethical aims of tax policy with nuanced understanding of the economic effects of tax policy and the psychology of tax compliance. It is not necessary, or perhaps even desirable, that all taxes be justified in the same way. A single fiscal system might combine forms of taxation justified on different grounds. For example, public goods that are inherently national in scope might be funded by income or consumption taxes assessed in light of ability to pay and adjusted to pursue distributive aims at the national level. Other taxes might follow the logic of the benefits principle or be derived from Pigouvian taxes.

References

Anderson, E. (1999) "What Is the Point of Equality?" *Ethics*, 109 (2), 287–337.
Bicchieri, C. (2006) *The Grammar of Society*. New York: Cambridge University Press, 140–141.
Buchanan, J. (1975) *The Limits of Liberty*. Chicago: The University of Chicago Press, 46–68.
Casal, S., C. Kogler, L. Mittone and E. Kirchler (2016) "Tax Compliance Depends on the Voice of Taxpayers," *Journal of Economic Psychology*, 65, 141–150.
Diamond, P. and E. Saez (2011) "The Case for a Progressive Tax: From Basic Research to Policy Recommendations," *Journal of Economic Perspectives*, 25 (4), 165–190.
Edgeworth, F. Y. (1897) "The Pure Theory of Taxation," *The Economic Journal*, 7 (25), 46–70.

Feldstein, M. (1995) "The Effect of Marginal Tax Rates on Taxable Income: A Panel Study of the 1986 Tax Reform Act," *The Journal of Political Economy*, 103 (3), 551–572.

Fried, B. (1999) "The Puzzling Case for Proportionate Taxation," *Chapman Law Review*, 2, 157–197.

Heath, J. (2006) "The Benefits of Cooperation," *Philosophy & Public Affairs*, 34 (4), 313–351.

Kaplow, L. (2008) *The Theory of Taxation and Public Economics*. Princeton, NJ: Princeton University Press.

Kirchler, E. (2007) *The Economic Psychology of Tax Behaviour*. Cambridge: Cambridge University Press, 167.

Kleinbard, E. (2011) "Stateless Income," *Florida Tax Review*, 11 (9), 699–774.

Kleinbard, E. (2013) "Through a Latte Darkly: Starbuck's Stateless Income Planning," *Tax Notes*, June 24, 1515–1535.

Lindsay, I. (2016) "Tax Fairness by Convention: A Defense of Horizontal Equity," *Florida Tax Review*, 19 (2), 79–119.

Loutzenhiser, G. (2016) *Tiley's Revenue Law*. 8th ed. Oxford: Hart Publishing, 175–177.

Mill, J. S. (1848) *Principles of Political Economy*. Volume II. London: John W. Parker, 346–366.

Mirrlees, J. (1971) "An Exploration in the Theory of Optimum Income Taxation," *The Review of Economic Studies*, 38 (2), 175–208.

Murphy, L. and T. Nagel (2002) *The Myth of Ownership*. Oxford: Oxford University Press.

Musgrave, R. (1959) *The Theory of Public Finance: A Study in Public Economy*. New York: McGraw-Hill Book Co. Inc.

OECD (2016) *Revenue Statistics 2016*. Paris: OECD Publishing.

Olson, K. (2010) "The Endowment Tax," *Philosophy & Public Affairs*, 38 (3), 240–271.

Ramsey, F. (1927) "A Contribution to the Theory of Taxation," *Economic Journal*, 37, 47–61.

Scheve, K. and D. Stasavage (2016) *Taxing the Rich: A History of Fiscal Fairness in the United States and Europe*. Princeton, NJ: Princeton University Press, 9–11.

Shaviro, D. (2009) *Decoding the U.S. Corporate Tax*. Washington, DC: The Urban Institute Press, 57–71.

Sidgwick, H. (1887) *The Principles of Political Economy*. London: Palgrave Macmillan.

Smith, A. (1776) *An Inquiry into the Nature and Causes of the Wealth of Nations*. Reprint 1904. Edwin Cannan (ed.). London: Methuen.

Tiebout, C. (1956) "A Pure Theory of Local Expenditures," *Journal of Political Economy*, 64 (5), 416–424.

Wicksell, K. (1958) "A New Principle of Just Taxation," in R. Musgrave and A. Peacock (eds.), *Classics in the Theory of Public Finance*. London: Palgrave Macmillan, 72–118.

14

THE ETHICS OF CENTRAL BANKING

François Claveau, Peter Dietsch, and Clément Fontan

Modern societies use a variety of institutions to pursue key collective objectives. Among these institutions, central banks form the apex of the payment system for each currency. As such, one can appropriately take central banks to be part of what Rawls (2001: §3–4) calls the 'basic structure of society' – that is, a society's 'main political and social institutions and the way they hang together as one system of cooperation'.

There is no historically unique template for central banks: what they are asked to do and how they interact with other institutions change through time. This evolution is attributable to shifts in the common understanding of how central banks can best contribute to key collective objectives. However, the general underlying objective itself stays the same: central banks are meant to serve the interests of the people in their political community, where the precise content of these interests is determined through democratic procedures.

In the late 1980s and early 1990s, the dominant understanding of central banks advocated policies in line with the 'central bank independence' (CBI) template. Yet, since the 2007–8 financial crisis, the effective functioning of central banks in advanced economies has diverged significantly from this template.

The goal of this chapter is to present three concerns that central banks as we know them today no longer promote the democratically determined common good of modern societies: first, their actions have serious unintended consequences; second, the interests of financial actors loom large in their decisions; and, finally, the concentration of monetary expertise around central banks does not provide the conditions for an effective error-correction mechanism on key issues. For reasons of space, we stipulate rather than argue that these developments conflict with either the expressed or the rational interests of modern democracies. By fleshing out these concerns, the chapter is meant as a preliminary step towards an updated understanding regarding the contributions central banks can and should make to our societies' basic structure.[1]

Central banking: the essentials

This preliminary section provides the conceptual background necessary to follow our subsequent discussion.

In a currency area, the central bank has a monopoly over the issuance of legal tender – this characteristic is what distinguishes it from all other institutions. Note that other institutions such as private banks 'create money', too, but central bank money has a special status: it must be accepted as a form of debt settlement by all members of the currency area (Pistor 2013).

This characteristic implies that the central bank can pursue two broad societal goals more effectively than most institutions: financial stability and price stability (Singleton 2010). First, it can act as a lender of last resort in the context of financial crises by creating liquidity. Second, it can manipulate the cost of credit and thereby control the general price level. In addition to these two basic goals, central banks sometimes have other responsibilities, such as promoting employment and supervising financial institutions.

Another characteristic of central banks that has varied over time is their degree of independence towards other state actors, especially towards elected officials. Before the 1990s, governments could typically ask central bankers to lower or raise their key interest rate. As the CBI template swept the world, various protections were put in place to ensure that central banks would not be subject to 'political' pressures in setting monetary policy (McNamara 2002).

The justification for this type of firewall is that a division of institutional labour mitigates credibility problems (Kydland and Prescott 1977; Barro and Gordon 1983; Rogoff 1985). The general reason why central bankers not shielded from elected officials have a credibility deficit is that, although they can *claim* that they will do what it takes to keep inflation low, they have incentives to spur inflation. Rational economic actors would not be systematically fooled by the promises of central bankers under these circumstances. The incentives for inflationary policies could stem from, for example, pressures by elected officials for inflation-induced economic growth towards the end of their term to increase their probability of re-election.

The CBI template not only promoted a high degree of operational independence of central banks but also defined their mandate more narrowly. Price stability became the focus of central banks. By contrast, financial stability was de-emphasised because of the pre-2007 conventional wisdom that technical improvements in finance coupled with price stability would greatly moderate financial fluctuations (Bordo and Jeanne 2002).

To accomplish their narrow mandates, central banks in the CBI era used a correspondingly narrow set of instruments. They chiefly relied on short-term open-market operations: central banks exchange with commercial banks an amount of liquidity for specific financial assets (mainly sovereign bonds). Under a repurchase agreement, the liquidity is later returned with interest and the asset recovered. Under the CBI paradigm, central banks' actions affected, indirectly but quite reliably, the whole array of interest rates in the economy.

From the perspective of how the basic institutions of society 'hang together as one system of cooperation' (Rawls 2001: §3), the CBI template implies that central banks must not consider how their policies contribute to societal objectives beyond price stability. Although societies have numerous objectives, central banks under CBI are asked to focus on optimising one variable: price stability. The government and other institutions must take monetary policy as a given when attempting to optimally serve other societal goals, such as limiting inequalities. As alluded to earlier, the CBI literature argues that a decentralised arrangement with independent central banks can best mitigate the credibility problems of monetary policy. This alleged gain comes at a cost, however: under the CBI template, there is little to no coordination between the different policy levers. One type of policy (e.g., monetary) can thus be detrimental to the objectives pursued with other policies (e.g., fiscal).

Since the 2007–8 financial crisis, the actual interventions of central banks in advanced economies no longer correspond to the CBI template. To save the economic system from collapse, central banks extended and intensified their interventions. In their role as lenders of last resort, they bailed out several financial institutions. They also upgraded their open-market operations in two ways. First, they extended them in size, range of collateral, and maturity. Second, they

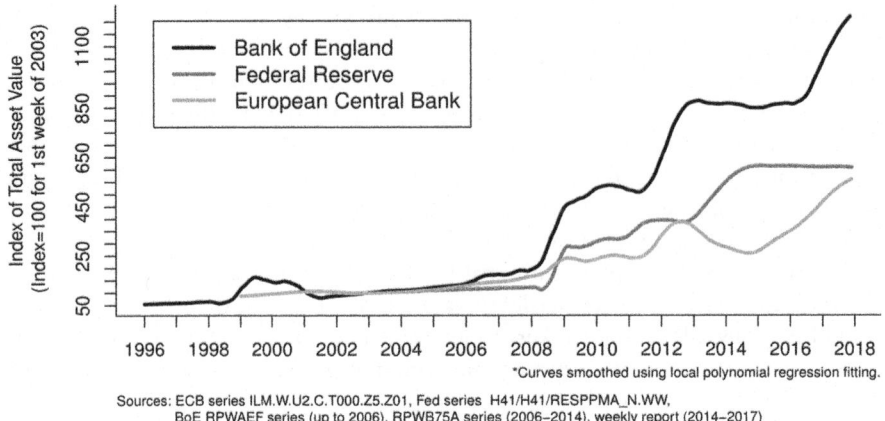

Index of Total Asset Value (Index=100 for 1st week of 2003)

— Bank of England
— Federal Reserve
— European Central Bank

*Curves smoothed using local polynomial regression fitting.

Sources: ECB series ILM.W.U2.C.T000.Z5.Z01, Fed series H41/H41/RESPPMA_N.WW,
BoE RPWAEF series (up to 2006), RPWB75A series (2006–2014), weekly report (2014–2017)

Figure 14.1 Total assets of three major central banks indexed at their early 2003 levels

launched quantitative easing programs – that is, the outright purchase (without repurchase agreement) of large amounts of financial assets on secondary markets. These measures are probably to be credited for stabilising financial markets and for mitigating deflationist tendencies. Although presented originally as 'temporary', they are for the most part still in place after almost ten years. Consequently, central bank policies clearly remain more significant than they were prior to the crisis, as is illustrated in Figure 14.1 by the growth in the asset value on major central bank balance sheets. Furthermore, many central banks were granted new responsibilities for micro- and macro-financial supervision in the aftermath of the crisis.

Does the institutional design of central banks today optimally serve democratically determined social objectives? We now discuss three reasons why one might worry that this is not the case.

First concern: distributive effects

Central bankers and monetary economists often use the term "unintended consequences" (e.g., White 2012) to describe certain side effects of monetary policy. In particular, should it not be a cause for concern if monetary policy contributes to growing inequalities in income and wealth? In order to limit the scope of our argument, two preliminary observations are in order.

First, it is important to distinguish two types of unintended consequences of central bank action. On the one hand, there are *unforeseen* consequences that fall within central bank mandates. Consider the argument by Austrian economists that credit-financed expansions will lead to a more pronounced boom and bust cycle (Hayek 1984), an idea confirmed by recent empirical work (e.g., Jordà *et al.* 2013). Today, one might thus worry that an economic recovery built on massive liquidity injections by central bank policies such as quantitative easing will drive us into the next round of financial instability (White 2012: 17).

If central bankers accepted that a consequence of this kind is likely, their mandate would give them a prima facie reason to adjust their policies accordingly. However, central bankers tend to hold (1) that these consequences are unlikely, (2) that they will be able to control them through countermeasures, *or* (3) that, all things considered, unconventional monetary policy is still warranted. (1) is what makes it an unforeseen consequence from their perspective. We will come back to these issues in the next section, but our focus here lies elsewhere.

On the other hand, there are *predictable but ignored* consequences of central bank actions. For example, central bankers know that unconventional monetary policies impact the distribution of income and wealth in a number of different ways, but they say that it is not their job to do anything about these effects.[2] Our goal here is to both enhance our understanding of these effects and ask whether they call for a more integrated approach to monetary policy and other policy fields, including fiscal policy.

The second limitation on the scope of our argument is the following. When central banks are criticised for not taking into account distributive considerations, in addition to pointing to their limited mandate, they sometimes add that a 'central bank with a clear mandate to safeguard price stability needs to act forcefully when push comes to shove. These distributional side-effects then need to be tolerated' (Mersch 2014). The common theme of this and similar statements by central bankers since 2008 is that their actions have been necessary to save the financial system from collapse.

While there is a kernel of truth to this idea, it applies only in very specific circumstances. When the financial crisis broke out and banks were threatening to go under, the urgency of the situation indeed meant that compromising on considerations of financial stability might have had even worse distributive consequences due to the unemployment created by a deeper and longer recession. However, as Hannoun (2012: 22) puts it,

> as crisis management gives way to crisis resolution, it is important that central banks highlight the limitations of their actions and the need for other policies to take over in order to ensure the necessary balance sheet repair and adjustment of the real economy.

The scope of this chapter is limited to times of crisis resolution, when public institutions – including central banks – dispose of the necessary *marge de manoeuvre* to adjust the policy mix in ways sensitive to a diverse set of policy objectives.

We now turn to one specific example of a predictable but ignored consequence. The relations between monetary policy and distributive justice are manifold. The goal of this section is to present them in a systematic framework that will help the formulation of adequate normative and institutional responses. To do so, we draw a basic distinction between two kinds of distributive questions that arise in the context of monetary policy. First, we consider what we call the *direct* distributive effects of monetary policy, which refer to consequences of central bank actions analysed in isolation from other policies. Second, when assessing what we call the *indirect* distributive effects of monetary policy, we look at the impact of monetary policy in conjunction with other policy variables.

In the first category, our analysis focuses on the unconventional monetary policy instruments deployed in the wake of the financial crisis (cf. Dietsch 2017), without implying that monetary policy does not have distributive effects in "normal times".[3] Here is a non-exhaustive[4] list of different kinds of inegalitarian consequences of recent unconventional monetary policy:

- The most significant distributive concern has been the impact of quantitative easing on the prices of financial assets (cf. White 2012; Group of Thirty 2015). Independently of whether one of the goals of quantitative easing is to stimulate higher consumption through rising asset prices, and independently of whether this policy is successful, it boosts the assets of the haves compared to the have-nots and thus arguably exacerbates inequalities (Domanski *et al.* 2016; Bank of England 2012).[5] The rallies of both stock markets and real estate markets in recent years, rallies that hardly reflect the outlook of economic fundamentals, have in part been stimulated by quantitative easing.

- Other unconventional policies, such as the long-term refinancing operations (LTROs) of the European Central Bank (ECB),[6] also tend to exacerbate inequalities. By offering low-risk arbitrage opportunities to banks, they boost profits of commercial banks without necessarily achieving their declared aim of boosting lending to the real economy.[7]
- In contrast to traditional open-market operations, since the crisis central banks have both switched from temporary to permanent ('outright') purchases and have expanded the asset classes they buy. The ECB, for instance, has launched a corporate sector purchase program (CSPP)[8] in order to stimulate lending for productive investment. While in the early days of the program only 4 per cent of the purchases took place on primary markets, studies show that even purchases on secondary markets bestow tangible benefits in terms of lower borrowing costs on those selected for the program, such as carmaker Volkswagen or arms-producer Thales (Corporate Europe Observatory 2016). Arguably, political decisions of this sort are incompatible with the independence, and thus limited democratic control, of a central bank.

Letting central banks ignore these distributive consequences and expecting governments to take corrective fiscal measures, even if – against the odds – it worked, could lead to a sub-optimal policy mix. Note that this leaves open the question of whether to ask central banks to be more sensitive to distributive issues in their policy formulation (Fontan *et al.* 2016) or to adjust other policy variables instead, notably through regulatory changes (Brunnermeier and Sannikov 2012: 377).

We now turn to the second category of *indirect* distributive effects of monetary policy. Monetary policy is not formulated in isolation, but it in part responds to decisions made in fiscal policy and different kinds of regulation that are not part of the central bank mandate. Conversely, these other policies are sensitive to monetary policy. Against this background, different policy *combinations* will have different consequences for distribution.

Consider first the impact monetary policy has on fiscal policy, before looking at the influence running the other way. In several countries, expansionary monetary policy in the wake of the crisis has been combined with fiscal austerity. Politics of austerity tend to exacerbate income inequalities. It is a legitimate question whether expansionary monetary policy has, at least in part, rendered fiscal austerity possible. Would governments have pursued growth-oriented policies under a less expansionary monetary policy regime? If there is a substitution effect between the two policy domains (Green and Lavery 2015: 906), and if monetary policy could and perhaps should have been normalised again more rapidly after the crisis (Hannoun 2012), then the omission to do so, via austerity, has an inegalitarian impact. Conversely, is there a sense in which austerity renders expansionary monetary policy necessary? On the plausible assumption that austerity will tend to dent employment and might prove deflationary, too, their mandates will indeed force central banks to compensate. A comprehensive assessment of the distributive impact of monetary policy will have to answer the questions raised in this paragraph and analyse monetary policy as one dimension of a combination of economic policies.

In sum, the first concern raised by the current contributions of central banks to societal objectives is that some objectives, especially distributional ones, are adversely affected by the new monetary policy, but the institutional configuration characterised by an absence of coordination is ill-suited to correct for these effects.

Second concern: central banking and finance

Since the 1970s, the literature on central bank independence (CBI) has focused on the independence towards political authorities. However, there is another aspect of the recent history of central banking that has not been seriously tackled by the literature: the operations of central banks in times of financialisation.[9] Financialisation is defined as the growth of the financial sector vis-à-vis the non-financial sector and the increasing dependence of the non-financial sector on the financial logic – for example, the growing importance of shareholder value in the operations of firms. As central banks play an interface role between financial markets and democratic states (Singleton 2010), financialisation and central bank activities mutually influence each other. In this section, we will first document the sociological and ideological connections of central bankers to financial markets, before arguing that central banking under financialisation is problematic because it suffers from a double bias in favour of financial actors' interests.

In a quantitative and historical study of professional biographies, Adolph (2013) emphasises two links between central bankers and the financial industry. First, the beliefs of central bankers who used to work in the financial industry are more likely to have been shaped by the latter (socialisation effect). For example, both Mark Carney and Mario Draghi worked for Goldman Sachs before becoming governor of the Bank of England and president of the ECB respectively. Second, when central bankers hope to be recruited by the financial industry upon leaving office, it is more likely that they send positive signals to their future employers when formulating policies (regulatory capture effect). The fact that central bankers' career trajectories are increasingly linked with the financial industry since the CBI era arguably is one of the drivers of financialisation.

While important, factors related to professional biographies cannot fully explain central banks' bias in favour of financial interests because different central banks with different compositions of their monetary committees have implemented similar monetary policies. To understand the reasons why financial actors are in a favourable position with respect to monetary policy, we must also remember that central banks rely on the smooth functioning of financial markets to implement and transmit their monetary policy to the real economy. Janet Yellen, the chairwoman of the Federal Reserve (Fed) from 2014 to 2018, said that although central banks 'work through the financial markets, our goal is to help Main Street and not Wall Street'.[10] While she might be right about the *intentionality* of central bank policies, financial institutions still enjoy leverage over monetary policy *outcomes* because central banks rely on the infrastructures of financial markets to implement their policies (Braun 2018; Gabor and Ban 2016).

Why did central bankers not try to disentangle their conduct of monetary policy from financial markets in order to decrease this leverage? One hypothesis is that operating monetary policy through financial markets allows them to further isolate central banks from political interference (Marcussen 2009; Krippner 2011). Adolph (2013: 314) suggests that there is an inverse correlation between the two faces of CBI: when central banks gain more independence towards political authorities, their independence towards financial players weakens, and *vice versa*.

Now that we have sketched the reasons why financial institutions are in an advantageous position, we will substantiate our claim that central banking under financialisation is problematic in two ways. On the one hand, central banks fuel the risky expansion of the financial sector in non-crisis times. In the run-up to the 2007–8 financial crisis, central bankers did not sufficiently control excessive credit and speculative bubbles. From 2001 to 2006, the Fed did not sufficiently 'lean against the wind' to tame the subprime financial bubble, but rather trusted the self-regulation of markets through the use of new financial instruments, such as derivatives and securitised financial products (Krippner 2011). On the other side of the Atlantic, the ECB feared that the financial fragmentation[11] of the Eurozone would impair its ability to implement its monetary policy. To promote financial integration, the ECB hence decided that the debt of any Eurozone country would be considered as identical collateral in its refinancing operations (Gabor and Ban 2016). By putting diverse countries such as Greece and Germany in the same basket, it encouraged financial operators to purchase more sovereign debt from peripheral countries, as it could be traded against liquidity at the ECB on a par with the more expensive debt from other member states. These perverse incentives partly explain both why many European banks became too big to fail (TBTF)[12] and the growth of public debt in the Eurozone periphery (Blyth 2013: chapter 3). Rather than making monetary policy more effective as central bankers had anticipated, financialisation ultimately weakened both the Fed's and the ECB's control over financial markets and was a major driver of the 2007 financial crisis.

On the other hand, since the crisis, central banks did not do enough to make the financial industry assume a fair share of the losses, nor to change the rules of the game to prevent future crises. First, when acting as lender of last resort, central banks should be wary about the risks of moral hazard[13] (Bagehot 1873) and attach conditions to their loans strict enough to have a deterrent effect for the future – nationalisations or forced mergers, for example. In 2007–8, central banks failed to prevent moral hazard when bailing-out TBTF institutions: they lent ample amounts of liquidity at low rates against risky assets without sufficient conditionality, thereby transferring credit risk from private institutions to public balance sheets (Cour-Thimann 2013). Moreover, central banks have an obligation to anticipate future financial crises and to make sure that their room for policy manoeuvre will be less constrained by TBTF financial institutions than it was during the last crisis. Thus far, central banks have not done nearly enough on this count: their attempts to re-regulate the financial sector have been too timid.

In addition, it can be argued that financialisation has pushed central bankers to unduly prolong their unconventional policies (Gabor and Ban 2016), exacerbating the problematic side effects discussed in the previous section. For example, it is plausible to think that in the absence of the strong reaction from financial markets to the mere mention of the possibility of reducing asset purchases by the Fed in May 2013, the Fed would have stopped its unconventional policies sooner and more decisively. Similarly, the persistent fragility of the Eurozone banking sector forced the ECB to renew its long-term refinancing operations (LTRO) in March 2016.

Finally, financialisation makes it more difficult for central bankers to ensure that the cheap liquidity provided to commercial banks is used to provide credit to the real economy. For example, in 2014, the ECB tried to impose some conditions on the use of liquidity by commercial banks.[14] However, it abandoned the conditionality component of its liquidity offers in March 2016, mainly because the banks were reluctant to respect the condition of lending to the real economy. This lack of conditions allows financial operators to use central bank liquidity to boost their profits without benefiting the economy at large.

In sum, central banking under financialisation has encountered two problems. First, central banks have fuelled financialisation dynamics when they failed to engage in sufficient prevention of financial imbalances. Second, financialisation and its consequences have constrained the post-crisis interventions of central banks. They weaken central bank efforts to control moral hazard and incite them to pursue their unconventional policies well beyond the immediate crisis.

Third concern: central banks as experts

Central banks are the dominant providers of research and expert opinion on central banking and monetary policy today. White (2005) provides ample evidence of the centrality of the Fed in the United States. For instance, he estimates in the early 2000s that 'the Fed employs full-time about 27 per cent more macro/money/banking economists than the top 50 US academic economics departments put together' (White 2005: 329). The centrality of the Fed is heightened by the tight links between the institution and economists in academia – for instance, through an extensive program of visiting scholars. There is also ample evidence that other central banks are major players in the research world:[15] Figure 14.2 shows that the fraction of articles signed

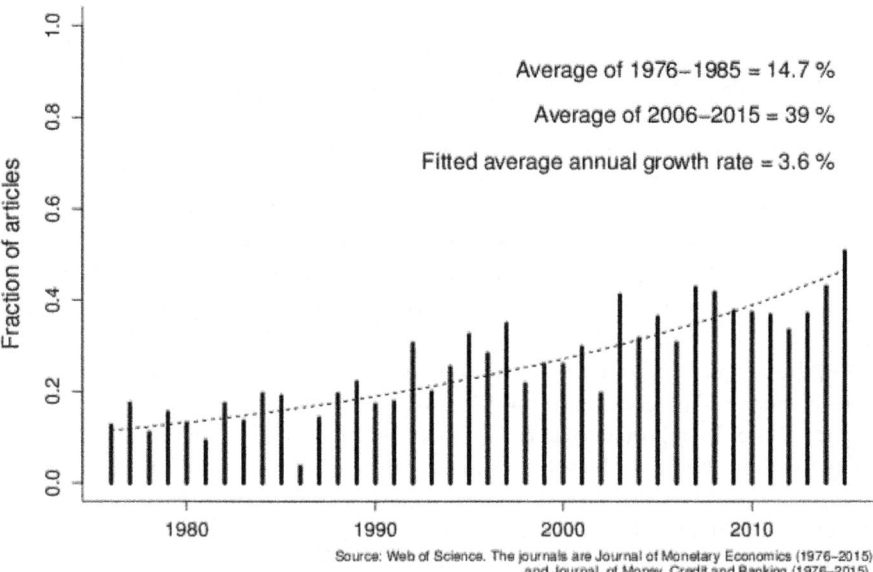

Average of 1976–1985 = 14.7 %

Average of 2006–2015 = 39 %

Fitted average annual growth rate = 3.6 %

Source: Web of Science. The journals are Journal of Monetary Economics (1976–2015)
and Journal of Money, Credit and Banking (1976–2015).

Figure 14.2   Fraction of articles in the two main specialised academic journals with at least one author working at a central bank

by at least one central bank employee in the two main academic journals on central banking and monetary policy has been growing at an average rate of 3.6 per cent since the late 1970s. In the last year in our corpus (2015), the percentage of articles signed by at least one central bank employee reached 50.6 per cent.

A core concern in the expert-layperson relationship is whether the expert is trustworthy (Goldman 2001). The general public relies on experts to provide them with reliable information. Experts must thus be worthy of being trusted as information providers. So, can the general public trust central bankers as experts on monetary matters?

A starting point in answering this question is to recognise that central bankers' dominant opinion on an important issue has failed us in the period prior to the financial crisis: the opinion that monetary policy should (almost) exclusively focus on price stability 'was fatally flawed' (Carney 2014: 14). But concluding from this fact that central banks cannot be trusted is premature. First, central bankers have corrected this erroneous belief. Second and more importantly, it would be too demanding to ask an expert community to be infallible. We should rather require that our reliance on the community's opinions in its domain of expertise be significantly more goal-conducive than relying on alternative sources.

Since directly assessing whether this condition holds is arguably beyond the layperson's grasp – indeed, we would ourselves be experts in the domain if we could directly judge the current reliability of alleged experts – we have to resort to a more indirect assessment. Because expert communities are fallible, our trust in them should be a function of whether they have a well-functioning mechanism to correct errors. From the literature in scientific methodology and philosophy, we have some knowledge of the general characteristics at the individual and collective levels that promote error correction. The question of whether the expertise of central banks is trustworthy can thus be converted into the question of whether they have an adequate error-correction mechanism. The simple three-part framework that we will use is inspired by Helen Longino's characteristics for procedural objectivity (Longino 1990).

First, error correction is more likely when the members of the community are *transparent* about both the claims they hold to be true and the standards they rely on to justify these beliefs, since being transparent on these matters allows one's beliefs to be effectively challenged. Central banks used to be opaque, but they have morphed into institutions cherishing transparency about certain aspects of their policy-making, in great part because the central banking community now believes that transparency promotes the effectiveness of monetary policy (Dincer and Eichengreen 2007). We can thus conclude that the central banking community possesses this first aspect of an error-correction mechanism to a far higher degree today than in previous periods. Yet, central banks are only *conditionally* transparent: the consensus is that they should control the flow of information to the extent that it promotes their policy objectives (Issing 2005).

Second, the adequacy of an error-correction mechanism hinges on the *sustained generation of varied lines of criticism*. The generation must be sustained because one successful blow is usually insufficient to unsettle important beliefs. Critiques must be varied so that no specific belief will be accepted without being probed. Let us look at the intensity and the variety of criticism in turn.

With their important research divisions and their extensive links to academic researchers, central banks have access to a sustained flow of novel research results. For instance, much of the research measuring the distributive effects of unconventional monetary policies has come out of central banks (e.g., Bank of England 2012; Saiki and Frost 2014; Domanski *et al.* 2016). Yet, a first caveat can be registered here. There is reason to worry that the structure of the community is such that the intensity of criticisms is muted. As we have seen, central banks are pivotal in the community; standard strategic considerations should lead agents who want to be fully recognised as members of the community to think twice before pursuing research that is likely to seriously challenge central tenets of the monetary policy consensus. Highly ranked central bankers have levers to silence some of the dissident voices. For instance, every research output, at the Fed and the ECB at least, has to go through an approval process before being made public. This process is officially meant to ensure 'the research is of high quality',[16] but it has been presented by a Fed employee as aiming 'to avoid statements in conflict with national monetary policy' (Fase and Vanthoor 2000: 32; for the ECB, see Mudge and Vauchez 2016: 161–2). For researchers that are not on a central bank's payroll, the influence is more indirect: being a black sheep diminishes the chances that one gets a share of the resources controlled by central banks (e.g., conference invitations, visiting scholarships), and the probability of publishing critical material in well-regarded journals is lowered when a large proportion of reviewers come from the incumbent institutions.

With respect to the *diversity* of criticism, the concern is twofold. First, central banks as regulators have incentives to channel resources towards research that is likely to help them better plan their interventions. They set research priorities accordingly – see, for instance, the Bank of England's One Bank Research Agenda (Bank of England 2015). Although this strategy is entirely understandable for a regulator, it can have the undesirable effect of limiting the scope of research. In particular, research that is not closely connected to a central bank's *current* mandate risks being underappreciated. Second, there is a vast literature documenting cases in the history of science 'where we can now see that even conscientious, well-intentioned scientists made problematic assumptions, adopted gender and racial stereotypes, or reasoned in ways that reflected and projected their own experiences, values and interests' (Intemann 2009: 255). We can thus worry about the diversity of criticism in the central banking community based on the low diversity of *its members*. The uniformity of governing bodies is most noticeable: out of 25 members of the ECB's Governing Council in early 2017, only 2 were women. Gender is only one dimension of member diversity that might be relevant. In the United States, the movement Fed Up has recently taken up the issue of member diversity with regards to ethnicity. One of its major claims is that the Fed is blind to the detrimental effects of its policies on specific ethnic groups. It asks both for a more diverse Board and for a Fed research program dedicated to these issues (WSJ Pro 2016).

In addition to transparency and sustained generation of varied criticisms, the last element of a well-functioning error-correction mechanism is the *willingness for belief revision*. Indeed, if most members of an epistemic community stubbornly stick to their opinions, error correction will not occur even if the first two elements are present. In the case of monetary economics, one must acknowledge that central banks' spokespersons have changed their minds on important issues since the financial crisis of 2007–8. They have, for instance, come to believe that 'extraordinary measures' such as quantitative easing could be a legitimate part of the toolbox and that financial stability can be enhanced by macroprudential interventions.[17]

Yet, we should be careful here: as members of an institution with privileges, we should expect the key players in the central banking community to be far less keen to revise their beliefs on other issues. The best example of such sensitive issues is the justification of central bank independence in the post-2007 era. In fact, the issue of independence illustrates well the interaction of the three elements of a well-functioning error mechanism and indicates that, as laypersons, we should not blindly trust central bankers as experts. Central bankers are *transparent* about their beliefs in independence and what they think justifies this belief: 'Extensive empirical evidence and theoretical analyses have shown that independent central banks are better capable of maintaining low inflation rates'.[18] Yet, while calls in the public sphere to reconsider independence have grown more vocal since the financial crisis, this issue is simply not a research topic in the epistemic community: from the approximately 10,000 research papers that have come out of central banks between 2008 and July 2017, only 5 studied the justifications for central bank independence.[19] This represents a clear defect in *criticism generation*. Furthermore, even if serious and sustained criticism existed with respect to central bank independence, we should expect a weak *willingness for belief revision* when it comes to the importance of independence. Central bankers have a vested interest in the *status quo* on this topic. There is thus a potential conflict of interest between their role as providers of information and the protection of their institutional status.

All in all, although the central banking community today comes closer than ever to having the characteristics of a "scientific" community (Marcussen 2009), it is prudent not to blindly trust them. Central banks could be asked to improve in some areas – for instance, on internal diversity – and our societies would also be better off if a serious counter-expertise could be organised. It is collectively unwise to concentrate expert credentials in a community that has vested interests.

Conclusion

This chapter is not meant to produce a clear-cut verdict on the social value of the current configuration of central banking, nor does it discuss potential remedies to the shortcomings of the status quo. Its goal has been to flesh out three concerns regarding this status quo and to offer guidance in thinking through these concerns. The ignored consequences of monetary policy – especially distributional ones – the undue influence of financial interests, and the oligopoly of opinion of central banks on monetary economics all highlight an important but typically overlooked fact about contemporary central banks. They are not 'neutral' institutions dedicated to a unique and merely technical objective. They are rather part of the main institutions created for our societies to flourish. As such, how they relate to other institutions should never be taken as settled, but be subject to democratic debate.

Notes

1 For our more detailed contribution to this topic, see Dietsch, Claveau, and Fontan (2018).
2 Peter Praet of the European Central Bank (ECB), for example, states that '[g]overnments have to take care of redistributive effects' (Praet 2015: 3).
3 See, for instance, Monnin (2014) on the link between inflation and inequality.
4 We bracket considerations of gender (Young 2018) and of international distribution (Reddy 2003) as well as environmental concerns; for the latter, see, for example, Volz (2017).
5 For a dissenting view, see Montecino and Epstein (2015), who claim that the inegalitarian effects get overestimated.
6 See www.ecb.europa.eu/press/pr/date/2011/html/pr111208_1.en.html (accessed February 22nd 2017).
7 Mario Draghi admits as much in his justification of ECB policy in his speech to the European Parliament on July 14, 2014.
8 See www.ecb.europa.eu/press/pr/date/2016/html/pr160421_1.en.html (accessed February 22nd 2017).
9 The issue of central banks' independence toward financial authorities has also been called 'financial dominance' (Hannoun 2012; Brunnermeier and Sannikov 2012).
10 See www.federalreserve.gov/newsevents/speech/yellen20140331a.htm (accessed February 27th 2017).
11 Financial fragmentation occurs when financial players do not enjoy similar access to credit within the same currency area.
12 The size of the Eurozone banking sector doubled between 2001 and 2007. European banks used periphery debt as collateral on repo markets to purchase US "subprime" financial assets. Therefore, in 2007, European banks were exposed to both the subprime crisis and risky peripheral debt.
13 Moral hazard occurs when the existence of a safety net, such as a central bank, encourages and/or sustains risky behaviour or activities.
14 Cf. the targeted long-term refinancing operations of the ECB (TLTROs).
15 For the ECB, see Mudge and Vauchez (2016) and internal reports (Goodfriend *et al.* 2004; Freedman *et al.* 2011). It is also clear that central banks strive to become even more important: for the ECB, see Freedman *et al.* (2011: 51); for the Bank of England, see Carney (2015).
16 See www.ecb.europa.eu/explainers/tell-me-more/html/research.en.html (accessed February 27th 2017).
17 That is, by measures designed to shore up the stability of the financial system through a variety of regulations.
18 See www.ecb.europa.eu/explainers/tell-me-more/html/ecb_independent.en.html (accessed February 27th 2017).
19 Data are from the BIS Research Hub (www.bis.org/cbhub/index.htm). The two most important outliers are Oritani (2010) and de Haan and Eijffinger (2016).

References

Adolph, Christopher. 2013. *Bankers, Bureaucrats, and Central Bank Politics: The Myth of Neutrality*. New York: Cambridge University Press.
Bagehot, Walter. 1873. *Lombard Street: A Description of the Money Market*. London: Henry S. King & Co.
Bank of England. 2012. *The Distributional Effects of Asset Purchases*. London: Bank of England, 73. www.bankofengland.co.uk/-/media/boe/files/quarterly-bulletin/2012/the-distributional-effects-of-asset-purchases.pdf?la=en&hash=2B755A0984858DB90078EB78313CFD58F509F63A.
Bank of England. 2015. *One Bank Research Agenda*. London: Bank of England.
Barro, Robert J., and David B. Gordon. 1983. "A Positive Theory of Monetary Policy in a Natural Rate Model." *Journal of Political Economy* 91 (4): 589–610.
Blyth, Mark. 2013. *Austerity: The History of a Dangerous Idea*. Oxford: Oxford University Press.
Bordo, Michael D., and Olivier Jeanne. 2002. "Monetary Policy and Asset Prices: Does 'Benign Neglect' Make Sense?" *International Finance* 5 (2): 139–164.

Braun, Benjamin. 2018. "Central Banking and the Infrastructural Power of Finance: The Case of ECB Support for Repo and Securitization Markets." *Socio-Economic Review.* https://doi.org/10.1093/ser/mwy008.

Brunnermeier, Markus K., and Yuliy Sannikov. 2012. "Redistributive Monetary Policy." In *The Changing Policy Landscape*, 331–84. Jackson Hole, Wyoming: Federal Reserve Bank of Kansas City.

Carney, Mark. 2014. "One Mission: One Bank: Promoting the Good of the People of the United Kingdom." Mais Lecture, Cass Business School, City University of London, March 18.

———. 2015. "Opening Remarks of the One Bank Research Agenda: Launch Conference." Bank of England, February 25.

Corporate Europe Observatory. 2016. "ECB's 'quantitative easing' Funds Multinationals and Climate Change." *CorporateEurope.org*, December 12.

Cour-Thimann, Philippine. 2013. "Monetary Policy and Redistribution: Information from Central Bank Balance Sheets in the Euro Area and the US." *Review of Economics* 64 (3): 293–324.

de Haan, Jakob, and Sylvester Eijffinger. 2016. "The Politics of Central Bank Independence." *DNB Working Paper*, no. 539. The Hague: De Nederlandsche Bank.

Dietsch, Peter. 2017. "Normative Dimension of Central Banking: How the Guardians of Financial Markets Affect Justice." In *Just Financial Markets: Finance in a Just Society*, edited by Lisa Herzog, 231–49. Oxford: Oxford University Press.

Dietsch, Peter, François Claveau, and Clément Fontan. 2018. *Do Central Banks Serve the People?* Cambridge: Polity Press.

Dincer, Nergiz N., and Barry Eichengreen. 2007. "Central Bank Transparency: Where, Why, and with What Effects?" *National Bureau of Economic Research Working Papers*, no. 13003.

Domanski, Dietrich, Michela Scatigna, and Anna Zabai. 2016. "Wealth Inequality and Monetary Policy." *SSRN Scholarly Paper ID 2744862*. Rochester, NY: Social Science Research Network.

Fase, Martin M.G., and Wim F.V. Vanthoor. 2000. *The Federal Reserve System Discussed: A Comparative Analysis.* Vienna: Société universitaire européenne de recherches financières.

Fontan, Clément, François Claveau, and Peter Dietsch. 2016. "Central Banking and Inequalities: Taking off the Blinders." *Politics, Philosophy & Economics* 15 (4): 319–57.

Freedman, Charles, Philip R. Lane, Rafael Repullo, and Klaus Schmidt-Hebbel. 2011. "External Evaluation of the Directorate General Research of the European Central Bank." Frankfurt: European Central Bank.

Gabor, Daniela, and Cornel Ban. 2016. "Banking on Bonds: The New Links Between States and Markets." *JCMS: Journal of Common Market Studies* 54 (3): 617–35.

Goldman, Alvin I. 2001. "Experts: Which Ones Should You Trust?" *Philosophy and Phenomenological Research* 63 (1): 85–110.

Goodfriend, Marvin, Reiner König, and Rafael Repullo. 2004. "External Evaluation of the Economic Research Activities of the European Central Bank." Frankfurt: European Central Bank.

Green, Jeremy, and Scott Lavery. 2015. "The Regressive Recovery: Distribution, Inequality and State Power in Britain's Post-Crisis Political Economy." *New Political Economy* 20 (6): 894–923.

Group of Thirty. 2015. *Fundamentals of Central Banking: Lessons from the Crisis.* Washington, DC: Group of Thirty.

Hannoun, Hervé. 2012. "Monetary Policy in the Crisis: Testing the Limits of Monetary Policy." Speech at the 47th SEACEN Governors' Conference, Seoul, Koreay, February 13.

Hayek, Friedrich August von. 1984. *Money, Capital and Fluctuation. Early Essays*, edited by Roy Mc-Cloughry. London: Routledge.

Intemann, Kristen. 2009. "Why Diversity Matters: Understanding and Applying the Diversity Component of the National Science Foundation's Broader Impacts Criterion." *Social Epistemology* 20 (3–4): 249–66.

Issing, Otmar. 2005. "Communication, Transparency, Accountability: Monetary Policy in the Twenty-First Century." *Federal Reserve Bank of St. Louis Review* 87 (2): 65–83.

Jordà, Òscar, and Moritz H.P. Schularick. 2013. "When Credit Bites Back." *Journal of Money, Credit and Banking* suppl. 45 (2): 3–28.

Krippner, Greta R. 2011. *Capitalizing on Crisis.* Cambridge, MA: Harvard University Press.

Kydland, Finn E., and Edward C. Prescott. 1977. "Rules Rather Than Discretion: The Inconsistency of Optimal Plans." *Journal of Political Economy* 85 (3): 473–91.

Longino, Helen E. 1990. *Science as Social Knowledge.* Princeton, NJ: Princeton University Press.

Marcussen, Martin. 2009. "Scientization of Central Banking: The Politics of A-Politicization." In *Central Banks in the Age of the Euro: Europeanization, Convergence, and Power*, edited by Kenneth Dyson and Martin Marcussen, 373–90. Oxford: Oxford University Press.

McNamara, Kathleen. 2002. "Rational Fictions: Central Bank Independence and the Social Logic of Delegation." *West European Politics* 25 (1): 47–76.

Mersch, Yves. 2014. "Monetary Policy and Economic Inequality." *At Corporate Credit Conference*. October 15. www.ecb.europa.eu/press/key/date/2014/html/sp141017_1.en.html.

Monnin, Pierre. 2014. "Inflation and Income Inequality in Developed Economies." *CEP Working Papers*. https://papers.ssrn.com/sol3/papers.cfm?abstract_id=2444710.

Montecino, Juan Antonio, and Gerald Epstein. 2015. "Did Quantitative Easing Increase Income Inequality?" *INET Working Paper*, no. 28.

Mudge, Stephanie L., and Antoine Vauchez. 2016. "Fielding Supranationalism: The European Central Bank as a Field Effect." *The Sociological Review Monographs* 64 (2): 146–69. doi:10.1002/2059-7932.12006.

Oritani, Yoshiharu. 2010. "Public Governance of Central Banks: An Approach from New Institutional Economics." *BIS Working Papers*. Basel: Bank of International Settlements.

Pistor, Katharina. 2013. "A Legal Theory of Finance." *Journal of Comparative Economics* 41 (2): 315–30.

Praet, Peter. 2015. "Peter Praet: Interview in Jornal de Negócios." www.bis.org/review/r150216b.pdf.

Rawls, John. 2001. *Justice as Fairness: A Restatement*. Cambridge, MA: Harvard University Press.

Reddy, Sanjay G. 2003. "Developing Just Monetary Arrangements." *Ethics & International Affairs* 17 (1): 81–93.

Rogoff, Kenneth S. 1985. "The Optimal Degree of Commitment to an Intermediate Monetary Target." *The Quarterly Journal of Economics* 100 (4): 1169–985.

Saiki, Ayako, and Jon Frost. 2014. "How Does Unconventional Monetary Policy Affect Inequality? Evidence from Japan." *DNB Working Paper*, no. 423. The Hague: De Nederlandsche Bank NV.

Singleton, John. 2010. *Central Banking in the Twentieth Century*. Cambridge: Cambridge University Press.

Volz, Ulrich. 2017. "On the Role of Central Banks in Enhancing Green Finance." *UN Inquiry Working Paper*, no. 17/01. London.

White, Lawrence H. 2005. "The Federal Reserve System's Influence on Research in Monetary Economics." *Econ Journal Watch* 2 (2): 325–54.

White, William R. 2012. "Ultra Easy Monetary Policy and the Law of Unintended Consequences." *FRB Dallas Working paper*, no. 126. www.williamwhite.ca/content/ultra-easy-monetary-policy-and-law-unintended-consequences.

WSJ Pro. 2016. "Transcript: Fed Officials Meet with Fed Up Activists at Jackson Hole." *Wall Street Journal*, August 26, sec. Economy. www.wsj.com/articles/transcript-fed-officials-meet-with-fed-up-activists-at-jackson-hole-1472234174.

Young, Brigitte. 2018. "Central Bank Policies, Inequality and Gendered Asset Bias." In *Handbook of the IPE of Gender*, edited by Juanita Elias and Adrianne Roberts. Cheltenham: Edward Elgar.

15

ETHICS AND FOREIGN POLICY

Michael Blake

The relationship between *public policy* and *foreign policy* is not an easy one to pin down.[1] Certainly, there are great similarities; both involve the use of collective power – both the coercive power of states, and the more diffuse power of social and political institutions – to achieve particular goals. Both are susceptible of being done well, or poorly, depending upon how these goals are met. And both, finally, are capable of being understood with reference to distinctly *ethical* sorts of values; both public policy and foreign policy can be justified (or condemned) by invoking a moralised account of the purposes such policy is designed to achieve, and the means with which those purposes are pursued.

They are distinct, though, in the nature of the *public* for whom the policy is intended. In most discussions of public policy, that set of people is assumed to be local; for domestic political decision-making, our focus is general on those within the domestic political community. Foreign policy, however, is distinguished precisely by the fact that it is brought to bear upon those who are *not* members of that domestic political community. We should not overstate this difference; foreign policy affects domestic citizens, just as domestic public policy has effects on the lives of foreign nationals. Still, the two forms of policy are to some degree distinct in whose lives they seek to alter. We have, further, comparatively little writing on the ethics of foreign policy; much of our ethical thinking here has subsumed the ethics of foreign policy under some other category of ethical inquiry. We have, for example, a great deal of writing on the ethics of war; we have long been interested in the question of when violence might be rightly used against a foreign political community.[2] We have also, in recent years, seen a great deal of writing on the justice of transnational institutions, including the formal legal institutions undergirding international trade.[3] The ethical analysis of foreign policy, however, requires us to think rather precisely about what it is that a domestic political community owes to those who are not its members – and to think about this not with reference to concepts such as the just war and international justice but with reference to the purposes animating our discussions of the ethics of statecraft more generally. What exactly is a state supposed to be *doing*, through its foreign policy? What sorts of values is it right to take as important ones, not simply as regards its own citizens, but as regards foreign persons and communities?[4]

This essay will not seek to offer a definitive answer to these questions; that would be impossible in this space, and would likely prove impossible in a much longer one. It will, instead, try to offer up a sense of the different ways in which policy-makers might begin to answer these questions. I will argue that our thinking about the ethics of foreign policy might have to begin with the question of which ethical value is most central in this context – and that this question may be a rather difficult one. I will try to abstract away from some related questions, in discussing these issues. I will be ignoring the morality of warfare and political violence – not because such questions are not important but only because most foreign policy uses means that are not (or at least not obviously) as violent as the means deployed in warfare; we have reason to avoid letting our discussion of foreign policy become reducible to the distinct discussion of legitimate violence. I will also be ignoring, to some degree, the increasingly significant literature on global justice. This literature tends to focus on the issue of whether the rules of global interaction are fair, and if not, what possibilities exist for rectification or resistance.

The question I ask here, instead, looks to the acts of an individual state, and simply accepts the current international system to be what it is. The line between these two questions is not sharp – the rules of the game, after all, are largely constructed in international politics by the rules made *within* the game.[5] I will, further, have occasion to note how some theorists of global justice might regard some particular question of foreign policy. Nevertheless, the two questions are rightly regarded as distinct; and our question will focus on what a state might rightly take as the purposes of its foreign policy, within the bounds of international society – and not on how international society should be reorganised in response to ethical concerns. I will assume, further, that the state seeking ethical guidance understands itself to be a liberal democracy. This assumption does not depend upon the proposition that only liberal democratic states are legitimate, but simply upon the fact that much of what I say here expands on moral notions prevalent in the public political cultures of liberal democratic states; I cannot say to what extent they will find echoes in other forms of political society. I will be ignoring, finally, the difficult and important question of how the ethical values discussed here ought to be balanced against other forms of value, including economic success and national security. These questions are important – indeed, central – ones for any political community; but they cannot be answered until we are clear on what the ethical values *are* against which these competing claims are to be weighed.

I will therefore be focusing on these questions: what value, or set of values, is that one that ought to be foremost in the thoughts of those seeking to justify a particular practice of foreign policy? If there is some ethical principle identifying particular goals as worthy – or particular means as permissible, or impermissible – what is that principle? To these questions, I think there are potentially any number of answers; here, though, I focus only on two, which have proven to be particularly important visions of what it is that a state ought to be focusing on in its design of foreign policy. These two answers are, put most simply, a concern with *equality*, and a concern with *toleration*. These notions are both powerful ones within the liberal democratic tradition; our thinking about domestic politics tends to defend the thought that both intolerance (rightly understood) and inequality (rightly understood) are incompatible with liberal justice. Neither of them is obviously implausible, as a guide for the design of foreign policy. My claim, however, is that we can derive significantly different conclusions about foreign policy, depending upon which of these values is taken as primary. More work needs to be done, then, to figure out which of these values is rightly understood as more significant – in this context – than its alternative.

Equality, toleration, and foreign policy

The notion of *equality*, as used here, focuses on the moral equality of human persons, and their equal right to be free from unjustified forms of disadvantage. It argues that the moral unit of account, in the international realm, is the human being, rather than the cultures or states in which such humans exist. This sort of framework is foundational for those who, in the literature on global justice, understand themselves to be cosmopolitans; for these figures, global institutions ought to regard any collective entity as having only derivative and conditional moral status.[6] This vision of equality also helps us understand the distinctively democratic vision of political ethics; the state's power, we think, must ultimately be derived from and justifiable to the rights of individual persons. We respect collective entities like states, that is, only when and to the extent that this helps us provide equal rights to human beings. This cosmopolitanism also animates some discussions about migration rights; cosmopolitans frequently defend the thought that states have no rights to exclude unwanted would-be migrants, since the human right to freely move over the world's surface constrains the desire of any state to exclude the unwanted.[7] A theorist using this moral notion to analyse foreign policy would, then, ask this question: does this particular policy help create a world in which all people are able to exercise the rights that are rightly ascribed to all persons? The evil that attracts our most immediate attention, for this view, is the deprivation for some people of particular rights – including rights to be free from particular forms of poverty and inequality.

The notion of *tolerance* also begins with the rights of persons – but focuses on the particular right to help create, and to live within, cultural and political structures that are taken as valuable by those individual persons. What this means is that this notion of tolerance tends to focus on the rights of foreign communities to decide for themselves how to use their collective power – rather than insisting that this power ought to be used in defence of egalitarian values.[8] In John Rawls's writings on international justice, this vision of liberalism is used to ground his rejection of cosmopolitanism; liberal democracies must give other societies the space within which to decide for themselves how to live together, how to balance competing goods, and how to understand the nature of political right. Rawls's ideas here include a notion of human rights, as a constraint on legitimate self-determination; these human rights, though, do not include an individual right to a particular distribution, nor do they include a right to democratic governance.[9] Rawls's contention is that it would be objectionably intolerant for a liberal democratic state to seek to undermine an illiberal state's right to rule – and that this notion of intolerance precludes either military action or foreign policy designed to pressure illiberal states into providing their citizens with democratic rights. In the literature on migration, similarly, those who oppose the concept of open borders tend to emphasise the collective rights of self-determination, on which the nation has the right to exclude those who are unwanted – not because the unwanted have no rights but because principled deference is owed to each society's choices about how to define itself and its membership.[10] The evil attracting our immediate attention, on this view, is imperialism and colonialism – the illegitimate usurpation by a powerful society of another society's right to self-determination.

These two notions are not, I should emphasise, rightly understood as competitors to each other; any plausible view of foreign policy would have to include, at some level, both of these values. (Most of us, after all, dislike both poverty *and* colonialism.) I make here only the more moderate claim that which value we take to be most central can have a significant impact in our conclusions about the ethics of public policy. These two moral notions pull, in some cases, in very different directions; and which one we take to be more central will determine the direction in which we are likely to go. We can see this by examining two potential areas in which the ethical analysis of foreign policy might prove important: the context of poverty relief, and that of human rights protection.

Equality and toleration, part 1: poverty relief

There are very few states – and very few philosophers – who have publicly endorsed the global prevalence of extreme poverty. Political leaders in wealthy societies have sometimes emphasised the ways in which poverty abroad can sometimes affect the interests of those at home; extreme poverty makes calls for radicalism and political violence more likely to be heard. Sometimes, though, political leaders have sought to address global poverty in terms of moral values, as President Obama did towards the end of his second term:

> And so today, we reaffirm our belief that in the 21st century, no child should go to bed hungry, and no child should die from a mosquito bite, and no one should be denied opportunity because of where they're born or what gender or religion they are, or the color of their skin or who they love. All of us are born equal and we're all connected. And if a schoolhouse door is closed to a young girl, then we're all diminished . . . So I may only have six months left in office, but I'm here to say that whoever the next president is, development has to remain a fundamental pillar of American foreign policy and a key part of our work to lift up lives not just overseas, but here in the United States. (Applause.) If you care about human dignity, if you care about reducing violence and terrorism, if you care about fighting climate change, if you care about addressing inequality and creating trade and prosperity that works for all and not just some, then you're going to have to pay attention to development. You're going to have to make an investment.[11]

This notion of poverty as anathema to dignity – and the related notion that the wealthy states of the world ought, through their foreign policy, to work against that poverty – is an attractive one. The more difficult questions, though, come about in our analysis of two related issues. First: what, exactly, *is* poverty, understood as the thing against which our foreign policy ought to be working? And, second: what sort of policies are those that we are rightly allowed to deploy against that poverty?

We will answer these questions differently, I think, depending upon whether our primary moral concern is the *equality* of persons or *toleration* of that which they have built. A state that takes its primary concern to be with the equality of persons, understood as individuals, will generally have a fairly expansive notion, both of what poverty is and of how it might be alleviated. On the first, we may take the work of Amartya Sen as exemplary.[12] Sen's analysis of poverty begins with the thought that our moral attention ought to be directed at the lack of freedom that is the result of a lack of material goods; those without money, to put things simply, will find it difficult or impossible to achieve states of affairs that are valuable, including physical survival and the ability to thrive during social or economic unrest. Sen's argument, however, notes that we have no good moral reason to worry about a lack of money as a unique form of evil, when there are other forms of social and economic circumstances that prevent us from achieving these valuable states of affairs; gender hierarchy, racial marginalisation, and caste structures broadly understood all have the ability to make a flourishing life more difficult to obtain. Sen's argument, then, entails that work against poverty demands alteration not simply in who owns what things but in how people understand their roles within society itself.

I use Sen as an exemplar of the egalitarian tradition for two reasons: first, because his work has been enormously influential – both in the academy and in practice – and, second, because that work consistently grounds itself on an image of the human person as entitled to the circumstances under which they are rightly understood as free. A state whose foreign policy is premised on the avoidance of poverty, on Sen's view, must work against all those forms of social institutions that undermine human freedom. Thus, the World Bank in 2012 – in a report showing the influence of Sen's ideas – argued that development out of poverty required that both states and transnational bodies work to increase respect for women's rights in Africa, in part through a decreased role for tribal and customary forms of self-governance among African tribal communities.[13] The thought, then, is that a foreign policy seeking to undermine the wrong of poverty must also undermine the wrong of marginalisation and unfreedom generally – and that these latter forms of wrongs may require a foreign policy intended to make it more difficult for existing communities to continue their current patterns of cultural and legal governance. A liberalism that begins with equality, most broadly, must approach the issue of poverty with the thought that working against poverty may legitimately involve undermining the political and social fabric of another society. Even those whose foreign policy does not depend upon Sen's expansive notion of poverty accept this general thought; Leif Wenar's analysis of oil-producing countries, for instance, entails that countries such as the United States ought to refuse to trade in oil from countries that routinely engage in domestic practices we regard as unrightful.[14] Wenar's chosen policy tool is a Clean Trade Act, on which countries must meet a particular standard of rights protection before we are morally permitted to purchase the oil that grounds that country's economy.

A foreign policy that begins with toleration, by contrast, may regard these policy conclusions as worrisome. John Rawls's Law of Peoples, for instance, regards the effort by a democratic country to sanction or pressure a non-democratic country into democratising to be an intolerant, and hence illiberal, action. More generally, though, Rawls's Law of Peoples would regard the thought that we may define poverty with reference to a particular vision of what counts as an objectionable lack of freedom – and then use foreign policy to undermine poverty so understood – as potentially a source of objectionable parochialism. The charge, here, is that we are unlikely from the outside to understand the ways in which a given society's practices are lived and understood by its members, and that our reactions might reflect our own ignorance and local values as to reflect universally valid principles of right. In distributive justice, Rawls argues that it would be objectionable for any society to seek to make another country revise its own economic system so as to more closely resemble our own; even Rawls's own distributive conclusions, so carefully defended over the course of his career, cannot for him serve as the basis of rightful foreign policy. This is not, of course, mere relativism; there are human rights, even in Rawls's system, that set the limits of membership in international society, and the liberal state need not actually think that illiberal states are as justifiable as liberal ones. The liberal state, however, would likely not be living up to its own values of tolerance were it to use the robust forms of foreign policy instruments described earlier. Rawls's attitude towards women's rights is complex, but it is worth noting in the present context that his Law of Peoples did not demand that women receive even formal legal rights in other societies; a consultation hierarchy that listened to women's concerns would be sufficient for membership in the society of peoples.[15] Thus, the recommendations from the World Bank Report would be, for Rawls, at the very least problematic; they would represent an effort by one democratic country to force the gender equality accepted (nominally) in that country upon an unwilling foreign community. More broadly, Rawls argued that neither global justice nor foreign policy requires us to seek global economic equality; we have an obligation, instead, to let foreign political communities decide for themselves upon the values they pursue, and if a given country chooses a pastoral economy over an industrial one, it is their right to do so – as it is their right to bear the economic costs that follow from making that choice. A liberalism like Rawls's, then, would constrain to some degree the right of individual states to decide upon the internal politics of other states, even when they are convinced that those politics are wrongful. Such a view of foreign policy would not demand respect for any society, no matter how wretched – Wenar's analysis, though it begins with equality, might be acceptable on Rawls's conception of international human rights – but it would have a standing reason to think that we ought to be moderate, both in how able we are to judge the internal practices of another society and in how free we are to act upon those judgements.

Equality and toleration, part 2: human rights

Human rights, as a legal concept, are the signature development of international law in the latter half of the twentieth century. The thought that we might be able to stand in judgement of another society's actions towards its own citizens – and to have that judgement backed up, potentially and sometimes in actuality, by force of arms – is a novel one, in historical context. I understand the function of human rights as being both a constraint on policy – whether domestic or foreign – and a justification for policy. That is: the fact that a given policy entails the violation of international human rights norms is a presumptive moral reason against that policy. The fact that some other country is violating those norms, moreover, creates in other states the moral right to do what is generally forbidden, including – in the limit case – the right to use military force.

If human rights are a legal fact, though, we might want to question the role for ethics; we have information about what these rights are, and so we must comply, and that compliance might not require the skills of a philosopher. This response is tempting, but wrong. Human rights are, despite their legal status, subject to an enormous amount of uncertainty, both as to their existence and to their relative weighting. On the former, we may note that Thomas Frank argued – in 1992 – that international law should be read as including a right to democratic governance; John Rawls, writing later in that decade, argued that international law neither did nor should include that right.[16] On the latter, we may note that different political communities – even those who are signatories to the most important human rights treaties – disagree quite profoundly about the importance of the right to free speech, especially blasphemous or offensive speech.[17] More generally, the simple fact remains that states can help to create new rights – or help to undermine existing ones – through their foreign policy; what states do can help create a new understanding of what states *ought* to do. When deciding what to do about human rights, then, what should the liberal state take as its ethical framework?

A view beginning with the equality of persons would likely begin by emphasising the universality of human rights. If, as President Obama argues earlier, human rights are grounded in dignity, and if all humans are alike in their moral title to be treated as creatures with dignity, then there can be no derogation by any particular culture or society from the demands of human rights. The work of Martha Nussbaum, in particular, has provided a robust vision of how this sort of egalitarianism would proceed.[18] Nussbaum provides a picture of cross-culturally valid forms of capability functioning – of aspects of life that ought to be included within a full human life – and argues that all persons ought to be provided with the tools needed to decide how to incorporate these freedoms into their lives. What this means, of course, is that all persons, male and female, ought to be provided with the tools to control their own bodies, their relationships, their physical and social environments, and so on. Nussbaum's conception of human rights is complex and powerful; for our purposes, it is enough to note that this conception of human rights permits states to act on behalf of the marginalised abroad, by working against those forms of oppression that would keep people from experiencing the forms of capability to which they are entitled. Nussbaum is aware that this might mean that some forms of cultural life will be rightly subjected to pressure, from other societies, for alteration. She responds, however, that the capabilities she discusses are susceptible of instantiation in a wide variety of different forms; we can maintain cultural diversity, and respect between cultures, so long as all cultures and all societies are able to provide people with the right forms of freedom. If the United States (for example) were to pressure China (for example) to respect particular human rights, that does not reflect a parochial belief in the superiority of the United States to China; rather, it reflects a moral belief that both the United States and China ought to develop their own forms of life within the bounds of moral right, and neither can cite its own cultural traditions as a reason to deviate from these bounds. None of this, of course, means that Nussbaum is committed to demanding any particular pattern of response to particular rights-abusers; she does not insist that there is only one valid foreign policy to be used against those who violate human rights. But she does insist that we are right to assert the universal validity of human rights; a respect for difference does not entail the obligation to respect those who violate human rights.

A foreign policy that began with toleration would echo some of these concerns; if human rights are to mean anything, they must mean that some states are able to use them to criticise the domestic acts of other states. A concern with toleration, however, would encourage us to notice certain facts about human rights as a practice that ought to be concerning. One of these is that human rights, as a practice, often involve the more powerful using them as a justification of acts undertaken against the less powerful. This is true both in the content of human rights law and in practices of enforcement. As regards content, we may note that Daniel Bell argues that Asian states – particularly those with a Confucian moral heritage – tend to prize filial loyalty more strongly than, for instance, the right of free political speech.[19] The fact that international human rights contain more concern with the former than with the latter reflects the fact that the international human rights tradition has often begun with Western notions of right and political justice, rather than with Asian ones. More broadly, though, there is a concern that the wealthy Westerners who have created the human rights tradition have not been willing to listen to the voices and traditions of Asians, preferring instead to think of them as moral inferiors in need of correction; Kishore Mahbubani, for instance, argues that even good-hearted Westerners are sometimes in the grip of fears of Oriental despotism, and therefore refuse to regard Asian forms of communal life as potential sources of value both for Asia and for the world.[20] These facts are coupled with concerns about the practice of enforcement; the more impoverished countries of the world are relatively unable to use international legal norms to actually change the behaviour of more wealthy states, while the more powerful states are able to use these norms selectively in the interests of domestic stakeholders. The International Court of Justice, for instance, has issued 39 indictments as of October 2016 – every one of them to a person of African descent.[21] The reasons for this pattern are complex, but reflect to a large degree the fact that the more wealthy signatories to the Rome Treaty would react poorly – if not violently – to the decision to subject their citizens to such an indictment. State officials in wealthy democracies are thus often insulated from liability for even grave abuses of human rights abroad. Even if, then, human rights are universally valid, we might have some worry about the decidedly non-universal way in which these rights actually link up to international politics.

The view of foreign policy that is premised upon toleration, then, might begin not by challenging the universality of some notion of human rights but by regarding those rights currently inscribed in law as an problematic basis for foreign policy. We have reason, this view might assert, to think that some of what we believe to be universally valid reflects local preference and tradition, rather than valid intercultural norm. We have reason, moreover, to worry that when a valid norm is used only by the powerful against the powerless, that norm might lose at least some of its moral power. We have reason, most broadly, to think that we might be subject to an enormous amount of bias in understanding and weighting the rights we value; to focus simply upon individuals' rights as we understand them, in isolation from the cultures and societies against whom our foreign policy is directed, risks intolerance in the name of moral right – a parochial insistence upon our own superiority, pressed by the powerful against the marginal.

Conclusions

What, though, can we learn from all the foregoing? One lesson, I think, is that values we often think mutually supportive in the domestic context might not sit together so neatly in the foreign context. Domestically, we might get tolerance and individual right as a sort of package deal, as it were; citizens are rightly understood as having individual rights, and these individual rights include a right to have one's form of life and personal decisions given some sort of tolerance. Individual right, that is, doesn't try to push up against toleration; instead, some of the rights we have are best understood with reference to ideas like toleration. In foreign policy, however, things are not quite so simple – and they are complex precisely because respecting foreign societies might mean ceasing to respect some subset of the rights held by foreign individuals. We might respect a country, that is, by refusing to act upon our own view of what legitimate government requires; we might, instead, respect foreign people, by refusing to take what the state says about the cultural relevance of its actions, and simply pushing that state to live up to what we believe to be rightful. Foreign policy, in short, requires us to get very clear indeed on what it is that we owe to outsiders – both as individuals and as societies.

I do not want to overstate the case here; it is true that even domestically we must sometimes choose between tolerance and equality, and it is equally true that internationally those theorists who begin with one value generally try to incorporate the latter. Rawls, as noted earlier, includes human rights as the limit of international toleration; Nussbaum relies on the notion that the rights she identifies are susceptible of multiple forms of realisation, such that cultural space is provided for self-determination; my own work has emphasised that we can be simultaneously confident in the truth of liberal democratic rights and modest in our claims to know what those rights demand. Nonetheless, these two values often lead us in different directions – tolerance towards forbearance, and deference towards the claims of foreign communities; equality towards agency, and a willingness to work for rights as we understand them. Both values, moreover, are powerful ones; even those of us who tend to rely upon one value must regard the other as a legitimate source of political guidance. We do not, finally, have any easily available meta-principle, with which we might rightly judge which of tolerance or equality ought to hold sway in a given dilemma; any such meta-principle would implicitly depend upon a particular view of which ethical value ought to be taken as basic for political reasoning. Even an appeal to democratic deliberation, for example, would require us to take a stand about why democracy matters, and whose deliberations ought to be dispositive – matters which can be resolved only through appeal to some notion of moral equality, which is the very notion we are seeking to illuminate. (Why would we value democratic deliberation, after all, except for some moral conviction about the moral equality of all those who participate in it?) We are, in short, stuck with irreducibly different moral norms, which will sometimes offer irreducibly different visions of what we ought to do.

What, then, is to be done? I can here offer only two ideas. The first is fairly bland: we have need for more guidance specifically about the ethical foundations of foreign policy. The literature on global justice is flourishing, and increasingly sophisticated; it would be good, though, if that literature was supplemented by more specific writing on ethics as applied to foreign policy.

The second, more helpful, thought, is that we might value and pursue those occasional bits of foreign policy guidance that would seem to be prized both for those who start with equality and for those who start with toleration.

I can offer here only two examples. The first deals with the practice of dumping cheap goods, produced with domestic subsidies, upon the markets of developing countries. This practice, which has been much condemned by Thomas Pogge, is still entirely too prevalent; a rich society uses tax revenue to produce a great deal of some commodity, and then sells the excess of that commodity at a price below market rate in some other country.[22] The wrongness of this practice is, we might say, overdetermined; a view beginning with equality would note that this practice tends to reduce the industrial base of the more impoverished country, making it more difficult for individuals within that country to ensure their continued security. If we rob that country of industry, after all, we rob it of jobs. A theorist who began with tolerance, in contrast, would likely begin by noting the ways in which this sort of practice undermines the ability of the impoverished society to determine its own economic future; self-determination requires some degree of collective freedom, and the wealthy country here uses its economic power to undermine that freedom for the less wealthy country. The second example is the trade in conflict commodities, whether diamonds or more contentious commodities, such as oil.[23] A theorist whose thought begins with equality would note simply the ways in which international trade can systematically incentivise the widespread violation of human rights. A theorist whose thoughts begin with tolerance, in contrast, would note the ways in which such conflicts often involve not simply individual oppression but also often collective oppression; conflict commodities emerge out of conflicts, after all, and many of these conflicts involve efforts from one powerful social group to oppress or annihilate some other social group.

If what I say here is correct, then, we may have some reason to prize those bits of ethical guidance that would seem to be correct on multiple visions of how to guide foreign policy. Philosophers generally avoid thinking about what it is that different theories agree about; our professional lives, at least, are often devoted to disagreement, and to the defence of one view over another. Our professional success, to be blunt, is premised on disagreeing with people, as a path towards defending our own distinct views. There is a place for this in writing about the ethics of foreign policy; we have reason to continue our collective search for an adequate theory here, and to defend the primacy of one value over others. There is, however, a greater *political* importance to be found in the fact of agreement. Ethics is, all too often, ignored entirely in discussions of foreign policy. Ethics is generally unwelcome; it prevents us from doing what we might want to do. We therefore often try to escape from these demands – by, among other things, rejecting the theories that ground these demands. In the present context, though, it might be good for us to make it harder for political leaders to do so, by emphasising that there are some ethical demands that seem to be demanded by *any* ethical theory – or, at least, any theory worth defending. All this, of course, is speculation; I am not well positioned to say how respect for ethics ought to be promoted among those who collectively determine foreign policy. I will be content, instead, if I have shown the need for a greater discussion of the ethics of foreign policy more generally.

Notes

1 I want to be clear that I do not think that foreign policy is necessarily a distinct field from public policy; this volume, after all, includes the former as a part of the latter. I only mean to note that, most of the time, public policy is assumed to be a domestic phenomenon.
2 The literature on justice in warfare is lengthy, and I cannot do justice to that literature here. See the chapter in this volume by Christopher Kutz for more details on how this literature has developed

3 The literature has now developed to the point that it has its own anthologies and overviews; see, for instance, Thom Brooks, ed., *The Global Justice Reader* (London: Wiley, 2008); Duncan Bell, ed., *Ethics and World Politics* (New York: Oxford University Press, 2010); and Gillian Brock and Darrel Moellendorf, eds., *Current Debates in Global Justice* (New York: Springer, 2005).

4 John Rawls's Law of Peoples is unusual precisely in that it purports to be an analysis of the ethics of foreign policy, rather than a theory of global justice. Nevertheless, Rawls's work here tends to focus on what principles could be agreed to by all reasonable peoples as a guide to their mutual interactions – rather than on the more direct question of what could justify the foreign policy of single state. See John Rawls, *The Law of Peoples* (Cambridge, MA: Harvard University Press, 1999); see also Michael Blake, *Justice and Foreign Policy* (Oxford: Oxford University Press, 2013).

5 Thus, Allen Buchanan argues that international lawbreaking might sometimes be justified as a method for the creation of novel and more ethically justifiable international legal rules. See Allen Buchanan, *Justice, Legitimacy, and Self-Determination* (Oxford: Oxford University Press, 2004).

6 The works of Thomas Pogge, Charles Beitz, Simon Caney, and Darrell Moellendorf are all canonical examples; each of these theorists develops views on which common humanity, rather than national self-determination, ought to be taken as basic for our theorising about global duties. See Thomas Pogge, *Realizing Rawls* (Ithaca, NY: Cornell University Press, 1989), and *Politics as Usual: What Lies Behind the Pro-Poor Rhetoric* (Cambridge: Policy Press, 2010); Charles Beitz, *Political Theory and International Relations* (Princeton, NJ: Princeton University Press, 1979); Simon Caney, *Justice Beyond Borders: A Global Political Theory* (Oxford: Oxford University Press, 2005); and Darrell Moellendorf, *Global Inequality Matters* (London: Palgrave MacMillan, 2009).

7 See, for instance, the cosmopolitan arguments of Joseph Carens, in his *The Ethics of Immigration* (Oxford: Oxford University Press, 2013); and of Kieran Oberman, "Immigration as a Human Right," in Sarah Fine and Lea Ypi, eds., *Migration in Political Theory* (Oxford: Oxford University Press, 2016).

8 Examples here include the theories of Michael Walzer, David Miller, and John Rawls. See Michael Walzer, *Spheres of Justice* (New York: Basic Books, 1986); David Miller, *National Responsibility and Global Justice* (Oxford: Oxford University Press, 2008); and John Rawls, *The Law of Peoples*.

9 See John Rawls, *The Law of Peoples*, 71–82.

10 See, in particular, David Miller, *Strangers in Our Midst: The Political Philosophy of Immigraton* (Oxford: Oxford University Press, 2016).

11 *Remarks by the President at the White House Summit on Global Development*, July 20, 2016. Available at https://obamawhitehouse.archives.gov/the-press-office/2016/07/20/remarks-president-white-house-summit-global-development.

12 Sen's view of poverty is laid out over the course of a number of books and articles; the most concise description of that view is likely found in his *Development as Freedom* (New York: Random House, 1999).

13 The 2012 World Bank Report on Gender Equality and Development focuses on women's agency as a site for development work; its recommendations are far-reaching, and include alterations in divorce law, increased access to contraception, and a reduction in the extent to which custom is taken as authoritative for dispute resolution in Africa. The report is available at https://siteresources.worldbank.org/INTWDR2012/Resources/7778105-1299699968583/7786210-1315936222006/Complete-Report.pdf.

14 Leif Wenar, *Blood Oil: Tyrants, Violence, and the Rules That Run the World* (Oxford: Oxford University Press, 2016).

15 John Rawls argues that women's human rights claims must be appropriately represented within the political apparatus of any society acting as a member of the society of peoples; Rawls does not, however, argue that these rights must include any democratic participatory rights for women themselves. See *The Law of Peoples*, 75–78.

16 See Thomas M. Franck, "The Emerging Right to Democratic Governance," 86(1) *American Journal of International Law* (January 1992); and John Rawls, *The Law of Peoples*.

17 Thus, in 2009, the United Nations Human Rights Council passed a resolution identifying the "defamation of religions" as a matter of human rights concern; the resolution was part of a wider package of initiatives designed to mark anti-religious speech – including, potentially, blasphemy – as legitimately controllable under international legal norms. The resolution is available at http://www2.ohchr.org/english/bodies/hrcouncil/docs/10session/A.HRC.10.L.11.pdf. These legal moves were met by opposition from many Western democracies, whose domestic constitutions generally favour the right to free speech over the right to be free from the experience of blasphemy.

18 See, most importantly, Martha Nussbaum, *Women and Human Development: The Capabilities Approach* (Cambridge: Cambridge University Press, 1999).

19 This fact is discussed in Daniel A. Bell's *East Meets West: Human Rights and Democracy in East Asia* (Princeton, NJ: Princeton University Press, 2000).

20 Kishore Mahbubai, *Can Asians Think?*, reprint edition (Singapore: Marshall Cavendish, 2007).

21 See Noah Feldman, "The International Criminal Court Is Too Focused on Africa," *Bloomberg.com*, October 26, 2016. Available at www.bloomberg.com/view/articles/2016-10-25/international-criminal-court-is-too-focused-on-africa

22 See Thomas Pogge, *World Poverty and Human Rights* (London: Polity Press, 2002).

23 See Leif Wenar, *Blood Oil*. For some worries about programs like Wenar's, see Jennifer Rubenstein, "The Misuse of Power, Not Bad Representation: Why It Is Beside the Point That No One Elected Oxfam," 22(2) *Journal of Political Philosophy* (June 2014) 204–230.

16

JUSTICE AND TRADE POLICY

Andrew Walton

What trade policy should we adopt? Should we have free trade or should we impose tariffs on imported goods? How should we respond when other countries impose tariffs on our exports? How should we protect intellectual property and how should we regulate foreign investment? Should we seek to harmonise production and labour standards with other countries? Should we impose lower tariffs on goods imported from developing countries? Should we impose trade sanctions on governments that violate the human rights of their citizens or engage in unjust wars? Few of these questions are new or particularly novel, but in a world of extensive global economic relations, they have considerable importance.

In this chapter I present a normative framework for addressing them. Broadly speaking, this requires exploring two theoretical matters. The first is: what moral principles are pertinent to formulating trade policy? We need to know, for example, whether a state's guiding consideration should be to enhance the lives of its citizens or whether it has duties to enhance the lives of citizens of other states or share the gains of trade fairly with other trading nations, or some combination, variant, or alternative to these ends. The second question is: how should these moral principles bear on trade policy? We need to know, for example, whether a demand to enhance the lives of individuals elsewhere asks us to shape our trade policy to this end or whether trade policy should be understood as part of a suite of policies that ought to realise this end together, but are not necessarily each directly tailored towards it.

Thus, I develop a framework for formulating trade policy by addressing these questions sequentially. In the first section, I introduce some terminology. In the second section, I discuss the moral principles pertinent to trade policy, canvassing recent arguments on this subject and clarifying some points of difference and disagreement between them. I indicate a position that I find plausible, but, for the purposes of the chapter, I proceed by identifying a moral principle concerned with improving the circumstances of the less advantaged globally that could be shared across different accounts of trade justice and is consistent with widely shared convictions that all countries, particularly currently wealthy liberal democracies, have duties to assist the very badly off in the world. In the third section, I consider how this demand ought to guide trade policy. Here I defend a position I call *policy-integrationism*, which holds that we should pursue such moral demands by arranging a suite of policies, or a 'basic structure', that combines to realise them, rather than focusing on whether any particular policy, such as trade policy, advances them directly. I mobilise this argument by exploring one live trade policy debate: the proposal that wealthy states ought to offer preferential terms of trade (e.g., reduced import tariffs) to developing countries that improve labour or living standards in their borders. The chapter endorses this proposal, but argues that analysis of it shows the importance of connecting trade with other policy areas.

Trade and trade policy

Before embarking on the major discussion of this chapter, it is useful to define some terms.

One common image suggested by the word 'trade' is two individuals exchanging goods. Perhaps A sells her pen to B for £1. Such an exchange can take place within or across the borders of a country. A similar exchange can occur between two states. For example, Country A might import a million pens produced in Country B, paying Country B £1 million for them. I shall refer to these kinds of interactions as 'transactions'.

I use this term to separate transactions from another image of 'trade' that takes a more structural form. Here the image of trade is a social practice with a set of rules to govern a regularised pattern of transactions. In the contemporary world, this practice is characterised by a large number of states forming agreements covering, among other things, tariff schedules across a range of industries, the protection of intellectual property, production standards, and means to settle disputes regarding trade conduct. I will use the term 'trade' for arrangements of this kind.

Within the terrain of trade, there are, at least, two areas of 'policy' that might be subjected to moral evaluation. First, we can consider the agreements and economic stances states make in relation to other states, such as the tariffs they impose on goods entering their country and the production standards they require these goods meet. I shall call this 'trade policy'. Second, we can consider the arrangements of a coordinating trade body, such as the World Trade Organization (WTO). These might include tariff and regulatory schedules the body demands countries adopt, negotiation protocol, and dispute settlement procedures. I shall call these 'trade rules'.

There are various ways in which transactions, trade policy, and trade rules connect and overlap. Trade rules may set parameters for transactions and it might be an aim of trade rules to harmonise trade policy. It may also be that what is defensible trade policy depends on the trade rules. Perhaps, for example, some trade policy is defensible only if a certain number of states adopt it and trade rules are an important means of ensuring this is the case. Nevertheless, it is useful to separate these various matters because it is possible to hold that different (even if, perhaps, overlapping) ethical considerations are pertinent to them. For instance, it can be argued that the concerns involved in transactions are largely duties that fall on specific actors – say, not to manipulate or exploit others – whereas the more systematic, organised nature of trade entails a collective duty to ensure *the practice* treats its participants fairly (cf. James 2005: 537).

Because it sits centrally in both prominent discussions of trade and the academic literature, trade policy (particularly that of wealthy states) will be my main focus in this chapter. With the terms delineated, we can now consider the first question posed in the introduction: what moral concerns might be thought pertinent to trade?

Justice and trade

There is a wide range of moral outlooks that might be thought to bear on trade and it is not possible to address them all here.[1] Instead, I shall outline four major lines of argument that I shall call the *basic rights conception*, the *exploitation conception*, the *trade fairness conception*, and the *global egalitarian conception*.[2] Following these summaries, I shall discuss some important points of difference between them.

The basic rights conception

The first account of moral principles pertinent to trade places emphasis on a set of basic rights its advocates believe all individuals hold. Accounts of these rights vary, but it is a widespread belief that all individuals hold various civil and political rights, rights to personal security, and rights to a certain level of social and economic opportunities or resources (cf. Shue 1996). Even those who deny the relevance of some moral principles to the international context accept that the protection and promotion of such rights is a universal demand that may have important bearing on global economic relations (cf. Blake 2001: 271; Nagel 2005: 131–132).[3]

It is worth noting that a list of basic rights owed to all persons may be quite extensive (cf. Cohen 2004). However, there is a trend in literature towards arguing that trade justice requires more than the protection and promotion of these rights. This trend has seen three prominent approaches to extending the moral demands pertinent to trade beyond it.

The exploitation conception

One such account focuses on the idea of exploitation. The conception has been most cogently developed by Risse (2007, 2012), Risse and Kurjanska (2008), and Risse and Wollner (2014). In essence, the view that runs across these texts is captured in Risse's objection to 'trade that comes at somebody's expense' (Risse 2012: 272). The thought here is that certain trade arrangements can take unfair advantage of certain actors and that such arrangements generate what amounts to 'ill-gotten gains' (Risse 2012: 272).

One instance of this worry concerns situations in which two countries are involved in trade, but the population of one country is oppressed. For example, they might be forced to work or have other human rights violated. In this case, Risse argues, any gains from trade that result from the oppression are tarnished and the 'conditions render trade partly constitutive of the oppression', giving 'the oppressed a complaint in fairness against the trading partner' (Risse 2007: 362). This concern aligns with the idea that the protection and promotion of basic rights are pertinent to trade, but adds a further objection focused on the distributions of trade's benefits that have emerged through such oppression.

Another version of this worry concerns the instances in which some actors benefit disproportionately from trade while others benefit too little. As Risse and Wollner (2014: 217–220) highlight, there are various ways in which the wrong here can be articulated. One account utilises some of the ideas canvassed in the previous section. It can be argued, for example, that an interaction (be it a transaction or trade) in which one actor had her rights violated and she receives less from the interaction as a result of this rights violation is wrong not only in the rights violation it involves but also in the distribution that results. Another account finds it objectionable if one actor is vulnerable and another actor utilises this vulnerability to benefit disproportionately from their interaction. Exploitation of these different kinds can involve a range of actors. An obvious case is companies that exploit the vulnerable position of potential workers, but it is also possible for wealthy states or large companies to exploit developing countries that desperately need to secure trade deals in order to provide opportunities or services for their populations. These concerns, Risse argues, give us reason to supplement our concern for basic rights with an anti-exploitation principle, which holds that it is objectionable if actors' 'contributions to the production of goods or the provision of services for export do not make them better off . . . to an extent warranted by the value of these contributions' (Risse 2012: 272).[4]

The trade fairness conception

The third view I will outline here places significance on the description of trade that I outlined in the introduction, as an ongoing system with a set of rules and regularised patterns of exchange. Aaron James argues that features of this kind classify trade as a 'social practice', specifically 'an international social practice of market reliance . . . in which countries mutually rely on common markets . . . for the sake of augmenting their national incomes' (James 2014: 178). A practice of this kind, James argues, generates 'requirements of structural equity', which demand that 'it distributes the benefits and burdens it creates according to a pattern that is reasonably acceptable to every country . . . affected' (James 2014: 179). It is in this way that James's view extends beyond a requirement to protect and promote basic rights and beyond anti-exploitation to a more egalitarian requirement of distributive justice.

Specifically, James contends that there are three moral principles particular to trade (cf. James 2012: 17–18; James 2014: 180–181). First, a principle of 'collective due care', which holds that states must protect people against the harms of trade, such as unemployment or wage suppression. Second, a principle of 'international relative gains', which holds that the increase in global wealth attributable to trade should be divided equally among trading nations, unless a greater share is given to poorer countries. This principle suggests something like the application of Rawls's difference principle (cf. Rawls 1971: 60–83) to distributing the gains of trade between trading states. Third, a 'principle of domestic relative gains', which holds that nations must distribute their share of the gains of trade fairly among their populations, either by dividing it equally or by dividing it unequally in a way that is beneficial to the worst off. This may mirror an application of the difference principle to how countries distribute their share internally.

The global egalitarian conception

The final conception to outline has some similarities to the *trade fairness conception*, but has a broader and more demanding understanding of these distributive requirements. The *global egalitarian conception* holds that we should distribute a wider set of resources or opportunities, including, but not limited to, the gains of trade, according to an egalitarian principle. For example, this could require that these goods are distributed so that all individuals or states have equal shares or allow inequalities that benefit the worse off, the latter reflecting a global difference principle that applies not directly to how we should distribute the gains of trade (as James's international relative gains principle does), but considers these gains part of a set of goods to which the principle should be applied together.

One version of this view is a global institutionalist account. On this account, the egalitarian distributive principle has bearing given the extent and nature of contemporary global relations. There is a similarity here to James's claim that egalitarian moral principles arise in the context of social practices of some kind. The difference is that the global egalitarian conception holds the relevant context to be a broader institutional context, such as the context of a global basic structure that, in a similar way to many states, regulates various aspects of political life, ranging from trade to environmental protection to war. It holds that it is the existence of such a basic structure that raises a requirement to distribute resources or opportunities fairly among those who live under it, perhaps because its affects are so profound and pervasive or because it is the relevant locus of reciprocal, coercive, or non-voluntary relations, and that, because our contemporary global architecture constitutes a basic structure, this requirement applies to our world (Beitz 1999; Walton 2009, 2014).

A somewhat different account is a non-institutional cosmopolitan view. On this account, the existence of institutional contexts is not pertinent to the application of a requirement to distribute resources or opportunities in an egalitarian fashion. Rather, individuals worldwide are entitled to an egalitarian share of resources or opportunities regardless of their institutional affiliations (Caney 2005: 102–147).

On either of these versions of the *global egalitarian conception*, transactions or trade takes a somewhat secondary role. To some extent, the argument for global egalitarian principles might be pressed regardless of their existence. Nevertheless, it is clear that such principles would have bearing on these matters. Because transactions and trade constitute certain kinds of opportunities and generate and distribute certain goods, there is a connection between them and the realisation of these principles. Thus, this final view amounts to positing that there is a broad egalitarian principle of distributive justice that pertains to trade.

Disagreements and a shared concern

Perhaps it will be clear that these conceptions are not necessarily in tension with one another, at least not completely. One could hold that the moral concerns pertinent to trade include respect for basic rights, a rejection of exploitation, and a demand that the gains of trade are distributed fairly. Nevertheless, there are certain ways in which these views come apart.

A main area of disagreement reflects a dispute that pervades the wider literature on global justice concerning the foundations of (certain) moral principles. Essentially, the main question here is: what "gives rise" to a requirement to distribute goods in an egalitarian fashion? As noted earlier, some views hold that certain kinds of social or institutional contexts must exist before this requirement has bearing. Non-institutional cosmopolitans disagree with this claim (cf. Caney 2005: 111). Advocates of the *basic rights conception* hold that the existence of some such context is important and that the relevant kind of context does not exist at the global level (Blake 2001; Nagel 2005). Advocates of the *exploitation conception*, the *trade fairness conception*, and the global institutionalist version of the *global egalitarian conception* agree about the importance of some such context existing, but claim that the relevant kind of context does exist at the global level. However, advocates of these views differ on what constitutes the relevant kind of context. Advocates of the *exploitation conception* and the *trade fairness conception* hold that it is trade that gives rise to such principles (cf. James 2012; Risse 2012), whereas advocates of the global institutionalist view hold that it is a global basic structure that gives rise to them (Walton 2009, 2014).

There are also disagreements on exactly which principles have bearing on trade. Although it is possible to hold a view that combines many of the concerns mentioned earlier, few authors do hold such a view. Those who endorse the *basic rights conception* generally do not endorse the concern for egalitarian principles, and many seem not to endorse the exploitation concern either. Some advocacy of the *exploitation conception* is partly in the vein of denying that broader egalitarian principles have bearing (cf. Risse & Wollner 2013: 393–400; Risse & Wollner 2014: 205–208). Meanwhile, James's argument for egalitarian principles of trade fairness is made (partly) in challenge to those who hold that only basic rights are pertinent to trade, and those who endorse broader global egalitarian principles (James 2012: 6–14) and those who endorse the *global egalitarian conception* tend to reject narrower egalitarian principles that concern only the distribution of gains from trade (Walton 2014, forthcoming).[5]

While resolving these disagreements and considering how they relate to other considerations, such as efficiency or national security, that might bear on trade are important tasks for articulating a complete theory of trade justice, I will set them aside here in order to explore the other question raised in the introduction: how should moral principles should be used to guide the formulation of trade policy? This question can be explored somewhat independently. For this reason, to avoid prejudicing the discussion towards a particular conception I focus on a moral concern that bears some relation to each of them. This concern is nicely expressed by Barry and Reddy as 'improving the level of advantage of less advantaged persons in the world' (Barry & Reddy 2008: 3). Although this does not stress the idea of basic rights directly, it follows the spirit of this conception in aiming to assist the badly off in the world, and it is a concern that the other conceptions also accept in some form or other. Thus, it can serve to consider how a principle should be used to shape trade policy.

Justice and trade policy

Although it might seem that this chapter has already begun considering how to theorise trade policy, it is important to see a gap between what has been discussed and this further question. Joseph Raz captures the essence of this gap in his comment that 'political theory can conveniently be divided into two parts: a political morality and a theory of institutions' (Raz 1986: 3). 'Political morality consists in the principles which should guide political action', Raz continues, and, then, these principles are 'the basis on which the theory of institutions constructs arguments for having political institutions of this character rather than that' (Raz 1986: 3). In short, we should separate two aspects of theorising. First, there is a task of determining the moral principles that give us the aims of justice. Second, there is a task of using these principles to guide a process of determining which institutions to adopt.

Occasionally these tasks are run together or the lines between them are blurred. It is plausible to believe that this assimilation has occurred in thinking about trade. It is quite straightforward to move from thinking that we should aim to improve the position of less-advantaged persons to the thought that trade policy should be used to promote this aim, especially if it would be a productive means of doing so. It is perhaps even easier to move between the idea that the gains of trade ought to be distributed in a fashion that treats trade's participants fairly and the idea that trade ought to be structured in a fashion that achieves this goal. But Raz's distinction should encourage us to see that articulating a theory of how principles should guide institutional design forms a necessary step between specifying a political morality and reaching conclusions about which policies we ought to adopt. There are various ways to approach this task. For the purposes of discussion here, I outline two.

The *policy-isolationist approach* holds that we ought to select policy by a criterion of which one best directly advances the moral standards of concern. Although I shall suggest that they do not fully adopt a *policy-isolationist approach*, the basic thrust of the position appears in Barry and Reddy's approach when they propose that a significant determinant of whether to select one policy or trade arrangement over another is 'whether it improves the level of advantage of less advantaged persons in the world to a greater extent' (Barry & Reddy 2008: 3). To see what this approach suggests, consider two trade policies. Trade Policy 1 is to set high trade tariffs on imports from countries where the less advantaged are particularly badly off. Trade Policy 2 is to set low tariffs on imports from these countries. Let us imagine that Trade Policy 1 more effectively enhances the position of those less-advantaged persons. The *policy-isolationist approach*, as captured by Barry and Reddy's proposal, would conclude that we should adopt Trade Policy 1.

This contrasts with the *policy-integrationist approach*, which holds that we ought to choose between trade policies by exploring how they combine with a wider array of policies and institutions to realise the moral standards of concern and selecting the set that would be most effective together. As an example, consider the two trade policies mentioned earlier. But now consider them alongside two aid policies. Aid Policy 1 gives low levels of aid to countries where the less advantaged are particularly badly off, and Aid Policy 2 gives high levels of aid to these countries. For the sake of argument, imagine that, when considered alone, Aid Policy 1 is more effective in improving the position of the less advantaged. But imagine that, through some type of compound effect, Trade Policy 1 and Aid Policy 1 combine more poorly than Trade Policy 2 and Aid Policy 2. Perhaps, for example, when only one policy area is considered, a cold shoulder approach is effective in improving the position of the less advantaged due to its symbolic tone, but when this approach is taken across a series of domains, it generates hostility and backlash. Meanwhile the more benevolent policies are ineffective in any individual case, but more effective when part of a comprehensive programme of friendly encouragement. The *policy-integrationist approach* places its focus on how policies work in conjunction in this fashion and selects the set that produces the best effects. In the suggested analysis, it recommends adopting Trade Policy 2 and Aid Policy 2, even though both of these policies seem sub-optimal when considered in isolation.

Although recent trade justice literature has offered various policy recommendations, my sense is that which of these approaches is employed has not been made explicit or defended. Thus, in what remains of this chapter, I shall now explore what arguments can be made in favour of each, beginning with the approach that I think is the more plausible.

Defending policy-integrationism

The case for *policy-integrationism* rests on the consideration that moral demands are commonly best addressed by multifaceted strategies that harness the combined effect of various policies. For this reason, assessing policies in isolation can misidentify good policy options, in a way that is avoided if we consider them in an integrationist fashion.

The plausibility of these claims can be demonstrated by working through some dimensions of a live policy debate in global trade concerning the following proposal:

> *Qualified market access*: Wealthy states ought to grant preferential market access (e.g., in the form of reduced trade tariffs) to developing countries that improve labour standards in their borders.[6]

The basic case for *qualified market access* is straightforward (cf. Stiglitz & Charlton 2005: 177; Barry & Reddy 2008: 30–33). Granting developing countries preferential access to the markets of wealthy states improves the former's economic prospects. It thereby sets an incentive and a realisable benefit to them. Meanwhile, tying this access to the improvements in labour standards means that obtaining this benefit moves alongside enhancement in wages, health and safety standards, and the protection of rights to collective bargaining and against forced or compulsory labour.[7] Improvements in these standards in developing countries plausibly would advance the position of the less advantaged in the world who currently work in low-paid, unsafe, unsanitary, and insecure jobs in these countries.

It is possible to argue that the focus of *qualified market access* should be broadened. Perhaps rather than labour standards, the proposal should focus on living standards, thereby ensuring improvements affect those outside employment or in less formal employment too. But the case for the proposal would hold in this guise as well.

The difficulty with the case begins to appear when the effects of it in practice are considered. As Stiglitz and Charlton (2005: 177–183, 191–193) note, the use and benefit of some existing trade preference schemes have been relatively low. There might be various reasons for this, but one appears to be a difficulty that faces developing countries' compliance with many WTO regulations: that adjusting to such regulations involves costs, including establishing new laws or conventions and their correlated accounting, monitoring, and enforcement systems. Although these sound like minor concerns, they tend to be quite significant for poorer countries, which require greater adjustments to comply with these regulations and whose legal and bureaucratic apparatuses are less developed.

Another argument is that using trade preference schemes linked to improving labour standards undermines one of the main economic advantages of developing countries (Barry & Reddy 2008: 36). Specifically, the thought is that developing countries have a comparative advantage grounded in the labour-intensive fashion they can produce goods given their lower labour standards. If labour standards are improved, production costs in these countries increase. The worry, then, is that they lose their comparative advantage and their goods are not competitive in international markets. There may also be a concern that it becomes unattractive for business to operate in these locations and these businesses relocate.

There is a way that both of these difficulties can be addressed. As Stiglitz and Charlton (2005: 204–208) note in relation to adjustment costs, it would be possible to offset these difficulties by programmes that offer developing countries assistance in reforming their systems. Similarly, as Barry and Reddy (2008: 37–40) note, it can be shown that there need be no loss in developing countries' comparative advantage if the additional production costs associated with improvements in labour standards are offset by wage subsidies, most plausibly financed by resource transfers from wealthier states.

But these points indicate precisely the case for *policy-integrationism*. When considered in isolation, it is not obvious that we should adopt *qualified market access*. Given the difficulties noted earlier, it is not clear that this proposal would be better than current trade policies (or free trade or symmetric market access) for improving the position of the less advantaged. Thus, a *policy-isolationist* approach would not have reason to endorse the proposal. But here we have an example of misidentifying good policy options. It is a misidentification because when considered in conjunction with supplementary policies, such as adjustment programmes or resource transfers, the case for adopting *qualified market access* as part of this set appears convincing. In short, it is through a *policy-integrationist* approach that the merits of the proposal and the most coherent policy selection become clear.

This point should not be particularly surprising. That the realisation of various aims typically requires using a range of often diverse policy levers is well established in other areas of public policy, particularly health care (cf. Wolff 2011: 128–146). It also has resonance with other areas of trade policy. For example, research on reducing child labour consistently shows that attempting to address the problem via one lever is less effective than adopting a multifaceted strategy (cf. Satz 2010: 162–169).

Making the point in general theoretical terms, John Rawls argues that we should 'distinguish between a single rule. . ., an institution. . ., and the basic structure of the social system as a whole' (Rawls 1971: 57). 'The reason for doing this', he argues, 'is that one or several rules of an arrangement may be unjust without the institution itself being so' – for example, when 'single rules and institutions are not by themselves sufficiently important' to affect or determine the quality of the overall system (Rawls 1971: 57).

What has been argued here supports Rawls's view by highlighting that, on many occasions, we cannot properly grasp whether a policy should be thought just without reflecting on how it combines with other policies. Given the way in which the realisation of moral demands depends on how multiple policies from a range of domains combine, it is valuable to think about responding to the moral concerns pertinent to trade by reflecting on how trade policy can be used as part of a suite of policies. We should, in short, approach trade policy selection by a method of *policy-integrationism*.

Alternatives to policy-integrationism

In what remains of this chapter, I will consider two lines of argument in the trade justice literature that might contest the *policy-integrationism* that has been defended earlier and point, rather, to a case for *policy-isolationism*.

The first argument concerns whether *policy-integrationism* is not properly sensitive to the nature of certain moral demands. Consider the case of forced labour. This practice remains disturbingly common and is present, despite being condemned, in global supply chains that are under the purview of our trade policy and trade rules (International Labour Organization 2017). We can imagine a trade policy that does not directly prohibit this practice. Perhaps our strategy for eradicating it is funnelled through our diplomatic policy, on the grounds, suggested earlier, that it is more effectively pursued this way than by tailoring trade policy to the end. Still, we may worry about such a trade policy. It might be argued that the structure of our normative concern with forced labour takes the form of a side constraint that ought to be respected, rather than a goal that ought to be promoted. In this regard, there might be a concern that the *policy-integrationism* approach is objectionably consequentialist, allowing or engaging in side-constraint violations, even if for the sake of maximising their protection overall. It may be thought that it is misaligned with what trade policy ought to regulate, focusing on how the combination of policies affects individuals overall rather than regulating the particular duties of particular actors towards particular others, such as those of companies to their workers. It could also be argued that focusing on the system rather than the particular components does not adequately take into account the nature of the wrong as it is experienced by those who suffer it or as it is perpetrated (cf. Goff forthcoming). In any of these ways, it might be argued that a *policy-isolationist* approach, focused on tailoring trade policy to regulate the precise duties of actors, is better attuned to the nature of, at least, some moral concerns pertinent to trade.

A response to these worries is to clarify that *policy-integrationism* should not be thought any more consequentialist than *policy-isolationism*. As noted earlier, it is a theory of how principles should be used to guide policy, not a theory of those principles. Thus, it is also concerned with regulating the particular duties of particular actors to other actors, if that is what the relevant moral principles demand. Its demarcating feature lies in holding that we should consider how these duties are regulated by a combination of policies, rather than by particular policies. What this position entails is not that our trade policy can engage in side-constraint violations or neglect the duties of companies to their workers if these wrongs are offset by the positives of our diplomatic policy. What it entails is that we should align our trade and diplomatic policies to ensure that these side constraints and duties are properly respected. If it endorses using diplomatic policy, rather than trade policy, to combat forced labour, that is because doing so ensures that we do not violate side constraints and that companies fulfil their duties to workers. The correct image, I think, is not one of doing the right thing 'on balance' but one of meeting the precise moral demands through whichever course of action best ensures they are met. In this respect, I think that concerns about the nature of relevant moral demands do not split, or, therefore, arbitrate between, the two approaches to policy formulation considered here.

A second line of argument to consider draws upon a theme mentioned in the foregoing discussion of conceptions of trade justice. A prominent argument in this literature is that different social practices have moral principles particular to them. It can also be thought that we should particularise how the policies or structures of these institutions are guided. Different arguments can be advanced for this view. It could be argued that trade is a separate or discrete domain of global politics, constituting a distinct social practice, that should be governed according to its own unique directives (cf. James 2012: 154–155). It can also be argued that the nature of current global politics in general is complex and patchwork and that to devise concrete guidance for any component, it makes practical and epistemic sense to think about its regulation in a particularised fashion rather than attempt to determine how an immense array of disjointed policies work together (cf. de Bres 2013). On these accounts perhaps there is reason to approach trade policy in a way that treats it more as a silo.

A response to this thought is to deny that trade can plausibly be treated as a separable sphere of global politics. Empirically, it can be argued that trade is very much entwined with other areas of policy, ranging from its connection to aid and resource transfers as discussed earlier to its connection to environmental protection in cap-and-trade emissions schemes and security in the use of economic sanctions to resolve civil and international conflicts (Walton 2014). This existing interconnection between domains suggests that it is both feasible and practical to formulate policy in an integrated fashion and, indeed, this is often deemed important in global politics because it is conducive to forming agreements to consider various domains of interstate relations simultaneously or as a unified package (cf. Caney 2012: 278–280) and it can help with enforcement and long-term cooperation (cf. Barry & Reddy 2008: 52–53). Normatively, it can be argued that the shape and effects of policies in these areas are pertinent to whether policies in other areas are just, because, for example, distributions of trade's benefits can be morally tarnished if they arise from injustices such as colonialism or the overuse of the world's resources or if they aggregate with the distributions of other goods to form significant overall inequalities between individuals or states (Walton forthcoming). In each of these respects, far from thinking that we should understand particularised normative principles or guidance as valuable for formulating trade policy, we should consider global politics integrated terrain that is more suited to *policy-integrationism*.

Conclusion

In essence, the central theme of this chapter is that thinking about justice in relation to trade and trade policy should not be limited to thinking about justice in relation to trade or trade policy alone. This theme emerged partly in discussion of the moral principles that bear on trade and was the main argument of how moral principles should be used to guide trade policy. As I noted, the point has bearing beyond trade. Insofar as health policy is one policy area among many that affect health and health is one moral concern among others in a theory of justice, formulating health policy is sensibly approached through consideration of its relation to these other matters. No doubt a similar argument can be made about policy for education, housing, labour markets, environmental protection, immigration, and so on, and this points in the direction of understanding these areas as components of a broader, cohesive whole. I have not had space to defend this more generalised thesis here. But the chapter has provided a rationale for this kind of integrationism that can be applied to these other areas and developed in this way, and, if nothing else, has shown why this framework is suitable for considering justice and trade policy.[8]

Notes

1 Another overview of the trade justice literature is de Bres (2016).
2 One account I do not consider is a libertarian account, which would hold that our rights to our person and property require allowing individuals to transact freely with each other (cf. Nozick 1974). This

view identifies no concern distinctive to trade and is not a major thread in current literature on the latter, so I set it aside.

3 Rawls (1999) also endorses this view. For an outline of the Rawlsian account see Walton (2015).

4 For discussion of how the gains of transactions can be divided fairly see Miller (2016).

5 Albeit with a slightly different focus, Christensen (2015) also argues that principles of trade justice must take account of broader moral concerns.

6 An overview of qualified market access and its application in the European Union's GSP+ scheme can be found in Herzog and Walton (2014). A version of the idea is also employed in fair trade (cf. Walton 2010). Thus, questions similar to those in this chapter can be asked about whether the aim of improving the position of the less advantaged gives individuals a reason to purchase fair trade goods, on which see Walton (2012, 2013).

7 The system may also reduce the incentive and feasibility of lowering labour standards to gain a comparative advantage.

8 For comments and discussion of the ideas in this chapter, I thank Derek Bell, Ali Emre Benli, Sarah Goff, Peter Jones, Beth Kahn, Graham Long, Erin Nash, Ian O'Flynn, Jo Swaffield, and an audience at the Newcastle University Political Philosophy Seminar Series.

References

Barry, C. & Reddy, S. (2008), *International Trade and Labor Standards: A Proposal for Linkage*. New York: Columbia University Press.

Beitz, C. (1999), *Political Theory and International Relations*. Princeton, NJ: Princeton University Press.

Blake, M. (2001), 'Distributive Justice, State Coercion, and Autonomy', *Philosophy & Public Affairs*, 30: 3, pp. 257–296.

Caney, S. (2005), *Justice Beyond Borders: A Global Political Theory*. Oxford: Oxford University Press.

———. (2012), 'Just Emissions', *Philosophy & Public Affairs*, 40: 4, pp. 255–300.

Christensen, J. (2015), 'Fair Trade, Formal Equality, and Preferential Treatment', *Social Theory and Practice*, 41: 3, pp. 505–526.

Cohen, J. (2004), 'Minimalism About Human Rights: The Most We Can Hope for?' *Journal of Political Philosophy*, 12: 2, pp. 190–213.

De Bres, H. (2013), 'Disaggregating Global Justice', *Social Theory and Practice*, 39: 3, pp. 432–435.

———. (2016), 'Justice and International Trade', *Philosophy Compass*, 11: 10, pp. 570–579.

Goff, S. (forthcoming), 'A Theory of Injustice in Global Trade, or: What We Can Learn About Injustice from Slavery in Global Supply Chains'.

Herzog, L. & Walton., A. (2014), 'Qualified Market Access and Inter-Disciplinarity', *Ethics and Global Politics*, 7: 2, pp. 83–94.

International Labour Organization (2017), 'International Labour Standards on Forced Labour', available at www.ilo.org/global/standards/subjects-covered-by-international-labour-standards/forced-labour/lang – en/index.htm. Accessed 28th February 2017.

James, A. (2005), 'Distributive Justice Without Sovereign Rule: The Case of Trade', *Social Theory and Practice*, 31: 4, pp. 533–559.

———. (2012), *Fairness in Practice: A Social Contract for a Global Economy*. Oxford: Oxford University Press.

——— (2014), 'A Theory of Fairness in Trade', *Moral Philosophy and Politics*, 1: 2, pp. 177–200.

Miller, D. (2017), 'Fair Trade: What Does It Mean and Why Does It Matter?' *Journal of Moral Philosophy*, 14: 3, pp. 249–269.

Nagel, T. (2005), 'The Problem of Global Justice', *Philosophy & Public Affairs*, 33: 2, pp. 113–147.

Nozick, R. (1974), *Anarchy, State, and Utopia*. Oxford: Blackwell.

Rawls, J. (1971), *A Theory of Justice: Original Edition*. Cambridge, MA: Harvard University Press.

———. (1999), *The Law of Peoples*. Cambridge, MA: Harvard University Press.

Raz, J. (1986), *The Morality of Freedom*. Oxford: Clarendon Press.

Risse, M. (2007), 'Fairness in Trade I: Obligations from Trading and the Pauper-Labour Argument', *Politics, Philosophy, and Economics*, 6: 3, pp. 355–377.

———. (2012), *On Global Justice*. Princeton, NJ: Princeton University Press.

Risse, M. & Kurjanska, M. (2008), 'Fairness in Trade II: Export Subsidies and the Fair Trade Movement', *Politics, Philosophy, and Economics*. 7: 1, pp. 29–56.

Risse, M. & Wollner, G. (2013), 'Critical Notice of Aaron James, *Fairness in Practice: A Social Contract for a Global Economy*', *Canadian Journal of Philosophy*, 43:3, pp. 382–401.

———— (2014), 'Three Images of Trade: On the Place of Trade in a Theory of Global Justice', *Moral Philosophy and Politics*, 1: 2, pp. 201–225.

Satz, D. (2010), *Why Some Things Should Not Be for Sale: The Moral Limits of Markets*. Oxford: Oxford University Press.

Shue, H. (1996), *Basic Rights: Subsistence, Affluence, and U.S. Foreign Policy*. Princeton, NJ: Princeton University Press.

Stiglitz, J. & Charlton, A. (2005), *Fair Trade for All: How Trade Can Promote Development*. Oxford: Oxford University Press.

Walton, A. (2009), 'Justice, Authority, and the World Order', *Journal of Global Ethics*, 5: 3, pp. 215–230.

————. (2010), 'What Is Fair Trade?' *Third World Quarterly*, 31: 3, pp. 431–447.

————. (2012), 'Consequentialism, Indirect Effects, and Fair Trade', *Utilitas*, 24: 1, pp. 126–138.

————. (2013), 'The Common Arguments for Fair Trade', *Political Studies*, 61: 3, pp. 691–706.

———— (2014), 'Do Moral Duties Arise from Global Trade?' *Moral Philosophy and Politics*, 1: 2, pp. 249–268.

————. (2015), 'Global Democracy in a Society of Peoples', *Critical Review of International Social and Political Philosophy*, 18: 6, pp. 577–598.

————. (forthcoming), 'Trade Justice: An Argument for Integrationist, Not Internal, Principles'.

Wolff, J. (2011), *Ethics and Public Policy: A Philosophical Inquiry*. London: Routledge.

17

DEMOCRATIC VALUES AND THE LIMITS OF WAR

Christopher Kutz

A democratic peace?

We live in an era of belligerent democracy, an unhappy sequel to the peaceful democratic transitions that unfolded across Latin America and Eastern Europe at the end of the twentieth century. Our current decade began with democratic aspirations voiced and dashed around the Mediterranean, and is ending with clearly authoritarian leaders claiming large democratic mandates. We live also in an era of democratic wars, when democratic states threaten and pursue violent conflict in the name of peaceable ends, ranging from democratisation to denuclearisation. We must therefore ask: does democracy as an ideal have an affinity for war?

It may seem an odd question, to be sure. For despite Churchill's famous quip – 'Democracy is the worst form of government, except for all those other forms that have been tried from time to time'[1] – democracy is seen as a source of both domestic and international flourishing. Democracy, understood roughly for now as a political system with wide suffrage, in which power is allocated to officials by popular election, can solve or help to solve a host of problems with stunning success. It solves the problem of revolutionary violence that condemns autocratic regimes, because mass politics can work at the ballot box rather than the streets. It can help solve the problem of famine, because the systems of free public communication and discussion that are essential to democratic politics are the backbone of the markets that have made democratic societies far richer than their competitors. It can help solve the problem of environmental despoliation, which occurs when those operating polluting factories (whether private citizens or the state) do not need to respond to harms visited upon a broad public. And democracy has been famously thought to help solve the problem of war, in the guise of the idea of the "peace among democratic nations" – an idea emerging with Immanuel Kant in the Enlightenment and given new energy with the wave of democratisation at the end of the twentieth century.

The "democratic peace" thesis, which holds that mature democracies rarely fight each other, has held up well as a correlation, even under sceptical scrutiny.[2] But closer scrutiny has also brought to light doubts about any broader, happy connection between war and democracy per se. Indeed, as political scientists Edward Mansfield and Jack Snyder have shown, emerging democracies are more likely than other kinds of states to go to war, often as a means of securing internal support and legitimacy (and in the process often stalling further democratic progress). Notable examples include France, Russia, Iran, and (former) Yugoslavia.[3] Meanwhile, mature democracies have shown great willingness to go to war against non-democracies, whether as part of colonialist and imperialist agendas, or for reasons of local or regional self-defence – think of the Spanish-American war, the Crimean War, the Iraq Wars, and the Balkan Wars. Democracy and war, it seems, are anything but adversaries. This is not news. Indeed, the "pro-democracy" or "freedom" agenda of G.W. Bush–era neo-conservatism came to be identified around the world as an expression of martial imperialism.

Discussions of the democratic peace thesis and the real purposes or effects of American "democracy promotion" are empirical questions. They are vital to politicians and international relations scholars. But philosophical, normative, questions about the relation between democracy and war, both civil and international, are equally urgent. Among those questions: how should we, as citizens, think about our responsibility for killing done in our name? Do democracies face special constraints in the kinds of weapons or tactics they can use, independent of the conventional law of war? Do democracies have a right or even an obligation to aid other peoples in achieving democratic governance, through force rather than example? Does the legal requirement that combatants be uniformed in order to be able to kill in war have any rationale beyond protecting civilians? What responsibilities do democratic revolutionaries have to property holders under the *ancien régime*?

As an ideal, democracy remains unchallenged, even unchallengeable. Twenty years ago, Francis Fukuyama declared 'the end of History', by which he meant that a history of grand ideological conflict had ended with the collapse of the Soviet empire, leaving only one governing philosophy in place: democratic liberalism, meaning popular control of political institutions, private property rights, and a market-dominated system of resource allocation.[4] Fukuyama was soon mocked for his declaration: even as the Cold War became a memory, geo-political conflict continued through decades defined by the resurgent tribalisms and post-nationalisms of the Balkans and Africa, as well as the broader contest between the forces of capitalist globalisation and anti-market Islamic fundamentalism. Even within the Western democracies, recent polling studies by political scientists Roberto Foa and Yascha Mounk suggest sharply declining support for democratic institutions among people under 45, with nearly a quarter of those between 16 and 24 agreeing that democratic institutions are a 'bad' or 'very bad' way to 'run this country'.[5]

Such negative views, doubtless grounded in cynicism about democratic institutions, are clearly rising, as is support for political parties clearly rejecting liberal equality- and rights-protecting values.[6] But even if history decisively has not ended, Fukuyama's central claim remains strong: within Western political thought, democracy has no extant challenger. The vocal authoritarianism of Putin, Orban, Erdogan, and Trump claims a democratic mandate, trumpeting vote counts.[7] On the broader global playing field, democracy's only remaining challengers are fundamentalism and Chinese-style managerial capitalism. The distance kept by the revolutionary Arab crowds from fundamentalism, especially in Egypt, makes the former an unwise bet; as to the latter, regardless of whether China can continue to suppress pro-democratic movements internally, its model represents a holding action at best, not a likely export.

Hegemony is a strong word, but it well describes the role of democracy within political theory, if not political practice. Political theorists compete with one another to offer more radical or fundamental forms of democracy for consumption and endorsement.[8] Legitimacy is defined in theoretical terms as the right to rule; the only evident source of that right is democracy, in one or another institutional form. The proto-democratic conception of the social contract, 'not worth the paper it's not printed on', to steal a line from Robert Nozick, has been replaced by demands for actual consent through universal suffrage and periodic elections.[9] What Bernard Williams called the 'Basic Legitimation Demand' can be met now only through the arrival of the people on the field of politics.[10]

My aim in this chapter is to introduce readers animated by the values of democracy to the ways in which those values can threaten to disrupt or subvert the delicate and incomplete historical achievement of finding ethical limits to war. This is not to argue against democracy, nor to challenge democracy's value as the ultimate ground of political legitimacy. Non-democracies fare far worse along these dimensions. Indeed, I argue that if we look to the values internal to democracy properly understood, as a kind of collective political agency manifesting mutual respect, we can provide surer footing for many of these concerns. As honest democrats, we must be prepared for an intimate critique of democracy in its relation to war, so that we can resist the temptation of too easily making the case for democracy's resort to violence.

My plan is as follows. First, I roughly sketch the central values and concerns of democracy, explaining why in my view democracy must be understood in terms of agency and mutual respect, not outcome or institution. Next, I offer a brief history of the ethical regulation of war, a history largely independent of democracy. But because democracy is now moral bedrock, I explore how we can justify, and to limit, war in democratic terms.

What is democracy?

Democracy refers to more than the institution of direct balloting and majoritarian-premised popular control over political office. More grandly, it names an ideal of universal and equal respect for all persons, for their right to direct themselves collectively and individually, including the right to get important decisions wrong. It attacks any claim of power founded in the unreason of tradition or force. The pre-requisites of effective democracy are the free movement of people and ideas, as well as institutions built to accommodate and – ideally – enhance the openness of each to the other, as we determine our projects together. Such institutions are the basis of the value of *security*: the confidence, embodied in such concrete institutions as police and fire departments, medical systems, armies and communications networks, that we will be able to execute the plans we make, to lead the lives we want to live. Closely linked to security is stability, and linked to both is dignity: the interest of each individual in having a life worth living, a life at least partly of one's own creation, proceeding along a predictable and self-planned path.[11] A final element in this constellation of democratic values is *community*: the good of living together, sharing tradition and meaning over past and future. So democracy, in its post-Enlightenment form, is essentially a humanism, committed to a politics of respect and recognition of individuals of equal worth, living lives of value, and with correlative claims to a say in common decisions about the use of collective resources, restrictions on individual liberty of action, and the meanings to be built into shared institutions.

Moral war without democracy

I will return in the next section to discuss democracy's peculiar relation to war. But first, it is worth looking quickly over the history of the theory of war. There are two general stories of the history of the ethics of war. Around the fifteenth century, with the preceding rise in a system of mutually recognised absolute sovereignty, begins to emerge a de-moralised picture of war, essentially as a prerogative of the sovereign who is not to be judged by any further terrestrial body, but only in the forum of victory. The second strand, already present in the medieval chivalric tradition, but gaining force with the professionalised militaries of the eighteenth century, is a professional ethic of the warrior. Both strands crystallise in the eighteenth century, the first in the work of Emerich de Vattel, the writer primarily responsible for the idea of "regular war" (*la guerre reglée*) or wars whose legitimacy comes from their form, rather than the justice of their cause. Vattel's work, which marks the essential break from a philosophical-theological tradition to a less normative "legal science," sets the scene for the theory of war that dominated thought from the Treaty of Utrecht to the end of the Cold War. This is the idea of a "regular war", or War in due form: a war waged between two public sovereigns, each asserting a right (to punish, to defend, and so on).[12] When a war is regular, although one may raise questions of justice concerning each side, actual judgement with withheld, and the two parties are permitted to contest until victory separates the righteous from the wrong.

The two strands, taken together, render the ethics of war as a peculiar form of cognitive dissonance: the internal morality of war, and the conduct of combatants, is heavily interlaced with norms and traditions of honour and protection of non-combatants, but surrounded by what is essentially an *external* amorality of international relations, where recourse to war is normal. Such a morality could barely claim to govern the period of Great Power warfare between sovereigns intent on maintaining geographical parity. And the ostensibly humanitarian rules of conduct did nothing to shield soldiers from trench gas in World War I, nor to shield civilians from area bombing in the second. The great break in this tradition followed World War II, with the UN charter and its restriction of war to self-defence, and the concomitant emergence of a conception of international human rights (which intersects in complex ways with international humanitarian law). While this intellectual and legal formation tilted again during the period of decolonisation of the 1960s and 1970s, providing (within the Additional Protocols) protection and combatant privileges for non-state actors, the system of state-centred legitimate violence remained generally intact. And the system, at least conceptually, has one great advantage: it permits a uniform set of humanitarian norms to apply to soldiers and civilians alike, with – in principle – gains in the reduction of suffering. Whatever the metaphysics of justice, the shift away from a view of soldiers and civilians as guilty of warmaking, and their location, instead, in a moral context seen as fully reciprocal, can offer them protection when they are most vulnerable.

Of course, any particular constellation of norms, laws, and historical understandings is unstable. It is remarkable that the regular war constellation endured as long as it did. But the instability now comes from new sources. The first source is the rise, connected intimately with the politics of the Middle East, of non-state-based violence, directed at both civilian and military targets. The second is the militarisation of human rights norms, under the aegis of humanitarian intervention. The first source has given rise to military conflicts embedded easily in a transnational conflict of basic values: religion and tradition versus modernity and markets. While of course the Cold War was also transnational and ideological, it was fundamentally state-based, and so the techniques of diplomacy and mutually advantageous trade could have some purchase over the conflict, as could the basic logic of deterrence. (Neither the USSR nor the US was, in the end, willing to gamble its own existence.) Conflicts between states and stateless (like al-Qaeda) or semi-stateless (like Hamas) forces take place out of the context of reciprocal threat and promise that can sustain a weak modicum of restraint. The end of reciprocity as a condition of war's constraint, as Mark Osiel has put it, entails on its own a need to rethink the foundations of humanitarian law.[13] To take one notorious example, treatment of captives is a problem of principle as well as practice, if one side, lacking a system of jails or justice, treats captives as objects of ransom (in a retreat to an older tradition), while the other finds itself tempted to discard in its entirety a legal regime crafted for a hierarchical and ordered military foe fighting a declared war in which victory or surrender is easily foreseen.[14] One may hope that non-reciprocal human rights norms of just treatment can fill what is far more than a gap, but that is hoping for a lot.

The rise of a muscular conception of human rights norms, backed by the willingness of nations and international organisations to deploy force, has also complicated the context of war. The change can of course be exaggerated. While there is a traditional rhetoric of absolute respect for the rights of sovereigns in their internal sphere, the rule is usually immediately qualified with an exception. Here is the great seventeenth-century Dutch natural law theorist Hugo Grotius, for example, echoing Suarez and de Vitoria:

> Though it is a rule established by the laws of nature and of social order, and a rule confirmed by all the records of history, that every sovereign is supreme judge in his own kingdom and over his own subjects, in whose disputes no foreign power can justly interfere. Yet where a Busiris, a Phalaris or a Thracian Diomede provoke their people to despair and resistance by unheard of cruelties, having themselves abandoned all the laws of nature, they lose the rights of independent sovereigns, and can no longer claim the privilege of the law of nations.[15]

Even with Vattel, the high-water mark conceptually of the system of independent states ('[A]ll states have a right to govern as they think proper, and no state has the smallest right to interfere in the rights of another') allows a qualified right of intervention against a flailing prince inflicting injury on his own people: 'But, if the prince, by violating the fundamental laws, gives his subjects a legal right to resist him . . . every foreign power has a right to succour an oppressed people who implore their assistance'.[16] The rhetorical tradition has, of course, a mirror in the practice of European states of interference in each other's affairs, frequently on the grounds of protecting religious minorities.[17] The masters of the field can be mined for nuggets endorsing cross-border interventions to rectify internal injustices. Grotius, for example, writes, 'If, however, the wrong is obvious, in case some [tyrant] should inflict upon his subjects such treatment as no one is warranted in inflicting, the exercise of the right vested in human society is not precluded'.[18]

The most robust conceptions of Westphalian sovereignty, as an absolute limit on external interference, have been more rhetoric than reality, including in Vattel's claim that the essence of nationhood lies in rights of non-interference.[19] But it is undeniable that conceptions of state autonomy have weakened, through a growing tradition of ostensible, and sometimes actual, humanitarian interventions. It is a tradition with admirable ideals if not always admirable integrity, encompassing Great Powers' interventions between Greece and Turkey in the 1820s, and Hitler's "protection" of the Sudeten Germans of Czechoslovakia, as well as the (so-far) better-judged intervention of NATO in Kosovo and Libya, and UN forces in East Timor.[20] (The problem, of course, is that virtually any territorial or resource control ambition in an under-governed region can be matched with a humanitarian concern.)

That said, the post-millennial politics of humanitarian intervention, under the rubric of the "Responsibility to Protect", or R2P, has caused a fundamental shift in post-WWII international conflicts. While the doctrine of R2P is, on its terms, limited to the prevention of civilian massacres – and while the practice remains extremely selective in its targets – the framework of international intervention has shifted, now to encompass the question of the prospects for reform in the targeted state. The effect is a gradual moralisation of international politics, a breaking of a fragile consensus around the limitation of the use of force to circumstances of strict self-defence. Many democratic idealists have been heartened by this shift, replacing the political realists' self-interested assessments of the costs and benefits of international interventions with a richer, cosmopolitan, and moral framework – even as they strive to separate their position from the neo-conservative emphasis on democracy growth. While the experience of Iraq has seemed to chasten the neo-conservative ambitions to remake the Middle East, and the politics of the Arab Spring of 2011 have further complicated the region, the reframing of conceptions of sovereignty and the triggers for intervention seem to have changed decisively.

Democracy and the problem of violence

The ethics of war as I have discussed it emerges from a state system and the concerns of reciprocity working to keep that system in external equilibrium; normative considerations internal to those states are irrelevant. One might therefore think that the problem of political violence is independent of the character of the state, for the place of political violence – incorporating both revolutionary and martial – in the origins and maintenance of states is universal. All states, democratic or not, honour their warrior-princes, their martyrs, and – in the modern age – their foot soldiers. Weber's classic definition of the state as the body claiming a monopoly on the legitimate violence presupposes the violence that lies at the origin of the state – if not as a matter of conceptual necessity, then as a matter of undisputed history.[21] Without violence (whether celebrated or shrouded in myths of origin), the circumstances of politics would not exist: a defined territory, a unifying system for resolving disputes between what is mine and thine, and common allegiance.

But we should be wary of fitting democratic states too easily into an international system that normalises collective violence. Democratic thought's invocation on the pacific virtues of shared deliberation and decision renders puzzling the ways in which modern democracies celebrate the uses they make of wars and violence, both in revolution and war. Violence – at least political violence – denies the voice and integrity of others, rejects their standing as equals in a shared dialogue about common causes and meanings – the essence of democratic self-government. And, indeed, mature democratic states have, over time, an outstanding record at rejecting violence in favour of dialogue, within their domestic spheres; the American Civil War stands out as an exception.[22] (The urge to democratic revolution also knows violence, of course, although the Eastern European and Tunisian experiences are encouraging models of recent, non-violent democratic revolution.) But the global record is less reassuring, whether as a product of colonialism, ideological conflict, or – most recently – a missionary conception of democracy, with the aim of seeding it as widely as possible. Democracies have, of course, the same instincts of self-defence as other regimes, as well as the same expansive capacity to understand the interests worth defending through resort to violence. Whether the trigger for war is naked colonialism, more subtle calculations of balances of power, the entanglements of treaties with democratic allies, or a universalist rhetoric of the defence of human rights, democracies use war as a routine and internally acceptable instrument of foreign policy.

And yet: the criminal law of the modern state, democratic and non-democratic, is virtually defined by the limits it places on private violence. With the exception of the homeowner's right of self-defence, there rests almost no license to its recourse. The restrictions of private law find their mirror in the law of nations: since the Kellogg-Briand pact of 1928, and further codified in the United Nations Charter, the right to war as a privilege of princes has been equally abrogated, left only in self-defence of territory or material interest.[23] One might well define the project of public international law as achieving for the international system something like the monopoly on violence exercised at the domestic level. Of course, the legal abolition of the right to non-defensive war has entailed nothing like its actual abolition, any more than its domestic abolition. If, in both cases, violence is now exercised in the face of the law, many are undeterred by law's sanction. Whether justified by tortured legal argument or simply executed in the teeth of the prohibition, violence, both private and political, persists.

At the international level, the ambivalence towards political violence lies in more than the gap between the abolitionist ideal and the reality of its exercise. It lies also in the laboured modern history of the doctrine of humanitarian intervention and its broader cousin, the Responsibility to Protect.[24] The doctrines are expansions of the right of national self- or other-defence, now including defence of persons and not just the state. Both have been and still are seen as a threat to the absolutism of Section 2(4) of the U.N. Charter, even if they give voice to an ideal of the protection of human dignity in their own form, existing only when exercised by the international community, or some substantial enough subset to claim legitimacy. It lies in the broad construal, accepted by international lawyers, of the right of military self-defence, extending beyond the right to defend territory to the right to protect one's nationals, wherever they are threatened, and the right to protect all the assets of national security, including electronic systems. And it lies in Additional Protocol II to the Geneva Convention (not universally accepted, to be sure), which grants the privilege of belligerency to insurgents fighting wars 'of national liberation'.[25] These doctrines and exceptions acknowledge that violence has the power to create and protect.

Of course truly self-defensive violence – violence justified to ward off violence – has the air of paradox. But it is only a debater's paradox, so long as one rejects the absolute prohibition on violence itself, and sees it instead as a cost to be minimised. But the ambivalence in democracies' reliance on violence is substantive. The ambivalence exists primarily across time, before and after the formation of what counts, in institutional terms, as a democracy. If democratic legitimacy resides, at first approximation, in the exercise of a universal franchise, then no acts preceding the exercise of franchise can claim *democratic* legitimacy. Thus, to justify its own origins, democratic theory must reach back into time, to link a group defined by its aspirations to its future status as popular assembly. The difficulty is that few or no rebellions or liberatory movements can actually define themselves in democratic terms, and hence can help themselves to democratic legitimacy only on terms of future credit. Put another way, the justification of the lives they take in revolutionary violence must come by the outcome such violence achieves, not any democratic process of its justification. Even the most velveteen of revolutions are not democratic in any institutionally meaningful sense.

To be sure, there are, indeed, distinctions among revolutionary movements: wider or narrower popular support, more or less dialogue-based ways of building that support; of greater or less attention to distinguishing non-combatants; greater or less independence from international interests. But it is fair to say, using history as our guide, that few revolutionary movements are likely to be fully respectful of the laws of war, grounded in essentially democratic politics – and triumphant. Historically, the democratic ambitions (both successful and failed) of the American, French, and Russian revolutions were largely independent of the military mobilisation or crowd violence that swept out the *anciens régimes*. At the other extreme stand the velvet revolutions of Eastern Europe, particularly in Poland and Czechoslovakia. Those revolutions, true, owe a great deal to popular mobilisation, democratic rhetoric, and – in Poland – genuine exercises in democratic votes. But even in these cases, success owed as much to the exogenous economic and political collapse of Soviet control as to the internal democratic practice of the revolutionaries. More generally, while contemporary revolutions – especially revolutions capable of winning the critical support of the democratic powers – will voice a democratic rhetoric, and will show their legitimacy through mass protest and mobilisation, their eventual legitimation comes after the risks have been run. Thus, if we are inclined to take revolutions as epitomes of popular will, we must leave behind the norm of democratic legitimacy.

An alternative is what has been called "performance legitimacy", or the legitimacy that accrues to any leader or group who delivers the goods of government, so to speak – namely, security, international status, and a functioning economic environment.[26] This is the basis for the legitimacy, such as it is, for many of the world's non-democratic states. If performance levels are high enough, then complaints about the lack of democratic legitimacy are tolerated, domestically and internationally.[27] But for groups at the margins of democracy, initiating new states themselves through revolution (often amid real performance incapacities), defending themselves from invaders despite non-democratic or non-existent domestic leadership, or projecting force into other states as a product of democratic transformation, neither performance nor democracy can provide. So what then is the proper source of legitimacy? What can distinguish the violence of all these struggles and transformations from pure murder and mayhem?

In my book, *On War and Democracy*,[28] I have attempted to argue that we must maintain our guard against the seductions of a particular understanding of democracy and its romance of collective agency. Democracy celebrates the politics of cooperation: the fusion of individual wills in crafting a common space. Put another way, it is the value of politics as such – the fusion of goals and wills in pursuit of a common system of civil life – that provides the legitimacy of non-state actors who are on the road to building democratic institutions. Democratic agency is a specific form of collective action, whereby agents orient themselves around shared goals and rules: voting, debating, supporting, rebelling, each with the thought, "I do this as part of what we do together".[29] Some forms of democratic, collective orientation are hierarchical, as when a subordinate follows the commands of a superior (or a superior issues those commands); sometimes it is collateral, as when we resolve together what we will do. The capacity to treat each other as collateral (mutual) authorities, and so to join our wills together, is if not uniquely human at least a distinctive feature of our humanity.[30]

This fusion of self in collective is the source of the violent threat posed by democracy. The very celebration of collective agency can lead to an overly permissive attitude towards collective violence. Seen no longer as an instrument of the king but instead an expression of popular will, democratic wars can seem to sanctify themselves. They offer a new form of "holy war", I have argued, one grounded in the comparative virtue of the democratic belligerent. But the temptation of democratic war rests on a misconception of democracy and the value of political agency: it takes democratic agency as something to be maximised rather than respected, as a value transferable from one state to another. The solution to the puzzle posed earlier, how democracy's irenic values can be reconciled with the ways democratic states rest on violence, comes from properly identifying the character of respect at the heart of democracy. Democratic values should be seen as constraints on both the forms and ends of collective violence, not as a new source of war's legitimacy.

Towards a democratic philosophy of war

I believe the proper task of the philosophy of war is to examine the clash between the demoralised legal and ethical modern conception of "regular war", with its conceptions of symmetry and its sharply bifurcated division of the *jus ad bellum* and the *jus in bello*, and the shift towards a borderless, re-moralised ethical framework for war. The further element is the need for the discussion of this clash to be rethought in the language of democratic legitimacy, which is the only active language we have now for working out a framework of fundamental ethical and political norms whose legitimacy lies beyond question. This is a different project than that of Jeffrey McMahan and Frances Kamm, whose aim is to locate war, democratic or not, within the broader space of deontological morality, and to define the values of individual liability and innocence that can, in their view, explain when lethal force is and is not justified.[31] Their project within the ethics of war has been influential and invaluable, in stressing the ways in which an ordinary, domestic morality of force and defence can be brought to bear on the topic of war. But my project, sketched here and laid out in my book, is distinct: it is to examine war's violence as essentially collective, and justifiable (if it is) only as the product of a form of collective political agency.

To take a simple example, a collection of individuals who raid an armoury to seize weapons are, variously, a conspiracy afoot, a rebellion, or a legitimate military operation. Their motives may be identical in all three cases: self-defence (or weakening an oppressive state). But the valence of their acts depends on the political context. The first act is one of criminality, the second one of martyred political idealism, the third a heroic act of war. Of course partisans will choose different labels for these acts — notoriously one person's traitor rebel is another's freedom fighter. But I believe we have to acknowledge that the metaphysical transformation of acts of collective violence, from criminality to legitimate war, goes beyond mere labels, and is anchored in an underlying recognition that political legitimacy can always find a ground in violence, and vice versa. A state's decision to equip its soldiers with uniforms accentuates the political character of their acts, but it does not create that character. In the case of democratic revolutionaries or resisters, the political quality comes from the will, not from the act of an invisible sovereign.

So how can democracy serve as both the source of legitimacy for mass violence and its resistance? At one level, if democracy is conceived as a value (like "goodness") then there is no puzzle: if democracy is an ultimate value in politics, then war and peace are instruments in its realisation. But if democracy's value is conceived instrumentally, then we should require a showing of evidence, as proof that it saves more lives than it takes (in, e.g., revolutionary efforts, or evangelical wars).[32] On the other side, if democracy is valued intrinsically, as the only way in which we can be both ruled and self-rulers, then its propensity for violence must be tamed.

Seeing violence as limited, but also in principle justifiable, by reference to democratic agency may seem to beg the question against philosophical pacifism, the view that resort to war can never be justified in political terms. I do take it as a given that wars and other forms of political violence are sometimes justifiable, that, for example, De Gaulle and Churchill were right while Pétain and Halifax were wrong in their decision to accept war. And regardless of whether the American, French, Chinese, South African, and Russian revolutions each took the best path to improving the well-being of the citizens concerned, I take it that in at least some of these cases, violent resistance was an appropriate response to colonial, feudal, and racist domination. While the just war tradition has attempted, by and large, to wrestle state violence within principled lines, it is fair to say that in its modern tradition, since Gentili and Grotius at least, it has been accepting of violence as an ordinary and permissible way of settling interstate disputes, whether flowing from an essentially theological conception of sovereign privileges, or from a political perspective. The comfort of the just war tradition with war (if not all wars) is easily documented.[33] Indeed, the tradition's conception of war as just punishment for injury done by another state has been an enormously pernicious force, in licensing a degree of violence that goes beyond the real justificatory core of any appeal to violence: self-defence. The justifications of self-defence end far short of the frontiers of actual wars, whose endpoints satisfy a range of concerns not linked directly to state survival.

The case for pacifism, like other forms of scepticism, seems to me rooted in a demand for justification of violence that is rational at its heart, and I cannot pretend confidence in the intuitions that deny its force. Given the dark record of war in achieving human goods, and the rarely run experiments in peaceful resistance, the case against pacifism seems to me weak as an empirical matter: it is a contest of "intuitions" about the state of the world we know, with its ready resort to war, versus one whose costs and benefits we can barely imagine, where aggression by some is resisted only non-violently. We can, therefore, bracket the question of pacifism, whether in fact, when one presses hard enough, any violence not self-evidently necessary and sufficient to prevent one's own personal demise (or the demise of those one cares about) can be justified.[34]

This is not to defend the easy acceptance of war, either in terms of a broad right of national self-defence, or in terms of a license to revolutionary violence. As I suggested earlier, we can accept that war, revolution, and anti-colonialist struggle are justified, at least when they are seen as the best possibility for avoiding or displacing occupation and oppression of various kinds. But to accept such violence is simply to report the fact that our ethics of politics, our meta-ethics of state violence, permits such violence that falls outside the frame of the state. Within the state, only that violence reasonably foreseeable as necessary to avoid immediate serious injury or death is permissible. But outside that frame, when the state is or has failed, we are more permissive, treating violent defence and emergence as birth- or growth-points for the state. This is a fixed point in our judgement, one that a theory must acknowledge, even if it works against it – and at the risk that the data point will anchor a *reductio ad absurdum* rather than mark the falling scales of toleration for violence.

Taking up a critical stance, then, entails two distinct but related tasks. The first is making sense of a political community's claim to be able to deploy violence in its name and for its ends, while restricting private violence among its members. This distinction between public and private violence (or between war and crime, in modern discussions) is fundamental to the nature of the state, sovereignty, and the conception of violence in human affairs. If a permission to use violence is seen to depend now on democratic credentials, then the link between democracy and force must be made clear. The second task is to define the limits of violence, in relation to not just the generic justification of self-defence but also the justifications presented by democracy itself. This is my central claim, adumbrated in my book: the conception of personhood that animates democracy demands a humility in the face of conflict, rather than the imperial assertiveness that has characterised so much democratic rhetoric, from the French Revolution to the Second Iraq War.

Our capacity for collateral authority and hence for collective action enables everything in human history, from shared harvest and hunts, to shared musical expression, to ritual, to shared deliberation, to revolution, to the construction of armies and parliaments, nuclear bombs and international treaties. The great irony of the military euphemism of "collateral damage" (referring to non-deliberately targeted death and destruction) is that our collateral capacity is our most precious value as persons. Such a capacity need not be exercised, obviously, in accordance with democratic norms – but it nonetheless lies at the root of democracy's claim to authority. The locus of democratic will lies in what I call "active community". Active community is built on a foundation of shared, intersecting, and competing loyalties. It defines not a people, not a state, and not a full community (in any communitarian sense), but it does reflect a body of people doing politics – in success or failure. The neo-Roman republican tradition resuscitated by Skinner and Pettit reflects a form of the ideal, in both its individual and collective forms. What is appealing about neo-Republicanism is the way in which a thin ideal, non-domination (regardless of whether it can be equally expressed in a liberal vocabulary), can be thickened into a quite comprehensive guide for the development of political institutions. The notion of a people, sovereign, that lies at the heart of the republican tradition has resources for explaining how political violence can be justified as democratic liberalism (or liberal democracy) – it is, in particular, the semi-collectivist character of republicanism that offers this promise, the ideal of a nation united.

Active community and the capacity for collective action define the substantial basis of democracy and are at the root of its value. But democracy's particular institutional structure is given by law, both domestic and international. Law is the skeleton of complex social institutions, the framework that makes possible the coordination over great spaces and times of plans for self-organisation. Since the egalitarian balance of voice in a democracy is such an idealisation, so distant from the messy imbalances of real power and privilege, democracies rest uniquely on law to maintain their character. This is the law not only of elections but also of governmental structure and the balance of institutional power. But, in a striking parallel to the role of violence, the role of law in democracies is equally Janus-faced. If law makes democracy possible, democracy can seem to make law unnecessary, by offering a separate claim to legitimacy hostile to the proceduralism inherent in democracies. Democracy, we might say, poses most strongly the question of the relation of legality and legitimacy to each other. Clearly they are not identical; legitimacy depends upon, but exceeds, legality. This is the insight of H.L.A. Hart and – quite differently – Carl Schmitt.[35] Legitimacy is instantiated, operationalised, and preserved through legality. Legality provides the "what" of legitimacy – the structure of the subject. But obviously legal forms can be abused, honoured in name but not principle, and so subvert legitimacy. More tendentiously, refusing to treat legal principles as (sometimes) evolving standards and instead insisting on their rigidity can undermine legitimacy by divorcing the form of government from its function (protecting public welfare). This is the point of those who insist on emergency delegations. But there are, of course, particular aspects of public life that depend on having sharp lines drawn (in a liberal democratic state, they include a commitment to democratic processes; basic human rights, including the right against torture and the right against undocumented detention; and free speech).

The more basic point, of course, is that the basis of the legitimacy of a state arises from the beliefs of its occupants – it is those beliefs, acceptances, and willingness to cooperate that give law its normativity and authority. That legitimacy, in both its normative and sociological senses, comes from community – from the consolidation of a group of people, living together, around a common set of norms. Community, in turn, is a product of collective agency, of individuals orienting their values and actions around one another, taking emotional and behavioural cues both from the groups as a whole and from leaders within that group.

For purposes of this inquiry, the dependence of democratic legitimacy on actual beliefs and practices means that even a relatively abstract account of war's character will be heavily inflected by changed social and technological developments. Just as the concept of regular war was undergirded by professional militias, and the humanitarian law of the twentieth century was grounded in the mass wars of that century, so too philosophical and ethical accounts of war must shift as both states and non-states turn increasingly to unmanned drones and (likely soon) autonomous weapons systems. Most poignantly for democracies, these technological shifts mean that citizens in democracies increasingly find themselves in wars with no democratic subjects (on their side) fighting. The decay of the concrete incentives of democratic accountability, grounded in demands of shared blood and treasure, makes all the more urgent a defence of the principles by which democracies must constrain their possibilities of violence.

Notes

1 Churchill apparently made the remark in 1947, after being voted out of office.
2 Edward D. Mansfield and Jack Snyder, *Electing to Fight: Why Emerging Democracies Go to War* (Cambridge, MA: The MIT Press, 2005).
3 See Mansfield and Snyder, Appendix.

4 Francis Fukuyama, "The End of History?" *The National Interest*, 16:3–18, 3 (1989).
5 Roberto Stefan Foa and Yascha Mounk, "The Democratic Disconnect," *Journal of Democracy*, 27:5–17, 8 (2016).
6 The remarkably strong showing of right-wing populist parties in France (the Front National took 34 per cent in the 2017 presidential elections) and Germany (13 per cent for the extreme right AfD party in the 2017 parliamentary elections) reflects rejections of universalist and cosmopolitan values by significant portions of the electorate.
7 For a discussion of authoritarianism's reliance on the rhetoric of democracy, see Steven Levitsky and Daniel Ziblatt, *How Democracies Die* (New York: Penguin Books, 2018). Hungary's prime minister Viktor Orban has declared the death of "the era of liberal democracy," but insists on the rebirth of "Christian democracy," understood as a culturally white and Christian state supported by the popular will. Marc Santora and Helene Bienvenu, "Secure in Hungary, Orban Readies for Battle in Brussels," *New York Times* (May 12, 2018). In the US, a signature feature of Donald Trump's campaign was that he, independently wealthy, could do the people's business without fear that his democratic mandate could be compromised by other elites.
8 See, for example, Benjamin Barber, *Strong Democracy* (Berkeley, CA: University of California Press, 1984), Drucilla Cornell, *Defending Ideals: War, Democracy, and Political Struggle* (New York: Routledge, 2004).
9 Robert Nozick, *Anarchy, State and Utopia* (New York: Basic Books, 1977), p. 287.
10 Bernard Williams, *In the Beginning Was the Deed: Realism and Moralism in Political Argument* (Princeton, NJ: Princeton University Press, 2005), p. 135.
11 I am referring to recent ideas of the idea of the good in liberal democratic theory. See John Rawls, *A Theory of Justice* (Cambridge, MA: Harvard University Press, rev. ed. 1999), esp. his discussion of a "thin theory of the good" as a basis for a common standard of assessment); and Ronald Dworkin's *Sovereign Virtue* (Cambridge, MA: Harvard University Press, 2000).
12 Emer de Vattel, *The Law of Nations* (1758), Bk, III, ch. iv, sec. 66. 'Since it is equally possible that either of the parties may have right on his side, – and since, in consequence of the independence of nations, that point is not to be decided by others (§ 40),—the condition of the two enemies is the same, while the war lasts'.
13 Mark Osiel, *The End of Reciprocity* (New York: Cambridge University Press, 2010).
14 One need not agree with the policies put in place to see the point in G.W. Bush White House counsel Alberto Gonzales's statement that the Geneva Convention conditions for prisoners of war, such as their right to recreation halls, seem "quaint" in application to al-Qaeda suspects. Obviously, the lesson is to discern a common principle of human treatment.
15 Grotius, *The Rights of War and Peace* [1625], Bk. II, Ch. 25, sec. 8 (trans. A.C. Campbell, 1901).
16 Vattel, Bk II, ch. 4, sec. 54.
17 See the nice account in Tonny Knudsen, "The History of Humanitarian Intervention: The Rule or the Exception?" accessed at http://zunia.org/uploads/media/knowledge/isa09_proceeding_3708011262835777.pdf.
18 Grotius, *Rights of War and Peace*, Book II, Ch.XXV, pp. 583–584.
19 See also Grotius, *Rights of War and Peace*, Book I, Ch.IV, pp. 157–158: 'the right to make war may be conceded against a king who openly shows himself the enemy of the whole people . . . for the will to govern and the will to destroy cannot coexist in the same person'.
20 Indeed, the nineteenth century is rife with examples of European military adventures under the banner of "preventing atrocities", especially in the Balkans – and it is a noteworthy feature of almost all the nineteenth- and indeed twentieth- and twenty-first-century incidents that the intervened-upon state is non-Christian.
21 Max Weber, "Politics as a Vocation" [1919]. Carl Schmitt famously argues (or asserts) that the suppressed foundation of every state is the power to protect friend from enemy. Schmitt, *The Concept of the Political* [1932].
22 Håvard Hegre et al., "Toward a Democratic Civil Peace? Democracy, Political Change, and Civil War, 1816–1992," *American Political Science Review*, 95: 33–48 (2001).
  It is a hard conceptual question whether the ante-bellum US really counted as a mature democracy, given the existence of slavery. But all historical measures of democracy are puzzling, since before the twentieth century virtually none accorded votes to at least half their adult citizens.
23 U.N. Charter 2(4); Kellogg-Briand Pact [1928]. See Oona Hathaway and Scott Shapiro, *The Internationalists: How a Radical Plan to Outlaw War Remade the World* (New York: Simon & Schuster, 2017).

24 At the domestic level, the ambivalence is reflected not just in the electoral uses of war but also (in the US anyway) in the celebration of vindictive violence in the criminal justice system.

25 Protocol Additional to the Geneva Conventions of 12 August 1949, and relating to the Protection of Victims of Non-International Armed Conflicts (Protocol II), 8 June 1977.

26 For the (widely used) concept of performance legitimacy, see, for example, Bruce Gilley, "The Determinants of State Legitimacy: Results for 72 Countries," *International Political Science Review*, 27: 47–71 (2006).

27 Of course there are dissidents both domestically and internationally who reject the legitimacy of performance-driven states as well.

28 *On War and Democracy* (Princeton, NJ: Princeton University Press, 2016).

29 My own account of collective agency is found in my *Complicity: Ethics and Law for a Collective Age* (Cambridge: Cambridge University Press, 2001). Two other principal accounts are those of Michael Bratman – for example, his *Shared Agency: A Planning Theory of Acting Together* (New York: Oxford University Press, 2014) – and Margaret Gilbert, *Joint Commitment: How We Make the Social World* (New York: Oxford University Press, 2015).

30 Fascinating recent empirical work by Michael Tomasello and his colleagues has pursued the idea that the capacity for complex cooperation is indeed uniquely human, although other primates share some of the relevant capacities. See his recent *A Natural History of Human Morality* (Cambridge, MA: Harvard University Press, 2016).

31 See, for example, Jeffrey McMahan, *Killing in War* (New York: Oxford University Press, 2011); and Frances Kamm, *Ethics for Enemies: Terror, Torture and War* (New York: Oxford University Press, 2013).

32 An extreme form of instrumentalism is found in Adam Przeworski, "Minimalist Conception of Democracy: A Defense," in *Democracy's Value*, ed. Ian Shapiro and Casiano Hacker-Cordòn (New York: Cambridge University Press, 1999). Przeworski treats democracy as essentially a low-violence way of distributing spoils in a regime. A more optimistic instrumentalism, in the Millian tradition, is found in Amartya Sen, *Development as Freedom* (New York: Knopf, 1999), where democracy is argued to drive social welfare gains, primarily through increased transparency and accountability.

33 See Michael Walzer, *Just and Unjust Wars* (New York: Basic Books, rev. ed., 2006).

34 For a powerful insistence that pacifism cannot be bracketed, but is fundamental to democratic politics, see Cheyney Ryan, "Pacifism," *Oxford Handbook on the Ethics of War*, ed. Seth Lazar and Helen Frowe (New York: Oxford University Press, 2016).

35 H.L.A. Hart, *The Concept of Law*, ed. Leslie Green (New York: Oxford University Press, 3rd. ed., 2012); Carl Schmitt, *The Crisis of Parliamentary Democracy* ([1923], Eng. trans. 1988).

PART III

Public policy, inclusion, and solidarity

18

THE POLITICAL ETHICS OF POLITICAL CAMPAIGNS

Dennis F. Thompson

Campaigns are an odd way to choose leaders. Corporations, universities, hospitals, and other organisations rely instead on search committees, trustee boards, outside consultants, and the like. Some of the most important public offices, such as judgeships, agency directorships, and cabinet positions, are made by appointment. It would be hard to argue that campaigns are necessary or desirable if the chief aim were to select the most qualified or the most deserving office holders according to any usual standard of merit. The political skills required for successful campaigning are only a small part of the qualifications needed for governing well, and in some respects what governing requires is the opposite of what campaigning requires (Gutmann and Thompson 2012).

What then is the democratic purpose of campaigns? I suggest that it is primarily to create conditions in which citizens can freely choose their leaders. Because the qualifications for these public offices are so varied and so contestable, we cannot specify in advance exactly the basis on which citizens should choose, and in any case we should expect that citizens may reasonably choose one leader over another for a variety of different reasons. If their choice is to produce a legitimate decision, they must be able to choose freely. The alternatives among which they choose are of course limited – arguably, too limited. But this constraint is imposed by the electoral system, which raises different ethical issues than campaign ethics (Thompson 2004).

Campaign ethics focuses on making the choice as free as possible within the constraints set by the electoral system. If making the choice as free as possible is the main purpose, what does free choice require? What criteria should we use to assess the extent to which campaigns promote free choice?

Recognising the limits of campaigns

Although political scientists no longer insist that campaigns have only 'minimal effects' (as the conventional wisdom in the field long held), they continue to find that campaigns largely reinforce attitudes that most voters had before the campaign started (Farrell and Schmitt-Beck 2002; Gardner 2009: 83–111; Erikson and Wlezien 2012). Most voters cast their vote on the basis of what political scientists call 'fundamentals' – such as the performance of the economy, partisan identification, and ideological compatibility (Campbell 2016). To protect their ability to cast their votes in this way is not only a more realistic aim of campaign ethics but also a more normatively acceptable aim. If voters were to so easily abandon long-held views about these fundamentals in the relatively brief period of a turbulent campaign, their choices would not likely be very well grounded. They would be the result of distortions created by the campaign.

Protecting voters from these distortions may be a modest aim, but the minimalist ethics of campaigns it suggests is nonetheless as important as it is neglected. (The approach here is also minimalist in another sense: it seeks to ground the ethics on a single principle, free choice, even though of course the electoral process may also be assessed by other principles as well.)

Some theorists favour more ambitious aims, and argue that campaigns should promote the purposes of deliberative democracy (Ackerman and Fishkin 2005; Bessette 2010; Orr 2013). Campaigns should enable citizens to reason together about the public good, and to learn from one another and their representatives through political discussion. Political scientists may be right about campaigns today, these theorists say, but surely campaigns could be made more deliberative in the future if we just try harder. Deliberative democracy is a normative theory, and should not defer so readily to empirical social science.

However, even a normative theory should pay attention to what is feasible (as the Kantian maxim counsels: 'ought' implies 'can'). More importantly, there are normative reasons to accept the limited role of campaigns in promoting deliberation (Thompson 2013). First, campaigns by their nature are strategic interactions, not deliberative exchanges. They do not function well if opponents are cooperating, rather than competing. They are supposed to provide voters with clear and distinct choices, which typically are highly partisan, and not best revealed through deliberative agreements.

The second problem with trying to make elections deliberative comes from the effect not on campaigns but on deliberation. Attempting to promote deliberation in campaigns discredits deliberation itself. Candidates and their supporters use reasons not primarily to reach agreement or encourage mutual respect, as deliberative democracy prescribes, but usually to gain advantage over opponents and to motivate their partisans, as campaign strategy requires. Under these conditions, attempts to encourage true deliberation are likely to give deliberation a bad name. Deliberative democrats should want to protect deliberation from campaigns. The aim of campaign ethics should be more protective than educative. (Deliberation may have a more important role in referendum campaigns, in which the people are directly making law.)

Protecting free choice

Given this limited function of campaigns and campaign ethics, what ethical standards should we use to assess the conduct of candidates? The standards should be directed towards protecting voters from practices that distort their free choice (Thompson 2004: 65–122). Voters are not free if they are led to believe false statements, or if they are pressured by irrational means to believe statements whether true or false. These two ways roughly correspond to Aristotle's modes of undermining free action: ignorance and compulsion (Aristotle 1963: III.1). An act is less free to the extent that it is done without knowledge of relevant information, or under pressures that act directly on the emotions rather than going through reason. Candidates and the media behave unethically when they interfere with the free choice of voters. They can do this in two ways (tracking the conditions of ignorance and compulsion): by providing misinformation, and by engaging in manipulation.

Candidates use many different techniques to misinform or manipulate (e.g., paying people not to vote, making fraudulent robo calls, initiating cybersquatting, and playing other dirty tricks), but I concentrate on communications – ads, speeches, and social media – because they illustrate most vividly the standards, and because they represent the largest expenditure of time and money.

Misinformation: distorting the content of the message

We should not expect candidates to provide all the information that might help their opponents or even the public. Full disclosure is not a standard to which we should hold candidates. But if we cannot expect candidates to be public educators, we can still demand that candidates be honest advocates. We can insist that they do not misinform voters. But misinforming is not as simple an act as it might seem. It takes several different forms.

Omissions

Communications can be true and relevant but still misleading because they omit essential facts. What you do not say can be as misleading as what you do say. One of the most disturbing kinds of omissions lies not in the content of the communication itself but in its context. What is too often omitted from an ad is who is paying for it. In US campaigns, there has been a dramatic decrease in the number of ads that do not disclose donors (Confessore 2014).

Why is this kind of omission objectionable? Should not voters judge the message, not the messenger? We usually regard it as a logical fallacy – ad hominem criticism – to attack the speaker instead of his or her arguments. If the argument is good (or bad), why should it matter who makes it?

The trouble is that in the case of most campaign ads, there are hardly any arguments. The effect of the ad depends largely on the credibility of the source. It is perfectly reasonable to want to know who is paying for it, if only to calibrate the level of one's suspicion.

Positive v. negative communications

Contrary to conventional wisdom, not all negative ads are harmful, and those that are harmful are not so because they are negative (Lau and Brown 2009; Elmelund-Præstekær and Svensson 2013). There is evidence that negative ads are more informative than positive ones (Sides et al. 2009). By their nature, negative ads have to be more specific and offer more evidence. Many negative ads actually increase turnout (although here the evidence is mixed).

But surely we want to object to some kinds of negative ads. In the final days of the Georgia Senate race in 2002, Saxby Chambliss ran an ad implying that his opponent Max Cleland was soft on terrorism because he voted against the Homeland Security bill (Gettleman 2002). The ad was objectionable not because it was negative but partly because it was misleading. Like a number of other senators, Cleland voted against the Homeland Security bill because it did not guarantee labour rights for federal workers in the new department. Cleland could hardly be said to be weak on national security issues: as a Vietnam veteran who lost both legs and an arm in the war, he consistently supported defence bills.

A further and more generalisable objection is not to this ad itself but to the fact that it was not effectively countered. Because it appeared so late in the campaign, Cleland was not able to respond with his own ad. At a critical moment on a sensitive issue, the content of the campaign was distorted, and the outcome affected by a particular charge that should not have had so much weight. Thus, the goal should be not to discourage negative ads but to make sure that there are adequate opportunities to respond to them. Candidates or others can then supply the missing facts to correct the misleading claims.

Half-truths v. flat-out lies

The director of 'Vote Leave', the successful 2016 campaign to get Britain to leave the European Union, has acknowledged that one of its most effective claims – that 'we send the EU £350m' every week – was an exaggeration (Cummings 2017). (About half is returned to the UK.) But the claim, he wrote in a post mortem on the campaign, was meant to provoke an argument by raising a real economic objection to remaining in the EU, which even the adjusted figure would support. He distinguished this kind of claim from 'flat-out lies', such as the prime minister's false assertion that under Brexit migrants would have to leave in six months if they did not have a job. We should not so easily excuse the exaggeration – misleading statements are not the best way to provoke productive arguments – but the distinction the director draws is important and increasingly relevant.

It used to be assumed that half-truths would be harder to counter than blatant lies. They seemed more insidious because they could not simply be denied or discredited by expert testimony. Outright lies, especially those involving publicly available facts or generally agreed-upon scientific findings, would be rare in a campaign. They could be easily challenged, would cast doubt on the credibility of the candidate, and ultimately prove counter-productive. It seemed perhaps less urgent for campaign ethics to condemn them.

But the 2016 presidential campaign in the US showed that a candidate can repeat falsehoods and make statements contrary to well-established scientific findings with apparently little or no cost. A Canadian newspaper compiled a systematic list of 560 falsehoods uttered by Donald Trump during the campaign, nearly all of which were contradicted by widely known facts or readily available public records (Dale and Talag 2016). Trump seems to have discovered a novel technique of disinformation: in addition to the familiar tactic of repeating a lie so often that it comes to be accepted as the truth, he multiplies the sheer number of lies, creating such a blizzard of untruth that, before any single lie can be exposed, another takes its place.

When the media environment is so fragmented and citizens rely on only sources that reinforce their prejudices, blatant lies go unchallenged, or if challenged, they persist, often even more firmly believed than before. The filters on which democratically healthy communication depends have been weakened, and the sources of truthful information have been deprived of much of their credibility.

Imbalances

Communications can be true and not misleading but still interfere with free choice. When the campaign is dominated by only a few issues or only a few voices, voters' attention and therefore their decision making are impoverished. They act with less information than they should have. This can happen in two ways – one involving issues, the other, influence.

Some *issues* such as a candidate's sexual misconduct or abuse of drugs even when relevant have a tendency to divert attention from other more important considerations. A kind of Gersham's law operates in a process in which the less relevant drives out the more relevant. Democratic accountability permits some exposure of the private lives of officials if such information is necessary for assessing past or likely future performance in office. This is the basis of a familiar 'relevance' standard: private conduct should be publicised to the extent that it is relevant to the performance in public office. But an often neglected point is that relevance is a matter of degree. The standard should not be interpreted as drawing a bright line between private and public life, which would allow the conduct to be publicised without limit once it has been deemed relevant. The standard, properly interpreted, seeks a proportionate balance between degree of relevance and extent of publicity (Thompson 2007).

Character is certainly relevant to the choice of political leaders – in some ways more relevant than positions on issues – but it is a special kind of character, which I call 'constitutional' (Thompson 2010). Constitutional character is the disposition to act, and to motivate others to act, according to the principles that constitute the democratic process. Constitutional virtues include sensitivity to the basic rights of citizenship, a respect for due process in the broadest sense, the sense of responsibility, tolerance of opposition, willingness to justify decisions, and a commitment to candour.

Some voices have more *influence* than they should because they have more resources than other citizens. In the US this is the result of a deeply flawed campaign finance system, and it violates principles of equality (though the Supreme Court has refused to accept this claim). However, the system can be shown also to violate a principle of free choice (Thompson 2004: 105–117). It creates an environment in which financial power shapes the conditions of choice in ways that citizens would reject if they had the opportunity. It is not that money should not have a role. It just should not dominate to the extent it does. It now distorts what voters hear and ultimately the conditions under which they choose.

Once we recognise that the underlying conflict in the reform debate is not simply between liberty and equality, we can take more seriously the possibility that free choice may be enhanced as well as constrained by campaign finance regulation. The constraining effects are emphasised by those who regard spending money on political causes as an expression of a free choice. Because money facilitates political speech, it enables some citizens to influence which candidates are nominated and what information voters receive. Any restriction on raising and spending money limits this influence and information. Money may also be necessary to counter another kind of influence – celebrity power – so prominent in the 2016 presidential election.

Yet the absence of such restrictions can also seriously undermine free choice. It can distort the information that voters receive and thereby make their choices less informed than they should be. The imbalance in political communication, the tilt towards the voices with more money, contributes to this distortion. So do the financial pressures on the media, which dilute the quality of political communication.

But distinct from the general problems of balance and quality is a further specific distortion, in which financial imbalance combines with informational omission. In a system of unregulated contributions and expenditures, voters cannot easily discover who is funding the candidates and for what purposes. They vote knowing little about the major contributors to whom the candidates are indebted and even less about what those contributors will ask of the candidates if they win. They cannot judge to what extent the candidate they vote for will represent their interests.

Thus from the perspective of campaign ethics, we should assess the regulation of campaign finance by balancing these various liberties, not simply by giving priority to the liberty to contribute and spend. Indeed, in the present system in most democracies, the latter liberty already tends to dominate, and balancing would call for greater limits on its scope.

Manipulation: distorting the mode of the message

The second way in which voters' choices can be undermined is by distorting not the content but the form of the communication. Candidates and their supporters try to manipulate voters. Manipulation involves a politician's attempt to influence your beliefs and actions (a) to serve his or her own ends, without regard to yours; and (b) with means that circumvent your rational faculties.

Manipulation is closely related to deception (including some of the types of misinforming already discussed). But not all manipulation is deceptive. Even when a manipulative act is deceptive, the manipulation adds a further distinct wrong to the act. Deception is typically a defensive, protective strategy: it is intended to deflect you from interfering with the deceiver's plans. Manipulation is more aggressive: it is intended to induce you to do the manipulator's bidding. It involves directly using another person only as a means. With deception, you obtain a kind of power similar to that of Hobbes's sovereign: the liberty to go your own way unimpeded. With manipulation, you acquire the kind of power that Machiavelli's prince exercised: the ability to make others go your way unaware.

Manipulation is therefore usually more insidious, and campaign ethics needs to pay special attention to it. How should we interpret the prohibition against the manipulator's short-circuiting of reason? It is unrealistic and undesirable to say that communications should never use emotional appeals that make claims that cooler heads would reject. That would take the passion —and the fun —out of politics.

But some kinds of appeals may go too far. Consider this test: manipulation is wrong when it exploits emotional reactions that are either (a) not morally respectable or (b) not psychologically controllable. If the message is false or misleading, that makes the manipulation worse. But even if the message is true, voters are still being used in ways that they cannot fully control, and for ends they may not agree with. They are being used as means only.

Going nuclear v. playing the race card

There is a plethora of manipulative ads, speeches, and tweets in recent elections, but step back and recall an ad that ran long ago in the early days of TV political advertising. It is the notorious daisy petal ad (officially known as 'Peace, Little Girl'), which the Democrats ran against Barry Goldwater in 1964 (Mann 2011). It actually ran only once, but it has become an icon in campaign advertising. It showed a young girl picking off the petals of a flower as a countdown to a nuclear launch and then an explosion are heard in the background.

In 1964, Goldwater's positions did seem more bellicose than Johnson's, more likely to risk nuclear war. In this respect the daisy petal ad might have accurately captured a relevant difference between the candidates at the time. But the powerful emotional appeal of the ad was designed to play on the most basic emotions of viewers and to evoke a response that went beyond any criticism of Goldwater that could be rationally justified. Goldwater certainly did not want a nuclear war any more than Johnson did.

But if this had been the only problem with the ad, we should not want to condemn it. It was manipulative, but at least the emotion it appealed to was morally admirable. It should be regarded as manipulative but not improperly so. The more serious problem was that the ad was also misleading: Johnson knew at the time that he intended to escalate the war in Vietnam. So the difference between the candidates was not so great after all. In this case, it is not the manipulation but the deception leading to misinformation that is objectionable.

Here is a contrasting example. The notorious Willy Horton ad run by the Republicans in 1988 more clearly fails the manipulation test (Museum 1988). As governor of Massachusetts, Michael Dukakis had supported prison reform, including a weekend release program that was widely thought to be successful. However, one of the convicts who received a weekend pass, Willy Horton, an African American, committed rape while he was out of prison.

The ad not only exaggerated the risks of the weekend release program but also was intended to exploit racial prejudices. It fails the proposed test – by playing on morally repugnant emotions. But is racial prejudice the only reason it fails? You might ask whether we should object if the ad had portrayed a white felon who had committed a crime while on release. Would that be objectionably manipulative too? Perhaps not as objectionably, but it would still fail on the first condition, that the reaction should be psychologically controllable.

October surprises

Information or announcements that come into the campaign at a point close to the election – so-called October surprises (Keller 2016) – count as another form of manipulation, because they do not allow time for responses and rational reflection and are therefore psychologically hard to resist. Some of the surprises are unavoidable – initiated by foreign powers (the release of the Iranian hostages) or mother nature (Hurricane Sandy in 2012). But others are deliberate and could be avoided (e.g., announcements of pending FBI investigations of candidates). Public opinion polls may also interfere with free choice by encouraging potential voters to base their decision to participate on what they see others doing rather than on their own autonomously determined reasons. To the extent that turnout is discouraged, the civic culture is impoverished, and the system of free choice eroded.

Social bots

In a major speech to Parliament in 2016, the German chancellor Angela Merkel called for a debate on the manipulation of public opinion by social bots (Copley 2016). A type of software program typically propagated on social network sites, social bots are designed to mimic human agents, often making users think the bot is a friend (or an enemy) and thereby winning their trust (or distrust) under false pretences. The bots are frequently used to spread false information and denigrating rumours. But even when employed for benign purposes, they should still be considered manipulative insofar as they deceive users about the communicator's identity in ways they cannot easily detect, and thereby circumvent their rational faculties only for the messenger's own ends. Germany's major political parties have pledged not to deploy bots in campaigns, but some experts warn that the anonymity of bots makes detection difficult, and in any case third parties might still use bots to try to discredit parties or politicians.

Denigration: distorting the system of free choice

So far the standards described here have focused on voters as individuals – prescribing what candidates should and should not do to enable a voter's choice to be more or less free. But a campaign might well support individual free choice but at the same time create an environment that makes the exercise of liberty more difficult – either for certain groups or for all citizens considered collectively. Candidates and their supporters distort the system of free choice when they denigrate individuals and groups. These failures could also be interpreted as violations of a principle of equality or equal respect, but in keeping with the minimalist framework proposed here I emphasise their effect on the free choice of those who are denigrated, and the practices that affect all participants who have to participate in a process that they would not choose.

Candidates who use racist and xenophobic rhetoric reveal serious character flaws and cause some citizens distress or fear. But they also degrade the campaign as a democratic practice. Although a campaign is a competition in which citizens choose sides, it is still part of a democratic process in which all citizens should have the freedom to participate on equal moral terms without fear of disrespect or implicit exclusion. Denigration is in this way a distinct wrong, even when it misleads and manipulates.

Campaign rhetoric does not have to be explicit to be denigrating. An especially insidious way to divide and denigrate citizens is the so-called dog whistle. The candidate makes a statement that seems to most listeners to make a legitimate (though perhaps disputable) point but that to others conveys a morally objectionable message. The candidate shows he agrees with the racists he is trying to reach, while preserving his respectability for the rest of the voters whom he doesn't want to offend.

On the campaign trail in 1980, Ronald Reagan gave a now infamous speech in Mississippi, where he told assembled supporters that 'I believe in states' rights . . . I believe we have distorted the balance of our government today by giving powers that were never intended to be given in the Constitution to that federal establishment' (*Neshoba Democrat* 2007). To some, this may have sounded like a statement on constitutional law. Yet to the residents of Neshoba County, where the speech was given, it was heard as an attack on what the immediate audience still viewed as an illegitimate federal imposition – the civil rights agenda. Not incidentally, the Neshoba County Fair was very close to the town of Philadelphia, Mississippi, where three civil rights activists were shot and killed in 1964. As one commentator wrote, Reagan 'was tapping out the code. It was understood that when politicians started chirping about "states' rights" to white people in places like Neshoba County they were saying that when it comes down to you and the blacks, we're with you' (Herbert 2007).

Even a simple request for information – asking for proof of citizenship – can send a denigrating message. The persistent demand to see Obama's birth certificate was intended to cast doubt on Obama's legitimacy, notably on racist grounds (Parker and Eder 2016). Ultimately, the demand lost its force with most citizens, partly because Obama himself mocked it (as at the White House Correspondents' Dinner in 2011). In this case humour was the best disinfectant for rhetorical offence.

Preventing denigration may take priority over providing information especially when the candidate's intention seems less to inform than to incite his followers. In the Netherlands, Geert Wilders, the far-right politician who was a leading contender to become prime minister, was convicted in 2016 of inciting discrimination and of insulting a group because he led a crowd at a political rally chanting, 'Fewer, fewer' to the question 'Do you want more or fewer Moroccans in this city and in the Netherlands?' (Siegal 2016). Wilders claimed he was only informing the public: 'Because I spoke the truth. I cannot take back the truth' (Transcript of Court Proceedings, 2016). His claim to be informing the public is obviously weak, as are most attempts to defend denigration by appealing to a supposed truth.

Designing institutional support

We should not underestimate the importance of clarifying and publicising ethical standards. That project can help create and sustain informal norms, which ultimately may be the most effective form of enforcement. Especially in the US, where the First Amendment reigns, informal pressures may often be one of the few ways to protect the free choice of some citizens from the abuse of free exercise of speech by others. But some changes in the institutions that affect campaigns should be considered. Here are a few examples (some admittedly quixotic).

Boards and commissions

Consider establishing a National Fact-Checking Board with a broad mandate to evaluate major speeches, ads, and debates of candidates. The Board would be nonpartisan, independent, and publicly funded. It could be modelled after the US Presidential Debate Commission, though with greater legal powers. Its mandate would go beyond pointing out misinformation; it would also be authorised to expose misleading statements, noting omissions, and criticising imbalances in the pattern of communication in the campaign. The Board would regularly publish reports, which the media regulated by the FCC would be required to air. With a large staff and respected professionals, the Board could over time build a reputation for fair and impartial appraisals of campaign conduct. Although voters do not pay much attention to fact checkers, elites do, and a Fact-Checking Board of this kind could by means of influence on opinion leaders have an indirect positive effect on campaign ethics In any case, we need to reaffirm what in the past seemed to go without saying – that truth telling is an essential standard of ethical campaigning.

Another commission, perhaps modelled after the Pulitzer Prize Committee or after a citizens' assembly, would award honours for exemplary campaign conduct. It would give special recognition to campaigns that consistently followed the ethical standards described here. Alternatively, the commission could announce ethical rankings – say, designating a campaign as a three-star enterprise, or a rally as a 90-point event. Any such recognition probably would have to be ongoing, revised from time to time, so that it could track the dynamics of the campaign.

Political parties

Political parties could develop new rules to control the conduct of their own candidates, and impose political penalties that might discourage the most egregious violations. Parties could strengthen their codes of conduct with more stringent sanctions (ACE 2012: 68–74, 80–81), which could range from expressions of disapproval to deregistration and withdrawal of financial support. Campaign managers guilty of violations would be black-listed, or in other ways blocked from working for party-endorsed candidates.

Public opinion

To avoid so-called October surprises, which do not give candidates time to respond or voters time to consider the implications, laws could restrict the kind of information released close to the election. Government agencies could be prevented from releasing reports or findings that could influence the outcome. Publication of public opinion surveys (and exit polls) could be more restricted than at present so as not to depress turnout and otherwise distort the final days of the campaign (16 EU countries already ban reporting of opinion polls close to the election; ACE 2013). Potential voters are less free if rather than deciding on their own, they make decisions about whether to vote only by considering whether others are voting.

Public forums

To control the tendencies towards civic disrespect and other forms of denigration, we could strengthen laws against defamation, carefully tailored for campaigns and focused on racial and other slurs by candidates or their official surrogates. There may be more room for regulation here than is commonly assumed (Marshall 2004; Rowbottom 2012).

In European countries, less encumbered than the US by deference to a constitutional provision like the First Amendment, offensive speech in campaigns can be prohibited if it denigrates groups and religions. In its 'fact sheet' on hate speech, the European Court of Human Rights (2016), while affirming the value of free expression, lists more than a dozen exceptions – such as ethnic, racial, and religious hate speech. (For a defence of regulating hate speech, see Waldron 2012.)

Campaign finance

The familiar reforms, especially public financing, could help make campaigns more ethical according to the standards described here (Campaign Finance Institute 2016; U.S. Library of Congress 2016). But some of the reforms should be specifically targeted to protecting voters' free choice by directing efforts more toward correcting imbalances than eliminating the influence of money, and more towards assisting voters in making decisions than in creating fair competition for candidates. Also, we should recognise that the length of campaigns may be just as important as the regulation of funding. Compared to the US, most other advanced democracies limit the campaign period (in some cases setting it as short as two weeks), and even without limits on spending do not experience the extreme forms of communication distortions seen in the US.

Strengthening civic obligations

Institutions alone cannot make campaigns more ethical. We can try to encourage politicians and their campaign managers to observe the minimal principles laid out earlier. But they are caught up in the heat of a campaign, and have an obligation to act zealously to support their own cause. To expect them to be notably public-spirited would be not only unrealistic but also in a professional sense unethical. It would be like expecting a defence lawyer to give equal weight to his client's interest in acquittal and the prosecutor's interest in conviction. The lawyer certainly has some obligations to the court (e.g., not to facilitate perjurious testimony), just as the campaign manager has an obligation not to encourage lies by his candidate. That is a higher standard than many managers now observe. But to find agents who have stronger obligations, we have to look beyond the campaigns themselves and turn to the media and ultimately to citizens.

Media

Even in an age of truthiness, the simple duty of truthfulness still has relevance. This traditional principle is still alive in many quarters of the professional world of journalism. It expresses not a commitment to pure objectivity or equal time but an obligation to report events and information as accurately and fairly as possible. The journalists who respect that obligation should be encouraged and praised. But they are under the increasing pressures of profit imperatives and special interests. No less disturbing is the fact that their role has been reduced by the fragmentation of the media and the rise of the Internet. Candidates and their supporters can use social media to bypass the traditional media completely and speak to the mass public directly.

These changes pose new challenges to journalists. How can journalists get the attention of the misinformed, who tend to read and watch only media that reinforce their mistaken views? When journalists do get the attention of these citizens, how can they overcome the widely shared distrust of so-called mainstream media? Some relatively innovative practices that journalists themselves have proposed may help (McBride and Rosenstiel 2014). Reporters and editors can be more transparent about their own processes of news gathering. They can show how they put together investigative reports, why they reject some information, why they trust some sources and not others. In short, they would write more stories about writing stories. A more far-reaching change would be to further develop what is called citizen journalism. Traditional media outlets could make more use of reports from what used to be called 'stringers' but who would now comprise thousands of volunteers throughout the polity and who would report and document events at times and places otherwise neglected. The sheer numbers might provide not only credibility but also reliability by means of what would be a form of crowd sourcing.

Social media are the source of much of what could be correctly called fake news, which has played an increasingly large role in campaigns. Sites like Facebook and Twitter – through their control over advertisers – could do much more to curtail the propagation of misinformation, misleading stories, and denigrating communication. But we should encourage another kind of fake news – the kind that T*he Daily Show, Last Week Tonight,* and other comedy outlets traffic in. Their 'journalists' make clear to their viewers that they are not simply reporting the news. But ironically much of what they present provides an accurate and often withering critique of their subjects, backed up with video clips that expose the inconsistencies and falsehoods of politicians (as well as the media).

Citizens

The duties of citizenship also become more challenging as politics become more polarised. The first duty of citizens in campaign ethics is simply to become better informed. There is actually plenty of accurate and diverse information available in campaigns, and citizens should try to look beyond sources that support only what they already think they believe. They should do so even if they do not intend to change their minds about fundamentals – and even when they should not do so. Some of the reforms already mentioned may enable citizens better to fulfil this duty, but ultimately any success depends on their own commitments and attitudes.

It may be too late to expect many current citizens to respect this duty, but surely it is not too late to try to help the next generation cultivate the dispositions and develop the knowledge necessary for responsible citizenship in democratic campaigns (Levinson 2012). That is why it is such an important part of any effort to make campaigns more ethical. Its importance also suggests a corollary: one of the most significant duties of current citizens is to try to ensure that the civic education of the next generation is more robust than theirs evidently has been.

Conclusion

In promoting campaign ethics, we should think less about how candidates can compete fairly or debate rationally, and more about what voters need to make decisions – what they need to exercise free choice. What voters need is not education about the common good but protection from misinformation and manipulation. This minimalist view of campaign ethics in effect adopts a political version of the Hippocratic oath: do no harm to voters' free choice.

Even so, we can have no confidence that politicians will soon rush to adopt the standards suggested here. Unless citizens themselves pay more attention to campaign ethics – and insist that candidates live up to their obligations to voters – the integrity of democratic campaigns will continue to suffer. Sooner or later, citizens will find ourselves supporting candidates like Luther Divine Knox, the Louisiana politician who once tried to run for governor of the state under a different name. In the hope of winning more votes, he went to court to change his legal name. His new name? 'None of the Above' (US Court 1979). If the integrity of our campaigns continues to deteriorate, we are likely to see – and perhaps even reluctantly welcome – many 'None of the Above's' on our ballots.

References

ACE Electoral Knowledge Network. (2012). *ACE encyclopaedia: Parties and candidates*, 2nd edition. Stockholm: ACE. Available online at: https://aceproject.org/ace-en/pdf/pc/view

ACE Electoral Knowledge Network. (2013). *ACE encyclopaedia: Media and elections*, 2nd edition. Stockholm: ACE. Available online at: https://aceproject.org/ace-en/pdf/me/view

Ackerman, Bruce and James S. Fishkin. (2005). *Deliberation day*. New Haven: Yale University Press.

Aristotle. (1963). *Works: Ethica nicomachea*, W.D. Ross ed. Oxford: Oxford University Press.

Bessette, Joseph. (2010). Should election campaigns be deliberative? *Election Law Journal* 93: 197–210.

Campaign Finance Institute. (2016). *Campaign finance bibliography*. Available online at: www.cfinst.org/about.aspx

Campbell, James E., ed. (2016). Elections in focus. *PS: Political Science & Politics* 49(4): 649–654 [see entire special issue].

Confessore, Nicholas. (2014). Secret money fueling a flood of political ads, *New York Times*, October 10, p. A1.

Copley, Caroline. (2016). Merkel fears social bots may manipulate German election, *Reuters Technology News*, November 24. Available online at: http://in.reuters.com/article/germany-merkel-socialbots-idINKBN13J1WR

Cummings, Dominic. (2017). On the referendum #21, *Dominic Cummings Blog*, January 19. Available online at https://dominiccummings.wordpress.com/2017/01/09/on-the-referendum-21-branching-histories-of-the-2016-referendum-and-the-frogs-before-the-storm-2/

Dale, D. and T. Talag. (2016). Donald Trump: The unauthorized database of false things, *Toronto Star*, November 4. Available online at: www.thestar.com/news/world/uselection/2016/11/04/donald-trump-the-unauthorized-database-of-false-things.html#analysis

Elmelund-Præstekær, Christian and Helle Mølgaard Svensson. (2013). Ebbs and flows of negative campaigning: A longitudinal study of the influence of contextual factors on Danish campaign rhetoric. *European Journal of Communication* 292: 230–239.

Erikson, Robert S. and Christopher Wlezien. (2012). *The timeline of presidential elections: How campaigns do and do not matter*. Chicago: University of Chicago Press.

European Court of Human Rights. (2016). *Fact sheet – hate speech*. Available online at: www.echr.coe.int/Documents/FS_Hate_speech_ENG.pdf

Farrell, David M. and Rüdiger Schmitt-Beck. (2002). *Do political campaigns matter?* New York: Routledge.

Gardner, James A. (2009). *What are campaigns for? The role of persuasion in electoral law and politics*. New York: Oxford University Press.

Gettleman, Jeffrey. (2002). Senator Cleland loses in an upset to Republican emphasizing defense, *New York Times*, November 6.

Gutmann, Amy and Dennis Thompson. (2012). *The spirit of compromise: Why governing demands it and campaigning undermines it*. Princeton, NJ: Princeton University Press.

Herbert, Bob. (2007). Righting Reagan's wrongs? *New York Times*, November 13, p. A29.

Keller, Jared. (2016). The strange history of the October surprise. *Smithsonian.com*. Available online at: www.smithsonianmag.com/history/strange-history-october-surprise-180960741/

Lau, Richard R. and Ivy Brown Rovner. (2009). Negative campaigning. *Annual Review of Political Science* 12: 285–306.

Levinson, Meira. (2012). *No citizen left behind*. Cambridge, MA: Harvard University Press.

Mann, Robert. (2011). *Daisy petals and mushroom clouds*. Baton Rouge: Louisiana State University Press.

Marshall, William P. (2004). False campaign speech and the first amendment. *University of Pennsylvania Law Review* 153: 285–323.

McBride, Kelly and Tom Rosenstiel, eds. (2014). *The new ethics of journalism*. Thousand Oaks CA: Sage.

Museum of the Moving Image. (1988). *Bush v. Dukakis; Willie Horton*. Available online at: www.livingroomcandidate.org/commercials/1988/willie-horton

Neshoba Democrat. (2007). Transcript of Ronald Reagan's 1980 Neshoba county fair speech, November 15. Available online at: http://neshobademocrat.com/Content/NEWS/News/Article/Transcript-of-Ronald-Reagan-s-1980-Neshoba-County-Fair-speech/2/297/15600

Orr, Graeme. (2013). Deliberation and electoral law. *Election Law Journal* 12(4): 421–434.

Parker, Ashley and Steve Eder. (2016). Inside the six weeks Donald Trump was a nonstop "birther", *New York Times*, July 2, p. A1.

Rowbottom, Jacob. (2012). Lies, manipulation and elections – controlling false campaign statements. *Oxford Journal of Legal Studies* 32(3): 507–535.

Sides, John, Keena Lipsitz and Matthew Grossmann. (2009). Do voters perceive negative campaigns as informative campaigns? *American Politics Research* 38(3): 502–530.

Siegal, Nina. (2016). Geert Wilders, Dutch politician, distracts from hate-speech trial with more vitriol, *New York Times*, October 31, p. A9.

Thompson, Dennis F. (2004). *Just elections: Creating a fair electoral process in the U.S.* Chicago: University of Chicago Press.

————. (2007). La vie privée des politiques. *Raison Publique* 6 (April): 61–72.

————. (2010). Constitutional character: Virtues and vices in presidential leadership. *Presidential Studies Quarterly* 40(1): 23–37.

————. (2013). Deliberate about, not in, elections. *Election Law Journal* 12(4): 372–385.

Transcript of Court Proceedings. (2016). Schiphol Netherlands, 2016. Available online at: https://gatesofvienna.net/2016/09/geert-wilders-on-trial-again-i-cannot-take-back-the-truth/, accessed August 11, 2018.

US Court of Appeal of Louisiana, First Circuit. (1979). *None of the Above* v. *Paul J. Hardy, William J. Guste, Jr. and Douglas Fowler*, 377 So. 2d 385.

US Library of Congress. (2016). *Regulation of campaign finance and free advertising: Austria, Canada, Finland, Israel, Japan, New Zealand, United Kingdom.* Available online at: www.loc.gov/law/help/campaign-finance-regulation/campaign-finance-regulations.pdf

Waldron, Jeremy. (2012). *The harm in hate speech.* Cambridge, MA: Harvard University Press.

19

SHOULD VOTING BE COMPULSORY? DEMOCRACY AND THE ETHICS OF VOTING

Annabelle Lever and Alexandru Volacu

The ethics of voting may seem a strange subject for a book on ethics and public policy. After all, one might think, once the state has ensured that all competent adults have legal rights to vote, is not the rest up to the conscience of voters? This intuitive way of thinking, however, ignores the way that the rules of voting are likely to reflect factual and normative assumptions about voters' behaviour, and may, in turn, affect what voters do. For example, many more people are likely to attend the polls if voting takes place at the weekend, rather than during the working week (Ballinger 2006, 20) and proportional representation is thought to boost turnout by 12 per cent (Margetts 2006, 29). Indeed, the differences among proportional systems affect the extent to which voters are encouraged to vote on local, as opposed to national, considerations, or to base their votes on strategic, as opposed to sincere, preferences. It is therefore difficult to distinguish sharply the questions of *whether and/or how* people should vote, given the rules in place, from the question of *what* those framing rules should be.[1]

Any normative evaluation of voting rules, and the moral duties that citizens have in respect to voting, cannot help but involve discussions on the nature and value of democracy. This becomes apparent when one considers contemporary debates about the politics and morality of compulsory voting. Compulsory voting (hereafter, 'CV') is often thought to be undemocratic because it imposes legal penalties on those who do not attend the polls at election time. However, there are many examples of CV in consolidated democracies, such as Australia (since 1924), Belgium (since 1893), Luxembourg (since 1919), and the Netherlands (between 1917 and 1967). In Latin America, CV has been an enduring electoral institution, even though it was introduced at an early stage of democratisation (as is the case of Bolivia and Uruguay) or during periods when the military exerted significant political power (as is the case of Brazil, Chile, Ecuador, and Peru). Moreover, its use has been energetically advocated by academics, 'think tanks' (Wertheimer 1975; Lijphart 1997; Hill 2002; Keaney and Rogers 2006; Birch 2009a, 2009b; Tin and Wieviorka 2011),[2] and even politicians, such as Barack Obama[3] or Geoffrey Hoon.[4] Thus, examining the arguments for and against the idea that CV is compatible with, and even necessary for, democracy enables us to investigate contemporary debates on the ethics of voting and their relationship to democratic principles and practice.

Democratic principles limit the ways we can evaluate competing arguments for CV. For example, democratic principles limit moralistic and paternalistic actions by the state, in the interests of protecting people's freedom and equality (J. Cohen 1996). They therefore limit the extent to which people can be forced to vote on moralistic or paternalistic grounds (Lever 2008; Maring 2016; Maskivker 2016). Democratic principles also constrain the arguments we can give against CV, because some forms of voluntary voting are incompatible with democratic ideas about what it is to treat people as free and equal. For example, we can imagine a system of voluntary voting in which citizens themselves have to organise elections, and take responsibility for ensuring that they are fair, as though elections were simply a private good, important only to the people who participate in them. Voluntary voting, then, is not intrinsically democratic. Nonetheless, this chapter shows, CV is generally at odds with democratic principles – whether we look at democracies in more idealistic or more realistic ways (Estlund 2008, 258–275). However, in unusual circumstances, CV may, perhaps, be justified.

Let's start by examining the case for CV as it is presented by Arend Lijphart, in his presidential address to the American Political Association, published in the *American Political Science Review* (Lijphart 1997). This article sparked the current interest in compulsory voting, and its strengths and weaknesses make it a particularly helpful guide to the political, as well as the moral, dimensions of voting.

Lijphart's argument for CV

Lijphart's case for compulsory voting can be summarised in the following four steps.

1   Low turnout at election time is a pervasive problem in most advanced democracies, and low turnout is associated with unequal turnout, because social groups do not abstain at the same rate (Lijphart 1997, 2–7). For example, the participation gap between manual and non-manual workers in Great Britain more than doubled: from around 5 per cent in 1997 to around 11 per cent in 2005. These results are not dissimilar in other countries (Birch 2009b). Moreover, as Ballinger notes, non-voting is now more common than voting in the 18–24 age group in the UK (Ballinger 2006, 14; Keaney and Rogers 2006, 11; more generally see Blais 2000, 49–54).

Low turnout is a concern for democracies, because it increases the probability that governments will be elected by a minority of the population – sometimes, by a very small minority of the population – thereby compromising the claims of governments to represent most people, and to be entitled to govern in their name. Unequal turnout is a concern, because it suggests that some groups – in particular, low-skilled workers and youngsters – are alienated from electoral politics in ways that cast doubt on the substantive fairness of electoral arrangements, and the representative character of government, however perfect they appear at first sight (Keaney and Rogers 2006; Lacroix 2007; Birch 2009b). Hence, concerns for the legitimacy, fairness, and stability of democratic government motivate Lijphart's case for compulsion. As Lijphart summarises the point, a 'crucially important reason to aim for maximum turnout is democratic legitimacy' (1997, 2, footnote 2).

2   While there are several potential cures for low turnout – such as weekend voting and proportional representation – Lijphart notes that none is as immediate and as successful at tackling both low and unequal turnout as CV (Lijphart 1997, 7–10; Birch 2009b; Hill 2006, 210–212).

3   According to Lijphart, it would be inconsistent with democratic principles to force voters to choose among candidates. However, he thinks, there is nothing immoral with forcing people to present themselves at the polls, and to tick off their names from a list, even if they do not wish to vote. 'Compulsory voting', on his view, should therefore be understood

as 'compulsory turnout' – as it was practised in the Netherlands between 1917 and 1967 (Gratschew 2004).

Given this understanding of CV as CT, it is surprising that Australia's apparently spectacular figures for electoral participation figure in arguments for compulsory *turnout* such as Lijphart's. Australia legally requires all registered voters to vote, unless granted a conscientious exemption – the terms of which are never made public (Hill 2002, 442–448; Ballinger 2006, 8 footnotes 18–19). Australia's form of compulsory voting is therefore inconsistent with freedom of conscience, as contemporary proponents of CV generally understand it, and appears, unfortunately, to assume that *secular* objections to voting cannot be conscientious. It would therefore be best to set the Australian case to one side when evaluating democratic arguments for compulsory voting, given that key features of Australian practice seem inconsistent with democratic principles.[5]

4   Finally, Lijphart argues that non-voters can be treated as free-riders, because they get the benefits of democratic elections, such as peaceful changes of power, and legitimate governments bound by norms of freedom and equality, but without making the effort to decide which of the available candidates for electoral office merits their support (Lijphart 1997, 11; Wertheimer 1975; Engelen 2007; Lacroix 2007). While it may be individually rational for each of us not to vote, and to leave others to do so, such behaviour is unfair, according to Lijphart and, if sufficiently widespread, can undermine the legitimacy of democratic government. Hence, he believes, compulsory voting is justified because no morally or politically significant liberties are threatened by a legal obligation to 'turnout', and the increases in voting, which compulsory turnout creates, can significantly remove the twin problems of low and unequal turnout.

Lijphart's arguments for compulsory voting are self-consciously democratic, reflecting the idea that legal compulsion can *protect* rather than *undermine* people's freedom, by combatting predictable failures of judgement and of will (Lacroix 2007; Engelen 2007; Satz 2010). Likewise, his assumptions about equality are self-consciously democratic, although few philosophers are likely to accept Lijphart's idea that treating people as equals always requires us to designate legal ceilings and floors which limit the ways in which people can differ (Lijphart 1997, 2; Young 1990; Bardon and Ceva in this volume).

Finally, what makes Lijphart's article notable is that it presents, in particularly pure form, two very different conceptions of the relationship between the ethics of voting and the justification for a legal duty to vote. On the first, Lijphart's argument is explicitly egalitarian and social-democratic – concerned with the way that rights to abstain can make it hard to pass social-democratic or redistributive economic policies in contemporary democracies. On the second, Lijphart's argument is concerned with the way that compulsory voting might further collective goods that are important to all democratic citizens, regardless of whether they support explicitly egalitarian or social-democratic forms of politics. Let's call the first argument the 'egalitarian' argument for CV, and the second argument the 'fairness' argument for CV. Contemporary proponents of compulsory voting tend to adopt one or both of these arguments, so their strengths and weaknesses can help us to evaluate the arguments in favour of compulsory voting.

The egalitarian argument for CV

On the egalitarian argument, compulsory voting is justified in order to promote voting by those who do not vote and who, Lijphart assumes, would benefit from more egalitarian policies than are currently favoured by those who do. This first argument for compulsory voting, therefore, assumes that democratic politics can involve quite sharp conflicts of interests among social groups – for example, around redistributive economic policies. Non-voters under voluntary voting, then, are likely to lose out in what is, in important respects, a zero-sum political game, although if they were forced to vote they might be expected to win, and to be capable of passing social-democratic policies, at least some of the time (Lijphart 1997, 4–5; see also Birch 2009a, 23; Hill 2006, 213–215).

However, unless the disadvantaged vote in a self-interested manner, when forced to vote, there will be no *egalitarian* case for CV on Lijphart's assumptions. Not-voting by the disadvantaged and altruistic voting are, from an egalitarian perspective, merely two different ways whereby the disadvantaged may perpetuate their disadvantaged situation, faced with the behaviour of the advantaged.[6] So, on the assumption that this disadvantage is unjust, and we need to remove it, the egalitarian argument for CV appears to assume that the disadvantaged are *morally required*, not just *permitted*, to vote in their self-interest.

But why suppose this? If the *advantaged* voted to alleviate disadvantage, there would be no egalitarian case for forcing the disadvantaged to participate electorally.[7] Perhaps egalitarians should therefore try to change the dispositions and behaviour of *voters*, and politicians, rather than trying to force non-voters to go to the polls? Indeed, from an egalitarian perspective, the political logic of compulsory voting is poor, because it seeks to get everyone to vote *regardless of whether they care about equality* (Lever 2010a).

Morally, too, the egalitarian case for CV is unpersuasive, even if we treat it as a remedial response to selfish or thoughtless voting by the advantaged. There is no egalitarian case for CV unless the disadvantaged vote their self-interest, which, if their disadvantaged position is unjust, they are morally entitled to do. But it does not follow from the fact that it is morally *permissible* for them to vote on self-interested grounds that it is morally *obligatory* to do so.

It is unlikely that the disadvantaged are morally required to treat the injustices from which they suffer as more important than other considerations (Shelby 2007). So, whether we look at the moral or the political dimensions of the egalitarian case for CV, it is hard to see why legitimate concerns for injustice and inequality require forcing non-voters to vote, let alone to 'turn out' at election time.

We might try to save the egalitarian argument by saying, 'but the duty of the disadvantaged is to vote for *justice*, not for their *self-interest*. It is only *because* voting for their self-interest will alleviate injustice that they have a duty to vote in their self-interest'. But *does* justice require us to vote, regardless of the choices we face? *Does* justice require us to vote regardless of the likely behaviour of our fellow voters, or of the other ways in which we might promote justice? *Should* injustice to disadvantaged non-voters take precedence over other moral concerns at election time? The most likely answer to these questions is 'no'. Hence, it is unclear that democratic citizens generally have a duty to vote, even if it might improve their situation, and that of others like them. The egalitarian case for compulsion takes seriously the conflicts of interest which can characterise, and undermine, democratic politics – that is a great part of its appeal. However, Lijphart's case for CV fails adequately to reflect the moral and political challenges posed by those very conflicts of interest.

The procedural, but egalitarian, case for CV

It is therefore worth considering if a *procedural* case for CV can be developed that would reflect the strengths and weaknesses of Lijphart's consequentialist egalitarian argument. For example, Lisa Hill suggests that the differential effects of coordination problems might explain the phenomenon of low and unequal voting, and provide a justification for CV, regardless of whether the disadvantaged vote in their self-interest (Hill 2006, 213–215; Hill 2010, 922–923; Birch 2009a, 23). According to Hill, high rates of turnout in and of themselves increase the chances of egalitarian social policies.[8] Compulsory voting may therefore be justified on egalitarian grounds even if current non-voters vote in ways that are ignorant, random, and counter-productive (Caplan 2008).

What makes this argument *procedural* as well as egalitarian is that CV is meant to respond to the unfair burdens on successful political action created by schemes of voluntary voting. Voluntary voting means that one is never sure whether one's political allies *will* vote, and this uncertainty can affect one's likelihood of voting. Such assurance and coordination problems, Hill plausibly maintains, are more difficult for poor than for rich people to overcome (Brennan and Hill 2014, 147–152, esp. 151). Hence, while elections under voluntary voting laws look fair, in practice they create procedural injustices that predictably disadvantage poorer social groups.

Potential voters can, indeed, be unfairly disadvantaged by apparently fair rules, as the procedurally egalitarian argument for CV maintains. For example, universal suffrage and majority rule may replicate, rather than remedy, morally arbitrary forms of power, because large, dispersed groups, such as consumers or workers, may find it harder to organise than smaller, more focused groups, such as producers and employers (Olson 1965). Likewise, freedoms of political association, expression, and choice offer insufficient protection for the freedom and equality of members of historically disadvantaged ascriptive groups – such as women, the members of racialised minorities, indigenous groups, and the disabled (Phillips 1995; Williams 1998; Mansbridge 1999). However, these well-known examples of the unequal burdens created by apparently fair electoral rules appear to *cross*, rather than to *track*, the difference between non-voters and voters. It is therefore unclear that – or how – compulsory voting will remedy them. Indeed, CV may exacerbate injustice in so far as non-voting is a response to a competitive political system that looks fair, but isn't.[9] Hence, the procedural arguments for compulsory voting on egalitarian grounds, which Hill and Birch try to develop, seem unlikely to circumvent the difficulties of more directly consequentialist arguments for CV.

The fairness argument for CV

The difficulties with the egalitarian argument for CV leave open the possibility that compulsory voting might be justified for reasons that are less intimately tied to facts about low and unequal turnout than Lijphart thought – hence the interest of Lijphart's second argument for CV, what we have called the 'fairness' argument for compulsion. The idea here is that 'nonvoting is a form [. . .] of free riding – and [. . .] free riding of any kind may be rational but is also selfish and immoral' (Lijphart 1997, 11). The appeal of this second argument for CV is obvious: if it works, it offers an argument for CV that anyone can accept, as long as they care about democracy. It is therefore independent of our political preferences, and of our views about how people ought to vote, or to behave more generally. It is irrelevant to the fairness argument whether the association between left-leaning politics and high turnout is as tight as Lijphart assumes; and it is irrelevant whether there are, in fact, other ways that might be as good at raising and equalising turnout, alone or in combination with other socio-political changes (Margetts 2006; Saunders 2010; Stone 2011; Lopez-Guerra 2014). The point of the fairness/collective goods argument is to combat *free riding* (on the assumption that it is morally wrong) and not simply to *improve* turnout. It is therefore concerned with the *assurance* of fairness that legal compulsion can provide, and with the public affirmation of (supposedly) public duties.

The fairness argument for compulsory voting, however, is at odds with the egalitarian argument for compulsion, so it is difficult to insist on *both* as justifications for compulsion. On the egalitarian argument for CV, non-voters are to be pitied and supported, because they are disadvantaged, marginalised, and excluded by an unfair political system. On the fairness argument, by contrast, non-voters are parasites, preying on the collectively beneficial efforts of voters. Proponents of compulsion must therefore decide which picture of non-voters they believe to be closest to the truth. Likewise, on the egalitarian case for CV, high turnout is desirable for partisan reasons – because low turnout is likely to disadvantage parties of the left. By contrast, on the fairness argument for CV, high turnout is a sufficiently important public good that we are justified in forcing people to vote. Proponents of CV, therefore, must also decide which of these strikes them as the most persuasive, given plausible ways of interpreting 'high' and 'low' turnout.

Democratic politics is a competitive as well as a cooperative affair (Lever 2010b, 915). However, Lijphart's egalitarian case for CV focuses solely on the competitive aspects of democracy, whereas the fairness argument for CV focuses solely on the cooperative ones. But if the combination of shared and conflicting interests makes it possible for us to envisage *political* solutions to our problems, then to ignore the ways that people can have conflicting, but also shared, interests risks depoliticising their situation in ways that are likely to undermine, rather than support, democracy. Hence the difficulty with the picture of non-voters and high turnout implied by the fairness argument for compulsion.

If non-voters are to be persuasively viewed as free-riders, they must be trying unfairly to benefit from the cooperative efforts of others – as though they were trying to jump a queue for the bus. Even setting aside cases where people do not vote for conscientious reasons, or because they are unsure who to vote for, this picture of non-voters is problematic. If there is no candidate at election time who you trust, or whose programme you support, then your failure to vote is an expression of disappointment, disgust, alienation, exasperation – perhaps also of confusion and ignorance – but not of a willingness to take advantage of others.[10]

There are normative problems with the fairness argument too. People are clearly entitled to abstain for conscientious reasons and may sometimes be morally obliged to do so (Brennan 2009; Hanna 2009). Non-voting on such grounds cannot be equated with unfairness or exploitation. Moreover, even when people are morally wrong to abstain, and even when that wrong consists in harming others,[11] it is odd to think of *voters* as the primary victims of harm (Lever 2010b, 914). Rather, it seems that when non-voting harms others, the primary victims are those who are unable to vote to protect their own interests – the young, the old, the ill, and those who are foreign. Non-voting may also harm some voters by letting them down, or making it harder for them to realise their legitimate ends. But even where this is so, these harms seem much less serious than those suffered by the voiceless and the voteless. So the fairness argument for CV seems to misrepresent the harm of abstention, when it is harmful, and wrongly to stigmatise behaviour that may not be morally wrong, or harmful, at all.

These problems arise because the fairness argument, as presently formulated, assumes that high turnout is democratically desirable, and a public good. It will be helpful, then, to look at the relationship between turnout and legitimacy more closely, and also to consider if it is possible to reformulate the fairness argument in order to avoid question-begging claims about the importance of high turnout.

High turnout and democratic legitimacy

Current ways of describing turnout for the purposes of cross-national comparisons use country-specific rates of turnout at national elections as their basis. They therefore imply that both the frequency of elections and their political importance are irrelevant to the ways we should classify elections as 'high' or 'low'. However, it is well known that countries such as the US or Switzerland have low rates of turnout at national elections, in part because they decide many more things electorally than other countries (Lijphart 1997, 8). Arguments for CV, therefore, need to explain why we should lump countries like the US and Switzerland into a category of 'low turnout' countries that includes Poland (a country with unusually low rates of voting at national elections), when citizens may be participating electorally to quite different extents.

Likewise, arguments for CV assume that rates of turnout should be measured and assessed irrespective of the interest and importance of the election in question, or of the ability of voters to remove incumbents. Indeed, countries which appeared to have low rates of turnout, such as the UK and the US, may have voters who are remarkably willing to vote, once one takes into account the advantages of incumbency.[12] In short, it is unclear that current ways of describing rates of turnout for cross-national purposes are adequately tracking morally and politically significant differences among people's willingness to participate politically, or to support democracy (more generally, see Rovensky 2008, especially 42–93).

Low turnout and legitimacy

But what of the idea that low turnout threatens democratic legitimacy? The reasons why high turnout can promote legitimacy reflect the idea that losers have reason to accept or 'consent' to an outcome that they did not want because 'it was a fair fight' (Weale 1999, 195–200). If legitimacy comes from winning a fair fight, however, it is the *fairness of the fight*, not the *level of turnout*, that is critical to legitimacy (Brennan 2016).

Even in non-ideal conditions, it is not evidently unfair that many of us have no chance of choosing a winning political coalition, or of being elected to political office, ourselves. Our views may be too idiosyncratic, speculative, or incoherent for us to form part of an electoral majority. As political professionals, or amateurs, we may lack political gifts, such as the gift of rhetoric, to which Walzer (1983) refers when arguing that some inequalities in politics are consistent with democratic government. We – and our favoured political candidates – may also lack the personality necessary for political success – being too impatient, or too accommodating for a given political climate, or a particular ideological context. As such we may have no reason to vote, while being willing to accept whoever is elected as legitimate, and willing to participate as amateurs in politics on occasion.

Injustice is neither a necessary nor a sufficient condition for low turnout in democratic politics, then. Politics is hard – often boring, frustrating, full of difficult things to learn, remember and apply; above all, it is time-consuming as democratic politics means persuading lots of people to support you, to trust you, and to make sacrifices for you with little, if any, external rewards (Weber 1919). Even following politics carefully and being well informed about it are likely to be distressing and unrewarding (compare Lijphart 1997; Lacroix 2007; Engelen 2007, 2009 on the 'undemanding' nature of CV). This is not because politicians are especially duplicitous or incompetent, but because democratic politics is tough, and the ability to change the world for the better may seem dishearteningly small compared to the need for change.[13]

The fairness argument for CV, then, will not work as long as it requires us to assume that high turnout is a public good, or necessary to democratic legitimacy. We could avoid this difficulty by frankly assuming that fairness requires us to vote for the common good and, therefore, to vote – absent compelling reasons to abstain. Although talk of a 'common good' has been condemned as populist and incoherent (Riker 1982) or as impossible to reconcile with the diversity of democratic interests and beliefs (Dahl 1989), the idea of a common good figures prominently in the literature on deliberative democracy, as well as in much contemporary liberal, republican, communitarian, and cosmopolitan thought. Moreover, there is nothing especially peculiar about the idea that large groups of people might have interests in common – interests in peace, security, prosperity, wisdom, well-being – which are consistent with treating each other as equals, and with taking seriously the moral claims of non-citizens. So, perhaps it is unfair not to vote for the common good, and it is *this* unfairness which, with generous exemptions for conscience and need, provides the best case for compulsory voting?

Voting and the common good

Citizens must bear the good of other citizens in mind while voting. It would be irresponsible and wrong not to do so, because our individual votes may contribute to the election of a government that will speak in our name, and that can bind us, domestically and internationally (Cohen 1996; Beerbohm 2012; Brennan 2016). However, it does not follow that we have a duty to *maximise* our common good, when voting, rather than to *satisfice*, or to secure a satisfactory level, of it. A duty to maximise our common good, after all, implies that nothing can be more important politically than advancing the ends we have in common. Such a position would be contentious even in ideal theory, and in non-ideal circumstances it seems deeply implausible, given that we may have urgent duties to remedy injustices inherited from the past at home and abroad (Lever 2017).

The familiar complaint that egalitarians may lack a reason to prefer 'levelling up' to 'levelling down' highlights the tensions between pursuit of our common ends and pursuit of equality, even when we have good reason to pursue both (Clayton and Williams 2002). Levelling up means that no one suffers from our efforts to improve the *welfare* of the disadvantaged, and is therefore Pareto-improving as compared to the *status quo*. However, raising up the bottom may do little to 'close the gap' in power, wealth, income, and status between the advantaged and the disadvantaged, although 'levelling down' generally implies a loss of collective well-being, and is therefore Pareto-suboptimal.

The fairness argument for compulsory voting, then, is difficult to square with democratic politics and morality. Some of these reasons reflect the difficulty of reconciling claims about the common good, or our shared interests, with concerns for their equality. Others reflect the difficulty of linking a democratic conception of the common good to the idea that not voting is free riding, and that high turnout is especially desirable. As such, the difficulties with the fairness case for CV illuminate the moral and political dilemmas of democratic politics and voting.

Epistemic arguments for CV

We have seen that it is difficult to justify CV on consequentialist grounds or deontological ones. It may therefore seem that we should abandon the effort to justify CV on explicitly *moral* or *political* grounds and, instead, look to *epistemic* ones – on the grounds that our interests in truth are distinct from, even if they may overlap with, our interests in morality. Some people suppose that democracy can, or should, be justified epistemically, based on the way that democratic institutions and practices improve the *quality* of political decisions, or 'track truth' in political matters (Talisse 2007; Misak 2008; Estlund 2008). However, you do not have to adopt such views to accept that democratic government has an important information-aggregating aspect, and to wonder, with Maskivker (2016), whether that informational aspect of democracy might generate compelling arguments for CV where distinctively moral or political ones fail.

However, it is unlikely that we can get such arguments to work. As we have seen, there is no democratic case for compulsory voting on the grounds that it is in people's interests to vote (even if it is), as this argument works only if the disadvantaged vote their self-interest. And we have just seen that neither high turnout nor the common good is able to save the fairness case for CV. It is unlikely, therefore, that people have a duty to provide information about their beliefs, interests, preferences, circumstances by *voting*, especially given that survey research, academic research, politically motivated research, citizen protests, and other communicative activities provide ways for eliciting, collecting, and using politically relevant information. Indeed, it is unclear how well voting reveals people's preferences (Hamlin and Jennings 2011) and, because there is usually more than one morally permissible way for voters to vote, it is unlikely that democratic elections will, or should, provide a consistent electoral 'message'. Hence, the reasons for rejecting Lijphart's arguments for compulsory voting suggest that epistemic arguments for compulsion are unlikely to be democratic either. This is not because epistemic democracy is an oxymoron – as Hill (2016, 8) implies, when referencing Saffon and Urbinati (2013) – simply that it is far harder to justify CV on democratic grounds than she believes.

Should countries with CV abandon it?

We have examined arguments for CV that purport to show that all democracies should adopt CV. However, their failure does not mean that CV may not sometimes be justified because it makes democratic government possible in circumstances where violent conflict is a real possibility, or in cases where democracies face difficult historical, geographical, or political situations.

Compulsory voting (especially with compulsory registration) helps to stabilise electoral turnout, and therefore to predict more accurately the likely effects of different electoral rules. It may therefore be a helpful device during transitions to democratic government, enabling political minorities to ensure that electoral arrangements adequately protect their interests, and reassuring political majorities that the risks of democratic politics are worth taking. It is possible that very high rates of turnout may also be necessary in order to construct a system of proportional representation that adequately reflects the profound social divisions within a country, or that enables it to cope with a combination of great size and diverse geographical and economic interests.

It is hard to know how powerful such context-specific arguments for CV might be – or others like them.[14] It is also hard to know what types of CV they would justify in practice, or for what duration. But, with these possibilities in mind, it is clearly premature to maintain that all countries with CV should abandon it even if, by 'abandon', one simply imagines a public statement that the relevant electoral law will no longer be enforced – as happened in Belgium.[15]

Conclusion

The ethics of voting have received relatively little attention from philosophers and political scientists, though they are far more complicated than one might have supposed. As we have seen, it is impossible to draw a sharp line between the principles that might justify adopting or rejecting compulsory voting and the evaluation of individual and collective behaviour within those rules. Resolving disputes about compulsory voting, therefore, requires us to decide when, if ever, people are morally entitled to vote on sectarian identities and interests, rather than for the 'common good' of their fellow citizens; when, if ever, they are morally entitled to vote on altruistic, rather than self-interested, concerns; and when, if ever, they may vote strategically, rather than sincerely. We do not yet have good answers to these questions. Above all, it is difficult to resolve disputes over the ethics of voting in general, and compulsory voting in particular, without relating the conceptions of rights, duty, freedom, and equality involved to those in other areas of moral and political philosophy, and to more empirical work on voting, on comparative public policy and political economy.

As a general rule, legal rights help to protect our interests, regardless of whether we ever exercise them. That is why it is so important *that* people have legal rights to vote even if, for conscientious reasons, they may never exercise them (Lever 2009, 225). However, what we can do with our right to vote depends on the behaviour of a great number of people we will never know, and whose interests may be quite different from our own. It is therefore hard to see what difference it makes whether we exercise our right to vote. A great deal, presumably, depends on who we are, how our interests differ from those of other people, and whether the rules of electoral competition counteract, or exacerbate, the conflicts of power and interest in our society.

Consequentialist arguments for and against compulsory voting, therefore, are likely to be persuasive only where they capture the specific structure and dynamics of a particular political setting, being too speculative or dependent on controversial assumptions to be persuasive otherwise. Non-consequentialist concerns with democracy, freedom, equality, rights, and duties are, therefore, likely to do much of the work in a philosophical evaluation of compulsory voting, and the ethics of voting more generally. As we have seen, these generally tell against compulsory voting as an expression of democratic values, interests, and duties, except in very particular circumstances. However, it is not easy to characterise 'voluntary voting' – or the alternative(s) to compulsory voting. Legal coercion is not the only obstacle to people's freedom, and democrats may differ in the importance that they attach to the others (Miller 2006). There is, therefore, much work to do in clarifying what forms of freedom and equality are necessary for democratic voting, and for the institutions, laws, and customs which protect and define it.

Acknowledgements

We would like to thank Alan Hamlin for his thoughtful comments on an earlier draft of this chapter, and Yoann Della Croce and Melis Akdag for research help. We are also grateful to the Fonds National Suisse for funding the research on which this chapter depends, as part of its grant for a project on democratic ethics.

Notes

1 This point has obvious affinities with G.A. Cohen's (1997) concern about the sharp distinction that Rawls (1971, 6–10) wished to draw between people's willingness to support and abide by the rules required for social justice and the way that they make personal decisions within those rules.
2 www.lemonde.fr/idees/article/2011/12/14/vive-le-vote-obligatoire_1618117_3232.html.
3 www.theguardian.com/us-news/2016/apr/10/barack-obama-praises-australias-mandatory-voting-rules.
4 www.theguardian.com/politics/2005/jul/04/uk.voterapathy.
5 Lacroix endorses the ECHR view that there is no violation of conscience when people are forced to vote, because they can always cast a blank vote (Lacroix 2007, 193). On those grounds, being forced to attend church would not violate my conscience, as long as I do not have to pray. This is clearly not a satisfactory interpretation of freedom of conscience.
6 However, morally they may be different (see Hanna 2009).
7 The argument here has affinities with GA Cohen's (2002).
8 Unfortunately, Hill appears to assume that politicians are interested only in whether people are likely to, rather than whether they are likely to vote (Hill 2016, 294). She also confuses a discussion by Kenworthy and Pontusson (2005, 456–459) of the 'Melzer-Richard model of the relationship between market inequality and redistribution' with the claim that in and of itself high turnout increases egalitarian social policies by government. Kenworthy and Pontusson's article is concerned with the best way

to measure 'market inequality'. It has 'no interest in, and nothing to say about, voting', as Pontusson confirmed in a private conversation.

9 For example, Nathan Hanna (2009) believes that people have a duty to abstain, rather than to vote, given current injustice.

10 If this point is correct, one of the difficulties with arguments for lotteries instead of elections as a way of determining who should govern is that they, too, tend to assume the cooperative aspects of democracy are more important than the competitive ones. However, for interesting efforts to get round these problems, and to combine lotteries with many of the main features of democratic elections, see Saunders (2010), Lopez-Guerra (2014), and Brennan (in Brennan and Hill 2014).

11 Not all moral wrongs are violations of rights, as we see in the case of ingratitude, unkindness, and selfishness.

12 For figures from the last US election, see www.rasmussenreports.com/public_content/political_commentary/commentary_by_kyle_kondik/incumbent_reelection_rates_higher_than_average_in_2016. As stated in the article, '393 of 435 House representatives, 29 of 34 senators, and five of 12 governors sought reelection (several of the governors were prohibited from seeking another term)'. For interesting discussions of French abstention, relative to the perceived importance of the election, see Didier Maus (2015) at www.partiradical.net/files/parti_radical/contenu/Actualites/Note-257.pdf.

13 This is a reason why deontological reasons to participate in politics, as well as virtue ethics, may be more important factors in political participation – especially over the long term – as compared to more straightforwardly consequentialist ones.

14 Mark N. Franklin, 'You Want to Vote Where Everyone Knows Your Name: Anonymity, Expressive Engagement and Turnout among Young Adults', unpublished paper, 2006, available online at www.lse.ac.uk/government/research/resgroups/PSPE/pdf/Franklin.pdf.

15 www.nrc.nl/buitenland/article2263399.ece/Belgie_vervolgt_niet-stemmers_niet_meer. Thanks to Dr Alex Voorhoeve for the link.

References

Ballinger, Chris. 2006. "Compulsory Turnout: A Solution to Disengagement?" In *Democracy and Voting*, edited by Chris Ballinger, 5–22. London: Hansard Society Democracy Series.

Beerbohm, Eric. 2012. *In Our Name: The Ethics of Democracy*. Princeton, NJ: Princeton University Press.

Birch, Sarah. 2009a. "The Case for Compulsory Voting." *Public Policy Research* 16 (1): 21–27.

Birch, Sarah. 2009b. *Full Participation: A Comparative Study of Compulsory Voting*. Manchester: Manchester University Press.

Blais, André. 2000. *To Vote or Not to Vote: The Merits and Limitations of Rational Choice Theory*. Pittsburgh: University of Pittsburgh Press.

Brennan, Jason. 2009. "Polluting the Polls: When Citizens Should Not Vote." *Australasian Journal of Philosophy* 87 (4):535–549.

Brennan, Jason. 2016. "The Ethics and Rationality of Voting." In *The Stanford Encyclopedia of Philosophy*, edited by Edward N. Zalta, Winter 2016 Edition. URL = <https://plato.stanford.edu/archives/win2016/entries/voting/>.

Brennan, Jason, Hill, Lisa. 2014. *Compulsory Voting: For and Against*. New York: Cambridge University Press.

Caplan, Bryan. 2008. *The Myth of the Rational Voter: Why Democracies Choose Bad Policies*. Princeton, NJ: Princeton University Press.

Clayton, Matthew, Williams, Andrew (eds.). 2002. *The Ideal of Equality*. Basingstoke: Palgrave Macmillan.

Cohen, Gerald Allan. 1997. "Where the Action Is: On the Site of Distributive Justice." *Philosophy and Public Affairs* 26 (1): 3–30.

Cohen, Gerald Allan. 2002. "The Pareto Argument for Inequality." In *The Ideal of Equality*, edited by Matthew Clayton and Andrew Williams, 162–181. Basingstoke: Palgrave Macmillan.

Cohen, Joshua. 1996. "Procedure and Substance in Deliberative Democracy." In *Democracy and Difference: Contesting the Boundaries of the Political*, edited by Seyla Benhabib, 95–119. Princeton, NJ: Princeton University Press.

Dahl, Robert. 1989. *Democracy and Its Critics*. New Haven: Yale University Press.

Engelen, Bart. 2007. "Why Compulsory Voting Can Enhance Democracy." *Acta Politica* 42 (1): 23–39.

Engelen, Bart. 2009. "Why Liberals Can Favour Compulsory Attendance." *Politics* 29 (3): 218–222.

Estlund, David. 2008. *Democratic Authority: A Philosophical Framework*. Princeton, NJ: Princeton University Press.

Gratschew, Maria. 2004. "Compulsory Voting in Western Europe." In *Voter Turnout in Western Europe Since 1945: A Regional Report*, edited by Rafael Lopez Pintor and Maria Gratschew, 25–31. Stockholm: International IDEA.

Hamlin, Alan, Jennings, Colin. 2011. "Expressive Political Behaviour: Foundations, Scope and Implications." *British Journal of Political Science* 41 (3): 645–670.

Hanna, Nathan. 2009. "An Argument for Voting Abstention." *Public Affairs Quarterly* 23 (4): 275–286.

Hill, Lisa. 2002. "Compulsory Voting: Residual Problems and Potential Solutions." *Australian Journal of Political Science* 37 (3): 437–455.

Hill, Lisa. 2006. "Low Voter Turnout in the United States: Is Compulsory Voting a Viable Solution?" *Journal of Theoretical Politics* 18 (2): 207–232.

Hill, Lisa. 2010. "On the Justifiability of Compulsory Voting: Reply to Lever." *British Journal of Political Science* 40 (4): 917–923.

Hill, Lisa. 2016. "Voting Turnout, Equality, Liberty and Representation: Epistemic Versus Procedural Democracy." *Critical Review of International Social and Political Philosophy* 19 (3): 283–300.

Keaney, Emily, Rogers, Ben. 2006. *A Citizen's Duty: Voter Inequality and the Case for Compulsory Turnout*. London: Institute for Public Policy Research.

Kenworthy, Lane, Pontusson, Jonas. 2005. "Rising Inequality and the Politics of Redistribution in Affluent Countries." *Perspectives on Politics* 3 (3): 449–471.

Lacroix, Justine. 2007. "A Liberal Defence of Compulsory Voting." *Politics* 27 (3): 190–195.

Lever, Annabelle. 2008. "'A Liberal Defence of Compulsory Voting': Some Reasons for Scepticism." *Politics* 28 (1): 61–64.

Lever, Annabelle. 2009. "Liberalism, Democracy and the Ethics of Voting." *Politics* 29 (3): 223–227.

Lever, Annabelle. 2010a. "Democracy and Voting: A Response to Lisa Hill." *British Journal of Political Science* 40 (4): 925–929.

Lever, Annabelle. 2010b. "Compulsory Voting: A Critical Perspective." *British Journal of Political Science* 40 (4): 897–915.

Lever, Annabelle. 2017. "Must We Vote for the Common Good?" In *Ethics in Politics. The Rights and Obligations of Individual Political Agents*, edited by Emily Crookston, David Killoren and Jonathan Trerise, 145–156. New York: Routledge.

Lijphart, Arend. 1997. "Unequal Participation: Democracy's Unresolved Dilemma." *American Political Science Review* 91 (1): 1–14.

Lopez-Guerra, Claudio. 2014. *Democracy and Disenfranchisement: The Morality of Electoral Exclusions*. Oxford: Oxford University Press.

Mansbridge, Jane. 1999. "Should Blacks Represent Blacks and Women Represent Women? A Contingent 'Yes'." *Journal of Politics* 61 (3): 628–657.

Margetts, Helen. 2006. "Citizens Cannot Be Compelled to Engage with Political Organisations." In *Democracy and Voting*, edited by Chris Ballinger, 29–35. London: Hansard Society Democracy Series.

Maring, Luke. 2016. "Why Does the Excellent Citizen Vote?" *Journal of Political Philosophy* 24 (2): 245–257.

Maskivker, Julie. 2016. "An Epistemic Justification for the Obligation to Vote." *Critical Review* 28 (2): 224–247.

Miller, David (ed.). 2006. *The Liberty Reader*. Edinburgh: Edinburgh University Press.

Misak, Cheryl. 2008. "A Culture of Justification: The Pragmatist's Epistemic Argument for Democracy." *Episteme: A Journal of Social Epistemology* 5 (1): 94–105.

Olson, Mancur. 1965. *The Logic of Collective Action*. Cambridge, MA: Harvard University Press.

Phillips, Anne. 1995. *The Politics of Presence*. Oxford: Oxford University Press.

Rawls, John. 1971 [1999]. *A Theory of Justice*, revised ed. Cambridge, MA: Belknap Press.

Riker, William. 1982. *Liberalism Against Populism: A Confrontation Between the Theory of Democracy and the Theory of Social Choice*. San Francisco: W. H. Freeman and Company.

Rovensky, Jan. 2008. "Voting: A Citizen's Right, or Duty? The Case Against Compulsory Voting." *Unpublished doctoral dissertation*, Faculty of Political Science, LUISS Guido Carli, Rome.

Saffon, Maria Paula, Urbinati, Nadia. 2013. "Procedural Democracy, the Bulwark of Equal Liberty." *Political Theory* 41 (3): 441–481.

Satz, Debra. 2010. *Why Some Things Should Not Be for Sale: The Moral Limits of Markets*. Oxford: Oxford University Press.

Saunders, Ben. 2010. "Democracy, Political Equality, and Majority Rule." *Ethics* 121 (1): 148–177.

Shelby, Tommie. 2007. "Justice, Deviance, and the Dark Ghetto." *Philosophy and Public Affairs* 35 (2): 126–160.

Stone, Peter. 2011. *The Luck of the Draw: The Role of Lotteries in Decision Making*. Oxford: Oxford University Press.

Talisse, Robert. 2007. *A Pragmatist Philosophy of Democracy*. London: Routledge.

Tin, Louis-Georges, Wieviorka, Michel. 2011. Vive le vote obligatoire! Pour enrayer la déliquescence de la démocratie, December 14, 2011, available at https://www.lemonde.fr/idees/article/2011/12/14/vive-le-vote-obligatoire_1618117_3232.html

Walzer, Michael. 1983. *Spheres of Justice: A Defense of Pluralism and Equality*. New York: Basic Books.

Weale, Albert. 1999. *Democracy*. Basingstoke: Palgrave Macmillan.

Weber, Max. 1919 [1946]. "Politics as a Vocation." In *From Max Weber: Essays in Sociology*, edited by H.H. Gerth and C. Wright Mills, 77–128. New York: Oxford University Press.

Wertheimer, Alan. 1975. "In Defense of Compulsory Voting." In *Participation in Politics*, edited by Roland Pennock and John Chapman, 276–296. New York: Lieber-Atherton.

Williams, Melissa. 1998. *Voice, Trust and Memory: Marginalised Groups and the Failure of Liberal Representation*. Princeton, NJ: Princeton University Press.

Young, Iris Marion. 1990. *Justice and the Politics of Difference*. Princeton, NJ: Princeton University Press.

20

THE ETHICS OF ANTI-CORRUPTION POLICIES

Emanuela Ceva and Maria Paola Ferretti

Introduction

The corruption of public officials and institutions is one of the most obvious problems that affects developed and developing countries alike. Because this view is largely shared, most current studies of this phenomenon – call it 'political corruption' – have been dedicated to either measuring or counteracting the negative political, social, and economic effects that this form of corruption may have in society.[1] As these studies have been proliferating, anti-corruption actions have been mainstreamed in many national and international agencies, with the EU, the OECD, the World Bank, and the UN at the forefront.

The theoretical significance and practical urgency of these studies and actions are beyond dispute. However, they have distracted the attention of commentators from a somewhat more basic analysis of this phenomenon. This analysis concerns the exact sense in which political corruption is *wrong*, besides the intuitive appeal of this judgement. This is an important drawback because the identification of relevant cases of political corruption depends on the outcomes of this analysis, which, as a consequence, has an important bearing on the development of anti-corruption policies by determining their target.

Most notably, this lacuna has resulted in the formulation of a multiplicity of actions that address a very heterogeneous set of issues, which includes such diverse phenomena as bribery, embezzlement, institutional malfunctioning, the inadequacy of political leaders, and clientelism – to name but a few examples.

To be sure, this situation is unsatisfactory because it lacks conceptual rigour and, therefore, it muddles important distinctions between different pathologies that may affect the public order. But it matters also for the design of anti-corruption strategies that risk either misfiring or being too vague by lacking a clear target and an account of the exact kind of wrong these strategies are meant to prevent and/or correct.

While this preoccupation holds across various institutional contexts, given the specific focus of this volume, we concentrate on the wrongness of political corruption as it occurs in a *democracy*. This is not to say that our considerations may not be extended to other forms of government; such an extension may be feasible, with some adjustments, and perhaps even desirable in order to come up with a general theory of the wrongness of political corruption that is true to the multifaceted nature of this phenomenon. However, this possible extension falls beyond our aims for the present chapter.

In our research on this topic, we have addressed this issue by offering a normative analysis of the wrongness of political corruption that is capable of explaining its distinguishing traits (see Ceva 2018; Ceva and Ferretti 2014, 2017, 2018; Ferretti 2018). In particular, we have developed a normative account of political corruption as a publicly unaccountable use of entrusted powers of office. In our view, politically relevant instances of corruption occur when a public official uses her entrusted power for the pursuit of an agenda whose rationale may not be publicly vindicated in accordance with the mandate on which the public officer ought to exercise the power associated with her institutional role. This form of corruption is inherently wrong in a politically relevant sense because it goes against the logic of publicity that undergirds the democratic public order. In this chapter, we draw on this research and expand it with a view to enhancing the identification of relevant instances of political corruption and the design of policies to counteract them.

In particular, in the second section, contra current 'institutionalist' analyses of corruption, we present our view of political corruption as a problem that affects the quality of both *public institutions* and the behaviour of *public officials*. In the third section, we explain why in a democracy political corruption is *inherently* wrong irrespective of whether it has negative social, political, or economic *consequences*. In the fourth section, we draw some normative implications for the development of a democratic ethics of anti-corruption. In the last section, we conclude.

Political corruption in a democracy

We focus on the *political* dimension of corruption as a pathology that affects the public order (Amundsen 1999). Standardly, the public order is the set of rules that is binding on individuals engaged in cooperative forms of social interaction. Political corruption is a form of vicious alteration of these rules. In order to understand in what it consists, we need a normative understanding of the public order that qualifies what a just set of rules is. This understanding is quite variable because it depends on a number of theoretical assumptions and contextual (including social and cultural) factors. Given the specific focus of this volume, the relevant theory of the public order is the theory proper of contemporary democratic societies.

This circumscription of the discussion is consistent with the invitation of some political theorists to make such a discussion dependent on an analysis of the social and political realities in which corruption thrives (see, e.g., Philp and David-Barret 2015). This approach is meant as an alternative to 'moralised' approaches that build on a general theory of institutions – grounded in either some idea of the common good (Sandel 2013) or an account of democratic legitimacy – and characterise corruption as a deviation from its normative dispositions (Warren 2004).

While we broadly agree with this 'realist' invitation, we also think that a normative assessment of political corruption requires a clear preliminary understanding of the conception of the public order and of the rationale of its constitutive institutions. From these we can derive the normative standards necessary for the identification of the conditions for the exercise of entrusted public power, attached to different institutional roles and governed by public rules, from which political corruption constitutes one vicious deviation.

So, to what account of the public order should we refer when we approach political corruption within a democratic framework? A recent attempt at characterising such an account comes from the perspective of 'institutional corruption' following the lead of Dennis Thompson (1993, 1995, 2005) and Lawrence Lessig (2013, 2014). Institutionalists have adopted a teleological perspective from which political corruption is problematic to the extent that it makes the public order dependent on partisan ends and, as a consequence, distracts public officials but also, more generally, citizens from the common good or some shared ends (see also Sandel 2013).

From this perspective, corruption is politically relevant when it manifests itself as a process of degradation of institutions that undermines their ability to achieve their purpose as well as their trustworthiness. The paradigmatic example is taken from democratic politics: the American electoral system and its dependency on the influence of private donors (Thompson 1993, 1995). The institution of democratic elections is itself corrupt in this case because it is made dependant on powers other than those on which it was designed to depend (e.g., finance v. popular sovereignty). Individual corruption has been less relevant to the institutionalists' concerns, except for when it causes the erosion of the functioning of institutions.

This institutionalist view is valuable as it captures an important aspect of why we should care about certain pervasive forms of political corruption. However, we also think that it is not fully satisfactory because, *inter alia*, it focuses exclusively on *systemic* forms of political corruption. In other words, this approach has the merit of attracting theoretical attention to phenomena of corruption that make the media headlines and are, understandably, of great concern for the civil society and governmental agencies alike.

But we contend that this approach risks overlooking the political salience of cases of *individual* corruption (see Ceva and Ferretti 2017, 2018). These are cases, for example, when a public official arbitrarily favours (even in one single occasion) a member of his religious group in the allocation of a job in order to increase this group's influence in a given sector of society. The political relevance of these cases, we suggest, should not be obfuscated by the practical opportunity to concentrate anti-corruption resources and deal with cases where the material damages of corruption (e.g., the impoverishment of a country) appear to be more obvious and urgent. We contend that only by understanding the wrongness that is inherent in politically relevant forms of corruption, rather than stopping at registering their negative consequences, we can start to take this problem seriously and in a systematic (rather than emergency-driven) manner.

This interpretative enhancement is an important analytical achievement in itself; but it is also a precondition for an enhanced design of anti-corruption policies. To limit these policies to dealing with the costs of political corruption entails an understanding of anti-corruption only as a remedial measure in response to the negative consequences of this phenomenon. Albeit necessary, this remedial function is not and should not be considered exhaustive of the scope of anti-corruption initiatives, which should, rather, be capable of going to the very roots of this phenomenon to engage with what makes it wrong essentially and fundamentally.

To this end, we have developed an alternative characterisation of political corruption that is apt to capture both its institutional and individual manifestations (see Ceva and Ferretti 2018). In our understanding, we have political corruption when a public official, entrusted with the public power either to make or to implement public rules, makes a publicly unaccountable use of that power.

This characterisation applies to cases in which such uses of power are systemic – that is, when they are entrenched in the very functioning of public institutions, as it may be the case of the private financing of electoral campaigns. But it also applies to more sporadic episodes of corruption that materialise through the occasional corrupt behaviour of an individual public official; an example is a public official who favours her husband in the attribution of a job in her office (nepotism).

So, for a case of corruption, whether institutional or individual, to be politically relevant it must see the involvement of at least one public official. Public officials are those citizens who occupy some legitimate role in a public institution and exercise power on public mandate.

They may be entrusted with either a law-making (e.g., elected political representatives) or a law-implementation function (e.g., civil servants). Corrupt public officials may thus operate within either such political institutions as parliaments or such other equally relevant public institutions as courts and hospitals.

Irrespective of the functions with which they are appointed, public officials must perform these functions in keeping with a mandate whose constitutive rules establish the officials' duties and the margins of discretion they have in fulfilling those duties. For example, rules of professional conduct regulate the behaviour of such professionals who work in public institutions as doctors. The duties that these rules establish pose legally binding constraints on the behaviour of public officials; violation of these rules is unlawful and may be prosecuted.

Public officials also retain some substantial margins for discretion on how to fulfil their duties. This discretion is a prerogative of all public officials that are called upon to exercise their capacity for judgement while they perform their functions; this is the case, for example, of judges but also, say, doctors, who have the discretion to decide what therapies are in the best interest of their patients (see Ceva and Ferretti 2014).

This discretion is not, however, itself unconstrained. In a democracy (but, in fact, in any system governed by the rule of law), public officials are expected to exercise their discretion in a way consistent with the mandate with which their public power was entrusted to them. So, were a public official asked why she made a certain decision, she should be able to answer publicly by reference to the rationale of her public function.

This concise account of public office is sufficient to see the special position that public officials occupy in society and the nature of the power with which they are entrusted. This position makes them vulnerable to political corruption. Public officials enjoy a significant margin for either altering or circumventing both the letter and the spirit of their mandate by using their power for the pursuit of an agenda other than that for which their power of office was entrusted to them.[2] This incoherence makes their use of power publicly unaccountable.

This publicly unaccountable use of power is a necessary condition for distinguishing political corruption from other instances of power abuse on the part of public officials. In our understanding, we have political corruption when a public official's agenda has a rationale that cannot be publicly vindicated with reference to the terms of that official's power mandare. In a democracy, those who act on public mandate are generally required to justify their actions publicly. This means that public officials must be capable, at least in principle, of explaining why they acted in certain ways on the basis of reasons that citizens may generally recognise as a ground for public action in keeping with (the letter or the spirit of) the rationale of the officials' mandate. To be true, any one official might never find herself in the position of having actually to provide this kind of justification. However, being in the position of providing it should be a regulative commitment that governs the behaviour of all those who exercise entrusted public power in a democracy. This is a direct entailment of the basic commitment to public accountability that is central to any democratic theory of the public order (see Ceva 2018).

Notice that the pursuit of such an agenda does not necessarily include seeking some kind of advantage that accrues to the corrupt official's material benefit. This agenda may include, for example, the favouring of a specific interest group for an improvement in either social status or political influence (as it may be the case of a politician who promises to prioritise in her agenda the allocation of public funds for improving the infrastructures in one particular neighbourhood in exchange for political support from the people who live there). But such items may also include the promotion of a cause that the public official shares with a certain group of people against the majority in society. This could be exemplified by a public official who favours male candidates in the allocation of jobs in the public sector motivated by the promotion of a conservative policy agenda based on the conviction that society benefits greatly from stay-at-home mothers. Surely, occurrences of this kind may be more difficult to pin down than those involving more obvious material private gains (as in the case of bribery). Nevertheless, their elusiveness does not make them any less publicly unaccountable.

This kind of publicly unaccountable use of power is what distinguishes these instances of political corruption from general forms of discrimination. Discriminatory behaviour may be the expression of some malicious personal intent or a form of chauvinism, or even the unintended consequence of carelessness or implicit bias. For this kind of behaviour to be considered an instance of political corruption, a necessary condition is a publicly unaccountable use of power in the sense we have explained.

Notice that the idea of public unaccountability does not necessarily entail that a public official's agenda is hidden. It might be common knowledge that a certain politician entertains clientelar relations with her voters and these relations may not even be unlawful. Nevertheless, these relations are corrupt because they respond to a patron/client logic that is extraneous to that of public accountability that ought to govern political interactions in a democracy and, therefore, may not be publicly vindicated.[3]

The publicly unaccountable connotation of the corrupt public official's use of power distinguishes political corruption also from other breaches of the official's duties that, although unlawful, may be publicly justified. That is the case, for instance, of public officials who use their power to question certain rules that they deem unjust, for example, through civil disobedience. Unlike civil disobedients, corrupt public officials may not act in formal breach of any law because they may be just going against the spirit of a rule without violating its letter, as is the case in many legal systems where nepotism is not unlawful. Nevertheless, their actions may not be publicly justified because they respond to a personal logic that cannot, unlike that of civil disobedients in some cases, withstand public scrutiny.[4]

In sum, political corruption defies a fundamental pillar of the democratic public order and can be viewed as a distinctively political problem that is irreducible to a matter of either professional ethics or personal morality. We think this is an interesting conclusion in its own right because it enhances our understating of a complex and widespread phenomenon. But this conclusion has also important implications for anti-corruption because it offers a tool to identify relevant cases of political corruption (beyond the standard references to bribes) as those that meet the conditions we have just discussed (including such elusive phenomena as clientelism and nepotism). This tool is important as it allows identifying specific targets for anti-corruption policies without either overstretching their domain (to include any instance of power abuse or political misbehaviour) or exaggerating their ambitions (by orienting them to an 'institutional big-bang' – see, e.g., Rothstein 2011).

The wrongness of political corruption

In the previous section we have presented our account of the forms of corruption that are politically problematic in a democracy. But why exactly should we treat these problems as a matter of serious concern that requires political intervention?

As already shown, the answer cannot refer to the unlawfulness of political corruption because while certain instances of this practice are outlawed (e.g., bribery), that is not necessarily the case (e.g., nepotism). A popular move consists in pointing the finger to the negative consequences of political corruption. So, political corruption may be wrong when it entails economic costs; it may have, for example, a negative impact on a country's development and growth. But this is not a generally valid argument because – in non-ideal conditions – certain specific instances of political corruption may have positive externalities. This happens, for example, when they work as an 'institutional grease' (see, e.g., Méon and Weill 2010; Pande 2008), or are beneficial to growth and development when they are, say, instrumental to speeding up certain bureaucratic processes that discourage foreign investments (see Nye 1967).

Political corruption may also have social and political costs. Especially when political corruption is widespread among public officials, it may impair the functioning of that institution and create an environment in which corruption is the price to pay to 'be part of the system'. The reiteration of corrupt relations over long periods of time and among a variety of agents may generate systemic corruption. In this case, it is difficult to disentangle specific causal and contributory responsibilities of individual public officials; it is the institution that is itself corrupt. Systemically corrupt institutions may result in a loss of the institutions' trustworthiness. This is an analysis that the institutionalist theories of corruption we have introduced earlier would endorse.[5]

These interpretations are successful in accounting for certain specific senses in which single episodes of political corruption may or may not be considered wrong. However, their implication is that certain contingent circumstances may discount the wrongness of political corruption, should negative consequences be absent. This implication is disappointing because it dismisses too quickly a general intuition that there is something wrong, at least *prima facie*, with political corruption, whenever it occurs.

What is more, from this purely consequentialist perspective, we are unable to give a general normative assessment of the wrongness of political corruption as an either individual or institutional *practice*. We must rely on a case-by-case evaluation informed by the actual or expected consequences of each relevant instance. Now, we might want to bite the bullet here, but the price we would thus pay is quite significant in terms of our capacity of both philosophical analysis and political guidance – with obvious implications for the justification and development of anti-corruption policies.

Is there a way in which we can make sense of the wrongness of political corruption in philosophically sound and action-guiding terms? We think that it is possible by building on our account of the corruption of public officials and institutions as a politically relevant problem. In particular, we think that in a democracy political corruption is inherently wrong because it consists in a violation of the kind of treatment owed to citizens.[6]

Whatever substantive view of democracy one may hold, it is a general presumption that one of the distinguishing features of this form of government is its capacity to treat all citizens as political equals in virtue of their bare status as right-holders (see, e.g., Christiano 2008). Citizens, so conceived, are the sources of political authority. Therefore, any use of entrusted public power must be publicly justifiable to them on grounds they all can accept as reasons for public action in consideration of this bare status of theirs.

There are many ways in which this status may be undermined and citizens' rights denied. One such way occurs anytime citizens' claims are either played up or hushed up for the arbitrary promotion of the official's agenda. In this sense, political corruption consists in a specific kind of mistreatment of citizens in their capacity as equal political agents and, therefore, it occurs in clear contradiction with the rationale of the democratic public order.

By using their power in a publicly unaccountable way, corrupt public officials unwarrantedly free themselves from the constraints that would normally apply to their actions. This is not only wrong from the perspective of either personal morality or professional ethics. The official's corrupt action is politically wrong because it occurs in violation of the rationale of the democratic public order (see Ceva and Ferretti 2014: 131, 2018). This is a more fundamental sense in which political corruption is inherently wrong as a practice. This sense is totally independent from the specific consequences of any single individual episode of corruption, if any.

Moreover, by their involvement in corrupt practices, certain citizens acquire a similarly privileged position from which they can influence public policies in a way that is congenial to them. Such a privileged position is in obvious contrast with the democratic commitment to the treatment of citizens as political equals that is owed to them as right-holders.

Consider the practice of patients making payments to health providers which are greater than official fees, or for such services as blood tests or emergency treatments that are supposed to be either subsidised by the National Health Service or, in fact, free. As a number of reports released by the European Commission (2013) and Transparency International (2006) show, such practices are common across Eastern Europe and many regions of Asia and Africa.[7] There is an obvious sense in which such practices are wrong to the extent that they produce distributive inequalities regarding access to certain public services (see Stokes et al. 2013). Many have regarded the distributive injustices that corruption causes as the most worrisome aspect of this phenomenon. Entire regions are impoverished because large amounts of public money and resources are channelled in the hand of a privileged few, thus causing the sharpening of inequalities between large portions of the population, high levels of organised crime, and a weaker rule of law.[8]

Those are very serious problems, whose relevance for national and international anti-corruption policies should not be downplayed. However, we argue that there is an even more fundamental sense in which such corrupt practices as those presented earlier are wrong in themselves. Notably, they constitute a violation of the kind of treatment that ought to be granted to all citizens because of a publicly unaccountable relation that certain citizens are in the position of establishing with corrupt public officials. This relation would be wrong even if it had no negative distributive consequences – for example, in the case in which the corrupt practices were so widespread that they happen to ensure that all people have access to whatever they need. But people in this scenario would have what they have as a matter of privilege and not as a matter of right (see Ceva 2018). To wit, they would be treated as clients rather than citizens. Thus, their political status as right-holders would be violated contrary to what democracy requires.

This reasoning illuminates the sense in which certain practices are inherently wrong in a democracy because they are instances of political corruption. What is more, it elucidates the general sense in which anyone who is interested in the quality of the democratic public order should be concerned with the corruption of public officials and institutions whenever it occurs and place anti-corruption policies at the centre of their agendas.

Refocusing anti-corruption

The understanding of political corruption as an inherent political wrong that violates the very foundations of the democratic public order has important implications for the design of anti-corruption strategies as well as for the state's responsibility to implement them.

From this latter perspective, the most far-reaching implication of our discussion is that the development of anti-corruption policies can be rightfully understood as a duty of the state. Because political corruption is inherently wrong, anti-corruption is not an option but a requirement, even in those cases in which no unlawful action has occurred.

We have brought to the fore an important sense in which citizens of a democratic society are wronged by corrupt public officials and institutions. This wrong, we have argued, consists in a violation of the treatment owed to citizens as political equals, a status that they possess in their capacity as the holders of democratic rights. Because granting this kind of treatment to citizens pertains to the very rationale of the democratic public order, in order for it to claim any authority over citizens, this kind of treatment must be ensured to all of them. As political corruption is a malicious violation of this commitment, the state has a positive duty to counteract it.

As for most states' positive duties, the duty of anti-corruption is pro tanto.[9] There might be specific circumstantial considerations – for example, of distributive justice – which might advise against acting on this duty. For example, this might be the case, in non-ideal conditions, when certain forms of patronage work as instruments to getting round procedural obstacles to hiring candidates for jobs in the public sector, who do not respond to certain formal requirements that are in fact irrelevant to the candidates' substantive capacity to perform. In cases like this one, there may be reasons to tolerate certain episodes of political corruption in view of their impact on citizens' employment opportunities. However, this is not to say that the wrongness of political corruption is discounted in these cases. In fact, we would be working with a non-ideal theory of anti-corruption and facing a 'dirty hands' scenario in which the state can still be said to fail to act on its anti-corruption duty. Political corruption retains its inherent wrongness as a practice and the general cogency of the state's pro tanto duty of anti-corruption is intact.

But what kind of anti-corruption policy is it the state's duty to develop? A first general consideration concerns the primary aim that such policies should pursue. They should be aimed at singling out forms of mistreatment of citizens and establishing an appropriate kind of political relation in their stead, one that is respondent to the commitments to political equality and publicity that political corruption invalidates. Therefore, anti-corruption policies should be *primarily* (albeit not exclusively) targeted at identifying and correcting the causes of political corruption rather than their consequences.

The state is certainly justified to act out of concern for the distributive inequalities that political corruption causes. For example, it may enact provisions to contain the impact of political corruption on the most vulnerable sections of the population. Think of those policies of forced redistribution developed to counteract the corruption of the judiciary. These policies aim to avoid that affluent citizens prevail in court litigation because they are in the position to bribe judges. However, the remedial efficacy of these initiatives is quite patchy and controversial. For example, certain studies have shown that once the total income of less affluent citizens rises, they become corruptors also (see Begović 2006).

Therefore, there is a reasonable ground to think that a more fundamental kind of action is required to identify and counteract, for example, the factors that make certain areas of the public sector vulnerable to such corrupt practices as clientelism (e.g., the health sector) or nepotism (e.g., as concerns hiring practices in public offices). These factors should inform indicators of political corruption, capable of tracking the economic, political, but also social and cultural determinants of this phenomenon across different contexts. Such indicators are irreducible to the standardised gathering and analysis of quantitative data concerning monetary losses, but should include such non-monetary factors as, for instance, the levels of social trust in institutions, access to public services, and the presence of a regulation for the use of private consultants in the public sector.[10]

Once relevant instances of political corruption are identified, an appropriate anti-corruption strategy should not be limited to the design of strict legal regulations for public offices (e.g., by specifying the boundaries for the exercise of the officials' discretion within a code of conduct); neither should it provide only for a tougher criminal prosecution of corrupt officials. Similarly, it does not seem sufficient to promote general mechanisms of institutional reform facing corrupt institutions. In fact, the implementation of the 'good governance standards' in cases of institutional corruption has proved to have modest success in counter-enacting this form of political corruption (see, e.g., Mungiu-Pippidi 2006; Rothstein 2011).

Many such measures, with special reference to the legal regulation and monitoring of public office, do not seem to have the capacity to counteract political corruption trans-contextually. A possible explanation concerns the different levels of entrenchment of certain corrupt practices in the political culture of some societies to which legal regulations may not be straightforwardly juxtaposed without an adequate preparation of the social substrate on which corruption grows. For example, in some countries 'particularism', or the different degrees of citizens' closeness to political power, rather than democratic impartiality governs social relations (Mungiu-Pippidi 2006). In these contexts, anti-corruption policies must primarily address the government's failure to sustain the rule of law. It is apparent that in circumstances of particularism a different kind of engagement with a society's political culture is required with respect to that appropriate for a democracy where the government fails to abide by the duty to treat citizens as political equals.

This explanation of the different trans-contextual success rates of anti-corruption formats is consistent with the recommendations put forward by such international organisations as the World Bank, the United Nations Office on Drugs and Crime, and the United Nations Development Programme. According to these agencies, national ownership in the design of anti-corruption strategies is generally linked to a more effective implementation of such strategies in comparison to formats that were developed in other socio-political contexts and then 'imported' in response to an imminent corruption crisis (UNO 2015; UNPD 2014).

We think that our account of the wrongness of political corruption can shed light on specific policies to get round such difficulties. From our position, it follows that, in order to establish the kind of treatment owed to citizens as the holders of democratic rights, anti-corruption policies must go beyond remedial measures of the kind outlined earlier. They must be capable of fostering a democratic public ethics through socio-political actions aimed at promoting democratic equality, publicity, and a diffused culture of anti-corruption.

For this reason we think that anti-corruption must have a multiplicity of entry-points in society (e.g., the media, schools, civil society's and professional corporations' as well as governmental initiatives) and rely on the synergy of a multiplicity of stakeholders. Educational programmes and public campaigns are crucial in order to develop and sustain a culture of anti-corruption that condemns practices of political corruption as wrong, irrespective of their material consequences.[11]

Additionally, it is important to fight the system of incentives (that underpins, e.g., the practice of smoothing administrative processes through the payment of bribes), which may obfuscate the wrongness of political corruption where specific instances of this phenomenon happen not to have any immediate and material negative consequences but, in fact, are perceived as an instrument to cope with social injustices and inefficiencies. This may be possible, for example, through a simplification of public administration processes, which may make it less crucial to rely on the personal favours of a crooked public official – for example, in order to obtain documents or have access to medical tests in a reasonable time. Actions of this kind may remove indirect incentives to corruption and counteract the tendency to discount the wrongness of corrupt practices as a means to cope with perceived injustices or inefficiencies in the provision of public services.[12]

To achieve these long-term objectives, anti-corruption requires the involvement of a number of diverse stakeholders with a commitment to promoting democratic equality and publicity. It is clear that the involvement of such non-state actors as NGOs and civil society organisations may contribute significantly to the capacity of the state to discharge its anti-corruption duties effectively. But it is an entailment of our argument that non-state actors cannot dispense the state from its anti-corruption duties by fulfilling them in its stead.

The kind of change we have outlined requires a transformation of the general perception of the tolerability of corruption associated with an increased public awareness of the inherent wrongness of this phenomenon. This suggests that targeted anti-corruption legal actions and institutional procedures may in fact work better in combination with broader interventions aimed at strengthening the capacity of citizens to hold public officials publicly accountable for their behaviour. Efforts to hold, where possible, public hearings, organise stakeholder consultations, and develop civic charters go in this direction. These latter are of particular importance because they consist in a formal statement of the commitment of a public institution to honour certain ethical standards, including the accessibility of information and procedures of grievance redress.

The stress on the importance of intervening on the corroboration of the democratic commitments to political equality and publicity in the fight against political corruption also calls for a discussion of anti-corruption from the perspective of individual responsibilities.

Our account of the wrongness of political corruption can justify a general perfect duty for individual public officials not to engage in corrupt practices. The grounds for this duty are germane to those that justify the state's anti-corruption duty. To wit, public officials have a negative duty not to violate citizens' status as political equals. This means that, for example, they ought to refrain from establishing clientelar relations; failures to act on this duty are punishable.

Can we also justify a general positive individual anti-corruption duty? Here the terrain becomes more slippery, but we want to suggest that our discussion of the role of public officials in a democratic society may lend support to the justification of some obligations that may substantiate such a duty. These include, for instance, an obligation to enforce codes of conduct and anti-corruption regulations in the workplace. Moreover, a positive anti-corruption duty could take the form of an obligation to report instances of corrupt behaviour. Take, for example, the practice of whistleblowing as a way of discharging this latter obligation (see Bocchiola and Ceva 2018).

Whistleblowing is the practice of reporting wrongdoings by someone who has or had privileged access to information within a legitimate organisation. This practice can be seen as an integral component of an anti-corruption strategy on two main counts. First, whistleblowing contributes to revealing episodes of political corruption, thus unmasking their underlying agendas. Second, by coming forward in the first person, public officials who decide to blow the whistle honour by their very action that commitment to publicity, which is the opposite of the unaccountability that characterises political corruption. Whistleblowers can thus be seen as acting on their democratic duty of public accountability. In this way, they also set an example of a model conduct that makes a direct contribution to an ethics of anti-corruption that is true to the ideals that undergird the democratic order.

Conclusion

Our discussion of anti-corruption has covered only some possible ways in which public officials and institutions can discharge their anti-corruption duties in a manner that is both true to the normative ideals that underpin the democratic public order and loyal to the rationale with which public power is entrusted to them. A comprehensive account of all such ways cannot possibly be given within the boundaries of a single book chapter.

Rather, we have tried to give a sense of the policy implications of our conceptual and normative account of political corruption in a democracy as a violation of the fundamental commitments to political equality and publicity. In this sense, as argued, political corruption is a specific kind of political wrong that may be predicated both on the quality of public institutions and on the behaviour of individual public officials. As they go against the rationale of the democratic public order, individual and institutional forms of political corruption are wrong in themselves even when they happen not to produce any negative material consequence.

We have also shown how this understanding of the inherent wrongness of political corruption has important implications both for identifying politically relevant instances of this phenomenon and for designing anti-corruption policies. Notably, a democratic ethics of anti-corruption requires the establishment of both institutional and individual responsibilities to ensure that citizens are treated as demanded by their status as the bearers of democratic rights and that public officials and institutions honour the democratic constraints of publicity.

Notes

1 For resources on the economic costs of corruption, see Wickberg (2013).
2 See also Kolstad (2012: 248; Kurer 2005: 23). For a discussion on the terms of the 'principal-agent problem', see Brehm and Gates (1997).
3 This specification distinguishes our position from Mark Warren's contention that the problematic feature of corruption in a democracy is that it implies the concealment of the actions of a corrupt agent from public scrutiny as a means to exclude those who have rightful claims to democratic inclusion (Warren 2004: 333). In our view, this concealment is not necessarily present in all acts of political corruption, whereas the absence of publicity is.
4 For a larger discussion see Ceva and Ferretti (2018).
5 For a discussion of the links between individual and institutional corruption see Ferretti (2018).
6 Ceva (2018) presents this form of mistreatment as an instance of relational injustice.
7 For a case-based illustration of this example, see Vian et al. (2015).
8 For a recent report on the costs of corruption in European countries see Rand Europe (2016).
9 For a discussion of the state's duties of anti-corruption as a set of pro tanto positive duties of relational justice, see Ceva (2018).
10 For a critique of the use of standardised anti-corruption measures see, for example, Rothstein (2011).
11 Such civil society-driven campaigns as 'Restarting the Future' (www.restartingthefuture.eu/about, last accessed: 29 August 2017) are already moving along these lines and promoting a multifaceted EU-wide anti-corruption initiative.
12 For a database on 'administrative simplification and reducing burdens' in OECD countries see: www.oecd.org/gov/regulatory-policy/administrative-simplification.html, last accessed: 29 August 2017.

References

Amundsen, I. (1999). Political Corruption: An Introduction to the Issues. *Chr. Michelsen Institute Development Studies and Human Rights*, WP 7, pp. 1–32.
Begović, B. (2006). *Economic Inequality and Corruption.* (http://pdc.ceu.hu/archive/00003699/01/economic_inequality_and_corruption.pdf, last accessed: 29 August 2017).
Bocchiola, M. and Ceva, E. (2018). *Is Whistleblowing a Duty?* Cambridge: Polity Press.
Brehm, J. and Gates, S. (1997). *Working, Shirking and Sabotage.* Ann Arbor: University of Michigan Press.
Ceva, E. (2018). Political Corruption as a Relational Injustice. *Social Philosophy & Policy*, 34, in press.
Ceva, E. and Ferretti, M.P. (2014). Liberal Democratic Institutions and the Damages of Political Corruption. *The Ethics Forum*, 9, pp. 126–45.
Ceva, E. and Ferretti, M.P. (2017). Political Corruption. *Philosophy Compass*, e12461.
Ceva, E. and Ferretti, M.P. (2018). Political Corruption, Individual Behaviour, and the Quality of Institutions. *Politics, Philosophy and Economics*, 17 (2), pp. 216–31.
Christiano, T. (2008). *The Constitution of Equality.* Oxford: Oxford University Press.
European Commission. (2013). *Study on Corruption in the Healthcare Sector.* HOME/2011/ISEC/PR/047-A2 (https://ec.europa.eu/home-affairs/what-is-new/news/news/2013/20131219_01_en, last accessed: 29 August 2017).

Ferretti, M.P. (2018). A Taxonomy of Institutional Corruption. *Social Philosophy & Policy*, 34, in press.

Kolstad, I. (2012). Corruption as a Violation of Distributed Ethical Obligations. *Journal of Global Ethics*, 8, pp. 239–50.

Kurer, O. (2005). Corruption: An Alternative Approach to Its Definition and Measurement. *Political Studies*, 53, pp. 222–39.

Lessig, L. (2013). "Institutional Corruption" Defined. *Journal of Law, Medicine and Ethics*, 41, pp. 553–5.

Lessig, L. (2014). What an Originalist Would Understand "Corruption" to Mean. *California Law Review*, 102, pp. 1–24.

Méon, P.G. and Weill, L. (2010). Is Corruption an Efficient Grease? *World Development*, 38, pp. 244–59.

Mungiu-Pippidi, A. (2006). Corruption: Diagnosis and Treatment. *Journal of Democracy*, 17, pp. 86–99.

Nye, J. (1967). Corruption and Political Development: A Cost-Benefit Analysis. *American Political Science Review*, 61: 417–27.

Pande, R. (2008). Understanding Political Corruption in Low Income Countries. In T. Paul Schultz and John Strauss, eds, *Handbook of Development Economics*, Volume 4, Amsterdam: Elsevier.

Philp, M. and David-Barrett, E. (2015). Realism About Political Corruption. *Annual Review of Political Science*, 18, pp. 387–402.

Rand Europe. (2016). *The Cost of Non-Europe in the Area of Organised Crime and Corruption*. Annex II – Corruption. Brussels: European Parliamentary Research Service. (www.europarl.europa.eu/RegData/etudes/STUD/2016/579319/EPRS_STU%282016%29579319_EN.pdf, last accessed: 20 February 2017).

Rothstein, B. (2011). Anti-Corruption: The Indirect "big bang" Approach. *Review of International Political Economy*, 18, pp. 228–50.

Sandel, M. (2013). *What Money Can't Buy: The Moral Limits of Markets*. London: Penguin Books.

Stokes, S. C., Dunning, T., Nazareno, M. and Brusco, V. (2013). *Brokers, Voters, and Clientelism: The Puzzle of Distributive Politics*. Cambridge: Cambridge University Press.

Thompson, D. (1993). Mediated Corruption: The Case of the Keating Five. *American Political Science Review*, 87, pp. 369–81.

Thompson, D. (1995). *Ethics in Congress*. Washington, DC: Brookings Institution Press.

Thompson, D. (2005). Two Concepts of Corruption: Making Electoral Campaigns Safe for Democracy. *George Washington Law Review*, 73, pp. 1036–69.

Transparency International. (2006). *Global Corruption Report 2006: Corruption and Health*. (www.transparency.org/whatwedo/publication/global_corruption_report_2006_corruption_and_health, last accessed: 29 August 2017).

UNDP. (2014). *Global Anti-Corruption Initiative* (GAIN) 2014–2017. (http://ba.one.un.org/content/dam/undp/library/Democratic%20Governance/Anti-corruption/globalanticorruption_final_web2.pdf, last accessed: 22 February 2017).

UNO. (2015). *National Anti-Corruption Strategies: A Practical Guide for Development and Implementation*. (www.unodc.org/documents/corruption/Publications/2015/National_Anti-Corruption_Strategies_-_A_Practical_Guide_for_Development_and_Implementation_E.pdf, last accessed: 22 February 2017).

Vian, T., Feeley, F. G., Domente, S., Negruta, A., Matei, A. and Habicht, J. (2015). Barriers to Universal Health Coverage in Republic of Moldova: A Policy Analysis of Formal and Informal Out-of-Pocket Payments. *BMC Health Service Res*, 15, pp. 319–38.

Warren, M. (2004). What Does Corruption Mean in a Democracy? *American Journal of Political Science*, 48 (2), pp. 328–43.

Wickberg, S. (2013). Literature Review on the Costs of Corruption to the Poor. *Transparency International*. (www.u4.no/publications/literature. . . costs-of-corruption. . . /3165, last accessed: 28 August 2017).

21

THE ETHICS OF ANTI-DISCRIMINATION POLICIES

Kasper Lippert-Rasmussen

Introduction

Many believe that discrimination is unjust or at least morally undesirable (cf. Eidelson 2015, 1).[1] Moreover, many believe that it is just and morally desirable, all things considered, to adopt anti-discrimination policies to deal with discrimination.[2] One important form of anti-discrimination policy is laws prohibiting employers from hiring or paying on racist or sexist grounds; affirmative action is another.

This chapter defines anti-discrimination policies and discrimination (second section) before distinguishing between various anti-discrimination policies (third section). The fourth section narrows the focus down to a specific kind of anti-discrimination policy, affirmative action, describing the policy in greater detail. The fifth section rebuts the reverse discrimination objection to affirmative action. The sixth and seventh sections critically examine other objections to affirmative action together with some of the main arguments in favour of affirmative action. The eighth section surveys three untraditional sites of anti-discrimination policies. The final section concludes. My main claims are: (1) that there are many different kinds of anti-discrimination policies; (2) of those, affirmative action is the most controversial; (3) yet it makes little sense to discuss the perfectly general question 'Is affirmative action justified?' – we must consider the specifics of each scheme; (4) nevertheless, the most common objections to affirmative action are problematic; (5) while some of the main arguments in favour identify important concerns; (6) albeit these concerns often support conflicting policies; (7) finally, that we should broaden our perspective on affirmative action to include untraditional sites, such as health, language, and housing.

Anti-discrimination policies and discrimination defined

For present purposes, I adopt the following definition:

> A policy is an anti-discrimination policy if, and only if, it is intended to: (a) eliminate or reduce discrimination, or (b) to counteract its negative effects on the discriminatees.

Whether something qualifies as an anti-discrimination policy according to this definition depends on the intention behind the policy, not its effects. A policy that reduces discrimination and is known to have this effect by policymakers but which is not adopted for this reason does not count as an anti-discrimination policy. Moreover, an anti-discrimination policy might be unsuccessful (e.g., might increase discrimination) because it strengthens people's dispositions to think of individuals as members of certain socially salient groups and to treat them differentially on that basis.[3]

Note also that 'is intended to eliminate or reduce discrimination' can be read intentionally as referring to the intention to eliminate or reduce something, *which the agent perceives* – perhaps mistakenly – to be discrimination. Alternatively, it can be read extensionally as the intention to eliminate or reduce the effects of something *which is* discrimination – even though the agent might not perceive it as such. I read the definition extensionally. According to my definition, say, a pre–civil rights movement employer who notes that certain biases result in fewer female than male applicants being hired and adopts a policy to counteract this tendency adopts an anti-discrimination policy, even if they have no concept of discrimination. Hence, to apply my definition of anti-discrimination policy, I should say what discrimination is (cp. Lippert-Rasmussen 2013, 13–46):

> X discriminates against Y relative to Z if, and only if, (1) X treats Y worse than Z; (2) this is (a) due to the fact that X believes that Y is a member of a certain socially salient group and believes that Z is not, or (b) explained in a certain way by the fact that Y is a member of a certain socially salient group and Z is not.[4]

A group is socially salient to the extent that perceived membership of it structures a wide range of social interactions. Racial groups are socially salient in a racist society in which race determines who gets to sit where in the bus, who can go to university, who can live in which neighbourhoods, and so forth. The group of people preferring Pepsi to Coca-Cola does not form a socially salient group, as the members of these two groups are very rarely treated differently. An employer might treat people who prefer Pepsi to Coca-Cola unfairly by idiosyncratically refusing to hire them, but this would not count as discrimination according to my definition.[5] More generally, a definition of discrimination focusing on socially salient groups fits standard lists of discriminatees quite well and, thus, aligns with which kinds of differential treatment we typically consider discriminatory. Moreover, discrimination so construed is morally significant due to the stigma and cumulative harms socially salient, disadvantageously treated groups experience and which often form a crucial background for moral complaints about discrimination (Lippert-Rasmussen 2013, 168–170).

Why is discrimination unjust? There are many different answers to this question. Some argue that discrimination, or at least some forms of discrimination, is disrespectful and for that reason unjust (Alexander 1992; Hellman 2008). Others believe that discrimination involves treating people unfairly, whether disrespectful or not. Others yet submit that discrimination is unjust because of its harmful effects (Lippert-Rasmussen 2006, 2013). And there are other accounts. Since this chapter is on the ethics of anti-discrimination policies – not the ethics of discrimination – I can largely bracket which of these accounts are correct. People can consistently disagree about what makes discrimination unjust, agree that discrimination is unjust, and agree on what ought to be done to eliminate or mitigate it.

Different types of anti-discrimination policies

There are many different anti-discrimination policies, which differ along several dimensions: (1) ends, (2) site, (3) means, (4) intended beneficiaries, and (5) agents. I explain and illustrate these dimensions ahead, some of which are morally significant, and all of which are politically important. I return to them in the fourth section to show how they offer a useful taxonomy over different kinds of affirmative action.

The first distinction is between policies aimed at eliminating the causes of discrimination and those aimed at preventing discrimination or mitigating its negative effects. Many anti-discrimination policies involve both, if for no other reason, because, typically, reducing the amount of discrimination will reduce its harmful effects. Analytically speaking, however, these two effects can be pried apart. An important example of eliminative anti-discrimination policies is the 'busing' of US school children implemented in the 1960s in view of *Brown v. Board of Education*. While partly intended to counteract the effects of the tendency of underfunding 'black' relative to 'white' schools, its primary aim was to eliminate the causes of discrimination through integration (cf. Suk 2018). A number of policies that legally forbid various forms of discrimination typically do not seek directly to weaken the causes of discrimination (e.g., implicit bias), seeking instead to counteract their effects, as in compensation to its victims.[6] Typically, however, the legal regulation of discrimination weakens the causes of discrimination in the long run, such as by creating gender-balanced workplaces and thereby weakening people's sexist biases.

The second dimension of anti-discrimination policies is site. Traditionally, anti-discrimination policies pertain to the labour market and education while not seeking to address private-sphere discrimination. Anti-discrimination policies rarely even indirectly address people discriminating on grounds of race or religion in their choice of partners, friends, or neighbours, despite anti-discrimination policies that would prevent these same people from discriminating against those with whom they do not want to associate in their private lives when acting as employers.

This asymmetric treatment of public and private discrimination requires justification. One putative justification is that public-sphere discrimination is more harmful than discrimination in the private sphere. This suggestion appears unpromising, however, as private discrimination (e.g., in relation to racially biased choice of partners) is a major causal factor underlying the reproduction of racial inequalities: 'If blacks and whites married each other without respect to race . . . racial inequality as such would vanish within a generation' (Wertheimer 2006, 957). A better justification might be that while discrimination in the private sphere is often as harmful as discrimination in the public sphere, the right to do wrong applies in the private sphere but not in the public sphere (cp. Waldron 1981). A third, pragmatic justification points to the difficulties in establishing that individual people discriminate racially in their choice of partner.

Three, anti-discrimination policies differ in terms of the means employed. For instance, an important distinction in anti-discrimination policies is the distinction between soft and hard goals. An example of a soft goal would be an aspiration of, say, a fire department to hire at least 20 per cent women over the next five years. Unlike with hard goals, there are no procedures in place actually ensuring that such goals be achieved. Rather, it is a goal involving no specific directives that, say, recruitment officers should bear in mind. Hard-goal anti-discrimination policies are generally thought to be harder to justify than soft-goal anti-discrimination policies.

Fourth, anti-discrimination policies differ in terms of the intended beneficiaries. Anti-discrimination policies typically seek to address discrimination against one particular group, thereby benefiting its members, as when the Americans with Disabilities Act from 1990 sought to address discrimination against disabled people only. Other policies have a broader scope, such as when a country implements policy to review the extent to which it complies with international anti-discrimination conventions. In principle, anti-discrimination policies could even partly be intended to benefit those who discriminate so as to counteract the inflated and harmful self-conception underpinning their discriminatory acts.

One particular issue in relation to the beneficiaries of anti-discrimination policies that has received a fair amount of attention is *intersectionality*. The concept was introduced to describe the situation of black women (Crenshaw 1989) enduring both racial and sexual discrimination. These two forms of discrimination interact in a complex manner, however, such that we cannot reduce the situation of black women as being that of suffering racist *and* sexist discrimination. Accordingly, anti-racist policies based on the experiences of the former and anti-sexist policies based on the distinct experiences of the latter often fail to address the situation of these women; indeed, they often exacerbate and fail to acknowledge it. Consider Crenshaw's analysis of *DeGraffenreid v. General Motors* (1977), where a group of female African Americans fired by GM sued the company on the grounds that the company's 'last hired, first fired' policy had a disparate impact on them; neither *qua* African Americans nor *qua* women, but *qua* African American women. GM had not hired any African American women prior to 1964. It had employed both African American men and white women before 1964, however, and the court accordingly found that the policy involves neither race nor sex discrimination, thus ruling in favour of GM and ignoring the distinct experience of African American women.

Presumably, similar claims about intersectionality apply to other groups (e.g., Muslim homosexuals) and to subgroups of black women (e.g., black lesbians). Hence, some people appeal to intersectionality to question an approach to discrimination that focuses on socially salient groups. The corollary seems to be scepticism about group-focused anti-discrimination policies (see second section). This strikes me as a misunderstanding; it is one thing to criticise our discrimination-related taxonomy of groups for being too coarse-grained, but it is another – and unwarranted – step to reject group-focused approaches to discrimination, however fine-grained, altogether. To motivate the latter, one must argue that any discriminatee's situation is unique.

Fifth, anti-discrimination policies differ in terms of agents. Anti-discrimination policies are typically enacted by the state, as in the regulation of discrimination by non-state agents. However, private companies can voluntarily adopt anti-discrimination policies. Even individual persons can do so in an extended sense of 'policy'; for example, I can adopt a policy to counteract tendencies that I suspect I have to give less weight to the testimony of women than to the testimony of men by granting extra attention to reasons why something to which a women testifies might be true and by giving extra attention to reasons why what a man testifies might be false (cf. Bishop and Trout 2005, 146–147).[7] While states initiate many anti-discrimination policies, state officials also discriminate. For instance, the use of risk assessment software that inaccurately rates offenders of some groups as being more likely to reoffend might well involve indirect discrimination (see endnote 4).[8] In such cases, a state anti-discrimination policy might consist of nothing more than repealing a discriminatory policy of its own.

Affirmative action

I now turn to a particular anti-discrimination policy, affirmative action: ' "Affirmative action" means positive steps taken to increase the representation of women and minorities in areas of employment, education, and culture from which they have been historically excluded' (Fullinwider 2013). While this characterisation can be improved (e.g., it seems possible to have affirmative action policies benefiting members of an excluded, numerical majority), it has the virtue of making the connection between affirmative action and anti-discrimination policies transparent.[9] Women and minorities have presumably been excluded from certain areas, and this exclusion has often been discriminatory in form.

As Fullinwider (2013, 1) notes, some forms of affirmative action generate 'intense controversy' due to the 'positive steps' qualification. By this, Fullinwider means steps extending beyond simply eliminating direct discrimination against women and minorities. An employer taking steps to eliminate sexist biases from influencing the evaluation of applicants by the hiring committee would simply involve the elimination of a particular source of direct discrimination against female applicants and, thus, merely amount to a 'negative step'. By 'direct discrimination', I mean discrimination satisfying 1 and 2a in my definition earlier. An example of 'positive steps' could be the implementation of a rule to the effect that every second person hired should be a woman. This goes beyond mere non-positive steps, as it might involve hiring female applicants instead of better-qualified male applicants, thus constituting a deviation from purely meritocratic hiring (see fourth section). The 'might' in the previous sentence is important. Suppose that two-thirds of the best-qualified applicants are women. The rule therefore does not require deviation from strict meritocratic norms. Nevertheless, this is a 'positive step' in that it could be a coincidence that it involves no disregard for meritocratic norms. Possibly, in most cases of affirmative action there is no happy harmony between merit in the standard sense and the relevant affirmative action measures. Hence, the agent of affirmative action seems engaged in direct discrimination against unusual discriminatees (e.g., white males). How can a directly discriminatory policy be an anti-discrimination policy? A response to this challenge is offered in the next section, which probes the sense in which affirmative action is directly discriminatory. Here, I focus on a different response – to wit, that affirmative action reduces or mitigates the effects of indirect discrimination.

How does affirmative action do so? We find a historical example in a 1971 US court case, *Griggs v. Duke Power*, where the Supreme Court (SC) ruled that even if the employer had no intention of excluding African Americans, requiring a high school diploma for promotion did not reflect any business necessity and was indirectly discriminatory against (i.e., had 'disparate impact' on) African American employees due to their being less likely as a result of past discrimination to have a high school diploma than white employees. *Griggs v. Duke Power* effectively positioned companies either to show that practices with disparate impact reflected business necessity or, alternatively, to adopt affirmative action measures to counteract disparate impact (Sabbagh 2007, 118–124).

Later SC cases in the 1970s upheld such voluntarily adopted affirmative action schemes. In *United Steelworkers v. Weber*, the SC sided with Kaiser Aluminium and Chemical Corp against a white employee, Brian Weber, who claimed that the company's affirmative action scheme violated his Civil Rights Act Title VII right against discrimination on the basis of race. The scheme meant that 50 per cent of craft training positions would go to black and 50 per cent to white employees despite the overwhelming majority of employees being white.[10]

Many regard affirmative action as a means of addressing indirect discrimination. The idea is this: suppose we live in a society with a lengthy history of discrimination against minorities. Even if all forms of direct discrimination against these groups had disappeared, they would still suffer from indirect discrimination, since society has been organised for years in a way that systematically disadvantages minorities. Suppose that much recruitment takes place through mouth-to-ear channels. Present employees inform friends and acquaintances about job openings. Since people are racially segregated, such recruitment indirectly discriminates against the formerly disadvantaged minority, since their members have lower employment rates. Since this disadvantage arguably reflects no direct discrimination on the part of employers, we cannot eliminate it by making direct discrimination illegal.[11] Hence, this is where affirmative action measures to improve the representation of formerly excluded groups enter the picture.[12]

Affirmative action policies differ along all five dimensions presented in the third section. First, while particular affirmative action schemes often seek to address particular forms of indirect discrimination, the more general affirmative action policy promoted by the state is intended to reduce discrimination in the long term. Second, most affirmative action policies target the labour market or university admissions. As described in the eighth section, however, it might be useful to expand our notion of the site of affirmative action. Third, the most drastic form of affirmative action is where the state makes (demanding) quotas legally mandatory. Much less drastic affirmative action measures are where a private company engages in outreach, such as efforts to ensure that potential minority applicants are aware of and encouraged to apply for a relevant position where the selection of the successful application is purely merit-based. Fourth, main beneficiaries of affirmative action schemes are racial or ethnic minorities, women, disabled people, linguistic minorities, Dalits, and so forth. Fifth, in most cases, the agents promoting affirmative action policies have been state agents (e.g., courts). Private companies are increasingly adopting non-legally required affirmative action schemes, however, although often for reasons not tied to the elimination of indirect discrimination.

The reverse discrimination objection to affirmative action

Some defend affirmative action as a means of counteracting discrimination. Others object that it constitutes discrimination against those whom it disfavours. If, say, being black counts as an advantage in relation to university admissions, not being black is a disadvantage assuming a constant number of admissions; and so, the objection goes, this means that affirmative action discriminates against – on the basis of race in this case. This renders affirmative action self-defeating; while intended to eliminate or at least mitigate discrimination, it merely constitutes a new form of discrimination. To some, this is a decisive objection. Call this *the reverse discrimination objection.*

The objection is widespread in popular culture but is also common in the philosophical literature. The core claim underlying it is found, for instance, in the following affirmative action dilemma articulated by Robert Fullinwider: 'if we do not use preferential hiring, we permit discrimination to exist. But preferential hiring is also discrimination. The dilemma is that whatever we do, we permit discrimination' (Fullinwider 1980, 156).

In the interest of clarity, I discuss the following version of the reverse discrimination argument:

1   If anything, that which justifies affirmative action is that it eliminates discrimination or mitigates its effects.
2   Affirmative action is in itself discrimination.
3   If it is true of a certain policy that that which, if anything, justifies the policy is that it eliminates a certain wrongful activity or mitigates its effects, then that policy is not justified if it itself involves the relevant kind of wrongful activity.
4   Thus, affirmative action is not justified.

This argument is weak. First, premise 3 is disputable. Even if a certain policy constitutes a wrong of the very kind the avoidance of which constitutes its rationale, it might be a less serious instance of that wrong, in which case it is an open question whether the policy might not be justified overall.

Second, and more seriously, 'discrimination premise 2' involves a different sense of 'discrimination' than premise 1. Or at least this is what reflective friends of affirmative action will say. Obviously, they must concede that affirmative action involves 'discrimination' in some sense. Affirmative action for women, say, involves treating men disadvantageously relative to women and in the generic sense of 'discrimination' in which one discriminates against someone if one treats them disadvantageously relative to others, because they are believed to have a certain property which those one does not treat disadvantageously do not have (cp. Lippert-Rasmussen 2013, 15). However, premise 1 does not employ discrimination in the generic sense. There are many contexts in which we do not think it wrongs people that they are being treated disadvantageously relative to others; for example, the courts do not wrong guilty people by treating them worse than those who are innocent. Hence, 'discrimination' in premise 1 must mean something akin to 'wrongful discrimination', which is more specific than generic discrimination. Moreover, the friends of affirmative action would say that it is discrimination only in the generic sense.

Ronald Dworkin (2003, 112), for instance, thinks that unjust discrimination is harmful, differential treatment involving the disrespectful view that the discriminatees are less worthy of respect. However, affirmative action does not involve any such view of those whom it disfavours (e.g., white males). Accordingly, Dworkin is entitled to resist the present objection on the grounds that, in his view, the sense of 'discrimination' that makes premise 2 true also renders premise 1 false.

While we might disagree with Dworkin about what makes discrimination unjust, we can presumably make an argumentative move similar to that one in response to the reverse discrimination objection. Some might object to this extrapolation of Dworkin's response (and indeed to Dworkin's response itself) on the grounds that discrimination in the generic sense – that is, treating some people worse than others 'simply on the basis of physical characteristics that have no relevance to the award given or to the burden imposed', such as race, religion, gender, or national origins – is in itself wrongful (Cohen and Sterba 2003, 24–25).

In reply, affirmative action proponents are likely to respond that regardless of whether the moral principle underlying this response is true, it is irrelevant to the justifiability of affirmative action. Justifications of affirmative action never assert that race, religion, gender, and/or national origins in themselves are the basis for differential treatment (cp. Nickel 2003, 4). It is not simply because women are women that, in a sexist society, we should adopt affirmative action schemes in their favour; rather, it is because being a woman in a sexist society renders it likely that one's opportunities diminish as a result of various unjust forms of discrimination. Hence, the real basis of differential treatment is whether individuals belong to a group whose members face unjust obstacles to equality of opportunity.

I conclude that, despite being very common, the reverse discrimination objection is flawed. This makes it interesting to explore some other less but still quite common objections to affirmative action.[13]

Other objections to affirmative action

This section surveys four alternative objections to affirmative action in the given order: (1) over/underinclusion, (2) bad faith, (3) meritocratic, and (4) stigma. The over/underinclusion objection submits that affirmative action is flawed in two ways (Goldman 1979): it is over-inclusive in that it invariably benefits members of a group that have generally been excluded but who are untypical, such as having come from rich families, and have not suffered from the relevant exclusion. Moreover, affirmative action schemes are invariably underinclusive; there are always groups that have been excluded by way of discrimination but for whom there are no affirmative action programs.[14] There are also groups that might not have suffered exclusion through discrimination but have suffered other injustices at least as bad. Charles Lawrence and Mari Matsuda (1997, 190–191) dismissively refer to this objection as the 'endless citings of the "poor white male from Appalachia"'.

On the face of it, the over/underinclusion objection is weak. For one thing, it is open for a defender of affirmative action to reply that there should be affirmative action schemes for non-included groups (Sterba 2009). Moreover, a feature of any feasible policy is that it is over/ underinclusive. While the legal system sometimes punishes innocents and lets the guilty go free, few would urge abolishing the legal system on those grounds. If so, why should affirmative action be abandoned in view of over/underinclusion?

Second, the bad faith objection points out that those defending affirmative action argue opportunistically and do not favour affirmative action for, say, white males in contexts where they need role models or might have experienced exclusion through discrimination. While some affirmative action supporters sometimes argue opportunistically, the same is true of some affirmative action critics; that is, they reject affirmative action because they condemn deviations from purely meritocratic standards and yet do not condemn giving preference to the children of former alumni (Cohen and Sterba 2003). The fatal flaw in the bad faith objection is that it is not an objection to affirmative action as such; rather, it is an objection directed at the coherence of the attitudes of someone who favours or opposes affirmative action.

Third, the meritocratic objection submits that affirmative action violates the claims of the best qualified. While this objection is more plausible than the previous two, it also has its limitations. For one thing, it is not an objection to all forms of affirmative action (e.g., it is not an objection to outreach). Moreover, some have argued that 'merits' should be understood in such a way that they reflect the fact that some have faced more obstacles in developing their merits and, thus, that many forms of affirmative action are compatible with meritocracy when merits are understood in a manner that involves 'leveling the playing field' (Mason 2006). Finally, many would deny that people have a claim that positions are filled on merit. Rather, merito-cratic norms are justified in terms of the good consequences of adopting them (Daniels 1978).

Fourth, the stigma objection asserts that affirmative action is wrong due to the stigma it creates for its intended beneficiaries (Cohen and Sterba 2003). Suppose that women, say, are hired partly on the basis of qualifications, partly on the basis of being women. In that case, many women actually hired will never know whether they would have been hired had there not been any affirmative action scheme in place and are, thus, likely to be seen – even by themselves – as less qualified than their male colleagues, ceteris paribus. If women are hired partly on the basis of gender in many contexts, this could result in women being stigmatised as less qualified than men.

While this objection has some force, it is also problematic, at least when used to defend a blanket rejection of affirmative action. Much hangs on the socio-psychology of stigma. On a purely rationalistic view of qualification stigma – that is, one according to which beliefs about someone's expected level of qualifications given that they belong to a certain group are correctly inferred from the available evidence, ceteris paribus – affirmative action schemes stigma-tise those hired on that basis as less qualified. According to a non-rationalistic view of stigma, however, factors such as the frequency with which one interacts with superiors belonging to a certain group (e.g., professors) will affect beliefs of the sort just mentioned, to a degree which is not warranted by its evidential weight. On this view, affirmative action might actually decrease stigma.

Another limitation of the stigma objection arises when stigma involves a kind of epistemic injustice. Suppose that being female gives you a marginal advantage in the hiring process due to an affirmative action scheme and that the resulting qualification-related stigma is out of proportion with this advantage. In that case, there might be an objection to affirmative action. It is one that is based on the unjust epistemic dispositions of those who stigmatise women, however, and the objection would disappear if we could school them out of the unjust epistemic dispositions.

There are obviously more than these four objections to affirmative action, and although I have expressed misgivings about all four objections, affirmative action schemes are sometimes unjustified. For one thing, they tend to be socially costly in the sense that they involve deviating from meritocratic norms and the costs this involves; for example, efficiency losses might outweigh the benefits brought by affirmative action in some cases.[15] Moreover, even the staunchest defenders of affirmative action concede that such schemes might be unjustified because they overcompensate; for example, setting aside 90 per cent of places at universities for women might be unfair to rejected male applicants, because such a scheme would go beyond counteracting the effects of discrimination or what is required to realise the long-term ambition to eliminate it.

Justifications for affirmative action

The failure of the reverse discrimination objection and problems with the four objections to affirmative action surveyed in the sixth section do not imply any positive justification for affirmative action. Is there? This section briefly expands and assesses the following four arguments in favour of affirmative action: (1) anti-discrimination, (2) equality of opportunity, (3) role model, (4) and diversity. In many contexts, these arguments support similar policies, but there are circumstances under which they involve conflicting recommendations.

Let us start with the anti-discrimination argument. The most obvious positive justification for affirmative action is that it eliminates or mitigates the effects of discrimination. This justification is very abstract, however, and can be specified in very different ways. In particular, the mere fact that something is bad (and that a certain means will reduce this badness) does not justify using these means. It might be bad that someone unjustly stole some of your property. One way of rectifying this might be by confiscating some of my property and giving it to you. But this does not justify doing so, and the fact that by taking my property one can rectify the injustice done to you might not even be a *pro tanto* reason for taking it (Fullinwider 2003, 74).

One important distinction here is that between the long-term effects of broad-scoped affirmative action policies (e.g., legislation imposing affirmative action duties on all employers) and the short-term effects of narrow-scoped affirmative action policies (e.g., an affirmative action scheme adopted by an individual company). While the former might plausibly be justified by appealing to how these policies reduce the amount of discrimination in the long run, the same cannot be said about the latter. The mere fact that one employer adopts an affirmative action scheme is likely to make only a very marginal contribution, if any at all, to the reduction of future discrimination.

Second, discrimination is often assumed to increase inequality of opportunity and, accordingly, that any anti-discrimination policy reduces inequality of opportunity; however, this is not necessarily so. While discrimination is an important source of inequality of opportunity, there are also others. For instance, even in the absence of any form of discrimination, socio-economic inequalities between groups will tend to leave young people from privileged groups better off opportunity-wise than those from non-privileged groups. Imagine a situation of a (socio-economically speaking better off) ethnic minority – say, Chinese people in Malaysia – whose members are subjected to racial discrimination favouring members of the socio-economically speaking worse-off majority. Here, anti-discrimination policies addressing racial discrimination against the Chinese look different depending on whether you take a discrimination perspective or one based on equality of opportunity.

Third, affirmative action is often defended by the need to have role models for underrepresented groups. If all professors are white males, this is likely to send the message that academia is not for women and blacks – and especially not black women. Moreover, it is likely to lead to an environment in which women and blacks feel unwelcome and will benefit less from teaching opportunities than white males. Unfortunately, the role model argument is often more hinted at than meticulously laid out. There are at least two respects in which this is so: the relevant empirical assumptions about role model psychology and the normative requirements pertaining to role models.

Regarding the former assumption, much hangs on the extent to which role model psychology is sensitive to whether students perceive the absence of group-identical role models as the effect of exclusion. German-speaking Belgians will rarely meet German-speaking role models at Belgian universities. Unlike African Americans who studied at nearly all-white US universities, however, they are likely to see this as simply reflecting how German-speaking Belgians constitute a tiny proportion of the Belgian population, in which case the absence of German-speaking role models might not detract from their motivation.

If the need for role models is insensitive to such facts, however, the argument then likely favours the much greater representation of German-speaking Belgians than a discrimination-based argument. The exact extent of this divergence depends on the second and normative assumption about role models, such as whether people have, say, a claim to be equally well-off with respect to group role models.

Fourth, in recent years, affirmative action schemes have increasingly been justified by appeals to the need for diversity along cultural, racial, and gender lines. This partly reflects the outcome of *Bakke v. Regent of California*, which was commonly seen as implying that non-quota affirmative action schemes might be legally permitted if narrowly tailored to the promotion of diversity and otherwise not. Obviously, one must be told in relation to what diversity is identified. This is not small potatoes, and while the proponents of the diversity-based argument usually think that diversity pertains to the very same categories as does discrimination, it is far from clear that there is a better-than-very-partial overlap here. While class is important to people's outlooks, the friends of anti-discrimination policies are rarely concerned with class-based indirect discrimination.

While diversity- and anti-discrimination-based arguments have similar implications regarding some of the standard cases to which they have been applied (e.g., the under-representation of women), the implications of the two arguments can diverge. Take diversity in South Africa. The South African population is classified as 2.5 per cent Asian. Suppose that South African Asians have a different outlook, statistically speaking, than other South Africans – an assumption that is similar to one often made about other groups in other contexts. If so, diversity-based arguments pertaining to workplaces would appear to support a much higher representation of Asian South Africans than an anti-discrimination argument.

In sum, while the four arguments in favour of affirmative action point to important concerns that in some contexts might justify affirmative action, in some contexts they will support conflicting policies. Furthermore, some of the arguments involve important unclarities that require resolution.

Untraditional sites of anti-discrimination policies

I have thus far focused on the traditional sites of anti-discrimination policies: higher education and the labour market. This focus is not mandated by my definition of anti-discrimination policies. This section considers three untraditional sites of anti-discrimination policies: (1) health, (2) discriminatory language, and (3) housing.

First, health is extremely important for one's opportunities. Moreover, many groups that are subjected to discrimination have worse health than groups not so subjected. In the US context, for instance, there was a 3.6-year difference in the life expectancies of black and white Americans in 2013 (down from 5.9 years in 1999) in favour of white Americans.[16] On one hypothesis, these health disparities owe to differences in socio-economic status, and discrimination is one determinant of socio-economic status.[17] Assuming this to be the case, there is conceptual room for affirmative action within health care. In the context of a welfare state, this would mean the modification of the universal health care principle in the interest of promoting the health of special groups. Indeed, with some qualifications, which I set aside here, Shlomi Segall (2013, 204) has defended 'radical affirmative action', which strives 'to assign priority to those whose need is caused by an ex ante worse-off health prospect, whether generated by social or natural factors'.[18]

Second, many biases surface in and are nourished by language. It is no coincidence that 'he' was generally the third-person pronoun used until recently and that many people are uncomfortable with using 'she' instead of 'he' in all contexts where they would normally and comfortably use 'he' even if unaware of the gender of the person to whom reference is being made. Political correctness is the view that we should cleanse our language of such discriminatory use of language. Indeed, it might be fruitful to see some forms of political correctness as affirmative action in terms of language. Think, for instance, of the 'Black is beautiful' slogan or the non-linguistic means of communication used by companies when they predominantly use white female and black (or Asian) male and female models to pose as company executives in their self-presentations. Like affirmative action in its more traditional sites, such kinds of affirmative action are not disrespectful to whites or white males *per se*. Because of the background – the predominance of Eurocentric aesthetic ideals and the overrepresentation of white males among company executives in North American and European companies – few are likely to think that the implicature of 'Black is beautiful' is that 'White is ugly' or to read into politically correct self-presentations by companies any message to the effect that white males have worse qualifications than females or non-whites.

Third, racial discrimination and religious discrimination often thrive on segregation in terms of housing. In an important study, Elizabeth Anderson (2010, 2) writes, 'Segregation of social groups is a principal cause of group inequality . . . It reinforces stigmatizing stereotypes about the disadvantaged and thus causes discrimination'. Few, however, would see desegregation policies as anti-discrimination policies. If Anderson's causal analysis is correct, however, anti-discrimination housing policies are no less important than anti-discrimination policies in other areas. Not all such policies need involve affirmative action; some might simply involve the merely negative step of eliminating direct discrimination against African Americans by financial institutions. However, other policies might take an affirmative action form. Interestingly, if the (intermediate) aim is to overcome segregation and that alone, we should be indifferent between 'affirmative action' for whites who move into 'black areas' (e.g., financial incentives of various kinds) and affirmative action for blacks moving into 'white areas'.[19] Indeed, one might imagine a combination of the two schemes such that the sum of local affirmative action schemes adds up to a race-neutral scheme, globally speaking.

While education and the labour market form the traditional sites of affirmative action, the three examples that I have given – others could be added – show that there are many other sites of anti-discrimination policies, including affirmative action.

Conclusion

I have focused on anti-discrimination policies assuming the form of affirmative action. My main reason for doing so is that affirmative action policies raise ethical issues, which are more interesting than anti-discrimination policies addressing direct discrimination. I have argued that affirmative action policies form a very diverse set of policies. Accordingly, 'Is affirmative action morally justified?' is a question that is posed at a level of generality which is too high. It does not plausibly allow for a negative or affirmative answer – only an 'it depends' answer. For instance, it is arguably not justified to make hard quotas for women in a situation where alternative means with fewer unintended, harmful side effects are available. That said, I have also argued that the most common objection to affirmative action – the reverse discrimination objection – fails across the board and that some of the main alternative objections to affirmative action are problematic in various ways as well. While noting that standard affirmative action schemes have social costs, most notably the deselection of those who are most qualified according to standard criteria, I took a more positive view of some of the main positive justifications for affirmative action – arguments, which, so I argued, often support similar affirmative action schemes but can support quite different policies under other circumstances in a way that often goes unnoticed. Finally, I suggested that the sites of anti-discrimination policies, including affirmative action, extend much beyond higher education and the labour market.[20]

Notes

1 I use the phrase 'unjust or at least morally undesirable' because, all things considered, justice is one of several factors determining what is morally desirable (i.e., morally permissible or morally required). In the interest of simplicity, I set this complication aside whenever possible.

2 The latter view is not justified simply because the former is. There might be a right to do wrong, in casu to discriminate. If so, we must possibly refrain from intervening to prevent certain kinds of morally undesirable forms of discrimination (Vallentyne 2006).

3 In part, this worry might motivate the resistance of some states (e.g., France) to adopt anti-discrimination policies requiring the state to classify its citizens along ethnic or racial lines (cf. Case and Givens 2014, 98).

4 I need 2b) to accommodate indirect discrimination. 2b) opens up for the possibility that X's beliefs about Y's group membership do not explain his treatment of Y qua being part of X's motivating reason. More generally, an act can be indirectly discriminatory in the sense I have in mind if it disadvantages members of a certain group relative to others and yet does not involve any objectionable mental states regarding the former group (Altman 2015; cp. Lippert-Rasmussen 2013, 72). That which is called 'indirect discrimination' in the European context is often referred to in the American context as 'disparate impact'. I use the two terms as synonyms.

5 Similarly, nepotism is the unfair, disadvantageous treatment of non-family members. Still, victims of nepotism do not normally think of themselves as victims of discrimination.

6 Implicit bias is 'relatively unconscious and relatively automatic features of prejudiced judgment and social behavior' (Brownstein 2015).

7 Cp. Fricker (2009) on testimonial injustice.

8 www.propublica.org/article/machine-bias-risk-assessments-in-criminal-sentencing.

9 For further discussion of the definition of affirmative action, see Lippert-Rasmussen (forthcoming, Chapter 1).

10 The 'black population ratio' of the town in which the relevant plant was located was 'four times the black plant ratio' (Ezorsky 1991, 46).

11 Similar reasoning applies to many other practices, such as the 'first hired, last fired' rule.

12 There is also a more pragmatic justification for affirmative action legislation. It is often difficult to prove discriminatory intent and in any case much more difficult than to show that a certain practice has disparate impact.

13 For a fuller assessment of a wider range of such arguments, see Lippert-Rasmussen (forthcoming).

14 While proponents of the over/underinclusion objection do not typically refer to intersectionality, possibly intersectionality might be part of the reason why affirmative action is over/underinclusive.
15 Admittedly, weighing the typically very diverse costs of affirmative action against its equally diverse benefits is very messy business. However, the challenge this represents is identical for friends and foes of affirmative action alike, who make claims about where the overall balance of benefits and harms of affirmative action lies.
16 www.cdc.gov/nchs/data/databriefs/db218.pdf.
17 www.nationalacademies.org/hmd/~/media/Files/Activity%20Files/SelectPops/Health Disparities/2011-FEB-24/Commissioned%20Paper%20by%20Lesley%20Russell.pdf.
18 Since natural factors do not seem to constitute 'exclusion', Segall's view is not a pure affirmative action view on Fullinwider's definition earlier.
19 Of course, desegregation will rarely be our only concern; for example, we might also have distributive concerns for worst-off individuals.
20 Previous versions of this chapter were presented at the Blavatnik School of Government, University of Oxford, and Department of Politics, University of Essex. I thank Andreas Albertsen, James Christensen, Søren Flinch Midtgaard, Kristian Kriegbaum Jensen, Timo Jütten, Lasse Nielsen, Tore Vincent Olsen, Tom Parr, Viki Pedersen, Tom Simpson, Jonathan Wolff, and the editors for helpful comments on a previous version of this chapter. In particular, I am indebted to Annabelle Lever for extensive, helpful written comments.

References

Alexander, L. (1992). "What Makes Wrongful Discrimination Wrong? Biases, Preferences, Stereotypes, and Proxies," *University of Pennsylvania Law Review*, 141, 149–219.
Altman, A. (2015). "Discrimination", *Stanford Encyclopedia*, https://plato.stanford.edu/entries/discrimination/#IndDis.
Anderson, E. (2010). *The Imperative of Integration*. Princeton, NJ: Princeton University Press.
Bishop, M. A. and Trout, J. D. (2005). *Epistemology and the Psychology of Human Judgment*. New York: Oxford University Press.
Brownstein, M. (2015). "Implicit Bias," *Stanford Encyclopedia*, https://plato.stanford.edu/entries/implicit-bias/.
Case, R. E. and Givens, T. E. (2014). *Legislating Equality: The Politics of Anti-Discrimination Politics in Europe*. Oxford: Oxford University Press.
Cohen, C. and Sterba, J. P. (2003). *Affirmative Action and Racial Preference*. New York: Oxford University Press.
Crenshaw, K. (1989). "Demarginalizing the Intersection of Race and Sex: A Black Feminist Critique of Antidiscrimination Doctrine, Feminist Theory and Antiracist Policies," *The University of Chicago Legal Forum*, 140, 139–167.
Daniels, N. (1978). "Merit and Meritocracy," *Philosophy & Public Affairs*, 7, 206–223.
Dworkin, R. (2003). "Bakke's Case: Are Quotas Unfair?" In Steven M. Cahn, *The Affirmative Action Debate*. New York: Routledge, 103–112.
Eidelson, B. (2015). *Discrimination and Disrespect*. Oxford: Oxford University Press.
Ezorsky, G. (1991). *Racism and Justice*. Ithaca, NY: Cornell University Press.
Fricker, M. (2009). *Epistemic Injustice*. Oxford: Oxford University Press.
Fullinwider, R. (1980). *The Reverse Discrimination Controversy*. Totowa, NJ: Rowman & Allanheld.
Fullinwider, R. (2003). "Preferential Hiring and Compensation." In Steven M. Cahn, *The Affirmative Action Debate*. New York: Routledge, 68–78.
Fullinwider, R. (2013). "Affirmative Action," *Stanford Encyclopedia*, http://plato.stanford.edu/entries/affirmative-action/.
Goldman, A. (1979). *Justice and Reverse Discrimination*. Princeton, NJ: Princeton University Press.
Hellman, D. (2008). *When Is Discrimination Wrong?* Cambridge, MA: Harvard University Press.
Lawrence, C. and Matsuda, M. (1997). *We Won't Go Back: Making the Case for Affirmative Action*. Boston: Houghton Mifflin.
Lippert-Rasmussen, K. (2006). "The Badness of Discrimination," *Ethical Theory and Moral Practice*, 9, 167–185.
Lippert-Rasmussen, K. (2013). *Born Free and Equal?* New York: Oxford University Press.

Lippert-Rasmussen, K. (forthcoming). *Making Sense of Affirmative Action*. New York: Oxford University Press.

Mason, A. (2006). *Levelling the Playing Field*. Oxford: Oxford University Press.

Nickel, J. (2003). "Discrimination and Morally Relevant Characteristics," In Steven M. Cahn, *The Affirmative Action Debate*. New York: Routledge, 3–4.

Sabbagh, D. (2007). *Equality and Transparency*. New York: Palgrave Macmillan.

Segall, S. (2013). *Equality of Opportunity*. Oxford: Oxford University Press.

Sterba, J. (2009). *Affirmative Action for the Future*. Ithaca: Cornell University Press.

Suk, J. (2018). "Anti-Discrimination Law and the Duty to Integrate." In Hugh Collins and Tarunabh Khaitan, *Foundations of Indirect Discrimination Law*. Oxford: Hart Publishing, 223–248.

Vallentyne, P. (2006). "Private Discrimination and Left-Libertarianism," *San Diego Law Review*, 43, 981–994.

Waldron, J. (1981). "A Right to Do Wrong," *Ethics*, 92(1), 21–39.

Wertheimer, A. (2006). "Reflections on Discrimination," *San Diego Law Review*, 43, 945–980.

22

RACE, RACISM, AND SOCIAL POLICY

Albert Atkin

Policy-making must always pay attention to race. That is the central claim of this chapter. To put the claim a little more broadly, I suggest that regardless of whether some particular policy debate is ostensibly "racial", policy-makers must attend to questions of race in their policy discussions. At a first pass, it might seem that a philosophical essay on race, racism, and social policy would do well to focus on a particular set of topics where matters of race seem to be most pertinent to policy – issues such as affirmative action, statistical profiling, or reparations, for instance. Indeed, this is the most common strategy, but the strategy for discussing race and policy that I pursue in this chapter is different and is motivated by three starting points or presuppositions: first, I maintain that philosophical and ethical reflection on social policy ought to be directed towards practical outcomes and real-world impact; second, I maintain that, unlike many current philosophical approaches to race and social policy, we must pay more attention to the *social dimensions* of race; and third, I argue that race is ubiquitous but frequently unnoticed, and as a result must be a relevant consideration for appropriately cautious policy-makers. I shall expand upon these three starting points in more detail ahead (in Part 1), but crucially they lead back to my central claim that race should always be a matter of consideration for policy-makers, regardless of how remote racial concerns may seem to be from the policy in question. I shall then (in Part 2) explain and support this central claim by introducing an example of the type of philosophical question about race that I think philosophers and policy-makers would do well to examine. In particular, I shall explore how the general racial question 'what is race?' is pertinent to policy consideration.

Part 1: starting points

As I have stated, the central claim I am making in this chapter is that public policy-makers must pay close attention to race, and I shall highlight how they might do this by examining an example question that policy would do to well attend to in Part 2. In this part of the chapter, however, I shall introduce some important starting points that lead me to make this claim about race, philosophy, and policy. In particular, I raise three important issues or questions here: first, how should philosophers be engaging and reflecting on matters of policy-making? Second, how should philosophers be engaging with public policy as it intersects with matters of race? And finally, why think (as I do) that proper philosophical engagement in public policy must have a special onus upon it to attend to the impact of race and racism? We'll look at each point in turn.

The first starting point for my concerns here, then, is with *how philosophers should be engaging with matters of public policy-making*. My own philosophical inclinations are broadly pragmatic and pragmatist, and as such, I am sympathetic to the idea that where philosophy and philosophers engage with social policy, they should do so by looking to the practical and pragmatic concerns of real policy-making rather than by becoming preoccupied with applying ethical theory to problems under laboratory conditions, so to speak. More specifically, I am most inclined towards an approach to philosophy and public policy found in Jonathan Wolff (2011), and Jonathan Wolff and Avner De-Shalit (2007), which Wolff characterises as "bottom-up" theorising. In simple terms, bottom-up theorising demands that we approach social policy questions by understanding the real practical problems that give rise to those questions. This is in contrast to a "top-down" approach, where we might start from a prior understanding of ethical theory and ask what a consistent application of that theory requires of our policy-making.

Wolff has various reasons for favouring a bottom-up approach to philosophical engagement with social policy, but I favour his approach because of three particular requirements it asks of us. First, the bottom-up approach requires that we accommodate the fact that the practical requirements of those problems that drive policy debate will change across the history of a policy area. As Wolff (2011, 7), borrowing from Joel Feinberg (1987, 18), notes, practical concerns mean that we are often engaged with *penultimate questions and problems* rather than with giving *final and ultimate answers*. In terms of race and racism, this will mean that our policy objectives are better framed and judged in terms of local and specific issues rather than with final goals in mind. Australians from the Aboriginal and Torres Straight Islander community experience many poor social outcomes primarily due to the racist and racialised settler colonialism of Australia, but the policies which affect these communities must focus primarily on, for instance, implementing clear interim targets for improving access to proper health care rather than focusing on larger-scale, more nebulous objectives, such as 'eradicating racism'. These are, of course, important final aims and ambitions for Australian society, but they are not the kind of objective by which to guide or judge interim policies in the face of appalling disparities in life expectancy, unacceptable child mortality rates, or troublingly high suicide and mental health problems among Aboriginal and Torres Strait Islander groups.

The second thing that a bottom-up approach to policy requires of us is, as already noted, that we focus on practice rather than theory. However, I take this practicalist dimension of bottom-up theorising to be especially important in philosophical deliberation on policy and race, and to have a much broader impact than mere appeals to attend to practice first. In particular, I take the practicalist requirement to mean that we must attend closely to real racial experiences, or rather, the experiences of the racialised, in our examination of policy. We can, for example, simply contrast a theory-first approach to affirmative action policy that looks at what our preferred ethical theories suggest about differential treatment with a practice-first approach that looks to current practices of affirmative action and intended outcomes. But I also take it that a practicalist approach means that we should pay especially close attention to the racialised experiences of those for whom race-based affirmative action policies are supposed to apply, and their experiences under the implementation of those policies.

Third, and finally, I take a bottom-up approach to require engagement with the fine detail of practical policy-making, and most importantly, familiarity with the context and history of particular policies. As Wolff puts it,

> [S]ome policies may simply be a reflection or hangover of value systems that are outmoded or should never have been accepted in the first place. But history can matter. Existing policies may be cobbled together to respond to previous historical

circumstances, including policy failure, and being aware of the history of a policy area can help us become sensitive to possible pitfalls with new recommendations.

(Wolff 2011, 7)

In matters of race and public policy, this third element requires that we pay very close attention to the *racial history and context* of particular policy-making. Now in certain cases – for instance, the bans on interracial marriage famously overturned in the 1967 *Loving v. Virginia* case (*Loving v. Virginia*, 388 US 1. [1967]) — the racial origin and context of particular policies are quite clear. In many other policy areas, however, the racial and racialised origin and context are less immediately apparent, and the importance for understanding the racial dimensions of current policy is frequently obscured. In Part 2 of this chapter, I will examine instances where the racial history of certain policies becomes particularly relevant, but for now it's enough to note that by adopting a bottom-up approach to philosophy and policy, we must always seek to understand the racial history of a policy area.

The second starting point for my concerns here is with how *philosophers should be engaging with public policy as it intersects with matters of race*. Unfortunately, this leads me into some rather negative and curmudgeonly reflection on current philosophical engagements with matters of policy and race. To be brief, proper engagement requires a much fuller understanding of the extensive social nature of race, racism, and the experiences of the racialised than we frequently see in philosophical engagement with race and policy. We shall return to this in discussion at various points in what follows ahead, but the concern is that race is ubiquitous and so intertwined with the nature and origin of the societies in which we live that we must attend to it by acknowledging and incorporating its social and structural nature, rather than by including it in our theorising as a thin and underspecified place-holder for colour-based differential treatment. In this respect, current philosophical reflections on race and public policy are frequently underwhelming. Nonetheless, my hope is that by showing why we might be concerned with current approaches that do not do proper work with race, we can begin to see how proper engagement should proceed.

The complaint here, then, is that where the interaction between race and the philosophy of public policy finds itself confined to particular topics, such as affirmative action, statistical profiling, and reparations, it is frequently under-explored. There is, of course, no reason why a focus on particular topics and racial matters cannot lead to important, insightful, and valuable work on race. Indeed, well-worked-out and full-blooded reflection on race exists in work on, for example, affirmative action (see Anderson 2010), or racial profiling (see Lever 2017). The problem, however, is that when focusing on specific debates with a racial dimension, race usually features as a rather ghostly and anaemic philosophical version of itself. To give some specific but common examples, race usually turns up in policy debates as either a "useful analogy", a "place-holder variable" for any dimension of inequality, or a "filter on some intuition pump" or other. Consider the following illustrative cases.

In various arguments on same-sex marriage or on animal experimentation, for example, race and racism are used as *useful analogies*. It is obvious, so the arguments go, that we shouldn't and don't insist on same-race marriage, and that the ethical reasoning here is transferable to debate on same-sex marriage (see, e.g., Wedgwood 1999, 240, or Rajczi 2008). Similarly, so the argument goes, the obvious immorality and impermissibility of racism are serviceable as an argument against animal experimentation and "speciesism" – 'speciesism and racism are sufficiently similar so that analogies between them cannot be blithely dismissed as category mistakes' (LaFollette and Shanks 1996, 42). Whatever we might think about the analogical reasoning in these cases, and I think there are serious problems, the problem is that policy debate on marriage equality or animal experimentation which uses race in this way pays too little regard to the deep structural dimensions of race, and the wide-ranging social impacts that accrue to racial difference.

Relatedly, race is often used as a *place-holder variable* for any dimension of differential treatment without paying full attention to what makes racial identity distinct. Discussion of statistical profiling, for example, usually frames itself in terms of criminal *racial* profiling (Risse and Zeckhauser 2004 or Risse 2007 are good examples), but there isn't often much sense that the positions that emerge from such philosophical reflection here would not have been served just as well by using some other dimension of individual social identity, such as gender, sexuality, or disability. Indeed, as Annabelle Lever notes,

> [T]his approach treats racial profiling as one example among many others of a general problem in egalitarian political philosophy, occasioned by the fact that treating people as equals does not always require, or permit, us to treat them the same.
>
> *(Lever 2017, 425)*

When properly understood, however, race presents a different and complicating set of considerations that do not hold of, say, sexuality or disability, and it is important that we understand just how significant the differences between race, gender, sexuality, and so forth are when it comes to examining race and policy. Indeed, Lever's own work on racial profiling is a good example of how we can take account of the deep structural elements of race – something Lever labels 'the social construction approach' (Lever 2017, 425) – when we engage with race and policy in specific areas of policy debate.

Finally, race is sometimes used as a *filter on an intuition pump*. An especially good example of this can be found in philosophical discussion of immigration, and especially in Michael Walzer's examination of how far nations are free to self-determine the make-up of their own population (1983, 42–48). For Walzer, racist and racial policies such as the White Australia policy (to which we shall return in Part 2) are simply to be used as test cases for how robust our intuitions about the nation's right to self-determine really are. The ethical and philosophical questions that arise from the racial elements of immigration are actually much deeper and far more socially complex than such a treatment can capture, and proper reflection needs to examine the ethical dimensions of race and racism in immigration policy in a much more thorough way (see Mendoza 2015 and Mendoza 2018).

Obviously, there are other ways in which race features in philosophical work on policy, but these three – as a useful analogy, a place-holder variable, or a filter on some intuition pump – are quite common. Now, as previously suggested, the concern here is with how philosophers should engage with race and policy, and the worry expressed in these three example cases is that treating race in these thin, under-explored ways leads to fruitless engagement between policy and race. In particular, such engagement leaves us with philosophical reflection on racial matters that fails to capture the impact and scale of race in a racialised society. Race must be handled in a much more complex and thoughtful way. Indeed, even in the discussion of these examples I mentioned work by Elizabeth Anderson, Annabelle Lever, and Jose Jorge Mendoza, which is among a growing body of philosophical engagement with questions of social policy that *does* engage with race in a deeper and more fruitful way.

The third and final starting point for my concerns here is with why we should think there is a special onus in philosophy and policy to engage with race. And in fact, the point here is the rather simple claim that race is a complex and ubiquitous social presence, but for large parts of society, almost completely unnoticed. It is helpful, I think, to divide this concern into two points: first, that contemporary society is founded upon and functions through a set of racial and racist structures and institutions; and second, that our society is geared to the normativity of whiteness.

To expand slightly, the reason these two points lead to the claim that race is ubiquitous but unnoticed is that, on the one hand, contemporary democratic societies are founded on a series of philosophical views which divide the world into racialised hierarchies. Charles Mills famously describes this in his book *The Racial Contract* (Mills 1997), and in later work notes the racism inherent the views of philosophers such as Hobbes, Locke, Rousseau, and Kant:

> Hobbes depictions of Native Americans as "savages" still in the (apparently real for them) state of nature; Locke's investments in the slave-trading Royal Africa Company, his role in writing the Carolina Constitution, and his representation of Native Americans and incompetent appropriators; Rousseau's limiting of contemporaneous savagery and his non-condemnation of African slavery; and (the easiest case) Kant's racial hierarchy.
>
> *(Mills 2017, 69)*

The racialised views of these figures (and others besides, including Hume, Hegel, John Stuart Mill, and Adam Smith) provide many of the philosophical foundations and justifications for organising contemporary society. Unsurprisingly, these racialised views find themselves everywhere embedded within the tools and institutions of our societies.

In terms of the normativity of whiteness, on the other hand, whiteness is both privileged by the ease with which it can navigate the racialised social structures made by and for white people (see Sullivan 2006), and made normative in virtue of treating race as something other groups in the hierarchy have as a result of failing to be white. This has the interesting effect of making white people largely unaware of the impact and presence of race at large, and seldom aware of their own race. As the black academic Patricia Williams notes,

> You need two chairs at the table: one for you and one for your blackness. For white people, moreover, racial denial tends to engender a profoundly invested disingenuousness, an innocence that amounts to the transgressive refusal to know. Again this is not to assign anything like blame, simply to observe the way in which we know race or don't.
>
> *(Williams 1997, 27)*

Between the overriding presence of racialised structures in society, and the normativity of whiteness, we can see the substance of the claim that race is ubiquitous, but largely unnoticed by large parts of society. In short, racial hierarchies are used to build and maintain society to the advantage of white people, but white people are invested in not seeing their own race, or its role in securing their position at the top of these hierarchies. Or to borrow a well-worn idiom, fish are the last to discover water.

The simultaneous ubiquity and invisibility (to the beneficiaries of racial privilege) of race are relevant to my concerns here, though, because, as mentioned, I take it to introduce a particular onus upon those considering philosophy and policy to attend to race. More specifically, philosophy as an academic discipline is remarkably white. Similarly, those in the position to develop and influence policy-making are remarkably white. It would be unsurprising, then, if somewhere between the whiteness of philosophy and the whiteness of policy-making, the ever-present impact and influence of race go unnoticed. For philosophers interested in policy, this means that the risk of passing race by without noticing its influence gives us reason to think some special provision must be made to ensure that race is not passed by, but instead properly attended to in policy deliberations.

These three starting points for considering race and public policy may seem fairly involved, but it should hopefully be clear why I take them to matter. Bottom-up theorising means getting to grips with the fine detail of policy at the real interface between policy-making and the racialised experiences of those it impacts upon. The proper way for philosophers to engage with race in matters of policy is not by treating race as a thin, abstracted theoretical tool but by attending to the complex social conditions that have given life to it, and which maintain it. And finally, because of the ubiquity of race and the whiteness of philosophy and policy-making, responsible reflection must ensure that race is not being missed, unnoticed, or merely given lip-service. This, I take it, is enough to at least give some sense of my claim that policy must always pay attention to race.

Part 2: race and policy

In the preceding section, I gave three starting points for my claim that philosophical engagement with social policy must always address race. In this part of the chapter I will try to give an extended example of the type of question about race that might very well play a role in guiding those engaging with race and policy. My particular concern will be with the importance of addressing the question 'what is race?'. There are other questions which we might easily identify as being important here – 'who defines racial membership?', or 'what are we using race for?', for instance. Obviously, these are all fairly general racial questions for philosophers reflecting on policy to engage with, and I certainly do not mean to suggest that asking general (non-policy-specific) questions about race is the only way to address the issue of race in policy. Indeed, throughout the preceding section I mentioned work by philosophers who are engaging with quite specific policy questions about race in what seems to me to be exactly the right spirit. Rather, what I am suggesting here is that regardless of whether we are not dealing directly with racial policy debates, such as race-based affirmative action or criminal racial profiling, there are important general racial questions that we must be aware of. The example used ahead – 'what is race?' – is, I think, the clearest example of why policy-makers must ask higher-level, more general questions about race.

What is race?

It is important that philosophers engaging with policy attend to the issue of what race is, and what type of conception of race they might be working with in policy deliberation. In many ways, this draws most directly upon the second starting point discussed in Part 1, where I suggested that race is a deep and complex socially constructed phenomenon, and that proper engagement with it in policy questions must attend to this dimension. Indeed, my complaint against much contemporary philosophical engagement with race and policy is that it frequently fails to do this. Here, though, I want to explore the relevance of raising this question by first contrasting two dimensions of our current understanding of race – the biological dimension, and the social dimension – before secondly, looking at some reasons why this difference matters to policy debate.

Biological race v. social race

Race is a curious and troublesome concept, and for all the reasons one might expect: it's hard to say precisely what it is or what makes someone one race rather than another; it is the foundation for some of the most unsavoury aspects of human behaviour and history, and so on. But it is made especially curious and troublesome because it has two elements, one *biological* and the other *social*. To be more precise, race is really a set of biological pretensions which ground a set of very real social constructions and constraints. This becomes troublesome in many discussions of race, however, because the biological pretensions and the social constraints frequently come apart, and the biological dimension tends to dominate our reflections upon race.

Race, viewed in biological terms, is best understood through the question of whether race as we understand it and use it has any substantial corollary in the biological sciences. As it happens, it doesn't, or at least this is what informed consensus suggests, but this doesn't stop a certain level of philosophical engagement and discussion of race in biological terms, not least because race as a concept has pretensions to be a robust scientific fact.

The idea that race and racial difference are a matter of biological fact is due in part to the origin of the modern concept in the enlightenment science of Linneaus (1758), Blumenbach (1795), and Kant (1775), among others. What we find among these thinkers is an essentialising view of race whereby the external bodily markers of race – skin colour, hair type, nose shape, and so on – come to be explained in terms of some deep underlying biological difference connected to breeding and ancestry. This construal of race in essentialist terms more or less gives us our modern concept, and even though we know that enlightenment scientific essentialism about race is empty, we still see contemporary questions about the underlying biology of race engaging racial difference in terms of genetic difference. Are races sub-species or, in much of the most recent debates about the biological reality of race, population clusters? General consensus is that whatever the biological sciences might suggest about human groups and populations, there is nothing to support the idea that race as ordinarily understood is a robust biological category (see, e.g., Lewontin 1972, Zack 2002, Hochman 2013, or Atkin 2017). Importantly, though, debate about whether race tracks some real biological category or is largely specious tends to be a core component of much philosophical reflection on race.

The other dimension to our contemporary view of race is that, partly because of the enlightenment's construal of race as a biologically robust category, it has been used to construct and justify a set of social conditions and constraints according to the racial categories it creates. This has led to different treatment and expectations for different races within society as a result. Looking at race in social terms, we see that being an Aboriginal and Torres Strait Islander in Australia, for example, is a matter of being subject to a set of specific social conditions and expectations in virtue of the perceived physiological and biological markers used to delineate Aboriginal and Torres Strait Islanders from other races in Australia. This is in contrast to the set of social conditions and expectations that white Australians are subject to in virtue of the perceived markers of whiteness. This manifests itself in terms of different social outcomes whereby white Australians have much better experiences in education and so much higher rates of educational attainment; white Australians have much better access to health care in the Australian health care system and so have remarkably higher life expectancy rates; and so on.

The sociocultural and historical practices surrounding the use of race and racial difference are, in many ways, the more important and interesting element of examining what race is. The biological pretensions of race are really nothing more than a flimsy justification for the deep differential treatment that manifests itself in the social reality of race. For this reason, then, it is important that we attend to the differences between race and racial categories as they arise from its social, rather than biological, dimension. To give an example of how this difference affects our understanding, consider the case of swimming in the United States:

> Black Americans are less likely to be able to swim than their white counterparts. Early (and specious) biological explanations of racial difference put this disparity down to underlying

physiological differences between the races. According to this claim, higher bone density, lower lung capacity, or even higher basal metabolic rate make black people less buoyant and so less capable at swimming (Allen and Nickel 1969). By taking account of the social dimensions of race in the United States, however, we see that black Americans are currently and historically more likely to live in areas where there is no proper access to swimming pools or functional swimming programs, and that even where there is access to usable pools and programs, black people have historically faced exclusion and discrimination in those venues. One upshot is that swimming is simply not part of black American culture (Wiltse 2014); another is that black Americans die from accidental drowning in proportionally higher numbers (Hastings et al. 2006). It should, I hope, be obvious, why policy-makers interested in doing something about higher rates of accidental drowning amongst black Americans would do well to avail themselves of the difference between the biological and social dimensions of race here.

Why does it matter to policy?

Turning to why policy-makers (and philosophers reflecting on policy-making) need to pay close attention to the difference between the biological and social dimensions of race, the example of black swimming in the US ought, I think, to be instructive. It is clear, in such a case, that a focus on the biological dimension would likely lead to one type of policy response, while a focus on the social dimension would likely lead to another. Moreover, it ought to be clear that the social dimension is probably the most pressing in this case. However, as much of the complaint in Part 1 suggests, there is a tendency among philosophers to focus on the thinner biological dimensions of race. The concern here, though, is with the claim that philosophers and policy-makers would do well to attend to the question 'what is race?' and to ensure that they are paying sufficient attention to the social dimension of race and racialisation. I want, then, to conclude this section by looking at two reasons for thinking that attending to this question (what is race?) in this way (by focusing on its social dimensions) matters to policy.

The first reason we should pay close attention to whether we are focusing on the biological or social dimensions of race is that too heavy a focus on biological questions and the biological pretensions of race has *a corrupting effect on policy-making*. An especially good example of how a focus on the biological dimensions of race corrupts policy-making is given in a recent paper by Tina Fernandes Botts (Botts 2017). Botts notes that there is a discernible shift in the Supreme Court of the United States' understanding of race from a social to a biological phenomenon. This she argues leads to a change in the court's understanding of when the Equal Protection clause applies, and a change in their general understanding of what counts as racial discrimination and to whom it applies. As Botts points out,

> [A]s the US Supreme Court's concept of race moves from being understood as a sociocultural/sociohistorical phenomenon to being understood as a purely biological phenomenon, there is a concomitant shift on the part of the Court from understanding racial discrimination as problematic because it reinforces the legacy and vestiges of American chattel slavery, to understanding racial discrimination as problematic per se.
>
> *(Botts 2017, 526)*

The effect of adopting this view of race as a putative biological category, she argues, is that Supreme Court decisions treat any attention to race or differential treatment of race as unconstitutional; why should black people *or* white people be excluded from some position or opportunity in society because of a biological fact over which they have no control? The knock-on effect on policy, however, is dramatic. Affirmative action programs in the United States, for example, are increasingly abandoned on the grounds of upheld cases of racial discrimination against excluded white applicants (e.g., *Gratz v. Bollinger*, 539 US 244 [2003]). Unfortunately, such reasoning by-passes the social dimension of race, where we can see quite clearly that racial discrimination is not simply any differential treatment on the basis of race, but should be properly understood as the product of America's long-standing cultural and historical disposition to treat black people as (considerably) less than the equal of white people.

What Botts shows us in her discussion of equal protection law in the United States is just how problematic a narrow focus on the biological dimension of race can be for policy debate. On a biological view of race, racial discrimination in the US is any form of differential treatment attributable to racial difference. On a social view of race, however, racial discrimination is differential treatment which compounds and reinvents the subjugation and oppression of black (and other non-white) Americans as part of the ongoing legacy of chattel slavery. Indeed, at a broader level, the corrupting effect of this focus on race as biological is shown in the overwhelming American political tendency towards race-neutral policy-making (Lieberman 2005), and tip-toeing around white discomfort with dissent towards white racial privilege.

The second reason why we should attend to the question 'what is race?' and ensure we are accounting for its social dimensions is that viewing race in biological terms often *masks the role that apparently non-racial policy has played in the social construction of race*. If we are to engage in bottom-up theorising about policy, to engage with race in its fullest and most socially robust sense, and to acknowledge the simultaneous ubiquity and hiddenness of race, we must be careful not to let a biological conception of race keep us ignorant of the sometimes hidden racial dimensions of policy areas. By way of illustration, consider the example of immigration policy.

If we treat race as a merely biological matter, and we view immigration policy as a matter of nations exercising their rights to control borders and population, it's not so straightforward to see how immigration policy is deeply racial. It's true, of course, that much populist sentiment about immigration is driven by barely concealed racism, but policy-making seldom makes explicit appeal to racial difference in demarcating acceptable immigration. Nonetheless, there is almost always the feeling that the practical application of immigration policy has the undertone of racial vetting, which is unsurprising given the role that immigration policies have played in the social construction of national identities, racial hierarchies, and the prescription of acceptable racial categories. At this point, though, we are looking at race in social (rather than biological) terms, and at the role immigration policy has played in the making and maintaining of race as a social category.

To elaborate, both the United States and Australia have, in the past, enforced anti-Chinese immigration policies – the US's *Chinese Exclusion Act* (1882) and Australia's *Immigration Restriction Act* (1901). In such instances, policy-makers were clearly intent upon determining the racial make-up of their countries, and imposing whiteness as a normative standard of acceptability. The political instigator of the Australian *Immigration Restriction Act* (1901), Prime Minister Edmund Barton, argued explicitly in Parliament that 'the doctrine of the equality of man was never intended to apply to the equality of the Englishman and the Chinaman', and in reflecting on the "success" of the policy in 1903, Australia's second prime minister, Alfred Deakin, stated that

> The alien coloured population is being steadily reduced. [. . .] A white Australia does
> not, by any means mean only the preservation of the complexion of the people of this

country. It means the multiplying of their homes, so that we may be able to occupy, use and defend every part of our continent; it means the maintenance of conditions of life fit for white men and white women; it means equal laws and opportunities for all.

(Quoted in Cook 1999, 179)

Viewing race socially, then, makes the racial nature of immigration policy clear. It is, and has long been, a tool for the construction and maintaining of racial hierarchies, and for the privileging of whiteness. Such reflection should, in turn, change the nature and impetus behind our philosophical engagement with immigration policy-making. We can no longer raise questions about immigration policy and freedom of association or governmental right to self-determination as though such matters are simply race-neutral. We should, instead, try to acknowledge and accommodate the racial nature of ethical questions about immigration in our public policy deliberation.

To give one illustration of how this might matter, once the social dimension of race in immigration is made clearer we can see how the "racial vetting" aspect of such policies has important social impacts upon existing racial groups within nations. Recent work on "linked fate" in the American Latinx[1] community, for instance, shows that the prominent "anti-Hispanic" sentiment of US immigration policy since 2001 creates a greater sense of linked fate among Latinx Americans (Vargas et al. 2017). We can think of "linked fate" as individual recognition of shared membership in, and so shared status, outcomes, and interests with, marginalised groups (Dawson 1994). As prominent immigration policies focus on the exclusion and removal of Latinx immigrants, Latinx Americans see their own social status as linked to those who are excluded. This has a direct impact upon the social status and position of Latinx Americans who feel that arguments for the exclusion of the Latinx immigrants they identify with simultaneously denigrate them as an economic burden and place them at odds with America's concept of itself. Such racial elements of immigration policy as these become clear, however, only once we start to analyse race more fully along its social, rather than biological, dimension.

The history of immigration policy in places such as Australia, then, makes for a relatively clear example of how treating race as biological rather than social can mask the role that policy has played in constructing racial hierarchies, and continues to play in maintaining those structures. It is not the only case we might have discussed here, and I would argue that when examined closely, much policy-making has been implicit in creating dominant racial structures, and by extension in maintaining structural racism.

We might have mentioned marriage policies, for example, by which the state has destabilised and devalued minority family structures and imposed white family structures as normative (Pinderhughes 2002). When viewed this way, it is unsurprising that state intervention into black families in the US or Aboriginal families in Australia is disproportionately high, given that such family structures here are deemed unorthodox or are pathologised in virtue of not being white. Relatedly, we might have mentioned adoption policy debates which frequently bypass the role that adoption has played, and still plays, in state control of racial groups, the assimilation of minorities, and in some cases the intended eradication of races. The primary tools by which Australia, during its own racial formation, controlled its Aboriginal population was through forced adoption programs and what has come to be known as 'the stolen generation' (Read 1983). Similarly, in post-Ceausescu Romania of the 1990s, Roma children were taken from their families and placed into international adoption programs, which, alongside the forced sterilisation of Roma women, was used as a means of controlling the Gypsy Roma population (Kligman 1998). It is unsurprising, then, that while children from racial minority groups are often overrepresented in foster and adoptive care systems, families from racial minorities are reluctant to take on the role of adoptive parents and are usually underrepresented in the system.

This puts much debate on adoption policy (and not just the ethics or politics of interracial adoption) in a different light.

We could continue by looking at, for instance, the racialised nature of education (Woodson 1933/1998) and the impact of education policy on people from minority groups (Derrington 2007). However, the general point here is that policy-making is itself part of the tool kit by which race is made, and through which oppressive racial hierarchies are maintained. It is part and parcel of what makes the practical racial experiences of the members of any given society. It is implicit in masking the influence of race for those at the top of any given racial hierarchy. Policy is one of the primary tools by which race is made ubiquitous, and it is one of the chief mechanisms by which race is hidden from and for white people. This means that without proper attention to the social dimension of race and its connection to social policy, our philosophical reflection on policy-making is at best severely hampered, and at worst remains complicit in maintaining racial privilege.

Conclusion

What I have tried to do in this chapter is, by showing my own starting points, motivate the claim that good policy-making (and philosophical engagement with it) must always pay attention to race. The argument is, I think, straightforward. The call to attend to practical concerns and social impacts in policy, the call to attend to the thick social construction of race, and the call to acknowledge that race is a prominent but unnoticed thread in our social fabric all seem to me to make the claim that race should always be a consideration for policy quite natural. The social dimension of race means policy is often an instrumental part of how race is made and maintained; the call to bottom-up theorising means we must look to the history and role that race plays when examining a policy's practical impact; and the simultaneous ubiquity and hiddenness of race means we must be especially vigilant in looking for the traces of race and racism in our social policy regardless of whether they seem to be there upon first inspection. I also take such a call to mean that the way that the philosophical examination of race and racial policy might proceed is different to more orthodox approaches. In particular, I think that much reflection on policy would do well to pause and ask the type of question about race and policy that I posed here with the question 'what is race?'. Engagement with race at the level of specific policy questions still seems to me to be viable, important, and pursuable in the right way, but engagement with race at this more general level for all policy reflection is crucial.

Note

1 "Latinx" is used here as a gender-neutral alternative to the term "Latino".

References

Allen, R.L. and Nickel, David. (1969). "The Negro and Learning to Swim: The Buoyancy Problem Related to Reported Biological Differences". *The Journal of Negro Education* 38(4): 404–411.

Anderson, Elizabeth. (2010). *The Imperative of Integration*. Princeton, NJ: Princeton University Press.

Atkin, Albert. (2017). "Race, Definition, and Science". In *The Oxford Handbook of Philosophy and Race*. Edited by Naomi Zack. 139–150. Oxford: Oxford University Press.

Barton, Edmund. (1901). "Immigration Restriction Bill". *House of Representatives, Debates*, 26 September, p. 5233.

Blumenbach, Johann Friederich. (1795). "On the Natural Variety of Mankind". In *Race and the Enlightenment*. Edited by Emmanuel Chukwudi Eze. Cambridge: Blackwell.

Cook, Ian. (1999). *Liberalism in Australia*. Oxford: Oxford University Press.

Dawson, Michael C. (1994). *Behind the Mule: Race and Class in African American Politics*. Princeton, NJ: Princeton University Press.

Derrington, C. (2007). "Fight, Flight and Playing White: An Examination of Coping Strategies Adopted by Gypsy Traveller Adolescents in English Secondary Schools". *International Journal of Education Research* 46(6): 357–367.

Feinberg, Joel. (1987). *Harm to Others*. New York: Oxford University Press.

Fernandes Botts, Tina. (2017). "The Concept of Race and Equal Protection Law". In *The Oxford Handbook of Philosophy and Race*. Edited by Naomi Zack. 526–536. Oxford: Oxford University Press.

Hastings, Donald, Sammy Zahran, and Sherry Cable. (2006). "Drowning in Inequalities: Swimming and Social Justice". *Journal of Black Studies* 36(6): 894–917.

Hochman, Adam. (2013). "Against the New Race Naturalism". *The Journal of Philosophy* 110(7): 331–351.

Kant, Immanuel. (1775). "Of the Different Races of Human Beings". In *Anthropology, History and Education*. Edited by Robert Louden, translated by G. Zoller and R. Louden. 82–97. Cambridge: Cambridge University Press.

Kligman, Gail. (1998). *The Politics of Duplicity: Controlling Reproduction in Ceausescu's Romania*. Berkeley, CA: University of California Press.

LaFollette, Hugh and Shanks, Niall. (1996). "The Origin of Speciesism". *Philosophy* 71(275): 41–61.

Lever, Annabelle. (2017). "Racial Profiling and the Political Philosophy of Race". In *The Oxford Handbook of Philosophy and Race*. Edited by Naomi Zack. 425–435. Oxford: Oxford University Press.

Lewontin, Richard D. (1972). "The Apportionment of Human Diversity". *Evolutionary Biology* 6: 381–398.

Lieberman, Robert. (2005). *Shaping Race Policy: The United States in Comparative Perspective*. Princeton, NJ: Princeton University Press.

Linneaus, Carolus. (1758). "Systema Naturae". In *Race and the Enlightenment*, Edited by Emmanuel Chukwudi Eze. Cambridge: Blackwell.

Mendoza, Jose Jorge. (2015). *The Moral and Political Philosophy of Immigration: Liberty, Security and Equality*. New York: Lexington.

Mendoza, Jose Jorge. (2018). "Philosophy of Race and the Ethics of Immigration". In *The Routledge Companion to the Philosophy of Race*. Edited by Paul Taylor, Linda Alcoff, and Luvell Anderson. New York: Routledge.

Mills, Charles. (1997). *The Racial Contract*. Ithaca, NY: Cornell University Press.

Mills, Charles. (2017). "Philosophy and the Racial Contract". In *The Oxford Handbook of Philosophy and Race*. Edited by Naomi Zack. 65–76. Oxford: Oxford University Press.

Pinderhughes, E. (2002). "African American Marriage in the 20th Century". *Family Process* 41(2): 269–282.

Rajczi, Alex. (2008). "A Populist Argument for Legalising Same-Sex Marriage". *The Monist* 94(3–4): 475–505.

Read, Peter. (1983). *The Stolen Generations: The Removal of Aboriginal Children in New South Wales 1883 to 1969*. NSW Ministry of Aboriginal Affairs, Occasional Paper No. 1. 1983.

Risse, Mathias. (2007). "Racial Profiling: A Reply to Two Critics". *Criminal Justice Ethics* 26(1): 4–19.

Risse, Mathias and Zeckhauser, Richard. (2004). "Racial Profiling". *Philosophy & Public Affairs* 32(2): 131–170.

Sullivan, Shannon. (2006). *Revealing Whiteness: The Unconscious Habits of Racial Privilege*. Bloomington, IN: Indiana University Press.

Vargas, Edward D. Sanchez, Gabriel, R. and Valdez Jr., Juan A. (2017). "Immigration Policies and Group Identity: How Immigrant Laws Affect Linked Fate among U.S. Latino Populations". *Journal of Race, Ethnicity and Politics* 2(1): 35–62.

Walzer, Michael. (1983). *Spheres of Justice: A Defense of Pluralism and Equality*. New York: Basic Books.

Wedgwood, Ralph. (1999). "The Fundamental Argument for Same-Sex Marriage". *The Journal of Political Philosophy* 7(3): 225–242.

Williams, Patricia. (1997). *Seeing a Color-blind Future: The Paradox of Race*. New York: The Noonday Press.

Wiltse, Jeff. (2014). "The Black White Swimming Disparity in America: A deadly Legacy of Swimming Pool Discrimination". *Journal of Sport and Social Issues* 38(4): 366–389.

Wolff, Jonathan. (2011). *Ethics and Public Policy: A Philosophical Inquiry*. London: Routledge.

Wolff, Jonathan and De-Shalit, Avner. (2007). *Disadvantage*. Oxford: Oxford University Press.

Woodson, Carter G. (1933/1998). *The Miseducation of the Negro*. Trenton, NJ: Africa World Press.

Zack, Naomi. (2002). *Philosophy of Science and Race*. New York: Routledge.

23

GENDER-EGALITARIAN POLICIES IN THE WORKPLACE AND THE FAMILY

Anca Gheaus[1]

Introduction

Gender justice is a worthy goal, for both liberal and democratic reasons.[2] This chapter looks at the question of how liberal democracies should design public policies that are informed by gender justice, with special attention to possible trade-offs between different ways of achieving this goal.

A large variety of policies can advance gender justice – directly or indirectly – with respect to many aspects of people's life. My focus is on policies that aim to improve fairness with respect to the gendered division of labour. They are of particular normative interest for several reasons. First, to redress injustices that result from women's and men's specialisation in different kinds of work it is necessary to aim at both the domestic and the economic spheres: gender-affecting policies in the family and in the workplace are intimately connected because women's main role in caregiving within the family deeply shapes their opportunities on the labour market, and some regulations of the labour market can either entrench or discourage the gendered division of labour at home. It is not clear whether policies concerning the gendered division of labour can simultaneously serve the best interests of both women and children in the absence of large and structural cultural or economic changes; the difficult question, in this case, is whether and at what cost we should pursue gender justice. Second, there is a debate on whether and how liberal states, which should take a neutral stance vis-à-vis citizens' conception of the good life, can legitimately enact such policies. Third, some of the policies discussed here are divisive among feminists, because they have the potential to set back legitimate interests of one or another socio-economic group of women.

I dedicate a section to each of these three issues; the next section contains a short discussion of "gender" followed by a brief exploration of gender justice. Some policies that advance gender justice are focused on the family: reforming marriage laws, making ectogenesis possible, providing more quality institutional childcare, and compensating stay-at-home spouses for care work. Other policies aim to reshape the workplace (there is obvious overlap): providing more quality institutional care, socialising children in ways that are free of gender norms, or actively socialising boys into care work, encouraging both parents to take equal parental leave, and introducing a universal basic income. They are briefly discussed in the third and fifth sections.

Gender justice and gender policies

According to a classical distinction, sex refers to the biological features of individuals while gender represents the social meanings associated with sex, including gender norms. Sex and gender map onto each other more or less perfectly because different norms regulate the behaviour of female and male individuals according to ideals concerning femininity and masculinity. I use "woman" for "female individual" and "man" for "male individual". The distinction between sex and gender is itself contentious (Mikkola 2016), and I use it for heuristic reasons, given the present interest in the division of labour between women and men. Note that a focus on women and men (understood as a sex rather than as a gender term) may obscure some areas of gender policies, such as those aiming to curb violence against gay and trans-sexual people and, more generally, eliminate homophobia, or policies concerning gay marriage and civil partnerships. The choice to follow the classical sex-gender distinction reflects my belief that there exist different concepts of gender justice, and it doesn't imply anything about the importance of other areas of gender policies.

Gender justice encompasses several *desiderata*, such as respecting women's rights over their bodies and their rights to make choices and ensuring that gender does not prevent or constrain their access to social institutions that distribute benefits. A full set of policies promoting gender justice will include protection from gender-motivated abuses of power, in both the public and the domestic sphere. In spite of their equal legal standing with men, women who live in economically advanced liberal democracies continue to be affected by several disadvantages: more often than men, they are subject to poverty, sexual and domestic violence, and particularly precarious forms of work in the pornography and prostitution industry, where they face coercion and high risks to bodily integrity (UN 2010). These disadvantages warrant the enactment of policies that prevent or mitigate their poverty, eliminate harassment and violence, and ensure that nobody is coerced into joining the pornography and prostitution industry and that its workers are protected against abuse. I leave to one side policies that address such injustices. I assume that their ethical justification is straightforward because they involve the infringement of individuals' economic rights or rights to bodily integrity and occupational freedom.

Instead, I focus on distributive inequalities that result from the gendered division of labour and on policies that can remedy them. By the gendered division of labour I refer to the fact that, on average, women do significantly more care work than men. By care here I understand the meeting of essential needs within personal relationships, especially when the care-receiver cannot meet the needs themselves (Bubeck 1995). Within paid work, caring professions are feminised and underpaid. Further, women tend to cluster at lower-rank jobs and have difficulties progressing in their career as fast as men. In particular, women in the EU are present in low proportions above the "glass-ceiling", as leaders in their professions – as CEOs, on managerial boards, as full professors in many academic disciplines, and so forth (Eurostat 2017). This phenomenon is closely connected with the enduring tradition of a gendered division of labour within the home, which consists in women leading care-centred lifestyles, looking after the household, children, and other family members. This has many undesirable effects for women: in spite of having joined the labour market massively in the past few decades, women continue to shoulder the bulk of unpaid domestic work and, on average, work longer hours than men when both paid work and unpaid domestic labour are taken into account (Hochschild and Machung 1989; UN 2010). Further, women's caring burden results in a weaker participation in the labour market; women are more likely than men to be unemployed permanently or temporarily, work part-time, and request paid or unpaid care leaves. This puts women at higher economic risks than men and thereby makes them financially dependent on their male spouses. Elderly women who have not been long enough in full-time employment and divorced women and their children are at particularly high risk of poverty. This can deter victims of domestic abuse from separating from their abusers. Finally, women who are absent from the labour market for a long time are deprived of those important non-monetary goods of work that, in our societies, are available only or mainly through paid work (Gheaus and Herzog 2016).

In contrast to cases that involve violations of rights to bodily integrity and various freedoms, the claim that the gendered division of labour is unjust – either in itself or due to its consequences – is controversial. Assuming that individuals have the right to make their own occupational choices, and engage voluntarily in different kinds of paid work and in different (even unequal) divisions of domestic labour, there is a strong *prima facie* reason to see the results of these choices as legitimate. Yet, as many feminists have argued, there are special reasons to be critical of the gendered division of labour. Some have to do with the fact that gender norms unduly influence women's choices by shaping their psychological and social identity. Therefore, preferences and choices largely shaped by gender norms may not be sufficiently autonomous and this would be a ground to protect women from their harmful consequences (Chambers 2004).

Other reasons concern inequalities between women and men that are generated by factors outside their control. Even if women's choices are autonomous – in spite of the role played by gender norms in the formation of their preference – it seems unfair that the cumulative result of gendered choices leads to unequal capability sets for women and men (Robeyns 2007). The gendered division of labour, which results from our socialisation in feminine and masculine social roles, triggers various social mechanisms responsible for women's lower opportunities on the labour market: explicit and implicit biases (Brownstein 2015) and statistical discrimination – all of which I discuss in the next section. Gender norms ultimately impose different costs on women's and men's pursuit of similar goals; for instance, women who want to rear children must forego their professional lives to a larger extent than men who want to rear children, and consequently face higher economic risks (Mason 2000). These considerations indicate that even if women are not coerced into a gendered division of labour, the ensuing inequalities are morally problematic.

Most generally, gender justice forbids inequalities that are the *mere* result of one's (real or perceived) sex. However, there is no consensus on what conditions must be in place for any inequalities of outcome between women and men to be legitimate: at the very least, women should enjoy equal opportunities to engage in the competition for socially available goods – that is, to compete unencumbered by socially created obstacles related to their sex (Radcliffe-Richards 2014). Others believe that gender justice requires more: for instance, equality of capabilities for women and men (Robeyns 2007). And some feminist scholars go as far as arguing that only equality of outcome can satisfy gender justice (Phillips 2004). Here I rely on an understanding of gender justice according to which 'A society is gender just only if the costs of a gender-neutral lifestyle are, all other things being equal, lower than, or at most equal to, the costs of gendered lifestyles' (Gheaus 2012, 10). A gender-neutral lifestyle is a lifestyle whose costs are not influenced by gender norms and is adopted by individuals on the basis of their gender-independent reasons to value its elements, and without social pressure. For instance, individuals who lead such lifestyles will choose to engage in caring activities or participate in the labour market because they have reason to value these activities *qua* human beings, rather than in virtue of norms that say that women should care and men should be breadwinners. The main reason behind this understanding of gender justice is that it is unfair that lifestyle options should be more or less costly for individuals due to their gender.

I assume (Gheaus 2012) that women and men will have equal reason to value care and participation in the labour market and that, absent any social pressure to the contrary, they are likely, on average, to engage in these activities equally. Thus, for example, in a gender-just society some women and some men will combine caring and paid work, while others may be full-time caregivers or breadwinners, but the total amount of unpaid care done by women and men will be roughly the same. In existing societies, the gender norms that shape the gendered division of labour most often result in lesser opportunities for women to access wealth, power, and status, but recent criticism has also pointed to the ways in which it sometimes disadvantages men (Benatar 2012; Brighouse and Swift 2014). For instance, men enjoy fewer opportunities than women to participate in child-rearing: they are less socialised into caring roles and social norms deter them from requiring parental leaves or joining caring professions. On this view, the effects of gender norms in general, and of the gendered division of labour in particular, could be unjust even if (implausibly) they were to disadvantage women and men equally. The assumption here is that the loss of valuable opportunities to goods in one significant area of life (e.g., work, or caring relationships) cannot be compensated by higher opportunities in another (Gheaus 2012).

Against this, some believe that justice, understood as comprehensive equality of opportunity, could be compatible – perhaps in an otherwise just world – with some kind of a gendered division of labour, insofar women and men really enjoyed equal overall life prospects (Arneson 1998). However, many feminists think that the gendered division of labour in the *real* world is at the root of much injustice. The foregoing principle of gender justice is part of a long feminist tradition according to which, in an ideally gender-just society, the default model of a worker is not the traditional breadwinner, who is assumed to be free from any caregiving duties (Okin 1989; Fraser 1994; Williams 2000), but, rather, a "universal caregiver" – a worker who spends part of her time caring for others. This involves a structural transformation of both the workplace and childcare institutions (Gornik and Meyers 2003) as well as of the way in which children are educated (Behrends and Schouten 2017). Gender neutrality,[3] in this chapter, refers to the ideal that, on average, women and men engage equally in paid work and care. According to some feminists (Schouten 2017), there is enough democratic support for gender egalitarianism to recommend it as a basis for policies that aim to dismantle the gendered division of labour.

Following my proposed understanding of gender justice, the main normative question concerning gender policies is how to identify policies that jointly satisfy the following conditions:

a   they make the costs of gender-neutral lifestyles more affordable to both women and men and
b   they can be permissibly enacted.

The next three sections review and offer some critical discussion of policies most often suggested by feminists.

Policies promoting gender justice

The gendered division of labour is difficult to prevent or dismantle because it creates path-dependent dynamics between women and their male life partners (especially when they have children together) as well as between female employees and (potential) employers. On the first count: since women tend to earn less, it is rational for them to specialise in caring once they have children, settling for part-time or otherwise less demanding jobs, while their male partners specialise in bread-winning. Once this choice is made, it is increasingly costly, at least economically, to outturn it (Allen 2008). On the second count: because women, more than men, are likely to leave their jobs in order to do care work at home, employers have economic reasons to prefer male over child-bearing-aged female employees, other things being equal; when they do this, employers engage in statistical discrimination. Statistical discrimination against child-bearing-aged women in the workplace is economically rational, in particular for jobs where worker retention is important, which also tend to be the more desirable jobs. A policy that could alleviate this would be to require employers to have – possibly subsidised – insurances against early loss of employees in which they have invested significant resources.

Statistical discrimination is not the only social mechanism that explains women's lesser opportunities on the labour market. Women's association with care feeds implicit (and explicit) biases against their leadership abilities (Steinpreis, Anders and Dawn Ritzke 1999) and prejudice concerning their motivation as workers. Further, gender norms that associate women with features that enable them to care well for others and men with competitiveness, assertiveness, and creativity may also explain women's susceptibility to stereotype threat – that is, the fear that others will perceive you in light of negative stereotypes associated with the group with which you identify, fear that tends to inadvertently confirm the existing stereotypes. If women suffer from stereotype threat when performing within the traditional "male" territory and, as a result, perform worse than they would otherwise perform (and worse than men), this can explain, to some extent, women's lower achievements in fields dominated by, and traditionally associated with, men (Stricker and Ward 2004).

Care work, then, and the qualities needed to do it well – attentiveness to other people's needs, empathy, cooperation, and other "soft" "feminine" virtues – seem to be at the root of the problem. Yet, we cannot eliminate this kind of work. We are all dependent on care at the beginning of our lives, most of us at the end of it, and some people continuously require substantial care from others. Reproductive work and, more generally, care work are socially necessary (Bubeck 1995; Kittay 1999; Folbre 2008).

But although we cannot do without care work, it is at least theoretically possible to reorganise society such that more of it is done in institutions. Turning childbearing and child-rearing into a public, rather than private, activity would amount to abolishing the family. Feminists have long argued that marriage is an essentially unjust institution and therefore we ought to be critical of it – rather than extend its privileges to gay people (Card 1996). One of the main feminist concerns with the traditional family is that it enrols women in procreation and child-rearing. Some feminists believe that the oppressive nature of the historical family is closely connected to the model of the "sentimental family", according to which the spouses are seen as forming a unit of emotional and economic interests (Okin 1982). On this model, the fact that one is the breadwinner and the other stays at home to look after the family does not appear inegalitarian: each contributes equally to the success of the family unit and women's "nature" makes them fit for domesticity. We know this model is problematic as a default social template, for at least two reasons: first, life-long home-making is often an unsatisfying lifestyle, but one which becomes increasingly difficult to abandon for individuals unless they receive active support. Second, a very significant proportion of marriages end in divorce; yet, former spouses continue to be co-parents – very often by sharing custody. Moreover, increasing numbers of individuals wish to form co-parenting units that are not organised around sexual/romantic relationships or even around common and fully integrated economic lives. Over the past decades feminist scholars have proposed reforms of the family law such that legal protection be given primarily to caring relationships (Fineman 1995; Brake 2010) and aimed at protecting those who are vulnerable either because they depend on other people's care or because they spend much of their time caring for others. Such a radically reformed family may be a more gender-just institution than traditional marriage since it would attribute to the state – rather than to a bread-winning spouse – the responsibility to protect caregivers' economic interests.

As Shulamith Firestone (1979) noted, the very act of gestation might be one root of women's domination. Besides its significant opportunity costs, gestation may be responsible for the symbolic association between women and the vulnerability that comes with their biological nurturing role. Firestone thought that a full feminist revolution would require ectogenesis. Even if we developed the technology necessary for ectogenesis, it is far from clear that (enough) people would want to use it, and, obviously, liberal states could not legitimately appeal to gender justice to ban natural procreation. But there seem to be sound reasons of gender justice to invest in the possibility of giving women this alternative to natural procreation (Smajdor 2012). At the same time, there may be child-centred considerations that speak against ectogenesis: if newborns come into the world already as part of a relationship with the birth mother (Gheaus 2018) and if this situation is in newborns' interest (Brighouse and Swift 2014), then it may be wrong, all things considered, to replace natural gestation with gestational machines.

Even more causally important then gestation is the fact that child-rearing takes place in the family rather than in public institutions. The thought that women's liberation is incompatible with the family as a site of child-rearing is as old as Plato. And some contemporary theories of justice acknowledge that the existence of the family also makes it difficult to realise the principle of fair equality of opportunity – a main desiderata of egalitarian justice (Rawls 1971, 1993; Munoz-Darde 1998). Yet, nobody advocates the abolition of the family as a site of child-rearing. Psychologists believe that children fare better with parents than raised in even good institutions (Waldfogel 2006), and philosophers see this as justifying an almost "no exit" clause from parenting (Alstott 2004). John Rawls believed that the family is a necessary institution, perhaps for the sake of the moral development of the next generation.

A particularly convincing account of why, on balance, we have decisive reason to keep the family was given by Harry Brighouse and Adam Swift (2014). They argue that child-rearing in small social units, by a limited number of adults who take continuous responsibility for, and provide continuous care to, children within intimate relationships, is more valuable than realising equality of opportunity. Indeed, it might be more important than gender equality. This is not only because we all start life as children but also because, for adults, families are the setting for enjoying the particularly valuable and unique goods made possible by the parent-child relationship, such as intimacy with children and taking responsibility for them.

The policy question, then, is how to reform the family to minimise its gender inegalitarian consequences. One approach aims at rectifying the unfair pay-offs of the gendered division of labour: the fact that most economic rewards go to full-time workers even though, in order to be as productive as they are, they rely on the unpaid work done at home by their spouses. Susan Moller Okin (1989) advocated a policy requiring employers to split the paycheck of wage-earning husbands between employees and their wives if the latter are not in paid employment (Okin 1989). This would address both the economic inequalities between spouses (and, in particular, shield women from the risk of poverty in case of divorce) and the power dynamics between them, by giving stay-at-home women more bargaining power. Others (Elgarte 2008; Baker 2008) think that one reason to support the introduction of a universal basic income is that it would enable individuals to undertake care work without the threats of poverty or dependence on, and possibly abuse from, their spouses. Okin's solution was criticised as a way to further entrench the gendered division of labour by giving women incentives to continue to do the bulk of the care work (Schwarzenbach 2007) and also for being inefficient (Kittay 1999), especially in changing the status of women as a social group associated with care work (Hirschman 2016). The same worries pertain to other direct cash transfers to those who opt out of the labour market in order to care for dependents (Gheaus 2008). Overall, this group of policies is attractive because they would rectify injustices suffered by some of the most vulnerable women. Against them speaks the consideration that they can further entrench the gendered division of labour unless a significant number of men will use the opportunities offered by these policies in order to do more care work.

A related, possibly more promising policy would be to try to compensate parents, especially those who do the hands-on care – that is, mostly mothers – for the loss in autonomy and economic opportunities that they incur by dint of raising children. Anne Alstott (2004) proposed the introduction of a 'caregiver's allowance' in the form of a voucher given to parents who provide hands-on care. The allowance could be used to pay for daycare in order to enable the parent to work in paid employment, or go towards retirement savings, or be invested in the parent's own education. The exact design of a fair policy of this kind will depend on an answer to the question of who should pay for the cost of having children – only parents, or both parents and non-parents (Olsaretti 2018)? If the former, perhaps the allowance could be subsidised by taxing parents who do not provide hands-on care and therefore do not incur the specific losses mentioned earlier. (This is a modification of Alstott's proposal; she believes the costs of childcare ought to be socialised.) Unlike the split paycheck, this policy need not incentivise women to stay away from the labour market.

Another kind of policy approach seeks to undo the gendered division of labour by freeing those women who are willing to join the labour market from caring duties. Barbara Bergmann (1998), for instance, argued that true feminist emancipation requires making available to women the same lifestyle that has so far been available to men: the possibility to join, and remain, in full-time employment without foregoing parenthood. This requires the creation of subsidised, good-quality, long-hours day-cares, kindergartens, and after-schools in order to make family life compatible with full-time employment for both parents. A variety of reasons support the subsidisation of caring institutions for all children from a very early age (Gheaus 2011). However, there may be an age limit above which it is beneficial for children to be institutionalised – studies suggest this limit is one (Waldfogel 2006). Moreover, there is a limit to how many hours children and parents can be away from each other while maintaining intimate and flourishing family relationships. If full gender justice can be achieved only at the price of sacrificing family life, then it seems we are facing a genuine conflict of values.[4]

It seems that the gendered division of labour can be dismantled without undue costs only if men, as well as women, engage in caregiving. Many feminists advocate a series of policies meant to incentivise this. Some concern early education: rearing children of both sexes as free as possible from gender norms that nudge them into different lifestyles (e.g., by giving them gender-neutral treatment, toys, and activities), and preparing both girls and boys for future caregiving. Jeff Behrends and Gina Schouten (2017) suggested a more radical policy according to which boys alone receive mandatory caregiving instruction, to offset the historical effects of gendered socialisation. Other policies are meant to promote gender-egalitarian parenting by introducing flexible hours for parents and designing parental leaves that encourage men to use them (Williams 2000; Gornick and Meyers 2003; Engster 2007; Schouten 2017).

With respect to parental leaves, in particular, feminists disagree on how to incentivise fathers to use the leave. Noting that a mere "use it or lose it" leave – splitting it between parents and not allowing one parent to transfer their leave to the other – is insufficient to motivate the majority of men to use their part of the leave, Harry Brighouse and Eric Olin Wright (2008) have defended a more radical policy. Their proposal is to make one's parent leave conditional on the other parent's use of leave, such that should the father fail to use his, the mother will also lack entitlement to hers. This has been criticised as illiberal, since it conditions one's person entitlement on another individual's behaviour, and is likely to backfire precisely on those women whose partners are so uninterested in gender neutrality that they will resist going on leave even if this means that their partner loses hers (Gheaus and Robeyns 2011). An overall better solution – although possibly less effective – is to make the leave the default option for both parents: just like mothers are allocated the leave automatically, so should the fathers – such that if they wish to opt out of this default scheme they would need to actively take steps to do so (Gheaus and Robeyns 2011). The main advantage of making parental leave the default option is that it counteracts to some extent the effect of gender norms that nudge men to always prioritise their careers over their family life.

Ideally, policies meant to fight the gendered division of labour or its effects would avoid setting back other important goals; but policies have unintended (yet foreseeable) consequences as well as intended ones, and hence they usually involve value trade-offs: some pitch gender neutrality against some individual freedoms. (Examples include, alongside the Brighouse-Olin-Wright leave, attempts to fight gender segregation by banning women-only playgrounds and playgroups to avoid discouraging men from caring.) Others involve possible tensions between carers' interests and children's interests, such as policies that nudge people into too much institutional care.

Gender policies and the liberal state

Policy design also has to take into account a more general question – namely, whether the enactment of a particular policy is compatible with the kind of neutrality that ought to be displayed by a liberal state.

On one view, policy design must be justified by appeal to consequentialist considerations. Policies that encourage women and men to share bread-winning and caring work within the family equally go against the expressed, and persistent, preferences of a significant group of women who have traditional gender values (Hakim 2000). This criticism, however, seems misguided given the following challenge to consequentialism in policy-making: citizens disagree in their conceptions of what constitutes a good life, and in a community in which we relate to each other as free and equal it is impermissible for the state to actively advance any controversial element of our conceptions of the good (Rawls 1993). By contrast, liberal states may and ought to enact policies that bring the society closer to realising justice – that is, to the satisfaction of its citizens' entitlements of justice. It is true that any particular policy is likely to favour the expressed interests of some social group or another. But this fact need not compromise a policy as illiberal, as long as the reason for enacting it is not that it supports any particular conception of the good but that it is just. Therefore, it is crucial to establish whether gender neutrality is a requirement of justice in order to determine the legitimacy of policies that promote it.

Citizens clearly have different views on whether women and men ought to play different social roles, and the gendered division of labour does not in itself violate anybody's rights, so appeal to the good of gender neutrality is, at least *prima facie*, the wrong type of reason to motivate a particular policy (Rawls 1993). Yet, as Okin (1989) has argued, the family is part of the basic structure of a society: it distributes benefits and burdens of social cooperation, has a basic educational role and deeply shapes people's future opportunities. These considerations seem to rule out some kinds of behaviours regulated by gender norms: for instance, humiliating forms of sexism that can undermine girls' self-respect – itself a primary good according to Rawls (Brake 2013). But surely not all types of gendered divisions of labour have this effect, and *pace* Okin (1994) it is possible for children to form a sense of justice even if they grow up in families regulated by gendered norms. Moreover, it is not clear that all institutions that are part of the basic structure of a society must be *internally* regulated by the principles of justice; rather, the interaction between the various parts of the basic structure must be such that it does not upset justice (Lloyd 1995). Therefore, it is difficult to see why justice could ban adult women and men from voluntarily stepping into traditional gender roles.

But is it permissible to merely *facilitate* gender neutrality by lowering the costs for choosing it for willing individuals, or even by nudging people into it – for instance, by implementing a number of the foregoing discussed policies? Some have argued that state-led gender-egalitarian interventions in the family are compatible with state neutrality because they are necessary for satisfying the demand of stability: in some societies there is enough democratic support for gender neutrality such that citizens would accept political interventions aimed at giving them a genuine option to lead gender-egalitarian lifestyles (Schouten 2017). Others support the same conclusion by noting that family interactions are already regulated by the state at entry, at exit, and through the stipulation of legal obligations between spouses; therefore, there is a strong *pro tanto* reason for the state to be concerned with how the family disrupts justice (Neufeld 2009). However, marriage and the family could, and should, be reformed into more liberal institutions (Fineman 1995; Brake 2010), which would make the inequalities resulting from any (enduring) gendered division of labour less problematic.

Another attempt to undermine the gendered division of labour proceeds by noting that care work is essential to social survival; this may indicate a restriction on the liberal right to occupational freedom. Diemut Bubeck (1999) suggested that care be understood as a duty of citizenship – much like national defence is in some societies. She advocated a mandatory "care corps" policy according to which all citizens spend some time of their adult life working in a public service that provides necessary care to those in need. This would make care work more equally shared. Sandrine Berges (2015) extended this argument to encompass housework as well as face-to-face caregiving. Bubeck's proposal seems unnecessarily restraining of individual liberty as long as there is enough voluntary supply of care work – just like drafting into the army seems problematically illiberal in societies where enough individuals volunteer to join a (perhaps professional) army. A more promising justification for such a scheme is to appeal to its educational value (Robeyns 2011).

Gender policy and competing feminist goals

Assuming that gender-egalitarian policies are justified, there still remains the problem that in current, distributively unjust societies, it may be very difficult to advance gender neutrality without unintentionally setting back the legitimate interests of some women who are among the most disadvantaged economically and socially. Policies that support caregiving in the home have been contentious among feminists because of their unintended negative effects on equality of opportunity between women and men in the workplace. This is true of policies that directly support care – such as the split paycheck, long parental leaves, and flexible working hours for parents (Cain Miller 2016) – and of policies that do so indirectly.

For instance, there is a feminist tradition of appealing to equality of opportunity as a *pro tanto* reason against a basic income: on the one hand, the basic income can advance the interests of some of the worst-off women, shielding full-time caregivers from poverty and giving them exit options from abusive relationships with spouses or employers (Elgarte 2008). On the other hand there is the worry that the basic income is likely to diminish women's participation in the labour market by making it affordable for more women to opt out of paid work and instead do even more unpaid care work. Over time, this would amplify statistical discrimination against women and entrench norms associating women with care, with a negative effect on women's opportunities on the labour market (Robeyns 2000; Gheaus 2008) and, possibly, on their access to positions of power and prestige. If this prediction is correct, and if equality of opportunity between women and men is a core element of gender justice, then there is a feminist case against the basic income (and other policies with similar consequences.)

Note, however, that the women whose opportunities would be lowered are likely to be the better-off women: statistical discrimination is particularly relevant for positions where workers' retention is important – that is, the better jobs which attract more educated women. Since in our societies education correlates positively with wealth and general privilege, a basic income is likely to set back the opportunities of the better-off women. According to the foregoing analysis, this effect would obtain as a side effect of protecting the options of women who are at the short end of economic distribution and social power: by giving them choices to opt out of the job market, which usually offers them only poorly remunerated, uninteresting jobs.

What should one make of this conflict? According to the most influential egalitarian views on social justice, the interests of the worst-off members of society should be given priority (Rawls 1971; Arneson 1998). Moreover, if poverty is feminised and women are at higher risk of abuses of power due to historical injustice against them, this suggests that feminists (as well as egalitarians) have good reason to favour, on balance, policies that protect worse-off women. A prioritarian principle should probably regulate a just society – that is, one where inequalities associated with different social positions are justified. The principle applies even more stringently to societies where inequalities of wealth, power, and status are unjustified. In such societies – that is, plausibly, most existing societies – the worse off are victims of injustice (Gheaus manuscript).

Conclusions

Gender-egalitarian policies meant to address the gendered division of labour and its inequality-generating effects work either by compensating caregivers or by aiming to dismantle the gendered division of labour. The former risks strengthening gender norms. The latter is effective only to the extent to which men are willing to engage in more caregiving; the policy's design must be sensitive to the possibility of negative effects on the interests of children. There is an ongoing debate concerning the legitimacy of enacting gender-egalitarian policies, at least as long as many individuals continue to embrace gender traditionalism.

A particular challenge is to design policies that avoid pitting against each other, on the one hand, the worst-off women's interests in economic sufficiency, independence, and freedom from exploitation and, on the other hand, the dismantling of the gendered division of labour and equal opportunities for women. The debate concerning a basic income, presented earlier, illustrates this problem. Where such conflicts cannot be avoided, any decision will reflect judgements about the relative importance and urgency of different goals. Providing sound judgements on these matters is, in my opinion, the most important way in which ethicists can contribute to public policy.

Notes

1 I am grateful to the editors for helpful feedback on this chapter. This project has received funding from the Ramon y Cajal Programme from the Spanish Government and from the European Research Council (ERC) under the European Union's Horizon 2020 Research and Innovation programme (Grant Agreement Number: 648610).

2 I discuss in depth the liberal case for gender justice. For the importance of gender justice, understood as justice towards women, in democratic theory see
   Pateman (1989).
3 Some authors call this position "gender egalitarianism"; this can be a bit misleading, given that feminists in general are interested in some kind of equality between women and men, but not all of them endorse gender neutrality in general or the dismantling of the gendered division of labour in particular.
4 Changing the norms and organisation of the workplace itself might allow workers to do some care during their job hours; yet, I assume that realising the goods of intimate relationships, which itself requires work, depends on sufficient time free from other responsibilities.

References

Allen, Anita. (2008). "Rationalising Oppression." *Journal of Power* 1(1):51–65.

Alstott, Anne. (2004). *No Exit: What Parents Owe Their Children and What Society Owes Parents*. Oxford: Oxford University Press.

Arneson, Richard. (1998). "What Sort of Sexual Equality Should Feminists Seek." *Journal of Contemporary Legal Issues* 21:21–36.

Baker, John. (2008). "All Things Considered, Should Feminists Embrace BI?" *Basic Income Studies* 3(3).

Behrends, Jeff and Gina Schouten. (2017). "Home Economics for Gender Justice? A Case for Gender-Differentiated Caregiving Education." *Ethical Theory and Moral Practice* 20(3):551–565.

Benatar, David. (2012). *The Second Sexism: Discrimination Against Men and Boys*. Hoboken, NJ: Wiley-Blackwell.

Berges, Sabrine. (2015). "Is Not Doing the Washing Up Like Draft Dodging? The Military Model for Resisting a Gender Based Labour Division." *Journal of Applied Philosophy* 34(3):301–314.

Bergmann, Barbara. (1998). "The Only Ticket to Equality: Total Androginy, Male Style." *Journal of Contemporary Legal Studies* 9:75–86.

Brake, Elisabeth. (2010). *Minimising Marriage*. Oxford: Oxford University Press.

Brake, Elisabeth. (2013). "Rereading Rawls on Self-Respect: Feminism, Family Law, and the Social Bases of Self-Respect." In Ruth Abbey (ed.) *Feminist Interpretations of Rawls*. University Park, PA: Penn State University Press, pp. 57–74.

Brighouse, Harry and Adam Swift. (2014). *Family Values*. Princeton, NJ: Princeton University Press.

Brighouse, Harry and Eric Olin-Wright. (2008). "Strong Gender Egalitarianism." *Politics and Society* 36:360–372.

Brownstein, Michael. (2015). "Implicit Bias." *Stanford Encyclopedia of Philosophy*.

Bubeck, Diemut. (1995). *Care, Gender, and Justice*. Oxford: Clarendon Press.

Bubeck, Diemut. (1999). "A Feminist Approach to Citizenship." In O. Hufton and Y. Kravaritou (eds.) *Gender and the Use of Time*. The Hague: Kluwer Academic Publishers, pp. 401–428.

Cain Miller, Claire. (2016). "When Family-Friendly Policies Backfire." *New York Times*, 26th of May 2016.

Card, Claudia. (1996). "Against Marriage and Motherhood." *Hypatia* 11(3): 1–23.

Chambers, Clare. (2004). "Are Breast Implants Better 'Than Female Genital Mutilation? Autonomy, Gender Equality and Nussbaum's Political Liberalism." *Critical Review of International Social and Political Philosophy* 7(3):1–33.

Elgarte, Julieta. (2008). "BI and the Gendered Division of Labour." *Basic Income Studies* 3(3).

Engster, Daniel. (2007). *The Heart of Justice: Care Ethics and Political Theory*. Oxford: Oxford University Press.

Eurostat. (2017). *Gender Statistics*. Accessed at http://ec.europa.eu/eurostat/statistics-explained/index.php/Gender_statistics. Last accessed on the 15th of November 2017.

Fineman, Marta. (1995). *The Neutered Mother, the Sexual Family and Other Twentieth Century Tragedies*. New York and London: Routledge.

Firestone, Shulamith. (1979). *The Dialectic of Sex: The Case for Feminist Revolution*. New York: Morrow.

Folbre, Nancy. (2008). *Valuing Children: Rethinking the Economics of the Family*. Cambridge, MA: Harvard University Press.

Fraser, Nancy. (1994). "After the Family Wage: Gender Equity and the Welfare State." *Political Theory* 22(4):591–618.

Gheaus, Anca. (2008). "Basic Income, Gender Justice and the Costs of Gender-Symmetrical Lifestyles." *Basic Income Studies* 3(3).

Gheaus, Anca. (2011). "Arguments for Nonparental Care for Children." *Social Theory and Practice* 37(3):483–509, 201.

Gheaus, Anca. (2012). "Gender Justice." *Journal of Ethics and Social Philosophy* 6:1–24.

Gheaus, Anca. (2018). "Biological Parenthood: Gestational, Not Genetic." *Australasian Journal of Philosophy* 96(2):225–240.

Gheaus, Anca. manuscript. "The Feminist Case Against Supporting Care."

Gheaus, Anca and Ingrid Robeyns. (2011). "Equality Promoting Parental Leave." *The Journal of Social Philosophy* 42(2):173–191.

Gheaus, Anca and Lisa Herzog. (2016). "The Goods of Work (Other Than Money!)." *Journal of Social Philosophy* 47(1):70–89.

Gornick, Janet and Marcia Meyers. (2003). *Families That Work. Policies for Reconciling Parenthood and Employment.* New York: Russell Sage Foundation.

Hakim, Susan. (2000). *Work-lifestyle Choices in the 21st Century: Preference Theory.* Oxford: Oxford University Press.

Hirschman, Nancy. (2016). "The Sexual Division of Labor and the Split Paycheck." *Hypatia* 31(3):651–667.

Hochschild, Arlie and Anne Machung. (1989). *The Second Shift: Working Parents and the Revolution at Home.* New York: Viking Penguin.

Kittay, Eva. (1999). *Love's Labor: Essays on Women, Equality, and Dependency.* New York: Routledge.

Lloyd, Susan. (1995). "Situating a Feminist Criticism of John Rawls's Political Liberalism." *Loyola of Los Angeles Law Review* 28:1319–1344.

Mason, Andrew. (2000). "Equality, Personal Responsibility, and Gender Socialisation." *Proceedings of the Aristotelian Society* 100(3):227–246.

Mikkola, Mari. (2016). "Feminist Perspectives on Sex and Gender." *The Stanford Encyclopedia of Philosophy.*

Munoz-Darde, Veronique. (1998). "Rawls, Justice in the Family and Justice of the Family." *The Philosophical Quarterly* 192(48):335–352.

Neufeld, Blain. (2009). "Coercion, the Basic Structure, and the Family." *Journal of Social Philosophy* 40:37–54.

Okin, Susan Moller. (1982). "Women and the Making of the Sentimental Family." *Philosophy and Public Affairs* 11(1):65–88.

Okin, Susan Moller. (1989). *Justice, Gender, and the Family.* New York: Basic Books.

Okin, Susan Moller. (1994). "Political Liberalism, Justice, and Gender." *Ethics* 105(1):23–43.

Olsaretti, Serena. (2018). "The Costs of Children." In Anca Gheaus, Gideon Calder and Jurgen De Wispelaere (eds.) *Routledge Handbook to Children and Childhood.* Routledge, pp. 339–350.

Pateman, Carole. (1989). *The Disorder of Women. Democracy, Feminism, and Political Theory.* Stanford: Stanford University Press.

Phillips, Anne. (2004). "Defending Equality of Outcome." *Journal of Political Philosophy* 12(1):1–19.

Radcliffe-Richards, Jeannette. (2014). "Only X%: The Problem of Sex Equality." *Journal of Practical Ethics* 2(1):44–67.

Rawls, John. (1971). *A Theory of Justice.* Cambridge, MA: Harvard University Press.

Rawls, John. (1993). *Political Liberalism.* New York: Columbia University Press.

Robeyns, Ingrid. (2000). "Hush Money or Emancipation Fee? A Gender Analysis of BI." In R. van der Veen and L. Groot (eds.) *BI on the Agenda: Policy Objectives and Political Chances.* Amsterdam: Amsterdam University Press, pp. 121–136.

Robeyns, Ingrid. (2007). "When Will Society Be Gender Just?" In J. Browne (ed.) *The Future of Gender.* Cambridge: Cambridge University Press.

Robeyns, Ingrid. (2011). "A Universal Duty to Care." In Axel Gosseries (ed.) *Arguing About Justice: Essays for Philippe van Parijs.* Louvain: Presses Universitaires de Louvain, pp. 283–290.

Schouten, Gina. (2017). "Citizenship, Reciprocity, and the Gendered Division of Labor: A Stability Argument for Gender Egalitarian Political Interventions." *Politics, Philosophy and Economics* 16(2):174–209.

Schwarzenbach, Sybil. (2007). "Civic Friendship: A Critique of Recent Care Theory." *Critical Review of International Social and Political Philosophy* 10(2):233–255.

Smajdor, Anna. (2012). "In Defense of Ectogenesis." *Cambridge Quarterly of Healthcare Ethics* 21:90–103.

Steinpreis, Rhea, Katie Anders and Dawn Ritzke. (1999). "The Impact of Gender on the Review of the Curricula Vitae of Job Applicants and Tenure Candidates: A National Empirical Study." *Sex Roles* 41(7):509–528.

Stricker, Lawrence and William Ward. (2004). "Stereotype Threat, Inquiring About Test Takers' Ethnicity and Gender, and Standardized Test Performance." *Journal of Applied Social Psychology* 34:665–693.

United Nations. (2010). *The World's Women: Trend and Statistics*, fifth edition. New York, NY: The United Nations.

Waldfogel, Jane. (2006). *What Children Need*. Cambridge, MA: Harvard University Press.

Williams, Joan. (2000). *Unbending Gender: Why Family and Work Conflict and What to Do About It*. New York: Oxford University Press.

24

DISABILITY, DEMOCRATIC EQUALITY, AND PUBLIC POLICY

Daniel Putnam

Introduction

Disability has recently become a central topic in discussions of distributive justice and social equality. This chapter provides an overview of the role of disability in these discussions, focusing on Rawlsian contractualism, luck egalitarianism, and democratic equality. It then proposes a novel interpretation of the claim that compensatory policies for disability undermine respect for persons. Even though compensatory policies are not intrinsically disrespectful, they carry a significant risk of undermining respect for persons by promoting stereotypes about people with disabilities that obscure the existence or full importance of their non-medical interests.

The chapter proceeds as follows. The first part distinguishes two very general ways of conceptualising disability: the medical model and the social model. The second and third parts trace the influence of these two models on discussions of disability within three approaches to justice: Rawlsian contractualism, luck egalitarianism, and relational egalitarianism. The fourth part focuses on one question that has been the subject of disagreement in these discussions – namely, whether compensating people with disabilities for the limitations associated with their impairments involves a failure of respect for persons. It suggests a novel answer to that question. Compensation may not be intrinsically disrespectful, but it carries a significant risk of promoting stereotypes about people with disabilities that indirectly undermine respect for persons by obscuring the existence or full importance of disabled people's non-medical interests. This entails a *pro tanto* reason of respect to prefer accommodation to compensation. Finally, I conclude with some thoughts about the recent debate over whether disability is "bad difference" or "mere difference". The basic idea is that we should distinguish the theoretical question of what descriptions are true of people with disabilities from the practical question of what descriptions should govern relationships between people of different ability statuses.

What is disability?

Let me begin by clarifying the scope of this chapter. This chapter focuses on physical disabilities. Although cognitive disabilities raise important questions of justice, it is beyond the scope of a single chapter to encompass both. Indeed, even within the category of physical disability, the conditions that are grouped together under that heading vary enormously with respect to both functional embodiment and phenomenology. To give just a few examples, blindness, deafness, rheumatoid arthritis, spinabifida, muscular dystrophy, cerebral palsy, and Parkinson's are all physical disabilities as that concept is generally understood. What if anything these different characteristics have in common is itself a matter of disagreement. Indeed, some dispute the philosophical utility of having a unified concept of disability in the first place (Beaudry 2016). Nonetheless, there are two characteristics that are generally associated with having a disability. The first is *impairment*: roughly, a physical or mental trait of the individual that represents a departure from species-typical functioning. The second is *limitation*: roughly, greater-than-average difficulty engaging in some or most human activities. To be sure, there is considerable disagreement about how to conceptualise both of these concepts (see, e.g., Shakespeare 2006; Tremain 2001; Amundson 2000; Wright 1983; Edwards 1997; Nordenfelt 1997). But the greatest controversies have centred on how to understand the relationship between impairment and limitations.

Here it is useful distinguish two general approaches to understanding disability: the *medical model* and the *social model* (for an overview, see Wasserman et al. 2011). Few would defend either of these models in their more extreme forms. Roughly, they mark endpoints on a continuum of views which differ in the degree to which they assign causal responsibility for disability-related disadvantage to the social environment as opposed to the impairment itself. According to the medical model, the limitations experienced by people with disabilities are primarily due to the functional characteristics of the impairment itself. This view suggests that the most obvious and direct way to respond to disability-related disadvantage is to correct the underlying impairment, just as the most obvious and direct response to illness is treatment of the underlying disease. Although the medical model has few explicit defenders, as many people with disabilities have themselves pointed out, it is the default way of understanding disability for many able-bodied people (UPIAS 1976). It also shapes many if not most representations of people with disabilities in popular culture (Hall 2015). For these reasons alone, it is worth making its presuppositions explicit.

A significant intellectual contribution of disability studies has been to articulate the social model of disability (Oliver 1990; Shakespeare 1998). Roughly put, the social model draws attention to the many ways in which the limitations experienced by people with disabilities are the product of an avoidably unaccommodating physical and social environment. One of the strongest political statements of the social model was enunciated by the Union of the Physically Impaired Against Segregation (1976), which identified 'contemporary social organization' (14) as the primary cause of disability-related disadvantage. Although many people regard this as a polemical overstatement (Shakespeare 2006), it is helpful in bringing out some of the morally relevant similarities between people with disabilities and other historically oppressed groups. This in turn points to a further distinction within the social model. The *minority group model* identifies stigma and deliberate exclusion as the principal causes of disability-related disadvantage. On this view, anti-discrimination protections are the most appropriate vehicle for securing justice for people with disabilities (Hahn 1997; Oliver 1990). A paradigm example of the minority group model being put into practice is the preamble to the Americans with Disabilities Act, which characterises people with disabilities as a 'discrete and insular minority' who have been 'subjected to a history of purposeful unequal treatment, and relegated to a position of political powerlessness in our society' (EEOC 1990, Section 2.7). By contrast, the *human variation model* focuses on the lack of fit between statistically unusual bodies and the social environment, where this mismatch need not be intentionally imposed or the product of overt disrespect (Scotch and Schriner 1997). On this view, reconstructing the social environment is the primary vehicle for securing justice for people with disabilities. The ADA incorporates this aspect of the social model in identifying reasonable accommodation as the appropriate form of protection against discrimination for people with disabilities.

The difference between the minority group model and the human variation model is primarily one of emphasis. They call attention to different ways in which the physical and social environment can fail to accommodate people with disabilities. Taken together, the medical model, the minority group model, and the human variation model underscore some of the major fault lines of normative disagreement about the implications of disability for ethics and public policy. In the next section, we will take a closer look at how disability has been understood in several prominent discussions about justice within the post-Rawlsian tradition. Needless to say, this overview will be selective and far from complete. I will focus on three approaches to justice that have received a great deal of attention in recent discussions, both in general and for their treatment of disability in particular: Rawlsian contractualism, luck egalitarianism, and democratic equality.

Disability in Rawlsian contractualism and luck egalitarianism

The publication of John Rawls's *A Theory of Justice* (1971) marked a watershed moment in the recent history of moral and political thought. Among other things, it revived substantive theorising about justice from a period in which disagreements about the content of morality were widely regarded by philosophers as fruitless on meta-ethical grounds. But Rawls had very little to say about people with disabilities. What he did say has been widely criticised. One line of criticism applies to the level at which the principles of justice are conceived and justified. Rawls conceived of principles of justice as applying only to 'normal and fully cooperating members of society', which he took to exclude 'temporary disabilities and also permanent disabilities or mental disorders so severe as to prevent people from being cooperating members of society in the usual sense' (1993, 20). Within his theory, this meant that laws and policies regulating disability would be settled at the subsequent, legislative stage. Unsurprisingly, this aspect of Rawlsian contractualism has been criticised. Some have argued that the best interpretation of the full cooperation requirement entails that many if not most people with disabilities are fully cooperating members of society (Hartley 2009; Stark 2009), while others have argued that the full cooperation requirement is not an essential feature of the original position (OP) and that the interests of people with disabilities can be adequately accounted for by a variation of the OP that dispenses with it (Richardson 2006). The fact that Rawlsian contractualism has some difficulty accommodating the interests of people with disabilities illustrates a more general challenge for contractarian or contractualist theories of justice, at least insofar as they depend on the idealising assumption that people are roughly equal in natural endowments or internal resources (Nussbaum 2006).

A second line of criticism takes aim at the substance of the principles of justice themselves. For Rawls, the metric of interpersonal comparisons is social primary goods: basic liberties, opportunities, and resources. But as Amartya Sen famously pointed out, two people can have equal shares of social primary goods and differ greatly in what they can do with those goods if one of the two has a significant disability (Sen 1980). Sen took this implication to support his own view that capabilities, or opportunities to achieve valuable functionings, are the proper currency of justice. Regardless of whether Sen is right about the currency question, the more general lesson is that when we ask how well off people are from the standpoint of justice, we should be sensitive to interpersonal variations in what people can do with the resources at their disposal, of which disability is one example. This is a straightforward implication of applying the human variation model to the first-order content of principles of justice.

Since the publication of *A Theory of Justice*, a family of approaches to egalitarian justice has taken centre stage which attaches fundamental normative significance to some interpretation of the distinction between *choice* and *circumstance*. Dubbed 'luck egalitarianism' by one of its critics (Anderson 1999, 289), these views share a core commitment to the idea that it is unjust when some people are made worse off through no fault or choice of their own (Arneson 1989; Cohen and Otsuka 2011; Dworkin 2000; Tan 2008; Lippert-Rasmussen 2015). Within discussions of luck egalitarianism, people with disabilities have figured primarily as *test cases* for different answers to the currency question. For example, in an influential article that inaugurated the luck egalitarian tradition, Ronald Dworkin presented people with disabilities as a puzzle for equality of resources. He argued that equality of resources can accommodate the claims of people with disabilities if it includes a hypothetical insurance scheme under which people with disabilities receive compensation equal to the amount by which the average person would insure herself against the possibility of ending up the disability in question (Dworkin 2000, 77–78). Similarly, the most discussed example of an individual person with a disability is Dickens's Tiny Tim, who combines a high level of welfare with a low level of "internal resources" (Dworkin 2000; Cohen and Otsuka 2011). The question raised by Tiny Tim was whether justice for people with disabilities requires that he be supplied with a wheelchair or whether it would be unjust to do so because that would require taking resources from people who by stipulation enjoy lower levels of welfare (Lippert-Rasmussen 2015, Section 4.4).

For our purposes, several points are worth emphasising about the luck egalitarian treatment of disability. The first is that luck egalitarianism, *as such*, does not contain a principled rationale for preferring accommodation to compensation or correction (Wolff 2009, 114–115). Regardless of whether disability is analysed as a welfare deficit or a deficit of internal resources, its normative significance consists in the fact that somebody is worse off than others through no fault or choice of her own. Given the core commitment of luck egalitarianism, it follows that there is a reason of justice in favour of whatever measures would most effectively mitigate that inequality. Compensation is the measure preferred by most luck egalitarians. Luck egalitarians could certainly defend accommodation or social construction instead of compensation. But the luck egalitarian argument for these alternative measures would presumably be instrumental, since nothing in the core commitment itself entails that one means is superior to another for mitigating unchosen inequalities.

Second, luck egalitarianism, *as such*, does not contain a principled rationale for distinguishing between equally unchosen disability-related disadvantages that reflect different causal contributions of the social environment. This is one implication of the recipient-oriented character of luck egalitarianism (Schemmel 2011). But there is a strong intuition that *collective responsibility* also matters: that it makes a difference, from the point of view of justice, whether otherwise identical patterns of unchosen disadvantage are intentionally imposed by institutions, merely foreseeably caused, merely uncorrected, and so on. To be clear, nothing in the core commitment of luck egalitarianism rules out the addition of a separate principle which ranks unchosen disadvantages according to the causal contribution of social institutions. But equally, nothing in luck egalitarians' core commitment provides any guidance on how to formulate such a principle, since it is exclusively concerned with the claimant's personal responsibility.

There is a more fundamental lesson here. It does not seem like an overstatement to say that at least until recently, luck egalitarianism, like Rawlsian contractualism, tended to analyse disability without serious consideration of the actual claims and concerns of people with disabilities. One consequence of this relative lack of attention is that luck egalitarianism has tended to tacitly incorporate the medical model, identifying compensation as the primary means of achieving justice for people with disabilities, while attributing no independent normative significance to the distinctions in collective responsibility on which the social model turns. To be sure, there are difficult methodological questions about how theorists of justice should take into account the claims advanced by real-world social movements (Fraser and Honneth 2003). But this incongruence in what considerations are identified as relevant and important raises a question about the practical applicability of luck egalitarianism to the policy challenges faced by actual people with disabilities.

Disability, democratic equality, and public policy

Both Rawlsian contractualism and luck egalitarianism stand in contrast with other areas of philosophy, where the concerns of people with disabilities have been treated as central. For example, there are a number of affinities between disability studies and recent work in feminist philosophy. Susan Sherwin has argued that medical authorities have often treated femaleness as a kind of disability (1992), while I.M. Young's "Throwing Like A Girl" makes the case that the male body is used as the standard for human functioning relative to which women's bodies are deemed deficient (1980). The idea that oppression often involves pathologising the bodies of people in the oppressed group represents a productive point of intersection between feminist philosophy, disability studies, and queer theory (Kafer 2005, 2013). At the same time, feminist philosophers writing from a disability perspective have also drawn attention to the ways in which mainstream philosophical feminism has tended to overlook the specific challenges faced by disabled women *qua* women (Asch and Fine 1988; Wendell 1989, 1996).

Within analytic political philosophy, one body of work that has been especially influenced by the social model of disability is *relational* or *democratic egalitarianism*. Perhaps more than any other text, Elizabeth Anderson's "What Is the Point of Equality?" (1999) introduced the social model to contemporary discussions of liberal egalitarianism. Although disability is not the primary focus of this piece, it includes a negative case against the luck egalitarian treatment of disability and a positive case for an alternative view. First, she argues that it is disrespectfully discriminatory to grant assistance to people with disabilities who are deemed not responsible for their condition while withholding assistance from those deemed responsible (Anderson 1999, 296). Second, with respect to disabled people who *are* granted assistance in the name of justice, she argues that the luck egalitarian rationale for doing so is inconsistent with respect for persons because it is based on *pity*, the judgement that they are defective simply in virtue of being the way they are (ibid.: 306). On these grounds, Anderson rejects luck egalitarianism as a credible theory of egalitarian justice. In its place she defends an interpretation of *democratic equality* under which justice requires all persons to have the capabilities they need to function as an equal citizen. For persons with disabilities, this implies that claims of justice are based on a demand for reasonable accommodation in public spaces and public accommodations. They are not claims to compensation for essentially private welfare or internal resource deficits (ibid.: 332).

In both its negative and positive aspects, Anderson's view can be seen as a rejection of the medical model of disability in favour of the social model. To that degree, democratic equality is arguably more responsive to the claims of justice advanced by the disability rights movement than either Rawlsian contractualism or luck egalitarianism. At the same time, it is also vulnerable to a number of objections. Two are worth underlining. First, it's not clear that compensation for disability is necessarily disrespectful or pitying. Among others, Linda Barclay makes a powerful case for the conclusion that it's not necessarily disrespectful to treat someone's unchosen circumstances, including her natural endowments, as grounds for compensation (2010). Second, there's a worry that Anderson's argument proves too much. If it's disrespectful to provide compensation to people with disabilities because that evinces pity, what about providing compensation to people who lose their homes in natural disasters? Indeed, is it *ever* permissible to compensate people for unchosen disadvantages if the respect objection to compensation for disability goes through? Perhaps there's something *special* about disability that distinguishes it from other kinds of unchosen disadvantages such that it is impermissibly disrespectful to compensate for the former but not for the latter. If so, an argument needs to be given to vindicate that premise.

Objections notwithstanding, Anderson's criticisms of luck egalitarianism initiated a lively conversation about the point of equality as a moral and political value that continues to this day. One author who explicitly takes up the project of integrating relational and distributive conceptions of equality with the aim of inferring concrete policy implications for people with disabilities is Jonathan Wolff (2009). In brief, he argues as follows. First, he defends the view that that justice requires every citizen to have *genuine opportunities for secure functionings*. This means, roughly, that every citizen enjoys reasonable access to valuable functionings free from undue risk of harm, where "functionings" include states of being, such as health, nutrition, education, and employment. This is the distributive component of his view. At the same time, Wolff argues that egalitarians should strive to create a *society of equals*, which implies that 'differences between people should be accepted' (ibid.: 116). This is the relational component of his view.

How can these two components be integrated into a conception of public policy for people with disabilities? Wolff begins by analysing disability as a condition in which a person's internal resources do not provide her with genuine opportunities for secure functionings *given* the social and material structure in which she lives *and* the external resources at her disposal. On this view, the impairment is the lack of internal resources and the limitation is the lack of genuine opportunities for secure functionings. Given this analysis of disability, there are in principle three different ways of mitigating the limitations associated with disability: increasing someone's internal resources (personal enhancement), increasing someone's external resources (compensation or targeted resource enhancement), and modifying the social and material structure (status enhancement). On Wolff's view, the relational commitment to a society in which people's differences are accepted generates several *pro tanto* reasons in favour of status enhancement as the means of mitigating disability-related disadvantage. In brief, status enhancement is non-stigmatising, since it does not identify individual beneficiaries; it is inclusive, 'welcoming people in their differences'; and it benefits everyone, by reducing the harms that would result from anyone's acquiring a disability (ibid.: 135).

There are several things to be said in favour of Wolff's approach. It is more fine-grained than other philosophical accounts of disability in distinguishing different ways of addressing disability-related disadvantage while indicating a principled rationale for preferring accommodation over other measures. It also incorporates some of the important insights of the social model by analysing disability as a relation between a person and the environment (human variation) and recognising the importance of reducing stigma (minority group). For these reasons, Wolff's account is a promising point of departure for specifying the policy implications of securing justice for people with disabilities. At the same time, a number of key ideas need to be filled in. For example, it's not clear what it means to create a society where "people are accepted in their differences". Furthermore, as with Anderson's claims about disrespect, there's a worry about proving too much: does Wolff's view entail a general *pro tanto* presumption against compensation as the means of addressing lack of genuine opportunities for secure functionings? If not, what's special about disability?

The next section takes a few steps towards filling in these gaps. In brief, the thought is that compensation carries a contingent but significant risk of promoting certain *stereotypes* about people with disabilities that indirectly undermine respect for persons.

Against compensating "the cripple"

Let me begin by saying what I mean by a "stereotype". Unsurprisingly, there is considerable disagreement about the metaphysical and normative status of stereotypes: what they are, and under what conditions they are harmful or wrong (Beeghly 2015; Brownstein and Saul 2016a, 2016b; Stangor 2000). But it is generally agreed that stereotypes have several features. First, they are *generalisations* to the effect that all or most members of some social group possess one or more attributes (Fricker 2007). Second, stereotypes are to some degree *resistant to revision* in light of the evidence. For example, someone who holds the stereotype that "all women are bad at math" will tend to hang onto that generalisation even if he meets a number of counter-examples. Third, from the perspective of someone who holds a stereotype, membership in the stereotyped group and the presence or absence of the associated attributes both tend to be *perceptually salient characteristics*. For example, someone who holds the stereotype that "black people are criminals" will see black people first and foremost *as black*: the fact that their skin has that colour will be the first thing she notices. And any characteristics that could be construed as evidence of criminality will also be very salient to her (Eberhardt et al. 2004).

Many stereotypes are morally benign. But not all. Consider the stereotype that people with disabilities lead miserable lives dominated by the experience of their impairment. Call this the stereotype of *the cripple*. Many people's perceptions of people with disabilities are to some degree coloured by that stereotype. This is reinforced by cultural representations in which people with disabilities are almost always depicted *as cripples*, if they are depicted at all (Jernigan 1974). Because this stereotype is so pervasive, when many people encounter a person with a disability, they perceive that person almost exclusively in terms of the needs they attribute to the relevant impairment: *as* a person who can't walk, *as* a person who can't see, and so forth. Indeed, the reduction of a whole person to a particular impairment is at the core of disability stigma (Asch and Wasserman 2005). Part of what gets lost in this reduction of a person to a particular impairment is a host of other characteristics, many of which ground important human interests. These include an interest in reasonable accommodation: having access to inclusive public spaces, working environments, and so on. But they also include the interests that just about any person has, regardless of disability: interests in having a satisfying career, rewarding interpersonal relationships, and all the rest. In short, by fixating people's attention on the impairment itself, the stereotype of *the cripple* obscures significant dimensions of disabled people's humanity. In that sense, it is a *humanity-obscuring stereotype*.

This brings us to respect for persons. It may be too strong to hold, as Raz does, that 'Respecting a person consists in giving appropriate weight to his interests' (1986, 188). But it is not too strong to hold that respect for persons entails giving appropriate weight to the interests of others. I fail to give appropriate weight to someone's interests if I recognise the existence and full importance of that person's interests but choose not to give them the weight they deserve in my reasoning about what to do. That would be *disrespect*. But I also fail to give appropriate weight to someone's interests if I don't recognise the existence or full importance of that person's interests in the first place. That would be a *failure of respect*. Because the stereotype of *the cripple* obscures important human interests belonging to people with disabilities, if it is widely circulating in society, it will tend to increase the incidence of epistemic failures of respect, relative to a situation in which people with disabilities are not routinely regarded *as cripples*. In practice, these epistemic failures of respect could manifest in many different ways. In face-to-face interactions, someone who is disposed to regard people with disabilities *as cripples* might solicitously draw attention to their impairments, perhaps wishing to help, but failing to register a preference to be left alone; in political situations, she might not support pro-disability laws and policies, or assume that prevention and correction are always more important than accommodation; and so on.

If it's true that the stereotype of *the cripple* has these consequences, then there is a *pro tanto* reason of respect against institutional arrangements that foreseeably increase the rate at which people with disabilities are regarded *as cripples*. Hence, the question is whether a policy of compensating people with disabilities will tend to promote the stereotype of *the cripple* in that sense. Clearly, one threshold question is what's meant by "compensation". As Wolff points out, it's not always clear what that means: often "compensation" seems to be a place-holder for 'whatever justice requires' (2009, 113). Presumably whether a given redistribution is an instance of compensation depends in part on the considerations that are taken to justify it. Very generally, I assume that if resources are being redistributed to a group of people *on the grounds that* they are worse off in some morally relevant respect, then it is appropriate to describe that redistribution as motivated at least in part by compensatory aims. If that's right, then the question is whether a policy of transferring resources to people with disabilities *on the grounds that* they are worse off in virtue of being disabled will tend to promote the stereotype of *the cripple*. Of course there is no general answer to that question. But it does not seem outlandish to think that in a society where the stereotype of *the cripple* is already in circulation – that is, in most societies – a formal policy of compensating people with disabilities on the grounds that they are *as such* worse off will tend to promote the idea that people with disabilities are defined first and foremost by the disadvantages linked to their impairments. For example, it will presumably be common knowledge among a large subset of the population that people with disabilities receive state compensation because of their impairments. This will tend to make impairments an intersubjectively salient characteristic, more than they already are. At the same time, it will invite people to locate the source of disability-related disadvantage in the "tragedy" of the impairment itself, rather than in features of the social, cultural, and physical environment. Because the stereotype of *the cripple* generates epistemic failures of respect in virtue of obscuring the wide range of human interests that people with disabilities have, it follows that whenever a policy of compensation can reasonably be expected to promote the stereotype of *the cripple*, it can reasonably be expected to promote epistemic failures of respect.

Several qualifications are in order. First, this is a weaker and more contingent argument against compensation than arguments which purport to show that compensation for disability is intrinsically disrespectful. I am not suggesting anything as strong as that. Instead, I am underlining a few concerns about the *social meaning* of compensation that should be taken into account when we ask how to weigh compensation against alternative policy responses to disability. Second, when compensation would in fact promote the stereotype of *the cripple*, it does not follow from this argument that there is a decisive reason not to compensate. Rather, this argument identifies a *pro tanto* "thumb on the scale" against compensation and in favour of other measures that would chip away at the stereotype of *the cripple*. Importantly, one such measure is status enhancement. A benefit of reconstructing the social environment to make it more accommodating of disability is that people with disabilities are thereby enabled to present as *counterstereotypical exemplars* – they are seen going to work, socialising with friends, going on dates, and so on, implicitly undercutting the vision of the "sad cripple" whose life revolves around the limitations associated with her impairment. Third, this argument applies in the first instance to disabilities that are perceptible in ordinary interpersonal contexts and hence triggers for the application of stereotypes. To be sure, this not to deny the significance of invisible disabilities (Davis 2005) – only to clarify the scope of the argument's conclusion.

In the previous section, we saw that one objection to respect-based arguments against compensation as the vehicle for mitigating disability-related disadvantage is that they prove too much. If there's a reason not to compensate people with disabilities because doing so would undermine respect for persons, does it follow that there's *always* a presumption against compensating people for being disadvantaged? In a word, no. This argument applies only when compensation would tend to promote humanity-obscuring stereotypes about the beneficiaries. Which compensation schemes will have that effect is of course an empirical question. But it seems unlikely that, for example, a policy of compensating people who lose their homes in natural disasters will promote humanity-obscuring stereotypes about the beneficiaries of that policy. Losing one's home in a natural disaster is not normally a characteristic that is salient in interpersonal contexts, as with many physical disabilities. Consequently, the beneficiaries of such a compensation scheme would not normally have to face the prospect of moving through the social world and having their humanity effaced because they are regarded by others as *merely disadvantaged*. More generally, there seems to be an important distinction between compensating people for incidental misfortunes and compensating people for *personal characteristics* – that is, for characteristics *of* the person: how one senses, how one's body functions, and so forth. The worry about humanity-obscuring stereotypes is especially pronounced when compensation is offered to a class of beneficiaries *on the basis of* personal characteristics that are already the object of humanity-obscuring stereotypes. Note that "on the basis of" is an important qualification. Compensating racial minorities for a history of unjust treatment would apply to a class of beneficiaries united by personal characteristics that are the object of humanity-obscuring stereotypes. But it would not apply to them *on the basis of* those personal characteristics, but rather on the basis of the unjust treatment those characteristics occasioned. By contrast, given the dominance of the medical model in the popular imagination, compensation for disability would plausibly be seen by many people as compensation for the personal characteristics themselves: for being blind, for being paraplegic, and so on. Insofar as that's the case, there is a real risk of promoting the stereotype of *the cripple*.

Conclusion

Now is a good time to take stock. The first part of this chapter distinguished the medical model of disability from the social model, as well as the minority group and human variation interpretations of the social model. The second part gave a critical overview of the treatment of disability in recent work on justice from the perspective of Rawlsian contractualism and luck egalitarianism, suggesting that the tacit acceptance of the medical model is part of the explanation for why the justice claims advanced by actual people with disabilities have been largely absent from these discussions. The third part discussed the treatment of disability within the democratic equality tradition, highlighting the influence of the social model while raising an objection to the putative link between compensation and lack of respect. The fourth part proposed one interpretation of the claim that compensation undermines respect for persons: namely, by promoting stereotypes which generate epistemic failures of respect.

In the space that remains, I want to suggest a connection between the preceding discussion of stereotypes and a current debate about the link between disability and well-being. In a recent article in *Ethics*, Elizabeth Barnes distinguishes two views about the link between disability and well-being (2014). According to what she calls the *bad difference view* of disability, being disabled is at least strongly correlated with being worse off, *and* this strong correlation would persist *even if* society were devoid of prejudice and as fully accommodating as possible. In contrast, the *mere difference view* is the denial of the bad difference view, along with its good-difference inverse. The current debate is about whether the mere difference view can be reconciled with the asymmetry of causing and preventing disability. Most people think that while it is permissible to prevent people from being disabled, it is generally impermissible to cause people to be disabled. At the very least, the two seem morally asymmetric. Barnes makes the case that proponents of the mere difference view can accommodate this intuitive asymmetry by appealing to non-welfarist considerations, like the wrongfulness of certain forms of interference. Against this, Guy Kahane and Julian Savulescu (2016) make the case that proponents of the mere difference view *are* saddled with a commitment to the moral symmetry of causing and preventing disability. From this, they infer a *reductio* of the mere difference view.

This debate raises a number of difficult issues which we cannot get into here. For now, I just want to underline what I take to be one of the main *motivations* for the mere difference view. Part of what motivates the mere difference view, I take it, is the recognition that constantly being seen as disadvantaged is *itself* a disadvantage. In particular, constantly being seen by others *as* a cripple means *not* being seen by others as having a host of other characteristics, including characteristics that generate important human interests. Insofar as a perception of the humanity-obscuring consequences of being regarded *as a cripple* is what motivates the mere difference view, the mere difference view is not fundamentally a claim about what descriptions of people with disabilities are *true*. Nor is it a claim about what follows from those descriptions. Rather, it is fundamentally a practical claim about what descriptions of people with disabilities should govern the interpersonal interactions between people with disabilities and their able-bodied counterparts.

If that distinction seems strange, consider the fact that a wide range of valuable interpersonal relationships are constituted in part by the considerations the parties *exclude* as reasons. This is one insight of the relational equality tradition (Viehoff 2014). For example, if you and I are friends, it would be inappropriate of me to treat the fact that you have more money than I do as a relevant consideration when deliberating about how much time to spend with you. Indeed, were I to do so, that would be strong evidence that I don't really regard you as a friend. If, on the other hand, I am a development officer at a non-profit and you are a prospective donor, it is not inappropriate for me to treat facts about your wealth as relevant considerations when it comes to allocating my time. Notice that the fundamental question here is not whether the consideration in question is true (whether you're wealthy). Nor is it, in any straightforward sense, a question about what follows from that consideration's being true. Rather, the fundamental question is what sorts of considerations it is appropriate to include or exclude from one's practical reasoning when relating to someone as a friend.

The fact that valuable interpersonal relationships are partly constituted by the considerations the parties exclude as reasons suggests that there is conceptual space for a reconciliation of the bad difference view and the motivation for the mere difference view. Suppose, for the sake of the argument, that the mere difference view is false. Instead, the bad difference view is true. Having a disability really does make people's lives go worse, and it would make their lives go worse even in a world where able-bodied people were inclusive and accommodating. This does not tell us anything about when it is appropriate to treat the bad difference view as a normative reason in the context of relationships between able-bodied people and people with disabilities. It may be true that in the specific context of deliberation about whether to cause or prevent disability, the bad difference view would indeed be an appropriate consideration to take into account. Needless to say, that is not the context most of us find ourselves in. And when we turn to other, more familiar contexts – relationships between friends, colleagues, clients, neighbours, and so on – it is far from clear that we need to rely on the bad difference view in order to respond appropriately to all the relevant reasons. It seems more likely that we can limit ourselves to context-specific considerations about what needs to be done to accommodate a particular individual's impairment, prescinding from global assessments of well-being. Moreover, given the prevalence of humanity-obscuring stereotypes like *the cripple*, there are positive reasons to set aside the bad difference view when engaging in ordinary human relationships between people who have disabilities and people who don't.

References

The Americans with Disabilities Act. (1990). Available at: Equal Opportunity Employment Commission <www.eeoc.gov/eeoc/history/35th/thelaw/ada.html>

Amundson, R. (2000). Against Normal Function. *Studies in History, Philosophy, Biology and Biomedical Science*, 31, pp. 33–53.

Anderson, E. (1999). What Is the Point of Equality? *Ethics*, 109, pp. 287–337.

Arneson, R. (1989). Equality and Equal Opportunity for Welfare. *Philosophical Studies*, 56, pp. 77–93.

Asch, A., and Fine, M. (1988). Introduction: Beyond Pedestals, in *Women with Disabilities: Essays in Psychology, Culture, and Politics*, M. Fine and A. Asch (eds.), Philadelphia: Temple University Press, pp. 1–37.

Asch, A., and Wasserman, D. (2005). Where Is the Sin in Synecdoche? Prenatal Testing and the Parent-Child Relationship, in *Quality of Life and Human Difference: Genetic Testing, Health Care, and Disability*, D. Wasserman, J. Bickenbach and R. Wachbroit (eds.), New York: Cambridge University Press, pp. 172–216.

Barclay, L. (2010). Disability, Respect, and Justice. *The Journal of Applied Philosophy*, 27, pp. 154–171.

Barnes, E. (2014). Valuing Disability, Causing Disability. *Ethics*, 125, pp. 88–113.

Beaudry, J. (2016). Beyond (Models of) Disability? *Journal of Medicine and Philosophy*, 41, pp. 210–228.

Beeghly, E. (2015). What Is a Stereotype? What Is Stereotyping? *Hypatia*, 30, pp. 675–691.

Brownstein, M. and Saul, J., eds. (2016a). *Implicit Bias & Philosophy: Volume I, Metaphysics and Epistemology*. Oxford: Oxford University Press.

Brownstein, M. and Saul, J., eds. (2016b). *Implicit Bias and Philosophy: Volume 2, Moral Responsibility, Structural Injustice, and Ethics*. Oxford: Oxford University Press.

Cohen, G.A. and Otsuka, M., ed. (2011). *On the Currency of Egalitarian Justice, and Other Essays in Political Philosophy*. Princeton, NJ: Princeton University Press.

Davis, N.A. (2005). Invisible Disability. *Ethics*, 116, pp. 153–213.

Dworkin, R. (2000). *Sovereign Virtue*. Cambridge, MA: Harvard University Press.

Eberhardt, J., Purdie, V., Goff, P. and Davies, P. (2004). Seeing Black: Race, Crime, and Visual Processing. *The Journal of Personality and Social Psychology*, 87, pp. 876–893.

Edwards, S. (1997). Dismantling the Disability/Handicap Distinction. *Journal of Medicine and Philosophy*, 22, pp. 589–606.

Fraser, N. and Honneth, A. (2003). *Redistribution or Recognition? A Political-Philosophical Exchange*. New York: Verso.

Fricker, M. (2007). *Epistemic Injustice: Power and the Ethics of Knowing*. Oxford: Oxford University Press.

Hahn, H. (1997). Advertising the Acceptably Employable Image: Disability and Capitalism. In *The Disability Studies Reader*, L.J. Davis (ed.). London: Routledge Kegan Paul, pp. 172–186.

Hall, A. (2015). *Literature and Disability*. London: Routledge.

Hartley, C. (2009). Justice for the Disabled: A Contractualist Approach. *Journal of Social Philosophy*, 40, pp. 17–36.

Jernigan, K. (1974). Blindness: Is Literature Against Us? Address to the Annual Convention of the National Federation for the Blind, July 3, 1974. Available at: <https://nfb.org/images/nfb/publications/convent/banque74.htm>

Kafer, A. (2005). Hiking Boots and Wheelchairs: Ecofeminism, the Body, and Physical Disability. In *Feminist Interventions in Ethics and Politics*, B. Andrew, J. Keller and L. Schwartzman (eds.). Lanham, MD: Rowman and Littlefield, pp. 131–150.

Kafer, A. (2013). *Feminist, Queer, Crip*. Bloomington: Indiana University Press.

Kahane, G. and Savulescu, G. (2016). Disability and Mere Difference. *Ethics*, 126, pp. 774–778.

Lippert-Rasmussen, K. (2015). *Luck Egalitarianism*. London: Bloomsbury.

Nordenfelt, L. (1997). The Importance of a Disability/Handicap Distinction. *Journal of Medicine and Philosophy*, 22, pp. 607–622.

Nussbaum, M. (2006). *Frontiers of Justice: Disability, Nationality, Species Membership*. Cambridge, MA: Harvard University Press.

Oliver, M. (1990). *The Politics of Disablement: A Sociological Approach*. London: St. Martin's.

Rawls, J. (1971). *A Theory of Justice*. Cambridge, MA: Harvard University Press.

Rawls, J. (1993). *Political Liberalism*. New York: Columbia University Press.

Raz, J. (1986). *The Morality of Freedom*. Oxford: Oxford University Press.

Richardson, H. (2006). Rawlsian Social-Contract Theory and the Severely Disabled. *The Journal of Ethics*, 10, pp. 419–462.

Schemmel, C. (2011). Distributive and Relational Equality. *Politics, Philosophy, and Economics*, 11, pp. 123–148.

Scotch, R.K. and Schriner, K. (1997). Disability as Human Variation: Implications for Policy. *The Annals of the American Academy of Political and Social Science*, 549, pp. 148–159.

Sen, A. (1980). Equality of What? In *The Tanner Lecture on Human Values*. Cambridge: Cambridge University Press, I, pp. 197–220.

Shakespeare, T. (1998). *The Disability Studies Reader: Social Science Perspectives*. London: Bloomsbury.

Shakespeare, T. (2006). *Disability Rights and Wrongs*. New York: Routledge.

Sherwin, S. (1992). *No Longer Patient: Feminist Ethics and Health Care*. Philadelphia, PA: Temple University Press.

Stangor, C., ed. (2000). *Stereotypes and Prejudice: Essential Readings*. Philadelphia, PA: Psychology Press.

Stark, C. (2009). Contractarianism and Cooperation. *Politics, Philosophy and Economics*, 8, pp. 73–99.

Tan, K. (2008). A Defense of Luck Egalitarianism. *The Journal of Philosophy*, 105, pp. 665–690.

Tremain, S. (2001). On the Government of Disability. *Social Theory and Practice*, 27, pp. 617–636.

UPIAS. (1976). *Fundamental Principles of Disability*. London: Union of the Physically Impaired Against Segregation.

Viehoff, D. (2014). Democratic Equality and Political Authority. *Philosophy and Public Affairs*, 42, pp. 337–375.

Wasserman, D., Asch, A., Blustein, J. and Putnam, D. (2011). Disability: Definitions, Models, Experience. *The Stanford Encyclopedia of Philosophy*. Published online. Available at: <https://plato.stanford.edu/entries/disability/>

Wendell, S. (1989). Toward a Feminist Theory of Disability. *Hypatia*, 4, pp. 104–124.

Wendell, S. (1996). *The Rejected Body: Feminist Philosophical Reflections on Disability*. London: Routledge.

Wolff, J. (2009). Disability Among Equals. In *Disability and Disadvantage*, K. Brownlee and A. Cureton (eds.). Oxford: Oxford University Press, pp. 112–137.

Wright, B. (1983). *Physical Disability: A Psychosocial Approach*, 2nd edition. New York: Harper & Row.

Young, I.M. (1980). Throwing Like a Girl: A Phenomenology of Feminine Body Comportment, Motility and Spatiality. *Human Studies*, 3, pp. 137–156.

25

THE ETHICS OF INDIGENOUS RIGHTS

*Teddy Harrison and Melissa S. Williams**

Representatives of settler states face a peculiar problem when trying to make public policies that apply to indigenous people. Indigenous peoples are distinct from other minority groups in having prior claims to land and governance, supported by pre-existing legal traditions. Even in democratic states, indigenous people can thus plausibly reject the legitimacy of the state's claim to have policy-making authority over them in the first place. This widens the scope of ethical contestation of public policy. Any public policy must be justified substantively and procedurally – that is, there must be an ethical justification of both the content of the policy and the procedure by which the policy was made. Yet justification at the substantive level of public policy presumes a prior justification of the legitimacy of the policy-making enterprise. This presumption of state legitimacy is challenged by many indigenous people, who point to the absence of an ethical grounding for the assertion of settler state sovereignty.

As two non-indigenous Canadian scholars of political science, we have chosen to focus this chapter on the ethics of state policy regarding indigenous people. This is itself partly an ethical decision, in that we do not consider ourselves situated in such a way as to be able to speak for indigenous people, nor do we presume to instruct indigenous people how to conduct their ethical struggle for decolonisation. We are better situated to offer critiques of state policy towards indigenous people, and an ethical framework to guide respectful engagement by non-indigenous policymakers with the claims brought forward by indigenous people. We have also focused our attention on the Canadian case, in part for the sake of simplicity (indigenous policy is already very complex) and in part because it is the case we know best. Indigenous claims are particular claims, based in a rootedness and connection to particular land.[1] It is therefore important to address them in a concrete context. However, we believe the lessons we draw from the Canadian case are relevant to other similar countries (e.g., the United States, Australia, and New Zealand, and the Nordic countries in relation to Sami people). One response to indigenous challenges to state legitimacy is to focus on carving out a sphere of self-determination for indigenous peoples, a principle affirmed in the United Nations Declaration on the Rights of Indigenous Peoples.[2] In this chapter, we take the existence of a right to self-determination to be settled from a moral point of view. Such a right is at its essence the right for indigenous

---

* Teddy Harrison is the lead author of this chapter and took primary responsibility for drafting it.

peoples to authoritatively regulate matters which affect themselves alone, without interference from non-indigenous authorities. There remain substantial challenges in conceptualising the right, particularly in agreeing on its scope in relation to state sovereignty. However, we contend that an ethical examination of state policy-making regarding indigenous peoples cannot be limited to determining the appropriate scope of self-determination. Even if a satisfactory degree of self-determination were available to indigenous people, important questions of public policy would remain at the state level.

In countries such as Canada, indigenous and non-indigenous people do not lead lives that can be neatly divided into separate spheres. More than half of all indigenous people live outside areas of indigenous jurisdiction, where their lives are inescapably linked to non-indigenous people through institutional, interactive, and familial ties. Elsewhere, Melissa Williams has argued that this makes Canada a 'community of shared fate'.[3] The futures of non-indigenous Canadians and the indigenous peoples of the territory are bound up together by relations of interdependence whether we like it or not. In Canada, because we are all here to stay, we do not have the choice to simply go our separate ways. The only choice we have is over how we choose to live together. If we turn to public policy, there are then two key questions. First, which choices must be made together, and which can be made separately? Secondly, how should joint decisions be made? The chapter is divided into two major sections. The first consists of a review of past policies, which we analyse according to five ideal-type normative orientations. This analysis helps to clarify the continued failures of state policy-makers to find an appropriate approach to policy regarding indigenous people. In the second section, we develop the idea of dual respect and the third normative space as an alternative framework to guide policy-making.

Part 1: a review of past policy

With the space available in this chapter, it is not possible to comprehensively catalogue the panoply of past state policies affecting indigenous people. Instead, we offer an ideal-type analysis of the normative orientations adopted by the state towards indigenous people when making public policy. We have discerned five such ideal types: eliminationism, paternalism, responsibilisation, legalism, and reconciliation. Like all ideal types, these are analytic constructs developed by emphasising particular aspects of our messy social reality. Actual policies will embody these types to greater or lesser degrees: some policies will fit neatly under a single ideal type, while others will combine two or more.

The first ideal type is eliminationism. The normative stance of eliminationism is quite simply that indigenous people should cease to exist *as indigenous*. According to Patrick Wolfe, settler colonialism *per se* follows a 'logic of elimination' that 'destroys to replace', combining a negative dimension – the destruction of pre-existing indigenous societies – with a positive element – the creation of 'a new colonial society on the expropriated land base'.[4] Because the negative dimension is required for the positive project of creating a colonial order, Wolfe argues that settler colonialism is *inherently* eliminatory.[5] Although physical genocide – the mass killing of indigenous people – is the clearest example of eliminationism, in historical practice the logic of elimination has more commonly produced a variety of less overtly violent policies. Wolfe identifies 'officially encouraged miscegenation, the breaking-down of native title into alienable individual freeholds, native citizenship, child abduction, religious conversion, [and] resocialization in total institutions such as missions or boarding schools' – all policies widely deployed in Canada.[6] It is important to note that a policy of assimilation is no less eliminationist than a policy of mass killing. Assimilationist policies are not analytically distinct, but are just that subset of eliminationist policies that combine the negative and positive aspects of the logic elimination in a single moment enacted upon indigenous subjects. Successful assimilation destroys the indigenous subject and replaces her with a settler-colonial subject. Early colonists were clear-eyed about this process. Richard Pratt, founder of Carlisle boarding school (the model for the modern residential school system), articulated the purpose as 'Kill the Indian in him and save the man'.[7] Indigenous critics of assimilation never forgot this lesson. Harold Cardinal described the 1969 White Paper, which proposed the abolition of distinct Indian Status in return for equal rights of citizenship, as 'a thinly disguised programme of extermination through assimilation'.[8]

The logic of elimination is clear to see in the policies of the Canadian settler state. During the first 100 years of confederation – termed the "Century of Dishonour" by Jonathon Milloy – Canadian policy was avowedly eliminationist.[9] Duncan Campbell Scott, deputy minister for Indian affairs from 1913 to 1932, declared that with the *Indian Act* 'our object is to continue until there is not a single Indian in Canada that has not been absorbed into the body politic, and there is no Indian question'.[10] This was the centrepiece of a broader legislative and administrative project of erasure of indigenous peoples that the Truth and Reconciliation Commission of Canada aptly described as cultural genocide.[11] The major purpose of residential schools was elimination through assimilation. Canada's first prime minister, John A. Macdonald, argued that schools must be residential in order to separate children from their families to ensure 'they will acquire the habits and modes of thought of white men' rather than becoming 'simply a savage who can read and write'.[12] Clearing indigenous people off the land and restricting them to reserves was another major element of the eliminationist strategy, literally erasing indigenous people from the map of Canada. Restrictive and sexist determinations of indigenous membership also served eliminationist functions. Because "Indian Status" was defined through male heads of household (fathers or husbands for women), many women and their children lost their status. Effectively, mixing of heritage was taken to erase or eliminate the indigeneity of individuals. As Wolfe argues, this is paradigmatic of settler-colonial eliminationism: the racialised construction of a category of "Indian" is designed to ensure the eventual elimination of that category, in order to free up access to land for settlers.[13]

The second ideal type is paternalism. Paternalist policy-making aims to promote the perceived well-being of indigenous people without regard for their autonomy. Paternalism can be ethically justified only if at least two conditions are met: (1) the objects of paternalist policy do not understand what is in their best interests and (2) the policy-makers do. These conditions are normally thought to obtain in the case of parents and children (hence the term "paternalism"), such that it is ethically appropriate for parents to make a host of decisions on behalf of their children to promote their well-being. However, neither condition applies in the case of indigenous people. There is no reason to suggest indigenous people are any less capable than others of understanding their own interests. There are, however, good reasons to think that non-indigenous policymakers are particularly poorly placed to have such an understanding. The record of purportedly well-meaning paternalist policies is very poor. Residential schools, for instance, were supposed to promote the well-being of indigenous people through providing a western-style education, but instead did tremendous harm. The structure of paternalist policy-making makes such an outcome likely because it licenses policymakers to ignore indigenous people's understandings of their own interests. Coupled with a general lack of knowledge of indigenous cultures and value systems, this has meant non-indigenous policy-makers imposing their own value systems on indigenous people.

Paternalism has been widespread in Canadian policies towards indigenous people. Under the *Indian Act*, indigenous people have been treated as wards of the state – that is, essentially as children under state care. The Act empowered non-indigenous administrators, including Indian agents and other bureaucratic officials, to regulate the minute details of indigenous people's lives. This paternalist power stands in an ambivalent relationship to eliminationism. Some paternalist measures explicitly aim at the preservation of distinct indigenous communities. For example, reserve land cannot be alienated, except to the Crown – a measure designed to ensure the preservation of a collective land base. The paternalism of this protection remains problematic – not least because governments have abused their control to alienate land for public and private purposes even when this was clearly *not* in the best interests of indigenous people[14] – but there is no necessary connection to eliminationism.

In practice, however, assimiliationist policies in Canada have regularly been a toxic combination of eliminationism and paternalism. Eurocentric assumptions of cultural superiority made policy-makers think indigenous people would be better off assimilated, and so they proceeded to force assimilation upon them. Residential schools were a particularly atrocious example, with separating children from their families and denying them access to their own language and culture justified as being in their best interests. The historic practice of "enfranchisement" followed a similar logic: indigenous people who met certain criteria (e.g., entering certain professions or attending university) lost their Indian status in exchange for gaining Canadian citizenship.

A third ideal type is "responsibilisation", a technique associated with market-based models of neoliberal governance.[15] Responsibilisation seeks to shift responsibility for solving problems to a lower level of authority – in Canada, this means away from the federal government to provincial or municipal governments, to indigenous communities, or to indigenous individuals. It is not merely the obverse of paternalism, in prioritising regard for autonomy over a concern for well-being. Instead, responsibilisation has been a strategy of governmentality deployed by the state in response to demands for indigenous self-determination. Since at least the 1950s, the federal government has repeatedly sought to shift its fiscal and administrative responsibility for indigenous people onto provincial governments or indigenous communities (with very limited success).[16] The most notable example of responsibilisation has been the transformation of indigenous demands for self-determination into administrative arrangements for "self-government". At its core, the assertion of the right to self-determination for indigenous peoples is a rejection of the assertion of Canadian sovereignty over them. Instead of addressing this challenge, Canadian policy-makers have developed of variety of models that incorporate a practice of self-government for indigenous people *within* the Canadian state, thus downloading responsibilities for governance onto indigenous communities without challenging the overall architecture of the Canadian state. Some of the models offer greater autonomy than others. Band councils under the *Indian Act*, for instance, have severely limited autonomy. By-laws still require the approval of a federal government minister, and the *Act* makes councils accountable to federal agencies, not to indigenous community members.[17] Yet even the most expansive modern treaties and self-government agreements maintain the assertion of underlying Crown sovereignty and subordinate indigenous governments to the Canadian state in a host of areas.

We term the fourth ideal type "legalism". By this we mean an approach that determines the parameters of policies affecting indigenous people through narrow legal reasoning, rather than more expansive political or normative argument. Although legalism has always been a factor in Canadian policy-making regarding indigenous people, it has played a leading role in driving the evolution of policy since the 1970s. A series of court decisions have supported the existence in Canadian law of a variety of Aboriginal rights and Aboriginal title to land, and have set forth important guidelines for policy, including the Crown's fiduciary duty to indigenous people and the honour of the Crown.[18] Because the courts have largely been more willing than politicians to recognise indigenous claims, indigenous people have strategically engaged with courts and government policy shifts have largely been reactions to court decisions. The *Calder* decision, for instance, opened up the policy space for the negotiation of modern treaties and land claim agreements; Canada engages in negotiation with indigenous groups largely because of the legal uncertainty created by the possible existence of Aboriginal title.

However, the reliance on narrow legal reasoning within the Canadian legal system severely limits the types of indigenous claims that can be advanced. Canadian courts are, for instance, constitutionally incapable of questioning the underlying assertion of Crown sovereignty (as it is also the basis for their legal authority). Although the *sui generis* nature of Aboriginal rights has stretched Canadian law, it still traps indigenous people into advancing claims within an alien rights discourse.[19] There are also some conclusions that are supportable only by legal reasoning. For instance, for a First Nations person to show the existence of an Aboriginal right, they must show the protected practice existed before contact with Europeans.[20] As Métis people did not exist before contact, the court devised an alternative test for Métis rights, which requires practices to have developed before the date of effective European control – but did not then apply this test to Aboriginal rights for First Nations people.[21] This apparent contradiction is supportable only within a framework of purely legal reasoning. More broadly, the legal tests for Aboriginal rights impose an essentialising and static conception of culture that is not accepted by indigenous people.

The final ideal type is reconciliation. The language of reconciliation dominates current discourse about the relationship between indigenous people and the settler state across a variety of domains: we have had a Truth and Reconciliation Commission, governments tout their commitment to reconciliation, and courts speak of reconciliation in the context of Aboriginal rights. Broadly speaking, reconciliation means bringing conflicting elements into harmony, or rendering them compatible with one another. The precise meaning, however, is contested – and the term is deployed in a variety of ways. The key elements of contestation are the conceptualisation of the conflict that needs reconciliation, and the placement of the burden of changing in order to achieve compatibility. The Truth and Reconciliation Commission presents an inclusive view, defining reconciliation as 'an ongoing process of establishing and maintaining respectful relationships'.[22] In practice, Canadian policy has deployed reconciliation in a more restrictive way. The Supreme Court has used the concept of reconciliation to infringe Aboriginal rights by balancing them against the interests of other Canadians.[23]

In the state paradigm, reconciliation is usually achieved by limiting or altering indigenous claims to fit within the state structure. This approach has been heavily criticised by indigenous scholars. Glen Coulthard argues that this form of reconciliation remains colonial because 'it remains structurally committed to the dispossession of Indigenous peoples of our lands and self-determining authority'.[24] Taiaiake Alfred argues that 'a façade of "reconciliation" is being used to buttress white supremacy, pacify and co-opt Indigenous leadership, and facilitate total access to Indigenous lands for resource development'.[25] If state reconciliation discourse is simply the latest new bottle for the old wine of assimiliationist policy, many indigenous scholars and activists urge turning to a program of resurgence that focuses on building up indigenous nationhood and restoring a nation-to-nation relationship between indigenous nations and settlers.

Part 2: the idea of dual respect and the third normative space

Through the history of Canadian policy regarding indigenous people, there is a recurring pattern of purportedly well-meaning reforms succeeding only in reproducing the underlying colonial order. Notoriously, the ironically named White Paper of 1969, which was ostensibly aimed at ending discriminatory treatment, in effect reasserted the normative superiority of non-indigenous ways of life and proposed to end any official recognition of indigeneity. 'To be an

Indian', the White Paper stated, 'is to lack power – the power to act as owner of your own lands, the power to spend your own money, and, too often, the power to change your own condition'.[26] The rise of legal Aboriginal rights may have had benefits for indigenous people, but it also traps claimants within a framework of underlying Crown sovereignty and an alien rights discourse.[27]

This pattern will repeat itself so long as the normative concepts used to evaluate and reform policy continue to be drawn exclusively from the liberal ethical system that underpins the colonial order; concepts like rights and sovereignty which are not rooted in indigenous norma-tive orders will always be a double-edged sword. Even the concept of reconciliation, which was introduced precisely to bridge indigenous and non-indigenous normative orders, has been implemented in such a way that it draws its content from the existing liberal legal order. In this way, it can be used to reject indigenous claims in the name of "reconciling" them with underlying Crown sovereignty.[28]

The concept of respect is a better starting point for evaluating policy because it has strong roots in both liberal and indigenous ethical systems. Respect has a central place in many indig-enous ethical systems – for instance, as one of the seven grandfather (or grandmother) teachings of the Anishinaabe people.[29] In fact, we have yet to encounter an indigenous ethical system in which respect is *not* a core value. Respect is also an important normative concept in liberal ethi-cal systems. Crucially, indigenous people have long emphasised the relevance of mutual respect in evaluating the relationship between indigenous people and settlers. Indigenous interpreta-tions of treaties often see them as grounded in a relationship of mutual respect, and the Truth and Reconciliation Commission used the concept of mutual respect as the basis for its vision of a renewed relationship.[30] In this chapter, we are primarily concerned with how the state can hold up its end of the bargain: how does the state support a relationship of mutual respect through its public policies regarding indigenous people? We contend that the Canadian state owes indigenous persons at least two distinct forms of respect: respect as bearers of the status of free and equal persons under law, including the rights of citizenship,[31] and respect *as indigenous* people.

The idea that the state must respect its citizens as free and equal persons is well entrenched in liberal states like Canada. There is also, by and large, a consensus among political theorists that this is a central component of state legitimacy. Although there is, of course, disagreement about how such respect can be instantiated, there is at least broad agreement on the goal of respecting all citizens as free and equal. Liberal political theorists work out the detailed requirements of equal respect in various ways. In practice, the constitutional order of Canada is another such formulation, providing as it does legal guarantees of rights to a variety of fundamental freedoms, to equality under the law, and to more specific rights designed to safeguard the equal enjoyment of fundamental freedoms. Our point here is not that Canada has found the correct answer but merely that it clearly recognises the challenge and provides a sophisticated, well-worked-out approach. If citizens wish to contest that approach, they can draw upon an equally sophisticated set of critiques and intellectual resources to imagine and pursue potential alternatives, without ever stepping outside the accepted paradigm of citizen respect.

Liberal theory and the Canadian state framework have much less to tell us about how to spe-cifically respect the indigeneity of indigenous people. Frequently, in fact, the Canadian state has denied that any particular respect for indigeneity is required (explicitly so, in the case of elimi-nationist policies). Even today, there is not a universal consensus that anything beyond basic citizen respect is necessary. However, the challenge of providing cross-cultural respect is as old as the settler-indigenous encounter. There is also good reason to think that early encounters, with nation-to-nation relationships worked out according to the protocols of both indigenous and settler ethical systems, came closer to achieving a relationship of mutual respect than later Canadian state policy.[32]

It might seem that a framework of liberal multiculturalism such as Will Kymlicka developed over two decades ago could be adequate to the task of realising respect for persons and respect for indigeneity simultaneously. Kymlicka's framework of "differentiated citizenship" for indigenous peoples and other cultural minorities began from the liberal premise that states owe respect to individuals as free and equal persons. His core argument was that the freedom of individuals requires that they enjoy a secure cultural context as the background condition for their capacity to exercise autonomy in making life choices, since it is culture that makes choice options meaningful to individuals. For indigenous peoples, national minorities, and immigrants, the dominance of the majority culture in shaping public norms threatens their cultural security and hence their autonomy. Respect for individuals therefore requires that the state accommodate minority cultures through a scheme of cultural rights that varies according to the qualities of the minority in question. For indigenous peoples and national minorities, cultural rights should include rights of collective autonomy or self-government. In the case of immigrants, accommodations or exemptions within existing legal frameworks are appropriate. Where practicable, language rights and rights of political representation are appropriate to all three types of cultural minorities.[33]

Although liberal multiculturalism goes some distance in expressing respect for indigenous peoples as bearers of distinct cultures, it is not sufficient as a framework of indigenous rights. First, indigenous peoples' rights of self-determination do not turn on their cultural difference from the majority population and place them in a *sui generis* relation to the settler–colonial state, one that cannot be assimilated to the position of other cultural minorities. Second, indigenous self-determination is understood as an inherent right, not a right bestowed on indigenous peoples by a benevolent state. The framework of liberal multiculturalism presupposes the basic legitimacy of the settler state's claim to sovereign authority over indigenous peoples without inquiring into the origins of this authority in the history of unjustifiable colonial domination. As Kymlicka has recently acknowledged, the background injustice of colonialism and the history of state domination of indigenous peoples cast the legitimacy of state authority into question. An adequate framework for indigenous rights 'must address these deeper issues, through some process of reconciling indigenous and settler sovereignties'.[34]

The key challenge in developing a model of cross-cultural respect within a framework that recognises indigenous rights of self-determination is that it cannot come solely from the intellectual resources of a single ethical system. In this case, that means that the Canadian state cannot develop an acceptable model of respect for indigeneity solely out of the Canadian constitutional framework or liberal political theory, even liberal multiculturalism. Instead, it must reach some sort of mutual understanding with indigenous modes of ethical thought and incorporate indigenous models of respectful relationships into its own policy-making. This going beyond oneself is particularly challenging for liberal thought with universalist aspirations. It requires an attitude of humility and a recognition that elements of our scheme of "universal" human rights may in fact be merely culturally specific formulations of underlying human interests.

It may be fruitful to understand the ethical failings of past policies as failures of respect. Some policies fail at one form of respect while delivering the other, while others fail to provide respect in either form. It is perhaps most egregious when Canada fails to provide respect to indigenous people even in its own terms, yet that has been the rule rather than the exception for most of Canadian history. Indigenous people were not considered to be citizens, and thus were explicitly not afforded the respect due to citizens as free and equal. This applied across a wide variety of policy domains, with indigenous people denied political participation, legal equality, freedom of movement, and even the ability to control basic details of their own lives.

Eliminationist policies clearly embody no respect for those they seek to sweep aside. Paternalist policies are a more complicated case. Paternalism towards indigenous people clearly does not evince citizen respect, in failing to treat them as free (by denying autonomy) or equal (to those whose autonomy is respected). In some cases, so-called paternalist policy-making was in fact an excuse for policies that respected neither the autonomy nor the well-being of indigenous people; in such cases, "paternalism" was merely a power-grab. State control of indigenous lands – ostensibly meant to protect indigenous people from unfair dealing – was often used to allocate reserve lands for use by non-indigenous peoples. In one high-profile case, Crown agents leased out a large part of the Musqueam reserve in Vancouver to create a golf course on unfavourable financial terms that were not disclosed to the Musqueam.[35]

In some cases, however, paternalist policies were designed in order to protect the indigeneity of indigenous people, as it was understood by governments. One example is the restriction on the sale of reserve property, designed to prevent the dissolution of reserves. While this may ultimately be a failed mode of cross-cultural respect, it was at least an attempt to respect indigeneity – at the cost of citizen respect.

Examples of the converse are easy to find: more recent Canadian policy has often sought to respect indigenous people as free and equal citizens at the cost of respecting indigeneity. The paradigm of this approach is provided by the 1969 White Paper, which proposed to respect indigenous people *only* as free and equal co-citizens while abolishing any attempts to respect a distinct indigeneity. The White Paper's core proposal was to abolish the *Indian Act*, the unjust and discriminatory policy through which the Canadian state governs the lives of indigenous people and treats them differently from all other Canadians. For example, for non-indigenous Canadians, most social policy domains, including education, health, and child welfare, are matters of provincial jurisdiction. Under the *Indian Act*, the federal government has jurisdiction over these matters as they pertain to indigenous people – and it allots fewer resources to them than any province allots to non-indigenous citizens, even though the needs in many indigenous communities are greater.[36] From this perspective, the White Paper's proposal to abolish the *Indian Act* might appear to be a good step towards respecting indigenous people as free and equal persons. Yet in abolishing the *Indian Act* the Canadian state would also have abolished the only legal framework through which it acknowledged the distinctive position of indigenous people within the constitutional order. This is why it met with such stiff opposition from indigenous leaders. Despite some progress in courts' interpretations of indigenous rights, Canada has not yet fashioned an alternative legal framework to respect indigenous persons as free and equal while also respecting indigeneity, and the pathologies of the *Indian Act* remain.

The battle over the White Paper marked a double turning point in Canadian indigenous policy. First, the government turned away from the history of explicitly denying citizen respect to indigenous people; respect as free and equal co-citizens was to be the baseline for future policy. In practice, this promise has yet to be realised. The discriminatory legislative framework of the *Indian Act* continues to govern the lives of many indigenous people. This includes the separate and unequal provision of social services, including education and health care. It also includes the lack of provision of basic services, such as clean drinking water, that most Canadians can take for granted. First Nation governance under the band council system is still subjected to paternalist control by the federal ministry. Beyond the legal discrimination sanctioned by the *Indian Act*, many indigenous people face systemic discrimination and overt racism in their interactions with the Canadian state. This can be seen clearly in the criminal justice system, where indigenous people are disproportionately the victims of violent crime, more likely to be incarcerated, and more likely to be subject to police violence.[37]

Second, the opposition to the White Paper mobilised by indigenous people made it clear that citizen respect was only the starting point; cross-cultural respect for indigeneity was also necessary. Nevertheless, the assimilationist thrust of 'white paper liberalism'[38] did not die with the White Paper. In a more subtle form of assimilation, indigenous claims have been distorted to become palatable within a (modified) model of citizen respect. Such models include Alan Cairn's *Citizens Plus*, which views indigenous people as citizens like any other, but with an additional package of rights.[39]

The approach of trying to incorporate indigenous concerns within a model of shared citizenship has been heavily criticised, with Gordon Christie calling it a sly form of colonial apology.[40] Regardless of whether we assent to that assessment, it does seem clear that existing discourses around both Aboriginal rights and reconciliation have failed to break out of the paradigm of citizen respect to offer something indigenous people themselves recognise as cross-cultural respect.

The two forms of respect are distinct in the sense that they are grounded in distinct normative systems. Thus, what determines the nature of respect comes from a system of liberal political ethics and indigenous ethical traditions respectively. In practice, the substantive requirements of each form of respect may overlap. Both forms of respect would clearly prohibit eliminationism, for example. There will be a further range over which the two forms of respect will be complementary, with actions required by one form of respect permitted (or perhaps simply considered supererogatory) by the other. Indigenous ethical systems often mandate respect for non-human animals over and above anything found in a liberal ethical system, but the liberal system does not mandate the opposite.[41] There may even be good reasons internal to one ethical system for endorsing complementary substantive elements of the other form of respect. This is clearly the case when a liberal commitment to civility supports engaging in indigenous protocols of respect and hospitality when framing cross-cultural dialogue.

Unfortunately, there will also be a range over which the two forms of respect generate conflicting prescriptions. One clear example of this conflict concerns forms of governance. The liberal model is now taken, almost universally, to require democratic governance, elections, and universal adult suffrage. Many indigenous ethical systems support other models of governance, which may be based on consensus but incorporate hereditary or gender-differentiated roles. Despite the imposition of elective band councils under the *Indian Act*, indigenous people in many communities continue to see hereditary chiefs as legitimate sources of authority.[42] For one example of gendered role differentiation, we can look to the Haudenosaunee (Iroquois). Traditional Iroquois society was firmly matrilineal: male chiefs were the political representatives of the confederacy, but they were chosen and could be impeached by the matrons (sometimes known as clan mothers). These powerful women controlled agriculture and the longhouses in which everyone lived.[43] Although the strong role for women may be attractive when compared to the colonially imposed patriarchy that followed, prescriptive gender roles – certainly those that exclude women from direct participation in political leadership – conflict with the liberal democratic model of politics. It is in these areas of conflict that it becomes most difficult to balance the competing demands of the two forms of respect.

Elsewhere, building on the work of Anishinaabe scholar John Borrows, Melissa Williams has developed a model of three normative spaces based on an interpretation of the two-row wampum treaty.[44] In general, the wampum belt, constructed of beads made from shells, is a traditional record of agreement between the Haudenosaunee people and other nations; wampum belts were used to represent and solemnise early agreements between indigenous peoples and the British Crown. The *Kaswentha*, or two-row wampum, was among these early representations of treaty relations between the Haudenosaunee and the British, and it is now frequently invoked as a model for a respectful relationship between indigenous and non-indigenous Canadians. The *Kaswentha* comprises five parallel rows of beads: two purple rows, and three white rows, one on the outer edge of each purple row and one separating the two purple rows. The purple rows are said to represent an indigenous canoe and European ship, sharing the same river (represented by the white beads) in a relationship of friendship, equality, and respect in which neither tries to steer the other's vessel.[45] The three normative spaces correspond roughly to the indigenous canoe, the European ship, and the river we share.

The first normative space is one 'governed *exclusively* by the norms and commitments affirmed by [indigenous] peoples themselves'.[46] The existence of such a space is part of the right to self-determination of indigenous peoples. The first normative space is, appropriately, the focus of much attention for indigenous peoples, both through efforts to establish a meaningful measure of self-government within the Canadian constitutional structure and through the movement for the resurgence of indigenous ways of living (regardless of the state). The first normative space is not, however, an appropriate field for state policy-making. If the state involves itself, it undermines the existence of this space, and turns any chance at meaningful self-government into an exercise of state paternalism or responsibilisation. Instead, state interaction with the first normative space must be limited to creating the constitutional space for the exercise of indigenous jurisdiction, and perhaps providing material support. Citizen respect does not seem to have a role to play in this normative space, and cross-cultural respect mandates a hands-off approach to policy-making.

The second normative space deals with individuals as citizens of Canada. It is a space 'governed by the norms expressed within Canadian institutions and practices of constitutional democracy, in all their pluralism and complexity'.[47] As such, it is also a space where the appropriate form of respect is citizen respect – that is, respect for one another as free and equal co-citizens. The norms of the second space thus must be the product of choices made by Canadian citizens through democratic institutions, and apply to all equally as citizens – ideally through a scheme of differentiated rights through which equality is reconciled with cultural and other forms of social difference. The second space is thus not merely a "European ship" to match the indigenous canoe of the first space, but is instead a distinctly Canadian multicultural space governed by liberal democratic norms, but drawing on diverse normative traditions for content. There is thus an ethically significant asymmetry between the first two normative spaces. While the survival of the first space requires the exclusion of outside normative authorities, the nature of the second space requires the *inclusion* of the voices of all members to generate authoritative norms.

The third normative space is the most significant for our analysis; in the metaphor, this is the river we all share and in which we interact *as indigenous and non-indigenous* Canadians. A third space is necessitated by the fact that we constitute a community of shared fate, and so inescapably will continue to live together in ethically significant relations. If those relations are not to be relations of domination, then the norms governing the relationship must be agreed upon by both parties equally. Agreement cannot be equal if the terms of discussion are dictated by one or the other normative tradition, and so agreement must come out of a process of cross-cultural dialogue. As such, this is a domain governed by the norms of cross-cultural respect first and foremost, albeit one in which the norms of citizen respect will also be in play. The boundaries of the first and second spaces can be determined only through discussion in the third normative space (and thus, the scope of the applicability of citizen respect).

The third space is thus a space of negotiation. Part of such negotiation will be over the nature of a nation-to-nation relationship between Canada and indigenous peoples. To be meaningful, such negotiations must start from a presumption of equal validity of indigenous and non-indigenous ethical systems, rather than operating *within* the ethical-legal system of the Canadian state from the start.[48] Reconciliation also finds its proper place in the third normative space. Here, as part of a project of mutually respectful cultural dialogue between partners on equal normative footing, negotiated reconciliation can live up to its potential in establishing and maintaining respectful relationships. Reconciliation discourse in Canada has seldom been located in the third normative space. In most cases, efforts at reconciliation are instead subordinated to the norms of the second normative space, and made to operate within the ethical structure of the Canadian state and its unjustified presumption of legitimate sovereign authority over indigenous peoples. In the worst cases, a legal version of reconciliation is used to directly circumscribe the first normative space and limit the scope of indigenous self-determination.

Conclusion

The idea of two forms of respect and the three normative spaces will not settle the specific questions of state policy towards indigenous people. It is our hope, however, that it provides a useful framework to help policy-makers understand the roots of the ethical failings of past policies. This framework should also help policy-makers to understand the work necessary to produce ethically acceptable policy. Most of the initial work will take place within the third normative space. It is only in the third normative space, through a real cross-cultural dialogue between indigenous and non-indigenous Canadians, that the groundwork can be laid for an ethical state policy towards indigenous peoples.

We began with two key questions: which decisions must be made together, and how should joint decisions be taken? It is not viable for one partner to unilaterally control the answers to these questions, as has been the case with the assertion and enforcement of state sovereignty over indigenous peoples. Instead, the answers to these questions must be worked out in dialogue between partners of equal normative standing. Such a dialogue must be governed by norms of cross-cultural respect, which cannot themselves be derived from a single normative system. Determining how to engage respectfully across cultures will be difficult, and there will likely be many failures along the way. The only way to know if one is being respectful will be to recursively check with one's dialogue partners.

Notes

1 Coulthard, *Red Skin, White Masks*, 13.
2 U.N. General Assembly, *United Nations Declaration on the Rights of Indigenous Peoples*, Article 3.
3 Williams, "Sharing the River," 104.
4 Wolfe, "Settler Colonialism and the Elimination of the Native," 387, 388.
5 Wolfe, "Settler Colonialism and the Elimination of the Native," 387.
6 Wolfe, "Settler Colonialism and the Elimination of the Native," 388.
7 Wolfe, "Settler Colonialism and the Elimination of the Native," 397.
8 Cardinal, *The Unjust Society*, 1.
9 Milloy, "Indian Act Colonialism."
10 Truth and Reconciliation Commission of Canada, *Honouring the Truth, Reconciling for the Future*, 54.
11 Truth and Reconciliation Commission of Canada, *Honouring the Truth, Reconciling for the Future*, 1.
12 Quoted in Truth and Reconciliation Commission of Canada, *Honouring the Truth, Reconciling for the Future*, 2.
13 Wolfe, "Settler Colonialism and the Elimination of the Native," 388, 400.
14 Guerin v. The Queen, 2 SCR.
15 Shamir, "The Age of Responsibilization," 7–9.

16 Comeau and Santin, "The First Canadians," 8.
17 Abele, "Like an Ill-Fitting Boot," 15–16, 24–25.
18 On Aboriginal Rights: R. v. Sparrow, 1 SCR; R. v. Van der Peet, 2 SCR; R. v. Powley, 2 SCR; on Aboriginal Title: Calder et al. v. Attorney-General of British Columbia; Tsilhqot'in Nation v. British Columbia, 2 SCR; on the fiduciary duty: Guerin v. The Queen, 2 SCR; on honour of the Crown Haida Nation v. British Columbia (Minister of Forests), 3 SCR.
19 Turpel, "Aboriginal Peoples and the Canadian Charter," 9–10; Turner, "This Is Not a Peace Pipe," 13.
20 R. v. Van der Peet, 2 SCR.
21 R. v. Powley, 2 SCR.
22 Truth and Reconciliation Commission of Canada, *Honouring the Truth, Reconciling for the Future*, 16.
23 McNeil, "Reconciliation and the Supreme Court," 9.
24 Coulthard, *Red Skin, White Masks*, 151.
25 Alfred, "Being and Becoming Indigenous." On indigenous resurgence, see also, for example, Corntassel, "Re-Envisioning Resurgence."; Simpson, "Indigenous Resurgence and Co-Resistance."; Napoleon, "Thinking About Indigenous Legal Orders."
26 Canada, *Statement of the Government of Canada on Indian Policy*, 1.
27 Turpel, "Aboriginal Peoples and the Canadian Charter," 9–10; Turner, "This Is Not a Peace Pipe," 13.
28 McNeil, "Reconciliation and the Supreme Court," 9.
29 Borrows, "Seven Gifts," 3.
30 Truth and Reconciliation Commission of Canada, *Honouring the Truth, Reconciling for the Future*.
31 Note, however, that because of the Canadian state's use of "enfranchisement" into Canadian citizenship as an instrument of assimilation, some indigenous people are wary of the language of citizenship to denote their relationship to Canada. See, for example, Henderson, "Sui Generis and Treaty Citizenship," 416–417.
32 As James Tully argues in Strange Multiplicity, chapter 4.
33 Kymlicka, *Liberalism, Community and Culture*, chapters 8–10; *Multicultural Citizenship*, chapter 2.
34 Kymlicka, "Liberal Multiculturalism as a Political Theory of State-Minority Relations," 84.
35 Guerin v. The Queen, 2 SCR.
36 For example, Blackstock, "The Canadian Human Rights Tribunal on First Nations Child Welfare."; Drummond and Rosenbluth, "The Debate on First Nations Education Funding."; Galloway, "Ottawa Still Failing to Provide Adequate Health Care on Reserves."
37 Perreault, "Violent Victimization of Aboriginal People in the Canadian Provinces, 2009"; Perreault, "The Incarceration of Aboriginal People in Adult Correctional Services"; Brennan, "Violent Victimization of Aboriginal Women in the Canadian Provincs, 2009."
38 Turner, "This Is Not a Peace Pipe," 15.
39 Cairns, *Citizens Plus*, 161.
40 Christie, "Book Review," 194.
41 Even if the record of permitting disrespectful and harmful treatment of the non-human under liberal systems is pretty poor, this is an area in which adding on a form of indigenous-inspired respect could be complementary rather than conflicting.
42 Coates, National Centre for First Nations Governance, and Canadian Electronic Library (Firm), *The Indian Act and the Future of Aboriginal Governance in Canada*.
43 Montour, "Iroquois Women's Rights with Respect to Matrimonial Property on Indian Reserves."
44 Williams, "Sharing the River."
45 See Borrows, "'Landed Citizenship," 335; Borrows, *Recovering Canada*, 125–127.
46 Williams, "Sharing the River," 108.
47 Williams, "Sharing the River," 108.
48 We are aware that this is a radical shift from existing state policy, but it seems to be a minimum requirement for legitimacy.

References

Abele, Frances. "Like an Ill-Fitting Boot: Government, Governance and Management Systems in the Contemporary Indian Act," Research Paper for the National Centre for First Nations Governance, June 2007. http://fngovernance.org/ncfng_research/frances_able.pdf.

Alfred, Taiaike. "Being and Becoming Indigenous: Resurgence Against Contemporary Colonialism," Narrm Orration, Melbourne, November 28, 2013. https://taiaiake.net/2013/12/13/being-and-becoming-indigenous-resurgence-against-contemporary-colonialism/.

Blackstock, Cindy. "The Canadian Human Rights Tribunal on First Nations Child Welfare: Why if Canada Wins, Equality and Justice Lose," *Child and Youth Services Review* 33: 187–194 (2010).

Borrows, John. "'Landed' Citizenship: Narratives of Aboriginal Political Participation," in Will Kymlicka and Wayne Norman, eds., *Citizenship in Diverse Societies*. Oxford: Oxford University Press, 2000.

Borrows, John. *Recovering Canada: The Resurgence of Indigenous Law*. Toronto: University of Toronto Press, 2002.

Borrows, John. "Seven Gifts: Revitalizing Living Laws Through Indigenous Legal Practice," *Lakehead Law Journal* 2(1): 1–13 (2016–17). https://llj.lakeheadu.ca/article/viewFile/1490/825.

Brennan, Shannon. "Violent Victimization of Aboriginal Women in the Canadian Provinces, 2009," Juristat, 2011. www.statcan.gc.ca/pub/85-002-x/2011001/article/11439-eng.htm.

Cairns, Alan C. *Citizens Plus: Aboriginal Peoples and the Canadian State*. Brenda and David McLean Canadian Studies Series. Vancouver: UBC Press, 2000.

Calder et al. v. Attorney-General of British Columbia (C January 31, 1973).

Canada, *Statement of the Government of Canada on Indian Policy* (The White Paper). Ottawa: Government of Canada, 1969. www.aadnc-aandc.gc.ca/DAM/DAM-INTER-HQ/STAGING/texte-text/cp1969_1100100010190_eng.pdf.

Cardinal, Harold. *The Unjust Society: The Tragedy of Canada's Indians*. Edmonton: Hurtig, 1969.

Christie, Gordon. "Book Review: Citizens Plus: Aboriginal Peoples and the Canadian State, by Alan C. Cairns; First Nations? Second Thoughts, by Tom Flanagan; A People's Dream: Aboriginal Self-Government in Canada, by Dan Russell," *Osgoode Hall Law Journal* 40(2): 189–200 (April 1, 2002).

Coates, Ken, National Centre for First Nations Governance, and Canadian Electronic Library (Firm). *The Indian Act and the Future of Aboriginal Governance in Canada*. Canadian Electronic Library. West Vancouver, BC: National Centre for First Nations Governance, 2008. http://myaccess.library.utoronto.ca/login?url=http://books.scholarsportal.info/viewdoc.html?id=/ebooks/ebooks0/gibson_cppc/2010-08-06/6/10385433.

Comeau, Pauline and Aldo Santin. *The First Canadians: A Profile of Canada's Native People Today*. Toronto: J. Lorimer, 1990. http://link.library.utoronto.ca/eir/EIRdetail.cfm?Resources__ID=604747&T=F.

Corntassel, Jeff. "Re-Envisioning Resurgence: Indigenous Pathways to Decolonization and Sustainable Self-Determination," *Decolonization, Indigeneity, Education & Society* 1(1): 86–101 (2012).

Coulthard, Glen Sean. *Red Skin, White Masks: Rejecting the Colonial Politics of Recognition*. Minneapolis: University of Minnesota Press, 2014.

Drummond, Don and Ellen Kachuk Rosenbluth. "The Debate on First Nations Education Funding: Mind the Gap," School of Policy Studies, Queen's University, Working Paper 49 (December 2013). http://education.chiefs-of-ontario.org/upload/documents/resources/funding/49-drummond-rosenbluth.pdf.

Galloway, Gloria. "Ottawa Still Failing to Provide Adequate Health Care on Reserves," *The Globe and Mail*, January 25, 2017. www.theglobeandmail.com/news/politics/ottawa-still-failing-to-provide-adequate-health-care-on-reserves-report/article33746065/.

Guerin v. The Queen, 2 SCR 335 (C 1984).

Haida Nation v. British Columbia (Minister of Forests), 3 SCR 511 (SCC 2004).

Henderson, James (Sákéj) Youngblood. "*Sui Generis* and Treaty Citizenship," *Citizenship Studies* 6(4): 415–440 (2002).

Kymlicka, Will. *Liberalism, Community and Culture*. Oxford: Oxford University Press, 1989.

Kymlicka, Will. *Multicultural Citizenship*. Oxford: Oxford University Press, 2005.

Kymlicka, Will. "Liberal Multiculturalism as a Political Theory of State-Minority Relations," *Political Theory* 46(1): 81–91 (2018).

McNeil, Kent. "Reconciliation and the Supreme Court: The Opposing Views of Chief Justices Lamer and McLachlin," *Indigenous Law Journal* 2(1) (January 7, 2017). http://jps.library.utoronto.ca/index.php/ilj/article/download/27699.

Milloy, John Sheridan. "Indian Act Colonialism: A Century of Dishonour, 1869–1969," Canadian Electronic Library. West Vancouver, BC: National Centre for First Nations Governance, 2008. http://myaccess.library.utoronto.ca/login?url=http://books.scholarsportal.info/viewdoc.html?id=/ebooks/ebooks0/gibson_cppc/2010-11-18/1/10418645.

Montour, Martha. "Iroquois Women's Rights with Respect to Matrimonial Property on Indian Reserves," in Martin J. Cannon and Lina Sunseri, eds., *Racism, Colonialism, and Indigeneity in Canada: A Reader*. Don Mills, ON: Oxford University Press, 2011, 80–84.

Napoleon, Val. "Thinking About Indigenous Legal Orders," in René Provost and Colleen Sheppard, eds., *Dialogues on Human Rights and Legal Pluralism*. Dordrecht: Springer, 2013, 229–246.

Perreault, Samuel. "The Incarceration of Aboriginal People in Adult Correctional Services," Juristat. Statistics Canada, June 2009.

———. "Violent Victimization of Aboriginal People in the Canadian Provinces, 2009," Juristat. Statistics Canada, March 11, 2011.

R. v. Powley, 2 SCR 207 (SCC 2003).

R. v. Sparrow, 1 SCR 1075 (C 1990).

R. v. Van der Peet, 2 SCR 507 (C 1996).

Shamir, Ronen. "The Age of Responsibilization: On Market-Embedded Morality," *Economy and Society* 37(1): 1–19 (2008).

Simpson, Leanne Betasamosake. "Indigenous Resurgence and Co-Resistance," *Critical Ethnic Studies* 2(2): 19–34 (2016).

Truth and Reconciliation Commission of Canada. *Honouring the Truth, Reconciling for the Future: Summary of the Final Report of the Truth and Reconciliation Commission of Canada*. [S.l.]: Truth and Reconciliation Commission of Canada, 2015. http://myaccess.library.utoronto.ca/login?url=http://site.ebrary.com/lib/utoronto/Top?id=11070416.

Tsilhqot'in Nation v. British Columbia, 2 SCR 257 (SCC 2014).

Tully, James. *Strange Multiplicity: Constitutionalism in an Age of Diversity*. Cambridge: Cambridge University Press, 1995.

Turner, Dale A. *This Is Not a Peace Pipe: Towards a Critical Indigenous Philosophy*. Toronto: University of Toronto Press, 2006.

Turpel, Mary Ellen. "Aboriginal Peoples and the Canadian Charter: Interpretive Monopolies, Cultural Differences," *Canadian Human Rights Yearbook* 1989–1990 3 (1989–1990).

UN General Assembly, *United Nations Declaration on the Rights of Indigenous Peoples*. Resolution adopted by the General Assembly, October 2, 2007, A/RES/61/295. www.refworld.org/docid/471355a82.html [accessed 23 February 2018].

Williams, Melissa S. "Sharing the River: Aboriginal Representation in Canadian Political Institutions," in David H. Laycock, eds., *Representation and Democratic Theory*. Vancouver: UBC Press, 2004. http://link.library.utoronto.ca/eir/EIRdetail.cfm?Resources__ID=605600&T=F.

Wolfe, Patrick. "Settler Colonialism and the Elimination of the Native," *Journal of Genocide Research* 8(4): 387–409 (2006). https://doi.org/10.1080/14623520601056240.

26

THE ETHICS OF REPARATIONS POLICIES

Alasia Nuti and Jennifer M. Page

Introduction

The normative reasons to repair past injustices have been the subject of much debate. Some scholars offer backward-looking justifications that do not hinge on whether past injustices affect present conditions (e.g., Miller 2007; Ridge 2003). Others instead point out that reparations are justified by forward-looking considerations of justice (e.g., Hendrix 1995; McCarthy 2004; Tan 2007; Valls 2007). However, questions of justification do not exhaust the range of pressing normative challenges that reparations raise. Normative reflection on the process of devising reparations programmes is as important and challenging as thinking about why reparations are owed.

Consider, for instance, the recent negotiation process between Japan and South Korea over the 'comfort system' that infamously forced women – mostly from Korea – to provide sexual services to Japanese soldiers before and during World War II.[1] Japan agreed to establish a 1 billion yen governmental fund for those few survivors who are still alive, officially recognised the involvement of the Japanese military in the sexual enslavement of the 'comfort women', and formally issued its 'most sincere apologies' for the abuses and trauma suffered by the women. South Korea, for its part, promised to consider the wrong as finally redressed and to not raise the 'issue' anymore in international forums. South Korea also agreed to negotiate the removal of a controversial statue representing the comfort women that was placed outside the Japanese embassy in Seoul. The agreement was welcomed and celebrated by both countries and their international partners as promoting the beginning of a new era in the relationship between Japan and South Korea, which has been strained by the unsettled imperial past (McCurry 2015). However, many South Koreans have opposed the agreement and, in particular, some survivors of the comfort system have vehemently criticised it as profoundly disrespectful because it was reached without their consultation (McCurry 2016). Moreover, non-Korean women from other territories occupied by Japan who were also sent to frontline brothels and forced to have sexual intercourse with Japanese soldiers have challenged the idea that the unjust past of the 'comfort women system' has been repaired through the bilateral agreement between Japan and South Korea. Without the inclusion of all those who were sexually enslaved by the Imperial Japanese Army, they argue, reparations will always remain incomplete.

It is not enough simply to pay reparations when they are owed. Further work must be done to grapple with the difficult ethical considerations that arise in devising reparations programmes. In this chapter, we identify three ethical challenges that seem to recur again and again at the implementation stage: (1) the problem of political instrumentalisation; (2) the problem of exclusion; and (3) the problem of inclusion. When the design of reparations programmes neglects ethical considerations such as these, their implementation is likely to leave the injustices in need of repair unscathed and – even worse – compound existing forms of exclusion, power imbalances, and marginalisation. Reasoning normatively about how to design reparations programmes should thus take centre stage in the ethics of reparations. As we argue, it is not possible to resolve the problems of political instrumentalisation, exclusion, and inclusion without bringing in reparations claimants as participants who play an active role in designing the reparations programmes that are to benefit them.

Two disclaimers before proceeding. First, like many reparations scholars, we find the UN's principles on reparations for human rights violations helpful in distinguishing between restitution (i.e., return to the status quo ante), compensation or redress (monetary or material transfer when restitution is not possible), and satisfaction (i.e., symbolic measures like apologies) (see "Basic Principles and Guidelines" 2005). A consensus seems to have emerged that reparations should include both material and symbolic forms of repair, and though we agree with this by and large, this essay does not meaningfully engage with the question as to the form that reparations should take. Second, and relatedly, the issues discussed in this chapter should not be regarded as exhausting all possible ethical concerns that the design of reparations programmes raises. By focusing on the three problems we've identified, we simply hope to show they are particularly pressing and, in this respect, exemplify the urgency of a serious normative engagement with the ethics of devising reparations programmes for past injustices.

The chapter proceeds as follows. The first section explores the problem of political instrumentalisation, which revolves around a worry expressed by reparation claimants and victims of injustice that reparations can seem to be a way for governments to legitimise their power rather than achieve justice. We argue that a necessary, although not sufficient, requirement that reparations programmes must meet to minimise this problem is the active involvement of claimants in the designing process. However, actively involving claimants is not a straightforward task. The second and third sections identify and discuss two ethical issues that arise in spite of there being some attempt to engage with those who suffered from past injustices. While the second section focuses on the problem of exclusion, which has to do with establishing the criteria for determining who has a valid reparations claim, the third section tackles the problem of inclusion, which arises because not all individuals with a potential claim to redress will be actively mobilised in making a reparations demand. In all three sections, our analysis is informed by real-world cases in liberal democratic societies. This approach allows our analysis to be guided by the problems that actual reparations claimants face, as well as to consider responses that are attentive to on-the-ground political circumstances.

The problem of political instrumentalisation

We tend to regard reparations programmes as measures that are always welcomed by those who have suffered from a past injustice or from their descendants. This is, however, a simplification of how reparations programmes have been historically received by their potential beneficiaries. Consider the Reparations Agreement between Israel and West Germany, which was signed on September 10, 1952, with the official intent to financially help Holocaust survivors who lived in Israel. Such an agreement is often regarded as exemplary, an early case in which reparations were paid, showing that the latter need not be regarded as a quixotic enterprise. Yet it is noteworthy that even this agreement was not enthusiastically received by everyone in the Israeli public. Both right-wing and left-wing organisations and parties criticised the agreement by arguing that accepting reparations from West Germany amounted to forgiving Germans for the crimes committed during the Holocaust, and rallies and protests took place before and after the agreement was signed (Segev 1993: 211–252). In other words, reparations programmes may meet with resistance not only from wrongdoers but also from potential beneficiaries.

Although some may consider beneficiaries' resistance to reparations an unfortunate yet inevitable feature of any attempt to repair past wrongdoing, often it signals a serious problem with the underlying and covert goals of specific reparations programmes. This occurs when governments use reparations not as a tool of justice but as a way to legitimise their authority and strengthen their power. Call this the *problem of political instrumentalisation*. To appreciate the seriousness of this problem and how it can forestall historical justice, consider the case of the Mothers of Plaza de Mayo who have relentlessly refused reparations from the Argentinian government for the 'disappearance' of their children during the 'Dirty War'.

The 'Dirty War' refers to the period between 1974 and 1983 in which the Argentinian military junta implemented a regime of state terrorism against citizens suspected of socialist allegiances. A still unclear yet shocking number of left-wing activists, guerrillas and militants, trade unionists, students, and journalists 'disappeared' after having been detained, tortured, and buried in unmarked graves or having had their corpses incinerated by the junta. Moreover, many of the children who were abducted with their parents or were born in detention centres did not come back to their families but were secretly adopted by military couples. The Madres' activism addressed how subsequent governments handled the atrocities committed during the period of the military junta (Moon 2012: 5). The two successive governments, led by Raul Alfonsín and Carlos Menem respectively, were equivocal when it came to holding the military junta accountable for their crimes. Although in 1985, Alfonsín's government started a series of trials for the members of the junta – culminating with the imprisonment of Jorge Videla, the Dirty War's architect – the government went on to introduce 'amnesty laws', stopping the very process of accountability that the government had put in place. During Menem's ten years as president of Argentina, not only were Alfonsín's amnesty laws were maintained but also pardons were granted to the members of the junta who were in jail, including Videla (Moon 2012: 6). In 1977, the mothers of the victims of the junta began mobilising and founded the grassroots association Madres de Plaza de Mayo both to gain information about the disappearance and location of their children and to press governments to prosecute the perpetrators. When Alfonsín's and later Menem's governments offered reparations to the Madres for the disappearance of their children, they strenuously rejected the proposal (Arditti 1999; Bouvard 1994).[2]

Recent accounts of reparations in the context of past injustices and violations of human rights have pointed out that there is an important link between reparations programmes and the legitimacy of state power. For instance, Steven Winter (2014: 7) argues that when wrongdoing was authorised by the state through direct sanction, permission, or toleration, the state ceases to properly function and its legitimate power is undermined and in need of repair. Reparations, so interpreted, become the way in which states attempt to 'repair the damage that authorized wrongdoing inflicts upon political legitimacy' (Winter 2014: 7). The Madres' refusal to accept reparations for the crimes perpetuated by the military junta was precisely a protest against the Argentinian state's intention to overcome its legitimacy deficit and strengthen its power simply by offering monetary and symbolic reparations for the 'disappearance' of their children. Their refusal expressed a normative stance on the very legitimacy of reparations programmes as a tool to restore the Argentinian state's political legitimacy. Had the Madres accepted reparations, other citizens may have regarded the Argentinian government as fully legitimate. By refusing reparations, the Madres were able to show that the governments succeeding the military junta did not have moral standing to pay redress. Given their shortcomings in addressing the crimes of the Dirty War, the governments could not acquire legitimacy merely through monetary means.

Of course, there may be cases in which a government's interest in improving perceptions of its legitimacy and the victims' interest in receiving redress align neatly, and the problem of political instrumentalisation does not arise. Winter's legitimacy-based theory of state redress is most definitely not an argument in favour of instrumentalist conduct by governments. The issue is rather when the potential beneficiaries feel they are being used as pawns in a government agenda over which they have no say. The case of the Madres in Argentina points to at least two warning signs to identify the problem of political instrumentalisation.

First, reparations programmes should not be advanced with the aim of imposing a 'top-down' and already-established interpretation of the unjust past, but as an opportunity to open a dialogue over it. As pointed out by Moon (2012: 8), the Madres perceived that accepting reparations would also have meant subscribing to the 'truth' about state terror and their children's disappearance that succeeding governments were trying to impose, such as Alfonsín's 'theory of the two evils', which regarded military terrorism and guerrilla opposition as equally responsible for crimes and wrongdoings. Before even starting to devise reparations programmes, an inclusive conversation about the meaning of unjust past events and the distribution of responsibilities should take place (Amighetti and Nuti 2015: 392). When, instead, the state makes reparations conditional on acceptance of its interpretation of past injustices – as in the Argentinian case – reparations programmes are more likely to be an instrument to legitimise and strengthen state power, rather than giving survivors, their families, and their descendants their due.

Second, reparations programmes cannot be conceived of as substitute for criminal justice. The Argentinian governments' attempts (especially during Menem's administration) to set up a redress programme addressed to the parents and children of the disappeared were combined with a reluctance to bring the perpetrators to justice. As part of their fight for accountability and retributive justice, the Madres refused to declare their disappeared children as 'dead' and to accept the exhumation of their corpses. Instead they demanded that their children be regarded as still living, a way of demonstrating that 'victims of injustice are not "dust and nothing" but retain a status and a presence as claimants on justice' (Booth 2011: 752). In Hebe de Bonafini's words, this demand 'question[ed] the system' as the Madres did not want to 'accept their [children's] deaths until someone [was] made responsible' (Bonafini 1990: 42; quoted in Moon 2012: 7). Indeed, the Madres held their last March of Resistance at Plaza de Mayo in 2005 when the Kirchner's administration repealed and declared unconstitutional the amnesty laws and pardons of previous governments. Only at that point, for the Madres, the government proved not to be an enemy of its people anymore.

In order to minimise the risk of the political instrumentalisation of reparations programmes, the direct involvement of their potential beneficiaries is necessary. It is only when potential beneficiaries are treated not as passive recipients of reparations but as invaluable actors in thinking about (i) what reparations programmes should aim for and (ii) how they should be devised that a fuller understanding of past wrongs can be gained. Moreover, engaging with potential beneficiaries helps put pressure on the state not to tender redress in an exchange for the punishment of those who are liable. Of course, the desideratum of the direct involvement of potential beneficiaries does not on its own guarantee that reparations programmes will not be tools of political legitimacy. There are many scenarios in which the bargaining power of beneficiaries is too insufficient to exercise influence on the state or not to be co-opted by it. However, if a reparations programme aims at being meaningfully legitimate, and not just as an instrument of a legitimacy project of the state, involving beneficiaries in deliberation from the beginning is invaluable. Carving out space for participation cannot itself overcome the problem of political instrumentalisation, but it can at least show respect for the would-be beneficiaries as persons with voices worthy of being heard. As such, their involvement is a necessary, although not sufficient, requirement that reparations programmes have to meet in order to defend against challenges to their legitimacy.

Nevertheless, the process of involving beneficiaries in the design of reparations programmes raises pressing ethical issues having to do both with the identification of who counts as a legitimate claimant and with potential disagreements within the community of beneficiaries. To such issues we now turn.

The problem of exclusion

If government officials take the time to listen to reparations claimants in designing reparations programmes, one thing that is apparent is that claimants are not content if they themselves receive monetary redress, yet perceive that there are others who are unfairly denied it. The *problem of exclusion* arises when a reparations programme is designed in a way that turns individuals away who are perceived as having valid claims. Even claimants with modest financial situations will often say that a payment is 'not about the money'; it is about justice being done. The problem of exclusion may cast suspicion on the government's motives and create the sense that the reparations programme's purpose is hush money, buying off select claimants as cheaply as possible. Indeed, a reparations programme accused of strategically excluding applicants may be seen as a political tool, and thus the problem of exclusion and the problem of political instrumentalisation go hand in hand.

Why would a government implement a reparations programme with too narrow a net, opening itself up to the problem of exclusion? Almost always, there are reasonable concerns on the part of the government about fraudulent claims. A filing process has to be devised whereby claimants demonstrate that they meet a predetermined set of criteria to be eligible for a payment. However, sometimes eligibility rules are determined before government officials have a good sense of how individuals were victimised, or before they are well acquainted with the specific characteristics of the reparations claimant class. If officials refuse to vary from the original eligibility criteria once more information emerges, this bureaucratic mentality may undermine the very purpose of a reparations programme.

Take the example of a US government-run uranium mining programme which conscripted around 1,500 Navajo men during the atomic era. Though the federal government knew about the health risks associated with radiation, it made no attempt to communicate this information in its cheerful recruitment efforts, making patriotic appeals and offering the men higher wages than they made farming and herding (Eichstaedt 1994: Ch. 5; Brugge and Goble 2003). All this was revealed in lawsuits filed by Navajo plaintiffs who developed radiation-related cancers. Congress resolved the matter legislatively with the 1990 Radiation Exposure Compensation Act (RECA), which consisted of an apology and a redress programme for the uranium miners and other Americans who contracted one of several identified cancerous diseases as a result of atomic weapons building and testing.

However, aspects of the RECA programme created a situation where relatively few uranium miners and families received redress. The programme required marriage records for deceased miners' widows. But in the 1930s and 1940s, Navajo marriages took place in traditional ceremonies and were undocumented. Moreover, a claimant needed to show employment records. However, for the uranium mining programme, the government's recordkeeping had been substandard;

uranium miners were often hired and paid without an official contract. On top of this, many of the uranium miners did not speak English (Eichstaedt 1994; Brugge and Goble 2003).

If a miner or surviving spouse cleared these hurdles and submitted a complete RECA application, there was still the matter as to how the application would be assessed. If a miner's medical records showed that he had one of the eligible cancers, his radiation exposure was then estimated based on how long he worked and what mine he worked in. Critics complained that Congress rejected the view, standard at the time, that radiation exposure at the level of 40 units would lead to increased risk; they instead went with the standard of 200 units for non-smokers and 500 units for smokers (Brugge and Goble 2003: 388–390). Critics also charged that the data for individual mines was imperfect, and that the sharpness of the RECA eligibility criteria did not square with the need to account for measurement error and uncertainty (Brugge and Goble 2003: 391). Indeed, relative to estimates, few uranium miners actually met RECA's eligibility criteria (Eichstaedt 1994: xi). As Stuart Udall, the former interior secretary and the uranium miners' attorney, put it, 'They've put these people in a bureaucratic legal maze designed to prevent compensation to Navajo miners. There's no pity for what happened to these people. No understanding. You have a compassionate programme administered in an utterly uncompassionate manner' (Schneider 1993).

In running a reparations programme, the government does have a legitimate interest in erecting safeguards against fraud. As much as a government should be wary about the filing process being too onerous, it would also undermine the purpose of the reparations programme if no attempt was made to distinguish between authentic and inauthentic claimants, and the programme was widely regarded as a gravy train. However, if the criteria are too stringent, this may undermine a reparations programme's aim. 'We believe that it is not possible to simultaneously apologize, set highly stringent criteria, and place the burden of proof on the victims, as did the 1990 RECA', wrote Doug Brugge and Rob Goble, who authored a critical evaluation of the RECA programme. 'Compensation should be a positive act of redress, an act of contrition, not a miserly and bureaucratic programme that views the recipients of the apology with suspicion' (Brugge and Goble 2003: 395). As an antidote, Brugge and Goble point to active collaboration with claimants:

> It is not reasonable to expect that the initial design of any compensation scheme will be perfect. But justice requires active collaboration with the persons who are seeking compensation to assure that the program is appropriate. Just as important is ongoing monitoring to assess whether or not the program is functioning as intended, and prompt adaptation of the program when problems are identified.
>
> *(Ibid.)*

Dissatisfaction with the RECA programme led to the formation of a 'Western States RECA Reform Coalition'. This grassroots movement successfully pushed for Congress to modify some of the requirements so that the administration of RECA would be a better fit with the original intent of the statute (Brugge and Goble 2003: 392). But no formal provisions were made around active collaboration going forward.

Presumably, government officials charged with the administration of the RECA programme simply did not know about traditional Navajo marriages, or realise that not all uranium miners were provided with formal contracts.[3] Active collaboration during the period when eligibility criteria were being designed would have shored up some of these issues pre-emptively, creating a more smoothly running programme that would have benefited both the claimants and the government officials charged with its administration. However, it is not only the goal of efficiency that is served. A claimant who has to gear up for a second battle to prove his or her eligibility after initially fighting for reparations may have the sense of being re-victimised and feel moral outrage. If we follow the traditional definition of justice as giving each person his or her due, a reparations programme that systematically turns away individuals with meritorious claim is unjust. Justice thus demands active collaboration in determining criteria that serve the goal of paying reparations to those for whose purpose the programme is being instituted.

The problem of inclusion

Typically, reparations programmes are preceded by mobilisation on the part of claimants who demand that the government pay redress: initiating a lawsuit against the government, pressuring the legislature to pass a redress bill, and in some cases, doing both. In the transition from a reparations movement to a reparations programme, the *problem of inclusion* naturally arises. The set of all possible reparations claimants is larger – sometimes much larger – than the set of claimants who are mobilised. It would be an issue for the government to make right only with those who are actively taking part in the reparations movement, ignoring the others. Yet at the same time, it may be problematic to assume that individuals who are not mobilised want the exact same thing as those who are.

Consider the ambitious healing programme undertaken by the government of Canada in response to thousands of lawsuits from former First Nations, Inuit, and Métis students of assimilationist residential schools. In interviews conducted by researchers, it was evident that many of the former residential school students – 'Survivors', as they are known – actively distrusted the Canadian government as a result of the physical, sexual, and cultural abuse they endured in the schools. Some Survivors who received reparations reported being unable to look at the check or open the envelope it was mailed in; others described it as 'blood money' (Reimer 2010: 52–53). One person sensed that the check meant, 'you've got your money now be quiet'. Another said she 'felt like a prostitute, like I sold my body' (Reimer 2010: 52).

Unfortunately, some Survivors who saw the money as a reminder of childhood trauma and sexual abuse were anxious to get rid of it as fast as possible, spending it on alcohol and drugs (Stout and Harp 2007: 31–33). As the authors of a 2007 report put out by the Aboriginal Healing Foundation assessed the matter, 'to the extent healing is already underway when a payment arrives, LSPs [lump-sum payments] can play a role in enabling or deepening opportunities to build upon it' whereas they '"accelerated and exacerbated the problems of individuals" who were not on a healing journey' (Reimer 2010: 776). It is possible to speculate that individuals already on a healing journey would be the ones mobilised in making a reparations claim, perceiving that the government's concrete acknowledgement of wrongdoing and accountability would help bring closure to past events. How then to include the voices and the needs of individuals who are not mobilised in making a reparations demand? Moreover, what if a redress movement consists of multiple mobilised factions making different, even contradictory, demands for the same harm?

The problem of inclusion refers to the set of issues that arise when governments pay reparations to a large group of claimants when (1) some did not play an active role in demanding redress, and (2) different subgroups are mobilised around different sets of redress-related aims. In examining the problem of exclusion, we saw that much of the burden rests on the reparations payee – in most cases the government – to be responsive to claimants as difficulties with the claim filing process and eligibility criteria emerge. With the problem of inclusion, it is still incumbent on government officials to take the issue seriously and design a reparations payment process in a way that is responsive to it. However, part of the burden nevertheless rests on the mobilised reparations claimants to legitimate their demand for redress to non-mobilised group members, as well as to think through the complicated issues of representation within groups of reparations claimants – that is, 'who can and should speak for whom?'.

Non-mobilised beneficiaries

Let us first turn to the issue of including non-mobilised beneficiaries and the Canadian residential schools redress programme, which again was set up in response to lawsuits from Survivors. The shape of a reparations movement often looks different if it aims at winning a lawsuit versus passing reparations legislation.[4] At least in theory, lawsuits are decided on their legal merits, detached from political considerations. Group members do not have to pour their energies into winning over public support for their cause – including the support of other group members who have not given much thought to the matter of redress. Rather, efforts are focused on building the strongest possible legal case: with lawyers, and usually not in full public view.[5]

However, imagine being a member of a victimised group who receives a letter in the mail informing you that you are potentially eligible for a government payment in recompense for trauma you endured decades earlier. Imagine that this is the first time you ever heard about the redress programme. You probably would not automatically assume that there are others with similar backgrounds to yours who had been fighting for redress for years or decades. It would make sense, being in such a position, to be sceptical of the government's aims, never having considered your experience as a compensable one. This perspective points to the importance of a highly visible redress movement that serves to educate previously non-mobilised group members about why redress is being sought, and encourage them to begin their 'healing journeys' by being a part of the redress movement itself. Mobilising group members is, of course, not the only reason for having a highly visible reparations movement: a movement can also educate the broader public about the original wrong and its structural effects, garner support for redress from non-group members, encourage (in the context of colonial injustices) settler-citizens to take responsibility for their individual and collective contributions to injustice, and pressure the government to enter into settlement talks and issue a formal apology. But ensuring that the redress movement is known to, and has broad legitimacy with, as many group members as possible is an underappreciated reason for building a reparations movement, regardless of whether a judicial or legislative strategy is decided on.

However, the onus is not only on group members to solve the problem of inclusion. Government officials can and should do more to include those unaware that redress is being fought for on their behalf. Here public hearings can play a positive role. Public hearings can take the form of a Truth and Reconciliation Commission, which is the route the Canadian government decided on. Alternatively, they might be held as part of a commission's mandate to investigate the injustice. Public hearings were an important aspect of the Japanese American internment redress movement, and interestingly, it was precisely because many white Americans denied that WWII internment had been wrong that the 'Commission on Wartime Relocation and Internment of Civilians' (CWRIC) was established. But as the chair of the Japanese American Citizens League's redress committee, John Tateishi, put it, his group supported the CWRIC because 'Japanese Americans really didn't know much about [the redress movement], and certainly members of the Congress didn't know and weren't convinced that the internment was wrong . . . before we could do anything we needed to educate the public' (Wolfe 2013: 206). Ultimately, the CWRIC hearings were crucial in 'organizing and energizing Japanese Americans to fight for redress' and creating a situation where even 'though Japanese American organisations advocated different paths and objectives, the Japanese American community agreed that redress was an appropriate goal' (Maki, Kitano, and Berthold 1999: 233, 235).

By contrast, the Truth and Reconciliation Commission of Canada took place concurrently with the monetary redress programme, rather than preceding it. Criticisms of Canada's Truth and Reconciliation Commission abound that have little to do with whether hearings came before or in conjunction with the disbursal of redress payments (see, e.g., Niezen 2013). Yet the latter nevertheless points to a missed opportunity. In holding public hearings before making a reparations determination, it becomes less likely that an eligibility letter is a would-be claim-ant's first acquaintance with the idea of reparations. It provides her with the opportunity to play a role in the reparations movement. To the actively mobilised claimant, reparations are more likely to be seen as the government symbolically acknowledging the wrong, and less likely to be seen as blood money.[6]

Holding public hearings is wise as the first stage in a government's address of the problem of inclusion, but it is nevertheless only a first stage. As we shall see shortly with the Chinese Canadian 'head tax' redress movement, the problem of inclusion is also relevant to determining the mode of redress. The sense of some Survivors was that the Canadian residential school sys-tem was not an appropriate context for individual reparations payments: 'the residential school experience is not an individual phenomenon' (Reimer 2010: xvi). Choosing between indi-vidual reparations payments and a group reparations programme should not be the task of the government alone, or by government officials in partnership with a small, self-selected number of group members. A deliberative democratic forum that brings together a diverse set of group members is the best way to assure that the mode of redress determined is viewed as legitimate by future reparations recipients (see Amighetti and Nuti 2015).

Finally, the problem of inclusion may be related to the problem of exclusion: if the claim filing process is difficult and there is the impression that the government is trying to turn indi-viduals away to save money, individuals not previously mobilised are more likely to view the reparations programme cynically. If a deliberative democratic forum is instituted, it may also be necessary to have it continue as the claims filing process is taking place as a way of providing ongoing feedback on the reasonableness of the eligibility and paperwork requirements.[7]

Non-unified redress movements

The final version of the problem of inclusion is this: when redress movements are not cohe-sive, and there are different groups who favour different tactics and have different goals, what responsibilities fall on government officials? What responsibilities fall on group members who find themselves in this situation?

Chinese Canadian head tax redress is a particularly salient illustration. Beginning in 1885, the Canadian government began charging Chinese immigrants $50 to enter the country – an amount that quickly increased to $100, and then $500 (Winter 2008: 122). Between 1923 and 1947, Canada forbade Chinese immigration altogether.[8] The redress movement began in 1983, when one head taxpayer approached his MP asking for assistance in obtaining a refund (Li 2008: 131). From there, Chinese Canadians began registering head tax certificates with the Chinese Canadian National Council (CCNC), an anti-racism organisation that agreed to advocate on behalf of head tax payers and families. Before long, 4,000 Chinese Canadians registered head tax certificates with the CCNC.

The redress movement spearheaded by the CCNC was broad, inclusive, and very visible, building 'media campaigns, public awareness initiatives, and community networks of sup-port' ('Chinese Head Tax and Exclusion Act Redress' 2003). Its leaders came from 'unions, churches, women's groups, other minority groups, aboriginal groups, Chinese community and other community groups'; 'thousands of ordinary people . . . signed petitions and sent in postcards' supporting redress at the bidding of the CCNC; and it organised 'Last Spike' events across Canada to raise awareness about the role of Chinese Canadian immigrants in constructing the Canadian Pacific Railway ('Chinese Head Tax and Exclusion Act Redress' 2003). However, the CCNC was very firm on three demands: (1) a formal apology from the Canadian government, (2) individual reparations, not just funds to the group, and (3) reparations to head tax families – that is, paying the children of head tax payers if their parent is deceased. This last point was crucial because the head tax, followed by 24 years of exclusion, caused families to be separated (Li 2008: 129; Winter 2008: 133).

Two decades after the redress movement began, public pressure was such that the Conservative party, following up on an election campaign promise, backed a private member bill that apologised for the unjust treatment that Chinese Canadians received. However, it proposed that redress take the form of an education foundation – to be negotiated with the National Congress of Chinese Canadians. Described as 'shadowy' and having 'no history of anti-racism activity' (James 2013: 39–40), the National Congress seemed to have a seat at the table for one reason. It was a group willing to accept an apology without individual reparations while claiming to represent Chinese Canadians.

It is true that not all Chinese Canadians supported the CCNC's goal of individual reparations. 'No group can claim to represent an entire community, especially one as large and diverse as the Chinese Canadian community', as the CCNC itself acknowledged ('Chinese Head Tax and Exclusion Act Redress' 2003). In the early 1990s, there had been tension between the CCNC and another group called the Toronto Chinese Head Tax Action Committee, which criticised the CCNC for being too insistent on individual payments (Li 2008: 131–132). However, the CCNC did see itself as being the legitimate representative of the 4,000 Chinese Canadians who had registered their head tax certificates with the organisation, and expressed its outrage that the bill set out exclusive negotiations with the National Congress. Many other organisations and media outlets were highly vocal in their disapproval of the bill, and it expired without passage.

Canadian government officials acted wrongly, no doubt, in strategically selecting an organisation to negotiate with based on its predetermined idea about how far redress should go. However, responsibility also falls on members of the National Congress. Given the prominence of the CCNC's redress campaign, and its formal claim to representing 4,000 head tax payers and families, it never should have agreed to exclusive negotiations with the Canadian government on the subject of redress. This does not mean, of course, that the CCNC should have agreed to exclusive negotiations had it been in the National Congress's position. Any organisation advocating for redress as part of a broader movement in which there is significant disagreement owes it to the community at large not to monopolise representation.[9]

Conclusion

It may seem that the most challenging ethical dilemmas about reparations arise when justifications for reparations programmes are discussed. In this chapter, we have shown that such an assumption is flawed because it neglects how the design of reparations programmes posits serious ethical issues. By looking at real-world cases, we have identified three problems that any reparations programmes for past wrongs should address: the problems of political instrumentalisation, exclusion, and inclusion. Reparations programmes should meet (at least) three *desiderata*: (1) they should be seen as legitimate by potential beneficiaries – that is, they should not be regarded as a mere political tool to legitimise the power of governments; (2) they should establish fair criteria to determine who can qualify as a proper claimant; (3) they should be as inclusive as possible. We have shown that reparations programmes are closer to incorporating such *desiderata* when they actively involve reparations claimants and deploy deliberative mechanisms to reach and engage with potential beneficiaries. Obviously, in this chapter we could focus on only three problems that the design of reparations programmes presents, and offer some preliminary indications as to which kinds of measures should be undertaken to minimise the problems we have identified. That being said, we hope to have shown that the process of designing reparations programmes should become more central to normative debates about reparations.

Notes

1 For an excellent account of the 'comfort women system', see Soh (2008).
2 N.B. The Madres split in two factions in 1986. The Mothers of the Plaza de Mayo-Linea Fundadora started to cooperate with the state for the search of the missing corpses and eventually accepted forms of redress, including memorials for their children. Conversely, the Asociacion Madres de Plaza de Mayo relentlessly rejected any type of collaboration with the state and refused any form of reparation. When referring to the Madres' refusal of reparations after 1986, our focus is mainly on the latter association. Note that the split among the Madres is an example of internal divisions within a group and the unwillingness of some to receive any form of reparations, issues we discuss in the third section.
3 Eichstaedt (1994) points to evidence of more deliberate obstructionism on the part of Justice Department officials.
4 That being said, published research on the RECA programme, which also responded to lawsuits, does not suggest that the problem of exclusion was an issue.
5 This is not to say that the Survivors acted wrongly in choosing a judicial rather than legislative redress strategy. Mobilised reparations claimants have to consider their chances of success in each venue, and proceed accordingly. Also, note that some reparations movements pursue legislative and judicial redress simultaneously, or one after the other strategy proves unfruitful.
6 If carefully designed, public hearings can work as the 'inclusion' stage of a deliberative democratic forum on what reparations should amount to (see Amighetti and Nuti 2015).
7 Amighetti and Nuti (2015) suggest that a deliberative democratic forum should also discuss issues of implementation.
8 The Chinese head tax and immigration ban were implemented in response to a belief expressed by white Canadians at the time that Chinese workers were taking jobs and driving down wages (James 2013). Chinese immigration was reinstated in the postwar period, but it was not until 1967 that Chinese immigrants were given the same treatment as immigrants of other nationalities (Li 2008: 129).
9 In the end, the Canadian government paid individual reparations to living head tax payers and surviving spouses, as well as funding educative and commemorative programmes, a programme it initiated in 2006 (Li 2008: 135). The redress programme notably did not include head tax payers' children.

References

Amighetti, S. and Nuti, A., 2015. Towards a Shared Redress: Achieving Historical Justice Through Democratic Deliberation. *Journal of Political Philosophy*, 23 (4), 385–405.

Arditti, R., 1999. *Searching for Life: The Grandmothers of the Plaza De Mayo and the Disappeared Children of Argentina*. Berkeley: University of California Press.

Basic Principles and Guidelines on the Right to a Remedy and Reparation [online], 2005. Available from: www.ohchr.org/EN/ProfessionalInterest/Pages/RemedyAndReparation.aspx [Accessed 24 Feb 2017].

Booth, W.J., 2011. 'From This Far Place': On Justice and Absence. *American Political Science Review*, 105 (4), 750–764.

Bouvard, M.G., 1994. *Revolutionizing Motherhood: The Mothers of the Plaza de Mayo*. Oxford: Rowman & Littlefield.

Brugge, D. and Goble, R., 2003. The Radiation Exposure Compensation Act: What Is Fair? *New Solutions*, 13 (4), 385–397.

Chinese Head Tax and Exclusion Act Redress Questions and Answers [online], 2003. *Ccnc.ca*. Available from: www.ccnc.ca/currentIssues/Redress-QA.doc [Accessed 19 Feb 2017].

de Bofanini, H., 1990. The Madres de Plaza de Mayo (Argentina). *Index on Censorship*, 19 (9): 42.

Eichstaedt, P., 1994. *If You Poison Us: Uranium and Native Americans*. Santa Fe: Red Crane Books.

Hendrix, B.A., 1995. Memory in Native American Land Claims. *Political Theory*, 33 (6), 763–785.

James, M., 2013. Neoliberal Heritage Redress. *In:* J. Henderson and P. Wakeham, eds. *Reconciling Canada: Critical Perspectives on the Culture of Redress*. Toronto: University of Toronto Press, 31–46.

Li, P., 2008. Reconciling with History: The Chinese-Canadian Head Tax Redress. *Journal of Chinese Overseas*, 4 (1), 127–140.

Maki, M.T., Kitano, H.H.L., and Berthold, S.M., 1999. *Achieving the Impossible Dream: How Japanese Americans Obtained Redress*. Urbana: University of Illinois Press.

McCarthy, T., 2004. Coming to Terms with Our Past, Part II: On the Morality and Politics of Reparations for Slavery. *Political Theory*, 32 (6), 750–772.

McCurry, J., 2015. Japan and South Korea Agree to Settle Wartime Sex Slaves Row. *The Guardian*, 28 Dec.

McCurry, J., 2016. Former Sex Slaves Reject Japan and South Korea's 'comfort women' Accord. *The Guardian*, 26 Jan.

Miller, D., 2007. *National Responsibility and Global Justice*. Oxford: Oxford University Press.

Moon, C., 2012. 'Who'll Pay Reparations on My Soul?' Compensation, Social Control and Social Suffering. *Social & Legal Studies*, 21 (2), 187–199.

Niezen, R., 2013. *Truth and Indignation: Canada's Truth and Reconciliation Commission on Indian Residential Schools*. Toronto: University of Toronto Press.

Reimer, G., 2010. *The Indian Residential Schools Settlement Agreement's Common Experience Payment and Healing: A Qualitative Study Exploring Impacts on Recipients*. Ottawa: Aboriginal Healing Foundation.

Ridge, M., 2003. Giving the Dead Their Due. *Ethics*, 114 (1), 38–59.

Schneider, K., 1993. A Valley of Death for the Navajo Uranium Miners. *New York Times*, 3 May.

Segev, T., 1993. *The Seventh Million*. New York: Picador.

Soh, C.S., 2008. *The Comfort Women: Sexual Violence and Postcolonial Memory in Korea and Japan*. Chicago: University of Chicago Press.

Stout, M.D., and Harp, R., 2007. *Lump Sum Compensation Payments Research Project: The Circle Rechecks Itself*. Ottawa: Aboriginal Healing Foundation.

Tan, K-C., 2007. Colonialism, Reparations, and Global Justice. *In:* J. Miller and R. Kumar, eds. *Reparations: Interdisciplinary Inquiries*. New York: Oxford University Press, 280–306.

Valls, A., 2007. Reconsidering the Case for Black Reparations. *In:* J. Miller and R. Kumar, eds. *Reparations: Interdisciplinary Inquiries*. New York: Oxford University Press, 114–129.

Winter, S., 2008. The Stakes of Inclusion: Chinese Canadian Head Tax Redress. *Canadian Journal of Political Science*, 41 (1), 119–141.

Winter, S., 2014. *Transitional Justice in Established Democracies*. London: Palgrave Macmillan.

Wolfe, S., 2013. *The Politics of Reparations and Apologies*. New York: Springer.

27

THE ETHICS OF ANTI-POVERTY POLICIES

Jonathan Wolff[1]

Few would deny that poverty is a social evil and that there are circumstances in which action should be taken to reduce or eliminate it at least in some of its forms. But how should we understand poverty? What's wrong with it? What anti-poverty policies are possible? How much should be the responsibility of private charity and how much for government to take action? And, critically, what ethical issues arise in the assessment of such policies? These are the questions that I shall discuss here, drawing on sources from both social policy and political philosophy. Ideally social and instructional arrangements should be designed so that poverty simply does not arise, but in the world as it is, I argue that anti-poverty policies should be selected both for their effectiveness in alleviating the harms of poverty and for the avoidance of stigma.

Understanding poverty

The most basic notion of poverty is relatively uncontroversial: not having enough money. But enough money for what, exactly? And is money the only relevant factor? Since a variety of answers can be given to both questions, the understanding of poverty is contested, for both conceptual and political reasons. A government that allows part of its population to live in avoidable poverty will be widely criticised, and therefore, any understanding of poverty is likely to be contested.

To take us back to the near beginnings of poverty research, I shall start with Benjamin Seebohm Rowntree's concept of 'primary poverty' (Rowntree 1901, viii). Rowntree defined primary poverty as the lack of the resources necessary to achieve 'physical efficiency' (viii), by which he meant a life with reasonable security against threats to health. Avoiding primary poverty would mean having the resources to live at the bare minimum of acceptable housing, nutrition, and clothing. Although no life is free from risks of illness, Rowntree seems to assume that there is a level of lack of access to shelter, food, or clothes that makes the risks much more severe. This defines the primary poverty line, and to measure poverty Rowntree calculated the income needed for different types of families to be able to achieve physical efficiency.

Two distinctions will be important to the analysis that follows. The first, between 'primary' and 'secondary' poverty, was introduced by Rowntree himself, but then was abandoned by him and rarely appears in poverty research. Yet I hope to show it is very helpful in understanding moral and policy debates about poverty. Rowntree deliberately set the primary poverty threshold very low, as he wanted to demonstrate to conservative opponents that poverty existed in the York of his day despite virtually full employment. Many of those in work could not achieve physical efficiency however careful they were with their money. Rowntree adds,

> And let us clearly understand what 'merely physical efficiency' means. A family living upon the scale allowed for it in this estimate must never spend a penny on railway fare or omnibus. They must never go into the country unless they walk. They must never purchase a halfpenny newspaper or spend a penny to buy a ticket for a popular concert. They must write no letters to absent children, for they cannot afford to pay the postage . . . The children must have no pocket money for dolls, marbles and sweets.
>
> *(Rowntree 1901, 133–134)*

Accordingly, Rowntree noted that many of the citizens of York had the resources to avoid primary poverty, but chose to put some of those resources to other purposes, good or bad. Thereby, he said, they suffered from secondary poverty. They could have achieved physical efficiency, but in practice did not, preferring to buy a stamp or putting money on a horse. Conceptually the idea of secondary poverty makes sense, but operationally it is difficult to judge whether people are failing to achieve physical efficiency. Rowntree left it to his inspectors to decide which families were living in 'obvious want and squalor' even though their financial resources made its avoidance possible. (For further discussion see Veit-Wilson 1986). In later work Rowntree adopted a single poverty line which included an allowance for modest leisure (Rowntree 1937). But the key moral question is whether if 'obvious want and squalor' could have been avoided by different spending choices, can there still be legitimate claims for assistance? I will return to this shortly.

The question of how money is, or could be, spent gives rise to a more familiar second distinction, between absolute and relative poverty. Absolute poverty can be understood along the lines of Rowntree's idea of primary poverty, while relative poverty was introduced in the following terms:

> Individuals, families and groups in the population can be said to be in poverty when they lack the resources to obtain the types of diet, participate in the activities and have the living conditions and amenities which are customary, or at least widely encouraged or approved, in the societies in which they belong. Their resources are so seriously below those commanded by the average individual or family that they are, in effect, excluded from ordinary living patterns, customs and activities.
>
> *(Townsend 1979, 31)*

Although the paragraph contains a number of distinct ideas – what is customary, or encouraged or approved, or average, or needed to avoid exclusion – Peter Townsend here is self-consciously reviving Adam Smith's remarks that in the England of his time, an ordinary artisan could not appear in public 'without shame' unless he was wearing a linen shirt and leather shoes (unlike Scotland, where wooden clogs were, at the time, acceptable, so Smith suggests) (Smith 1976 [1776], 869–872). I will gloss the idea of relative poverty as not having enough to 'fit in'.

How, then, are we to find a measure of relative poverty to operationalise this definition? In the social policy literature, there are at least three broad attempts to try to find a measure of relative poverty. One defines poverty in terms of relative income: a common measure is 60 per cent of median income after housing costs (Joseph Rowntree Foundation 2009). Of course, any precise number feels arbitrary but if you fall this far below the median it will be hard to afford what is normal for your society. A second looks at standard of living. In *Breadline Britain*, for example, Mack and Lansley (2015) propose a concept of 'deprivation poverty' (46) consisting of lacking 3 or more of 25 listed necessities (defined by a majority of people in a survey regarding them as necessities). Such necessities include, at the highest priority: heating to keep the home adequately warm; a damp-free home; two meals a day; ability to visit friends and family in hospital or other institutions; and ability to replace or repair broken electrical goods. A third approach to measuring relative poverty simply asks whether a person is subjectively poor (Narayan et al. 2000; cf. Bradshaw and Finch 2003).

Each measure has its attractions, but also well-known defects. On the relative income account poverty could, according to the measure, decline simply because median income is falling. Objectively we might think of this as a situation in which more people are being sucked into poverty, but given that poverty is defined relative to the median, poverty, as measured, could be falling (Shaw 1988; cf. Hull 2007). Politicians, however, tend to be much more frustrated by the reverse problem. When all incomes are rising, but low incomes less so than median incomes, poverty will be recorded as increasing.

Consequently, the standard of living approach may seem more reasonable, but it will not necessarily track what worries us about poverty. Some people voluntarily adopt what others regard as a low standard of living despite having the income for higher consumption levels. Others maintain a decent standard of living by rapidly running down savings, or going into debt.

Finally, the subjective measure is subject to various forms of self-deception or adaptive preferences (Sen 1980). Some people in poverty do not regard themselves as poor compared to others: 'I saw two women who were eating food they had found in the garbage. This is poverty!' (quoted in Narayan et al. 2000, 72). Others regard themselves as poor, despite reasonable income and living standard, because they treat the more affluent as the relevant comparison class (Runciman 1966).

There is, therefore, an imperfect correlation between these measures (Bradshaw and Finch 2003). In Wolff and De-Shalit (2007) it was conjectured that it would be reasonable to consider someone as poor if they met two out of the three conditions. Someone above the income threshold but experiencing a poor standard of living and feeling poor is likely to have debts to service or exceptional expenses. Someone achieving the standard of living but with a low income and feeling poor is likely to be running down savings or acquiring debts. Someone who doesn't feel poor but has low income and low standard of living is likely to be experiencing adaptive preferences, adjusting preferences to circumstances. However, it is important to note that the 'two out of three' criterion was speculative rather than based on empirical research.

These three approaches are different ways of measuring relative poverty. But what is it, precisely, that they are trying to measure? The quotation from Townsend provides the basic idea: not having enough to fit in. Yet Rowntree's account of secondary poverty suggests that some people do spend their money on fitting in, even at the expense of their health. In his early study of York, he spent time explaining why people with little money nevertheless sought out the pleasures of companionship at the pub (Rowntree 1901, 311–312). Later, in 1937, in response to the putative objection that poor people wasted their money drinking, smoking, and going to the cinema he wrote,

> [W]orking people are just as human as those with more money. They cannot live just on a 'fodder basis'. They crave for relaxation and recreation just as the rest of us do. But . . . they can only get these things by going short of something which is essential to physical fitness, and so they go short . . . They pay dearly for their pleasures!
>
> *(1937, 126–127)*

In the context of considering minimum wages for women Rowntree suggests that a woman living alone, unlike a married woman, has a need for nice clothes for evening and weekends, 'as a girl who cannot dress nicely will be seriously handicapped in the matter of marriage' (Rowntree 1937, 108). In an earlier edition of the same work he said that 'a girl engaged in a monotonous repetitive job in a factory, for fifty hours a week, is in absolute need of some recreation in the evenings' (Rowntree 1919, 120).[2]

In thinking about how people choose to spend their money a division between personal, social, and goods that maintain one's status (I will call them 'fitting-in goods') is helpful. A personal good can be enjoyed independently of social context, such as a warm, dry bed, or tasty food. A social good is one that is used in connection with relationships to others. Rowntree's stamp for a letter, or birthday presents, and a night in the pub all fall into this category. Fitting-in goods are those needed for self-respect, such as Smith's leather shoes and linen shirt. Goods can fall into more than one category, such as a child's school trip. Its educational aspect is a personal good. The pleasure of a trip with one's friends is a social good. And the humiliation of not being able to afford to go reveals its status or fitting-in function (Ridge 2002, 74–82).

Studies have shown that many people even with low incomes can feel compelled to spend significant sums of money on fitting-in goods. The clichéd examples for children are having the right brand of trainers (Ridge 2002, 73), or this season's football kit. Dorling points out the increasing importance of a foreign holiday (Dorling 2010). But the need to spend money to fit in is a global phenomenon. For example, one leading cause of financial difficulty in South Africa has been the expense of elaborate funerals, which became an increasing strain, in addition to the emotional burden, when deaths from HIV-related causes were at their height (Collins et al. 2009, 75–86).

The immediate point of these examples is to explore why individuals put themselves into secondary poverty. Rowntree himself fully understood that a human life involves more than physical efficiency. He included tea as a necessity, even though it has no nutritional value. The occasional 'treat' and a social life are part of what it is to be a human being. Adam Smith was also clearly sympathetic to the need to purchase the necessary status goods to fit in. In fact, Smith discussed leather shoes and linen shirts in the context of sales tax, and possible exemptions for necessities. Smith argued that leather shoes and linen shirts had become necessities in England. And the issue is still with us today. The leading example in the UK is the notorious court case to determine whether Jaffa Cakes are a chocolate biscuit, and hence a luxury good, subject to VAT, or, as the judges rule, a cake, regarded as a necessity (Edmonds 2017; cf. H.R. Revenue and Customs 2015).

It is interesting – and counter-intuitive – that cake is regarded as a necessity. One possibility is that birthday cakes are rightly considered necessities, but as it would be impossible to implement a distinction between birthday cakes and other cakes, all are considered necessities. Alternatively, it might be thought that the occasional luxury is a necessity for any decent human life, and therefore it is important to have some luxury goods available to those on a tight budget. Other explanations, about nutritional value, are also possible.

Broadly, though, there is no mystery why people put themselves in secondary poverty. Narayan et al. write, 'The maintenance of cultural identity and social norms of solidarity helps poor people to continue to believe in their own humanity, despite inhuman conditions' (Narayan et al. 2000, 4–5). Ridge points out that for young people wearing the right clothes improves their confidence, with further beneficial effects (Ridge 2002, 70). Going to a nail bar or a barber or a pub or a betting shop is a way in which poorer individuals can have their humanity reaffirmed, simply by being treated with the courtesy due to any paying customer. Because of the near universal association of (avoidable) poverty and shame (Walker 2014), some poor people will take steps to avoid the appearance of poverty, even at great cost to other aspects of their lives.

Rowntree's comment about the need to dress nicely in order not to be 'seriously handicapped in the matter of marriage' is also important. Dressing correctly is not simply a matter of pride; it can help avoid other problems, such as being rejected at the interview stage for jobs, or for children, being bullied at school. In terms I have used elsewhere, not looking right can be a corrosive disadvantage, leading to other substantial problems (Wolff and De-Shalit 2007).

Poverty and capability deprivation

In order to bring more structure to the issues it will be helpful to introduce Amartya Sen's account of capability deprivation (Sen 1980, 1983, 1999). The key concepts in this approach are 'functionings' and 'capability'. A functioning is what someone is or does: has adequate nutrition, shelter, and clothing, or meaningful work, or lives a long life, or has self-respect, or has a supportive social network. A capability is a person's ability to achieve a functioning and, critically for Sen and Nussbaum (Nussbaum 2000, 2010), will include capabilities to achieve functionings that the person chooses not to achieve. For example, a person may have the capability for religious practice (religious freedom), in that were they to want to worship any God they would be able to do so, but, being an atheist choose not to. Nevertheless, this person may rightly value the capability for freedom of worship.

Sen conceives of a person's capability set as a set of the alternative sets of functionings that he or she could achieve (Sen 1980). To illustrate with a simple case, suppose someone in difficult circumstances has enough money to buy either a nourishing meal or a warm bed for the night, but not both. In that case the person is faced with a choice of two distinct functioning sets (meal and no bed, or bed and no meal). The person's capability set is the set of those two functioning sets, and he or she has to make a difficult choice between them. For Sen, the normal situation for any individual requires a choice between different functioning sets, for even if money is unlimited time is not. But in this case the position is extremely stark, as it will be for anyone with highly constrained financial resources. In the worst cases of poverty an individual will not be able to achieve any functioning to an acceptable degree, which corresponds to Rowntree's understanding of primary poverty. Secondary poverty can be understood as:

1   Having a very limited capability set that forces a choice between physical efficiency, or something else you value (a modest social life, perhaps, or a linen shirt).
2   Making choices that threaten your physical efficiency.

Interestingly we can see a partial convergence between secondary poverty and relative poverty once 'fitting in' is added as a potential functioning. Those in relative poverty do not have the resources both to achieve physical efficiency and to fit in. This limited capability set is also all that is available to those in secondary poverty, who nevertheless chose to fit in (or do something else they value) rather than achieve physical efficiency.

It is tempting, therefore, to attempt to define poverty as capability deprivation. A person in poverty lacks an adequate capability set and either cannot securely achieve any valuable functioning (absolute and primary poverty), or has to make a difficult choice between different functioning sets, failing to achieve at least one critical functioning (secondary and relative poverty). However, taking this approach has a radical consequence. Although lack of financial resources is an important source of capability deprivation, it is not the only source. A woman, or a member of a minority race, may find that the impediment to capability lies in discriminatory laws or customs, independently of anything to do with resource possession. A disabled person may also suffer from reduced capability, independently of limited financial resources. It would be odd to say that a person with above average financial resources but nevertheless a diminished capability set is poor.

Accordingly, it is problematic to define poverty as capability deprivation. Sen has given a good account of what we might call 'an impoverished life',[3] but, as understood in a tradition of thought that reaches back more than 100 years, poverty is linked specifically to lack of financial resources. Abandoning this approach and replacing it with a definition of poverty purely in terms of capability deprivation creates problems related to measurement and trend analysis, as well as taking the definition away from the ordinary meaning of the term (see Lister 2004, 18–19; Wolff et al. 2015). A compromise might be to define poverty in terms of 'capability deprivation caused by lack of income'. Or, better, to accommodate the fact that some goods can be provided directly by the state, to say 'capability deprivation caused by lack of external resources'. Consider, for example, two societies, one in which education and health care are free at the point of consumption and the other in which they have to be paid for privately. It is clear that the same income will yield different capability sets in the different societies. The variability can be dealt with either by having a different poverty line in the two societies or by putting a value on access to public services and adding it to the value of a person's external resources. Whichever route is taken, defining poverty in terms of capability deprivation caused by the lack of external resources utilises the insights of the capability approach without abandoning the link between poverty and resources.

Yet this does not go far enough. Elsewhere I have argued that people's opportunities in life depend on the interaction of their 'personal resources' (strengths, skills, education, etc.), their 'external resources' (income, wealth, entitlement to services, etc.), and the social, legal, material, and cultural structure in which they live. In principle, it is possible to improve individuals' opportunities, and hence their capability set, by doing any of (1) improving their personal resources (2) augmenting their external resources, or (3) changing the social structure (Wolff 2002, Wolff and De-Shalit 2007). It may seem wrong, therefore, to say that a low capability set is ever caused simply by the lack of external resources. Rather it is caused by the combination of their personal resources, external resources, and the social structure.

Hence there is a tension in the understanding of poverty: ordinary language pushes us towards the idea that it is to be understood as capability deprivation caused by lack of external resources, whereas philosophical analysis suggests that such a mono-causal understanding of capability deprivation is too simplistic. Perhaps a compromise is to say that poverty is a form of capability deprivation that could be remedied in the short to medium term by provision of external resources. But this faces the obvious problem that in practice not all poverty can be remedied. Nevertheless, I will adopt it here as a working understanding, while accepting that the distinction between poverty and an impoverished life is not clear cut.

The wrong of poverty

One of the questions listed at the start of this chapter was 'what's wrong with poverty?'. Does anything more need to be said? A life that faces the diminished capability sets associated with poverty is a diminished life. It is commonly argued that people in poverty will have difficulty salvaging their basic humanity, their dignity, or their self-respect (Jones 1990). As Narayan et al. point out, people in poverty find themselves without voice or power (Narayan et al. 2000, 4). Hennie Lotter makes the interesting observation that only human beings are ever described as living in poverty (Lotter 2011, 22). Animals can suffer but are not described as living in poverty, which indicates that poverty is some sort of degraded humanity. All these charges are plausible and go some way to explaining why poverty is morally challenging. Poverty, understood this way, is a serious injustice from a wide range of moral positions, not only those based in the egalitarian tradition. On most philosophical views (we will return to this ahead) it is clear that governments have an obligation to try to prevent people falling into poverty, and to help people to escape poverty on a permanent basis, where possible. Few governments have ever shirked that responsibility entirely, but it is clear that many could do more and some are currently moving in the wrong direction.

Anti-poverty policies

What, then, should government do to try to eliminate poverty? There are many conventional strategies currently in use around the world. Most obviously there are attempts to boost the income of the working poor, such as minimum wage or income support. Some training programmes try to prepare people for better paid employment. Redistributive transfer payments from the wealthier to the less wealthy, such as welfare support for unemployment or disability, are common, as are individual payments to all who qualify, independent of wealth, like child support or tax breaks for those with children. Provision in kind includes important goods to those who qualify, such as subsidised housing, and those that provide goods for all, including the poor, such as free health care and education, subsidised public transport, access to parks and beaches, museums and libraries, and so on. Other, more experimental proposals, include capital grants, unconditional basic income, and the state becoming the employer of last resort (for discussion of many possible policies see Atkinson 2015).

Some policies require significant redistribution, and there will also be a question of where the burden should fall. This, though important, is often hidden. For example, while anti-poverty campaigners are generally in favour of income support for low-paid workers, note that the burden of income support falls on the general taxpayer, whereas if minimum wages were higher the cost would fall on the employer, and then to consumers or investors. When the employer is a large, highly profitable company, in effect income support is the mechanism by which the general taxpayer unwittingly subsidises investors' profits.[4] Alternatively policies of rapid economic growth, relying on trickle-down of wealth to lift people out of poverty, have been effective on a mass scale in China, for example, and do not require redistribution in any obvious sense. But the scope for such policies is obviously limited, and there are environmental costs to consider too.

In assessing different policies clearly there are economic questions to be asked in terms of effectiveness. But these questions can be subtle. For example, raising incomes will not necessarily improve capability sets. As society gets wealthier what counts as 'fitting in' may well become more expensive, especially if the non-poor wish to maintain their distinction from the poor through their conspicuous spending habits. Low-income individuals may remain just as excluded as before if the cost of fitting in increases. Let us call the phenomenon of spending additional money on ever more expensive fitting-in goods 'diverted status spending'. If diverted status spending takes place on any significant scale, those affected may continue to suffer from poor housing and nutrition, simply in order to avoid the appearance of looking poor, even as their incomes rise.[5]

Hence to avoid relative poverty it is important to ensure that the inequalities of income and wealth between those towards the bottom and those living a 'typical' life are not too severe. This, of course, is the motivation of the measure of poverty as 60 per cent of median income after housing costs. And it seems very unlikely that reduction in poverty so understood can be achieved without redistribution or some other deliberate anti-poverty policy. However, redistribution is always second-best. Ideally part of the routine functioning of the economy and social structure should ensure that no one falls into poverty, but given how far away we are from that goal, redistribution seems critical.

Nevertheless, we have noted that raising income, under some circumstances, will not always improve the capability sets of people on low incomes because it can simply make self-respect more expensive to achieve. In such cases an alternative way of improving the capability sets of people classified as poor is to spend money on public services rather than raising income. Some, with libertarian sympathies, may object to the alleged paternalism in the provision of public goods, but we can see here that the rationale is the effectiveness of a policy, rather than the superiority of one conception of the good over another. An important anti-poverty strategy can be to take at least some necessities out of discretionary spending, as is common with education and health care. Subsidised housing, effective cheap public transport, and affordable childcare are other similar strategies. Although these changes will not register as an improvement according to the '60 per cent of median' measure of poverty, they do, nevertheless, provide resources that improve the capability sets of poor people, and hence reduce poverty according to the underlying definition.

Equally, bearing in mind that much of the secondary poverty observed by Rowntree was a matter of people spending money on social goods, the government can also make these cheaper by providing community centres, evening classes, public parks, sports facilities, and so on. Yet to preserve individual choice, autonomy, and self-respect, there needs to be a limit to public provision, and retention of significant scope for discretionary spending. The general theoretical point is not that all goods should be provided by the state but that a particular amount of money will go further in terms of capability provision under some social conditions than others, and some social arrangements make diverted status spending less likely to soak up additional resources designed to tackle poverty.

It is also worth returning to the concept of 'corrosive disadvantage' introduced earlier, as well as 'fertile functioning', which is where the possession of an advantage brings cumulative benefits. Generally social policy should avoid the formation of corrosive disadvantages and encourage the generation of fertile functionings. For example, breakfast clubs at schools not only provide nutrition but also put children in a better position to learn. Insisting on a cheap school uniform and heavily subsidised school trips makes it easier for children from low-income families to fit in, and thereby take better advantage of their educational opportunities, freer from anxiety. Taxing unhealthy consumption choices (e.g., minimum alcohol pricing) could also be considered, yet there is a real need to be careful, as an analogue of diverted status spending is possible, especially where the goods involved have an addictive quality. It could be that putting up the price of alcohol simply means that there is less money to spend on other things, such as nutritious food, rather than reducing alcohol consumption. Various 'nudge'-style policies could be considered, to incentivise behaviour that improves capability sets (Sunstein and Thaler 2008).

In terms of corrosive disadvantage, theorists have pointed to spending patterns that reinforce poverty. Bannerjee and Duflo, for example, report that the fruit vendors of Chennai borrow working capital each day at an extortionate rate of interest, but also drink many cups of tea. They calculate that if vendors cut down their tea by just two cups a day for three days, they could reduce their borrowing with miraculous cumulative effects (Banerjee and Duflo 2011, 190–191). But such concerns are nothing new. Mayhew in 1861 made similar comments regarding the costermongers of London, who behaved in virtually the same way. A literature has sprung up in behavioural economics to try to understand why people under such pressure make such apparently irrational decisions (Mullainathan and Shafir 2013), although whether they really are so irrational can be questioned, given the importance of social and fitting-in goods (Wolff 2017; Sheehy-Skeffington and Rea 2017). Such considerations must be considered when designing and assessing the likely effects of anti-policy policies.

Ethical assessment of anti-poverty policies

Some will question whether poverty alleviation is the duty of the state as distinct from that of private individuals (Nozick 1974). The philosophical mainstream has not accepted Nozick's position, favouring Rawls's argument that one's place in the distribution of natural and social fortunes is 'arbitrary from a moral point of view', and those favoured by fortune owe support, as a matter of justice, to those who are worse off, and particularly to those towards the bottom of the distribution (Rawls 1971, 1999). Nevertheless, libertarian criticisms of equality have led many egalitarians to focus hard on the distinction between those who are poor for reasons beyond their control and those who are poor as a result of their freely made choices. This has given rise to what is now generally called 'luck egalitarianism', introduced by Dworkin (1981a, 1981b; see also Cohen 1989; Arneson 1989), which at its heart is a distinction between 'option luck', which is the result of choice, and 'brute luck', which concerns those things beyond an individual's control.

The general luck egalitarian position is that justice requires complete remedy for bad brute luck, but no compensation for bad option luck. Luck egalitarians argue that those who have made choices that turn out badly are responsible for their own misfortune, and society has no duty in justice to help (even if some individuals may choose to do so as a matter of charity). This clearly has implications for anti-poverty policies, for some policies, so it is claimed, provide benefits for those who are perfectly capable of overcoming their poverty for themselves, but, for their own reasons, have chosen not to or are poor as a result of their own choices. On the luck egalitarian view the claims of those in a position to help themselves should be dismissed, at least from the standpoint of justice. Luck egalitarianism's concern for individual responsibility, therefore, will rule some potential anti-poverty policies morally acceptable (sickness pay, perhaps) but others (unconditional grants) morally unacceptable.

It cannot be denied that this theory resonates with some common intuitions about desert and justice. However, it has a number of unfortunate aspects. First, it resurrects older debates about the distinction between the deserving and underserving poor, individualising responsibility and paying no attention to the structural factors that are so fateful for individual lives (see, e.g., I.M. Young 1990). Second, and relatedly, it presumes that the distinction between free choice and circumstances outside one's control is clear. Third, it requires a social test for distinguishing between those who are responsible for their low income and those who are in poverty through no fault of their own. Any such test is likely to be humiliating and costly, and hence in conflict with the values of equality, respect, generosity, and efficiency (Wolff 1998, 2010; Anderson 1999). This is exactly what we see in cases where benefit claimants have to go through the charade of applying for jobs that they have no hope of attaining, as a condition of continuing to receive benefits.

Nevertheless, objecting to the luck egalitarian distinction between brute luck and option luck does not mean abandoning the idea of responsibility. An alternative approach has been suggested by Alexander Brown, who argues that we should reconceive responsibility as a type of virtue of character that can be fostered or impeded by different social arrangements, for the benefit of individual and society (Brown 2009). It is an empirical question which policies will facilitate the growth of this virtue, but it is not at all obvious that punishing people for their alleged imprudent choices would have the desired effect.

However, from the point of view of anti-poverty policies we are left in something of a dilemma. The motivation behind luck egalitarianism, and other theories that emphasise responsibility or desert, pushes in the direction of highly conditional welfare benefits, which have the disadvantages outlined earlier. Unconditional benefits, however, are thought to take away incentives to work and to encourage free riding, with consequent destructive effects on the morale and motivation of 'hard-working families' who feel exploited and let down by the system. It is, however, an empirical question whether this is a true dilemma. It is possible that if decent, well-paid jobs are available, free riding in the form of voluntary unemployment would be low, as most people prefer to work than to remain unemployed, at least in their middle years. Indeed, Paul Gomberg has argued that a primary injustice in the contemporary world is that, through unemployment or under-employment, many people are excluded from the opportunity to make a wider contribution to the lives of others (Gomberg 2007).

A further issue is the level of benefits available to welfare claimants, and the other regulations that govern their claims. Typically benefits are kept at a low level, and will leave claimants and their families with very limited capability sets, to the point of remaining in relative poverty. In many countries declaring any income will mean that benefits are significantly reduced or forfeited altogether, and so in the absence of access to a decently paid job, claimants have no way of overcoming poverty by legal means. Those who earn money in the informal economy and do not declare it are breaking the law, and are colloquially known as 'benefit cheats', reviled by the national press, and subject to criminal charges if caught. Of course, organised welfare fraud does exist, but for many people in this category their motivation is simply to bring about a modest improvement over their existing capability deprivation: the need to buy a birthday present for a child, or to have the occasional night out, as described by Rowntree. Any government that wishes to overcome the effects of poverty needs to consider the relation between welfare benefits and small supplementary earnings. Punitive arrangement will mean that claimants are faced with the choice of grinding poverty if they live within the law, or, if they earn money cash in hand, somewhat lesser poverty, but with the threat of arrest, disgrace, and imprisonment hanging over their heads.

Conclusion

The ultimate goal of anti-poverty policy should be to aim for social arrangements in which poverty simply does not arise. In the circumstances of the world as we find it the arguments of this chapter push in the direction of reasonably generous benefits, many of which are provided unconditionally, and are not significantly reduced when a small additional income is generated from additional resources. Yet at the same time I have also argued for significant social resources to be devoted to the public sector, supplying goods for all, free at the point of consumption. In turn, these policies will require a higher tax rate than we currently see in some countries, and hence will be very difficult politically. Nevertheless, the ethical imperative to set up social and economic institutions that lead to routes out of poverty is clear. The difficulty is marshalling the political will to introduce the needed reforms, especially at a time when many governments are seeking, if anything, to reduce taxes or to spend budgets on other supposed priorities.

Notes

1 I would like to thank audiences at UCL, Frankfurt, Paris, and Oxford for comments that have transformed this chapter. I would also like to thank Andrei Poama and Annabelle Lever for their help in conceiving and formulating this project, as well as their insightful comments, which have led to many improvements.

2 Note that this remark was deleted in the 1937 edition of *The Human Needs of Labour*, but replaced with a general reference to recreation and the need for money for holidays as well as the by-then compulsory unemployment insurance (Rowntree 1937, 109–110).
3 I thank Fran Bennett for this formulation.
4 I owe this point to Lucy Parker.
5 Although rather different in focus, this argument is influenced by Hirsch (1977) and Frank (1999).

References

Anderson, Elizabeth. 1999. 'What Is the Point of Equality?' *Ethics*, 109, pp. 287–337.
Arneson, Richard. 1989. 'Equality and Equal Opportunity for Welfare', *Philosophical Studies*, 56, pp. 77–93.
Atkinson, A.J. 2015. *Inequality*, Cambridge, MA: Harvard University Press.
Banerjee, Abhijit, and Duflo, Esther. 2011. *Poor Economics*, New York: Public Affairs.
Bradshaw, Jonathan, and Finch, Naomi. 2003. 'Overlaps in Dimensions of Poverty', *Journal of Social Policy*, 32, pp. 513–525.
Brown, Alexander. 2009. *Personal Responsibility: Why It Matters*, London: Continuum.
Cohen, G.A. 1989. 'On the Currency of Egalitarian Justice', *Ethics*, 99, pp. 906–944.
Collins, Daryl, Morduch, Jonathan, Rutherford, Stuart, and Ruthven, Orlanda. 2009. *Portfolios of the Poor*, Princeton, NJ: Princeton University Press.
Dorling, Danny. 2010. *Injustice*, Bristol: Policy Press.
Dworkin, Ronald. 1981a. 'What Is Equality? Part 1: Equality of Welfare', *Philosophy & Public Affairs*, 10, pp. 228–240.
Dworkin, Ronald. 1981b. 'What Is Equality? Part 2: Equality of Resources', *Philosophy & Public Affairs*, 10, pp. 283–345.
Edmonds, Davis. 2017. 'Cake or Biscuit? Why Jaffa Cakes Excite Philosophers'. www.bbc.co.uk/news/magazine-38985820 (Viewed September 15th, 2017).
Frank, Robert. 1999. *Luxury Fever*, Princeton, NJ: Princeton University Press.
Gomberg, Paul. 2007. *How to Make Opportunity Equal*, London: Routledge.
Hirsch, Fred. 1977. *Social Limits to Growth*, Oxford: Basil Blackwell.
H.R. Revenue and Customs. 2015. 'VAT Notice 701/14 Food'. www.gov.uk/government/publications/vat-notice-70114-food/vat-notice-70114-food#confectionery (Viewed January 17th, 2017).
Hull, Richard. 2007. *Deprivation and Freedom*, London: Routledge.
Jones, John D. 1990. *Poverty and the Human Condition: A Philosophical Inquiry*, Lewiston, New York: Edwin Mellen Press.
Joseph Rowntree Foundation. 2009. *Reporting Poverty in the UK*, York: Joseph Rowntree Foundation.
Lister, Ruth. 2004. *Poverty*, Cambridge: Policy.
Lotter, H.P. 2011. *Poverty Ethics and Justice*, Cardiff: University of Wales Press.
Mack, Joanna, and Lansley, Stewart. 2015. *Breadline Britain*, London: Oneworld.
Mayhew, Robert. 1861. *London Labour and the London Poor*, London: Griffin Bohn and Co.
Mullainathan, Sendhil, and Shafir, Elder. 2013. *Scarcity*, New York: Henry Holt.
Narayan, D., Patel, R., Schafft, K., Rademacher, A., and Koch-Schulte, S. 2000. *Voices of the Poor: Vol. 1, Can Anyone Hear Us?* New York: Oxford University Press for the World Bank.
Nozick, Robert. 1974. *Anarchy, State, and Utopia*, New York: Basic Books.
Nussbaum, Martha. 2000. *Women and Human Development*, Cambridge: Cambridge University Press.
Nussbaum, Martha. 2010. *Creating Capabilities*, Cambridge, MA: Harvard University Press.
Rawls, John. 1971 [1999]. *A Theory of Justice*, Cambridge, MA: Harvard University Press.
Ridge, Tess. 2002. *Childhood Poverty and Social Exclusion: From a Child's Perspective*, Bristol: Policy Press.
Rowntree, Benjamin Seebohm. 1901. *Poverty: A Study of Town Life*, London: Palgrave Macmillan.
Rowntree, Benjamin Seebohm. 1919. *The Human Needs of Labour*, London: Nelson.
Rowntree, Benjamin Seebohm. 1937. *The Human Needs of Labour*, revised edition, London: Longmans.
Runciman, W.G. 1966. *Relative Deprivation and Social Justice*, London: Routledge and Kegan Paul.
Sen, Amartya. 1980. 'Equality of What?' in *Tanner Lectures on Human Values, Vol. i.*, ed. S.M. McMurrin, Salt Lake City: University of Utah Press, pp. 195–220.
Sen, Amartya. 1983. 'Poor, Relatively Speaking', *Oxford Economic Papers*, 35, pp. 153–169.
Sen, Amartya. 1999. *Development as Freedom*, Oxford: Clarendon Press.
Shaw, Brenda. 1988. 'Poverty: Absolute or Relative', *Journal of Applied Philosophy*, 5, pp. 27–36.

Sheehy-Skeffington, Jennifer, and Rea, Jessica 2017. *How Poverty Affects People's Decision-Making Processes*, York: Joseph Rowntree Foundation.

Smith, Adam. 1976 [1776]. *An Inquiry into the Nature and Causes of the Wealth of Nations*, republished, R.H Campbell and A.S. Skinner, eds., Oxford: Oxford University Press.

Sunstein, Cass, and Thaler, Richard. 2008. *Nudge*, New Haven, CA: Yale University Press.

Townsend, P. 1979. *Poverty in the United Kingdom: A Survey of Household Resources and Standards of Living*, Harmondsworth: Penguin Books.

VeitWilson, J. H. 1986. 'Paradigms of Poverty: A Rehabilitation of B.S. Rowntree', *Journal of Social Policy*, 15, pp. 69–99.

Walker, Robert. 2014. *The Shame of Poverty*, Oxford: Oxford University Press.

Wolff, Jonathan. 1998. 'Fairness, Respect and the Egalitarian Ethos', *Philosophy and Public Affairs*, 27, pp. 97–122.

Wolff, Jonathan. 2002. 'Addressing Disadvantage and the Human Good', *Journal of Applied Philosophy*, 19, pp. 217–218.

Wolff, Jonathan. 2010. 'Fairness, Respect and the Egalitarian Ethos Revisited', *The Journal of Ethics*, 14, pp. 335–350.

Wolff, Jonathan. 2017. 'Forms of Differential Social Inclusion', *Social Philosophy and Policy*, 34, pp. 164–185.

Wolff, Jonathan, and De-Shalit, Avner. 2007. *Disadvantage*, Oxford: Oxford University Press.

Wolff, Jonathan, Lamb, Edward, and Zur-Szpiro Eliana. 2015. *Poverty: A Philosophical Review*, York: Joseph Rowntree Foundation.

Young, Iris Marion. 1990. *Justice and the Politics of Difference*, Princeton, NJ: Princeton University Press.

28

THE DEMOCRATIC ETHICS OF A MINIMUM INCOME

Stuart White

Introduction

Should a democratic state ensure individuals access to at least a minimally decent income? If so, why? On what terms should this minimum income be available? Should receipt of the income be conditional on actively seeking a job or other employment-related activity? Recent years have seen a shift towards greater 'conditionality' in 'welfare policy' in many nations. Is this consistent with the values of a democratic society, or does it contradict them? This chapter aims to provide the reader with an introduction to the debate over this central social policy question. There is a strong argument, at the level of democratic ethics, for a qualified form of conditionality. However, there are also strong arguments against it that we need to consider.

The chapter is structured as follows. In the first section I clarify what I mean in this chapter by a right to a minimum income and I set out why a democratic ethics supports the institution of such a right. The second section then presents arguments from within democratic ethics for making access to a minimum income conditional on employment-related activity (at least for those safely judged to be 'able to work'). One argument appeals to the value of reciprocity, understood as a democratic norm of fair cooperation between equal citizens, and a second argument is grounded in paternalism. The third section then reviews some objections to the democratic case for conditionality. The fourth section presents arguments for an unconditional 'basic income'. The last section concludes.

A right to a minimum income?

The focus of this chapter is the responsibility of the democratic state to make available to its members a *minimum income*. A minimum income is here understood as an income that is sufficient to meet the individual's basic needs and, thus, sufficient for a minimally decent standard of living. This is unlikely to be the same for all members of the community. Due to health conditions and disabilities, for example, some people will have higher living costs than others and so will require more income to have a minimally decent standard of living. One core aim of social policy in a democratic society is to design the distributional structure of the society so that all have reasonable access to a minimum income, appropriately adjusted in level to individual circumstances. Individuals may be said to have a *right to a minimum income* in this sense: they have a right of reasonable access to a minimum income.

The idea of a minimum income can be distinguished from the idea of a *basic income*. This term refers to a payment from the community: (a) to each individual; (b) that is not subject to a test of means (i.e., is not dependent on wealth or income from other sources); and (c) that is not subject to any test of willingness to get a job or otherwise engage in productive activity (Van Parijs 1995; Van Parijs and Vanderborght 2017). Such an income is 'basic' in the sense that it represents, within the community, a universal base on which individuals can build further income – for example, from employment. A basic income in this sense is not necessarily a minimum income. As just defined the basic income might be below, at, or even above the level that is sufficient to provide a minimum income for many citizens. Moreover, even if the basic income suffices to cover the basic needs of many citizens, it may not be high enough, for example, to cover the needs of those with specific disabilities.

Note also that while a basic income is by definition unconditional with respect to job-related activity, this is not the case with what I have called the right to a minimum income. The right to a minimum income, as defined earlier, is a right of 'reasonable access' to a minimum income. One way to secure reasonable access is indeed to simply pay everyone a high enough income without any job-related or similar conditions. But this is not necessarily the only form that 'reasonable access' can take. For example, if someone is able to take a job, and a job is made available to them that is not degrading in the terms, conditions, and content of the work, and it pays a wage that is equitable and at least sufficient to meet their basic needs, then this job offer arguably constitutes reasonable access to a minimum income. Thus, in principle, a democratic state might satisfy the right to a minimum income, at least for some of its members, by making sufficient (and sufficiently good) jobs available to them rather than by directly giving them the income. Direct payment of income would then apply to the extent that people don't have the capacity or opportunity to take up a job of this kind.

In addition, a basic income is not subject to any test of means, whereas, on the face of it, there is nothing in the definition of the right to a minimum income that would rule out means-testing. At least on first sight it looks as if the democratic state could satisfy the right if it establishes a system of means- or income-related transfers in which it tops up what people acquire themselves just enough to ensure they have a minimum income. If the individual's circumstances change, so that he or she receives more pre-transfer income, then the state correspondingly cuts back its own top-up. Finally, while a basic income is paid to the individual, social policy aimed at satisfying the commitment to a minimum income might take the household as the relevant unit for assessing eligibility for support. The policy regime might focus on the household's overall income and pay transfers according to how much income and/or wealth the household as a whole has. I draw out these distinctions just to make clear that the relation between the right to a minimum income and provision of a basic income is an open one. A democratic state might institutionalise the right to a minimum income using a basic income, but how far it does so (if at all) is an open question.

Why, though, should a democratic state institute a right to a minimum income? Why is such a right required as a matter of democratic ethics? Democratic ethics, as I use this term here, has both a procedural and substantive dimension. Procedurally, it requires that all members of a political community have the effective opportunity to participate, as equals, in the democratic political process, to help determine the laws and policies to which they will be subject. Substantively, it requires that the rules under which we live and cooperate together reflect and support an ideal of mutual respect between free and equal persons. Roughly speaking, these correspond to two aspects of what Rousseau termed the 'general will': (a) that laws ideally come from all of the people and (b) that in making laws citizens mutually respect their interests, including material interests, as free and equal members of the community (Rousseau 1994).[1]

Considering first the procedural dimension of democratic ethics, we can discern the *political inclusion argument* for a right to a minimum income. Those who lack reasonable access to a minimum income are, as a result, significantly constrained in their opportunity to participate politically and to participate on an equal footing. Their political inclusion is compromised. By instituting a right to a minimum income, the state thereby helps secure the conditions for political inclusion.

Turning to the second dimension of democratic ethics, we can discern an *economic fairness argument* for a right to a minimum income. The rules of the economic system must accord with the ideal of mutual respect between free and equal persons (Rawls 1999). This has major implications for the kinds of rules we may regard as intrinsically fair. For an economic system to be fair by such a standard, it is necessary – not sufficient, but certainly necessary – that it assure each member of society of reasonable access to a decent minimum of income. If the basic structure of the economy has the predictable effect of denying people reasonable access to this minimum, while others get more than this minimum, then their status as free and equal members of the society is compromised.[2] The resulting deprivation is, in itself, a failure to recognise their status as properly free and equal because it requires them to sacrifice their most basic material interests for the benefit of less urgent interests on the part of others. And such deprivation threatens to undermine their freedom and equality in social relationships by making them more vulnerable to marginalisation and domination by others (Goodin 1986).

If, however, the right to a minimum income is plausibly grounded in a democratic ethics, we can see from the foregoing groundwork how there remain some important questions as to how to implement this commitment in policy terms. Should the policy regime apply means-testing? If there is means-testing, should it take the individual or the household as the relevant unit for assessing need? What kinds of adjustments to payments will be necessary to suit individual circumstances? Should receipt of a minimum income be conditional on job-related or similar activity? Even if one has accepted that a democratic ethics demands a right to a minimum income, these (and other) questions remain. How should a democratic society answer them? For illustrative purposes, we will focus in the remainder of this chapter on the question of making minimum income conditional on job-related and similar activity.

The democratic case for conditionality: reciprocity and paternalism

Democratic ethics is centred on a norm of mutual respect between free and equal people. This basic norm arguably implies a *reciprocity principle* that those who share in the goods and services created through the labour of others have an obligation to make a contribution to the production of these goods and services in return: to return good for the good that they receive. To share in the fruits of others' productive efforts without making a reciprocal productive contribution when one is so able (and has sufficient opportunity) is arguably to take unfair advantage of others and so, in one sense of the term, to exploit them. It is to assert a kind of privileged position in relation to others, and thus runs counter to the spirit of mutual respect between equals (White 2003). In elaborating his conception of 'justice as fairness', John Rawls captures this principle when he claims that 'all citizens are to do their part in society's cooperative work' (Rawls 2001, p. 179).

The reciprocity principle does not require, however, that people make productive contributions in strict proportion to what they are able to consume. Were the principle understood as requiring such a strict proportionality it would disadvantage those who have less ability to contribute. This contradicts the idea of egalitarian social cooperation. Rather, the principle should be understood as entailing an obligation to 'do one's bit' productively, to make a reasonable contribution given one's ability and opportunity to do so. The reciprocity principle in this sense has frequently been affirmed by radical egalitarian thinkers (White 2003, pp. 53–58).

What implications does the reciprocity principle have for the way a democratic society structures the right to a minimum income? First recall the points made earlier, that the right in question here is, fundamentally, a right of reasonable access to a minimum income, and that reasonable access does not necessarily rule out work-related conditions on receiving a minimum income. The next point is that if a minimum income is provided without any work-related condition, then some individuals might receive a minimum income, and so make a claim on goods and services produced by others, without making any appropriate productive contribution of their own in return even though they have the capacity and opportunity to do so. If we wish to prevent this reciprocity failure, then an obvious response is to make a minimum income conditional on behaviour that promotes a reciprocating productive contribution. For (and only for) those safely judged to be capable of doing a job, we might make eligibility for any public transfers conditional on job-related activity. Concretely, this will involve making cash benefits to the unemployed conditional on active job search or training or even work itself.

In addition to the reciprocity-based argument for conditionality, a democratic ethics might also incorporate a *paternalist* argument. Paternalism refers to proposed justification of state coercion of the individual on the grounds that this will serve the individual's own welfare (Dworkin 1971). It is not a question of preventing unfairness to others, as with the reciprocity-based argument, but of preventing 'harm to self'. The argument, then, is that conditionality rules will work to serve the interests of those receiving state transfers. For example, it might be argued that rules requiring active job search can work against unemployed workers becoming discouraged and withdrawing from the labour market, which would harm their long-term interests. Justifications for conditionality are sometimes put forward in explicitly paternalist terms (Mead 1992).

A first objection to the putative paternalist case for conditionality is that paternalism is inherently incompatible with democratic ethics. According to this objection, paternalist legislation necessarily involves one group of citizens claiming superior judgement over what is good for the individual rather than allowing individuals, as free and equal persons, to make their own judgements. However, while some paternalist arguments do have this quality, they need not do so. Gerald Dworkin has argued that we can understand paternalism in terms of collective self-paternalism (Dworkin 1971, pp. 120–123; see also Gutmann and Thompson 1996, pp. 261–272; Conly 2013). Each of us can see that there are some decisions we might make that have serious and irreversible consequences, and we can see that we might sometimes lack the ability to act on our better judgement. Knowing that we have these vulnerabilities, we will find it rational to impose constraints on our immediate freedom of action as a kind of 'insurance'. For example, I might endorse the judgement that I should put on a seat-belt when in a car. At the same time, I foresee that on some occasions I will fail to put the seat-belt on. Anticipating this, I agree to a law that requires me to put the seat-belt on. This is not a case of others overriding my judgement of what is best for me to do, but of my using the law to help me act more consistently with my own judgement about what it is best for me to do. Of course, there may be many cases where people disagree about whether a law is helpful in this way. But in some cases a significant majority will think the law is helpful in this way and, if so, there are grounds, in terms of democratic ethics, for this law.[3] If we accept this general justification of paternalism, we can go on to ask whether it might apply in the case of income support and conditionality. We would have to ask whether most people agree it is in their interest to look for a job if unemployed, and if so, whether they also support a conditionality rule that requires this of them – not of others but of themselves – when unemployed.

Here, then, are two kinds of arguments that can be made for conditionality, consistent with democratic ethics: the reciprocity-based argument and (more tentatively in terms of democratic ethics) the paternalist argument.

The democratic case against conditionality 1: fair reciprocity

There is also a strong case against conditionality, however, from the standpoint of democratic ethics. A first argument takes us back to the reciprocity principle. As indicated earlier, in the framework of democratic ethics this principle is understood as one element in a conception of mutual respect between free and equal parties. We have an obligation, under the reciprocity principle, to 'do our bit' in productive work *as part of* an economic and social system that expresses such respect. But what if the economy isn't sufficiently just in other major respects? In this case, the obligations of reciprocity arguably do not apply, or apply to the same extent, at least for those disadvantaged by background injustice. In consequence, the reciprocity-based argument for conditionality in the income support system no longer applies or applies to the same extent. It may then be inherently unfair to apply conditionality to disadvantaged workers; indeed, doing so might have the effect of consolidating the unjust disadvantage they suffer.

To elaborate, what matters is not reciprocity in isolation but fair reciprocity, reciprocity in the context of wider fairness in the economic and social system (White 2000, 2003, 2017; see also Gutmann and Thompson 1996, pp. 273–306).[4] The wider fairness concern sets some important conditions on the application of the reciprocity principle – and, in turn, on the application of conditionality (insofar as this is supported by the reciprocity principle). What are these *conditions of fair reciprocity*?

A first condition is that there must be *equity and consistency in the application of reciprocity-based work obligations*. Within the income support system itself, obligations must be applied equally to all: 'like cases treated alike'. In addition, people getting income via the 'welfare' system and those getting an income from asset ownership should be treated equitably under the reciprocity principle. If someone is living off the income from an asset, this may not be connected to any productive contribution he or she has personally made (e.g., if the wealth is inherited). In this case, the person gets an income in violation of the reciprocity principle. If society tries to stop reciprocity failure in the income support system, then equity surely requires that it do the same with respect to asset incomes – for example, by taxing away the relevant assets.

Equity in the application of the reciprocity principle has further aspects. One is that any enforcement of work-related obligations through the income support system must give those subject to these requirements adequate due process rights to contest decisions about their eligibility, not least because of problems of implicit bias in the way rules are applied (Brownstein and Saul 2016). As the recent controversy in the UK over new conditionality rules applied to the benefits of disabled people shows, this is a hugely important requirement (see Butler 2015, and discussion at the blog sites of 'Bendygirl' and Sue Marsh). In addition to due process rights, work-related conditions must not in themselves be degrading to the individual. For example, requiring people to 'work for their benefits', where this involves their working full-time in a role that is ordinarily paid a wage that exceeds their benefits, is degrading. Finally, much work in our society happens outside of an employment or market context. In particular, a great deal of care work – for example, for children – is performed outside of the formal economy, largely by women.[5] This work also crucially helps society meet the needs of its members and should count in satisfaction of the reciprocity principle (Cochrane et al 2010; Shelby 2016, p. 180). Conditionality rules that make no or inadequate allowance for the work people perform as unpaid carers are not treating carers equitably with others.

A second general condition of fair reciprocity is that there is *sufficient fairness in the opportunity and reward structures of the economy*. As suggested earlier, our obligation to 'do our bit', as an expression of fairness, applies in a society that treats us sufficiently fairly in other respects. If, however, society denies us a sufficiently fair level of economic opportunity and/or reward, then the obligation does not apply, or apply to the same extent. We are not obliged, as a matter of fairness, to 'do our bit' in the context of an economy that fundamentally works to 'do us down'. Tommie Shelby makes this point in his discussion of whether work obligations apply to the black ghetto poor in the US:

> [J]ob opportunities for low-skilled workers are severely limited and the jobs that are available are often menial, dead-end service positions that pay wages too low to provide adequate economic security for a family. Now it might be replied that if the ghetto poor do not want to take these low-wage jobs they should develop their skills . . . As is widely known, however, the quality of education available to ghetto residents is generally so substandard that most cannot get a basic education there, let alone proper preparation for college. . . . This lack of equal educational opportunity, which in turn creates an unfair employment opportunity scheme, vitiates any obligation to work.
>
> *(Shelby 2007, pp. 146–147)*

Shelby does not claim that the ghetto poor have no duties in such a situation. He argues that they have 'natural duties' to others, which include the duty to help to create just social structures (Shelby 2007, pp. 144–159). But specifically 'civic obligations', which are a matter of reciprocity to one's fellow citizens in the context of a cooperative scheme between equals, do not apply when the cooperative scheme is seriously unfair (to those who are disadvantaged by this unfairness). If these obligations do not apply, then they cannot ground a case for conditionality in the income support system. Further, the effect of conditionality might well be to consolidate or worsen the unjust disadvantage that some individuals face. This may be because of the inherent burden of the conditionality requirements themselves in reducing freedom of action; because the need to meet them can weaken the market power of disadvantaged workers; and, as Shelby argues, because of the possible 'expressive harm' that work conditions stigmatise and demean those subject to them (Shelby 2016, pp. 197–200). Far from violating fairness, the choice not to work in this context, by those subjected to serious structural injustice, is a legitimate, self-respecting form of dissent against unfairness, as Shelby argues with respect to the black ghetto poor in the US (Shelby 2016, pp. 175–200).

To recap, then, while there is a reciprocity-based case for conditionality in the income support system, this case must be approached in a way that is sensitive to broader concerns of fairness: what matters is fair reciprocity. Reciprocity-based work obligations must be enforced, therefore, if they are enforced, (a) in a way that is equitable and consistent and (b) against a background of economic institutions that are in other ways sufficiently just in terms of the structure of opportunities and rewards. When these conditions of fair reciprocity are not met, the reciprocity-based work obligations do not apply, or apply to the same extent; and efforts to enforce these putative obligations are then unjust and can work in various ways to deepen the deprivation that disadvantaged individuals face. In this crucial sense, 'conditionality is conditional'.[6]

A question that we always have to ask as democratic citizens, therefore, is whether our society meets the conditions of fair reciprocity. Are we doing what is necessary to apply the reciprocity principle equitably and consistently? Are we applying it in an economic system that offers sufficiently fair opportunities and rewards? My own judgement is that many advanced capitalist countries, such as the US and the UK, currently do not meet the conditions of fair reciprocity and that the conditionality currently a feature of the income support systems in these countries is correspondingly unfair (at least for many of those who are subject to it).

I have focused on the reciprocity-based argument for conditionality. What about the paternalist argument? Paternalist arguments appeal to the way conditionality supposedly promotes the good of those subject to it. But if these rules are pressuring individuals into work on unfair terms, will they reliably work to their good? Whatever good is generated by the conditionality policy for the individual concerned has to be set against the bad (including the dignitary harm) of his or her being pressured into employment on unfair terms. For this reason, the paternalist argument for conditionality is also likely to fail where society does not satisfy the conditions of fair reciprocity. In addition, in democratic ethics paternalism is properly understood as collective self-paternalism, an idea that is premised on shared risk and common vulnerability to imprudent choices in the risk context. In many real-world societies, however, the politics of 'welfare' does not exhibit shared risk and a sense of common vulnerability but rather involves racial, gender, and class inequalities that may in turn support patronising and demeaning judgements about what is supposedly good for others (Shelby 2016, pp. 199–200).

The democratic case against conditionality 2: 'predistribution' and basic income

One of the key arguments for conditionality appeals to a reciprocity principle which holds that we have an obligation to contribute to production of goods and services if we share in the fruits of others' labours (and if we have capacity and adequate opportunity to make such a contribution). However, not all the resources that societies have are a product of the labour of their current members. Some resources exist prior to the labour of current members of society. These include, for example, natural resources – for short, 'land'. They also include the resources produced by past generations that are an inheritance to the present generation.[7] If fairness requires that we apply the reciprocity principle to the distribution of resources produced by the labour of current fellow members of society, what about these resources? Given that they are not the product of labour by current fellow citizens, perhaps they fall outside the remit of the reciprocity principle? Before we consider the fair basis for distributing the fruits of our fellows' labours, perhaps we should first establish a fair basis for what we might call the 'predistribution' of these external assets, such as land (Robertson 2004)? The reciprocity principle then properly applies to the distribution of the economic product generated over and above this predistribution of external assets.

In libertarian political philosophy the just predistribution of these assets is understood as the problem of 'justice in acquisition' (Nozick 1974, pp. 15–151). Assuming that the assets are initially unowned by anyone, the question is: Under what conditions are individuals justified in appropriating an asset as their private property? Robert Nozick argues that individuals justifiably appropriate resources in this way so long as nobody is harmed as a result, by which he appears to mean that as a result nobody suffers lower welfare than they would in a world where all assets remain unowned (Wolff 1991, pp. 107–112). However, this proposed principle of just acquisition can be criticised on a number of grounds. It sets a very low threshold of justification for private acquisition and, as a result, allows for very unequal initial distributions of assets that, in turn, will make for highly unequal economic outcomes (Cohen 1995, pp. 67–91). An alternative approach that seems more consistent with the democratic ideal of mutual respect between free and equal people is to stipulate that each individual has a right to an initially equal share of these external assets: a principle of equal division (Steiner 1994). On this view, every person has a right to an equal share of inherited and natural external assets and, because it applies to these assets in particular, the right stands outside the scope of the reciprocity principle.

Is this principle of equal division practicable, however? If we imagine a group of people arriving on a previously uninhabited planet it is easy to see how the equal division idea applies to them in the first instance. But what happens as new generations get born? Do we have to literally redivide the land every time a new person appears? That doesn't seem feasible. There is, however, a more feasible possibility that seems to capture what was crucial in the equal division idea. Instead of literally dividing up the assets we might instead give everyone a right to an equal share of the *market value* of these assets. For example, we can imagine the community standing as the formal owner of all land and leasing out use-rights to the land in a competitive auction.[8] The return on this commonly owned asset then becomes a fund to which each individual has an equal claim. The rental return on the land can be paid out to all on a uniform basis.

This payment can take different forms. The community could pay it out as 'benefits in kind' – for example, as specific goods and services like health care or education that are available to all. Another possibility is to pay it out as a lump-sum capital grant. This is the option supported by Thomas Paine in his 1797 pamphlet, *Agrarian Justice* (Paine 1987). A third option is payment as a regular income. So, for example, each year every individual might receive a cash sum from the community representing his or her share of the return on the relevant assets. This is sometimes called a 'social dividend'. We currently see something like this in Alaska (Widerquist and Howard 2012). Revenues from the sale of mineral rights are invested by the Alaskan state in the Alaska Permanent Fund, and each year every Alaskan citizen receives a cheque representing his or her share of the return on this investment fund. Many nations today have sovereign wealth funds that could in principle be used in a similar way (Cummine 2016). A similar outcome can be achieved if the state taxes the value of the assets in question and uses this taxation to fund payments to individuals.

This *external asset dividend*, as we might call it, can thus take the form of a basic income as defined in the first section: a uniform income paid to each person with no work-related condition attached. A basic income in this sense is not necessarily a minimum income: it might be below the level sufficient to meet a person's basic needs. (In Alaska, the dividend has recently been in the region of $1,000–$2,000 per person per year.) Nevertheless, even if a basic income is below the minimum income level, it provides people with a partial minimum income. More-over, as we have seen, the rationale for the basic income seems to place it outside the scope of the reciprocity principle. So this is an income that apparently ought not to be linked to any job-related conditionality (at least on reciprocity-based grounds). Thus, even if conditionality ought to apply to some of the income necessary to meet basic needs, it looks like it ought not to apply to this basic income. If the basic income is high enough, then individuals will have a right to a minimum income – or an income that is even higher – that is apparently not properly subject to conditionality at all.

There are at least two objections to the foregoing argument for a basic income, however. One is that the proposal is, in fact, too paternalist. Recall that basic income is only one option for paying out the external assets dividend. Compared to paying the dividend as 'benefits in kind', one might argue that basic income is the less paternalistic option, leaving individuals with more discretion as to what they use the dividend for rather than requiring them to take it in the form of specific goods and services. But compared to the capital grant option, under which individuals get a lump sum on reaching adulthood, basic income looks more paternalistic. Indi-viduals can always turn their capital grant into a guaranteed income flow through an annuity and so, in a sense, the capital grant encompasses a basic income. But individuals have the freedom to use their capital grant in other ways – for example, to make major initial investments in a business. If we stipulate that the external asset dividend take the form of a basic income, which may not be 'mortgaged' to support major investments of these kinds, then we are denying individuals the freedom to use their share of society's external assets in this way. What justifies this?

One reasonable worry with the capital grant policy is what Anne Alstott and Bruce Ackerman, proponents of the policy, call 'stakeblowing' (Ackerman and Alstott 1999): that individuals may invest their capital grants, and then, due to imprudence or bad luck, lose their capital. This will then place them permanently in a weaker position in the economy, lacking the relative security that comes with independent asset ownership and a flow of asset income. However, perhaps here we can usefully return to Dworkin's theory of justified paternalism (see the first section). Given the risk of stakeblowing, and what it implies, we can plausibly argue that reasonable individuals would in fact agree to limit how far they take their external asset dividend as capital rather than as income (Van Parijs 1995, pp. 45–48; White 2015). Perhaps they would not wish completely to restrict their freedom to 'capitalise' their external asset dividend. But a reasonable balancing of pros and cons will support some restriction and this supports paying a non-trivial share of the external asset dividend as a (non-mortgageable) basic income.

A second objection to the foregoing argument for a basic income focuses on the underlying principle of equal division. The intuition behind equal division, and making this unconditional with respect to work-related activity, is that the assets are not the product of the labour of current members of society and so apparently not covered by the reciprocity principle. However, some argue that an equal and unconditional division of these assets can nevertheless be exploitative. Gijs van Donselaar has made this argument in a particularly compelling way (van Donselaar 2009). To capture van Donselaar's key point, imagine that we have a simple scenario with two people, assumed to have the same productive ability, and an external asset, land, of which there are four units. Left to herself, Smith would choose to use three of the four units to grow corn; we may say that she has an 'independent interest' in three units of land. Left to himself, Jones would choose to use one unit of land (also to grow corn), so he has an independent interest in one unit of land. Note that, given their respective independent interests in land, there is actually no underlying scarcity of land in this case. Both could use land as they want without impairing the other's desire to use land. However, imagine that, having read the foregoing argument, a legislator insists that Smith and Jones each be given equal shares of the available land (two units each). Now there is scarcity. Specifically, Jones has more land than he needs, relative to his independent interest in land (in one unit), and Smith has less land than she needs, relative to her independent interest (in three units). This creates an opportunity for trade. Jones can offer Smith access to the 'surplus' unit of land he has in return for a share of what Smith produces with it (thereby reducing the amount Jones has to work to get the corn he desires). Given Smith's and Jones's preferences, there will typically be some price at which trade will happen. Relative to the baseline in which each of them gets land in accordance with his or her independent interests, Jones is thus made better off by equal division and Smith is made worse off by it (because she now has to pay some of her output of corn to access the third unit of land). Van Donselaar argues that this is unfair because it amounts to a form of 'parasitism': equal division means that one party is made worse off by the other's presence, while one benefits from the other's presence. There is thus a basic failure of mutual benefit here, a failure that clearly recalls the original concern with reciprocity that we discussed in setting out the case for conditionality. In van Donselaar's view, fairness requires not equal division of external assets like land but a division that tracks individuals' independent interests in using external assets. Against a background of an equal presumption of access to external assets, those with less interest in using the assets should not be able to take advantage of the greater enthusiasm of others.

In response to van Donselaar's powerful criticism, one might argue that the concern to prevent 'parasitism' is trumped by other moral considerations, such as the need to secure individuals' effective liberty and bargaining power by means of a basic income (Pateman 2004; Raventós 2007). However, even if we accept van Donselaar's claim, it does not necessarily wholly defeat the policy of basic income. What matters fundamentally in van Donselaar's analysis is that individuals have independent interests in using external assets. In the foregoing example, we presented the individuals' independent interests as interests in making *productive use* of assets (the use of land to grow corn). However, people can have independent interests that are not productive (or productive in this standard sense). So far as land is concerned, for example, someone can have an independent interest related to aesthetic appreciation or simply in holding land as a space in which one is free to act (Waldron 1993). We should not conclude, therefore, that the implication of van Donselaar's argument is that people have rights to an initial share of external assets only in proportion to their willingness to make productive use of them. People can have an independent interest in these assets even if they are entirely lacking a productive interest. Of course, this does not (necessarily) save the principle of equal division. But it suggests that, even on the basis of van Donselaar's argument, those with little interest in production in the usual sense will have *some* independent interest in these assets, and so, by extension, will have a right to some, perhaps non-trivial, share of any external asset dividend (Widerquist 2006).[9] Thus, van Donselaar's argument certainly complicates the case for a basic income, but it does not necessarily eliminate the argument for everyone receiving some basic income (as a share in their society's external asset dividend fund).

Conclusion

Democratic ethics suggests there is a right to a minimum income as a matter of political inclusion and intrinsic economic fairness. However, this leaves open numerous questions of policy design. One such question is whether the receipt of income transfers from the state, to help secure a minimum income, should be conditional on work-related activity (for those who have capacity and adequate opportunity to work).

Exploring this design question, we have seen that there are arguments from within a framework of democratic ethics for conditionality. These are arguments of reciprocity and paternalism. However, the arguments are not conclusive. The fair and equitable application of the reciprocity principle is crucial to the case for conditionality. The failure of many societies to meet the conditions of fair reciprocity implies that conditionality is unfair in these societies, at least for those individuals most disadvantaged by their background injustice. In addition, even under ideal conditions, there is a strong argument that individuals have a right to some income that is not properly conditional on any work-related activity as a way of securing their fair share of inherited and natural assets. This basic income will contribute something towards a minimum income.

As noted, there are many other design questions, such as the use of means-testing in a system of minimum income provision. Although we have not had the space to address these directly here, I hope that the discussion indicates in broad terms how we – as democratic citizens – might approach them.

Notes

1 Rousseau's own conception of political citizenship excludes women, but I believe we can and should detach his underlying conception of democratic community from this feature of his thought.
2 What matters is that we can predict, on the basis of the best evidence we have, that under specific rules some proportion of citizens will face poverty (we need not be able to predict exactly whom).
3 Ideally there should be unanimity on the law's usefulness. But this seems too stringent and I suggest that a reasonable supermajority suffices to make a paternalist law justifiable on the grounds of self-paternalism. Nevertheless, democratic ethics requires us to be sensitive to the position of those who have particularly strong reasons of conscience against such a law – for example, possibly by allowing an 'exemption' for those with profound religious objections.
4 The idea of fair reciprocity represents my effort to integrate the idea that citizens have work obligations with egalitarian values; see White (2003) for a full statement. For another, distinct approach that attempts this integration see Stancyk (2012, forthcoming).
5 There is a role here for democratic procedures to identify other, agreed forms of non-market contribution that count in satisfaction of the reciprocity principle.
6 I believe I owe this phrase to Declan Gaffney.
7 If members of the current generation have a duty to maintain to some degree the value of inherited assets for future generations, and this requires labour to offset depreciation, then we should make an adjustment to our estimation of the 'labour-independent' inherited asset stock to allow for this labour.
8 In a fuller discussion we would consider how far some such resources should be kept available for use on a non-market basis – for example, as part of a 'commons' with shared rules of use.
9 This argument is weakened, however, if some of the asset is made available in other ways that serve the non-productive independent interest (e.g., as a non-marketised 'commons'). See van Donselaar (2015).

References

Ackerman, Bruce, and Alstott, Anne, 1999. *The Stakeholder Society*. New Haven: Yale University Press.
Bendygirl (Franklin, Kaliya), *Benefit Scrounging Scum*, http://benefitscroungingscum.blogspot.co.uk/
Brownstein, Michael, and Saul, Jennifer, eds., 2016. *Implicit Bias in Philosophy: Volume 2: Moral Responsibility, Structural Injustice, and Ethics*. Oxford: Oxford University Press.
Butler, Patrick, 'Thousands Have Died After being Bound Fit for Work', *The Guardian*, 27 August 2015. www. theguardian.com/society/2015/aug/27/thousands-died-after-fit-for-work-assessment-dwp-figures
Cochrane, Clare, Haddad, Moussa, Fooks, Louie, and Garton, Jane, 2010. *Something for Nothing: Challenging Negative Attitudes to People Living in Poverty*. Oxford: Oxfam. http://policy-practice.oxfam.org.uk/ publications/something-for-nothing-changing-negative-attitudes-to-people-living-in-poverty-114046
Cohen, G.A., 1995. *Self-Ownership, Freedom, and Equality*. Oxford: Oxford University Press.
Conly, Sarah, 2013. *Against Autonomy: Justifying Coercive Paternalism*. Cambridge: Cambridge University Press.
Cummine, Angela, 2016. *Citizens' Wealth: Why (and How) Sovereign Wealth Funds Should Managed by the People for the People*. New Haven: Yale University Press.
Dworkin, Gerald, 1971. 'Paternalism', in Richard A. Wasserstrom, ed., *Morality and the Law*. Belmost: CA, Wadsworth, pp. 107–126.
Goodin, Robert E., 1986. *Protecting the Vulnerable: A Reanalysis of Our Social Responsibilities*. Chicago: University of Chicago Press.
Gutmann, Amy, and Thompson, Dennis, 1996. *Democracy and Disagreement: Why Moral Conflict Cannot Be Avoided in Politics, and What Should Be Done About It*. Cambridge, MA: Harvard University Press.
Marsh, Sue, *Diary of a Benefit Scrounger*, http://diaryofabenefitscrounger.blogspot.co.uk/
Mead, Lawrence, 1992. *The New Politics of Poverty: The Nonworking Poor in America*. New York: Basic Books.
Nozick, Robert, 1974. *Anarchy, State, and Utopia*. Oxford: Blackwell.
Paine, Tom, 1987 [1797]. 'Agrarian Justice', in Michael Foot and Isaac Kramnick, eds., *The Thomas Paine Reader*. Harmondsworth: Penguin, pp. 471–489.
Pateman, Carole, 2004. 'Democratizing Citizenship: Some Advantages of a Basic Income', *Politics & Society* 32 (1), pp. 89–105.
Raventós, Daniel, 2007. *Basic Income: The Material Conditions of Freedom*. London: Pluto.
Rawls, John, 1999 [1971]. *A Theory of Justice: Revised Edition*. Cambridge, MA: Harvard University Press.

————, 2001. *Justice as Fairness: A Restatement*. Cambridge, MA: Harvard University Press.

Robertson, James, 2004. 'Towards Land Value Taxation', paper for Local Government Conference, Oxford. www.jamesrobertson.com/article/lvt.htm Accessed April 18 2017.

Rousseau, Jean-Jacques, trans. by Christopher Betts, 1994 [1762]. *The Social Contract*. Oxford: Oxford University Press.

Shelby, Tommie, 2007. 'Justice, Deviance, and the Dark Ghetto', *Philosophy and Public Affairs* 35 (2), pp. 126–160.

————, 2016. *Dark Ghettos: Injustice, Dissent, and Reform*. Cambridge, MA: Harvard University Press.

Stancyk, Lucas, 2012. 'Productive Justice', *Philosophy and Public Affairs* 40 (3), pp. 144–164.

————, forthcoming, *From Each: A Theory of Productive Justice*.

Steiner, Hillel, 1994. *An Essay on Rights*. Oxford: Blackwell.

van Donselaar, Gijs, 2009. *The Right to Exploit: Freedom, Parasitism, Basic Income*. Oxford: Oxford University Press.

————, 2015. 'In the Company of the Funny Sunny Surfer off Malibu: A Response to Michael Howard (and Some Others)', *Analyse & Kritik* 37, pp. 305–317.

Van Parijs, Philippe, 1995. *Real Freedom for All: What (if Anything) Can Justify Capitalism?* Oxford: Oxford University Press.

Van Parijs, Philippe, and Vanderborght, Yannick, 2017. *Basic Income: A Radical Proposal for a Free Society and a Sane Economy*. Cambridge, MA: Harvard University Press.

Waldron, Jeremy, 1993. 'Homelessness and the Issue of Freedom', in Jeremy Waldron, ed., *Liberal Rights*. Cambridge: Cambridge University Press, pp. 309–338.

White, Stuart, 2000. 'Social Rights and the Social Contract: Political Theory and the New Welfare Politics', *British Journal of Political Science* 30 (2), pp. 507–532.

————, 2003. *The Civic Minimum: On the Rights and Obligations of Economic Citizenship*. Oxford: Oxford University Press.

————, 2015. 'Basic Capital in the Egalitarian Toolkit?' *Journal of Applied Philosophy* 32 (4), pp. 417–431.

————, 2017. 'Should a Minimum Income Be Unconditional?' in Stefano Civaterese Matteucci and Simon Halliday, eds., *Social Rights in Europe in an Age of Austerity*. London: Routledge, pp. 181–196.

Widerquist, Karl, 2006. 'Who Exploits Who?' *Political Studies* 54 (3), pp. 444–464.

Widerquist, Karl, and Howard, Michael W., 2012. *Alaska's Permanent Fund Dividend: Examining Its Suitability as a Model*. Basingstoke: Palgrave Macmillan.

Wolff, Jonathan, 1991. *Robert Nozick: Property, Justice and the Minimal State*. Oxford: Blackwell.

29

PUBLIC ENGAGEMENT IN HEALTH POLICY

Mapping aims and approaches

Matthew S. McCoy and Ezekiel J. Emanuel[1]

Introduction

In 2017, a panel convened by US National Academies of Science and Medicine published a report on the science, ethics, and governance of human genome editing. Human genome editing, as defined by the report, refers to a 'suite of methods' used 'for making precise additions, deletions, and alterations to the genome – an organism's complete set of genetic material'.[2] Though clinical applications of genome editing to treat disease and disability hold great promise, they also raise ethical concerns. These concerns are especially pronounced in the context of germline genome editing, which creates changes to the genome that can be inherited by future generations.

The National Academies report laid out principles and recommendations for the governance of human genome editing in the US and other countries. Notably, the report included an entire chapter and five separate recommendations addressing the need for public engagement in various aspects of the regulation and oversight of human genome editing. These recommendations included that 'public participation should be incorporated into the policy-making process for human genome editing' and that 'extensive and inclusive public participation should proceed clinical trials for any extension of human genome editing beyond treatment or prevention of disease and disabilities'.[3]

By all appearances, the report displayed a deep commitment to the practice of public engagement. Yet shortly following its release, the report came under attack for failing to recommend a substantial *enough* role for the public in fundamental policy decisions about the future of human genome editing. Writing on *Scientific American's* blog, Jim Kozubek accused the report's authors of failing to include the 'crucial recommendation' that the public should have a say in the decision of whether human genome editing should move forward at all.[4] The director of the Center for Genetics and Society echoed Kozubek's sentiments, arguing that the report gives scientists and policymakers a 'green light for proceeding with efforts . . . to engineer the genes and traits that are passed on to future children and generations' but 'excludes the public from participation in deciding whether human germline modification is acceptable in the first place'.[5]

The episode was striking – less for the disagreements it highlighted than for the shared assumptions it revealed. Not long ago, a call for multiple layers of public engagement in the regulation and oversight of a complex emerging medical technology might have seemed radical. Indeed, a 2005 National Academies report on embryonic stem-cell research, a similarly controversial issue, did not include the phrase "public engagement" or any of its familiar variants.[6] But by 2017, no one appeared to question the notion that there ought to be a substantial degree of public engagement in policy decisions about the future of human genome editing. The only thing left to debate, it seemed, was just how much public engagement there ought to be.

The discussion around the human genome editing report reflects the state of a larger conversation about the role of public engagement in health policy. Today, there is a growing consensus among policymakers, civil society leaders, scholars, and other stakeholders that the public ought to be substantially involved in a range of health policy decisions. This trend is reflected in the activities of government agencies and institutions across the globe, which involve members of the public in a range of policy decisions related to health care and research.[7] Unfortunately, the proliferation of opportunities for public engagement in health policy has outpaced careful theorising about the normative foundations of the practice. As a result, despite widespread embrace of the idea that public engagement in health policy making is a good thing, there is little certainty about why it is a good thing, and there remains a striking lack of clarity about what the specific goal (or goals) of engagement ought to be. As calls for public engagement in health policy continue to multiply, this lack of normative clarity presents a barrier to rational policy development in this area.

Our goal in this chapter is to shed light on the normative foundations of public engagement in health policy making, focusing in particular on justifications for public engagement that appeal to democratic values. We are not the first to undertake this task, but two features of our approach distinguish it from most previous efforts. First, we pay particular attention to clarifying the relationship between public engagement mechanisms and traditional institutions of representative democracy – namely, elected legislatures and agencies run by professional administrators. Proponents of public engagement in health policy often move too quickly from the widely accepted premise that democracy requires popular control over government to the more controversial conclusion that democracy requires direct public involvement in the work of agencies and institutions responsible for policy development, failing to reckon with the fact that democratic states already have institutions in place to channel popular input into policy-making and oversight processes.[8] This approach is flawed for several reasons, not least of which is that it fails to offer practical guidance to policy-makers considering how to implement public engagement mechanisms in the context of a representative democracy.

Taking this contextualised approach to describing the place of public engagement in a representative democracy yields the second distinctive feature of our account. Drawing on a theory of participatory governance developed by Archon Fung,[9] we suggest that public engagement mechanisms are best viewed as means of shoring up different weak points in the representative policy-making process. Because different weak points have distinct features, the ways in which they can be addressed by public engagement are varied. Thus, while some have sought to locate a single or primary aim for public engagement in health policy making, we defend a more pluralistic approach. Analysing policy examples of resource allocation, health care reform, and emergency preparedness and response, we demonstrate that there are multiple defensible aims for public engagement in health policy and that each is best served by a different approach. We show that there is no one-size-fits-all approach to be had, and that different desiderata of public engagement activities – such as being widely inclusive and being deliberative – are often in tension with each other.

Clarifications

The term "public engagement" is itself somewhat ambiguous, as is its relationship to terms like "public consultation" and "public deliberation". We follow Rowe and Frewer in defining public engagement broadly as 'the practice of involving members of the public in the agenda-setting, decision-making, and policy-forming activities of organizations and institutions responsible for policy development'.[10,11] We also follow Rowe and Frewer in using the term "public consultation" to denote a particular type of public engagement marked by the one-way flow of information from members of the public to the sponsors of the engagement initiative, typically public officials. We use the term "public deliberation" to denote a type of public engagement in which information flows bi-directionally between sponsors and the public (and between members of the public themselves) in some type of structured dialogue. Unlike public consultation, which is designed to elicit more or less "raw" ideas and opinions from the public, public deliberation is typically intended to refine the ideas of the participating public.[12]

While it useful to distinguish consultation and deliberation in principle, it is important to recognise that elements of the two types can be combined in practice. For instance, as part of its Voice of the Patient initiative, the US Food and Drug Administration (FDA) holds public meetings with representatives of different patient populations.[13] The meetings combine in-depth exchanges between small panels of patients and FDA officials (deliberation) with polling questions directed to a larger audience (consultation). In addition to these hybrid models, there are forms of public engagement which are largely consultative but with some opportunities for dialogue between sponsors and the public. Town hall meetings hosted by public officials serve primarily as an opportunity for citizens to express their concerns to officials. But citizens can also use the meetings to ask questions of officials and to engage in brief exchanges.

Some have suggested that highly structured, deliberative methods of public engagement are categorically preferable to these more consultative methods, given that the former are thought to generate more reasoned and reflective feedback.[14] As we will show, however, both deliberative and consultative methods of engagement have strengths and limitations. By focusing our analysis on the broad category of public engagement, we mean to allow for the possibility that either type of public engagement may be well suited to a particular policy context.

Theory

Justifications of public engagement in health policy making often appeal to democratic values. In particular, many proponents claim that public engagement in health policy is justified because it advances democratic legitimacy. The strongest version of this claim is that public engagement is necessary for achieving democratic legitimacy. As the authors of one study put it, 'engagement of a large number of citizens of diverse perspectives is required for legitimate health-policy development'.[15] A weaker version of the claim – one that treats legitimacy as a quality that varies by degree rather than a threshold concept – is that public engagement necessarily makes the democratic policy-making process more legitimate, even if that process is somewhat legitimate without public engagement.[16] These claims contain an important kernel of truth in that there is a link between democratic legitimacy and public engagement. But whereas that link is sometimes treated as categorical, we argue that it is contingent on certain factors that do not exist in every context. In short, we argue, public engagement is not always needed to achieve or enhance democratic legitimacy; understanding when and why it serves this function is a crucial step towards understanding the oft-cited but under-theorised legitimacy-based rationales for public engagement in health policy making.

To clarify the relationship between public engagement and democratic legitimacy, we need to begin with a working definition of democratic legitimacy. For present purposes, we will assume that democratic legitimacy requires that citizens exercise control over their government, directing its actions in accordance with their own values and interests.[17] Some democratic theorists might wish to elaborate on this account. For instance, deliberative democrats might insist that legitimacy requires that popular control be exercised discursively.[18] But the notion that democratic legitimacy requires popular control is fundamental to most accounts of democracy. A government that was not subject to popular control might pass wise and just laws, but it would not be democratic. Realising the democratic ideal requires 'giving kratos to the demos, power to the people'.[19]

On this understanding of democracy, one argument for justifying public engagement on the basis of democratic legitimacy would be the following:

> Democratic legitimacy requires popular control over government.
>
> Citizens cannot exercise popular control over government unless they are directly engaged in the work of the agencies and institutions responsible for policy development.
>
> Thus, achieving democratic legitimacy requires public engagement in the work of the agencies and institutions responsible for policy development.

If successful, this argument would ground a categorical legitimacy-based claim for public engagement in health policy making and, indeed, in other policy areas as well. The difficulty with the argument is that its second premise is not widely accepted. There are compelling reasons why modern democratic states do not function as direct democracies, in which citizens themselves bear primary responsibility for policy development. Regardless of whether most citizens would desire this level of involvement in government, the scale and complexity of modern democratic states make direct democracy practically difficult. Instead, modern democratic states function as representative democracies, in which citizens delegate the tasks of governing to elected lawmakers and professional administrators. In such a system, at least in principle, citizens exercise control over government not by carrying out its essential functions but by selecting the individuals who do and holding them to account. Rather than rejecting the ideal that democracy requires popular control over government, representative democracy provides a set of institutions for realising that ideal on the scale of modern states.[20]

Of course, one could reject the basic idea of representative democracy on the grounds that representative institutions do not actually enable popular control. However, it seems unlikely that most proponents of public engagement in health policy would want to defend their position via an attack on the normative foundations of representative democracy. More importantly, there are good prima facie reasons for preferring representative democracy to other forms democratic control. Some of these reasons are practical. In most democratic countries there is a cultural preference for representative democracy. Moreover, despite its shortcomings, some of which we discuss ahead, representative democracy has shown itself to be a feasible means of democratic control on the scale of modern states. There are also moral reasons that can be offered in support of representative democracy, chief among which is that a one-person, one-vote system is a good way of instantiating political equality among citizens. If this is correct, the second premise of the foregoing argument is too strong. Not only is representative democracy a means of enabling popular control over government, but also it is one supported by practical and moral reasons.

What about the more modest argument, suggested earlier, which appeals to the notion that legitimacy varies by degree in a political system? That argument might be formulated as follows:

> We should strive to make government as legitimate as possible.
>
> Increasing the degree of popular control over government increases democratic legitimacy.
>
> Public engagement in the work of the agencies and institutions responsible for policy development increases popular control over government.
>
> Thus we ought to pursue public engagement in the work of the agencies and institutions responsible for policy development.

Unfortunately, this argument's first and third premises raise questions. With respect to the first premise, even if one grants that democratic legitimacy is an important value, it does not follow that we ought to try to maximise that value, come what may. Implementing additional mechanisms for enabling popular control over government comes with costs. In particular, public engagement activities involve both significant financial costs and opportunity costs for the participating public.[21] If representative institutions already enable a reasonable degree of popular control, it is not clear that these additional costs would be justified.[22] With respect to the third premise, even if one accepts that we ought to try to maximise democratic legitimacy at all costs, it is not clear that the best way to realise this goal is by multiplying mechanisms of popular control. Rather than amplifying a clear signal of the popular will, using multiple mechanisms to enable popular input into the policy-making process could result in competing signals, eroding rather than strengthening popular control.

A weakness of both of these arguments is that they fail to reckon with the central role of representative institutions in modern democracies, and thus move too quickly from the notion that there ought to be popular control over government to the conclusion that popular control ought to be exercised by way of public engagement. This way of arguing not only muddles the legitimacy-based rationales for public engagement in health policy making but also offers little practical guidance to the government sponsors of public engagement activities who are typically operating in the context of representative institutions. To make the case for public engagement in a representative democracy, it isn't enough to show that democratic legitimacy requires popular control of the policy-making process. One must show when and why existing institutions fail to realise this goal and how public engagement can help.

One way of answering these questions has been suggested by Archon Fung, who argues that various types of public engagement can be used not to replace representative institutions, nor to add to representative institutions when those institutions are working well, but to address particular deficits that can arise in the representative policy process. Fung summarises that process as follows:

> [C]itizens have (1) interests and (2) preferences over policy options that they think will advance those interests. They (3) signal these preferences to government by voting in periodic elections for parties and politicians whose programs most closely match their preferences. These electoral signals generate mandates for representative politicians to make (5) policies to advance these interests. Under the separation of powers between legislative and executive functions, (6) agencies staffed by professional administrators are charged with executing these policies, which generate (7) outcomes that advance the (1) interests that begin this process.[23]

Under ideal conditions – including, among other things, a well-informed citizenry, electoral competition among candidates with clearly defined policy positions, and competent administrators – the representative policy process enables citizens to exercise control over government, directing its essential functions in accordance with their values and interests. Under such conditions, there may be little need for an additional element of public engagement to enable popular control over government. Indeed, as noted earlier, introducing public engagement into a well-functioning representative policy-making process might be regarded as an unjustified expense at best and a distortion of the representative process at worst.

In the real world, of course, ideal conditions rarely obtain: citizens are lamentably ill-informed about basic aspects of policy and politics; campaigns are conducted in soundbites rather than reasoned exchanges over competing policy positions; administrators often lack the resources they need to successfully implement the policies they are charged with enacting; and so on. As a result of these and other challenges, links in the chain of the representative policy-making process can stress and break.

Fung notes several characteristically weak links in the chain. First, owing to ignorance, irrationality, or a general lack of interest in the political process, citizens may have unclear or unstable preferences about which policies are likely to advance their interests in a particular area. Thus, even if citizens do elect politicians who pass their preferred policies, those policies will not reliably advance citizens' underlying interests. Under these conditions, even though citizens do influence the policy-making process, they exert only what Pettit calls 'wayward influence' rather than control towards achieving some desired end.[24]

Second, even if citizens have coherent preferences, periodic elections provide infrequent and blunt signals of those preferences to politicians.[25] Thus, even a politician acting in good faith who endeavours to be responsive to the preferences of her constituents may not know what those preferences are. Third, even if voters form coherent preferences and politicians legislate accordingly, it is possible that administrators will fail to implement policies in a way that delivers desired results. One common source of failure, which Fung notes, is that in some policy areas, achieving a desired result depends on coordination with private actors in the economic sphere. Without buy-in from these actors, even skilled administrators may be limited in their ability to deliver results.

Against this backdrop, Fung argues that one way to conceptualise the place of public engagement in a representative democracy is as a means of supplementing the representative policy process to address these and other deficits. On this account, public engagement is justified on the grounds that it advances democratic legitimacy, not in every case but in those circumstances where it serves the type of reinforcing function Fung describes. The argument might be formulated as follows:

Democratic legitimacy requires popular control over government.

In representative democracies, popular control is exercised primarily via the representative policy process.

However, the representative policy process can suffer from deficits.

In some circumstances, public engagement can address these deficits and help to reestablish popular control over government.

Where it serves this reinforcing function, public engagement advances democratic legitimacy.

Thus, there are some circumstances in which we ought to pursue public engagement.

Like the previous arguments, this one grounds the case for public engagement in the value of democratic legitimacy. However, the justification offered by this argument is contingent rather than categorical. Public engagement does not always advance democratic legitimacy and hence is not always justified; rather, it is justified in those contexts where it serves a particular democracy-reinforcing function.

In addition to grounding the link between democratic legitimacy and public engagement in a more plausible and nuanced way than competing accounts, this account has a second important benefit. Because it ties the value of public engagement activities to their potential to address particular problems in the representative policy process, it provides a framework for articulating the possible aims of public engagement. With these aims in mind, planners and policymakers have a set of standards that can be used to measure the benefits of one approach to public engagement against another.

Applications

We've argued that public engagement can be justified as means of addressing deficits in the representative policy process. In this section, we apply that idea to particular issues in health policy making. The individual examples show that there are areas of health policy in which public engagement activities can be used to address breakdowns in the representative policy process and thus vindicate the idea that public engagement can enhance the legitimacy of health policy development. Taken together, however, the examples show that an approach to public engagement that might be useful in addressing one deficit in the representative policy process will likely be ill-suited to addressing another.

Resource allocation

The representative policy process depends on citizens being able to translate their interests and values into corresponding policy preferences. Where the contours of a given policy issue are clear and well understood by the public, we can expect this process of translation to work well.[26] However, where issues are technically complex, where the trade-offs at stake are unclear, or where people are uninformed or misinformed, difficulties can arise. One area where such difficulties are likely to arise is in decision making about the allocation of scarce health care resources.

The need to set limits on health care spending is acutely felt in publicly funded health insurance programs. Decisions about which interventions should be included in a basket of covered services require trade-offs that pit competing interests and values against one another. And in most cases, there will be multiple morally permissible ways to set coverage priorities, all of which will privilege some interests and values over others. Deciding on one coverage scheme over another will depend on which values are deemed to be most important. And in recent years, there has been increasing interest in soliciting the public's values in making these decisions.[27]

The difficulty is that even if policy-makers want public values to inform coverage decisions, most citizens lack clear views on which to draw. Those with limited experience in the health care system may not know how to value certain benefits against others. Preferences that citizens do have regarding benefits may be coloured by misinformation or confusion. Infamously, in the debates leading up to the passage of the Patient Protection and Affordable Care Act (ACA) in the US, a provision that would allow Medicare to reimburse providers for conducting consultations about end-of-life care was widely mischaracterised as establishing federal "death panels".

Understandably, many citizens voiced opposition to the notion of death panels, but those same citizens may have endorsed the benefit had they understood it. Finally, even if citizens do understand benefits well, they may have unrealistic or unstable preferences about how these benefits should be combined. For instance, citizens might wish for unfettered access to the newest and most expensive therapies with no out-of-pocket costs and without a higher tax burden: a set of desires which are not jointly realisable.

These challenges have been keenly observed by proponents of public engagement, who have sought to demonstrate that certain types of public deliberation can help people to form more coherent views about allocating health care resources. One well-known approach to public deliberation that has been used in this context is the "citizens' jury". Citizens' juries involve a panel of 10–20 lay participants, recruited to be demographically representative of their community.[28] Lenaghan describes the process of a citizens' jury as follows:

> They are brought together for four days with a team of two moderators. They are fully briefed about the background to the question, through written information and oral evidence from witnesses. Jurors scrutinise the information, cross examine the witnesses and discuss different aspects of the question in small groups and plenary sessions.[29]

Lenaghan describes five citizens' juries commissioned by local health authorities in the UK, which addressed broad questions such as 'What are the most important criteria for setting spending priorities?'[30] To make these questions concrete, jurors were asked to allocate imaginary budgets across different benefit areas, and then had their intuitions tested by case studies that illuminated the implications of coverage decisions.

Another mechanism for encouraging deliberation about coverage policy is the Choosing Health Plans Altogether (CHAT) tool, developed by Goold and Danis.[31] The CHAT tool utilises a game-like structure, built around a board divided into different health benefit categories. Participants in the exercise distribute a limited number of markers across the board to indicate which benefits they would like included in the insurance package. Participants lack the markers to maximise each benefit area and are thus forced to make trade-offs in designing a benefits package. The exercise takes place in two rounds. First, participants choose benefits individually to suit their needs and the needs of their family. Second, the group works together to choose a benefits package that they believe will best suit the needs of the broader community. To help participants appreciate the implications of their choices, they are assigned random health event cards that 'contain stories of illness episodes and explain the consequences of the benefit choices in relation to these events'.[32]

Public engagement mechanisms like citizens' juries and the CHAT tool have been shown to help ordinary citizens articulate informed, clear, and stable preferences with respect to complicated issues like health benefit design. But while these mechanisms have the clear virtue of enabling an uncommon degree of reflection on a difficult policy issue, they also have limitations. An unavoidable limitation of highly structured, deliberative exercises like citizens' juries or the CHAT game is that they must be restricted to a relatively small number of participants to enable sufficient opportunities for debate and deliberation. Additionally, in order to ensure focused deliberation, the sponsors of these activities significantly shape the conduct of the exercise – they pre-select the question(s) to be addressed; they select sources of authoritative information; they structure the rules of deliberation. All of these features help to ensure that the deliberation stays on track, but increase the risk that sponsors will bias the results of the deliberation.

Ultimately, these highly structured deliberative exercises do not solve the challenge of uninformed or unstable preferences in the broader public; they solve the problem for a small subset of citizens.[33] This raises significant questions about how the results of the deliberations should be incorporated in the policy-making process. In principle, a legislature could delegate policymaking authority to a citizens' jury, imbuing the jury's decision with the force of law. So far as we know, however, citizens' juries are rarely given this type of authority in practice. And indeed, as scholars have suggested, there are reasons for avoiding vesting citizens' juries with such authority, chief among which is that they lack bonds of accountability and authorisation to the broader population that would be subject to their decision.[34] This leaves citizens' juries to influence the policy-making process in indirect ways. One way in which citizens' juries might influence the policy process is through media coverage of their activities. Thus, small-scale deliberation might be the catalyst for broader deliberation at a societal level. Though this is sometimes touted as an effect of deliberative exercises, there is little evidence to support it.[35] Another way in which public deliberation might influence the policy-making process is by officials citing the results of public deliberations as a source of democratic justification for their decisions. Ultimately, however, officials will turn to this justification only where citizens' juries already have wide social acceptance.

Health care reform

There are no doubt areas of health policy in which citizens will have unclear or unstable preferences that might be improved through public deliberation. In other areas, however, the challenge is not that citizens do not have clear preferences but that elections provide an insufficient means of communicating their preferences to officials. An example of the latter challenge occurred after the 2016 federal elections in the US. Having won control of the presidency while retaining control of both branches of the legislature, Republicans were poised to repeal the ACA, which had been passed under the previous Democratic administration and had extended and strengthened insurance coverage for tens of millions in the US.

Following the elections, evidence from polls showed that the majority of Americans did not want to see the ACA repealed.[36] Nonetheless, relying solely on the election results to gauge public temperament, Republican lawmakers could perhaps assume that they had received a mandate to repeal the health care law. Alternatively, lawmakers might suspect that their constituents wished to see the ACA upheld, but harbour their own reasons – for example, ideological commitments, party loyalty, a desire to appease donors – for wanting to undo the law. Either way, election results alone gave no clear signal of popular preferences with respect the health care law, allowing a situation in which lawmakers' behaviour could become untethered from the wishes of their constituents.

These circumstances created an opportunity in which public engagement mechanisms could be used to send a focused signal of citizens' views about the ACA to their representatives. Unlike the examples of highly structured deliberation discussed earlier, the types of public engagement employed in this context were primarily consultative in nature, serving not to refine citizens' inchoate opinions about a policy matter they knew little about but to signal clear preferences to their representatives. Citizens communicated their views about the law via petitions and submissions to open comment forums. However, the most notable form of public engagement that took place involved a series of town hall meetings hosted by members of Congress. In what became a major news story, dozens of town hall meetings hosted by lawmakers were packed with constituents explaining the ways in which they had come to depend on the ACA and expressing their anger about Republican plans to repeal the law.

The character of the often "tumultuous" town hall meetings was quite different than the controlled environment of a citizens' jury.[37] Whereas citizens' juries and similar mechanisms for facilitating public deliberation involve small groups of participants, carefully selected to mirror the demographic characteristics of residents in a given jurisdiction, the town hall meetings operated with an open-door policy and typically drew large crowds – sometimes more than could be accommodated in meeting rooms. Whereas citizens' juries are structured to focus on a particular question, the citizens who attended the town hall meetings set the agenda. That the meetings were dominated by discussion of Republican plans for the health care law was not the sponsors' choice but the attendees'. Whereas citizens' juries are designed to refine opinions, the town halls functioned to communicate constituents' strongly held views to their representatives.

As others have noted, all of these features make town hall meetings ineffective forums for careful deliberation about policy issues.[38] But these same features made town hall meetings effective mechanisms for amplifying the concerns of citizens, and for holding elected officials accountable. At a town hall meeting in Wisconsin, for instance, constituents got their representative to commit to maintaining popular provisions of the ACA.[39] Regardless of whether they are honoured, these sorts of commitments, made in public in response to questioning from constituents, can function as important measures for holding politicians accountable in subsequent elections. Additionally, though the town hall meetings were not deliberative in the same way that citizens' juries are deliberative, they attracted a great deal of media coverage and commentary, and in this regard, arguably made an important contribution to deliberation at a societal level.

Against the tendency to treat highly structured forms of public deliberation as the gold standard of public engagement, the example of the town hall meetings shows the value of a more nuanced account of the relationship between democratic legitimacy and public engagement. There is more than one way in which public engagement can contribute to democratic legitimacy. And what makes a particular approach to public engagement inappropriate in one context can be a virtue in another.

Emergency preparedness and response

The representative policy process can also suffer when administrators lack the expertise or resources they require to carry out policies they are charged with enacting. As noted, this type of failure is especially likely to occur when success in a particular policy area depends on cooperation from community-based and private-sector actors. Arguably, a number of health policy areas have these characteristics. One such area that has received increasing attention is public health emergency preparedness and response. As one commentator put it, 'the process of actually preparing a community for an emergency is essentially a social undertaking that involves creating and strengthening relationships, partnerships, and collaborations throughout the community'.[40]

The importance of community partnerships has long been recognised as an important component of public health planning. As a 2003 Institute of Medicine (IOM) report on the future of public health noted, 'all partners who can contribute to action as a public health system should be encouraged to assess their roles and responsibilities, consider changes, and devise ways to better collaborate with other partners'.[41] In light of this goal, the report recommended 'a new generation of intersectoral partnerships that also draw on the perspectives and resources of diverse communities and actively engage them in health action'.[42] Arguably, however, the need for this kind of partnership and coordination is even greater in the context of public health emergencies, where the capacity of public health agencies is likely to be taxed, and where a coordinated and rapid response is essential to crisis management. This point was emphasised by two recent IOM reports, and has been reflected in the emergency planning activities of a number of American cities and states.[43]

Public engagement to develop the "social infrastructure" for emergency preparedness and response has a different aim and requires different approaches than the examples of public engagement discussed earlier. Rather than aiming at deliberative preference articulation or the communication of citizen preferences to elected officials, public engagement in this context is geared towards collective planning and agreement on the roles and responsibilities of different actors during a public health emergency. As Ruth Gaare Bernheim rightly notes, achieving this aim requires more than town hall meetings or one-off consultations; it requires long-term trust and relationship building between government, private-sector, and community-based actors.[44] One component of a public engagement strategy in this context might simply be public communication from government officials to the public about the available resources during a public health emergency. Another component might be a kind of joint strategising between public health officials and community members about how challenges might be handled. Gaare Bernheim offers planning for how to deal with deaths if normal funeral services have to be suspended as an example of a problem that community members and public health officials might work to solve together.[45]

While citizens' juries and similar mechanisms typically involve lay people with no vested interest in the topic under deliberation, the sorts of public engagement activities employed in emergency planning tend to involve a mix of laypersons and representatives of different community groups and organisations, including community health clinics, schools, advocacy organisations, and faith-based organisations.[46] Involving these sorts of "vested stakeholders" in a citizens' jury would rightly be thought to bias the results of that exercise and undermine the extent to which its output could be interpreted as indicative of broader community values. However, in the context of emergency planning, where the aim of public engagement is to forge understanding and agreement on the roles that different actors will play in a crisis, there is good reason to involve stakeholders with knowledge of and connections to different social groups.

Conclusion

We have argued that that public engagement in health policy can be justified as a means of advancing democratic legitimacy, not categorically but in circumstances in which it can be plausibly shown to address a deficit in the representative policy process. Amid growing calls for public engagement in health policy making, our argument has two lessons worth emphasising. First, before implementing public engagement activities, policymakers and planners should clearly identify the particular problem or deficit they hope to address via public engagement. Is the goal to develop an understanding of what policies citizens would regard as advancing their interests and values if they had the wherewithal to carefully analyse those problems? Is the goal to build trust and collaboration between the public and officials to enable joint planning? Without some clear idea of how public engagement will enhance the legitimacy of the policy-making process, there can be no way of knowing which approach and which particular mechanisms of public engagement, if any, should be employed. The second lesson is that choosing a particular approach to public engagement involves making trade-offs. A public engagement mechanism cannot be maximally inclusive and ensure adequate opportunities for reasoned deliberation; it cannot be both carefully structured to focus on a particular set of questions and allow members of the public themselves to set the agenda. Having a clearer sense of the aims of public engagement can help policy-makers navigate these trade-offs, but it does not eliminate the need to make them.

Notes

1 Work on this chapter was completed while Matthew S. McCoy was a Caroline Miles Visiting Scholar at the Ethox Centre, University of Oxford.
2 Engineering National Academies of Sciences, *Human Genome Editing: Science, Ethics, and Governance*, 2017, 1, www.nap.edu/catalog/24623/human-genome-editing-science-ethics-and-governance.
3 National Academies of Sciences, *Human Genome Editing*.
4 Jim Kozubek, "The Public Should Have a Say in Allowing Modification of Our Germline Genetic Code," *Scientific American Blog Network*, accessed May 4, 2017, https://blogs.scientificamerican.com/guest-blog/the-public-should-have-a-say-in-allowing-modification-of-our-germline-genetic-code/.
5 Ibid.
6 Institute of Medicine and National Research Council, *Guidelines for Human Embryonic Stem Cell Research*, 2005, www.nap.edu/catalog/11278/guidelines-for-human-embryonic-stem-cell-research.
7 Julia Abelson et al., "Public Deliberation in Health Policy and Bioethics: Mapping an Emerging, Interdisciplinary Field," *Journal of Public Deliberation* 9, no. 1 (April 30, 2013).
8 A notable exception is Albert Weale, "Democratic Values, Public Consultation and Health Priorities: A Political Science Perspective," in *Equity in Health and Healthcare*, ed. Adam Oliver (London: Nuffield Trust, 2003).
9 Archon Fung, "Democratizing the Policy Process," in *The Oxford Handbook of Public Policy*, eds. Michael Moran, Martin Rein, and Robert E. Goodin (Oxford, UK: Oxford University Press, 2008).
10 Gene Rowe and Lynn J. Frewer, "A Typology of Public Engagement Mechanisms," *Science, Technology & Human Values* 30, no. 2 (April 1, 2005): 251–90.
11 We use the terms "public participation" and "public involvement" roughly interchangeably with "public engagement".
12 Rowe and Frewer, "A Typology of Public Engagement Mechanisms."
13 Center for Drug Evaluation and Research, "The Voice of the Patient: A Series of Reports from FDA's Patient-Focused Drug Development Initiative," WebContent, accessed May 13, 2017, www.fda.gov/forindustry/userfees/prescriptiondruguserfee/ucm368342.htm.
14 Presidential Commission for the Study of Bioethical Issues, "Bioethics for Every Generation: Deliberation and Education in Health, Science, and Technology," May 2016. https://bioethicsarchive.georgetown.edu/pcsbi/node/5678.html
15 Jeff Nisker et al., "Theatre as a Public Engagement Tool for Health-Policy Development," *Health Policy* 78, no. 2–3 (October 2006): 258–71.
16 Chris Degeling, Stacy M. Carter, and Lucie Rychetnik, "Which Public and Why Deliberate? – A Scoping Review of Public Deliberation in Public Health and Health Policy Research," *Social Science & Medicine* 131 (April 2015): 114–21.
17 Philip Pettit, "Varieties of Public Representation," in *Political Representation*, ed. Ian Shapiro et al. (Cambridge: Cambridge University Press, 2010).
18 Cohen, Joshua, "Deliberation and Democratic Legitimacy," in *Deliberative Democracy: Essays on Reason and Politics*, ed. James Bohman and William Rehg (Cambridge, MA: The MIT Press, 1997).
19 Pettit, "Varieties of Public Representation," 61.
20 Ibid.
21 Craig Mitton et al., "Public Participation in Health Care Priority Setting: A Scoping Review," *Health Policy* 91, no. 3 (August 2009): 219–28.
22 George Klosko, "Review Essay: Democracy and Liberty: Extending the Paradigm," *The Review of Politics* 67, no. 1 (2005): 135–52.
23 Fung, "Democratizing the Policy Process," 671.
24 Philip Pettit, *On the People's Terms: A Republican Theory and Model of Democracy* (Cambridge: Cambridge University Press, 2012).
25 Fung, "Democratizing the Policy Process."
26 Fung cites abortion and wealth redistribution as examples.
27 Craig Mitton et al., "Integrating Public Input into Healthcare Priority-Setting Decisions," *Evidence & Policy: A Journal of Research, Debate and Practice* 7, no. 3 (August 1, 2011): 327–43, doi:10.1332/174426411X591762; WHO, "Making Fair Choices on the Path to Universal Health Coverage," 2014.
28 J. Lenaghan, "Involving the Public in Rationing Decisions. The Experience of Citizens Juries," *Health Policy* 49, no. 1–2 (October 1999): 45–61.

29 Ibid, 50.

30 Ibid, 52.

31 Susan Dorr Goold et al., "Choosing Healthplans All Together: A Deliberative Exercise for Allocating Limited Health Care Resources," *Journal of Health Politics, Policy and Law* 30, no. 4 (August 2005).

32 Marion Danis et al., "Eliciting Health Insurance Benefit Choices of Low Income Groups," *Economic and Political Weekly* 42, no. 32 (August 11, 2007): 3331–9.

33 Similarly, as Lever rightly notes, deliberative forums can have educative benefits insofar as they teach participants how to deliberate effectively. But it is less clear that they serve as a mechanism for "reskilling" the broader population that does not participate. Annabelle Lever, "Democracy, Deliberation and Public Service Reform," in *The Future of Public Service Reform*, ed. Henry Kippin and Gerry Stoker (London: Bloomsbury, 2013).

34 John Parkinson, "Hearing Voices: Negotiating Representation Claims in Public Deliberation," *The British Journal of Politics & International Relations* 6, no. 3 (August 1, 2004): 370–88; Weale, "Democratic Values, Public Consultation and Health Priorities: A Political Science Perspective."

35 Presidential Commission for the Study of Bioethical Issues, "Bioethics for Every Generation: Deliberation and Education in Health, Science, and Technology." 2016.

36 Jessica Estepa, "Poll: Majority of Americans Want to Keep Obamacare," *USA TODAY*, March 7, 2017, www.usatoday.com/story/news/politics/onpolitics/2017/03/07/poll-majority-americans-want-to-keep-obamacare/98854446/.

37 Matt Flegenheimer and Thomas Kaplan, "Republicans Charge into Resistance at Tumultuous Town Halls," *The New York Times*, February 18, 2017, www.nytimes.com/2017/02/18/us/politics/town-hall-protests-obamacare.html.

38 Ruth Gaare Bernheim, "Public Engagement in Emergency Preparedness Planning and Response," in *Emergency Ethics: Public Health Preparedness and Response*, ed. Bruce Jennings et al. (Oxford, New York: Oxford University Press, 2016).

39 Thomas Kaplan, "Angry Town Hall Meetings on Health Care Law, and Few Answers," *The New York Times*, February 13, 2017, www.nytimes.com/2017/02/13/us/politics/affordable-care-act-sensenbrenner-republicans.html.

40 Gaare Bernheim, "Public Engagement in Emergency Preparedness Planning and Response," 172.

41 Ibid., 173.

42 Ibid.

43 Institute of Medicine, *Guidance for Establishing Crisis Standards of Care for Use in Disaster Situations: A Letter Report*, 2009, www.nap.edu/catalog/12749/guidance-for-establishing-crisis-standards-of-care-for-use-in-disaster-situations; "Crisis Standards of Care: A Systems Framework for Catastrophic Disaster Response" (Institute of Medicine, March 21, 2012), www.nationalacademies.org/hmd/Reports/2012/Crisis-Standards-of-Care-A-Systems-Framework-for-Catastrophic-Disaster-Response.aspx.

44 Gaare Bernheim, "Public Engagement in Emergency Preparedness Planning and Response."

45 Ibid.

46 Institute of Medicine, *Engaging the Public in Critical Disaster Planning and Decision Making: Workshop Summary*, 2013, www.nap.edu/catalog/18396/engaging-the-public-in-critical-disaster-planning-and-decision-making.

30

THE ETHICS OF DEATH POLICIES

Søren Holm

Introduction

Modern states formulate policies in a range of areas that directly or indirectly determine which of the citizens[1] of the state will die, and under what circumstances deaths caused by the state, its agencies, or its citizens are legitimate and justified. Let us call such policies 'death policies'.

Some death policies are direct. Rules of engagement in war, policy on capital punishment, policy on police or citizen use of lethal force, and policy on euthanasia are direct death policies. They determine in which situations it is legally legitimate to kill another human being directly.

Most death policies are, however, indirect. They do not specify when or whom the state or citizens can kill directly, but they do instead indirectly determine who will die and who will live. Many resource allocation policies are indirect death policies because the allocation of resources also allocates risks of accidents, illness, effective help, and ultimately death between different groups of citizens. Many environmental and zoning policies allocate risks of environmental exposures or susceptibility to disaster in a similar way and are also indirect death policies. Indirect death policies are often not conceptualised as death policies, partly because they allocate death implicitly and indirectly, partly because the 'victims' of the policies are often difficult to identify and therefore not as salient as identifiable victims. The loss of a 'statistical life' does not have the same impact as the loss of someone with a name and a face.

This chapter will analyse the specific ethical issues raised by death policies. It will first analyse the general question of whether death should be given particular weight in policy-making, and then analyse two case studies of current death policies in health care (1) resource allocation as a typical example of an indirect death policy, and (2) policy on assistance in dying as an example of a mixed policy with both direct and indirect effects. In the analyses it will be assumed that the policy-making takes place within a democratic society where policy processes must, at least to some extent, take account of the interests and perceptions of citizens. The analyses do not assume a perfect democracy but just a reasonably well-functioning democracy.

The reason for choosing case studies from health care is primarily pragmatic. The policies in this area are public and reasonably transparent, and the causal link between the policies and death is relatively clear and can be explicated without resorting to complex models. The results of the analysis are, however, likely to be transferable to other areas of policy-making since the issues and considerations are perfectly general. Trade-offs between lowering the risk of death and achieving other policy objectives occur in areas such as traffic policy, environmental protection, zoning policy and building regulations, and public health policy, and many others.

Does death matter?

A basic assumption in distinguishing between death policies and other policies is that there is something distinctive about death – that death is not just one among many other benefits and costs. Seen from the point of view of orthodox economic theory this assumption does not make much sense. There are many techniques for putting a monetary value on life, or on life years, and although the estimates generated for the monetary value of a life saved or lost differ widely between different contexts and different estimation techniques (Doucouliagos et al. 2014; Mrozek and Taylor 2002; Viscusi and Aldy 2003), a value can be generated and put into the formula for calculating the cost/benefit ratio of a particular policy or policy proposal. Seen from this perspective there are no in principle difficulties in comparing policies that have death as one of the outcomes with other policies. It may be difficult in practice – for example, because it is difficult to agree on the correct monetary value of a life or of life years – but it is not difficult in principle.

However, seen from the point of view of moral theory death has some peculiar features. Death is not compensatable ex-post, and it falls within the class of irreversible harms. In the following we will analyse both of these features.

It is usually possible to compensate people for their losses, and the central economic tool of potential Pareto optimality relies on compensation being possible. In order for us to consider whether a particular social change is Pareto-optimal is has to be possible for the winners (those who benefit from the change) to compensate the losers (those who experience a loss as a result of the change). If compensation is not possible in principle the Pareto optimality framework cannot be applied (Pareto 1971).

Some believe that each life has an infinite value and that that in itself completely precludes compensation for loss of life. For those who hold that view, the economic evaluation of and choice between outcomes that involve death will always be deeply problematic.[2] Some have drawn the conclusion that when choosing between two actions the number of lives saved/deaths caused by each does not matter (Taurek 1977), whereas others have disputed this strongly and even labelled it 'innumerate ethics' (Parfit 1978; Kamm 1985). This debate, which often involves more and more contrived trolley cases to elicit less and less reliable intuitions, is still ongoing (Kamm 2015; Rakowski 1994). Although trolley problems are of great interest to philosophers, they are problematic as a guide to public policy because they abstract away or bracket many of the contextual factors that are relevant to the public policy-maker who most often has to make decisions not about what track the runaway trolley should be directed onto when it has started rolling but about the design of the trolley system and the amount of money to be spent on automatic emergency brake systems.

However, a problem still occurs for those who think that compensation is possible because either (1) the value of a life is not infinite and can be estimated, or (2) even though there is no way to compare the value of lives objectively from a third-party perspective, each person can legitimately put a value on his or her own life. The problem is that although this gives us a way of providing just compensation to a person ex ante – that is, prior to his or her death – we cannot compensate people ex-post because they can derive no benefit from the compensation.

We can see this in a typical trolley example, where I as the conductor of the trolley choose to kill you to save five other people (Thomson 1976). These five other people who have been saved are good people and want the situation ex-post to be not only potentially Pareto-optimal but also actually Pareto-optimal, so they decide that they have to compensate you for the loss of your life. They calculate the amount necessary to provide full compensation using the best current estimates of the value of a life, and pay the money to . . . Who should they pay the money to, to effect full compensation? They can't pay the money to you, since you are no longer here, which means that you are no longer able to benefit from any monetary transfer.[3] They could pay the money to your family, but that would not compensate you, the person who is dead. The five good people who survived when the trolley was redirected might of course decide that your family should also be compensated to achieve full, actual Pareto optimality, but that would be a compensation for their loss, not for yours.

This problem is the flip side of the much more discussed problem of whether it is possible to harm the dead. This problem has, for instance, been discussed in relation to consent for post mortem organ donation, or genetic research using material from people who are long dead (Holm 2001; Masterton et al. 2010; Spital and Taylor 2007). If we accept the argument that it is not possible to harm the dead because they have no interests that can be harmed or choices that can be frustrated, then we also have to accept that it is not possible to benefit them either, and therefore not possible to compensate them for their death.

So, in cases where we cannot identify who will die long enough in advance to offer them compensation while they are alive, we cannot even in theory compensate for death.

A slightly less special feature of the harm caused by death is that it belongs to the class of harms that are irreversible. Some harms are fully reversible both in principle and in practice – for example, simple pecuniary losses – some can be partly reversed or remediated but still leave a residue or remnant of harm, and some are irreversible – once you have harmed the person the harm cannot be undone. A harm that is irreversible can still be compensatable – for example, I may have caused you to have a small scar but may still be able to compensate for this by paying you a finite sum of money, but as we saw earlier death is compensatable only ex ante, not ex-post. In the policy context we may have at least two reasons to treat policies distributing irreversible harms differently from policies distributing reversible harms only. The first reason is that if we later find that our policy was problematic in some way – for instance, because it did not produce the benefits it was predicted to produce – we cannot undo the harm we have caused to some citizens. The second is that a policy causing irreversible harm leaves an indelible mark that persists, even if the policy turns out to be effective.

There is also another peculiarity about death which is worth noting. Every human being dies once, and only once.[4] Being resuscitated is not really being brought back from death; it is just the process leading to death being reversed before death has irreversibly occurred. The 'once, and only once' then has the interesting implication that talking about interventions or policies saving lives is potentially quite misleading. Persons can have their lives saved a potentially infinite number of times, until succumbing to the condition or event that actually kills them. Think, for instance, of a situation where you are paralysed from the neck down, with no spontaneous respiratory effort and completely ventilator-dependent. How many times does the ventilator treatment save your life? Only once, or with every single breath it produces?[5] 'Once' is a tempting answer, but let's imagine that the tracheal tube becomes dislodged and you become unconscious before someone notices the problem and repositions the tube. Has your life been saved for a second time or has it not? The quite complex questions of the proper analysis and ascription of causality in these examples are beyond the scope of this chapter (but see von Wright 1971 on causal ascription). Suffice it to say that it is not obvious that it would be absurd to claim that your life is saved 12 times every minute – each time the machine inflates your lungs – by the ventilator. This casts doubt on the value in counting instances of life saving, or conversely instances of death. Perhaps what is really at stake is not life saving but death postponement.

It is finally obvious that death has particular public salience. A road traffic accident which leads to death is much more newsworthy than one that leads 'only' to severe injury, and the media pay much closer attention to the number of soldiers and civilians killed in a particular conflict than they do to the number severely injured. These are examples of violent deaths, and it is probably true that violent deaths have some extra salience because of the drama introduced by the violence component. But even non-violent deaths seem to be more salient than other catastrophic events that happen to people. If we take media attention as a proxy for public salience it is evident that crises, events, and normal conditions in low-income countries get much more attention when deaths can be attributed to them than when they cause just immense suffering (Joye 2009). Public salience is not in itself a good reason to pursue any particular policy, but it does give the policy-maker a perfectly understandable reason to attend to the issue that the public finds interesting and important.

Death and other injuries

There is an unresolved debate in the literature concerning whether death as an injury is *sui generis* or whether it is commensurable with other injuries. Can we weigh death against other injuries? On one side of the debate stand philosophers mostly supporting some form of consequentialism and on the other side philosophers who for the most part align themselves with some form of deontology, although they are joined by some consequentialists with non-standard valuations of life (Harris 1985, 1988). Both sides have some stock idealised cases designed to elicit moral intuitions that lend support to their argument. Those who argue that death is incommensurable with other types of injuries will, for instance, ask us to consider whether alleviating a large number of mild headaches could ever outweigh causing one death. And those who argue for commensurability may ask us to consider whether relieving the extreme suffering of a large number of people is not worth causing just one death.

It is difficult to see how this debate can be resolved despite the very considerable amount of philosophical energy that has been expended on it.

The only certainties that have emerged from this debate are the following. First, that commensurability is important to consequentialist theory. It is probably possible to design a functioning consequentialist theory without commensurability, but much easier to design one if commensurability can be assumed. Second, that commensurability is not strictly incompatible with deontological theories, but that many deontological theorists dislike the idea. And third, that at the level of non-theoretical intuitions most people seem to operate with some kind of triviality threshold – that is, the idea that there are instances of genuine injury and suffering that should be ignored when considering causing or allowing death, simply because even though they are genuine instances the amount of injury and suffering is so small that it is something we all have to bear (and therefore incommensurate with unbearable injuries and sufferings). The three frameworks mentioned do not come close to exhausting the field of moral theories and frameworks, but they are the three within which discussions of commensurability have had most prominence. A Sartrean existentialist or an (Neo-)Aristotelean virtue theorist will, if asked, provide an analysis of commensurability, but it is not an issue that arises as prominently and centrally within their theoretical frameworks as it does for consequentialists and deontologists.

Resource allocation as an indirect death policy

We can imagine health care systems where explicit resource allocation decisions are not necessary. In a system where there is no third-party payment – that is, no state provision, no health insurance, and no organised charity – and where all health care is paid for directly by the recipients of that care there is no need for explicit resource allocation within the system. There will be an allocation of financial resources in society and that allocation will directly determine access to health care. Each person will have to make decisions about how to allocate his or her own resources between health care and other areas of expenditure, but there will be no allocation decisions made within the system.

We can also imagine a system with third-party payment and no need for resource allocation. If the available resources are sufficient to meet all legitimate claims for health care there is no need for resource allocation,[6] since all persons/patients can get all the health care they need.

Resource allocation is, however, necessary in a health care system with third-party payment if the available resources are insufficient to meet all legitimate claims. This disparity between resources and legitimate claims is a feature of all presently existing health care systems, and this entails that they all incorporate implicit or explicit procedures for resource allocation.

A common form of explicit resource allocation in health care is allocation by precise indication – that is, making access to an intervention I conditional on fulfilling a set of criteria C1–Cn that will usually include a specific diagnosis, a specific stage of the disease, a specific general health state, and so forth. The criteria are set so that the group of patients delineated by the criteria includes some but not all of those who could derive net health benefit from being provided with I. Such a resource allocation is a type of rationing, refusing some patients access to beneficial treatment. This is, for instance, the type of recommendation that the English National Institute for Health and Care Excellence (NICE) usually provides when it approves a new expensive treatment for use in the National Health Service, and the approach used by many US health maintenance organizations when issuing guidance to their providers on choice of treatment. The process for setting such criteria has been the object of sustained theoretical and practical attention and a full account of this debate is beyond the scope of this chapter. However, it is possible to discern a division between two fundamentally different ideas about what the process should aim to achieve and how it should be configured (Holm 1998). On the one hand we have philosophers and health care economists who advocate for an algorithmic process. We define a goal for the health care system, we develop instruments to measure whether the goal has been achieved, and we allocate resources to maximise goal achievement. The criteria are thus, at least in principle, decided through an algorithmic process where the only value-laden decision is the decision about the goal of the health care system. The most prominent example of this approach is the idea that resource allocation in health care should be driven by the goal of maximising the number of quality adjusted life years (QALY) produced by the system (Williams 1996).[7] On the other hand we have philosophers and social scientists who argue that such an algorithmic process is (a) not implementable in practice, and (b) not desirable since our health care system has many potentially conflicting goals and the questions about justice in health care allocation cannot be reduced to goal maximisation. What we should do is therefore to devise resource allocation processes that allow all stakeholders to influence the decision in an open and transparent way and reach a decision on criteria which is legitimated by the process. The most prominent example of this approach is the Accountability for Reasonableness framework (Daniels and Sabin 1998, 2008).

The reason for allocating resources in this way is most commonly stated as being either (1) that it maximises the amount of health or welfare produced given the resource constraints – for instance, by maximising the number of quality adjusted life years gained, (2) that it reflects a socially acceptable cost/utility threshold – that is, that those who are excluded from receiving the intervention would be too costly to treat relative to the health benefit they would get, (3) that it reflects a socially acceptable minimum threshold of benefit – that is, that those who are excluded from receiving the intervention would not receive sufficient benefit to cross the benefit threshold, or (4) some combination of 1–3 (see, e.g., NICE 2008). All three options for justification of a resource allocation involve implicit or explicit value judgements. As discussed earlier deciding on a goal for the health care system involves a value judgement, as does deciding whether a cost/utility threshold or a minimal benefit threshold is 'socially acceptable'.

If a resource allocation excludes people from receiving interventions that are life-saving/life-prolonging then the resource allocation is an indirect death policy. It indirectly decides which of the citizens of the state should die (and when) and which should live.

This is perhaps easiest to see if we think about a very high-level resource allocation decision. In a country with many remote and sparsely populated islands there is presumably a minimum number of inhabitants on any given island that is necessary to justify the health care system employing a resident health care professional on that island. A decision-maker could plausibly justify a policy stating that only islands with a population > 200 will get a resident nurse and only islands with a population > 500 will also get a resident doctor.[8] Unless our hypothetical country has extremely favourable weather conditions so that fast medical evacuations are always possible from all islands, the reasonable and on the face of it justifiable policy decision about the allocation of health care professionals is then a death policy. Some people on some islands who could have been saved if their island had had a resident health care professional or if they lived in a big city on the mainland will die because they do not receive the care they need in time, and they would counterfactually have survived if the policy had allocated a health care professional to their island.

There are many very similar actual examples from health care planning. Decisions about which vaccines to offer in the standard childhood vaccination program involve balancing costs against lives saved and illness averted, as do decisions about acceptable response times for ambulances, the target number of patients for each general practitioner, and the number of intensive care beds to be built for a given population.

Perhaps even more common are decisions to restrict access to particular very expensive life-saving/life-extending drugs to the group of patients who will get the largest benefits from the drug. This type of allocation policy follows almost automatically when policies are decided on the basis of cost-utility or cost-benefit calculations. Costs will usually be relatively fixed and unrelated to individual benefits.[9] Among the excluded patients in the penumbra of the group that fulfils the criteria there will often be patients who are either (1) equally likely to benefit, but not to the same extent – for example, who will not get six months of life extension but only three, or (2) less likely to benefit, but still with some non-negligible likelihood.

Although this is not the stated aim of the policy, it does indirectly lead to a situation where some people die earlier than they would otherwise have done, and some might not have died at all from the specific condition if they had been treated, making the policy an indirect death policy.

Are such indirect death policies justifiable? Let us assume for the sake of argument that explicit resource allocation policies within a health care system are justifiable. That is, that if all legitimate claims cannot be met within the available resources then it is justifiable to have policies that exclude some people from benefits to which they have a prior, legitimate claim. And let us further assume that one part of the justifiability relies on such policies being consistent with requirements of justice. This gives rise to two specific questions for indirect death policies: (1) can indirect death policies ever be justified, and (2) if indirect death policies can be justified should they be treated differently than resource allocation policies that involve only the allocation of suffering and/or disability, but not death?

It seems intuitively plausible that resource allocation involving the indirect allocation of death should be justifiable, because if it is not we implicitly commit ourselves to use all of our health care resources on life saving and life extension. There will always be a possible life saving or life extension that we can spend our available resources on, and those who 'merely' suffer would never get a look in.

More theoretically we can also see that such policies must be in principle justifiable, since we would need to allocate our resources even in a health care system exclusively focused on life saving and life extension. If not all can be saved we need a procedure to decide who should be saved. We may of course choose a procedure where expected benefit or cost-benefit plays no role – for example, random allocation between legitimate claims – but such an allocation policy would still be an allocation policy and thereby an indirect death policy.[10]

This entails that we are forced to consider the second question – that is, whether indirect death allocation policies should be treated differently than other allocation policies. Is death as an outcome so much more important than suffering or disability that we should give higher priority to life saving and life extension than to the alleviation of suffering or the prevention or cure of disabling conditions?

We have earlier discussed the common 'triviality' intuition that some suffering is so small that it should not count when weighed against even a single death, but the question here is not about trivial levels of suffering. The question is whether life saving and life extension should be given higher priority when balanced against significant, non-trivial suffering.

Let us first note that many individuals are willing personally to trade off life time against other valuable things, including the alleviation of suffering. We should not draw too much from this fact, since many of the situations where people make such choices are tragic situations where there is no good outcome to be had. The choice is between outcomes that are all, seen from the point of the chooser, bad outcomes. But nevertheless, the existence of these personal trade-offs shows that there are many people who do not believe that life extension is lexically ranked above the alleviation of suffering, for them. A similar kind of trade-off occurs when persons choose assistance in dying as preferable to continued suffering. However, allocation policies that are indirect death policies are almost always not exclusively about the allocation of death and suffering within lives but about the allocation of death and suffering between persons, and it is not obvious that a personal willingness to trade off within your own life is equivalent to an acceptance of a public trade-off between lives.

This, unfortunately, seems to bring us back to the unresolved general philosophical problem about commensurability between death and other injuries discussed earlier. If death and other injuries are fundamentally incommensurable there can be no principle-based interpersonal trade-offs between them. If, however, we assume commensurability the question of the weight to be given to death and to suffering in allocation decisions remains an important question. Here the facts that death is irreversible and uncompensatable ex-post may provide some reason to give some extra weight to death as a negative outcome of policy, compared to injury and suffering which may be irreversible but are in principle compensatable.

Assistance in dying as a direct death policy

More and more jurisdictions are now explicitly legalising some form of assisted dying. These include the Netherlands, Belgium, Luxembourg, Switzerland, Colombia, Canada, and the US states of Vermont, Montana, Washington State, Oregon, and California. Usually what is legalised is some form of physician-assisted dying, either physician-assisted suicide or physician-performed voluntary euthanasia or both. The in principle legalisation of these practices is often combined with criteria for exactly who can legitimately be provided with assistance in dying. These policies are direct death policies given the definition provided in the introduction, as is of course the complete prohibition of these practices that existed earlier, or a possible complete liberalisation allowing for assisted suicide on demand. The policies directly decide under what circumstances, if any, someone can legally assist or cause the dying of another person.

But assistance-in-dying policies are also at the same time indirect death policies. This feature of the policies is perhaps more philosophically interesting. By making certain options in dying legally available they change the choice architecture and 'incentive structure' for everyone who either knows that they are dying or who wants to die. An enforced legal prohibition of assistance in dying creates a strong disincentive to seek such assistance, it limits the opportunities for finding assistance, and it may even mean that people never contemplate assisted dying as a realistic option open to them. If that is true then lifting the prohibition will lead to many more people actively contemplating assisted dying and some of them choosing it as their preferred choice for how they want to die. Some of these will fall within the specific legal criteria in a particular jurisdiction and will be able to access assistance, whereas others will fall outside of the criteria. There is, however, a problem in discussing the indirect effects of a legalisation of assisted dying and that is that the empirical evidence base is at the same time limited and contested, and that the interpretation of the available data often seems to depend very much on the initial views of the person interpreting them (Holm 2015; Rodgers et al. 2016).

The move from complete prohibition of assistance in dying to legalisation based on specific criteria raises two issues, one related to the direct effect and one related to the indirect effect.

In relation to the direct effect we can always ask whether the chosen policy correctly identifies the cases where assistance in dying is justifiable. There are essentially two main justifications for allowing assistance in dying: (1) respect for self-determination, and (2) relief of suffering. In the classical case of a patient with irremediable suffering who wants to die the two sources of justification work together. But they may also come apart – for instance, in cases where there is suffering, but a loss of decision-making capacity, and in cases where there is a strong desire to die, but no suffering (except, perhaps, the suffering caused by the frustration of the desire). In so far as any given policy depends on both justifications for the setting of criteria for access to assistance in dying it is thereby inherently unstable. For any given restrictive criterion based on the need for a certain level of self-determination there is always an open question along the lines of 'this criterion unfairly discriminates against those who have a justified claim based on suffering', and vice versa if the criterion restricts according to suffering by requiring some particular degree or kind of suffering. Any policy, except complete prohibition, must resolve this tension. We cannot have a policy based exclusively on considerations of suffering, since that would entail assisting those who passed the suffering threshold but who did not want assistance. A policy based exclusively on self-determination – that is, where it is exclusively the expressed desire to die that matters for the decision to allow assistance – is possible, but not completely unproblematic. There seems to be something strange about a completely isolated wish or desire to die – that is, a wish or desire that is not linked either to the person's current state of being or to what the person thinks will happen after death. Someone who when asked, 'Why do you want to die?' would answer only, 'Because I do' and would not provide any further reasons or justifications would come across as distinctly odd. This oddness might not in itself be a reason to prohibit assistance, but it could be a reason for not obliging any person or profession to provide the assistance. Any policy giving weight to self-determination will also have to solve the problem of deciding a threshold for the level of decisional competence/capacity at which the expressed wish to die should be taken as valid and acted upon.

In relation to the indirect effects we can ask whether, given that the option is available, some people will choose to ask for assistance in dying because they feel that they have to. Or to put the point differently will there be people who have a strong preference for continued life who nevertheless choose to ask for assistance in dying, not because they suffer but because the choice architecture and incentive structure they face make assistance in dying the rational choice?[11] And if there will be such people, should we worry about it? John Harris argues that we should not worry. In a recent short article he writes in his usual forthright style,

> Many objectors to medically-assisted death emphasise their concern to protect the vulnerable. I yield to none in my concern for the vulnerable. But there are two groups of vulnerable people to whom we owe concern, respect and protection. *One consists of those who might be pressured into requesting death.* The others are those, like Tony Nicklinson, who are cruelly denied the death they seek. We are surely not entitled to abandon one group of vulnerable people in favour of another. We have somehow to protect both.
>
> *Those who might be encouraged to die are and remain free to refuse. They are not victims unless they make themselves victims.* Those seeking assisted death are the more vulnerable because they are truly coerced, absolutely prevented from obtaining the remedy they seek. They seek death and are denied it: these are genuinely coerced and are certainly the victims of tyranny.
>
> *(Harris 2015, pp. 141–2, my emphasis)*

The argument here seems to be that if a person is pressured into requesting death this is a minor ethical problem because he or she is not "truly" or "genuinely coerced", and where genuine coercion seems to be implicitly defined as legal and/or physical coercion only. This seems a rather strange argument to make for a philosopher who among his first papers counts one entitled 'The Marxist Conception of Violence' (Harris 1974). The Marxist analysis of the violence that workers suffer at the hand of the bourgeoisie makes the exact point that it is better for each worker, and therefore the rational choice of each worker, to agree to work in exploitative conditions. But the analysis also leads to the rather obvious point that this does not mean that each worker is not exploited or not a victim of the capitalist system. The worker is in a social position where he is coerced to accept an offer to work on unjust terms. He may choose which factory owner to work for, but he does not have the effective power to choose not to work.

Or to return to the question of assistance in dying, let us imagine an old and frail widower who is told by his children that they will no longer visit or support him because he is a drain on the family resources and depriving his children and grandchildren of their just inheritance, and that he furthermore has a moral duty to die. It is of course true that this person is free to refuse, even if his family has been waging this campaign for several months. But he is free to choose only in the sense that he is not being legally or physically coerced. His family is exerting plenty of social and emotional coercive power, and if he finally caves in and asks for assistance in dying it borders on disrespect to say that he has made himself a victim. He is a victim whose vulnerabilities were ruthlessly exploited by his family and he was truly and genuinely coerced.

And, following from the Marxist conception of violence, and the more general principle that states can be responsible for harm caused by both commission and omission, an assisted dying policy that did not contain protections for people coerced into asking for assisted dying would be ethically deficient. If such a deficient policy was implemented anyone coerced into asking for assisted dying, while not actually wanting to die, would be just as much a victim of tyranny as those who cannot have assistance when they genuinely need and want it. Harris is therefore exactly right when he states that in formulating an assisted dying policy, 'We have somehow to protect both'! Designing such protection is not straightforward since it would have to protect without obstructing the access to assistance for those whose desire to die is non-coerced.

A more remote indirect effect arises in relation to the specific legalisation of assistance in dying in the form of euthanasia – that is, where some other person, most often a medical doctor, actively kills the person receiving assistance. It has been suggested in the literature that a moral duty to die arises in certain circumstances – for instance, a patient may have a duty to die if life-prolonging expensive medical treatment will leave the family of the patient destitute (Hardwig 1997). More recently Cohen has suggested that obligations to die are not strictly duties but instances of forced supererogation – that is, moral actions that you ought to do, but where you are not blameworthy if you do not act on the ought (Cohen 2015).[12] In a context where euthanasia is effectively prohibited the only way to discharge such a duty is by suicide, and you would not have a duty to be killed, on the 'ought implies can' principle. You cannot have a duty to be killed if you cannot find someone who can and will kill you. However, as soon as euthanasia is legalised it generates a duty to be killed for anyone who has a duty to die.

Conclusion

The formulation and evaluation of death policies raise questions that actualise fundamental disagreements between different ethical theories and fundamental issues in political philosophy. For some there is nothing special about death – it is just the last event that occurs in a person's life, although in many cases not the last thing that happens in the narrative account of that life. For others death is a special event, completely unlike other events that occur in a person's life. The public decision-maker has to navigate between these two incompatible conceptualisations of death and its importance. This, in practice, requires more than a sound grasp of ethical and political theories. It requires practical wisdom and an understanding that thinking about death policies purely in terms of numbers of statistical lives lost or gained is problematic. Death policies allocate death between real people with real lives.

Notes

1 Citizen is used throughout the chapter as a shorthand for 'someone affected by the policy' and may include citizens, residents, and/or aliens.
2 Except perhaps when two policy proposals both entail the same number of predicted deaths. However, when analysing policy alternatives under the assumption that life has infinite value we have to keep in mind that mathematically $\infty \times n = \infty$ for all positive values of n. This means that it could be argued that the number of deaths becomes irrelevant, since already one death leads to an infinite loss, and this loss does not increase for larger numbers of deaths.
3 We might note in passing that within certain religious frameworks compensation would be possible. In a Catholic context the five good people could, for instance, pay for perpetual prayers to be said for the soul of the departed, which would help it by shortening its time in purgatory and thus provide a benefit to the dead person.
4 This is what makes any instance of true 'resurrection from the dead' at the same time implausible and astonishing.
5 This is not a purely theoretical issue, as exemplified in the heading of a BBC news story about recurring cardiac arrests and resuscitation: "Wednesbury Man Who 'Died' 27 Times Praises Hospital Staff" (BBC 2017).

6 Delineating the class of 'legitimate claims for health care' is beyond the scope of this chapter.
7 In a very similar way the WHO measures health system and public health performance in terms of disability adjusted life years (DALY) lost.
8 The numbers are plucked out of thin air and merely intended to illustrate that it is plausible that there are a number of island inhabitants below which a state would be justified in not providing resident health care.
9 Many pharmaceutical products are priced according to 'value-based pricing', and there will therefore often be a relation between costs and average benefit, because the firm marketing the drug wants to extract the maximum price that the health care system in question is willing to pay for a given benefit (Sussex et al. 2013). But although the average benefit is an aggregate measure of individual benefits, the price for the treatment of any given individual is not directly related to the benefit that accrues to that specific individual.
10 Random allocation of benefits is rare as an explicit policy, but random allocation of punishment has historically been used in a few instances, such as 'decimation' – that is, the execution of every tenth man when a whole military unit had deserted on the battle ground or refused to obey orders (see Duxbury 2002 for an in-depth exploration of decimation and other positive and negative applications of randomness in law).
11 This is not a slippery slope–type argument but a simple result of the fact that the legalisation of assisted dying will, in itself, change what is the rational thing to do in certain situations. One of the intended effects of a legal prohibition of a particular kind of act is precisely to change the pay-off from performing the act, making it less rational to choose the act.
12 It is beyond the scope of this chapter to explore whether there actually is a 'duty to die'.

References

BBC. Wednesbury man who 'died' 27 times praises hospital staff. 18 February 2017 www.bbc.co.uk/news/uk-england-birmingham-39015109
Cohen, Shlomo. (2015). "Forced supererogation." *European Journal of Philosophy* 23, no. 4: 1006–1024.
Daniels, Norman, and James Sabin. (1998). "The ethics of accountability in managed care reform." *Health Affairs* 17, no. 5: 50–64.
Daniels, Norman, and James E. Sabin. (2008). *Setting limits fairly: Learning to share resources for health*. New York: Oxford University Press.
Doucouliagos, Hristos, T. D. Stanley, and W. Kip Viscusi. (2014). "Publication selection and the income elasticity of the value of a statistical life." *Journal of Health Economics* 33: 67–75.
Duxbury, Neil. (2002). *Random justice: On lotteries and legal decision-making*. Oxford: Oxford University.
Hardwig, John. (1997). "Is there a duty to die?" *Hastings Center Report* 27, no. 2: 34–42.
Harris, John. (1974). "The Marxist conception of violence." *Philosophy & Public Affairs*, pp. 192–220.
Harris, John. (1985). *The value of life: An introduction to medical ethics*. New York: Routledge.
Harris, John. (1988). "More and better justice." *Royal Institute of Philosophy Supplements* 23: 75–96.
Harris, John. (2015). *Cancelling our captivity*. In: Colin Brewer & Michael Irwin (eds.). *'I'll See Myself Out, Thank You' – Thirty personal views in support of assisted suicide*. Newbould on Stour: Skyscraper Publications, pp. 139–144.
Holm, Søren. (1998). "Goodbye to the simple solutions: The second phase of priority setting in health care." *British Medical Journal* 317: 1000–1001.
Holm, Søren. (2001). "The privacy of Tutankhamen – utilising the genetic information in stored tissue samples." *Theoretical Medicine and Bioethics* 22, no. 5: 437–449.
Holm, Søren. (2015). "The debate about physician assistance in dying: 40 years of unrivalled progress in medical ethics?" *Journal of Medical Ethics* 41, no. 1: 40–43.
Joye, Stijn. (2009). "The hierarchy of global suffering: A critical discourse analysis of television news reporting on foreign natural disasters." *Journal of International Communication* 15, no. 2: 45–61.
Kamm, Frances Myrna. (1985). "Equal treatment and equal chances." *Philosophy & Public Affairs* 177–194.
Kamm, Frances Myrna. (2015). *The trolley problem mysteries*. Oxford: Oxford University Press.
Masterton, Malin, Mats G. Hansson, and Anna T. Höglund. (2010). "In search of the missing subject: Narrative identity and posthumous wronging." *Studies in History and Philosophy of Science Part C: Studies in History and Philosophy of Biological and Biomedical Sciences* 41, no. 4: 340–346.

Mrozek, Janusz R., and Laura O. Taylor. (2002). "What determines the value of life? A meta-analysis." *Journal of Policy Analysis and Management* 21, no. 2: 253–270.

National Institute for Health and Care Excellence (NICE). Social Value Judgements – Principles for the development of Nice Guidance (2. Ed.). National Institute for Health and Care Excellence, 2008. www.nice.org.uk/Media/Default/About/what-we-do/Research-and-development/Social-Value-Judgements-principles-for-the-development-of-NICE-guidance.pdf

Pareto, Vilfredo. (1971). *Manual of political economy*. London: Palgrave Macmillan.

Parfit, Derek. (1978). "Innumerate ethics." *Philosophy & Public Affairs* 285–301.

Rakowski, Eric. (1994). "The aggregation problem." *Hastings Center Report* 24, no. 4: 33–36.

Rodgers, Mark, Alison Booth, Gill Norman, and Amanda Sowden. (2016). "Research priorities relating to the debate on assisted dying: what do we still need to know? Results of a modified Delphi technique." *BMJ Open* 6, no. 6: e012213.

Spital, Aaron, and James Stacey Taylor. (2007). "Routine recovery of cadaveric organs for transplantation: Consistent, fair, and life-saving." *Clinical Journal of the American Society of Nephrology* 2, no. 2: 300–303.

Sussex, Jon, Adrian Towse, and Nancy Devlin. (2013). "Operationalizing value-based pricing of medicines." *Pharmacoeconomics* 31, no. 1: 1–10.

Taurek, John M. (1977). "Should the numbers count?" *Philosophy & Public Affairs* 293–316.

Thomson, Judith Jarvis. (1976). "Killing, letting die, and the trolley problem." *The Monist* 59, no. 2: 204–217.

Viscusi, W. Kip, and Joseph E. Aldy. (2003). "The value of a statistical life: A critical review of market estimates throughout the world." *Journal of risk and uncertainty* 27, no. 1: 5–76.

Williams, Alan. (1996). "QALYs and ethics: A health economist's perspective." *Social Science & Medicine* 43, no. 12: 1795–1804.

Von Wright, Georg Henrik. (1971). *Explanation and understanding*. Ithaca, NY: Cornell University Press.

PART IV

Public policy, diversity, and sustainability

31

THE ETHICS OF FAMILY REUNIFICATION

Iseult Honohan

The ethics of immigration

Are states justified in exercising controls on entry and residence – or in discriminating among would-be entrants? For some, democratic political communities are thought to have the right to determine admission and membership on a variety of grounds that include: protecting communitarian identity (Walzer 1983), respecting freedom of association (Wellman 2008), preserving a common public culture (Miller 2005), recognising associative ownership of public institutions (Pevnick 2011), and protecting from costs of jurisdictional responsibility (Blake 2013). For others, principles of freedom, equality, democracy, or human rights imply, if not complete freedom of movement across borders, strong constraints on state controls over those borders (Carens 2013; Cole 2000; Abizadeh 2008; Oberman 2016). There is thus no agreement about what liberal or democratic principles imply for the right of political communities to exclude (Cole and Wellman 2011).

In the practical world of public policy, it is largely taken for granted that states have rights to control entry and residence. Even if it is accepted that democratic political communities can limit the numbers of those who enter, we can still ask whether states have complete discretion or should favour certain kinds of applicants over others. Thus it is widely thought unacceptable to select on the basis of race, ethnicity, or religion.[1] But certain categories of migrants are acknowledged to have particularly strong claims, and this is reflected in international law. In addition to refugees, these include family members of citizens (and, to varying degrees, of resident immigrants). For this chapter I assume a general right of states to control borders, without which the issue of priority for families in admission would not arise. The second section outlines current trends in family migration policies. The third section reviews recent debates on the nature and value of the family. The fourth section analyses arguments for family reunification and outlines an alternative view. The fifth section addresses some objections concerning integration, costs to others, and feasibility. The final section concludes.

Family migration today

In practice, family reunification constitutes a substantial though controversial and declining element of migration. In member countries of the Organisation for Economic Co-operation and

Development (OECD), this constituted 30 per cent of all migration in 2015, declining from 40 per cent in 2008 (OECD 2016, 18). A higher level has been sustained in the US, which has more inclusive policies for citizens and some provision for permanent residents. While the majority of sponsors are men, women (mostly spouses) constitute two-thirds of all family migration, and children and other dependents account for most of the remainder.

Family reunification is supported by international conventions that include the right to family life, embodied in many written documents. Thus articles 12 and 16 of the Universal Declaration of Human Rights declare the right to found a family and to respect for one's family life, and article 8 of the European Convention on Human Rights lays down an obligation for states to respect the family life of all individuals present in their territory, be they nationals or aliens. Yet these do not constitute a right to family reunification as such (although the latter has been interpreted as including a right to family migration by the European Court of Human Rights).

The high proportion of family migration, rather than reflecting universally generous family admission, is a result of increasing constraints on other avenues for migration. Indeed policies display a tension between recognising families and the aims of many states to limit the numbers entailed. Thus provisions vary greatly across countries, and apply differently between citizens and immigrants and among categories of immigrants. The European Union grants mobility rights to the families of citizens, and in 2003 adopted a directive on the Right to Family Reunification for third-country nationals (Directive 2003/86/EC). A UN Convention on Protection of Rights of all Migrant Workers and Members of Their Family was ratified in 2003 (though without being ratified by any net immigration country).[2]

With the increasing politicisation of migration in the twenty-first century, family reunification policies in receiving countries have, along with economic migration and refugee policies, been subject to considerable change. Along with some expansion to include same-sex marriage and civil partnerships in some countries and across the EU, conditions for entry on family grounds have tended to become more restrictive in the OECD overall, particularly in European states. Increasingly entry is limited to the nuclear family, consisting of spouses and minor children, although some countries include dependent ascending relatives and even adult siblings. Even for nuclear families, admission has become more conditional, often including long prior residence periods, high minimum age, income and employment requirements for resident migrants and even citizens, additional requirements and restrictions for spouses and children who are entering, and low age limits for dependent children. In particular a number of countries have stringent pre-entry language and cultural integration tests for joining family members, and only some take steps to support their preparation or to foster the process of integration for family members after entry (Strik et al. 2013). High income requirements in particular make it more difficult for women, who constitute an increasing proportion of initial migration but have lower average earnings, to be joined by their spouses and children. In contrast, schemes for immigrants with particularly valued skills or capital to invest often guarantee immediate family entry.

Such policy developments reflect less a reduced respect for family life so much as increased concerns about the numbers, economic contribution or costs, and social and political integration of family migrants. Although the empirical evidence of the impact of family migrants, as of immigrants in general, is highly contested, many states want to limit numbers when demographic, economic, environmental, political, and social factors are seen to lead to increasing demand for entry to wealthy countries. More important than numbers is the perceived character of migration. In policy debates, family migration is characterised as economically inefficient, favouring those who are less skilled, and leading to an increasing burden on public resources. Thus it has been argued that more migration should be based on skill-points schemes (Macedo

2007). In addition, the effect of family reunification policies on integration and social cohesion, formerly seen as positive, has come to be seen more negatively (Bonjour and Kraler 2015).

So, according to one comparative assessment, MIPEX 2015, which provides indicators on migration policy, in 2015 only about half of the 38 countries included had policies on family reunification for migrants that ranked as 'slightly favourable' or 'favourable' to migrant family reunification (MIPEX 2015).[3]

The ethics of the family

The assessment of priority for family admissions should first be set in the context of recent debates about the value of the family and its status in society. As a legal relationship based on marriage or genetic descent, state recognition of the family has been subject to increasing criticism. In the first place the traditional basis of the family in heterosexual monogamous marriage has been increasingly questioned; in response, marriage has come to be interpreted more expansively to include same-sex unions, and some of the status formerly associated with it is now granted to partners with or without formal marriage or civil partnership. In addition, the centrality of marriage to the family (when bearing and rearing children no longer closely track marriage) has been queried. Finally, independently of issues about marriage, it is also questioned what (if anything) is special about the family, and whether the state should recognise families or a wider range of relationships, or simply treat all equally as individuals.

Two prominent lines of approach are relevant here. The first argues for removing or reforming the status of marriage; the second debates the nature and value of the family independently of marriage.

The first approach criticises the legally established status of marriage as treating other relationships (whether different- or same-sex, or of friendship) unequally (Brake 2012).[4] One argument suggests that marriage should have no privileged legal status, and that features currently associated with it, such as cohabitation, joint property-owning, and parenting, should be disaggregated and recognised separately where appropriate (Chambers 2013). Others propose redefining the relevant relationships more broadly, to include, for example, any non-dependent caring relationships between adults without restrictions on sex, gender, number of parties, amatory relationship, or rights exchanged, in a status of 'minimal marriage' with a variable set of commitments (Brake 2012, 156). Still others have emphasised the significance of affectionate care (with or without material caregiving) or a particular personal concern for the well-being of partners (Metz 2010).

A second line of approach aims to locate the value of the family in parental care, rather than in relationships between independent adults, whether romantic, sexual, or broader caregiving (Archard 2010; Gheaus 2012; Brennan and Cameron 2016).

However families are defined, favouring them may be open to the criticism of privileging certain kinds of relationships over others. Families may be seen to reinforce social inequality through the transmission of privilege, by not only transfers of wealth or provision of private education but also other kinds of advantages that parents can convey. In assessing legitimate and illegitimate family partiality Brighouse and Swift (2014) articulate one of the most considered accounts of what may be essential and valuable in family life. They argue that children, who are vulnerable and dependent, have a fundamental interest in growing up with continuous material and affective care by at least one parent figure in order to become well-adjusted and autonomous adults. (They define parents as those in an established relationship of care rather than in biological terms.) In addition to care and love children need parental authority. The proper exercise of both requires continuity and an overriding interest in the good of the child.

But, as well as a responsibility, parents may be seen as having an interest in exercising authority in a relationship of fiduciary care with their children.[5]

Thus they argue that there are certain distinctive 'familial goods' intrinsic to family relationships, valuable in themselves and important in developing and sustaining democratic citizens. These can be distinguished conceptually from those aspects of parenting that confer unjustified advantage.

Despite differences in emphases, these arguments on family can all be seen as highlighting the centrality to human development and flourishing of continuing caring relationships with different levels and kinds of dependence. They provide reasons for refocusing the concept of the family away from legal contract or genetic descent towards continuing intimate relationships of care involving personal attachment (whether more broadly, or more specifically as parental relationships with children) and seeing these as having intrinsic value, and a precondition of minimum characteristics of democratic citizenship.[6]

We should note here that conceiving of 'family' in terms of responsibility for personal care (with or without the provision of material care) shifts our understanding of these relationships from being primarily voluntary or a matter of individual interest solely of the carers. Such relationships and their commitments are at least in part involuntary (with the partial exception of spouses or romantic partners). Parents may or may not choose to have children, but they do not normally choose the children that they parent; children do not choose their parents.

But once established, the relationship and its responsibilities are experienced strongly in the context of (inter-) dependency of different kinds – material and psychological. Thus these relationships involve assuming responsibilities as well as exercising privileges. 'Care-giving is Janus-faced. While care-giving can be burdensome (a responsibility to be discharged), it can also be among our most meaningful and rewarding work (a right to be exercised)' (Kittay 2009, 69; Scheffler 2001). The particular attachment involved in care in this sense is well expressed by Eva Kittay as 'attending to those interests of another that the person in need of care cannot reasonably be expected to satisfy on his or her own, and to attend to these interests for the sake of the one in need of care' (Kittay 2009, 70). In other words, it is not just care *for* but also care *about* the person for his/her own sake that is involved (Darwall 2002, 13). This implies a low degree of substitutability in such relationships.

In addition, while Brighouse and Swift focus on parental care in childhood, it may be argued that the relevant relationships are epitomised in spouses and may extend across a lifetime. Even if certain kinds of care are latent at some points, they become salient at times of heightened dependency, when a person may find themselves the primary person responsible for care of a partner, elderly parents, or grandchildren. As the locus of relatively permanent or durable relations and concern that presumptively extend across a lifetime, the family is distinct from friendships and other collaborative partnerships, which, though they may sometimes rise to this level of personal commitment, represent a wide spectrum, and cannot all be understood in this way.

So we may see the value of the family as based in a fundamental human interest in establishing and living in intimate relationships of affection and support – that is, *giving and receiving* care potentially across a lifetime, and especially in those parts of our lives that involve necessary dependency, including childhood and old age. If there is a right to family life – it is to discharge the special obligations that arise in these particular relations, where the exact obligations will vary with relationships, circumstances, and need.

Family reunification in migration

The diverse approaches outlined earlier are partially reflected in recent philosophical debates about family reunification preference in immigration. It has been argued that there is no basis for preferring families over other close relationships, and that such preference violates liberal neutrality by favouring one conception of the good life over others. But family migration has also been justified on the liberal basis of freedom of association. Finally, it has been argued that it is the particular kind of relationship of care between family members that warrants giving them preference in admission.

Matthew Lister argues that the principle of freedom of association provides a strong justification for family reunification. This challenges arguments that justify sovereign rights of self-governing communities to control admission on precisely this basis (Wellman 2008). Lister argues that, if accepted, the principle applies most forcefully to intimate relationships, as essential to the development of an individual's sense of autonomy and sense of justice and an interest of all citizens of a liberal society (Lister 2010, 721–3). He sees the family as the most intimate of associations, which extended living together is intrinsic to sustaining – unlike other relationships, where temporary visits may be adequate (Lister 2010, 736). For Lister, the family's freedom of association rights override any claims of the state, a large, anonymous organisation, which, moreover, being primarily involuntary, does not qualify as an association for the purpose of freedom of association. If someone is excluded from the state, they may not easily find an alternative, which restricts the legitimate powers of the state (or democratic majorities) to exclude, compared with smaller private associations (Lister 2010, 733–4). Thus, he concludes, states must allow family reunification if they are not to violate the fundamental rights of their citizens. Freedom of association at the state level cannot justify limiting family entry, even though this means allowing some significant level of immigration (Lister 2010, 735). This does not include other kinds of relationships that could be accommodated on the basis of temporary visits.

But it has been argued that this account does not specify clearly enough what counts as a family or intimate relations (Yong 2016; Ferracioli 2016). Lister suggests there is a core common understanding of a family as (two) parents and their dependent children. Beyond this, he declares that states will have different conceptions of family and how extended this may be, which is subject to democratic deliberation (Lister 2010, 743). But, as Yong points out, even within a society there will be different accounts of the scope of family concern; leaving this to be defined democratically does not establish the solid liberal basis for family priority that Lister's initial argument suggests (Yong 2016, 69–70).

More broadly, it may be that freedom of association itself – to the extent that it implies voluntary association – does not capture the kinds of family relationships that entail responsibilities of care, which, as noted earlier, are to some extent experienced as involuntary.

In contrast to Lister, Luara Ferracioli argues that there is nothing unique about romantic or familial relationships to allow a liberal state to give them priority in migration over other kinds of relationships, and doing so would violate liberal neutrality by privileging a particular perfectionist conception of the good (Ferracioli 2016, 2). While primarily identifying a dilemma for those liberals who accept both states' rights to control admissions and the priority of family members, she sets out strong objections to priority for family reunification. A liberal society that privileges families is seen as disrespecting other kinds of close relationships. Certain kinds of friendship and artistic collaboration, for example, may be more intimate or caring and have a stronger claim to live together than some instantiations of family relationships (e.g., of long separated siblings, or estranged spouses). As much as family, these enduring and valued relationships give meaning to the participants' lives, and are not easily substitutable – thus they equally require living in proximity (Ferracioli 2016, 23).

This account identifies the importance of particular personal relationships, but does not capture the elements of dependence and responsibility for care (personal or material) that distinguish relationships whose maintenance requires close proximity over an extended period from, for example, artistic collaborations, where temporary visits may be sufficient. If instead we recognise 'family' as based in partly involuntarily acquired responsibilities of dependency and care, this differentiates them from other relationships, and justifies their particular need to live together.

Moreover, to avoid allowing subjective attachments of citizens from imposing costs on others, Ferracioli inserts a proviso that the broader relationships in question be socially valued. Yong again points out that, in the likely absence of agreement across society on which relationships are to be so valued, this undermines the basis of the justification offered (Yong 2016, 66–7).

Yong comes closer to the account of family relationships as involving distinctive goods that I am outlining here. He seeks to articulate a more precise understanding of the substance of relationships that warrant admission by distinguishing intimacy of form, characteristic of many relationships involving regular face-to-face contact, from intimacy of content, limited to relationships where intimacy is the primary goal of the association (Yong 2016, 70). For Yong, it is the most significant relationships, characterised by both kinds of intimacy, as family relationships that involve material and personal care that need continuing proximity and particularly warrant admission. This gives no priority to marriage or biological descent as such, but to dependent-carer relationships through periods of exceptional dependency, as quintessentially in childhood, where (following Brighouse and Swift) Yong sees a child as needing care from an adult committed to his or her well-being and development through a sense of personal attachment. This applies also in cases of adult dependents, if maintaining the person's care at a threshold of a minimally good life would otherwise be jeopardised, even if material care could be otherwise provided, since a context of personal attachment may be central to the provision of care. These needs are so fundamental that entry for the dependent in an established relationship with a citizen or permanent resident is a matter of human rights (Yong 2016, 74). Yong suggests further that intimate relationships between relatively independent adults may also be essential to their full development of personal autonomy and sense of justice such that, on a different basis, as a matter of justice *within* society – what citizens owe to fellow citizens – they also should be admitted (Yong 2016, 77). While Yong's argument recognises the centrality of established relationships of dependence and care, it does not emphasise the distinctively enduring nature of the relationships and their responsibilities.

Yong sees his account as expansive insofar as it requires that 'all non-citizen independent adults joined in intimate caring relationship with a receiving state's citizens and residents be granted preferential immigration eligibility' (Yong 2016, 79), but restrictive in so far as it does not favour marriage or any biological relations per se. Consistent with this being only contingently a defence of family migration schemes, Yong acknowledges that it does not apply to a child with whom a caring relationship has not yet been established (Yong 2016, 82). It can also be argued that it does not support the admission of a partner for marriage with whom the citizen has not yet established any direct relationship.

We may note that there is underlying disagreement among these authors on the nature of the claim for admission – whether it is based on justice within a society or a matter of human rights. For Lister and Ferracioli the warranted claim is as one of a citizen who wishes to be joined by family, on the ground of reciprocity among citizens.[7] In contrast, for Yong, there are two different kinds of reasons to admit – human rights or global justice in the case of the dependent non-citizen who enters, as well as social or domestic justice based on reciprocity among citizens for the person who wishes to be joined by an independent intimate partner.[8]

But a state can be considered to have a *prima facie* universalist obligation to admit family members in order to allow those who are subject to its authority on a continuing basis to pursue family life and the agent-specific obligations of care to one another that are entailed without giving such priority to citizen claims. The claim to family reunification applies to citizens and to long-term resident non-citizens alike, as in both cases their opportunity to pursue family life is fundamentally determined by the provisions of the state. But it does apply differently to those claiming from 'inside' the country and those claiming from 'outside' the country: the 'outsider' has a claim to live with his or her family but not so clearly that this should be in *this* country. The 'insider' who claims to be joined, however, should not have to suffer unreasonable costs by having to leave simply in order to live with his or her family (in cases where this is even a possibility). The latter's claim, however, is not a stronger claim of a citizen, but applies to all persons who are subject on a continuous basis to the jurisdiction of the state (Benton 2014).

This supports reunification for family members in intrinsically caring relationships of particular kinds of intimacy and dependency – this may be primarily of spouses and parents with minor children, but will also include, for example, elderly parents who receive care from adult children, or who give care to minor grandchildren. These should be admitted without significant costs, waiting times, or other conditions that risk undermining these relationships. It will in principle exclude independent adult siblings and more extended family members. But it also provides some basis for considering claims of other family members in individual cases of need for care.

Objections

A number of objections to prioritising family migration, especially on this reconceived version, should be considered: its impact on integration and on others with competing claims, and its feasibility as a basis for policy.[9]

a. Integration

Social cohesion and the integration of immigrants are central issues in early twenty-first-century politics, and family migration has been central to these debates. Social integration may be considered a prerequisite for a sustainable liberal democracy, where citizens see themselves as sharing in common a society, economy, and polity. Democracy is weakened when society is deeply unequal or divided among hostile social groups, or when some feel alienated from it. But 'integration' is a rather broad and fuzzy concept, particularly as it is used in political contexts. While concern for integration initially addressed the provision of economic opportunities and acceptance of migrants by the host society as much as the obligations of migrants, from the late 1990s concerns about social cohesion, cultural identity, social order, and security led to political demands for policies aimed at ensuring greater integration of migrants into society, focusing more on the problems of migrant diversity than the other dimensions, and addressing this by requiring competence and practices of migrants in social and political life (Entzinger 2014; Wievorka 2014).

There are contrasting views on the impact of family migration on integration. On the one hand states – and the European Union in particular – have supported family reunification as a 'vehicle to integration', through increasing stability and social connections in migrants' lives. Thus it may encourage male migrants to re-skill, and the participation of children in schools may provide a link to social networks. But there has also been evidence – for example, in Germany – that language and cognitive skills of children with immigrant mothers fall behind their peers, and that family migrants have lower rates of employment than other categories of migrant. (For an overview, see Bonjour and Kraler 2015.)

This evidence emerges, however, in a context where existing policies may contribute to difficulties in integration, for example, in long waiting periods for reunification and in application processes that can have a negative impact even if families are ultimately admitted. Integration is increasingly expected before families come, with pre-entry tests of language and cultural integration (in 2016 in Austria, France, Germany, Denmark, Netherlands, and the UK; of these, only Germany provided funded courses abroad).[10] Indeed such requirements have been criticised as a matter more of controlling entry than of fostering integration (Kostakopoulou and Ripoll Servent 2016). Similarly support to assist integration after families arrive is varied in terms of paid language courses, access to the labour market, and other aspects.

With this in mind, it can be said that the empirical evidence on the impact of family migration on integration is inconclusive (Bonjour and Kraler 2015, 1423).

In any case, if family unity is important for the development and flourishing of citizens as has been suggested here, moreover, it is a very stringent requirement, and implies that the focus of policy should be on fostering family integration rather than limiting family entry.

b. Costs to other migrants and to citizens

Even if family claims are substantial, how do they compare with those of other migrants, including refugees and those seeking to improve their economic condition? If states are entitled to limit immigrant numbers, it can be argued that the more family migrants there are, the fewer refugees may be admitted (Gibney 2004). Refugees have been widely agreed to have a particularly strong claim since they otherwise lack fundamental state protection. While Matthew Gibney has argued that broader family claims should be seen as less urgent (Gibney 2004, 243), Yong suggests that dependent family members have a claim that ranks equally with that of refugees (Yong 2016, 81).

Is it possible to compare the claims of refugees and family migrants? It may be that we can acknowledge the strength of each of the claims of family members and refugees, without there being any easy way of ranking them.[11]

On the one hand, it may be argued that meeting the needs of refugees is more urgent and represents an absolute claim. But this is primarily a claim to securing protection, not necessarily to entry and residence in a particular state. If refugees can be protected only by admitting them, then they should take priority. But there are extensive debates as to how refugees are best to be protected – by admission by the state at whose borders they first arrive, or by a system of shared responsibility among states, with quotas based on wealth, capacity to accommodate, and other factors, by supporting states near to the refugees' origins in accommodating them, or by addressing the root cause of their rights violation and displacement. Likewise it is often argued that many economic migrants would be better served if global poverty were addressed through more international development and greater justice in international trade than by migration. Yet, in the absence of any settled agreement or policy reforms in these areas, and with rising pressure caused by climate change and other factors, admission to wealthier states may continue to appear the most immediate route for refugees and economic migrants alike to secure improvement in their position, and states should be seen as having responsibilities of different levels of stringency to refugees and economic migrants.

Nonetheless, in the case of family migrants (as relatively narrowly defined here), it seems much clearer in principle that admission is the appropriate response: it is clearer that coming to live in this country with a family member is the primary need, and it is therefore clearer which state has the duty to admit. These claims may also be relatively urgent, insofar as delays of years undermine the relationship of spouses and the possibility of parenting and being parented.

In any case, the account of family reunification outlined here, based not on marriage or genetic descent but on existing relationships of care, supports less inclusive policies than currently make family reunification such a large proportion of migration in the US, for example, where adult siblings of citizens are given a high level of priority. While not defined in terms of the nuclear family, this account provides more clearly for the reunification of spouses and of minor children with parents, or of adults with dependent adults, ascending or descending, than more extended family connections. It may be noted also that the arguments outlined here also seem not to provide a strong basis for what is classed as 'family formation' – entry at or before marriage, at least in cases where no relationship already exists. There may be independent grounds for allowing migration in such cases but it seems less easy to justify on these grounds.[12]

It may also be argued that family migration should not place excessive costs on other members of the receiving society. Thus, for Lister, while family claims overcome state rights to exclude, it may nonetheless be reasonable to require citizens to guarantee economic support for their entering family members.[13] This implies that reunification constitutes primarily a benefit to the family member and primarily a cost to the rest of society. While any entrant imposes certain costs on society (e.g., of jurisdiction; Blake 2013), the economic cost-contribution balance of migrants is a contested issue.[14] Looking specifically at family migration (and apart from the contested lower immediate economic contribution to the labour market), joining family members may be seen as making other social contributions, and by absorbing costs that could otherwise fall to society – in terms of domestic care, and the material and psychological physical support of their family members, especially in the case of spouses and ascending relatives, where grandparents may play a significant part in the upbringing of children.

Finally, it should be borne in mind that recognising families in migration policy does not always involve setting family reunification candidates *against* refugees, economic migrants, and others. Family relationships and their recognition arise within these categories too, and, while given more or less consideration in current immigration policies, are currently subject to significant similar pressures (on refugees, see ELENA 2016). The argument in this chapter is, therefore, relevant also to their claims.[15]

c. Criteria for implementing policies

There remains a challenge in translating this understanding of the family into criteria that can be applied to policy. In the absence of the clear dividing line provided by traditionally documented legal statuses, can these ideas of intimate care-based family relationships provide a basis for determining claims to admission?

There is a tension between the increasingly flexible and pluralist social understanding of family and states' interest in clear (and generally narrower) criteria. Marriage and genetic descent have the apparent advantage of being clearly documented. But even in current migration regimes, where marriage 'becomes a door opener and springboard for those wishing to reach the First World' (Beck Gersheim 2011), certificates alone are not taken to constitute evidence of a genuine marriage, so that, on the one hand, additional proof of the continuity and reality of the relationship is often required for entry, and, on the other, some countries recognise more informal partnerships. As Ferracioli and Yong agree, similar evidence of a continuing relationship could be sought in the case of other relationships. It is possible to envisage this being done with no greater levels of intrusion or incentive to fraud than current provisions – for example, through evidence of the custody of a child, or undertaking joint commitments and shared lives between partners (Ferracioli 2016, 19–20; Yong 2016, 80). This may be possible to extend on a case-by-case basis to other family members in care-dependent relationships. Thus Australia has a specific visa status for family members caring for a relative, wider than regular family reunification categories. Key family relations constitute an identifiable category, albeit one that may be fuzzy around the edges (Lindauer forthcoming).

Conclusion

The value of family relationships in the sense outlined here and their fundamental role in personal development and flourishing of democratic citizens provide good reasons for democratic states to allow families to live together. This is not a duty owed to fellow citizens but a duty to those who are in continuing subjection to political authority of the state.

Even if democratic states are considered to have the right to control admissions, the admission of family members (thus reconceived) is justified as supporting the intrinsic value of family life, understood in terms of continuing intimate relationships with responsibilities of care with particular others, rather than biological or legal relationships, or other kinds of relatively intimate relationships. Those in the position of parents have an interest in and a particular responsibility to care for their children when young, and there are distinct but comparable interests and responsibilities of care among adults in long-term committed relationships that imply a clear and fundamental interest in living together, as a necessary condition for realising many of the intrinsic and non-substitutable goods of family life.

This entails a different definition of family members with a claim to entry than those currently applied in either the US or Europe, for example. Rather than doubting the significance of the family or the strength of the claim to unity, in a democratic society this should be granted equally to all long-term residents who are under continuing subjection to the authority of the state. This is required both for equal treatment and to foster the development of personal and political autonomy of democratic citizens.

Even if it is naïve to expect that states will admit all who count as family members in this view, the importance of such relationships suggests that states, who acknowledge the importance of family in increasingly granting family reunification rights to skilled workers, investors, and other categories of preferred immigrants, have a duty to recognise the claims of all those under their jurisdiction with respect to family admission, rather than implementing stratified regimes that are inclusive for some but increasingly restrictive and conditional for many.

Notes

1 But see Fine (2016) on the persistence of these grounds in migration policies.
2 For details of provisions by country for each category of family migrant, see OECD (2016) Annexe 4.A.4. In the EU policies still differentiate between mobile EU citizens, EU citizens in their state of origin, third-country nationals (non-EU citizens), and refugees, constituting what has been described as a tiered system of egalitarian communitarianism for EU citizens, but restrictive collectivism for non-EU citizens (Kostakopoulou and Ripoll Servent 2016). See also Block (2015). The 2003 EU Directive does not apply in Denmark, Ireland, or the United Kingdom, although they are subject to European Court judgements on family migration rights of EU citizens and their non-EU family members. The trend is towards more restriction, as a central part of RAISE legislation proposed to reduce immigration in the US in August 2017 focuses on narrowing the definition of family (Gellat 2017), as does an initial draft of the migration regime envisaged in the United Kingdom after Brexit (Guardian 2017).
3 These are the two highest points on a six-point scale measuring policy favourability to family migration on the combined dimensions of: persons eligible, conditions for admission, security of status, and associated rights.
4 Another line of criticism addresses problems of freedom and inequality of participants within marriage, which is set aside in this discussion. (See further Brake 2012; Chambers 2013; and Gheaus this volume.)

5 This does not, for most of the authors cited, entail any general right to become or be a parent.
6 Families can be seen as central to moral education that develops autonomy, reciprocity, and responsibility essential to democratic citizenship.
7 While Ferracioli sees reunification as justified principally on grounds of reciprocity, she accepts that there could be a human rights claim in the specific case of a child in an existing relationship to join a parent, given that society already recognises state support for parental childcare (Ferracioli 2016, 28).
8 Note that none of these accounts relies on an analogy between family and ethnic relationships as a basis for preference.
9 The interpretation and significance of each of these issues depend partly on the contested questions of whether (a) the level of migration that can be accommodated is a fixed quantity and (b) this level is exceeded by the numbers of those currently seeking to enter. These questions cannot be addressed within the scope of this chapter.
10 See Bech et al. (2017) for policy variation among Scandinavian countries.
11 See Honohan (2009) for more detailed discussion.
12 For a human rights argument for migration that includes rights to migrate in order to form romantic relationships, see Oberman (2016).
13 Lister accepts, for example, the US requirement of 125 per cent of poverty level, evidence of financial support, and limits to state benefits for entrants (Lister 2010, 739).
14 Another contested issue is the effect on low-paid members of the existing community, but it may be argued that this refers to low-skills migration, not to family migration per se, so will not be addressed here.
15 A question needing further consideration is whether family policies should vary between categories of migrants – whether refugee family admission should be more inclusive, as, for example, extended families of refugees from persecution are often subsequently targeted.

Bibliography

Abizadeh, A. (2008). 'Democratic Theory and Border Coercion: No Right to Unilaterally Control Your Own Borders', *Political Theory*, 36 (1), 37–65.
Archard, D. (2010). *A Liberal Defence of the Family*. Basingstoke: Palgrave Macmillan.
Bech, E., Borevi, K. and Mouritsen, P. (2017). 'A "Civic Turn" in Scandinavian Family Migration Policies? Comparing Denmark, Norway and Sweden', *Comparative Migration Studies*, 5 (9), doi.org/10.1186/s40878-017-0052-4
Beck Gersheim, E. (2011). 'Migration and Marriage: Examples of Border Artistry and Cultures of Migration?' *Nordic Journal of Migration Research* 2 (1), 60–68.
Benton, M. (2014). 'The Problem of Denizenship: A Non-Domination Framework', *Critical Review of International Social and Political Philosophy*, 17 (1), 49–69.
Blake, M. (2013). 'Immigration, Jurisdiction, and Exclusion', *Philosophy and Public Affairs*, 41, 103–130.
Block, L. (2015). 'Regulating Membership: Explaining Restriction and Stratification of Family Migration in Europe', *Journal of Family Issues*, 36 (11), 1433–1452.
Bonjour, S. and Kraler, A. (2015). 'Introduction: Family Migration as an Integration Issue? Policy Perspectives and Academic Insights', *Journal of Family Issues*, 36 (11), 1407–1432.
Brake, E. (2012). *Minimizing Marriage: Marriage, Morality, and the Law*. Oxford: Oxford University Press.
Brake, E. (ed.). (2016). *After Marriage*. Oxford: Oxford University Press.
Brennan, S. and Cameron, B. (2016). 'Is Marriage Bad for Children? Rethinking the Connection Between Having Children, Romantic Love, and Marriage', in E. Brake (ed.), *After Marriage*. Oxford: Oxford University Press.
Brighouse, H. and Swift, A. (2014). *Family Values: The Ethics of Parent-Child Relationships*. Princeton, NJ: Princeton University Press.
Carens, J. (2013). *The Ethics of Immigration*. Cambridge: Cambridge University Press.
Chambers, C. (2013). 'The Marriage-Free State', *Proceedings of the Aristotelian Society*, 113 (2), 123–143.
Cole, P. (2000). *Philosophies of Exclusion*. Edinburgh: Edinburgh University Press.
Cole, P. and Wellman, C. (2011). *Debating the Ethics of Immigration: Is There a Right to Exclude?* Oxford: Oxford University Press.
Darwall, S. (2002). *Welfare and Rational Care*. Princeton, NJ: Princeton University Press.
Entzinger, H. (2014). 'The Growing Gap Between Facts and Discourse on Immigrant Integration in the Netherlands', *Identities: Global Studies in Culture and Power*, 21 (6), 693–707.

European Legal Network on Asylum (ELENA). (2016). *An Information Note on Family Reunification for Beneficiaries of International Protection in Europe*. Brussels: European Council on Refugees and Exlies (ECRE). Available at www.ecre.org/wp-content/uploads/2016/06/Family-Reunification-note_ ECRE_June-2016.pdf [last accessed 19 March 2017].

Ferracioli, L. (2016). 'Family Migration Schemes and Liberal Neutrality: A Dilemma', *Journal of Moral Philosophy*, 13 (5), 553–557.

Fine, S. (2010). 'Freedom of Association Is Not the Answer', *Ethics*, 120 (2), 338–356.

Fine, S. (2016). 'Immigration and Discrimination', in S. Fine and L. Ypi (eds.), *Migration in Political Theory: The Ethics of Movement and Membership*. Oxford: Oxford University Press.

Gellat, J. (2017). 'The RAISE Act: Dramatic Change to Family Immigration, Less so for the Employment-Based System'. Available at www.migrationpolicy.org/news/raise-act-dramatic-change-family-immigration-less-so-employment-based-system [last accessed 6 September 2017].

Gheaus, A. (2012). 'Is the Family Uniquely Valuable?' *Ethics and Social Welfare*, 6 (2), 102–131.

Gibney, M. (2004). *The Ethics and Politics of Asylum*. Cambridge: Cambridge University Press.

Guardian. (2017). 'Post-Brexit Immigration: 10 Key Points from the Home Office Document'. Available at www.theguardian.com/uk-news/ng-interactive/2017/sep/05/post-brexit-immigration-10-key-points-from-the-home-office-document [last accessed 6 September 2017].

Honohan, I. (2009). 'Rethinking the Claim to Family Reunification in Migration', *Political Studies*, 57 (4), 765–787.

Kittay, E. (2009). 'The Moral Harm of Migrant Care Work: Realising a Global Right to Care', *Philosophical Topics*, 37 (1), 53–73.

Kostakopoulou, D. and Ripoll-Servent, A. (2016). 'The Rule of Life: Family Reunification in EU Mobility and Migration Laws', in M. Fletcher, E. Herlin-Karnell and C. Matera (eds.), *The European Union as an Area of Freedom, Security and Justice*. Abingdon: Routledge, 246–262.

Lindauer, M. (forthcoming) 'In Defense of a Category-Based System', *Journal of Moral Philosophy*.

Lister, M. (2010). 'Immigration, Association and the Family', *Law and Philosophy*, 29 (x), 719–745.

Macedo, S. (2007). 'The Moral Dilemma of U.S. Immigration Policy', in C. Swain (ed.), *Debating Immigration*. Cambridge: Cambridge University Press, 63–82.

Metz, T. (2010). *Untying the Knot: Marriage, the State, and the Case for Their Divorce*. Princeton, NJ: Princeton University Press.

Migration Policy Group. 'Indicators on Integration 2015: Family Reunion'. Available at www.mipex.eu/family-reunion [last accessed 19 March 2017].

Miller, D. (2005). 'Immigration: The Case for Limits', in A. Cohen and C. Wellman (eds.), *Contemporary Debates in Applied Ethics*. Malden, MA: Blackwell Publishing, 193–206. Available at www.migration-policy.org/news/raise-act-dramatic-change-family-immigration-less-so-employment-based-system.

Oberman, K. (2016). 'Immigration as a Human Right', in S. Fine and L. Ypi (eds.), *Migration in Political Theory: The Ethics of Movement and Membership*. Oxford: Oxford University Press, 32–56.

OECD. (2016). *International Migration Outlook 2016*. Paris: OECD Publishing. Available at http://dx.doi. org/10.1787/migr_outlook-2016-en.

Pevnick, R. (2011). *Immigration and the Constraints of Justice: Between Open Borders and Absolute Sovereignty*. Cambridge: Cambridge University Press.

Scheffler, S. (2001). *Boundaries and Allegiances*. Oxford: Oxford University Press.

Strik, T., de Hart, B. and Nissen, E. (2013). *Family Reunification: A Barrier or Facilitator of Integration? A Comparative Study*. Nijmegen: Wolf Legal Publishers. Available at https://emnbelgium.be/sites/default/files/publications/familyreunification-web.pdf [last accessed 25 February 2017].

Walzer, M. (1983). *Spheres of Justice*. New York: Basic Books.

Wellman, C. (2008). 'Immigration and Freedom of Association', *Ethics*, 119 (1), 109–141.

Wieviorka, M. (2014). 'A Critique of Integration', *Identities: Global Studies in Culture and Power*, 21 (6), 633–641.

Yong, C. (2016). 'Caring Relationships and Family Migration Schemes', in A. Sager (ed.), *The Ethics and Politics of Migration: Core Issues and Emerging Trends*. London: Rowman and Littlefield International, 61–83.

32

ARE CIVIC INTEGRATION TESTS JUSTIFIABLE?

A three-step test

Bouke de Vries

Introduction

In recent decades, many liberal democracies have made it easier for rich and highly skilled foreigners to become residents and citizens.[1] This trend has not been matched for other groups of would-be residents and would-be citizens, especially those from low GDP and non-EU countries. Not only are many members of these groups required to meet financial and/or age requirements, but also several liberal democracies nowadays require them to pass language- and civic integration tests.[2]

This chapter focuses on the latter type of test. Its aim is twofold: (1) to propose a three-step test for determining whether civic integration tests are justifiable and (2) to show that there are good grounds for doubting whether civic integration tests can pass these steps. By 'civic integration tests', I mean standardised written exams that determine whether non-citizens can gain entry, long-term residence, and/or citizenship within a given society. Such tests are meant to promote and/or provide evidence of their ability to become (long-term) members of the society or to join its political community.

To avoid confusion, it should be noted that the term 'civic integration tests' constitutes a *pars pro toto* in the following ways. First, while it might be thought that the adjective 'civic' singles out citizenship tests, the term is often construed broadly within academic and political discourses to include tests for gaining entry to a country (i.e., pre-entry tests) and for gaining long-term residence in it (i.e., permanent residence tests). In this chapter, I adopt this broader definition. This means that, in asking whether civic integration tests are justifiable, I am interested in whether it is ever morally permissible for states to make these various legal statuses *conditional* on the passing of tests. Second, not all questions that appear on civic integration tests tend to be 'civic' in the sense of being related to the (would-be) host society's politico-legal structure. While many questions asked on these tests fall into this category, especially those asked on citizenship tests,[3] questions about a country's social norms, cultural accomplishments, and/or geography are also sometimes included.

As civic integration tests have become a common feature of immigration regimes, the question of whether they are justifiable has gained political saliency. Over the past two decades, many European countries have followed the example of the US[4] by introducing citizenship tests, including Germany, the Netherlands, Denmark, the United Kingdom, Austria, Estonia, Lithuania, and Hungary.[5] In addition to this, several have introduced permanent residence tests (e.g., Austria, Denmark, Germany, the Netherlands, and the United Kingdom)[6] and pre-entry tests (e.g., Germany, the Netherlands, and Denmark).[7]

Before asking when, if ever, civic integration tests are morally justifiable, it is important to get a clearer sense of the kinds of questions that appear on these tests. This will be our next aim.

What do civic integration tests test?

Broadly five different categories of questions can be distinguished: questions about civics, geography, culture (both high and low), societal norms (both formal and informal), and the immigrant's personal beliefs and dispositions. Consider these in the order stated.

Civics

By 'civic questions', I mean questions about a country's political and judicial system, including the various rights and duties that its citizen and non-citizen residents possess. For example, on the British citizenship and permanent residence test (the 'Life in the UK Test'),[8] the following questions might appear:

'What is the judiciary responsible for?'

    A Deciding whether a person is guilty
    B Looking after a jury
    C Interpreting the law
    D Putting people in prison[9]

'What is the official report that contains everything said in Parliament called?'

    A Hansard
    B The Domesday Book
    C The Government press
    D The Government report[10]

On the German citizenship or *Einbürgerungstest*, civic questions may include the following:

'Which of the following constitutes a fundamental right [Grundrecht] in Germany?'

    A Possession of arms
    B Right to use force [Faustrecht]
    C Freedom of expression
    D The right to take justice into one's own hand [Selbstjustiz][11]

'What fundamental right does article 1 of German constitutional law [Grundgesetz] guarantee?'

    A The inviolability of human dignity
    B The right to life
    C Freedom of religion
    D Freedom of expression[12]

And on the Dutch pre-entry test, the 'Basic Civic Integration Examination Abroad' (Basisexamen inburgering in het buitenland), immigrants may be presented with two pictures and asked to identify the parliament (second chamber),[13] as well as to select the correct voting age from two options (18 or 21).[14]

Geography

Geographical questions focus on a country's rivers, lakes, mountains, and cities, and so on. For example, those applying for US citizenship test might be asked the following:

- 'Name one of the two longest rivers in the United States'.
- 'What ocean is on the West Coast of the United States?'[15]

Applicants to the Life in the UK Test may face the following question:

'Where is Loch Lomond located?'

    A Scotland
    B England
    C Northern Ireland
    D Wales[16]

And those sitting the Dutch pre-entry test may have to know the following:

'In which part of the world is the Netherlands located?'

    A Europe
    B South America[17]

Culture

Questions about a country's culture often cover both high and low (or folk) culture. An example of the former can be found in the following question from the German *Einbürgerungstest*:

'On which holiday do people in Germany wear brightly coloured costumes and masks?'

    A Rose Monday [Rosenmontag]
    B First of May [Maifeiertag]
    C Oktoberfest
    D Pentecost[18]

Or the following question from the Life from the UK Test:

'Who was the first Briton to win the Olympic gold medal in the 10,000 meters?'

    A Bradley Wiggins
    B Mo Farah
    C Sir Chris Hoy
    D David Weir[19]

For questions about high culture, one might consider the following question from the same test:

'Which play was written by Shakespeare?'

A Before the Dawn
B Come, Walk with me
C Hamlet
D Freedom of Love[20]

Or the following question from the Dutch pre-entry test:

'Who made this painting [a picture is shown of *The Night Watch*]?'

A Rembrandt van Rijn
B William of Orange[21]

Note that cultural questions need not focus exclusively on the cultures of majorities, but may also include questions about minority cultures, such as those of historical communities (e.g., Native American tribes in the US) or those of more recently settled immigrants. For example, applicants to the Life in the UK test might be asked the following:

'What celebrates the end of Ramadan?'

A Hanukkah
B Eid ul Adha
C Eid al-Fitr
D Vaisakhi[22]

And the following:

'How long does Diwali normally last for?'

A 5 days
B 8 days
C 7 days
D 3 days[23]

Norms

Questions about the norms of the (would-be) host country may cover both formal and informal norms. Examples of the former can be found in the following questions from the German *Einbürgerungstest*:

'When do the official quiet hours [gesetzliche Nachtruhe] begin in Germany?'

A When the sun sets
B At 22.00
C When the neighbours go to bed
D At midnight[24]

'A young woman wants to get her driving license. She is anxious about the exam because German is not her mother tongue. Which of the following statements is correct?'

A She must have lived at least ten years in Germany before she can do a driving test.

B It might be possible for her to do the theoretical exam in her mother tongue, as the test is offered in more than ten different languages. It is possible to choose from more than ten different languages.

C She is not allowed to have a driving license unless she speaks German.

D She must obtain her driving license in a country in which she speaks the language.[25]

Some of these questions seem addressed to would-be residents and would-be citizens with illiberal values and beliefs. Consider the following question from the same test:

'In Germany . . .'

A One is only allowed to be married to one partner at a time.

B One is allowed to have several partners simultaneously.

C One is not allowed to re-marry when one has been married before.

D A woman is not allowed to re-marry when her husband dies.[26]

Or the following question from the Dutch pre-entry test:

'Is discrimination against homosexuals legal or illegal in the Netherlands?'

A Legal

B Illegal[27]

Examples of questions about informal norms can be found in the following question from an older version of the British citizenship test:

'You spill someone's pint in the pub. What usually happens next?'

A You would offer to buy the person another pint.

B You would offer to dry their wet shirt with your own.

C You may need to prepare for a fight in the car park.[28]

Or the following question from the Dutch pre-entry test:

'Do people in the Netherlands shake each other's hand at a job interview or do they sit down straightaway?'

A They sit down straightaway.

B They shake each other's hand first.[29]

Personal beliefs and dispositions

While most of the questions that appear on civic integration tests can be subsumed under these categories, there have been cases where applicants were quizzed over their *personal* beliefs and dispositions as well. The most well-known examples of this can be found in the citizenship test of Baden-Württemberg (a German *Land*) before the federal government in Germany introduced nationwide citizenship tests. Questions on this test included the following:

Imagine that your adult son comes to you and declares that he is a homosexual and would like to live with another man. How would you react?

Your daughter applies for a job in Germany but she is rejected. Later, you discover that a
black African from Somalia got the job. How would you react?

Some people accuse the Jews of being responsible for all the evil in the world, and even state
they were behind the September 11 attacks. Do you believe in such statements?

Your adult daughter or your spouse would like to dress like other German girls and women.
Would you try to prevent this? If yes, by which means?[30]

Can civic integration tests be morally justified?

Now that we have a sense of the kinds of questions that appear on civic integration tests, we
are able to consider whether such tests are morally justifiable. In addressing this question, I will
assume that the benchmark for determining the justifiability of such tests is one where the
state simply abandons such tests rather than replaces them with more informal interviews with
immigration officers. As such interviews have greater potential for discrimination and bias (and
may be more difficult to appeal), it might well be true that civic integration tests are preferable
to this alternative.[31] However, the philosophically more interesting question here is whether
civic integration tests can be justified when they are *not* replaced with alternatives that are more
problematic from a moral point of view.

Without ruling out this possibility entirely, I will argue ahead that vindicating civic integration tests is a notoriously difficult task, one that is unlikely to be met. To show the difficulties
involved, it is necessary to explicate the costs that civic integration tests can impose on would-
be citizens and would-be residents.

The potential costs of civic integration tests

These costs can be substantial. Insofar as people are unable to pass their pre-entry or permanent
residence test, or even take these tests in the first place because they cannot afford the registration fee, they might be unable to join, or remain with, friends or family members (even if it is
possible in principle to live with their nearest and dearest in another country, there might be
significant costs to moving there). Other reasons for wanting to become a resident of, or remain
in, a country may include the fact that it has superior employment opportunities and/or cultural
or religious significance. Finally, to the extent that individuals are already residing in the country, whether as regular or irregular immigrants, they may have grown attached to their place of
residence (or the country more generally) and/or to the people living there.[32]

Things are generally better for those with permanent residence permits. However, even for
these individuals, there may be considerable costs when citizenship tests preclude them from
becoming citizens of the host country. While they are more secure in their residence status,
they do not usually enjoy the right to return to the host country that citizens possess, the right
to diplomatic protection abroad, or the right to vote and run for office in national elections
(and sometimes in local elections as well). Accordingly, when civic integration tests are an
insurmountable obstacle to naturalisation, this may not only render people vulnerable to exploitation and domination[33] but also undermine the state's democracy legitimacy by excluding
groups from the demos who have been ruled by it for an extensive period. (Though it might
be thought that the solution to these problems is to give non-citizen residents more robust
[political] rights, insofar as this does not happen, citizenship tests will continue to carry the
aforementioned costs.) Finally, in addition to conferring distinct legal entitlements, citizenship
may be important to individuals because of its symbolic significance by signalling full inclusion
within the society.

Yet it is not just the inability to pass civic integration tests that may prove costly. Even when people manage to pass their civic integration test eventually, the *delay* with which this happens may already burden them. These burdens can be social (because of delayed reunification with loved ones), financial (think of those who have to take the test multiple times), and/or psychological (the higher the costs of being denied entry, permanent residence, or citizenship, the more stressful the preparation for, and sitting of, these tests will typically be). Besides undermining their well-being, such burdens may adversely affect the autonomy of the applicants – as well as the autonomy and well-being of those close to them – by rendering it difficult for them to make long-term plans. Finally, the fact that those without (permanent) residence permits and citizenship enjoy fewer legal protections may render them especially vulnerable to domination and exploitation.

This is not to suggest that everyone, or even most applicants, will be affected by these problems. Especially when civic integration tests are cheap and easy, they might impose few costs on people (this holds true at least when people are decent enough learners). In fact, some might enjoy the process of studying for the exam and regard its completion as a symbolically valuable rite of passage. Nonetheless, insofar as it is true that state policies ought to be justifiable to the very last individual affected by them[34] – as I assume here – it seems that the significant costs that civic integration tests impose on some groups cannot be simply discounted.

A three-step test

In light of the aforementioned costs, it seems that civic integration tests will be justifiable *if and only if* the following criteria are satisfied: (1) the relevant tests should promote legitimate goals; (2) there should not be any superior alternatives to their use; and (3) their expected benefits should outweigh their costs.

As we will see ahead, there are good reasons for doubting whether civic integration tests can pass this three-step test.

Step 1: do civic integration tests promote legitimate goals?

The most obvious condition on which the justifiability of civic integration tests depends is their ability to *promote legitimate goals*. Whereas a wide variety of goals have been suggested as potentially legitimate, I will focus here on the ones that I consider the weightiest: (a) the transmission of political knowledge; (b) the transmission of knowledge of formal and informal norms; and (c) the exclusion of anti-liberal and/or anti-democratic individuals. My contention will be that all these goals are legitimate under certain conditions. However, as I go on to show, there are reasons for doubting whether civic integration tests do much to realise them, especially (c).

POLITICAL KNOWLEDGE

One reason why many people deem civic integration tests valuable is that they believe that such tests can promote the applicant's political knowledge.[35] While it might be questioned whether such tests are a very effective vehicle for transmitting political knowledge (I say more about this ahead), the ambition to transmit it seems legitimate. To see this, it should be noted that having knowledge of the political system of one's (would-be) host country and of the possibilities for political participation will typically make it easier for applicants to capitalise on their political rights, such as their rights to vote in national and/or local elections and to run for political office. This may not only render them less vulnerable to exploitation and domination but also benefit the wider society by making these individuals better equipped to share in the burden of holding those in power accountable.[36] Furthermore, by testing them over the (liberal democratic) values that undergird the political system of their (would-be) host society, this group may be more likely to take knowledge of the fundamental normative principles that they are expected to respect. (Observe that these reasons for requiring [would-be] immigrants to pass civic integration tests may similarly justify mandatory civic education classes in schools for resident and citizen children, which explains why these requirements are often defended in tandem.)[37]

In passing, it bears emphasising that it might be pertinent to transmit political knowledge not just to would-be citizens but also to would-be (permanent) residents. Though the right to participate in national elections is generally the preserve of citizens, there are some exceptions to this, such as New Zealand.[38] And even when non-citizen residents lack the right to vote or run in national elections, many countries allow them to do so in local or municipal elections (this is the case within the EU).[39] Finally, even when non-citizen residents lack political rights altogether, for them to have political knowledge can still be valuable by fostering their ability to exert political power in *informal* ways – for example, through lobbying, protesting, or organising marches.

KNOWLEDGE OF FORMAL AND INFORMAL NORMS

Another reason why civic integration tests are often valued is that they are believed to promote the applicants' knowledge of formal norms – for example, laws – and informal norms – for example, social etiquette – within the (would-be) host society. Such knowledge is valuable because it fosters people's ability to participate within the relevant society.[40] By 'participate', I mean that it becomes easier for them to engage in a range of activities. These include, but are not limited to: navigating the housing market, job market, and consumer market, partaking in voluntary associations and social movements, and interacting with members of the society on a more informal basis. Since all these activities are norm-governed, having knowledge of the formal and informal norms of the (would-be) host country can be expected to have a positive effect on people's integration. (Of course, whether civic integration tests are effective in transmitting such knowledge is another issue, to which I turn ahead.)

Promoting applicants' ability to participate within the (would-be) host society might benefit a variety of groups. Most obviously, these include the applicants themselves; not only can such participation be valuable in and of itself but also it will typically have various instrumental benefits for these individuals. Their ability to earn a decent – or more than decent – income will often hinge on their ability to participate within the (would-be) host society's economy. Furthermore, unless they have the skills and knowledge to socialise within this society, it might be difficult for them to make new friends, find partners, and/or join various voluntary associations or social movements that may enrich their lives. Another group with stakes in their successful integration consists of any (dependent) family members that they might have, who may have particularly strong interests in their socio-economic integration. Yet another group consists of existing residents and citizens, who might benefit financially from the successful integration of immigrants through the latter's contributions to the economy, socially through their love and companionship, and culturally through any valuable cultural or religious practices that these individuals might bring with them.[41]

Besides these benefits, Andrew Mason has hypothesised (building on Floyd Allport's social contact theory) that regular interaction with the native population may play an important role in fostering mutual respect and trust among different cultural, religious, and ethnic groups.[42]

414

If correct, this would benefit all members of the society, especially when it is true – as Robert Putnam has argued[43] – that immigration and ethnic diversity can have (temporary) corrosive effects on support for welfare expenditure.

A third ground on which civic integration tests have been defended is their possible role in excluding anti-liberal and/or anti-democratic individuals from membership of the society or of its political community. By 'anti-liberal and/or anti-democratic individuals', I mean those who reject basic liberal rights, such as freedom of conscience, freedom of association, and free speech and/or democratic procedures for political decision-making (while the question of exactly when someone qualifies as anti-democratic and/or anti-liberal is contested, it should be noted that there are individuals who unequivocally fall into these categories, such as jihadists and neo-Nazis). In order to exclude these groups, it might be considered useful, if not necessary, for civic integration tests to ask questions about the applicant' moral and political beliefs and dispositions, such as those included on the now replaced citizenship test of Baden-Württemberg (see the section 'What Do Civic Integration Tests Test?').

Ahead, I raise doubts about the effectiveness of using civic integration tests for such exclusionary purposes. For now, it should be noted that unlike the previous goals, the moral legitimacy of attempts to exclude anti-democratic and/or anti-liberal individuals has been called into question. Whereas some authors believe that preventing people from becoming (permanent) residents or citizens can never be a legitimate goal of civic integration tests,[44] James Hampshire has argued that it might be when necessary for maintaining a reasonably just society.[45] This view is predicated on the assumption that there are limits to the number of "bigots" and "puritanical zealots" that liberal democracies can tolerate without endangering basic rights and freedoms;[46] when the influence of these individuals becomes too strong, liberal democratic institutions will be undermined. Accordingly, insofar as civic integration tests can help to avert this outcome by excluding anti-liberal and/or anti-democratic individuals, such tests might be justifiable.

I believe this is plausible. Even if excluding these individuals is morally problematic, it seems that that the demise of liberal democracy will often constitute a greater evil, as such a demise means that at least some groups of citizens will be denied fundamental liberties. This might not only affect more individuals but also take a greater toll of their autonomy and well-being compared to the autonomy and well-being costs that those who are denied (permanent) residence or citizenship incur. Furthermore, to the extent that liberal nationalism can be vindicated (for arguments in favour see the work of David Miller[47] and Yael Tamir),[48] the interests of existing citizens would need to be given greater weight than those of non-citizens.

While the foregoing goals can be legitimate under certain conditions, then, it is often unclear, if not dubious, whether civic integration tests do much to realise these goals. This is most obvious when the tests are poorly designed, which might be due to the fact that they contain ambiguous questions; questions with false answers; questions with no unequivocally correct answer; or questions with multiple correct answers where only one is accepted. Consider two examples from the foregoing list. Whereas the desired answer to the question "in which part of the world is the Netherlands located" is "Europe", the fact that this country has overseas territories in South America suggests that option (b) should be counted correct as well. Similarly, it is debatable whether there is a single correct answer to the question of what usually happens next in a British pub after one spills someone's pint.[49]

Even when the questions are well designed and test knowledge that is relevant to the foregoing goals, however, it might be doubted whether civic integration tests will make significant contributions to the realisation of these goals. Given that most of these tests ask multiple-choice questions selected from pre-circulated lists, there is significant risk that applicants will study for them by rote.[50] This is problematic, as such studying makes it (especially) unlikely that the applicants will absorb the relevant material or retain this knowledge. Whereas asking open questions might go some way towards solving this problem, it raises several new ones. First, it increases the risk of biased assessments by requiring a greater degree of judgement on the part of the examiner. Second, it raises the costs of such tests, as assessing open questions will require more time and resources than multiple-choice questions (this is true especially when the latter can be marked by machines or computers). As far as questions about personal beliefs and dispositions are concerned, moreover, it seems easy for applicants to *pretend* that they possess the relevant liberal democratic beliefs and values. Since words will often be cheap compared to the costs of failing civic integration tests, such lies are likely to be common.

Apart from the fact that the tests might do little to inculcate political knowledge or knowledge of the (would-be) host society's formal and informal norms, failing them may mean that individuals will not acquire knowledge of these topics they would have gained otherwise. Those who are unable to pass their pre-entry exam, for example, will not gain the knowledge of the would-be host society they would have acquired had they been admitted. This is so because simply by living and participating in the society, people often learn a great deal about its political, legal, and social structures (for the same reason, individuals who are forced to leave the country because they have failed their permanent residence exam may not acquire knowledge of the society they would have attained had they been able to stay).

Finally, even were civic integration tests an effective means for excluding unreasonable would-be citizens and would-be residents, it is unclear whether their exclusion would do much to protect liberal democracy. There are at least three reasons for this. First, it seems that even when permanent residents are prevented from becoming citizens, their (conditional) right to remain gives them plenty of opportunities to act in ways that undermine their host society's liberal democratic institutions (e.g., by trying to convince other members of the society of their anti-liberal and anti-democratic views through speeches, demonstrations, and/or the distribution of written material). Second, states that seek to deny citizenship to anti-liberal and/or anti-democratic individuals might cause this group to feel alienated, which in turn may cause them to become more radical (the same might apply to groups who sympathise with these individuals). Third, by living under institutions that treat them as free and equal, some people with anti-liberal and/or anti-democratic views might become more hospitable towards liberal democracy over time. Though these mechanisms are conjectural, the fact that they are not implausible means that those who seek to justify civic integration tests on grounds that this will protect liberal democratic institutions need to address them *in addition* to facing the arduous task of showing that such tests can reliably identify anti-liberal and/or anti-democratic individuals.

Step 2: are there better alternatives to civic integration tests?

So far, I have questioned whether civic integration tests are an effective means for promoting the aforementioned goals. Even if they are, however, this is not enough for such tests to be justifiable. Given that they can impose substantial costs on individuals (see the section 'The

Potential Costs of Civic Integration Tests'), it is also necessary that there be no superior alternatives. By this, I mean that no policies could be implemented that satisfy one of the following sets of criteria:

a   All other things equal, the relevant policies realise the goals of civic integration tests more efficiently (i.e., they achieve the same results with fewer resources)

or

b   The relevant policies realise the goals of civic integration tests equally efficiently but do so in ways that better respect the autonomy and well-being of the applicants.

While there are no empirical studies on this issue, there is reason to believe that such alternatives will often exist. Here are some possible candidates:

1   When applicants are required to take integration classes already, the money spent on civic integration tests (which includes the money invested in their development and assessment, the updating of questions, and the logistics behind the test-taking) might be used to improve the quality of these classes. This could be done, for instances, by reducing the number of students per class, providing teachers with additional training, and/or purchasing better classroom materials (e.g., visual aids). During these classes, applicants might be taught not just about the (would-be) host country's political structure and formal and informal norms but also about the (liberal democratic) values that undergird its various institutions.

2   When no civic integration classes are currently offered by the state, the budget for civic integration tests might be used to provide them. Alternatively – or in addition – this money could be used to inform people about their (would-be) host society in other ways – for example, by developing educational videos that applicants need to watch as part of their application procedure. To maximise the effectiveness of these videos, states might translate them into different languages and/or tailor them to different cultural backgrounds.

3   Indeed, even when civic integration tests are replaced with *mandatory* civic integration classes, forcing people to attend such classes might still better respect their autonomy. While many (would-be) immigrants are on busy schedules, the costs of such mandatory attendance may be outweighed by the much greater costs that some of these individuals will incur when they are denied entry to the would-be host country; when they are forced to leave the host country; or when they are prevented from joining its political community. Furthermore, states could offer applicants some leeway in terms of when they attend the relevant classes.

4   Rather than denying (permanent) residence or citizenship to applicants who fail their civic integration tests, states might deny them benefits that are more respectful of their autonomy. Mason gives the example of denying those who fail their citizenship test the possibility of obtaining a full driving license (which allows people to drive on their own and to rent cars).[51] While withholding this particular benefit may be unreasonable – those in more rural areas often depend heavily on their car for mobility, as do those living in urban areas with poor public transport – there might be other benefits that respect people's autonomy better *without* significantly diminishing their willingness to study for their civic integration tests. For example, fines could be imposed on those who fail their permanent residence exam. Provided that the amounts charged are sensitive to people's ability to pay, such penalties show greater concern for people's autonomy than forcing them to leave the host country.

5   States could use (part of) the money spent on civic integration tests for increased vetting of applicants. Such vetting may be a more reliable way of finding out whether applicants have anti-liberal and/or anti-democratic beliefs and dispositions than using civic integration tests, given the ease with which test-takers can lie about their personal beliefs and dispositions (see earlier).

Step 3: do the expected benefits of civic integration tests outweigh their costs?

In the unlikely event that civic integration tests pass the previous two steps, a final hurdle must be cleared: its defenders ought to show that the expected benefits of such tests outweigh their potential costs. Here too, there are reasons to doubt that this can be done.

To vindicate this claim, let us first consider cases where it is most evident that any benefits of civic integration tests fail to outweigh the burdens they impose on would-be citizens and would-be (permanent) residents, and possibly other groups as well.

Case 1: It would be a severe injustice to require refugees (i.e., those whose human rights cannot be adequately protected within the country from which they have fled) to pass pre-entry tests, given the dire circumstances in which these individuals find themselves. For the same reasons, it would be unjust to require individuals to pass a permanent residence test when a return to their country of origin would pose a clear threat to their safety.

Case 2: It would also seem problematic to require individuals to do a permanent residence test or citizenship test when they have spent a considerable part of their childhood within the relevant country. For one thing, the fact that they have spent many of their formative years there means that they will often be well equipped to live and work within the society, especially when they have gone through its education system. For another, the fact that their lives and self-conception will typically have been shaped heavily by the society (which means that they have significant stakes in the ability to become a resident or citizen of it,[52] especially when there is no other country in which they have lived as many years), along with the fact that they cannot be held responsible for not being a resident or citizen, suggests that they have moral claims to be admitted as residents or citizens *without* having to undergo such tests.

Case 3: More controversial – but, I believe, still plausible – is the view that it is objectionable to require those with very strong and enduring emotional ties to existing citizens or permanent residents to pass a pre-entry or permanent residence test. Such individuals might include spouses, children, and non-relatives with whom people are in close and persistent non-amorous relationships. Besides the fact that the physical and emotional well-being of this group might be bound up with their ability to (continue to) live with those who are already citizens of, or permanent residents in, the country (even if one is not a cosmopolitan, such interests should arguably carry some weight), the fact that the interests of *existing* members of the society are implicated suggests that states may owe it to the latter to exempt these individuals from pre-entry or permanent residence tests.

Case 4: Lastly, there are strong reasons – decisive ones in my view – against requiring those with learning difficulties or disabilities to pass permanent residence or citizenship tests (and arguably pre-entry tests as well). The fact that no matter how hard they try, it will often be extremely difficult for these individuals to pass such tests suggests that it would be *unfair* to require them to do so. In addition to this, such requirements might *stigmatise* existing citizens and residents with learning difficulties or disabilities. This is the case when the mass exclusion of (would-be) immigrants with learning difficulties and disabilities conveys that those who have these impairments are somehow less valued members of the society.

The reasons *against* requiring individuals to pass civic integration tests in order to become (permanent) residents or citizens seem strongest in the cases just mentioned. However, even if none of the foregoing conditions obtains, it is doubtful that the benefits that civic integration tests might bring can justify their costs. As we have seen, making (continued) residence or citizenship conditional on the passing of a test can leave people vulnerable to domination and exploitation. In the case of citizenship tests, furthermore, it might create democratic deficits by involuntarily excluding from the national – and possibly local – demos those who have resided within the society for long periods. Finally, when such tests preclude people from joining a country, remaining in it, or becoming a citizen of it, they may impose substantial social, emotional, and/or financial costs not only on those who take them but also on their nearest and dearest, as well as on members of the wider society.

When set against the uncertain and seemingly small potential benefits of civic integration tests, there is good reason for being sceptical about the justifiability of such tests. As indicated, it is most improbable that civic integration tests can reliably exclude individuals with anti-liberal and/or anti-democratic beliefs and dispositions. And while they might help to transmit valuable knowledge, by incentivising people to familiarise themselves with useful political, legal, and social facts, the added value of this incentive seems low. This is so *especially* when states use the money that they would have spent on these tests to spread this knowledge in the other ways I proposed (which seem to be more efficient and/or more respectful of people's autonomy). Yet even when states do not take any alternative measures, it appears that simply by living and participating within a society, people will usually gather a great deal of knowledge about it already, particularly with respect to its formal and informal norms.[53] Hence, the benefits that civic integration tests might bring are unlikely to justify their costs.

Conclusion

Given the substantial costs that civic integration tests can impose on would-be (permanent) residents and would-be citizens, as well as on other groups (e.g., friends and family members, the wider society), this chapter has suggested that such tests are justifiable *if and only if* the following criteria are satisfied: (1) the relevant tests should promote legitimate goals; (2) there should not be any superior alternatives to their use; and (3) their expected benefits should outweigh their costs. After identifying three potentially legitimate goals that civic integration tests might serve – namely, the transmission of political knowledge, the transmission of knowledge of formal and informal norms, and the exclusion of anti-liberal and/or anti-democratic individuals – I showed that it is dubious whether these criteria are ever jointly satisfied. Thus, civic integration tests seem very difficult to defend.

Notes

1 Ayelet Shachar, "Picking Winners: Olympic Citizenship and the Global Race for Talent," *The Yale Law Journal* 120 (2011): 2088–2139.

2 Sarah Goodman, *Immigration and Membership Politics in Western Europe* (New York: Cambridge University Press, 2014); Christian Joppke, "Civic Integration in Western Europe: Three Debates," *West European Politics* 40, no. 6 (November 2, 2017): 1153–1176, https://doi.org/10.1080/01402382.2017.1303252

3 Ines Michalowski, "Citizenship Tests in Five Countries: An Expression of Political Liberalism?" Working Paper (WZB Discussion Paper, 2009), www.econstor.eu/handle/10419/49769

4 'Origins of the Naturalization Civics Test', USCIS, accessed 23 August 2018, https://www.uscis.gov/history-and-genealogy/history-and-genealogy-news/origins-naturalization-civics-test.

5 Goodman, *Immigration and Membership Politics in Western Europe*; Sarah Goodman, "Lost and Found: An Empirical Foundation for Applying the Liberal Test," in *How Liberal Are Citizenship Tests?* ed. Christian Joppke and Rainer Baubock, EUI Working Papers (Florence, 2010), http://cadmus.eui. eu//handle/1814/13956.

6 Iseult Honohan, "Civic Integration: The Acceptable Face of Assimilation?" in *The Ethics and Politics of Immigration: Core Issues and Emerging Trends*, ed. Alex Sager, Reprint edition (London; New York: Rowman & Littlefield International, 2016), 145–158.

7 Joppke, "Civic Integration in Western Europe."

8 For a comprehensive analysis of this test, see the excellent Thom Brooks. 2016. Becoming British, UK Citizenship Examined. Biteback Publishing.

9 'Can You Pass the Citizenship Test?', Lifeintheuktests.co.uk (blog), accessed 23 August 2018, https:// lifeintheuktests.co.uk/life-in-the-uk-test/.

10 'Can You Pass the Citizenship Test?'

11 'Alle 300 Fragen Und Antworten Zum Einbürgerungstest Der Bundesrepublik Deutschland', accessed 23 August 2018, https://www.einbuergerungstest-online.eu/fragen/.

12 'Alle 300 Fragen Und Antworten Zum Einbürgerungstest Der Bundesrepublik Deutschland'.

13 '100 Examenvragen Bij Het Fotoboek En de Film Naar Nederland', accessed 23 August 2018, http:// cdn.naarnederland.nl/naarnederland/examen/data/NN-fotoboek-2014-herzien-wijzigingen-web.pdf.

14 '100 Examenvragen Bij Het Fotoboek En de Film Naar Nederland'.

15 '100 Civics Questions and Answers with MP3 Audio (English Version)', USCIS, accessed 23 August 2018, https://www.uscis.gov/citizenship/teachers/educational-products/100-civics-questions-and-answers-mp3-audio-english-version.

16 'Can You Pass the Citizenship Test?'

17 '100 Examenvragen Bij Het Fotoboek En de Film Naar Nederland'.

18 'Alle 300 Fragen Und Antworten Zum Einbürgerungstest Der Bundesrepublik Deutschland'.

19 'Can You Pass the Citizenship Test?'

20 'Can You Pass the Citizenship Test?'

21 '100 Examenvragen Bij Het Fotoboek En de Film Naar Nederland'.

22 'Can You Pass the Citizenship Test?'

23 'Can You Pass the Citizenship Test?'

24 'Alle 300 Fragen Und Antworten Zum Einbürgerungstest Der Bundesrepublik Deutschland'.

25 'Alle 300 Fragen Und Antworten Zum Einbürgerungstest Der Bundesrepublik Deutschland'.

26 'Alle 300 Fragen Und Antworten Zum Einbürgerungstest Der Bundesrepublik Deutschland'.

27 '100 Examenvragen Bij Het Fotoboek En de Film Naar Nederland'.

28 Liav Orgad, "Illiberal Liberalism Cultural Restrictions on Migration and Access to Citizenship in Europe," *The American Journal of Comparative Law* 58, no. 1 (2010): 93.

29 '100 Examenvragen Bij Het Fotoboek En de Film Naar Nederland'.

30 Orgad, "Illiberal Liberalism Cultural Restrictions on Migration and Access to Citizenship in Europe," 67.

31 Compare Christian Joppke, "How Liberal Are Citizenship Tests?" in *How Liberal Are Citizenship Tests?* EUI Working Papers, 2010, http://eudo-citizenship.eu/docs/RSCAS_2010_41.pdf.

32 For a defence of a social membership account of the right to stay in a country, see Joseph H. *Carens, Immigrants and the Right to Stay* (Cambridge, MA: The MIT Press, 2010).

33 Compare Honohan, "Civic Integration: The Acceptable Face of Assimilation?"

34 This is a basic assumption of liberal philosophy. See Jeremy Waldron, *Liberal Rights: Collected Papers 1981–1991* (Cambridge: Cambridge University Press, 1993), 37.

35 See, for example, Hansen, "Citizenship Tests: An Unapologetic Defense."

36 Andrew Mason, "Citizenship Tests: Can They Be a Just Compromise?" *Journal of Social Philosophy* 45, no. 2 (2014): 139.

37 For a defence of such a two-pronged approach, see Hansen, "Citizenship Tests: An Unapologetic Defense."

38 'Enrol and Vote from Overseas', Electoral Commission, accessed 23 August 2018, https://www.elec tions.org.nz/voters/get-ready-enrol-and-vote/enrol-and-vote-overseas.

39 'Municipal Elections', Your Europe – Citizens, accessed 23 August 2018, https://europa.eu/ youreurope/citizens/residence/elections-abroad/municipal-elections/index_en.htm.

40 See, for example, Mason, "Citizenship Tests," 139–40.

41 Compare Mason 2014, 139 and Robert E. Goodin, "Liberal Multiculturalism: Protective and Polyglot," *Political Theory* 34, no. 3 (2006): 289–303.

42 Mason, "Citizenship Tests," 150.
43 Putnam Robert D., "E Pluribus Unum: Diversity and Community in the Twenty-First Century the 2006 Johan Skytte Prize Lecture," *Scandinavian Political Studies* 30, no. 2 (June 15, 2007): 137–74, https://doi.org/10.1111/j.1467-9477.2007.00176.x.
44 See, for example, Sergio Carrera and Elspeth Guild, "Are Integration Tests Liberal? The 'Universalistic Democratic Principles' as Illiberal Exceptionalism," in *How Liberal Are Citizenship Tests?* ed. Christian Joppke and Rainer Baubock, EUI Working Papers (Florence, 2010), 29–34, http://cadmus.eui.eu//handle/1814/13956.
45 James Hampshire, "Liberalism and Citizenship Acquisition: How Easy Should Naturalisation Be?" *Journal of Ethnic and Migration Studies* 37, no. 6 (July 1, 2011): 953–71, https://doi.org/10.1080/1369183X.2011.576197.
46 Hampshire, 965; see also Christian Joppke, "How Liberal Are Citizenship Tests? A Rejoinder," in *How Liberal Are Citizenship Tests?* ed. Christian Joppke and Rainer Baubock, EUI Working Papers (Florence, 2010), 39–41, http://cadmus.eui.eu//handle/1814/13956.
47 David Miller, "Reasonable Partiality Towards Compatriots," *Ethical Theory and Moral Practice* 8, no. 1/2 (2005): 63–81, https://doi.org/10.2307/27504338.
48 Yael Tamir, *Liberal Nationalism*, Revised edition (Princeton, NJ: Princeton University Press, 1995).
49 For a more detailed discussion, see Orgad, "Illiberal Liberalism Cultural Restrictions on Migration and Access to Citizenship in Europe."
50 Mason, "Citizenship Tests," 152.
51 Mason, 141.
52 For a defence of a stakeholder principle of political membership, see Rainer Baubock, "Stakeholder Citizenship and Transnational Political Participation: A Normative Evaluation of External Voting," *Fordham Law Review* 75, no. 5 (January 1, 2007): 2393.
53 Orgad, "Illiberal Liberalism Cultural Restrictions on Migration and Access to Citizenship in Europe," 21.

33

THE ETHICS OF LANGUAGE POLICIES

Astrid von Busekist

Language policies are unique compared to other public policies given that linguistic disenfranchisement is impossible (e.g., as opposed to religious disenfranchisement).[1]

Firstly because interactions between institutions and their members (or their would-be members – think of immigrants) always occur through specific languages: institutions regulate linguistic public rights and duties, and therefore linguistic hands-off policies cannot exist. Secondly because language is a collective good in its own way,[2] primarily because states cannot distribute language the same way they distribute health care, social security, or housing,[3] despite the fact that languages are important social and common goods. But states can and do distribute "access rights" and services related to (minority) language(s) via instrumental or accommodationist policies.[4]

Language policies include the ways institutions shape the linguistic structures of a society in general, and the claims of individual speakers or linguistic groups to change existing language arrangements or legislations; the ways states or institutions impose official language(s); manage language diversity in multilingual settings; legislate on international linguistic rules (e.g., in the EU);[5] and lay out preferential treatments to protect speakers of vulnerable language communities.

To some scholars languages are comparable to primary social goods individuals should be able to enjoy in much the same way as other goods or liberties. To others language determines all our social interactions because it is a token of identification with a culture, large or small. True equality (of opportunities, participation, access to goods) is hence possible only if individuals have a significant context of choice in their own linguistic surroundings. The former look at the equal liberty and rights of individual speakers (with language belonging to principles of democracy and justice), and the latter look at communities of speakers (and the moral importance of belonging to a language community).

This chapter aims to clarify why language policies are the substructure of a variety of important democratic requirements and hence why fair and ethical language policies matter for democratic polities. In a nutshell: without language skills, access to various spheres – political as well as socio-economic – is hindered. Without access to these spheres of citizenship, no political, social, and economic rights and duties can be properly exercised, and no rights claims can be properly voiced.

My general claim is that language skills are politically enabling not goods per se.[6] Language is a political enabling skill meant to connect people and to interact meaningfully within democratic polities.[7] The literature identifies two potentially contradictory principles regarding linguistic democracy: identity-related claims, and utility- or efficiency-related linguistic claims as bases for ethical and democratic language policies. In my view, ethical language policies should be designed to sustain these two claims simultaneously against the background of a set of democratic values – for example, participation, recognition, parity of esteem, non-domination, and self-government.

I will first briefly lay out the (divergent) normative assumptions about the political value of languages. They roughly revolve around two poles, concerned with identity-related claims on the one hand, and efficiency-related claims, often sustained by utilitarian principles, on the other hand. Somewhere in between, the "linguistic justice" paradigm, most prominently defended by Philippe Van Parijs,[8] is an attempt to bridge the divisions (first section). I will then show how these analyses implicitly draw on the notion of *burden* – vulnerable speakers or speech communities are burdened in asymmetrical language situations – without reflecting properly on the precise nature of the burden. I will argue that the type of burden and the type of linguistic constellation matter, and hence general claims (e.g., about domination or self-esteem) are limited in scope and often depend on specific situations and contexts. On the one hand our moral judgement of asymmetrical situations should be, to some extent at least, context-dependent; on the other hand different assumptions about burden lead to different normative approaches and policy designs (second section). I will conclude (last section) by arguing that the literature is not always clear about the political preferences that inspire normative prescriptions for language policies. Different types of political or moral desiderata (autonomy, liberty, non-domination, security, self-government, mobility, employability) call for different justifications of language policies and lead to different shapes of language constellations.[9]

Identity and efficiency

As I have pointed out earlier, scholars dealing with language issues are quite divided about the way we should democratically recognise language groups, communities, and individual speakers. Either we value identity-related claims or we value utility-related claims.[10]

The fact that language is a tool to connect as many people as possible for some and an identity vector for others, or rather that there exists a hierarchy between these two conceptions,[11] leads to different ethical, moral, and political claims. For team one, those who believe that language is intrinsically linked to something precious, worthy of being publicly defended and protected[12] – our personal and political identity – the state has a moral duty to accommodate this quest for (collective) recognition.[13] Each of us should have access to a significant realm of choices and opportunities within our own "societal culture" (education, employment, office). If specific cultures are different from the general linguistic culture (official or national language), institutions should confer linguistic rights to individual members of minority or vulnerable communities. Note that these accommodation policies, in the eyes of their most vocal proponent, Will Kymlicka, apply only to "historical minorities", much less so to immigrant communities.[14] In his approach, the holder of protection rights is nevertheless the individual, as it is assumed that her citizenship rights are dependent upon her identity as a speaker.[15] More and more scholars, although with different paths of justification and looking at different types of constituencies – local and communal rather than national – argue that immigrants should be granted the same privileges.[16]

A second subset of the literature argues that language communities should be granted collective rights – that communities should benefit from rights related to their collective minority/vulnerable status. There are multiple ramifications of this thesis. Firstly, it is not a classical liberal take on language policies, as it is not foremost concerned with individuals. The idea is that one cannot remedy or rectify linguistic injustice (which is often a result of socio-economic inequalities, large power structures) without granting collective rights (not necessarily territorialized). Here restorative justice mechanisms would typically compensate forceful assimilation into majority (often colonial) languages. Linguistic genocide, "linguicide", is the most radical way of framing the necessary resistance to hegemonic language policies. Insofar as language is power, a "colonisation of the minds", Anglo-American globalisation is equated with a human rights violation.[17]

A third and related way of staging identity-related issues draws on ecology or environmental ethics. Linguistic diversity is considered a global public good. The fact that languages die every day is considered a moral loss for humanity and an injustice for its speakers as they are deprived of their genuine cultural relationship to their environment. However, active language survival policies come with a price, comparable to the cost of protecting dying species;[18] and as they are often framed as an 'ought', to be implemented coercively and against the will of their speakers, they are illiberal.[19]

The defence of language as a primordial sign of identity – individual and collective – and strong advocacy for diversity as a value conceals important problems for policy-makers: should diversity trump mobility and employability? Democratic deliberation and participation? How are we to manage political problems that cut across different language communities while enhancing participation, valuing democratic procedures, and protecting individual rights?

These are the questions another set of scholars asks – for example, those committed to efficiency. Most of them are consequentialists, and they rightfully believe that languages are foremost tools to connect people. The discussion on efficiency can lead to two possible outcomes: *lingua franca* policies – in order to achieve efficient integrated political practices reaching constituencies beyond specific linguistic repertoires, in the EU for example, and in which everyone can take part, we need a either one common language or *coordinated* language policies – for example, a system that connects our different repertoires without necessarily choosing a lingua franca. Neither is a priori incompatible with political fairness, nor hostile towards identity-related claims or the value of diversity. Both are compatible with either territoriality or non-territoriality.[20] Interestingly, although coordination games are desirable, as argued forcefully by economist François Grin,[21] for example, the proponents of coordination often end up defending lingua franca policies, although not always to the exclusion of language diversity. This is the case for Abram de Swaan,[22] Reinhard Selten, Jonathan Pool, and David Laitin,[23] who argue that language communities engage in – or should engage in – a cost-benefit analysis with compensations, trade-offs, and "side payments" in order to evaluate what they are ready to give up – or demand – in exchange for being able to communicate with other groups than their native community.[24] The rationale underlying this approach is the following: languages are collective goods produced by coordination, and their utility is conceptually dependent on their utility for other speakers: languages are utile for me only if they are utile for a sufficient number of other speakers[25] as I engage in learning another language only if I expect to be able to communicate with other speakers (this what de Swaan would call anticipated probability and profitability.

Another in my view more promising way of looking at efficiency asks what kind of efficiency we are aiming for. Is it to support democracy, social justice, non-domination, self-government, and equal chances and opportunities? How can or should these democratic goals be severed from identity-related claims? In the case of conflict between democratic values and identity-related claims (the legitimate quest for diversity and linguistic autonomy), we must ask how and why identity claims should be traded off against democratic imperatives. The answer here is instrumental again, but in another way, leaning rather on democratic equality among individuals than on the utility of language networks: language disadvantages are said to be detrimental to democratic equality and therefore to democratic participation;[26] and the argument in favour of common (national or supra-national) languages is made to foster a healthy participatory "talk-centric" democracy.[27]

This is a pragmatic argument about the advantages of sharing a language that goes well with what I have said earlier: access to a common language is the substructure for other democratic values and interests. Imposing a common language may be (transitionally) detrimental to minority language groups, but overriding democratic interests exist in insisting on a common language or common languages: employability, equality, autonomy, non-domination, mobility, and access to relevant social services count among these principles. Common language proficiency is desirable both for citizens and for newcomers[28] as they can interact autonomously and take part in the political culture of the state, and for the state because it fosters cooperation and solidarity and ensures the sustainability of the a *political* culture. In other words the need to master a common languages is not an independent or exclusive goal (it is *not* a moral ought), nor should it be detrimental to minority, regional, or native tongues, but should serve as a gateway to autonomy and self-government. Speaking a common language is empirically relevant. Consider two examples: from an individual point of view, intermediary social institutions where speakers *should* have maximum control over their own fate (interaction with immigration administration, parents at their children's schools, the workplace, neighbourhood councils, possibly local democracy, neighbourhood or town councils), lack of language proficiency excludes individuals and families, newcomers, residents, and citizens alike. As we know, participation does not only occur through classical political channels: it is shaped by and through intermediary associations and local institutions that are the ones migrants in particular are first in contact with and where they most they need some (linguistic) skills to be able to communicate. From the point of view of the state, the importance of language skills is reflected in the language component most states require in their citizenship tests. Mastery of the official language(s) and culture is a tangible sign of migrants' willingness to become members of the political community, of sharing in the national common good.[29] States expect social solidarity and educational and cultural benefits through mastery of the national language(s), as well as economic benefits. Most scholars agree that these tests do not cross the line of discriminatory or exclusionary practices,[30] except when other, non-language-related values[31] are tested along with, or during, language tests,[32] and except when language tests are "pre-entry barriers".[33]

Burdens and opportunities

I have so far made a distinction between identity-related claims and utility-related claims. Both claims are taken very seriously in the realm of linguistic justice. The most prominent author in this field, Philippe Van Parijs, has dedicated his work to combining identity claims and efficiency claims fairly. I will first say a few words on his theory and mention some objections to his model, and then show why I believe that the notion of burden is under-theorised.

Van Parijs argues for 'cooperative linguistic justice'[34] relying on two main principles: a global lingua franca (English) and coercive territorial protection for national languages. The two principles are of a different nature and are justified for different reasons: the first principle is pragmatic and presentist. It is at once rational and desirable to opt for English as lingua franca, and

English is already our lingua franca, or, to put it otherwise: an aggregation of independent interests has led to English being our global lingua franca without our explicit consent. We should nevertheless actively encourage English for our own best interest and for the sake of democracy. This is our "duty" in Van Parijs's words:[35] in order to communicate across borders and despite linguistic diversity we need a common ground, language, so that a violation of rights in one place is now felt throughout the world as Kant would put it. The means to achieve this are quite simple: we need to equalise the cost-benefit ratio of learning languages.[36] Van Parijs is aware that Anglophones benefiting from their "mother-tongue blessing" will not pay (via taxes) for the language training of non-native English speakers (via subsidies), the only fair way to jointly foot the bill of language acquisition.

But Van Parijs is also committed to identity-related claims. He clearly combines these identity claims with democratic requisites – namely, parity of esteem (a way of acknowledging the dignity of speakers), which he derives from Rawlsian principles: the "maximin principle" and "social support for self-respect",[37] and which are best protected and achieved through linguistic territoriality. Every language should be "a Queen" in its own territory in order to minimise feelings of disparity of esteem experienced by (communities of) speakers who do not master English and whose languages are now in a lower, colonial, position vis-à-vis English. Territorial language regimes provide language stability and language security (small languages are protected on their territory), and for territoriality to be efficient, it is mandatory that all speak the official language in its territory of reference. This coercive regime has boundaries but these are to be decided upon by democratic procedures if its members collectively desire to claim territorial rights. In this model, undoubtedly ingenious, a global demos capable of addressing global concerns in the same language (global justice) coexists with a variety of local demoi sensitive to the identity of individual speakers and communities. It is a combination of cooperation, coordination, efficiency, and recognition.

The main objections to Van Parijs's model can be summarised under four headings.

First, the territoriality principle in fact reproduces a rather classical nationalistic model of language rationalisation within a territory, unconvincing for principled reasons (how could we possibly defend global justice and argue in favour of territorial boundaries that are to a great extent arbitrary?), but also for empirical reasons (there are more languages than territories, and there are no unilingual territories, so how should we deal with immigrant communities?). Second, the key role language plays in arguing speakers' disparity of esteem may be real, but the subjective feelings of humiliation, lack of recognition, and even lack of autonomy are not necessarily the result of injustices or politically unfair practices.[38] Third, a global lingua franca as well as territorial language communities is not immune to power relations, neither in the coming about of language constellations (Anglo-American hegemonic culture and economy), nor in the perpetuation of linguistic inequalities or access to literacy for the least well off. Finally Van Parijs's preference for coercive territorial regimes may end up being illiberal, despite the fact that territoriality theoretically depends on the collective desire of the speakers.

The only solution – quite unrealistic – would be to argue for a procedural model of language regimes, in which linguistic preferences are morally neutral: citizens would vote for their preferred language in a non-outcome-oriented way.[39] But as we have already pointed out, states "speak", hands-off policies are hardly possible. And more importantly: what would the relevant constituency be? The recent debates in Spain have shown that the Catalonian vote in favour of Catalonian territoriality is – for many Castilian speakers within Catalonia – unjustifiable.

The dividing line between those who argue in favour of identity-related claims and efficiency-related claims – I believe that ethical policies must in some way combine the two elements – is maybe less to be drawn between a specific awareness regarding dignity, parity of esteem, and social support for self-respect on the one hand, and political-democratic efficiency on the other hand.

I would like to suggest that an alternative reading looks at *language burden*. In a nutshell: either small and vulnerable languages are a burden for their speakers (exclusion, non-participation, symbolic and material costs of learning the lingua franca, humiliation, disparity of esteem), or they are not; they are simply an arbitrary result of birthplace, but need not be conceived as a burden, and may even offer opportunities for innovation in coordinated language policies.

The story goes like this: small and vulnerable languages are a burden, much like socio-economic endowments are morally arbitrary, and therefore they need to be compensated (through equalising costs of learning, territoriality, a Rawlsian difference principle). This is what most authors recommend: managing the burden through institutions and practices in the light of desirable democratic requisites. (a) By learning languages upwards and switching into the bigger language,[40] (b) by conferring rights to small language communities,[41] (c) by encouraging a lingua franca alongside territorially protected small languages,[42] or (d) a combination of the foregoing.

If we agree on my premise that language policies are the substructure for other democratic requirements, we need to explain the exact nature of the burden in order to find out how to fix it. Yet most scholars fail to explain the nature of the burden: different burdens call for different policy answers. Note that none of the options ahead excludes a lingua franca regime, but maybe not of the kind Van Parijs has in mind.

If the burden is on *equality and democratic participation*, the policy answer should be equalising situations, opportunities, and encouraging equal participation. Is this possible only in the lingua franca plus territoriality model? One may argue that democratic participation (local or global) is not necessarily determined by linguistic skills, although a common language is desirable. Firstly social multilingualism as well as groups of multilingual social translators may do the job. Secondly, citizens can participate and have access to social and political services in their language *and* (an idiosyncratic variety of) English. "Open English"[43] would be then an alternative to English as a lingua franca.[44] Open English has no real centre (neither the UK nor the US is such a centre, and therefore neither the UK nor the US is a hegemonic provider of language-related culture); it is a "hybrid" language[45] with very little *a priori* norms;[46] it is contextual, situational, and dynamic. It is also universal in the sense that every speaker has to learn it – even, to a certain extent, native speakers of norm-English, because of the amount of idiosyncrasies:[47] there are hence as many languages as speakers. Open English is a multilingual, *sui generis* language and would fix, in part at least, asymmetric language situations. Thirdly, linguistic disadvantages can be compensated, either instrumentally by providing translation services and incentives, or more substantially by offering a proper (free of charge) language training that 'grants equal access to democratic opportunity'[48] without hindering recognition and parity of esteem. Lastly, there are many ways to be informed and to participate in other languages than the official or common one.

If the burden is on *autonomy and liberty*, the answer is different. For *individuals*, autonomy is supposed to heavily rely on language skills, firstly because they enable them to make significant life choices within a community with whom they share a (verbal and non-verbal) understanding of the identity of their community, and secondly because access to the social, the political, and the market spheres are dependent on the ability to communicate with the relevant offices and administrations, and to claim rights. For language *communities*, autonomy serves different purposes: it is rather about sharing and protecting a political public culture (carried by a specific language typically in sub-state entities, such as in Québec, where the survival of French is endangered), and setting the grounds for self-government within a mutually intelligible context of debate and decision-making. Autonomy is hence an identity-related claim *and* a tool for efficient democratic government. But in the identity version, it is because individual speakers claim recognition that states should (territorially) accommodate them. In the democratic efficiency version (e.g., Rainer Bauböck's "stakeholder model"),[49] individual language rights are not the building blocks for territorial language regimes; it is rather because of the collective value people assign to their languages that (territorial) linguistic regimes are the result of self-governing powers meant to alter, influence, and shift language preferences. This, in turn, means that specific demoi should have the right, for democratic self-governing reasons, to design their language policies in the way they deem fit and fair. Note that a common language is neither a necessary nor a sufficient resource for self-government, nor for lively democratic deliberation.[50] Self-government is the independent variable we are looking at (language is merely the tool), whereas language (as an identity marker) is the dependent variable.[51] Therefore the burden on autonomy justifies coercive territorial regimes only in so far as coercion is the result of democratic self-government.[52] *Caeteris paribus*, the burden on autonomy justifies lingua franca regimes only in so far as autonomous self-governing polities have an equal say in designing the global regime and the terms of global justice. But this is obviously empirically untrue. Language communities are not equal partners in designing global justice regimes: industrialised countries with high numbers of literacy, a good educational system with language training, and skilled workers are clearly ahead of all the others. In other words, if the burden is on autonomy, the burden needs to be referred to the relevant spheres and to the relevant constituencies.

If the burden is on *diversity, non-domination* (and exclusion), the answer is different still. If language diversity is a value, then diversity should be upheld by all means (e.g., as in the EU, where 'equal respect [is] due to all cultures and languages' according to the European Council),[53] regardless of the efficiency model, and regardless of its consequences on domination and exclusion. If diversity is not valued *per se* but is expected to be traded off against mutually intelligible common languages or a lingua franca, then the lingua franca model plus territorial or personal arrangements may be the best option. Van Parijs is indeed ready to give up local diversity for inter-local diversity. But is territoriality plus lingua franca really the best answer to combat exclusion and to foster global justice? Language economists have convincingly shown that the reduction in the number of official languages in the EU (24) would (a) exclude a vast amount of citizens from access to EU politics, (b) be detrimental to the least well off – for example, the most vulnerable social groups and the weakest members in terms of language skills – and (c) that

> that the current full multilingual policy of the EU, based on translation and interpreting, is not only the most effective language policy among the alternative options usually put forward in the literature; it is also (and it will be for the foreseeable future) the only one that is truly inclusive.[54]

If that is so, there is no reason to give up diversity for inclusionary and non-domination reasons, and there is no reason at all to adopt a lingua franca 'for Europe and the world'.[55]

Language burdens are in reality opportunities in this approach if treated in the right way. And the relevant question is not how we should compensate the least well off linguistically while sharing global concerns and encouraging global justice in a global language, but how to assess a normative claim that is not empirically fully worked out.

Conclusion: political language policies, a contextual approach

I have shown that linguistic justice scholars work with the notion of burden on small and vulnerable languages, but that they do not always disentangle the nature of the burden and hence the political and normative conclusions that flow from the type of burden one is concerned with.

I will conclude by arguing that we are not always clear about the political preferences that inspire normative prescriptions for language policies. *Just* language policies are not necessarily *democratic* language policies. Democratic policies are not equivalent to liberal or republican language policies: they have different normative starting points. Secondly, I believe that there is no one all-encompassing, normative answer to the challenges of linguistic diversity. The best solution is, as often, a second-best solution, mindful of different empirical situations and existing political regimes, power structures, and sensitivity to 'politics against domination'.[56]

The question then is rather which legitimate political principle or which policy outcome is best served by the different approaches to linguistic justice or ethical language policies in specific locations.

As I have argued the literature can be usefully organised according to the value authors confer to either identity or political efficiency or a combination of both.[57] Say identity is important but should be acknowledged in one way or another by political efficiency. No regime respectful of individual rights and democratic constitutionalism can disregard identity (e.g., the quest for recognition and parity of esteem: in seeking respect, dissenters convey that their private preferences are indeed the business of the community).

If we now cross these two principles with political preferences (liberalism, democracy, republicanism, nationalism in broad strokes), what kinds of policies do we get?

I have argued (a) that it is illiberal to secure or sustain languages (and hence language communities) without the explicit consent of their members;[58] (b) that it is non-democratic to impose coercive territorial language regimes without the consent of the relevant constituency;[59] (c) that it runs against the non-domination principle that individuals should be coerced into learning a language they do not wish to learn; (d) but that it is desirable for economic and political reasons (employability, mobility, integration of migrants) that people speak a common language within a given territory; (e) that it is desirable for a democratic polity to function with a maximum amount of participation: the demos designs the laws, and the demos is the author of the laws, and therefore the laws are legitimate and justifiable to everyone; (e) that positive liberty but also (liberal) nationalism requires that demoi identify with their polity (shared public culture, solidarity, belonging), and therefore must uphold, or be committed to, a public sphere that is intelligible for all; (f) that a global lingua franca enhances awareness of global injustice, encourages a global civil society, and lessens inequality of opportunities and global exclusion.[60]

If you are a *liberal egalitarian*, you would go for non-coercive territorial protection plus a regime of multiple *linguae francae*; if you are a *utilitarian liberal* you would opt for either the territorial or the personality principle combined with a lingua franca regime; if you are a *liberal* or a *cultural nationalist*, you would opt for acknowledging and protecting diversity via language rights for vulnerable historical communities, the personality principle, and a combination of *linguae francae*; if you are a *nationalist*, you would go for coercive territoriality, and maybe for a non-coercive lingua franca regime for utilitarian reasons; if you are a *democrat*, you would opt for the procedural model: self-government and autonomy in designing language policies (most probably a territoriality of consent); a lingua franca regime would be acceptable only under the same conditions of global consent between demoi; if you are a *republican*, you would go for any options that prevent domination (territoriality, self-government, equal recognition, equal opportunities, possibly an additional lingua franca regime for utilitarian reasons); if you are a liberal committed to global justice and parity of esteem (this seems to be a *sui generis* category), you will opt for coercive territoriality and encourage English as a lingua franca; if you are an *illiberal ecologist*, you would protect diversity at all costs, regardless of the desire of speakers.

This is an analytical and probably too systematic way of ordering preferences. But it does show that a combination of a global language (English) and (coercive) territoriality is only one way of designing ethical language policies. The trade-off between territoriality (versus diversity)[61] and a lingua franca (versus global injustice and domination) is not satisfying without more empirical evidence and without a clear statement about the burdens we wish to alleviate within a hierarchy of given political preferences.

In short, different types of political or moral desiderata (autonomy, liberty, non-domination, security, self-government, mobility, employability) call for different justifications of language policies and design different language constellations. I believe that non-coercive territorial regimes (even if they may empirically promote majority languages), combined with a set of *lingua francae*, is the best solution. People should have a say in their linguistic preferences and collectively decide on the minority languages they wish to protect domestically on the one hand, and they should be able to freely choose the language or the languages they would like to learn for global, inter-regional communication on the other hand.

This solution has the following advantages. The language constellation (in the EU and globally) would remain dynamic: (a) English is not the only European/global lingua franca, and if we refrain from actively encouraging English, there is a chance that other languages will acquire the same status English enjoys today; and (b) as people are free in their language choices, the language combinations of each individual, and of each polity collectively, encourage aggregate diversity without hindering international communication.

The constellation would also be fairer because it would be less exclusive (see the European data).[62] It would lastly be advantageous for intra- and extra-European communication: people need to master other languages than English in order to sustain a global and free system of linguistic exchanges. Coordination policies within the EU or within regional institutions would be able to decide on working languages relevant for their respective constituencies while guaranteeing inter-regional connections. Multilingual speakers and translators are relevant facilitators in this coordination game.

Notes

1 A. Patten, "Liberal Neutrality and Language Policy", *Philosophy and Public Affairs* 31/4, 2003, 356–386, 366.; R. Brubaker, "Language, Religion and the Politics of Difference", *Nations and Nationalism* 19/1, 2013, 1–20, 1.

2 A. de Swaan has argued that languages are non-excludable 'hypercollective public goods' with positive network externalities in *Words of the World*, Cambridge, Polity Press, 2001.

3 Y. Peled, "Language, Rights and the Language of Language Rights: The Need for a Conceptual Framework in the Political Theory of Language Policy", *Journal of Language and Politics* 10/3, 2011, 436–456, 445.

4 R. Meylaerts, "Translational Justice in a Multilingual World", *Meta* 56/4, 2011, 743–757; G. González Núñez, "Translation Policy in a Linguistically Diverse World", *Journal on Ethnopolitics and Minority Issues in Europe* 15/1, 2016, 1–18.

5 A. von Busekist, "Language and Politics", in B. Badie, D. Bergschlosser, L. Morlino eds., *International Encyclopedia of Political Science*, 8 vol., London, Sage, 2011, 2070–2072.

6 B. Boudou, A. von Busekist, "Language Proficiency and Migration: An Argument Against Testing", in M. Gazzola, B. A. Wickström, T. Templin eds., *Language Policy and Linguistic Justice: Economics, Philosophical and Sociolinguistics Approaches*, Berlin, Springer, 2017.

7 B. Boudou, A. von Busekist, art. cit.

8 P. Van Parijs, *Linguistic Justice for Europe and the World*, Oxford, Oxford University Press, 2011.

9 D. Laitin, R. Reich, "A Liberal Democratic Approach to Language Justice," in A. Patten, W. Kymlicka, eds., *Language Rights and Political Theory*, Oxford, Oxford University Press, 2003, 80–104.

10 Interestingly, De Schutter and Robichaud write identity "interests" when referring to scholars who argue that identity claims matter in linguistic demands and regulations. I believe, however, that the concept of interest is a way of slightly twisting the debate by stretching the identity category beyond its scope. The authors list a number of "identity interests" among which are autonomy, context of

choice and opportunities, self-realization; whereas non-identity interests are efficiency, democracy, and equality of opportunity. I fail to understand how one would have non-identity interests realised without prior or simultaneous realisation of identity interests. H. De Schutter, D. Robichaud, "Van Parijsian Linguistic Justice – Context, Analysis and Critiques", in Van Parijs and his Critics eds., *Linguistic Justice: Critical Review of International Social and Political Philosophy*, Taylor & Francis, 18/2, 2015, 87–112.

11 D. Laitin, "What Is a Language Community?" *American Journal of Political Science* 44/1, 2000, 142–155; J. Pool, "The Official Language Problem", *The American Political Science Review*, 85/2, 1991, 495–514; A. de Swaan, "Why Is This in English?" Schuman Lecture, Universiteit Maastricht, 2000 retrieved here: http://wwwdeswaan.com/engels/from_our_archives/WhyEnglish.htm

12 D. Réaume, "Official Language Rights: Intrinsic Value and the Protection of Difference", in W. Kymlicka, W. Norman, eds., *Citizenship in Diverse Societies*, Oxford, Oxford University Press, 2000.

13 S. May, *Language and Minority Rights: Ethnicity, Nationalism and the Politics of Language* (2nd Edition), New York/London, Routledge, 2012.

14 W. Kymlicka, *Politics in the Vernacular: Nationalism, Multiculturalism and Citizenship*, Oxford, Oxford University Press, 2001. An addendum in W. Kymlicka, K. Banting, "Immigration, Multiculturalism, and the Welfare State", *Ethics and International Affairs* 20/3, 2006, 281–304.

15 The difference Kymlicka makes between external protections and internal restrictions is redundant: external protections are indeed meant to protect minorities from the tyranny of the majority and to ensure equality of rights for all as spelled out by a constitutional democracy. Individual members are assumed to be rationally committed to protect their particular societal culture (by aggregated preference); external restrictions (meant to protect individual members from group pressure) on the other hand are a simple restatement of the generally applicable law.

16 C. Joppke, "Beyond National Models: Civic Integration Policies for Immigrants in Western Europe", *West European Politics* 30/1, 2007, 1–22; A. Shorten, "Linguistic Competence and Citizenship Acquisition", in G. Calder, P. Cole, J. Seglow eds., *Citizenship Acquisition and National Belonging: Migration, Membership and the Liberal Democratic State*, New York, Palgrave Macmillan, 2010; C. M. Rodriguez, "Language and Participation", *California Law Review*, 94/3, May, 2006, 687–767.

17 T. Skutnabb-Kangas, R. Phillipson, "Linguicide", in *The Encyclopedia of Language and Linguistics*, Aberdeen, Pergamon Press & Aberdeen University Press, 1994, 2211–2212.

18 Idil Boran, "Global Linguistic Diversity, Public Goods and the Principle of Fairness", in W. Kymlicka, A. Patten, eds., *Language Rights and Political Theory*, op. cit, contra A. de Swaan, "Endangered Languages, Sociolinguistics, and Linguistic Sentimentalism", *European Review*, Cambridge, Cambridge University Press, 12/4, October 2004, 567–580.

19 A. Musschenga, "Intrinsic Value as a Reason for the Preservation of Minority Cultures", *Ethical Theory and Moral Practice*, 1, 201–225.

20 A. von Busekist, "Idealism or Pragmatism: Ad hoc Multilingualism and Open English", in F. Grin, P. Kraus, eds., *The Politics of Multilingualism: Linguistic Governance, Globalisation and Europeanisation*, Amsterdam, John Benjamins, 2017.

21 F. Grin, "L'anglais comme lingua franca: questions de coût et d'équité. Commentaire sur l'article de Philippe Van Parijs", *Économie publique*, 15/2, 2004, 33–41 and "Diversity as Paradigm, Analytical Device, and Policy Goal", in W. Kymlicka, A. Patten eds., *Language Rights and Political Theory*, op. cit., 169–188.

22 A. de Swaan, *Words of the World*, London, Polity Press, 2001.

23 R. Selten, J. Pool, "The Distribution of Foreign Language Skills as a Game Equilibrium", in R. Selten ed., *Game Equilibrium Models*, Vol. 4, Berlin, Springer, 1991, 64–87.

24 J. Fidrmuc, V. Ginsburgh, S. Weber, "Le français, deuxième langue de l'Union européenne?" *Économie publique* 15/2, 2004, 43–63 and V. Ginsburg, S. Weber, *How Many Languages Do We Need? The Economics of Linguistic Diversity*, New Haven, Princeton University Press, 2011.

25 E. Lagerspetz, "On Language Rights", in *Ethical Theory and Moral Practice*, Alphen, Netherlands, Kluwer Academic Publishers, Vol. 1, 1998, 181–199.

26 B. Barry has argued this forcefully regarding Welsh, Culture and Equality: An Egalitarian Critique of Multiculturalism, London, Polity Press, 2001. D. Weinstock is less severe towards minority languages, "Can parity of self-esteem serve as the basis of the principle of linguistic territoriality?", in H. De Schutter, D. Robichaud, op. cit., 199–211.

27 J. Dryzek, *Discursive Democracy: Politics, Policy, and Political Science*, Cambridge, Cambridge University Press, 1990.

28 A. Blackledge, "As a Country We Do Expect: The Further Extension of Language Testing Regimes in the United Kingdom", *Language Assessment Quarterly* 6/1, 2009, 6–16; L. M. Kahn, "Immigration, Skills and the Labor Market: International Evidence", *Journal of Popular Economy* 17/3, 2004, 501–534.

29 S. W. Goodman, "Controlling Immigration through Language and Country Knowkedge Requirements", *West European Politics* 34/2, 2011, 235–255.

30 C. Joppke in R. Bauböck, C. Joppke, eds., *How Liberal Are Citizenship Tests?* Florence, European University Institute, 2010 (EUI Working Papers RSCAS 2010/41, p. 39sq.

Interestingly, Special Eurobarometer 437 (Discrimination in the EU in 2015), http://ec.europa.eu/COMMFrontOffice/publicopinion/index.cfm/Survey/getSurveyDetail/instruments/SPECIAL/surveyKy/2077, does not mention language as a factor of discrimination.

31 In France, for example, the would-be citizen has to 'justify her assimilation into the French community – namely, by adhesion to the essential principles and values of the French Republic'. (Le demandeur doit aussi justifier de son assimilation à la communauté française, notamment par l'adhésion aux principes et valeurs essentiels de la République et par une connaissance suffisante de la langue, l'histoire, la culture et la société françaises, ainsi que les droits et devoirs qui lui sont conférés par la nationalité française. L'assimilation est vérifiée lors d'un entretien individuel avec un agent de la préfecture ou du consulat. Le gouvernement a implementé un test special, dit Test de Nationalité, qui consiste en 12 questions à choix multiple, qui vont être posées à tous les candidats.) See the French government website detailing the requirements for successful language testing. https://www.immigration.interieur.gouv.fr/Accueil-et-accompagnement/La-nationalite-francaise/Les-conditions-et-modalites-de-l-acquisition-de-la-nationalite-francaise

32 These are "covert" (versus "overt") language policies. See H. Schiffman, *Linguistic Culture and Language Policy*, London, Routledge, 2012, 149–150; E. Goldberg Shohamy, *Language Policy: Hidden Agendas and New Approaches*, New York: Psychology Press, 2006; D. C. *Johnson, Language Policy*, London, Palgrave Macmillan, 2013, 10–11.

Women who were wearing headscarves typically failed to live up to secularist standards, for example, in France (2010), as well as in the Netherlands (2006), were denied citizenship. See K. Groenendijk, R. van Oers, "How Liberal Tests Are Does Not Merely Depend on Their Content, But Also Their Effects", in Bauböck, Joppke, EUI Working Paper RSCAS 2010/41, op. cit.; H. Alaoui, J. Pélabay quote an example of a veiled woman who, despite a flawless accent, has less of a chance than 'white' and apparently secular Canadians with a very heavy accent; Table ronde AFSP, "La Communauté libérale", Paris, Oral Communication, 2013.

33 See B. Boudou, A. von Busekist, art. cit.

34 P. Van Parijs, Linguistic Justice for Europe and for the World, op. cit., 53.

35 P. Van Parijs, *Linguistic Justice for Europe and for the World*, op. cit., 31.

36 P. Van Parijs, "Must Europe Be Belgian? On Democratic Citizenship in Multilingual Polities", in C. McKinnon, I. Hampsher-Monk, eds., *The Demands of Citizenship*, London, New York, Continuum, 2000, 235–253; "The Ground Floor of the World: On the Socioeconomic Consequences of Linguistic Globalization", *International Political Science Review*, 21/2, 2000, 217–233; "Europe's Three Language Problems", in D. Castiglione, C. Longman, eds., *The Challenges of Multilingualism in Law and Politics*, Oxford: Hart Publishing, 2006.

37 On social support for self-respect: J. Rawls, *A Theory of Justice*, Cambridge, MA, Harvard University Press, 1971, Ch. VII, Sect. 67, 386sq; Sect. 26–28; *Political Liberalism*, Columbia University Press, 2005, Part 3, Lect. VIII, Sect. 6 pg. 318sq.

38 As argued by A. Stilz, "Language, Dignity, and Territory", H. De Schutter, D. Rbichaud op. cit., 178–190.

39 D. Laitin and R. Reich, art. cit., 80–104.

40 A. de Swaan, *Words of the World*, op. cit.

41 W. Kymlicka, *Politics in the Vernacular*, op. cit.; S. May, *Language and Minority Rights. Ethnicity*, op.cit.; P. Van Parijs, *Linguistic Justice for Europe and for the World*, op. cit., 2011; D. Réaume, "Official Language Rights: Intrinsic Value and the Protection of Difference", in W. Kymlicka, W. Norman, eds., *Citizenship in Diverse Societies*, op.cit.

42 P. Van Parijs, *Linguistic Justice for Europe and for the World*, op. cit.

43 R. M. Bhatt, "World Englishes", *Annual Review of Anthropology*, 30, 2001, 527–550; B. B. Kachru, "World Englishes and English Using Communities", *Annual Review of Applied Linguistics* 17, 1997, 66–87.

44 S. May, "The Problem with English(es) and Linguistic (in)justice. Addressing the Limits of Liberal Egalitarian Accounts of Language", in H. De Schutter, D. Robichaud, op.cit., 131–148.

45 S. Canagarajah, "Lingua Franca English, Multilingual Communities, and Language Acquisition", *The Modern Language Journal*, 91, Focus Issue, 2007, 924–939.

46 J. House, "English as Lingua Franca: A Threat to Multilingualism?" *Journal of Sociolinguistics* 7/4, 2003, 556–578.

47 A. Firth, "The Discursive Accomplishment of Normality. On 'lingua franca' English and Conversation Analysis", *Journal of Pragmatics*, 26, 1996, 237–259.

48 A. Shorten, "Linguistic Competence and Citizenship Acquisition", art. cit., 117–118.

49 R. Bauböck, "Morphing the Demos into the Right Shape: Normative Principles for Enfranchizing Resident Aliens and Expatriate Citizens", *Democratization* 22/5, 2015, 820–839.

50 This would caeteris paribus contradict the argument that a global lingua franca fosters global democracy, or, to a lesser extent, global justice.

51 B. Boudou, A. von Busekist, "Language Proficiency and Migration: An Argument Against Testing", chap. cit.

52 D. Weinstock, art. cit., 199–211.

53 Decision No 1934/2000/EC of the European Parliament and of the Council of July 17, 2000, on the European Year of Languages 2001, retrieved here: http://eur-lex.europa.eu/legal-content/GA/TXT/?uri=celex:32000D1934.

54 M. Gazzola, "Language Policy and Linguistic Justice in the European Union: The Socio-Economic Effects of Multilingualism", ELF Working Papers Series, #15, www.elf.unige.ch.
    Others argue that the self-fulfilling prophecy of English as a lingua franca is fundamentally flawed. English is neither the language of international politics and higher education nor a world language: only 14 per cent of EU citizens speak English, only 21 per cent master English on a "fairly good level" as a second language in the member states, and only 7 per cent to 8 per cent of the world population speak English. See M. Gazzola, "The Linguistic Implications of Academic Performance Indicators: General Trends and Case Study", *International Journal of the Sociology of Language*, 216, 2012, 131–156.

55 P. Van Paris, *Linguistic Justice for Europe and for the World*, op. cit.

56 I. Shapiro, *Politics Against Domination*, Cambridge, MA, Harvard University Press, 2016.

57 This is a very classical way of ordering the literature.

58 Contra R. Phillipson, "Lingua Franca or Lingua Frankensteinia? English in European Integration and Globalization", *World Englishes* 27/2, 2008, 250–267; "English as Threat or Opportunity in European Higher Education", 2013, retrieved here: www. researchgate. net/publication/265794097_English_as_threat_or_opportunity_in_European_higher_education.

59 R. Bauböck, "The Political Value of Languages", in H. De Schutter, D. Robichaud, op. cit., 212–223.

60 D. Archibugi, M. Cellini, "Democracy and Global Governance. The Internal and External Levers", IRPPS Working paper 69/2015.

61 P. Van Parijs, "Linguistic Diversity as Curse and as By-Product", in X. Arzoz ed., *Respecting Linguistic Diversity in the European Union*, Amsterdam, John Benjamins Publishing Company, 2007, 17–46.

62 M. Gazzola, "Language Policy and Linguistic Justice in the European Union: The Socio-Economic Effects of Multilingualism", op. cit.

34

THE ETHICS OF TOLERATION AND RELIGIOUS ACCOMMODATIONS

Aurélia Bardon and Emanuela Ceva

Introduction

The idea of toleration plays a paramount role in liberal theorising with regard to the normative characterisation of the public policies for the accommodation of minority claims in a democracy. This is the case in general, given the multicultural connotation of contemporary societies, and with regard to the policies for the accommodation of religious diversity in particular. Ready-to-hand examples include the debates surrounding the scope and place of religious practices (e.g., ritual animal slaughter) and symbols (e.g., the Muslim hijab or the Christian cross) in a liberal democratic polity, as well as those concerning the tensions between the contours of legitimate satire and respect for religious diversity (e.g., the case of Danish cartoons on the prophet Mohammed, but also the recent attack on Charlie Hebdo).

It is not surprising, therefore, to notice a wide scholarly – both conceptual and normative – interest in the idea of toleration as a fundamental political ideal (not only as a personal moral virtue); nor is it infrequent in contemporary societies to hear political appeals to developing public policies that are inspired by that idea (Cohen 2004; Creppell et al. 2008; Galeotti 2001; Walzer 1997). However, this generalised attention should not distract from some conceptual uncertainties and normative controversies concerning the boundaries and implications of the idea of toleration within a liberal theory of democracy.[1]

Standardly, liberal scholars have defined toleration as consisting of three necessary components: (1) the tolerator's negative judgement towards an object of toleration; (2) her power to interfere with what to which she objects; and (3) her reasons for non-interfering with it (Forst 2007; see also Cohen 2004).

Each of these components has been widely debated. Should we conceive of the tolerator's negative judgement as resting only on moral bases (disapproval), or can it also involve more simple considerations of either taste or preference (dislike) (Heyd 1996)? Should we look only at cases where the tolerator's power to interfere is actual or do counterfactual considerations matter too (Forst 2007)? How should we make sense of the different kinds of reasons for toleration – whether epistemological (fallibilism, scepticism), practical (prudence), or moral (value commitments)?[2]

In this chapter, we do not aspire to rehearse the many discussions that have developed around these conceptual issues (Oberdiek 2001). We take the concept of toleration as just presented at face value (with all its conceptual uncertainties), but we engage with a further cluster of questions that concerns the normative status of this idea and its implications for the development of public policies for the accommodation of diversities within a (broadly conceived) liberal democratic framework.

The main issue, from this perspective, is whether toleration, as a liberal political ideal, is best conceptualised as forbearance of what one either disapproves or dislikes. This issue is problematic because it risks making toleration redundant as a normative political ideal that shapes public policies in liberal democracies: if toleration equals forbearance, is it not made redundant by the basic liberal commitment to political neutrality?[3]

In order to vindicate a political role for the idea of toleration, some have reinterpreted it as embodying a more positive attitude of recognition of diversities that overcomes neutrality (Galeotti 2002). But, so conceived, does the positive connotation that toleration receives not collide with the inherent negativity that derives from the kind of judgement on the basis of which the tolerator is presupposed to be prima facie moved (Jones 2006)?

These questions are of general philosophical and political interest as parts of an investigation of the normative grounds of liberal democratic polities. But they acquire special importance when they are brought to bear on one of the main challenges with which contemporary liberal democracies are unescapably faced – the accommodation of religious diversity. Certainly, there are many more or less problematic sources of diversity that liberal democracies must confront; these include culture, gender, ethnicity, ethics – just to name a few examples. But an even random look at the headlines of any newspaper worldwide is sufficient to realise that the challenges of religious diversity are a social constant and a matter of political urgency virtually anywhere.

The social relevance and political urgency of these challenges prompt a further set of more specific questions concerning the idea of religious toleration. What do we tolerate when we tolerate religion? Does the traditional liberal commitment to toleration demand the accommodation of religious diversity in a democracy? What public policies should be developed to accommodate religious diversity in a tolerant manner? Are we justified in singling out religion as an object of special protection in liberal democracies?

To address these two sets of questions, we devote this chapter to the pursuit of a twofold aim. First, we offer a general discussion of the idea of toleration as the normative ground for the accommodation of religious diversity in a liberal democracy. Second, we draw the specific implications of this analysis for the design of public policies capable of making sense of the challenges raised by a plurality of religious claims.

In keeping with this twofold aim, the chapter is divided into two parts. The first part revolves around the general question of what it means to develop tolerant public policies. The second part addresses the more specific issue of the kinds of policies that toleration demands when it comes to the accommodation of religious diversity in particular.

The ethics of toleration: what does it mean to tolerate?

Toleration is a relational ideal. It characterises a relation between a subject *B* who takes exception with some feature *Z* of *A* but, although *B* could interfere against *Z*, she decides not to do so.[4] Accordingly, the core of toleration consists in someone's deliberate refraining from acting on the basis of his or her negative judgement.

So understood, toleration may qualify horizontal moral relations between peers as well as political ones. These latter have been typically presented as consisting in the state's non-interference with citizens' beliefs and practices.

In this sense, from a liberal perspective, political appeals to toleration have been standardly grounded in the normative characterisation of the vertical relations that occur in pre-modern politics. Although the sovereign has the power to decide on – say – religious matters and to implement her decisions through coercion, a commitment to toleration motivates her to waive this power and let citizens abide by their beliefs of faith, much as they are contrary to the sovereign's own beliefs.

It is apparent that this characterisation sits uncomfortably with the vindication of toleration as a political ideal that qualifies normatively state-citizens relations in contemporary liberal democracies (Heyd 2008). It is a defining feature of the liberal state that certain spheres of individual action – including religion – are immune to the state's interference. These spheres of personal freedom are protected by rights, whose distribution across the citizenry is the subject matter of justice.

Those who hold public office simply lack the prerogative to make use of their entrusted public power to interfere negatively with individuals' spheres of personal freedom – within limits that are standardly associated with some understanding of the harm principle and needs of action coordination. More generally, those who hold political power are not authorised to act on the basis of their individual negative judgement of the uses that citizens make of their rights.

Think, for example, of one of the domains to which claims of toleration have traditionally applied: the domain of religion. It is a basic tenet of an important stream of liberalism that the state is duty-bound to protect citizens' rights to live by their religious beliefs and practices independently of the state's or other citizens' evaluations of the merits of such beliefs and practices. To the extent that the state is neutral in this sense, its action may not be informed by the judgement of citizens' religious beliefs and practices. From this it follows that the state may not be the subject of relations of toleration. To wit, in contemporary liberal democratic societies, citizens enjoy religious freedom (alongside such other basic freedoms as that of conscience, thought, expression, or association) as a matter of right, not as an entailment of toleration.

On this ground, some commentators have come to the conclusion that the conceptual space for toleration as a political ideal within the boundaries of liberal democracies is exhausted by the commitment to protecting individual freedom. This commitment requires public policies that ensure that all citizens be treated neutrally, in a way that is responsive to their equal status as "bare citizens", as the holders of democratic rights. This general status applies to all of them equally and impartially – that is, independently of the variable specific statuses they have in virtue of either their convictions or group belongings. On this ground toleration can easily be set aside as a normative basis of the development of public policies.[5]

Needless to say, toleration may still retain its importance as a personal virtue and, as such, characterise political relations that hold horizontally *between* citizens (Jones 2007). However, from this perspective, appeals to toleration appear conceptually and normatively redundant to qualify state-citizens relations normatively.

In order not to bite the bullet in response to this qualm, a way forward consists in rethinking the conception of toleration in a way that questions its semantic reduction to the sphere of liberal neutrality. Such an alternative conception builds on abjuring the standard liberal conviction that the instantiation of a difference-blind public sphere is the best solution to prevent the rise of discrimination by granting every citizen a basic set of rights and opportunities.

This idea can be questioned on the grounds that contemporary liberal democratic societies are in fact characterised by social dynamics of marginalisation and stigmatisation of diversities that are easily turned into discriminatory practices. In other words, liberal democratic societies are certainly characterised by their commitment to realising political neutrality. But this is an aspiration. The social fabric of any liberal democracy is in fact dominated by a mainstream that dictates the general standards of social and political acceptability of a good plan of life as well as of what counts as a legitimate variation with respect to it. As a result, certain differences that are perceived as compatible with the mainstream are largely tolerated (e.g., vegetarianism, Christian minority churches); other differences that question some social standards are rejected by the antibodies of the mainstream and, as a result, stigmatised or marginalised (e.g., queerness, Muslim animal ritual slaughter) (Galeotti 2002).

This situation has been arguably caused by the liberal political commitment to neutrality. Therefore, it cannot possibly be remedied by reference to this ideal. This is where the normative space for a new conception of toleration opens up. From this point of view, toleration should be reinterpreted as the commitment to taking positive actions to correct these dynamics of stigmatisation and marginalisation of differences, and the exclusion of minority beliefs and practices from the liberal mainstream (Creppell 2003; Deveaux 2000; Galeotti 2002).

So understood, toleration does not merely require forbearing what to which we object; toleration requires, rather, recognition of the object of our dislike or disapproval as belonging to the domain of legitimate differences, notwithstanding the persistence of our dislike or disapproval. In more directly political terms, toleration does not boil down to a state's neutrality and non-interference with citizens' individual freedom. Toleration is a matter of public recognition of a variety of legitimate – albeit controversial – ways of life, grounded in different beliefs and generating different practices. In this sense, unlike toleration as forbearance, toleration as recognition is not primarily a property of the relations between the state and individual citizens. The relations between majority and minority groups are relevant too and so is the kind of treatment that the liberal state ought to grant to citizens in virtue of their status as members of such groups.[6]

Moreover, as seen, toleration as forbearance requires public policies that are essentially aimed at the protection of individual rights (including sanctions for those who trespass on them). On the other hand, toleration as recognition justifies a more positive kind of action of the part of a liberal and democratic state. Notably, in this interpretation, tolerant public policies could include affirmative actions addressed to compensate certain minorities for past and current discriminations (e.g., quotas for certain politically underrepresented groups). But they could also include symbolic interventions aimed at promoting a change of perception of certain differences as extraneous to the mainstream (e.g., advertisement campaigns).

These policy implications show a potential tension in this conception of toleration. Its positive connotation may, in fact, look problematic *qua* incompatible with the negative judgement that is necessarily presupposed in relations of toleration; as anticipated, we can tolerate, strictly speaking, only what to which we object (otherwise we have either indifference or, in fact, acceptance). The concern is thus whether we can still properly speak of toleration when this idea takes the positive connotation of the recognition of the equal legitimacy of different identities and lifestyles (Jones 2006).

So we can see that the distinction between these two conceptions of toleration as forbearance and recognition matters both conceptually and practically in view of its public policy implications for the accommodation of religious diversity. If we interpret toleration as forbearance, the tolerant state has a duty to protect the different spheres of individual religious freedom. Discharging this duty requires difference-blind public policies that do not directly discriminate religious believers or the members of a particular religious minority. If, on the other hand, we interpret toleration as recognition, the tolerant state has a duty to correct and remedy the discriminations and marginalisation that members of minority religious groups have suffered. The fulfilment of this duty requires the public recognition of different religious ways of life and, possibly, special minority group rights.

Many contemporary societies have opted for a sort of middle ground between these two lines of policy-making: the accommodation of religious diversity. Accommodation refers to a type of policy that grants some kind of differential treatment to members of religious minorities – for example, through the concession of exemptions from generally applicable laws. Accommodation, therefore, goes beyond mere forbearance as it aims to make it easier for religious believers to practise their religion whenever it conflicts with generally applicable rules. But accommodation does not require the positive connotation of some policies of recognition – for example, those that demand special group representation. Notably, policies of accommodation are meant primarily to facilitate the exercise of the individual right to religious freedom; they are not meant to respond to the stigmatisation, exclusion, or lack of representation of religious minorities. Resorts to policies of accommodation are not immune to controversies, however. We devote the next part of the chapter to discuss some such controversies as concern the accommodation of religious diversity.

From toleration to accommodation: how should we tolerate?

As emerges from the foregoing discussion, in contemporary liberal democracies, the hard question is not whether we should tolerate religious diversity but what it actually means to tolerate it: what form should toleration of religious diversity take in practice?

In line with the criticism of policies of toleration as forbearance we have discussed in the previous section, the mere absence of persecution of religious minorities might not suffice. Moreover, as the defenders of the idea of toleration as recognition have shown, difference-blind policies can have indirect discriminatory effects for religious believers, which may make it excessively burdensome for some individuals to abide by their religious beliefs and perform their religious practices. To illustrate, say that there is a good and neutral reason for prohibiting the carrying of knives in certain situations – for instance, in schools: it is necessary for public safety. But this prohibition affects Sikhs, who have a religious commitment to wear a religious dagger, the kirpan, at all times, more than it affects other citizens. Does tolerating Sikhism mean that a special treatment of their situation is required? Should Sikhs be allowed to wear the kirpan even when the carrying of knives is normally prohibited? If so, what are the boundaries of this differential treatment? Consider that even where there is a legal exemption from the prohibition of carrying knives in public, Sikhs are not allowed to wear the kirpan in prison or on airplanes (Jones 2017: 172).

The toleration of religion is not an all-or-nothing decision; it requires a thorough evaluation of particular situations and the careful balancing of competing interests. These are the dilemmas that policies for the accommodation of religious diversity face in contemporary liberal democracies.

But first, a clarification: what is a policy of accommodation? To accommodate religion means to modify or suspend rules for certain groups of people or for certain institutions, 'specifically for the purpose of facilitating the free exercise of religion' (McConnell 1985: 3–4). What those who demand policies of religious accommodation challenge is not necessarily the general legitimacy of the rule but its application to some religious believers in particular (Cohen 2015: 187).

To illustrate, consider exemptions as a particular form of accommodation: individuals or institutions are exempted when the rule simply does not apply to them. Exemptions are common legal tools in contemporary liberal democracies, used especially in the domain of health and disability. They are also widely used to respond to demands of religious believers: the Catholic Church is exempted from anti-discrimination law and can hire men exclusively; special menus are provided in prisons for inmates with religious dietary restrictions; Sikhs are exempted from wearing a helmet when riding a motorcycle; some religious believers have been exempted from mandatory vaccination, when it clashes with their religious beliefs.[7]

When neutral laws are more burdensome for some citizens than for others because of their religious commitments, is the development of policies of accommodation the appropriate tolerant response? In this part of the chapter, we examine two main questions concerning the accommodation of religious diversity: the question of the justification of accommodation (a) and the question of the object of accommodation (b).

a. The justification of accommodation

Should we accommodate? And if so, *why* should we accommodate? Is accommodation the right kind of tolerant response to the unequal effects of difference-blind laws? There are three possible arguments in response to the question of the justification of accommodation: (i) the sceptical argument, (ii) the equality argument, and (iii) the special right argument.

i. The sceptical argument

The sceptical argument denies that there is any compelling justification for granting exemptions to religious believers, provided that the law is legitimate and publicly justified (Barry 2001; Dworkin 2013; Leiter 2013). All laws necessarily have different impacts on different people (Barry 2001: 34). It is most likely the case that religious believers are more affected than non-believers by the disestablishment of religion. Similarly, it is most likely the case that uniform regulations affect more those citizens who want to wear some particular dress for cultural or religious commitments, or for fashion or aesthetic preferences. Taxation is less burdensome for those who are naturally generous and traffic regulations for those who do not drive. Sceptics therefore argue that unequal effects do not necessarily mean unequal or unfair treatment, and so, on their own, they provide insufficient grounds to justify exemptions.[8]

What matters, then, is not the effects of the law but its justification: 'Either the case for the law (or some version of it) is strong enough to rule out exemptions, or the case that can be made for exemptions is strong enough to suggest that there should be no law anyway' (Barry 2001: 39). There are two main claims supporting scepticism about exemptions. The first claim concerns the generality of the law in any liberal democracy. To the extent that a law is legitimate and neutrally justified, it should be the same for all citizens. The second claim is more specific and it aims at avoiding the objection of the proliferation of exemptions. If exemptions were granted for religious reasons, we might have to grant exemptions for moral non-religious reasons as well, and maybe even for non-moral projects and mere preferences (May 2017). Ultimately, when the state grants exemptions, it necessarily singles out certain claims as being more valuable than others; this, according to sceptics, is necessarily unfair.

ii. The equality argument

The equality argument provides a first way to justify accommodations, including exemptions. This argument is based on a comparative approach. It suggests that difference-blind rules might disadvantage certain citizens more than others, and so they can indirectly entail unequal treatment. Following this argument, accommodations are justified because they are a way to guarantee fair and equal opportunities for all citizens (Quong 2006; Patten 2017) or equal respect of all citizens (Ceva 2011).

To evaluate whether an accommodation is required, then, one has to look at the burdens imposed on religious believers whose freedom of religion has been limited by a particular rule, and to compare them with the burdens – for example, on a person's integrity – imposed by the same rule on other citizens: are (some) religious believers more burdened than others because of their religion? In other words, are they indirectly discriminated?

In Western societies, for example, schools are open from Mondays to Fridays: days of work and days of rest are the same for all schoolteachers. Jewish and Christian schoolteachers are not affected by this provision, but Muslim schoolteachers are. It just happens to be the case that one of the days they are expected to work is considered a religious holiday in Islam, but not in Judaism or Christianity. The burdens imposed by the generally applicable rules regarding weekly days of rest are heavier for Muslims than for non-Muslims.[9] Accommodation is justified in this case to re-establish equality and make sure that all citizens have equal opportunities to combine their professional duties and religious commitments.

iii. The special right argument

The special right argument is another way to justify religious accommodation. It is based on a non-comparative approach. Accommodation is justified when a law imposes an excessive burden on something that deserves some special degree of protection.

This argument presupposes "the specialness thesis". There are two ways in which religion can be said to be special.[10] In the special right argument, religion is special in the sense that it should be specially protected – that is, it belongs to a category of claims that are worthy of a special type of protection that claims that do not belong to this category do not deserve. Limitations on the free exercise of religion, then, require a particularly high degree of justification. On the other hand, the second interpretation of the specialness thesis says that religion is uniquely special – that is, that *only* religion is worthy of special treatment. This uniqueness thesis is compatible with the special right argument, but it is not necessarily implied by it. It might be that the normatively relevant category in the special right argument is that of religion, in which case religion is uniquely *and* specially protected; but it might also be that the relevant category is that of deep moral commitments, in which case religious moral commitments are specially but not uniquely protected (all conscientious commitments qualify).[11]

In its most common version, the special right argument identifies conscience as requiring special protection.[12] It is, for instance, the claim defended by Martha Nussbaum: there should be special protection of freedom of conscience – that is, religious claims might be specially protected to the extent that they are conscientious claims, but secular conscientious claims will be equally protected (Nussbaum 2008).

Based on the special right argument, accommodations are justified independently of how other citizens are treated. The focus of the argument is not on how burdensome a particular rule is for some religious citizens compared to other citizens who do not share the same religious commitments; rather, the focus is on how burdensome and how necessary or justified a particular rule is.

Slaughtering regulations, for instance, impose that animals are stunned before they are killed. These regulations are particularly burdensome for those who believe the meat they consume has to come from animals that have been slaughtered in a traditional way incompatible with these regulations. The special right argument looks at the burden that the regulation entails for those citizens, and at the same time asks to what extent the rule itself is justified and necessary.

Evaluating accommodations based on the special right argument therefore requires evaluating and balancing the interests of the citizens and those of the state: the stronger the interests of the state, the weaker the claim for an exemption. As opposed to general rights, special rights 'place much more powerful and general constraints on government' (Dworkin 2013: 131). This raises the justificatory level for generally applicable rules. On this account, it is easier to limit general rights than it is to limit special rights. For many advocates of the special right argument, then, limitations on freedom of religion or freedom of conscience are legitimate only when a compelling state interest is at stake (Nussbaum 2008: 169).

The main issue for the advocates of the special right argument lies with the assessment of the different claims. On the one hand, the claims, burdens, and interests of citizens must be assessed: how should we evaluate the severity of the burden imposed on citizens? What should count as a 'substantial burden' (Greenawalt 2008: 205)? If the accommodation claim is based on religious beliefs, how should we assess such beliefs and when do they justify an accommodation (Billingham 2017)? On the other hand, the interests that the state has in having the rule, and in having a uniform application of the rule, also have to be assessed: how important is the rule that causes a substantial burden on some citizens? Is there a sufficient and neutral justification for this rule? Is it necessary that the rule apply to every single citizen? What counts as a compelling state interest (Greenawalt 2008: 214–232)?

In sum, the equality and the special right arguments provide two different reasons to justify policies of religious accommodation as instances of toleration. The equality approach justifies accommodation in cases of *unequal* burdens. Policies of accommodation require that the burdens of compliance with a certain law be measured for different citizens. Policies of accommodation are means to re-establish equality of treatment. On the other hand, the special right approach justifies accommodation in cases of *excessive* burdens for citizens that are assessed independently of the burdens of others.[13] These two arguments are not mutually exclusive, but they appeal to two distinct ways to justify why policies of accommodation should be developed. In this sense, they offer different views of what it means to tolerate religious diversity in practice.

b. The object of accommodation

Our discussion so far has concerned the *reasons* for toleration through the accommodation of religious diversity. A further important issue regards the *object* of toleration through policies of religious accommodation: *what* should we accommodate when we tolerate religious diversity? What is it exactly that we are trying to protect or that we consider worthy of protection when we accommodate? The problem comes up in both the equality and the special right arguments: what is it exactly that we think we should equalise? What is it exactly that we think deserves some kind of special protection?

There are two dimensions to this question: (i) What is the normatively relevant dimension of religion that we want to protect through accommodation? And (ii) are we accommodating individual religious believers or religious groups?

i. Should we accommodate religion or something else?

Most of us have a strong moral intuition that religion is something that should be protected. But why is this the case? What is it exactly that we are we trying to protect when we protect religion and, therefore, accommodate religious diversity? Political theorists fall in one of the following two camps in this debate: those who believe that religion should be uniquely protected (advocates of the uniqueness thesis), and those who believe that it should not be uniquely protected (egalitarians).[14]

The uniqueness thesis raises the issue of the specialness of religion in a second sense with respect to that identified in our foregoing discussion. If religious diversity is singled out for special treatment, then it means that what the state is trying to protect is religion itself or some special religious good. The argument is based on the idea that religion is distinctly and intrinsically valuable: 'religion is unlike other human activities' (Laycock 1990: 16) and 'no such institutions are as important to the process of developing, transmitting, communicating, and enforcing concepts of morality and justice as are the churches' (McConnell 1985: 18). Religion is also unique in the sense that it might be true and superior to all forms of secular power. 'Religious claims – if true – are prior to and of greater dignity than the claims of the state. If there is a God, His authority necessarily transcends the authority of nations; that, in part, is what we mean by "God"' (McConnell 1985: 15).

The uniqueness of religion is a built-in characteristic of how McConnell and others define the concept:[15] ultimately religious authority transcends secular authority. This is what justifies the unique and special treatment of religion and, therefore, the accommodation of religious diversity as an instance of toleration.

For egalitarians, on the other hand, the state has no reason to protect religion in itself and, therefore, no reason to treat religious diversity as a special addressee of accommodation policies (with respect to other forms of diversity). Rather, the state should protect a category of claims that are particularly valuable for citizens and that include, but are not limited to, religious claims. In other words, religious claims are protected but not *as* religious. Different interpretations of this broader category of protection-worthy claims have been offered: what ultimately must be protected are claims of conscience (Ceva 2017; Nussbaum 2008; Leiter 2013), deep commitments (Eisgruber & Sager 2007), meaning-giving beliefs (Maclure & Taylor 2011), special commitments (Patten 2014), or commitments that are central for an individual to live with integrity (Bou-Habib 2006; Laborde 2017; Seglow 2017).

Egalitarians therefore argue that the category of religion is underinclusive; many secular claims are just as important and valuable for citizens as religious ones, and they should be protected in exactly the same way. If we give special menus to inmates who cannot eat pork for religious reasons, we should equally give special menus to inmates who are committed to vegetarianism for secular moral reasons. If an exemption from military service is granted for those who are pacifist for religious reasons, then the same exemption should be granted for secular pacifists.[16]

ii. Should we accommodate individuals or groups?

Depending on what is identified as the normatively relevant dimension of claims that deserve protection, accommodations can be granted to individuals exclusively, or to groups too. From this perspective, a particularly important object of group accommodation is religious institutions. Individual and institutional accommodations serve different purposes (McConnell 1985: 26–27). Individual accommodation is meant to make it easier for religious believers to live according to what they see as their religious duties. Institutional accommodation, on the other hand, is meant to guarantee the autonomy of religious institutions (Smith 2016): to what extent should religious institutions, such as churches, schools, hospitals or even for-profit corporations, be subject to state laws? Should exemptions be granted when these laws clash with some of the religious beliefs that are central to the identity of the religious institution? Familiar cases include churches that want to hire men exclusively, religious adoption agencies that refuse to place children with homosexual couples, or religious hospitals that refuse to perform abortions.

This question has become particularly salient in recent discussions on law and religion, especially through two US Supreme Court cases. In the *Hosanna-Tabor* case (2012), for example, the Supreme Court confirmed that religious schools are exempted from anti-discrimination laws: the ministerial exception does not apply exclusively to churches. In *Burwell v. Hobby Lobby* (2014), the court went even further when it decided that business corporations are also protected by freedom of religion. An exemption from providing coverage for contraception was granted to Hobby Lobby because providing it would violate 'the sincerely held religious beliefs of the companies' owners' (Hobby Lobby, Opinion of the Court: 1). Both *Hosanna-Tabor* and *Hobby Lobby* assume that freedom of religion applies not only to individuals but also to religious institutions; they represent a "corporate turn" in freedom of religion, from an individual liberty to a corporate liberty (Flanders et al. 2016).

It has been objected that this corporate turn is based on a problematic understanding of corporate personhood (Cohen 2015; Shorten 2015). What does it mean for a group to have a religious objection to a law? What does it mean to say that religious institutions have a right to religious freedom, or that they are burdened by particular laws? And which institutions exactly should count as religious institutions? Ultimately the issue raised by institutional religious freedom is that of sovereignty and legal jurisdiction. By demanding autonomy, religious institutions contest the authority of the state in the religious domain and claim that they are themselves 'non-state legal sovereigns' (Cohen 2015: 195).

Interestingly, the idea of institutional religious freedom rests on the uniqueness thesis: it is the unique value of religion that justifies the need for autonomy. Because they emphasise the value of religion for individuals rather than the value of religion in itself, egalitarian theories cannot provide any ground for policies that revolve around institutional religious freedom.[17]

Conclusion

Toleration is a buzzword of contemporary liberal democracies and it is very often appealed to as the morally appropriate response to diversity. Our societies are characterised by an ever-growing diversity of conceptions of the good life, religions, cultures, languages, and identities. These are unavoidably the object of deep disagreements among individuals and groups.

In response to such disagreements, toleration demands – in a basic sense – that different individuals and groups put up with each other. But, on a more demanding understanding of this idea, a commitment to toleration may entail the recognition of the equal legitimacy of this diversity.

While there is a general consensus that toleration is required in either of these interpretations, a great degree of uncertainty concerns the ways in which we should *tolerate in practice*: what does it mean to tolerate? How should we tolerate? What is the object of toleration? And what are the limits of toleration?

This chapter has provided a critical discussion of some of these questions as they emerge with reference to an especially controversial object of toleration – that is, religious diversity. We have discussed the key conceptions of toleration that shape scholarly and political debates. In particular, we have shown how different normative considerations about toleration and about how to manage religious diversity have different implications in terms of public policy. This suggests that there are many different ways to tolerate.

The resort to accommodation, including in some cases the use of exemptions, is one possible option, which corresponds to one particular understanding of what it means to be tolerant and of what it is that we should tolerate.

Notably, our discussion has offered a general framework for thinking about toleration through the development of policies of religious accommodation. To be true, this is not sufficient to decide *when* we should accommodate in particular cases. Contextual considerations apply, for instance, to the evaluation of the costs of religious accommodation, especially in terms of shifting burdens on others (Jones 2016). These are specific considerations that are certainly central to policy-making. However, their discussion must necessarily be left to a case-by-case discussion rather than general philosophical analysis.

Notes

1 A liberal democratic framework has been the locus classicus of the debate on toleration. However, recent contributions to the discussion of this ideal have emerged from the neo-republican tradition too – see, notably, Laborde (2008, 2017). While drawing a dividing line between these two traditions is not a straightforward operation, in this chapter, we concentrate on liberal democracies primarily given the prominence of the references to this form of government both in the philosophical and political debate on religious toleration. For a multifaceted discussion, see Laborde and Bardon (2017).
2 Examples include, respectively, Popper (1987); Barry (1995); Gray (2002); Forst (2003); Galeotti (2002). For a general discussion, see Mendus (2009).
3 For one of the most influential presentations of toleration as forbearance see Horton (2011). For the charge of redundancy see Heyd (2008); Jones (2003; 2007); Meckled-Garcia (2001); Newey (1999, 2001).
4 See, among others, King (1997); Cohen (2004); and McKinnon (2006).
5 Along these lines of argument, some have argued that in a liberal democracy appeals to toleration should make way to those to respect as an appropriate normative ground for policy-making in liberal democratic societies – see, for example, Carter (2013), Ceva (2015), and Rossi (2013). For a discussion of toleration as a provisional arrangement on the way to realising political neutrality, see Galeotti (2015).
6 See Deveaux (2000); Galeotti (2002). A critical voice may be found in Horton (2011).
7 For a general discussion of different issues of differential treatment, see Calder and Ceva (2010).
8 Sceptics focus more specifically on the question of exemptions. Leiter, for instance, has called his argument the "No Exemptions" approach (2013: 100–108). But some forms of accommodation might be compatible with the sceptical argument.
9 See *Ahmad v. Inner London Education Authority*. For a discussion of this case, see Peter Jones (1994).
10 Alan Patten has proposed a similar distinction between two versions of the specialness thesis (Patten 2017: 212–213).
11 The second version of the specialness thesis (the uniqueness thesis) is discussed in this chapter in b(i).
12 It is what Jonathan Seglow has called the 'argument from conscience' (Seglow 2011: 56–59).
13 The distinction between the equality argument and the special right argument corresponds to the distinction between, respectively, accommodation claimed under discrimination law and accommodation claimed under human rights law (see Jones 2017).
14 On egalitarian theories of religious freedom, see Laborde (2014).
15 The idea of a God is central in McConnell's definition, and so it provides a basis for the uniqueness only of monotheistic religions.
16 The US Supreme Court adopted a broad interpretation of "religion", in line with egalitarianism, in the landmark cases *United States v. Seeger (1965)* and *Welsh v. United States* (1970) regarding whether secular conscientious objectors should be exempted from military service: a religious belief was interpreted as a 'sincere and meaningful belief occupying in the life of its possessor a place parallel to that filled by the God of those admittedly qualified for the exemption' (*United States v. Seeger*), and so it was concluded that exemptions from military service could be granted on non-religious grounds.
17 Egalitarian theorists can still justify accommodation for religious groups as groups, and not specifically because they are religious groups. Sager (2016) has defended such an argument to justify the right of churches to discriminate.

References

Ahmad v. inner London education authority.
Barry, B. (1995). *Justice as Impartiality.* Oxford: Clarendon Press.

Barry, B. (2001). *Culture and Equality*. Cambridge: Polity Press.

Billingham, P. (2017). How Should Claims for Religious Exemptions Be Weighed? *Oxford Journal of Law and Religion* 6(1): 1–23.

Bou-Habib, P. (2006). A Theory of Religious Accommodation. *Journal of Applied Philosophy* 23(1): 109–126.

Burwell v. Hobby Lobby 573 U.S. ___ (2014).

Calder, G., and Ceva, E. (2010). (eds.). *Diversity in Europe. Dilemmas of Differential Treatment in Theories and Practice*. London: Routledge.

Carter, I. (2013). Are Toleration and Respect Compatible? *Journal of Applied Philosophy* 30: 195–208.

Ceva, E. (2011). Self-Legislation, Respect and the Reconciliation of Minority Claims. *Journal of Applied Philosophy* 28(1): 14–28.

Ceva, E. (2015). Why Toleration Is Not the Appropriate Response to Dissenting Minorities' Claims. *European Journal of Philosophy* 23(3): 633–651.

Ceva, E. (2017). How Should We Respect Conscience? In: C. Laborde and A. Bardon, eds, *Religion in Liberal Political Philosophy*. Oxford: Oxford University Press.

Cohen, A.J. (2004). What Toleration Is. *Ethics* 115: 68–95.

Cohen, J.L. (2015). Freedom of Religion, Inc.: Whose Sovereignty? *Netherlands Journal of Legal Philosophy* 44(3): 169–210.

Creppell, I. (2003). *Toleration and Identity: Foundations of Early Modern Thought*. London: Routledge.

Creppell, I., Hardin, R., and Macedo, S. (2008). (eds). *Toleration on Trial*. Lanham: Lexington Book.

Deveaux, M. (2000). *Cultural Pluralism and Dilemmas of Justice*. Ithaca, NY: Cornell University Press.

Dworkin, R. (2013). *Religion Without God*. Cambridge, MA: Harvard University Press.

Eisgruber, C., and Sager, L. (2007). *Religious Freedom and the Constitution*. Cambridge, MA: Harvard University Press.

Flanders, C., Schwartzman, M., and Robinson, Z. (2016). Introduction. In: C. Flanders, M. Schwartzman and Z. Robinson, eds., *The Rise of Corporate Religious Liberty*. Oxford: Oxford University Press. xiii–xxv.

Forst, R. (2003). *Toleranz im Konflikt. Geschichte, Gehalt und Gegenwart eines umstrittenen Begriffs*. Frankfurt/Main: Suhrkamp.

Forst, R. (2007). Toleration. In: E. Zalta, ed., *Stanford Encyclopedia of Philosophy* http://plato.stanford.edu/entries/toleration/.

Galeotti, A.E. (2001). Do We Need Toleration as a Moral Virtue? *Res Publica* 7: 273–292.

Galeotti, A.E. (2002). *Toleration as Recognition*. Cambridge: Cambridge University Press.

Galeotti, A.E. (2015). The Range of Toleration. *Philosophy & Social Criticism* 41: 93–110.

Gray, J. (2002). *Two Faces of Liberalism*. New York: The New Press.

Greenawalt, K. (2008). *Religion and the Constitution*. Volume 1. Princeton, NJ: Princeton University Press.

Heyd, D. (1996). (ed.), *Toleration: An Elusive Virtue*. Princeton, NJ: Princeton University Press.

Heyd, D. (2008). Is Toleration a Political Virtue? In: M.S. Williams and J. Waldron, eds., *NOMOS XLVIII: Toleration and Its Limits*. New York: New York University Press. 171–194.

Horton, J. (2011). Why the Traditional Conception of Toleration Still Matters. *Critical Review of International Social and Political Philosophy* 3: 289–305.

Hosanna-Tabor Evangelical Lutheran Church & School v. Equal Employment Opportunity Commission 565 U.S. ___ (2012).

Jones, P. (1994). Bearing the Consequences of Belief. *Journal of Political Philosophy* 2(1): 24–43.

Jones, P. (2003). Toleration and Neutrality: Compatible Ideals? In: D. Castiglione and C. McKinnon, eds., *Toleration, Neutrality and Democracy*. Dordrecht: Kluwer. 97–110.

Jones, P. (2006). Toleration, Recognition and Identity. *The Journal of Political Philosophy* 14(2): 123–143.

Jones, P. (2007). Making Sense of Political Toleration. *British Journal of Political Science* 37(3): 383–402.

Jones, P. (2016). Accommodating Religion and Shifting Burdens. *Criminal Law and Philosophy* 10(3): 515–536.

Jones, P. (2017). Religious Exemption and Distributive Justice. In: C. Laborde and A. Bardon, eds., *Religion in Liberal Political Philosophy*. Oxford: Oxford University Press. 163–176.

King, P. (1997). *Toleration*. London: Routledge.

Laborde, C. (2008). *Critical Republicanism*. Oxford: Oxford University Press.

Laborde, C. (2014). Equal Liberty, Non-Establishment and Religious Freedom. *Legal Theory* 20(1): 52–77.

Laborde, C. (2017). *Liberalism's Religion*. Cambridge, MA: Harvard University Press.

Laborde, C., and Bardon, A. (2017). (eds.). *Religion in Liberal Political Philosophy*. Oxford: Oxford University Press.

Laycock, D. (1990). The Remnants of Free Exercise. *The Supreme Court Review* 1–68.

Leiter, B. (2013). *Why Tolerate Religion?* Princeton, NJ: Princeton University Press.

Maclure, J., and Taylor, C. (2011). *Secularism and Freedom of Conscience*. Cambridge, MA: Harvard University Press.

May, S.C. (2017). Exemptions for Conscience. In: C. Laborde and A. Bardon, eds., *Religion in Liberal Political Philosophy*. Oxford: Oxford University Press. 191–203.

McConnell, M. (1985). Accommodation of Religion. *The Supreme Court Review* 1–59.

McKinnon, C. (2006). *Toleration. A Critical Introduction*. London: Routledge.

Meckled-Garcia, S. (2001). Toleration and Neutrality: Incompatible Ideals? *Res Publica* 7: 293–313.

Mendus, S. (2009). (ed.). *Justifying Toleration: Conceptual and Historical Perspectives*. Cambridge: Cambridge University Press.

Newey, G. (1999). *Virtue, Reason and Toleration: The Place of Toleration in Ethical and Political Philosophy*. Edinburgh: Edinburgh University Press.

Newey, G. (2001). Is Democratic Toleration a Rubber Duck? *Res Publica* 7: 315–336.

Nussbaum, M. (2008). *Liberty of Conscience*. New York: Basic Books.

Oberdiek, H. (2001). *Tolerance: Between Forbearance and Acceptance*. Lanham, MD: Rowman & Littlefield.

Patten, A. (2014). *Equal Recognition*. Princeton, NJ: Princeton University Press.

Patten, A. (2017). Religious Exemptions and Fairness. In: C. Laborde and A. Bardon, eds, *Religion in Liberal Political Philosophy*. Oxford: Oxford University Press. 204–219.

Popper, K. (1987). Toleration and Intellectual Responsibility. In: S. Mendus and D. Edwards, eds., *On Toleration*. Oxford: Clarendon Press. 97–110.

Quong, J. (2006). Cultural Exemptions, Expensive Tastes and Equal Opportunities. *Journal of Applied Philosophy* 23(1): 53–71.

Rossi, E. (2013). Can Tolerance Be Grounded in Equal Respect? *European Journal of Political Theory* 12(3): 240–252.

Sager, L. (2016). Why Churches (and, Possibly, the Tarpon Bay Women's Blue Water Fishing Club) Can Discriminate. In: C. Flanders, M. Schwartzman, and Z. Robinson, eds., *The Rise of Corporate Religious Liberty*. Oxford: Oxford University Press. 77–101.

Seglow, J. (2011). Theories of Religious Exemptions. In: G. Calder and E. Ceva, eds., *Diversity in Europe*. London: Routledge.

Seglow, J. (2017). Religious Accommodation: Responsibility, Integrity, and Self-Respect. In: C. Laborde and A. Bardon, eds, *Religion in Liberal Political Philosophy*. Oxford: Oxford University Press. 177–190.

Shorten, A. (2015). Are There Rights to Institutional Exemptions? *Journal of Social Philosophy* 46(2): 242–263.

Smith, S.D. (2016). The Jurisdictional Conception of Church Autonomy. In: C. Flanders, M. Schwartzman and Z. Robinson, eds., *The Rise of Corporate Religious Liberty*. Oxford: Oxford University Press. 19–37.

United States v. Seeger 380 U.S. 163 (1965).

Walzer, M. (1997). *On Toleration*. New Haven, CO: Yale University Press.

Welsh v. United states 398 U.S. 333 (1970).

35

FREEDOM AND DESTINY

How new technologies are influencing the ethics and policy of abortion

Giulia Cavaliere and John Harris

Introduction: the continuing relevance of abortion for ethics and public policy

Abortion has almost certainly been practised as long as long as pregnancies have been unwanted. In modern bioethics abortion has for several decades been at the forefront of controversies in ethics and public policy. At the time of writing, the landmark English case of *R. v. Bourne* (1938), which brought abortion from dark alleys to the English Central Criminal Court, has just passed its seventy-fifth anniversary. Despite this longevity, the controversy surrounding abortion has not aged well. Abortion continues to be a matter of debate both in the context of public policy and in ethics. The controversy takes also more tangible forms of expression. Almost each time an abortion law or a modification of an existing law is considered, people fill the streets and demonstrate to make policy-makers hear their voices. For instance, in Poland during autumn of 2016, Polish women and men went on strike and demonstrated against a new abortion law that was at the time discussed in the parliament. The law would have *de facto* banned and criminalised all terminations, with women risking conviction for a period of up to five years in prison and doctors liable for prosecution and prison for assisting women (Davies 2016a). Black-clothed women went out in the streets as a sign of mourning the loss of reproductive rights and the feared death of women undergoing backstreet abortions. A few days later, after the government U-turn on this proposal, they started to demonstrate again as the new proposed law banned abortion in cases of severe congenital malformations, which had been allowed in Poland up until then (Davies 2016b). In the United States, one of the first moves of President Donald Trump was to sign legislation that repealed a rule issued in the final days of Barack Obama's administration (2016), which prohibited states from cutting government funding to organisations such as Planned Parenthood and others that perform or facilitate abortions.[1] The new law *de facto* nullifies an existing rule, which was finalised in the last days of the Obama administration (after the election of Donald Trump), that barred withholding federal funding from organisations providing services related to sexually transmitted diseases, contraception, cervical and breast screening, pregnancy care, and so forth, regardless of whether these organisations provided services such as abortions (Hirschfeld Davies 2017). While conservatives and pro-life groups praised this move, people filled the streets to demonstrate against this new bill. This time they were not wearing black, but crimson robes and white bonnets to invoke some of the characters of Margaret Atwood's dystopic novel *The Handmaid's Tale*[2] (Hauser 2017).

The controversy surrounding abortion remains live and highly visible globally. Discussions of the right to have an abortion or of the interests engaged in having an abortion[3] impact broader questions concerning the moral and legal status of the foetus; the right to self-determination of women; their reproductive health and care; the appropriate role of the medical professional, *telos* of medicine; and finally the appropriateness of the state enforcing "morality". These discussions engage passionately held views and beliefs, and involve a number of different stakeholders (Cavaliere 2017a).

What threatens the Pandora's box that abortion has the potential to unseal is the fact that for some people, foetuses are equal to persons and hence deserve the same rights as existing persons (i.e., the full moral status view) or have the potential to become fully developed persons and hence, by virtue of this potential, deserve legal protection and moral respect (i.e., the potentiality view).[4] Others are moved more by the belief that women should be free to decide what happens to their bodies in matters of procreation and no other citizens,[5] nor the state, should be allowed to interfere with this right (a moral and legal principle that, in the next sections, we refer to as reproductive freedom).

Some are more engaged by the question of the duties of health professionals to their patients and to their employers, whether, for example, conscientious objection to services regarded as legitimate by professional bodies AMA and BMA, for example, or which are legal and routinely provided (e.g., by the UK's NHS) is legitimate.

A further question concerns the role of the state in regulating matters of moral concern and the degree of state involvement in discussions about ethics (i.e., a conflict between liberal and communitarian views on the role of the state). In this chapter, we discuss only some of these questions, including the scope and relevance of reproductive freedom, the appropriate rights and duties of health care professionals (HCPs) and whether they should be allowed to conscientiously object to participating in an abortion, and the appropriate role of the state in matters of ethics.[6] These are the questions that, figuratively, bring us from the armchair to the "streets" to write this chapter, not least because writing and speaking are often a form of activism (Harris 1980).

The agenda

In this chapter, we situate abortion in historical and contemporary struggles regarding women's rights and responsibilities and in particular in the effects of science and technology on the nature of the debate and in the ability of states to regulate reproduction for good or ill.

We then describe some contemporary regulatory approaches, and we briefly illustrate a recent case in which the right to have an abortion was at the centre of the ethical and legislative debate in Northern Ireland, the issues of which turned on the availability of new drugs, on their safety, and on the use of the Internet. In the third section, using the Northern Ireland case, we address the question of reproductive freedom and the role of the state. In the fourth section, we reflect on the role and rights of health care professionals in the abortion debate and on the question of conscientious objections and moral complicity. Lastly, we argue that new technologies (e.g., abortion drugs) might affect access to terminations in countries where the right to abortion is either not recognised or severely constrained.

Women's struggles, women's rights, and reproductive destinies

While *the debate* on the ethics and governance of abortion dates back to landmark cases such *R. v. Bourne* (1938) in the United Kingdom or *Roe v. Wade* in the United States (1973), *the practice* of abortion has a much longer history.

The history of abortion goes hand in hand with other struggles that have been forced on women by centuries of prejudice and discrimination, such as the fight for the right to vote and the right to paid employment and to freedom from dependence on the state and the family (Ford 2017). As the example of the United States shows, cutting funding to abortion clinics means also curtailing women's reproductive rights to other forms of care.[7] Women were working for much longer than they were paid and they were bearers of duties for much longer than they were of rights. The fight for reproductive liberty is the fight against the imposition on women of reproductive duties for the benefit of others while denying women the most fundamental reproductive rights to protect themselves.

Women's 'liberation' – access to an education (which is one of the biggest single factors in falling birth rates),[8] the right to work, and indeed basic equal opportunities in all fields – depends on their ability to control fertility, including by abortion. Reproductive liberty frees women from economic dependency on their fathers, brothers, and husbands; the vote allows women to have some say in policies that concern them directly and indirectly; being able to terminate a pregnancy finally allows women to take control over their reproductive destinies on which most of the other liberties for women depend.

Unsafe, "backstreet" abortions have been practised for centuries and have been compared to a 'persistent, preventable pandemic' (Grimes et al. 2006, p. 1908). In countries where abortion is prohibited altogether, allowed only to save a woman's life, or still severely restricted in multiple ways, backstreet abortions have allowed women to take control over their bodies and over their reproductive destinies, but at very high costs. They put women's physical and mental health and even their lives at risk, especially in developing countries (Shah and Åhman 2010).

The regulation of abortion varies greatly among countries, and a detailed account of the existing regulations worldwide is beyond the scope of this contribution. In the next section, we outline some exemplifying policy approaches in order to show how nations have severely restricted access to abortion either directly through statutory limitations or indirectly through geographical and economic limitations.

Abortion laws yesterday and today

The United States represents an interesting case from a public policy and ethics perspective, as while abortions are legal, there are several statutory restrictions that limit in practice access to this practice. *Roe v. Wade* (1973) legalised abortion nationwide and gave the framework for coherent legislation across all states (Ely 1973). A second landmark case, *Planned Parenthood v. Casey* (1992), upheld the right to abortion, but, at the same time, granted to each state a certain degree of discretion to enact restrictions that do not constitute an "undue burden" for women seeking terminations (Wharton et al. 2006). What constitutes "undue burden" is currently a matter of both interpretation and dispute (Robertson 2011; Wharton et al. 2006), and, since *Planned Parenthood v. Casey*, states have passed laws that restrict abortion in various ways. For instance, some states bar late-term abortions, while others mandate performing ultrasound scans, listening to the foetus heartbeat, and counselling regarding the risks of the procedure and the available alternatives (Gold and Nash 2012; Robertson 2011; Sanger 2008); others require parental notifications for minors, or waiting periods (Dennis et al. 2009), which force women to go to the clinic multiple times (Gold and Nash 2012). In addition to these legal limitations, other geographical and economic limitations impinge on the right to abortion and in practice restrict severely the feasibility of accessing abortions. For instance, not all states have abortion clinics, which absence forces women to travel to other states and to bear the costs of the journey; and the right to have an abortion is also restricted indirectly through economic limitations: federal funding for abortion through Medicaid is allowed only when the woman's life is at risk, and in the event of rape or incest since the Hyde Amendment (1976) (Guttmacher Institute 2017a), and several states restrict insurance coverage of abortion (Guttmacher Institute 2017b).

Besides Malta, Andorra, and the Vatican State, many European countries allow abortions, but restrictions, even if generally less severe than in the United States, apply in these countries too (Boland and Katzive 2008). For instance, abortions in Ireland are permitted only to save a woman's life, while in Poland, abortions are allowed only if the life or the health of the woman is at risk, if the foetus has severe malformations, or if the pregnancy is the result of rape or incest (Boland and Katzive 2008). In Italy, where abortions are allowed on demand since 1978 (194/78 Law), and in other European countries, time limitations apply and women can terminate unwanted pregnancies up until 12 weeks after conception. The right to have an abortion in Italy, however, is indirectly curtailed as the 194 Law allows gynaecologists and obstetricians[9] to conscientiously object to performing the procedure[10] (Minerva 2014). In the United Kingdom, abortions are permitted by the 1967 Abortion Act, which allows the procedure in England, Wales, and Scotland, but not in Northern Ireland, where abortions are regulated by the Offences against Person Act 1861 (sections 58 and 59) and the Criminal Justice Act (Northern Ireland) 1945 (sections 25 and 26) (Bloomer and Fegan 2014). There, abortions can be lawfully performed only if the physical and mental health of the woman is in danger (Boland and Katzive 2008).

A recent case involving a 15-year-old girl and her mother in Northern Ireland stirred new controversy and echoed unresolved moral and legal questions that characterise the abortion debate from its inception. The mother of a 15-year-old girl is currently threatened with criminal conviction, as, in 2013, she helped her daughter to procure abortion pills online, which eventually led to the termination of the girl's pregnancy. The 15-year-old had the abortion voluntarily and is not being prosecuted (neither is the 16-year-old boy who fathered the child and who committed a criminal offence because the 15-year-old could not legally consent to sex). Her mother on the other hand faces up to ten years in prison for breaching the Offences against Person Act 1861 (Gentleman 2017). The abortion was brought to the attention of the court as a general practitioner working in the clinic where the young adolescent sought medical advice after taking the abortion pills reported the mother and daughter to the authorities. This case raises several moral and legal questions: a first question concerns women's right to reproductive freedom, a moral and legal principle that we discuss at length in the next section (Harris 1992, 1998); a second question concerns the duty of the health care professional and, especially, of those health care professionals that have strongly held moral views against abortion; a third question concerns the use of abortions pills available online and how new "technologies" (broadly conceived) change the moral landscape of the debate on abortion – how, in other words, they can be both liberating and potentially bearers of new responsibilities.

Why does the right to abortion matter? Reproductive freedom and the democratic presumption[11]

In this section, we primarily address the issues of human rights and reproductive liberty in the decision to prosecute the mother of a 15-year-old girl, who, as the Public Prosecution Service

(PPS) of Northern Ireland puts it, as 'parent and guardian responsible for the well-being of her daughter . . . procured potentially harmful medication and allowed her daughter to take a potentially dangerous course of medication without the proper medical involvement and supervision', even though, as the PPS also admits, her daughter had been made pregnant by a 16-year-old boy who in doing so had committed what the PPS accepts to have been a criminal act against the 15-year-old victim (see ahead).

The concept of reproductive liberty

One of the presumptions of liberal democracies is that the freedom of citizens should not be interfered with unless good and sufficient justification can be produced for so doing. The presumption is that citizens should be free to make their own choices in the light of their own values, regardless of whether these choices and values are acceptable to the majority. Only serious real and present danger, either to other citizens or to society or significantly damaging to the public interest, is sufficient to rebut this presumption. If anything less than this high standard is accepted liberty is dead.

This presumption is sometimes expressed as saying that citizens should enjoy the maximum liberty which is compatible with a like liberty for all. This way of putting the liberal presumption acknowledges that one legitimate limitation of the liberty of the individual is where its exercise limits the liberty of others, or threatens others with significant harm. The alternative to a presumption of liberty is what John Stuart Mill and Alexis de Tocqueville think of in terms of the "tyranny of the majority" (Mill 1979; Tocqueville 1835). To avoid this tyranny the presumption in favour of liberty can be rebutted only by showing that the exercise of liberty for some either infringes the like liberty for others or causes real and present dangers of significant harm either to individuals or to society. It is not enough that others are made uncomfortable by its exercise, nor that they do not like it, nor that they find it repellent.

Upholding liberty, safeguarding a free society, is not cost-free. One of the costs is that citizens must be prepared to accept that others must be free to do things that they themselves would not do or would not wish to do, and even things that make them uncomfortable or which they find repugnant. The liberty to do only those things of which the majority approve is no liberty at all.

What consenting adults do in private is (almost always) their own affair. The exceptions must establish serious harm to others or society. Where, as in the present case, a 15-year-old is legally incapable of giving valid consent to sexual intercourse she has been the victim of a sexual offence. But even if she had not been the victim of a crime, her reproductive liberty and privacy – that is, her right to privacy and family life (as protected by Articles 3 and 8 of the European Convention on Human Rights) – should operate to protect her right to end a pregnancy, certainly at this early stage. (Lever 2013). These rights are protected in England, Wales, and Scotland with respect to the accessibility of safe and lawful abortions for those in this or an equivalent position to this child. It is unconscionable and indefensible that they are not similarly legally protected in Northern Ireland. That they are not is clearly a violation of the human rights of both mother and daughter and of the democratic presumption in favour of freedom to which we have referred. It is also a violation of the principle of "equal protection" of the law and of the principle that access to public services provided by the state, like the National Health Service (NHS) in the United Kingdom, either should be provided to all citizens or, at the very least, should not be selectively provided to some citizens (in this case the citizens of England, Scotland, and Wales) but not to other citizens of the relevant state, which, in this case, is the United Kingdom of England, Scotland, Wales, and Northern Ireland.

The denial of reproductive liberty

The burden of proof is not on those who defend liberty but on those who would deny it. Those who would exercise reproductive liberty do not have to show what good it would do; rather those who would curtail freedom have to show not simply that it is unpopular, or undesirable, or undesired, not even that it is illegal in a particular jurisdiction, but that it is seriously harmful to others or to society and that these harms are real and present, not future and speculative.

In most democracies (though not all) there is a presumption in favour of liberty. As the American legal theorist Joel Feinberg put it in 1984 in his book *The Moral Limits of the Criminal Law,*

> Whenever a legislator is faced with a choice between imposing a legal duty on citizens or leaving them at liberty, other things being equal, he should leave individuals free to make their own choices. Liberty should be the norm; coercion always needs some special justification. It is legitimate for the state to prohibit conduct that causes serious private harm, or the unreasonable risk of such harm, or harm to important public institutions and practices. In short, state interference with a citizen's behaviour tends to be morally justified when it is reasonably necessary (that is, when there are reasonable grounds for taking it to be necessary as well as effective) to prevent harm or the unreasonable risk of harm to parties other than the person interfered with.
>
> *(Feinberg 1984, pp. 9–11)*

If drastic and punitive measures are occasioned by the facts of this case they would be justified against prosecution of the mother and those who would bring such a prosecution. The termination of pregnancy was in this case successful, and no harm was done; what is the point of this prosecution? The burden of justifying their actions falls on those who would deny liberty, even if the locally applicable law also denies it, not on those who would exercise it. If this is right, the presumption must be in favour of the liberty to access reproductive technologies whether as means of founding families or as means of preventing the founding of families unless good and sufficient reasons can be shown against so doing.

Reproductive liberty as a fundamental human right

But more than being a simple exercise of liberty or personal preference, reproductive liberty has a serious claim to be a dimension of a fundamental human right – however characterised. If it involved the exercise of a bare preference, like drinking coffee or playing tennis, its free exercise would still be a fundamental entitlement. However, if it can be shown to involve more than an assertion of an entitlement to exercise freedom of choice, but that it also involves the claim to exercise a choice that is part of a fundamental or basic human right, then the arguments against its exercise (and certainly the decision to apply criminal sanctions that carry substantial prison terms) must be proportionately stronger and the harms that are claimed to result from its exercise must be proportionately greater. There can be no question that reproductive liberty has a good claim to be part of such a fundamental right.

As Ronald Dworkin (1977) has persuasively argued, making use of this distinction between liberty as licence and liberty as dignity or liberty as a bare freedom and liberty as a basic right,

> If freedom to choose . . . (something) is simply something that we all want, like air conditioning or lobsters, then we are not entitled to hang on to these freedoms in the face of what we concede to be the rights of others to an equal share of respect and

resources. But if we can say, not simply that we want these freedoms, but that we are ourselves entitled to them, then we have established at least a basis for demanding a compromise.

(Dworkin 1977, p. 267)

Dworkin (1993) has defined reproductive liberty or procreative autonomy as 'a right to control their own role in procreation unless the state has a compelling reason for denying them that control' (Dworkin 1993, p. 148). The availability of termination of pregnancy in the United Kingdom (except Northern Ireland) demonstrates that the reasons cannot be compelling, although they might be politically expedient.

Neither nature nor the gods protect early embryos

One additional reason is provided by the absurdity of punitive measures to protect the early embryo from its own mother. We now know that for every successful pregnancy, which results in a live birth, many[12] early embryos will be lost or "miscarry". Many of these embryos will be lost because of genetic abnormalities but some would have been viable. How are we to think of the decision to attempt to have a child in the light of these facts? One obvious and inescapable conclusion is that God and/or Nature (depending on one's beliefs) are profligate with embryonic life, particularly in the early weeks. The sacrifice of embryos is an inescapable and inevitable part of the process of procreation. It may not be intentional sacrifice, and it may not attend every pregnancy, but the loss of many millions of embryos is the inevitable consequence of the vast majority of pregnancies. For everyone who knows the facts, it is conscious, knowing, and therefore deliberate sacrifice; and for everyone, it is part of the true description of what they do in having or attempting to have children or even in having unprotected intercourse. This high rate of loss is motiveless and inevitable. How much better then is having a good reason to end a particular pregnancy, in the present case, that good reason (good both in the sense of "moral" and in the sense of "sufficient") is the protection of the life opportunities, health, and peace of mind of an abused 15-year-old girl?

Evolution of rights

The key idea of reproductive liberty is surely respect for autonomy and for the values which underlie the importance attached to procreation (Harris 1998, 2003, 2005). These values see procreation and founding a family as involving the freedom to choose one's own lifestyle and express, through actions as well as through words, the deeply held beliefs and the morality which families share and seek to pass on to future generations. Implicit in this defence of reproductive liberty and in that of others, such as Ronald Dworkin, is the idea that such liberty must extend to the use of technology and methods of reproduction not envisaged by Adam and Eve, nor by Acts of Parliament passed in 1861. The legal theorist Antje Pedain (2005) has made this implication explicit, and elaborates this approach:

> Harris insists that human rights extend to the use of new technologies which expand our powers, options and ability to affect another person's fate and condition in ways and by means which were previously unknown.
>
> While it initially appears that this assumption might require some argument, on reflection this is not so. Technical advances often change the way in which we exercise our rights and freedoms, and thus broaden the practical scope of these rights.

Freedom of movement now extends to moving around by car or plane, and not just by foot, boat or bike, and may tomorrow encompass flying to Mars in a rocket. Freedom of speech now extends to the distribution of newspapers, television, and internet chatrooms, and not just to speaking at public assemblies and the like. If fundamental rights and freedoms were not capable of protecting new ways of exercising them, their scope of application would shrink over time in that, with the advances of technology, the right in question would only cover some, instead of all instances of exercising the protected activity. The only way to prevent such a gradual erosion of fundamental rights and freedoms is to expand their range of application along with the changes of technology.

Consequently, Harris is right in saying that the presumption of liberty applies not only to procreative techniques that achieve outcomes which, if circumstances were different, sexual procreation could achieve, but also to the use of techniques which may eventually enable prospective parents to achieve outcomes beyond what is possible by "natural" sexual procreation (for instance, the exchange of single defective genes for non-defective ones in embryos, and the creation of embryos by cloning or by combining genes from more than two existing human beings). Any restriction of this liberty requires a sufficiently weighty reason, and it is in this context that the important aspects in which the new forms of exercising a fundamental right differ from the ones which were previously known can and must be taken into account.

(*Pedain 2005, pp. 507–509*)

Pedain's apposite insistence that the law must move with the development of science and technology, no less than with public and private morality, highlights the pointlessness, and indeed the wickedness, of this prosecution based on a law enacted in 1861. To describe the actions of the mother and daughter in this case as 'unlawfully procuring . . . a poison or other noxious thing' (Offences Against The Person Act 1861) fits neither the facts of this case nor the current state of scientific knowledge and safe methods of termination of pregnancy, nor the obvious good intentions of the mother and daughter.

The operation of reproductive liberty in this context

Any suggestion[13] that it might be wrong to do something to or for the benefit of children because they are not in a position to consent is simply absurd. If decisions could not be made for children, unless and until they could consent to those decisions themselves, they would never grow up not to be children. Indeed, they would not live long at all. All sorts of decisions are routinely made for children. Their parents (usually) or guardians or those charged with their care (hopefully) dress them, feed them, talk to them, play with them, hug and kiss and cuddle them, sleep with them, eat with them, travel with them, educate them, and try to teach them the difference between right and wrong.

In the present case there are strong arguments to suggest that forcing this 15-year-old to continue with a pregnancy is manifestly against her interests as well as a violation of her rights, not least her right to equal protection of the law. Further, a regulatory regime which prosecutes the use of *mifepristone* and *misoprostal* for home abortion without medical supervision, in a context where medical supervision is not only not available but also illegal, and when millions of fellow citizens can use both methods of abortion safely and without risking prosecution, surely constitutes a denial of the equal protection of the law to all citizens.

The *prima facie* evidence of at worst prejudicial and at best highly selective and discriminatory priorities of the PPS also requires attention. The PPS argument contains a number of inconsistencies which seem to amount to *prima facie* prejudice and unfair discrimination, absent any supporting evidence.

In paragraph 11 of Michael Agnew's[14] evidence as presented to the court in this case, he states,

> Consideration was given to the fact that there was some evidence that the practice of acquiring abortifacient drugs on the internet for administration in Northern Ireland was not uncommon. It was considered that it was in the public interest to deter such practices given the unregulated nature of the activity and the potential risks posed to those taking the medication.
>
> *(JR76 2017)*[15]

This is a sweeping and entirely unsupported reference to '*the potential risks posed to those taking the medication*' and to 'the public interest'. What are those risks, and where is the evidence either that they exist or as to their nature, extent, or severity?[16] What of the public interest in protecting underage girls from abusive relationships and pregnancy? On the basis of this, on the face of it entirely unsupported, piece of speculation (both as to the extent of the practice of supplying abortifacient drugs on the Internet and as to the nature and extent of any alleged dangers) the PPS has instigated the prosecution of a vulnerable mother attempting to protect her daughter from the consequences of what the PPS themselves admit to have been '*a crime*' (paragraph 19) and an '*abusive relationship*' (paragraph 20). Finally, it is surely excessive, to say the least, for the PPS (even if it is admitted that it might be '*in the public interest to deter such practices given the unregulated nature of the activity*') to attempt to focus the majesty of the law and the burdens of deterrence on the victims of those practices rather than those primarily responsible for them.

Conscientious objections and moral complicity

Within this debate one of the most discussed questions is whether health care professionals (HCPs) should be granted the right to refuse to terminate an unwanted pregnancy (when the termination would be safe and legal) on grounds of the morality of this practice. Proponents of granting this right argue that allowing HCPs to refuse to perform abortions respects their moral integrity (Pellegrino 2002; Wicclair2011, 2017), and that personal values and beliefs should be tolerated in the name of the plurality of moral views that characterises democratic societies (Benn 2005; Sulmasy 2017). The problem with granting this right to HCPs, however, is that the exercise of this right *may* generate a clash with other relevant moral and legal rights (and their exercise): indeed, granting one group (e.g., HCPs) a moral right can significantly impinge on the exercise of other rights by another group (e.g., women), and vice versa.

Matters of disagreement are not only as to whether HCPs should be granted a right to refuse to perform abortions but also as to whether this right should be absolute or subjected to limitations that depend on the context and on the ability of others to exercise their rights.

The right to refuse to perform an abortion has different implications in countries where there is a sufficient number of HCPs that perform abortions to allow women to freely exercise their right to have an abortion and in countries (e.g., Italy) where the number of HCPs that perform abortions is so low that women's right to have an abortion is significantly constrained (Giubilini 2014; Lalli 2011; Minerva 2017). Social and political contexts matter, even in matters of morality. A democratic commitment to reproductive freedom entails that HPCs' right to refuse to perform an abortion cannot be absolute, but limited in scope and actualisation depending on the context where it is exercised.

Countries that allow both the right to have an abortion and the right of HCPs to refuse to perform it have sought a solution of compromise between these competing moral and legal rights (Cavaliere 2017b; Gutmann and Thompson 2012). Even if they allow HPCs to conscientiously object to carry out abortions themselves, they require them to facilitate access to this practice by informing women that an abortion may be a relevant medical option and by referring them to non-objector colleagues. This view, dubbed by Brock (2008) as 'conventional compromise' (Brock 2008, p. 194), seeks to find a compromise between competing moral rights and interests, and 'balances the profession's obligations to its patients with protecting the individual professional's moral integrity' (Brock 2008, p. 196). The problem with the conventional compromise is that it generates the dilemma of complicity in (what is believed to be) a morally reprehensible act[17] (Charo 2005; Brock 2008). However, as in the case of countries where there is no sufficient number of HCPs that perform abortions to allow women to exercise their right, a commitment to reproductive freedom should trump HCPs' right to refuse to perform abortions in contexts where the economic and emotional costs of a referral are too high.

Bypassing the clash? How new technologies can change the scene

In the previous sections, we have argued that the policy and ethics of abortion generate a clash of competing moral views, or, as Charo (2005) puts it, 'culture wars' (Charo 2005, p. 2472). Whether one believes that women's reproductive freedom should be granted a higher moral importance than HCPs' right to refuse to allow the exercise of such freedom, and that laws banning abortion represent an undue violation of such freedom, the legislation of many countries does not reflect these views. For this reason, in this last section, we propose an alternative that may represent a way forward for the clashes of moral views described earlier.

Unwanted pregnancies can be terminated surgically, but also medically – that is, by taking two different medications: mifepristone and misoprostol. Mifeprestone is a synthetic steroid that blocks the action of progesterone, a hormone that is necessary to maintain a pregnancy. Mifestrone alters the uterine lining (endometrium), induces bleeding, and causes the uterine lining to shed. This medication is used in conjunction with another pill that contains misoprostol, which causes the cervix to soften and the contraction of the uterus, thereby facilitating the expulsion of the uterine content. In countries that allow medical abortions, these pills are normally administered by HCPs, but they can also be purchased online at specific websites for women living in countries where abortions are either forbidden by law or difficult to access. They are safe and effective up to 24 weeks of gestation (Royal College of Obstetricians and Gynaecologists 2011, Recommendation 7.18, Section 7.2 "Medical Methods of Abortion", p. 68).

Abortion pills can represent an alternative for women who live in countries with statutory bans on abortion or with regulations that restrict access to this practice. They may be a way to respect women's reproductive freedom even in contexts where either the law or the personal views of HCPs curtail such freedom. In countries where abortion is banned, such as in Northern Ireland, women could purchase these pills online and subsequently see a doctor in case of necessity. In countries like Italy or the United States where abortion is allowed but access to this practice is severely restricted, women could circumvent these obstacles. It must be clear that abortion pills (if they are the only available option) do not represent an optimal alternative as women should be given the choice of having a surgical abortion or of having a medical abortion under the supervision of an HCP (e.g., it is prescribed in England, Scotland, and Wales). These pills allow women to exercise their reproductive freedom and take control over their reproductive destinies only partially – only, in other words, in an imperfect world. Some will still think that "there ought to be a law against accessing abortion pills" and that failure to enact one makes all complicit. But where there are powerful arguments for and against tolerance is not complicity. Rather, as Oscar Wilde said, 'selfishness is not living as one wishes to live. It is asking other people to live as one wishes to live' (Wilde 2001, p. 156).

As our defence of reproductive freedom highlights, the fight for the freedom and destiny of women is an ongoing struggle that will certainly not end with the online purchase of safe early abortion and with it significant control of reproductive destiny. But this possibility, perhaps because online access to information and products of all types on the Internet is virtually unstoppable, may represent a compromise that all parties can live with.

Notes

1 President Donald Trump was able to overturn Obama's rule under the 1996 Congressional Review Act (CRA), which allows lawmakers to nullify regulations within 60 days of enactment.
2 *The Handmaid's Tale* is a dystopian novel that takes place in the fictional state of Gilead (a Christian theocracy established in the United States after overthrowing the government). There, a group of high-ranking officials deals with low fertility rates by enslaving women and forcing them to bear their children. These fertile women are referred to as handmaids and are forced to wear crimson robes and white bonnets. Those demonstrating in the United States dressed as handmaids to express their anger against the government and to protest against attempts to limit their reproductive rights.
3 For the purposes of this essay, we regard the entitlement or not to terminate a pregnancy in particular circumstances as a matter of balancing the rights and interests engaged in any particular case.
4 For discussion of moral status and potentiality see John Harris *The Value of Life*, Routledge, London 1985. Chapter 1, pp. 7–28.
5 Lever (2013) links the right to have an abortion to the right to privacy that is so fundamental in democratic societies.
6 While there are of course many approaches to the ethics of abortion not all are equally valid. It will be clear to those reading this essay precisely what we believe to be the most coherent and valid approach.
7 Planned Parenthood and other groups advocate and provide not only abortion services but also services related to contraception, pregnancy care, screenings for cervical, ovarian, and breast cancer, and so forth.
8 www.earth-policy.org/data_highlights/2011/highlights13. www.weforum.org/agenda/2015/11/the-relationship-between-womens-education-and-fertility/. Both items accessed 7th August 2017.
9 In Italy abortion is performed by gynaecologists and obstetricians and not by GPs, as in some other countries.
10 Data about gynaecologists who conscientiously object to performing abortions is staggering. The latest data from the Italian Ministry of Health (Ministero Della Salute) reports that 70 per cent of gynaecologists are objectors. While this data reports the national average, the number of objectors per region varies significantly, and in some regions (e.g., Abruzzo, Molise, and the Autonomous Province of Bolzano), it peaks to 90 per cent and over (Ministero della Salute 2016).
11 The arguments of this section were originally presented in an affidavit submitted by John Harris as a "philosopher's brief" in support of a judicial review known as JR76 (Application 16/122207) in the High Court of Northern Ireland.
12 The literature puts this at a figure of three embryos lost for every live birth: see Charles E. Boklage (1990) and Henri Leridon (1977).
13 Here the argument follows lines set out elsewhere (Harris 2003).
14 Michael Agnew was the official speaking for the PPS in this case.
15 In the High Court of Justice in Northern Ireland. In the divisional court, in the matter of an application for judicial review by JR76. And in the matter of a decision of the director of public prosecutions. 2017. From the affidavit of Professor John Harris.
16 There is significant evidence to the contrary; see Royal College of Obstetricians and Gynaecologists (2011, Recommendation 7.18, Section 7.2 "Medical Methods of Abortion", p. 68) as discussed ahead.

17 It must be noted that it is not only abortion that raises the question of complicity. This question is present also in another contexts: in debates on pharmacists' duties with respect to the emergency hormonal contraceptive pill (Ceva and Moratti 2013); in debates on stem cell research (Devolder 2010) and on euthanasia (Trigg 2017), and so forth.

References

Benn, P. (2005). The role of conscience in medical ethics. In: Athanassoulis, N. (ed.), *Philosophical Reflections on Medical Ethics*. Basingstoke: Palgrave Macmillan, pp. 160–179.

Bloomer, F. and Fegan, E. (2014). Critiquing recent abortion law and policy in Northern Ireland. *Critical Social Policy*, 34(1), pp. 109–120.

Boklage, C. E. (1990). Survival probability of human conceptions from fertilization to term. *International Journal of Fertility*, 35(2), pp. 75–94.

Boland, R., & Katzive, L. (2008). Developments in laws on induced abortion: 1998–2007. *International Family Planning Perspectives*, 34(3), pp. 110–120.

Brock, D. W. (2008). Conscientious refusal by physicians and pharmacists: Who is obligated to do what, and why? *Theoretical Medicine and Bioethics*, 29(3), pp. 187–200.

Cavaliere, G. (2017a). Genome editing and assisted reproduction: Curing embryos, society or prospective parents? *Medicine, Health Care and Philosophy*, https://doi.org/10.1007/s11019-017-9793-y

Cavaliere, G. (2017b). A 14-day limit for bioethics: The debate over human embryo research. *BMC Medical Ethics*, 18(1), pp. 1–12.

Ceva, E., and Moratti, S. (2013). Whose self-determination? Barriers to access to emergency hormonal contraception in Italy. *Kennedy Institute of Ethics Journal*, 23(2), pp. 139–167.

Charo, R. A. (2005). The celestial fire of conscience – refusing to deliver medical care. *New England Journal of Medicine*, 352(24), pp. 2471–2473.

Davies, C. (2016a). Polish women strike over planned abortion ban. *The Guardian*. Available at: www.theguardian.com/world/2016/oct/03/polish-women-strike-over-planned-abortion-ban [Accessed 02.08.2017].

Davies, C. (2016b). Polish women vow to step up pressure over abortion restrictions. *The Guardian*. Available at: www.theguardian.com/world/2016/oct/25/polish-women-step-up-pressure-abortion-restrictions. [Accessed 02.08.2017].

Dennis, A., Henshaw, S. K., Joyce, T. J., Finer, L. B., and Blanchard, K. (2009). *The Impact of Laws Requiring Parental Involvement for Abortion: A Literature Review*. New York: Guttmacher Institute.

Devolder, K. (2010). Complicity in stem cell research: The case of induced pluripotent stem cells. *Human Reproduction*, 25(9), pp. 2175–2180.

Dworkin, R. (1977). *Taking Rights Seriously*. London: Duckworth.

Dworkin, R. (1993). *Life's Dominion*. London: Harper Collins.

Ely, J. H. (1973). The wages of crying wolf: A comment on Roe v. Wade. *The Yale Law Journal*, 82(5), pp. 920–949.

Feinberg, J. (1984). *The Moral Limits of the Criminal Law*. Oxford: Oxford University Press.

Ford, L. (2017). Family, fertility and feminism: Landmarks in women's rights. *The Guardian*. Available at: www.theguardian.com/global-development/2017/jul/27/families-fertility-feminism-landmarks-in-womens-rights-timeline. [Accessed 07.09.2017].

Gentleman, A. (2017). Woman who bought abortion pills for daughter can challenge prosecution. *The Guardian*. Available at: www.theguardian.com/world/2017/jan/26/ulster-woman-who-bought-abortion-pills-for-daughter-can-challenge-prosecution. [Accessed 02.08.2017].

Giubilini, A. (2014). The paradox of conscientious objection and the anemic concept of 'conscience': Downplaying the role of moral integrity in health care. *Kennedy Institute of Ethics Journal*, 24(2), pp. 159–185.

Gold, R., and Nash, E. (2012). Troubling trend: More states hostile to abortion rights as middle ground shrinks. *Guttmacher Policy Review*, 15(1), pp. 14–19.

Grimes, D. A., Benson, J., Singh, S., Romero, M., Ganatra, B., Okonofua, F. E., and Shah, I. H. (2006). Unsafe abortion: The preventable pandemic. *The Lancet*, 368(9550), pp. 1908–1919.

Gutmann, A., and Thompson, D. (2012). *The Spirit of Compromise: Why Governing Demands It and Campaigning Undermines It*. Princeton, NJ: Princeton University Press.

Guttmacher Institute. (2017a). *State Funding of Abortion Under Medicaid*. Available at: www.guttmacher. org/state-policy/explore/state-funding-abortion-under-medicaid. [Accessed 02.08.2017].

Guttmacher Institute. (2017b). *Restricting Insurance Coverage of Abortion*. Available at: www.guttmacher. org/state-policy/explore/restricting-insurance-coverage-abortion. [Accessed 02.08.2017].

Harris, J. (1980). *Violence and Responsibility*. New York: Routledge and Kegan Paul.

Harris, J. (1992). *Wonderwoman & Superman: Ethics & Human Biotechnology*. Oxford: Oxford University Press. Publication link: 08265e9c-8afa-4753-bb10-ea149d5555be. [Accessed 02.08.2017].

Harris, J. (1998). Rights and Reproductive Choice. In: J. Harris and S. Holm, eds., *The Future of Human Reproduction: Choice and Regulation*. Oxford: Oxford University Press, pp. 5–37.

Harris, J. (2003). Reproductive Choice. In *Encyclopaedia of the Human Genome*. London: Nature Publishing Group Reference.

Harris, J. (2005). Reproductive Liberty, Disease and Disability. *Reproductive Medicine Online*, 10(1), pp. 13–16.

Hauser, C. (2017). A Handmaid's tale of protest. *The New York Times*. Available at: www.nytimes. com/2017/06/30/us/handmaids-protests-abortion.html?mcubz=2 [Accessed 02.08.2017].

Hirschfeld Davies, J. (2017). Trump signs law taking aim at Planned Parenthood funding. *The New York Times*. Available at: www.nytimes.com/2017/04/13/us/politics/planned-parenthood-trump. html?mcubz=2 [Accessed 02.08.2017].

Lalli, C. (2011). *C'è chi dice no. Dalla leva all'aborto. Come cambia l'obiezione di coscienza*. Milano: Il Saggiatore.

Leridon, H. (1977). *Human Fertility: The Basic Components*. Chicago: University of Chicago Press.

Lever, A. (2013). *A Democratic Conception of Privacy*. Bloomington: AuthorHouse.

Mill, J. S. (1979). *On Liberty*. New York: Penguin. (Original work published 1859).

Minerva, F. (2014). Conscientious objection in Italy. *Journal of Medical Ethics*, 41, pp. 170–173.

Minerva, F. (2017). Conscientious objection, complicity in wrongdoing, and a not-so-moderate approach. *Cambridge Quarterly of Healthcare Ethics*, 26(1), pp. 109–119.

Ministero della Salute. (2016). *Relazione del Ministro della Salute sulla attuazione della legge contenente norme per la tutela sociale della maternità e per l'interruzione volontaria di gravidanza (Legge 194/78)*. Roma: MinisteroItalianodella Salute.

Offences Against The Person Act (1861). Paragraphs 58 and 59. Available at: www.irishstatutebook.ie/eli/ 1861/act/100/enacted/en/print [Accessed 12.09.2018].

Pedain, A. (2005). On Cloning (book review). *The Cambridge Law Journal*, 64(2), pp. 507–509.

Pellegrino, E. D. (2002). The physician's conscience, conscience clauses, and religious belief: A catholic perspective. *Fordham Urban Law Journal*, 30, pp. 221–244.

Robertson, J. A. (2011). Abortion and technology: Sonograms, fetal pain, viability, and early prenatal diagnosis. *University of Pennsylvania Journal of Constitutional Law*, 14(2), pp. 327–390.

Royal College of Obstetricians and Gynaecologists. (2011). *The Care of Women Requesting Induced Abortion. Evidence-Based Clinical Guideline No. 7*, 3rd revised edition. London: RCOG Press. Available at: www.rcog.org.uk/globalassets/documents/guidelines/abortion-guideline_web_1.pdf [Accessed 02.08.2017].

Sanger, C. (2008). Seeing and believing: Mandatory ultrasound and the path to a protected choice. *UCLA Law Review*, 56, pp. 351–408.

Shah, I., and Åhman, E. (2010). Unsafe abortion in 2008: Global and regional levels and trends. *Reproductive Health Matters*, 18(36), pp. 90–101.

Sulmasy, D. P. (2017). Tolerance, professional judgment, and the discretionary space of the physician. *Cambridge Quarterly of Healthcare Ethics*, 26(1), pp. 18–31.

Tocqueville, A. (1835). *Democracy in America*. London: Saunders & Otley.

Trigg, R. (2017). Conscientious objection and "Effective Referral". *Cambridge Quarterly of Healthcare Ethics*, 26(1), pp. 32–43.

Wharton, L. J., Frietsche, S., and Kolbert, K. (2006). Preserving the core of roe: Reflections on planned parenthood v. Casey. *Yale Journal of Law& Feminism*, 18(2), pp. 317–387.

Wicclair, M. (2011). *Conscientious Objection in Health Care: An Ethical Analysis*. Cambridge: Cambridge University Press.

Wicclair, M. (2017). Conscientious objection in healthcare and moral integrity. *Cambridge Quarterly of Healthcare Ethics*, 26(1), pp. 7–17.

Wilde, O. (2001). *The Soul of Man Under Socialism*. London: Penguin. (Original work published: 1891).

36

TOWARDS A DEMOCRATIC ETHICS OF YOUTH POLICIES

Juliana Bidadanure

Introduction

In 2016, Australian columnist Bernard Salt made the headlines for his rant on millennials. Young people, he argued, are wasteful and lazy, which explains why they cannot get on the property ladder like the previous generation:

> I have seen young people order smashed avocado with crumbled feta on five-grain toasted bread at \$22 a pop and more. I can afford to eat this for lunch because I am middle-aged and have raised my family. But how can young people afford to eat like this? Shouldn't they be economizing by eating at home? How often are they eating out? Twenty-two dollars several times a week could go towards a deposit on a house.
>
> *(Salt 2016)*

The article would be quite honestly funny if it was not so symptomatic of an embedded discourse on youth. The generation born in the 1980s has been described as the 'entitlement generation', 'generation me', and the 'dumbest generation' (Twenge 2006; Bauerlein 2008). Seventy per cent of Americans consider today's young people to be less virtuous and industrious than their elders (Taylor et al. 2009: 8). The avocado story thus epitomises the lens of incomprehension, condescension, and suspicion through which young generations are often seen.

'Brunch is the opiate of the masses' – millennial Brigid Delaney responded for the *Guardian* – 'we are not going out for brunch instead of buying houses: we are brunching because we cannot afford to buy houses' (Delaney 2016). Young adults have been hit disproportionally hard by the 2007 financial crisis, and by the austerity politics that followed. European countries struggle with high rates of youth unemployment, as high as 50 per cent in Greece and Spain, but often two to four times as high as for older age groups in other European countries. Young adults are overrepresented among the 'Precariat' – a growing class of individuals without income or occupational security (Standing 2011). They often start their lives ridden with university debts in countries like the US or the UK where generations of students before them often enjoyed a tuition-free higher education.

Youth policy is defined as a strategic plan to ensure good living conditions and opportunities for the young population of a country (Denstad 2009: 13). What counts as a 'good

460

living standard' and 'adequate opportunities for the young', however, is far from self-evident. A political community may be feeling as though it is granting more than enough opportunities for its youth while in fact denying them a *fair* range of opportunities. For instance, negative stereotypes of the young as entitled and wasteful can prevent political communities from understanding the urgency of the socio-economic difficulties young adults face. This is even more probable when young adults are comparatively disenfranchised: young adults are far less likely to vote or even to be registered for the elections, and they are also underrepresented in the legislature. As a result, youth issues are handled by older age groups often from a condescending 'we know what's best for you' perspective (Furlong and Cartmel in Berry 2012: 16).

This chapter proposes to sketch the contours of a *democratic ethics of youth policies*. Drawing on theories of justice between co-existing generations, I shed some light onto the distributive question of what counts as an adequate set of opportunities for the young. But while doing this, I also explore democratic barriers that often prevent political communities from answering these questions adequately. There is a tendency in the existing literature on intergenerational justice, and also on distributive justice in general, to consider distributive questions in abstraction from democratic ethics. I will use this chapter to bring the two together – articulating distributive issues of justice between overlapping generations with questions of democratic ethics, and offering some mechanisms to reduce the intergenerational democratic deficit.

In the section that follows, I give an overview of the existing core questions that shape issues of justice between co-existing generations. I present the state of existing research on the question and offer my own account. In the third section, I attempt to translate one principle of age-group justice – lifespan sufficiency – into recommendations for youth policies. I show that one can hardly accomplish this task without deliberative procedures to settle on what counts as 'enough' opportunities for the young. Lastly, in the fourth section, I highlight a number of democratic barriers to an adequate answering of these questions and identify some potential responses to youth political marginalisation.

Before moving into the rest of the chapter, it is important to clarify what we mean by *youth* and *young adults*. In this chapter, I will typically have a broad understanding of the category – starting at around 16 years old and ending at 35 years old. What makes this age bracket relevant from my perspective is first that it includes the age category used to describe youth unemployment – which tends to be typically higher than for other age groups and extends from 16 to 25 years old (although in some countries it starts at 15 or ends at 24). I go all the way to 35 years old for two main reasons. First, in contexts of job scarcity, the category affected by chronic unemployment tends to go beyond 25 years old to at least 30 years old. Moreover, some of the negative effects associated with youth unemployment are visible in older young adults who tend to be dependent on their families for longer and sometimes delay their move out of the family home until their thirties. Second, I am also interested in the young as a politically marginalised category. Typically, the age group that is invisible from parliaments is not just young adults below 25 years old but also adults of up to 35 years old. So this 16–35-year-old age range captures some of the significant structural vulnerabilities that I want to discuss in this chapter.

What we owe the young: some lessons from the literature on justice between generations

Alongside child-policies and old-age policies, youth policies are a subset of age policies. In order to get a better sense of what ensuring adequate opportunities for young adults may mean, we must thus reflect upon what age-group justice requires. For instance, we may want to establish how scarce resources – such as health care, education, housing, income, and the associated opportunities they render possible – ought to be distributed between age groups. One way to approach this question is to ask which inequalities (if any) in opportunities and outcomes between age groups are acceptable. If inequalities between age groups are wrong, then perhaps one goal of age policies is to redress inequalities (in opportunities or well-being or resources) between age groups; or more positively to promote equality (of some sort) between age groups. On the contrary, perhaps equality between age groups is not a goal that we should pursue, even if we are otherwise egalitarian, because age is special in a relevant manner.

As a society, we seem to widely contend that some inequalities between age groups are acceptable. For instance, we tolerate inequalities in voting rights between children and adults; we sometimes give preferential loans or educational benefits exclusively to young adults; we may give free access to some public transportation to people over a certain age; we may prevent seniors in some fields from keeping their job after a certain age; and we may also reserve some costly healthcare resources to those younger than a certain age. Age, in short, is often used as a criterion for assigning benefits and burdens in society and for rationing scarce resources. We only need to compare this unequal treatment by age to a similar unequal treatment based on race, for instance, to see that age feels special. It is morally unacceptable to ration resources (educational opportunities, health care resources, housing, etc.) by race because that would violate the basic principle that each member of a community ought to be treated as a moral equal – whose fundamental interests matter just as much as those of others. So what is so special about age that such instances of unequal treatment and rationing often appear more justifiable?

Age groups are stages of life – we grow out of them. I may be denied some social goods as a young adult but granted some rights later as an older member of a community – say, the right to an unconditional old-age cash payment. Differential treatment between age groups is special in that, if institutions remain stable over time, the young will benefit from the social goods afforded to older members of a community when they need it. In this way, age inequalities fundamentally differ from gender or racial inequalities: while the latter are inequalities between persons over time, inequalities between age groups are just temporary. This is important because it means that inequalities between age groups do not necessarily undermine the basic principle of equal moral worth mentioned earlier. If we conceive of persons through time, unequal treatments between age groups are compatible with a perfectly equal treatment of diachronic persons.

This common-sense view explains in part why we often approach issues of inequalities between age groups, and even issues of age discrimination, with more leniency than we do other social inequalities (Bidadanure 2017). And to an extent, it makes sense. The young may be subject to higher risks of unemployment, they may be poorer, more likely to be financially dependent on their families, and less likely to vote; but they will grow out of young adulthood – they will gain the skills, competences, experience, and financial security that will then make them less likely overall to be unemployed and dependent as they grow older.

However, there are at least three reasons to challenge this common-sense view that inequalities between age groups are not concerning. Highlighting those reasons will help us identify a frame for thinking through issues of age-group justice.

First, we cannot always assume that inequalities between age groups will be temporary. It is true that young adults of all generations tend to be more vulnerable to unemployment than older age groups, and so youth unemployment is in part an age issue. But when labour market vulnerabilities are exacerbated by a crisis, the cohort that is young at that particular time may be *scarred* in the long run, such that they may remain comparatively more likely to be unemployed or underpaid even after they have aged. When jobs are scarce, new entrants have to accept lower wages in order to find a job; then there is a lack of a catch-up on earnings, so they remain low because of the point at which they entered the labour market. Similarly, the lack of valued work experience causes a decline in ambitions and self-confidence, which in turn sends negative signals to employers. This leads to further experiences of unemployment and a slowdown in job progression, and it explains why such workers often suffer from low earnings. As a result of this series of scarring effects, 'when the difficulties disappear, the cohorts who faced these problems continue to suffer from long-term consequences of past handicaps' (Chauvel 2010: 84).

As scarring effects illustrate, we have to assume that inequalities between age groups can create inequalities between cohorts. In such cases, the age inequality becomes a cohort inequality issue. And, contrary to age membership, birth cohort membership is not temporary. One important modification to the common-sense view we started with is thus that we need to distribute resources between age groups with an eye to ensuring that policies are sustainable over time and promote generational equity. We want to ensure that a particular age group – let's say the young – does not become a disadvantaged birth cohort through inequitable, short-sighted, or unsustainable policy-making.

There is a second reason to be concerned about inequalities between age groups. Surely, particular instances of differential treatment by age fall short of the basic principle that all members of a community should be treated as equals – even if persons end up being treated fairly over time. One example is ageist age discrimination (Bidadanure 2017). Think of a case where a 50-year-old is denied a job based on the stereotype that older people cannot get work done properly. Or think of a society that is leaving its senior citizens in miserable retirement homes while allowing its younger citizens to thrive; or the reverse – a society that leaves its youth vulnerable to exploitation and abuse by older age groups. Surely here, the inequality in treatment between age groups strikes us as incompatible with a community of individuals able to stand as equals, even if all generations one after the other are subject to the same treatment at the relevant point in their life.

This important concern about age inequalities is best grounded on relational egalitarianism (Bidadanure 2016). Relational egalitarians are concerned with whether members of a community are able to appear without shame, whether they are respected, and whether minority groups are recognised or, on the contrary, whether they are victims of exclusive norms and are marginalised or demonised. This sets limits on the extent to which we may tolerate inequalities between age groups in a community, even if those inequalities are temporary and equitable over time. Politicians should register how different age groups stand in front of each other and design policies to prevent some being widely vilified as lazy and politically marginalised – say, the young – or others being stigmatised as burdens on the economy, infantilised, or segregated in mass – say, the very elderly. The politically infantilising narrative on young adults as fundamentally unable to rule and the exclusionary stereotype that older people are fundamentally incapable of meaningfully contributing to their communities are some of the culturally oppressive norms that egalitarians should register and combat.

A third and last ground for concern in the face of age inequalities is when they result from unreasonable or imprudent life course planning. For instance, imagine that we denied the young of different generations quality education consistently over time while giving access to such education to older age groups. This would be compatible with equality over time, and it would perhaps not threaten their equal status from a relational egalitarian perspective. After all, it would merely be a different way than current to distribute educational resources over the life course. And yet, this would, rightly I think, strike us as an inadequate distribution of resources over the life course. Having access to educational resources early in life enables one to enjoy the fruits of such education for many more years of one's life than the alternative.

Learning to read or write later in life would enable us to lead only a section of our life with such skills and the related opportunities. It thus does not seem to be the best way to distribute those resources. Another example is that we may systematically deny older age groups access to income support. Again, this would be compatible with equality over time, if we were applying the policy consistently for successive generations, but we would be likely to think that this falls short of even the most basic commitment to sufficiency. Leaving entire parts of our existence, especially when disability risks are much increased, without access to sufficient resources may make it impossible for us to live in dignity for important parts of our existence.

The concerns expressed here have been cashed out in terms of *lifespan prudence* by philosopher Norman Daniels (1988). To establish how resources must be distributed between age groups, we need to think about what makes a life as a whole go well. Thinking about the best distribution of resources intra-personally can help us think more clearly about the fairest distribution of resources between age groups. We all have different conceptions of what a good life entails, but we need to find some common ground from which a government may decide how more or less scarce resources (like health care, education, or income) must be distributed between different stages of life. Norman Daniels has argued that institutions should be "prudent" in the sense that they must make people's lives as a whole go as well as possible as determined by appeal to a procedure – the prudential lifespan account (PLA). Planners in the PLA are placed behind a veil of ignorance so they have no knowledge of their age. They are asked to distribute a given bundle of resources (their diachronic fair share) throughout their lives so as to maximise lifespan utility. For Daniels, by telling us what the most prudent distribution of resources looks like, the procedure helps us figure out which instances of differential treatment are acceptable eventually. Note that distributive equality between age group here does not need to be the baseline in any way. The most prudent distribution may in fact be fairly unequal synchronically.

There are two plausible conclusions that I draw in other work from this prudential procedure (Bidadanure 2016; Bidadanure forthcoming). First, we would want to distribute our bundle of resources to ensure that we would always have enough. Let us call this the lifespan sufficiency requirement. Daniels's formulation of this principle is that we must distribute resources between age groups in a way that ensures an *age-sensitive normal opportunity range* throughout people's lives. Second, we would want to make sure that resources are made available early in the life course when having access to those resources may make our life as a whole go better. I call this the lifespan efficiency requirement – resources should be invested early in the lifespan when it increases diachronic returns. If we will ensure a life of better overall quality by securing early access to educational resources or preventive health programmes, for instance, then we ought to do it. The resulting imbalance in spending between stages of lives, and so between age groups, would be justified.

Our search for standards to establish which inequalities between age groups matter has given us at least three ways to think about age-group justice. Age policies must be sustainable over time and compatible with generational equity between birth cohorts. They must be designed prudently – people at different stages of their lives must have enough at any point, and they must have access to some central benefits sufficiently early in life to maximise lifespan returns. Last, age policies must ensure that all adult members of a community are able to stand as equals, without marginalisation, demonisation, or other forms of anti-egalitarian exclusion and oppression.

Having sketched this framework does not give us a theory of youth policies. I would have to say much more about how inequalities *within* an age group must be dealt with, for instance. An important role of youth policies (at least from an egalitarian perspective) is to reduce social inequalities within an age group. This means that any plausible account of youth policies must be intersectional – it must pay attention to the various ways in which gender, race, and class make the experience of youth fundamentally diverse – even if the young as an age group and generation are subjected to common trends and can be jointly disadvantaged in some respect.

This said – I want to focus here on the difficult task of thinking about what any of those broad principles of age-group justice mean in practice for the design of youth policies. For lack of space, I will focus primarily on the implications of one of those principles – lifespan sufficiency. I take this principle to be particularly difficult to translate into concrete policies and I hope it will serve as an illustration of the broader problem of translating abstract political theory into the practice of policy design. One of the conclusions that I will draw is that we can hardly convert the sufficiency principle into youth policy guidelines without appealing to a democratic procedure of some kind involving all age groups, especially those most directly concerned. The successive section will highlight various ways in which an intergenerational polity can become insufficiently democratic, and why it matters for the realisation of adequate youth policy.

The sufficiency example

What does it mean for the young to have enough? Based on what I have identified as *lifespan sufficiency*, from a Danielsian perspective, institutions must make it possible for young people to enjoy an *age-relative normal opportunity range* – that is, a range of opportunities that are adequate for young people in a particular society at a given time to enjoy. Identifying this youth normal range would help us answer the question that motivates this chapter: what does it mean to provide 'adequate opportunities' for the young?[1]

Sociologists most often define young adulthood as the transition from childhood to adulthood. It is a process, which typically involves seeking economic and spatial independence from one's parents. The normal opportunity range describes the 'array of reasonable life plans' people are likely to make for themselves. The plan to leave the family household seems to be among those 'reasonable' plans. In their book on disadvantage, Jonathan Wolff and Avner De-Shalit discuss the phenomenon of 'planning blight' which occurs when people facing uncertainty in terms of income, employment, or housing put off reasonable plans that they importantly value, such as founding a family or leaving home (Wolff and De-Shalit 2007: 69). So perhaps one of the implications of the lifespan sufficiency principle is that governments should help ensure that the young are able to gain parental independence at a normal age, if they want to.

Two important remarks are needed at this point. First, saying that it is reasonable for young adults to aspire to independence does not amount to assuming that the individualist western model of family structure is necessarily reasonable or preferable. I am merely arguing that in a society where young adults massively value spatial and economic independence from their parents, it seems important to render this opportunity accessible to those who could not afford it on their own. Second, note that there are many different ways to ensure such opportunity – an unconditional basic income for the young, a means-tested minimum income for young adults whose families cannot finance their aspiration to spatial independence, a job guarantee to significantly reduce long-term youth unemployment, and decently paid training options for the young, may all count as possible pathways to achieve this end.

The opportunity to leave the parental household by a *normal* age can therefore be taken to be one of the important opportunities to provide, for those who want it. Let me thus use this key opportunity as the main example in this section. To shed some light onto how the age-relative normal opportunity range may be implemented, let's ask *at which age* young people should be able to leave the parental household. For this purpose, we can consider a series of possible indicators that may guide us in deciding what should count as the age at which a state should seek to facilitate the opportunity for the young to gain independence from their parents.

First, we can derive the youth normal age from the average or median age at which young people leave home in a given time and place. Indeed, what is 'fair' on the age-relative normal opportunity range principle is for the young to have access to the opportunities that are 'normal' for a given society at a given time. In France and the UK, the average age at which young people leave the parental home is about 24 years old (Eurostat 2009: 29). If we index the range to the empirical average, then it seems that what we owe the young is to ensure that they do not have to depend on their families for much longer than age 24 if they want to leave the family home. This has important implications for how housing and income benefits should be designed.

However, it is important to note that indexing the sufficiency requirement to the average age means that, if it became normal for young people to be unpaid or poor for longer, and thus dependent for longer, then the state's obligation would be to give young people the substantive opportunity to leave home at the new (later) normal time. In Italy, Portugal, Spain, and Poland, for instance, the average age for people to leave the family home is closer to 30 years old (Eurostat 2009: 29). Does that mean that young people should have access to the opportunity to leave their home at that later age in those countries?

One may rightly worry that this appeal to what *is* to establish what *should be* is normatively problematic. Nancy Jecker (1992), for instance, has raised many criticisms against the strong reliance on normality:

> Although the history of ethics teaches that *ought* statements cannot be derived from *is* statements, this does little to deter such appeals. For, despite ourselves, we tend to think that what is ought to be. The upshot of this is that those attuned to the added force that appeals to nature give often refer to *is* statements in order to lend support to *ought* statements.
>
> *(Jecker 1992: 270)*

The important added value of Daniels's appeal to the age-relative opportunity range, however, is that it allows us to make *some* comparisons between what is owed to the young and what is owed to older members of a community. It would not be fair to deny the elderly the necessary resources to live decently (both absolutely, with respect to their humanity, and relatively, with respect to their age) in order to provide a more than normal, or ideal, level of functioning to the young. The appeal to normality is helpful, in other words, to set *some* limits fairly. Moreover, we can and should always push the boundaries of what counts as a 'normal' range of opportunities for an age group at a given time. If there is widespread youth unemployment and precariousness, or during an economic recession, what the young are able to do is considerably reduced. So rather than, or in addition to, using the empirical norm to set the threshold fairly, we could index the normal range on the *cultural norm*. Even when prolonged dependency is becoming more common (in the average sense), it may still not be viewed as what 'should' be. For instance, prolonged dependency may be shameful and stigmatised.

Louis Chauvel's (2010) sociological study of French young people is an illuminating example in this context. According to Chauvel (2010: 75–78), three stages of young adulthood have emerged in young adults' processes of socialisation in France. The first stage brings together those under 25 years old and involves the first experiences of transition to adulthood. The second stage refers to the steps of partial independence through the labour market and occurs between 25 and 30 years old. This second stage is also characterised by long-term dependence on parents for economic support – mainly because wages do not match the costs of the housing market. The third stage involves those who failed to gain independence in the previous stages. Chauvel identifies this third stage as correlated with a situation of never-ending dependence on family (until 35 or later). This stage is made all the more difficult when economic dependence after 25 years old is viewed as abnormal (Chauvel 2010: 76).

So perhaps we could appeal to the stigma attached to the third stage of youth to set the age by which the state should ensure that the young are able to leave home. The stigma attached to prolonged dependency in Stage 3 is evidence that it is not perceived as a normal phenomenon. One underpinning reason for why we may care about both the empirical and the cultural norm in a given society is that it may have an important impact on the social basis of self-respect. Young people who are not able to leave home by the normal age often suffer from low self-esteem and status. We may thus consider that the normal opportunity range principle requires that institutions end the third (abnormal) stage of youth by the age that is considered normal at a given time in a given society, as indicated by cultural reactions to it. This way, for instance, in France, we could focus our efforts on providing substantive opportunities for independence for the young in Stages 2 and 3 while ignoring familial dependency in Stage 1 as largely unproblematic. Interestingly, the absence of individualised 'revenu minimum' for the young under 25 years old in France was partly justified in this manner. It was seen as quite normal for the young under 25 years old to be dependent on their parents for shelter, the argument went, so the denial of income support to those under the age of 25 was also seen as acceptable (Bidadanure 2012).

But there are very serious problems with this appeal to the cultural norm too. Prolonged dependence on one's family after 25 may be stigmatised, but perhaps if we give the new phenomenon a generation or two it becomes perceived as normal. For instance, nearly half of young adults in the US now return home after having moved out (Goldfarb 2014: 54). As Sally Goldfarb claims, while the phenomenon is new, expectations have already changed in such way that it is now unrealistic for parents to expect their children to become independent upon reaching adulthood (Goldfarb 2014: 54). We may thus consider that parental dependency is normal and, as a result, that institutions do not have to secure such opportunity. After all, in a society where it is normal to be dependent for longer, the young's self-respect may not be affected. But typically, when a social norm is creating stigma and shame around a lifestyle, we ought to question the social norm rather than simply assume that there is something wrong with the lifestyle. So is the cultural norm really a good basis for deciding which opportunities should be promoted? Surely the average and the cultural norms are indicators that can help us think about what counts as adequate opportunities for the young. But they are not sufficient bases and should be approached critically.

What the case of family independence has illustrated so far is that the age-relative normal opportunity range can guide us in different ways depending on the indexes we use to determine what counts as normal. For instance, the normal opportunity principle will not necessarily instruct that the young be given the required resources to be independent from their families, if they need and want it, at least before 25 years old. But it will require that they have access to the necessary resources to be autonomous after an age where it becomes unreasonable to expect a young adult to depend on one's family for survival. I have tried to suggest, however, that the appeal to empirical and social norms may give too much weight to the contingencies of current practices. It may provide useful indications as to what counts as 'not enough' in a given society at a given time, but it does not tell us much about what else we may do for the young, once the quite minimal threshold is met.

Another way to set the threshold would be to look at what the young themselves say they want, or actually do, when they have the resources required to make a choice. In fact, when young adults have access to income from their families, early departures tend to be common (Furlong and Cartmel 2007: 62). This may lead us to consider that the young should be able to leave home at 20 years old, for instance, even if most cannot until much later, and even if dependency on one's family is not stigmatised until much later. Surveys of youth values and interests here can help. But the deeper point here seems to be that issues of age policies are necessarily comparative and deliberative. What I mean is that it is necessary to think about what being young in a particular context means, and also about what growing old means, to establish what counts as an adequate set of opportunities for the young. Those questions will find different answers in different temporal, geographic, and democratic contexts – they require careful deliberations including members of different age groups.

At the very least, it seems that the young must take an active part in this discussion. And from that perspective, the critical under-representation of young adults under 30 years old in parliaments and the relative disenfranchisement of young adults are both concerning phenomena. Procedurally, it seems much harder to get a clear sense of what may count as a reasonable range of opportunities for the young in their absence. If we remember Daniels's planners, they were placed behind a veil of ignorance. The least we can do in our societies to determine what counts as a reasonable opportunity set is to ensure that each age group is represented in the discussions. Let me now spend some time introducing some democratic barriers to just youth policy-making, and some potential remedies.

Democratic barriers to just youth policies

In earlier sections, we distinguished inequalities between age groups from inequalities between birth cohorts. In identifying democratic barriers to just intergenerational policies, it is important to refer to this distinction once again (Bellamy et al. 2018). To illustrate this, think of the following examples. It may be considered a barrier to adequate democratic representation if young adults below the age of 21 years old cannot vote, or if young adults below the age of 35 years old cannot run for presidential office. We may make the case that 16–21-year-olds should be allowed to vote, and that any adult member of a community should be allowed to run for office. The debate here would probably be about competence, autonomy, and critical abilities at different ages. This first case is really about age.

At the other end, it may also be considered a barrier to democratic representation if young cohorts are outnumbered by older cohorts and never get to enjoy the political power of those over 50. This could happen due both to the ageing of the electorate and to the young's low voting turnout – voting turnouts tend to be vastly correlated with age (Berry 2012: 34). We could make the case that majoritarian democratic institutions may be unable to protect the interests of younger cohorts in ageing societies and that we ought to remedy any serious democratic deficit between generations. Here, we would also be worrying about the young's political marginalisation, but as a birth cohort.

The distinction between age groups and birth cohorts is important and helpful, and some issues fall neatly in one or the other. As we just discussed, the question of whether 16-year-olds should have the right to vote, for instance, is largely about age membership, whereas the demographic imbalance between smaller and larger generations is largely a cohortal issue. But, of course, many political issues can be understood only by appeal to both cohort and age effects jointly. An important zone of overlap, for instance, has to do with lower rates of participation in the young. The question here is to know whether it can be explained by appeal to age effects alone (in which case the disengaged will end up re-engaging at normal rates as they age), or by appeal to cohort effects (lower rates of participation could have to do with a generational change in attitude and have a continuing impact on voting behaviours in the long run). In fact, recent studies suggest that we must appeal to both age and cohort effects to understand youth disengagement (Sloam 2012).

As such, the socio-economic disadvantage of the young is not necessarily directly an issue of democratic ethics. After all, those inequalities may be matters of distributive justice on some conceptions of what we owe each other, but they may be procedurally fair. However, the comparative socio-economic disadvantage of the young can be viewed with suspicion from a democratic perspective in light of their marginalisation in formal politics both as an age group and as a birth cohort. As the various issues I have just discussed make clear, there can exist both age and cohort democratic imbalances at the level of electoral and representative institutions.

So what is the state of the democratic deficit exactly? In many OECD countries, young cohorts have definitely become comparatively disenfranchised. The problem is not necessarily that older generations are trying to marginalise younger generations. But with their higher number and voting turnout rates, they often find themselves in a privileged position to shape political outcomes with their values and interests. A particularly striking example of this is the Brexit referendum in the UK, where over 70 per cent of the 18–24 age group voted Remain and more than 60 per cent of voters over the age of 65 years old voted Leave. Given the outcome of the referendum, this is a good example of a case where the values and perceived interests of older age groups have determined the political outcome, even if younger cohorts will be affected by the results of the election for longer than older cohorts.

The phenomenon of youth marginalisation is reinforced by the fact that the young tend to have fewer political rights than older age groups. These age-based inequalities in basic rights are meant to capture unequal levels of competence, but they are not unproblematic. Politicians can easily manipulate children and we justify the disenfranchisement of children by the need to protect them from becoming vulnerable targets around election times. But it is not clear that such reasons stand when it comes to older teenagers and young adults. The young have a high stake in many of the core policy areas communities vote on – housing, education, the environment, pensions, and income support. So their relative de jure exclusion from voting has to be questioned. The unequal representation of different age groups in parliaments is an example of the de facto (rather than de jure) exclusion of young adults from formal politics (for more on de jure and de facto exclusion of youth, see Bellamy et al. 2018). The gap between the global average age of a parliamentarian and the median age of the global population is almost 30 years (Inter-Parliamentary Union 2012). Representatives of less than 30 years old in fact make up less than 2 per cent of two-thirds of single and lower houses at the global level, while three-quarters of upper houses do not elect young parliamentarians at all (Inter-Parliamentary Union 2014).

If our discussion of the requirements of youth policies in previous sections has made anything clear, it is that it is probably inadequate to attempt to solve difficult questions about the comparative opportunities each age group should have access to in the abstract, especially when it comes to establishing what counts as 'enough' for each age groups. If this is true, we should worry about the under-representation of youth interests through voting and in parliaments. Which possible mechanisms could help us re-engage the young in order to ensure a more procedurally fair treatment of issues of age-group justice? Re-enfranchising the young seems like one of the central solutions to this problem. Both lowering the voting age to 16 years old and making voting compulsory (hoping it will boost youth voting rates) are potential solutions. Youth participation can also be fostered more simply by implementing easier voting systems and by making voting registration simpler or automatic.

An interesting policy to correct the under-representation of young people in parliaments is the introduction of youth quotas in the legislatures (Bidadanure 2015). The presence of young MPs can be expected to have at least two kinds of impacts on decision-making. The first is substantive. Regardless of their party membership, young MPs can be expected to contribute to expanding the available party policy packages through pushing for the better inclusion of youth concerns in political agendas. Bringing in more young persons in parliaments can also increase the likeliness that misconceptions about young people will be challenged. Quotas can prevent the important risk that policies and debates become driven by disrespectful misrepresentations, if conducted solely within some age groups and in exclusion of others. The second potential impact of youth quotas is more symbolic. Youth quotas would signal to society and young people that their contribution is valued and that they are considered with equal respect. Youth quotas may thus act as a strong symbolic gesture to re-engage youth in politics, with a potential impact on their future participation.

Conclusion

In this chapter, I have highlighted some requirements of age-group justice and its implications for youth policy. I have suggested that abstract principles of distributive justice cannot give us specific answers on what counts as an adequate set of opportunities for the young. As illustrated by the example of sufficiency, those principles often give us a frame to set the terms of the debate, but they do not tell us precisely what the young, or any other age groups, are specifically owed. This is where deliberations that involve different age groups are particularly important. In this context, the political marginalisation of the young is particularly worrying – youth policy is far too often made for the young without the young. We must find remedies against those democratic barriers to a just youth polity, and I have suggested that re-enfranchising the young and asserting their political equality through quotas in parliaments are some of the solutions to consider.

Note

1 The arguments in this section are further developed in my forthcoming book with Oxford University Press on age-group justice.

References

Bauerlein, M. (2008) *The Dumbest Generation: How the Digital Age Stupefied Young Americans and Jeopardizes Our Future.* New York: Jeremy P. Tarcher/Penguin.

Berry, C. (2012) *The Rise of Gerontocracy? Addressing the Intergenerational Democratic Deficit.* London: Intergenerational Foundation.

Bidadanure, J. (2012) Short-Sightedness in Youth Welfare Provision: The Case of RSA in France. *Intergenerational Justice Review* 1: 22–28.

Bidadanure, J. (2015) Better Procedures for Fairer Outcomes: Can Youth Quotas in Parliaments Increase Our Chances of Meeting the Demands of Intergenerational Justice. In *Youth Quotas and Other Forms of Youth Participation in Ageing Societies,* edited by Joerg Tremmel et al. London: Springer, pp. 37–55.

Bidadanure, J. (2016) Making Sense of Age-Group Justice: A Time for Relational Equality? *Politics, Economics and Philosophy* 15(3): 234–260.

Bidadanure, J. (2017) Discrimination and Age. In *The Routledge Handbook on the Ethics of Discrimination,* edited by Kasper Lippert-Rasmussen. Oxon: Routledge, pp. 243–253.

Bidadanure, J. (forthcoming) *Justice Across Ages: Treating Young and Old as Equals.* Oxford: Oxford University Press.

Bellamy, R., Merkel, W., Bhargava, R., Bidadanure, J., et al. (2018). Challenges of Inequality to Democracy. In *Rethinking Society for the 21st Century: Report of the International Panel on Social Progress*, edited by IPSP. Cambridge: Cambridge University Press, pp. 563–596.

Chauvel, L. (2010) The Long-Term Destabilization of Youth, Scarring Effects, and the Future of the Welfare Regime in Post-Trente Glorieuses France. *French Politics, Culture & Society* 28 (3): pp. 74–96.

Daniels, N. (1988) *Am I My Parents' Keeper? An Essay on Justice Between the Young and the Old*. Oxford: Oxford University Press.

Delaney, B. (2016) Baby Boomers Have Already Taken All the Houses, Now They're Coming for Our Brunch. *The Guardian*, 17 October. https://www.theguardian.com/commentisfree/2016/oct/17/baby-boomers-have-already-taken-all-the-houses-now-theyre-coming-for-our-brunch

Denstad, F.Y. (2009). *Youth Policy Manual: How to Develop a National Youth Strategy*. Strasbourg: Council of Europe Publishing.

Eurostat (2009). *Youth in Europe: A Statistical Portrait*. Luxembourg: European Commission.

Furlong, A., and F. Cartmel (2007) Changing Patterns of Dependency. In *Young People and Social Change: New Perspectives*. Maidenhead: McGraw-Hill/Open University Press, pp. 53–70.

Goldfarb, S. (2014) Who Pays for the 'Boomerang Generation'? *Harvard Journal of Law and Gender* 37: pp. 45–106.

Inter-Parliamentary Union (2012). *Global Parliamentary Report: Facts and Figures*. Geneva: Inter-Parliamentary Union/United Nations Development Programme.

Inter-Parliamentary Union (2014) *Youth Participation in National Parliaments*. Geneva: Inter-Parliamentary Union.

Jecker, N. (1992) Appeals to Nature in Theories of Age-Group Justice. In *Aging and Ethics: Philosophical Problems in Gerontology*, edited by Nancy Jecker, pp. 269–283. Clifton, NJ: Humana Press.

Salt, B. (2016) Moralizers We Need You, *The Australian*, 15–16 October. https://www.theaustralian.com.au/life/weekend-australian-magazine/moralisers-we-need-you/news-story/6bdb24f77572be68330bd306c14ee8a3

Sloam, J. (2012) Introduction: Youth, Citizenship and Politics. *Parliamentary Affairs* 65 (1): pp. 4–12.

Standing, G. (2011) *The Precariat: The New Dangerous Class*. London: Bloomsbury.

Taylor, P., R. Morin, K. Parker, D. Cohn, and W. Wang. 2009. *Forty Years after Woodstock, a Gentler Generation Gap*. Washington DC: Pew Research Center. http://www.pewsocialtrends.org/files/2010/10/after-woodstock-gentler-generation-gap.pdf

Twenge, J. (2006) *Generation Me: Why Today's Young Americans Are More Confident, Assertive, Entitled – and More Miserable Than Ever Before*. New York: The Free Press.

Wolff, J., and A. De-Shalit (2007) *Disadvantage*. Oxford: Oxford University Press.

37

MEASURING INTERGENERATIONAL JUSTICE FOR PUBLIC POLICY

Pieter Vanhuysse and Jörg Tremmel

Introduction

Population ageing – widespread across rich democracies – has led to a renewed popular and academic interest in the notion of justice between generations (Gosseries 2002; Tremmel 2009; Vanhuysse and Goerres 2012). Applied to public policy, this notion leads to questions of the long-term affordability of public programmes, such as health care and pensions, and more generally the persistence of current consumption patterns. These policy problems have been exacerbated as a result of the changing age composition of society through the second demographic transition, which is characterised by the combination of low fertility and increasing life expectancy (Gál/Monostori 2016, 3). The political economy literature dealing with public policies for different generations puts forward three main propositions: (1) currently older generations receive more overall public transfers, and currently young and working-aged generations much less, than generations that were old in past decades (Kotlikoff and Burns 2012); (2) older persons receive more on average than children (e.g., Vanhuysse 2013, 2014); and (3) the ratio of public resources that go to the elderly has increased relatively to the amount of resources going to young people (Preston 1984). Some observers assume that the key intermediary mechanism for these fiscal cost developments is political participation: the larger share of elderly voters that comes with population ageing tends to mobilise politically and electorally proportionately more than younger age groups in pursuit of their policy interests. This then leads to fears of 'grey power', 'gerontocracy' (Sinn and Uebelmesser 2002), grey 'electoral majorities' (Sanderson and Scherbov 2007), or 'pro-elderly bias' (Tepe and Vanhuysse 2009, 2010). Some even speak of 'generational storms' or 'clashes' (Kotlikoff and Burns 2012). Clearly, population ageing makes sober and informed analysis of the intergenerational justice of public policies both urgent and timely.

The aim of this chapter is to examine issues of public spending across generations in a way that combines economics (and the literature on economic indicators in particular) with normative accounts of justice. Theories of intergenerational justice have to specify who (recipients) should get how much (pattern or scope) of what (currency or distribuendum) by whom (providers). We do not intend to put forward a full theory of intergenerational justice here (for overviews, see Tremmel 2009; Gosseries/Meyer 2009). Rather, we follow an intuitive yardstick principle of justice based on the notion of a fair balance of benefits received *relative* to contributions given to society, as applied to generations (see also Sabbagh and Vanhuysse 2010). The intuition is that it is unjust that generations who contribute to the same degree to society (often, the public budget) do not benefit to the same degree from public spending. Similarly, it seems unjust if those who contribute more benefit less than others who contribute less. Note that we do not discuss currencies of intergenerational justice outside the realm of public spending in cash and kind.[1] We limit our discussion to financial resource transfers between age groups and between cohorts that come with a public policy which is, in turn, influenced by demographic change.

With regard to public spending, two different concepts of 'generation' are relevant (e.g., Goerres and Vanhuysse 2012; Tremmel 2009, ch. 3). First, when we want to evaluate inter-generational justice over *complete lives*, we need the concept of *(birth) cohorts*. These are groups of people who were born in the same year or narrow range of years (e.g., 1970–1975). Cohort members, by virtue of ageing together at the same period in history, have shared distinct eco-nomic experiences and have thus benefited or been harmed ('scarred') by specific public poli-cies but also by external events outside the ambit of public policy (e.g., deep recessions for the worse or technological progress for the better).[2] Second, when we want to make a snapshot analysis of intergenerational justice at a *given moment* in time, *age groups* combine people of the same (narrow) age bracket at a particular moment. Age group members find themselves in the same stage in the life cycle, which is politically relevant because public policies tend to institu-tionalise the life course, proscribing and inhibiting certain behaviours. Another moral intuition driving our analysis of intergenerational justice is that it is not *prima facie* problematic that at one given point in time different age groups receive an unequal treatment from the state. But if such inequalities are perpetuated across different birth cohorts over the entire life cycle, then we do end up with intergenerational inequities.

This chapter is structured as follows. The second section outlines the lexis diagram, a heu-ristic tool that serves to illustrate and thereby to explain the comparisons between 'generations' (age groups and cohorts) that underlie most metrics for intergenerational justice with regard to the domain of public policy. The third section exemplifies the age group approach, with a focus on the 'elderly-bias indicator of social spending' (EBiSS) as one prominent synchronic metric to measure justice between age groups for public policy. The fourth section supplements this with a discussion of metrics that employ diachronic comparison of cohorts. Generational accounting will be discussed to illustrate the cohort viewpoint. The fifth section connects the empirical findings with the general debate about intergenerational justice. The chapter argues that there are strong empirical indications that the baby boomer generation is unfairly treating younger generations in terms of both the age group metric (e.g., in Italy, Japan, and Poland) and the cohort metric (e.g., in France, Italy, and Spain). We conclude with some reform proposals in the final section.

Comparing generations

Obviously, all methods and indices measuring intergenerational justice draw comparisons between providing generations and recipient generations, but what they conceptionalise var-ies greatly. The complexity of comparing generations can be illustrated by a Lexis diagram, a two-dimensional diagram showing the relationship between periods and cohorts (Figure 37.1).

In the Lexis diagram, the vertical axis shows the age of cohorts, and the horizontal axis shows the flow of time. The diagonal line that starts above the birth year of a certain cohort represents its life course. For instance, the cohort born in 1950 is symbolised by the diagonal line that starts in that year; it is 10 years old in 1960, 20 years old in 1970, and so on. Comparisons can

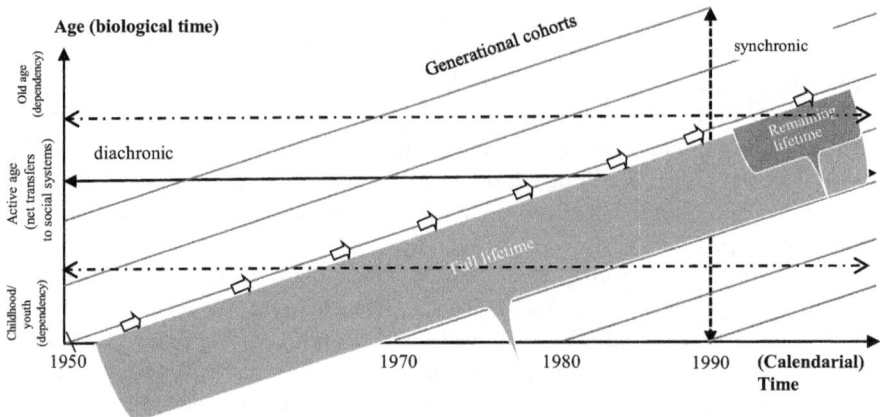

Figure 37.1 Lexis diagram

be drawn between people either of different ages at a certain point in time (age group comparisons), or of the same age at different points in time (cohort comparisons). The dotted vertical line above the year 1990 represents a synchronic comparison, a 'snapshot', between people that were 'young' and 'old' in the year 1990. 'Young' and 'old' can designate different age intervals – for instance, 'old' can designate 'all people currently between 65–90 years of age'. Often, the age brackets that are of interest are established by legal requirements in a society, such as the legal retirement age. But the object of analysis can also be a single year age group (e.g., all people 80 years of age at the time of the snapshot). For instance, if we are interested in the wealth distribution by age in a specific country, we look at the wealth distribution of people in their twenties, thirties, forties, fifties, and so on at time t_0 (e.g., in the year 2010). A diachronic comparison, by contrast, compares people of the same age at different points in time. For instance, if the question at hand is whether people in their twenties were wealthier or less wealthy in different decades (2000s, 1990s, 1980s, and so on), one must apply a diachronic comparison.

A sophisticated form of a diachronic comparison is a comparison of life courses of (at least) two generations (Tremmel 2009). A life course analysis in itself is a longitudinal study. It analyses either a specific part of the life course (often: the remaining lifetime) or the full life course. Consider the cohort born in 1950 in the Lexis diagram. As these individuals move through time they can be subjected to a life course analysis. However, as long as this life course analysis is not compared with the life course analysis of another cohort – say, the 1960-born cohort – we have just a longitudinal study in which individuals are monitored over a relatively long period of time, but not a comparison between generations.

The EBiSS as measure of age-group justice

The overall pro-elderly bias in social spending (henceforth EBiSS) is a pragmatic and empirical metric to compare age groups with regard to public policy transfers across 29 OECD countries (Vanhuysse 2013).[3] The analysis is synchronic (an internationally comparable snapshot of how different *age groups* are treated at one point in time), not diachronic (it does not follow cohorts over time). The unit of analysis is countries. The recipients are both the elderly and the non-elderly (in relation to each other); the providers are all taxpayers, including future taxpayers, if social expenditures are partly financed by borrowing. The methodology and data presented here stem from Vanhuysse 2013 (for previous such approaches, see, e.g., Lynch 2006; Tepe and Vanhuysse 2010). On the *elderly*-oriented spending side, the EBiSS numerator includes old-age-related benefits in cash and in kind, survivors' benefits in cash and in kind, disability pensions, occupational injury and disease-related pensions, and early retirement for labour market reasons. On the *non-elderly* spending side, the EBiSS denominator includes family benefits in cash and in kind, active labour market programs, income maintenance cash benefits, unemployment compensation and severance pay cash benefits, and all education spending. To control for demographic structure, the resulting elderly/non-elderly social spending ratio has been adjusted by means of each country's old-age support ratio (the number of persons aged 20–64 over the number of persons aged 65 or more).[4] Since public health spending, a major elderly-oriented spending item everywhere, has not been incorporated into these EBiSS calculations, the EBiSS as defined here almost certainly *underestimates* the pro-elderly bias of welfare state spending.

As Figure 37.1 shows, the least pro-elderly biased welfare states in the years following the global economic crisis were New Zealand, South Korea, Canada, Ireland, and Denmark. The rest of Europe is more strongly represented at the other end of the spectrum. EU member states occupy eight of the ten highest EBiSS positions. Poland was the most pro-elderly biased welfare state in the sample. The Polish welfare state spent on average 8.7 times as much on each elderly Pole as it spent on each non-elderly Pole in the late 2000s. Following at some distance, Greece and Italy (EBiSS values around 7), Slovakia (around 6.5), then Czech Republic, Slovenia and Japan (around 5.5) were all positioned on the high-EBiSS side of the spectrum as well (Figure 37.2).

The connection between demographic structure and pro-elderly policy bias is spurious. Figure 37.1 shows that of the OECD's four demographically oldest societies, Italy and Japan

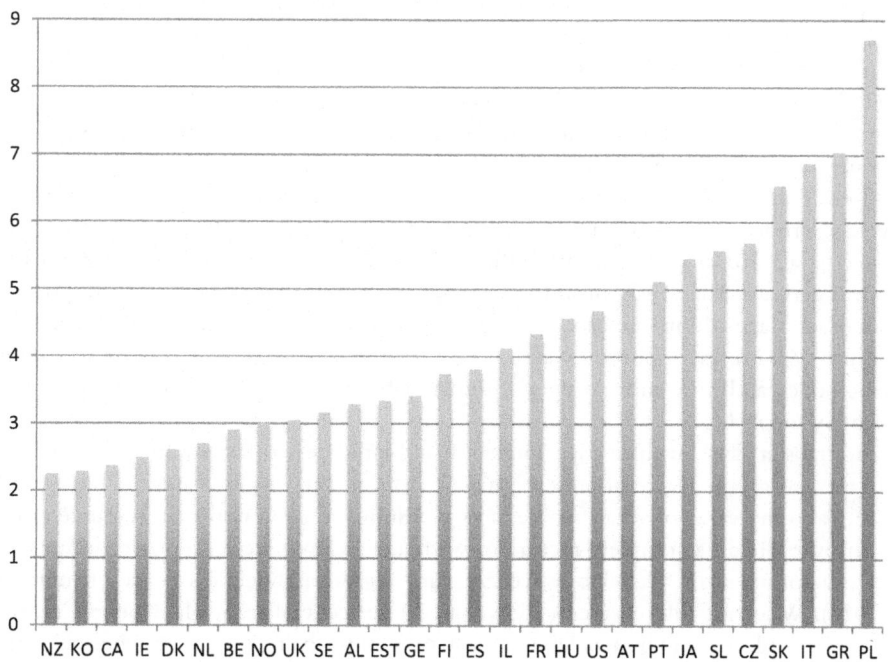

Figure 37.2   Elderly-bias indicator of social spending (EBiSS), 2009–2010 or latest

Source: Computations by P. Vanhuysse following Vanhuysse (2013).

had a high level of pro-elderly social spending bias at the end of the 2000s, with values of respectively around 7 and 5.5. But Germany and Sweden, also demographically old societies, showed relatively low pro-elderly bias, with EBiSS values of respectively around 3.5 and 3. Conversely, the Irish and Belgian welfare states spent respectively 2.5 and three times as much on average per each elderly citizen as per non-elderly citizen, even though Ireland was a demographically young society, whereas Belgium was a much older society. In the demographically old Greece, the state spent seven times more for every elderly Greek as it spent for every non-elderly Greek. But in comparably old Sweden, the state spent only three times more.

Demography is *not* destiny as regards the pro-elderly bias of European welfare states. Instead, it is policy choices as determined by long-standing governance cultures that drive EBiSS patterns. Together with three Southern countries (Greece, Italy, and Portugal), Slovenia, the Czech Republic, Slovakia, and (especially) Poland (which, around 2009–2010, still counts as a 'young-to-middle-aged' society) have the most pro-elderly biased welfare states according to the EBiSS measure. This can be explained largely as a result of legacies of early post-communist transition, such as the need to compensate pensioners for the loss of their savings through (hyper-)inflation in the early 1990s, 'familializing' state approaches towards mothers and children, and policy-induced, historically unprecedented exit into early and disability pensions.[5]

Of course, EBiSS figures refer purely to *public* spending efforts. Working-age groups spend very significant time and financial resources caring for both older and, much less visibly, younger generations within family settings. Once one includes also private cash and, most crucially, time transfers in addition to public policies, conclusions differ radically. Gal et al. (2018) show that European welfare states, as welfare *states*, are indeed pro-elderly biased: public policies predominantly serve the elderly today. But at the same time, European societies, as *societies*, transfer more than twice as many resources on average to each child as to each older person, because families transfer resources too, notably cash and time. In line with pro-elderly welfare studies (Lynch 2006; Tepe and Vanhuysse 2010; Vanhuysse 2013), and the results in Figure 37.1, older Europeans (defined as those who are net resource-dependent in later life) are found to receive on average more than twice as much in net public transfers as children (defined as those who are net resource-dependent in early life): 37 per cent of the average prime-earnings income in their country, compared to 15 per cent for children. But Gal et al. (2018) show that limiting the analysis of intergenerational resource transfers to public transfers alone seriously misinforms about actual resources received during resource-dependent life stages. If private cash transfers are also taken into account, the picture changes significantly. And more importantly still, if in a third step we expand our currency of justice in public policy and now add transfers of unpaid labour (time), the original proportions are quite simply *inverted*.

Public transfer data on their own might by and large be satisfactory for snapshot evaluations of the age-group justice of policies (what *states* do). But this indicates the importance of estimating also the value of what families accomplish in cash and non-cash resource transfers, if the aim is to obtain a complete picture of what age groups give each other within *societies*. Europe is a continent of 'pro-elderly welfare states *and* strongly child-oriented families' (Gal et al. 2018). Whereas children receive less than 40 per cent of what older people receive in public transfers alone, children receive almost two-and-a-half times *more* when all transfers are combined (Gal et al. 2018). Of course, the observation that families, not states, are the main source of transfers for children in Europe today shifts us from an intergenerational to an intra-generational perspective, as it brings class (and gender) back in. In the (comparative) absence of universal state provision for children, richer families (women) will be able to spend many more resources per capita on their own children than poorer families (Gal et al. 2018). The recent social investment and early human capital paradigm in social policy thus still has much scope for expanding in order to complement these massive family investments made in children and compensate for class inequalities and diverging destinies based on the accident of birth (Vanhuysse 2015b).

Fiscal deficit accounting as a metric for cohort justice

In this section, the second meaning of the notion 'generation' – *cohorts* – comes to the fore. One often employed method for justice between cohorts[6] is fiscal gap accounting, developed in the early 1990s (Auerbach et al. 1991, 1994; Blanchard et al. 1990; Blanchard 1993) to analyse the fiscal treatment of current and future cohorts. The name of this method (or ensemble of methods) is still disputed.[7] In fiscal gap accounting, the distinction between explicit and implicit debt is key. While indicators such as public debt or annual public deficit measure fiscal policy in a narrow sense, these new methods aim to measure the fiscal public policy (e.g., public pension policy or public health policy) in a broader sense, adding an implicit deficit perspective to the traditional explicit indicators. Fiscal gap accounting first determines how many taxes, social security contributions, levies, and fees each average individual of today's cohorts will pay to the state in each year of his or her remaining lifetime. Secondly, it calculates the transfers (e.g., pension scheme, health insurance benefits, nursing care insurance benefits, children's benefits, welfare support, public education services, public goods) each individual will receive from the state in the years of his or her statistically remaining lifespan. Thirdly, the balance between payments and transfers is calculated for each cohort (Figure 37.3).

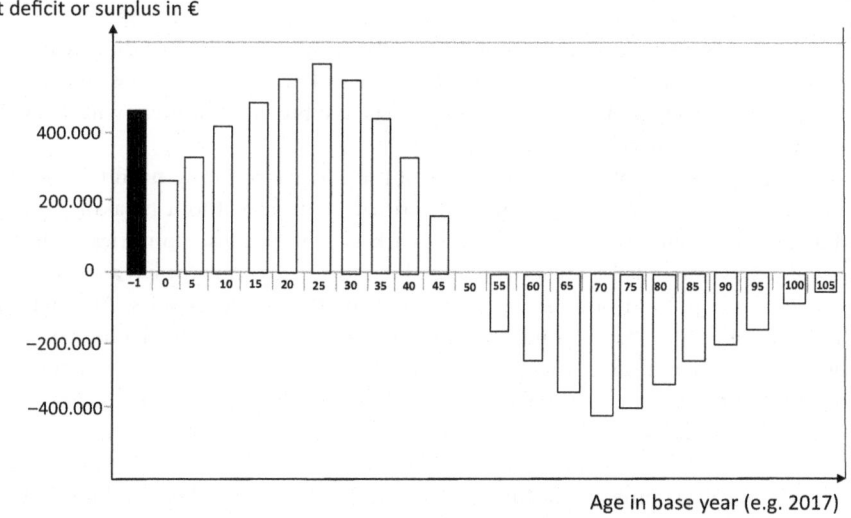

Figure 37.3 Cohort accounts for remaining lifetime and for entire lifetime (exemplary)

Source: Computations by J. Tremmel.

No sound comparison can be drawn between the presently living cohorts (transparent bars) because a 70-year-old will obviously receive more money from the state than he will pay in his remaining lifetime, because he is already a pensioner. Instead, this method relies on comparing the net transfer payments of a newly born child to those of an average individual that will be born in the future (black bar) as both agents' accounts are observed over their entire life cycle. In a second step, these profiles (often not only age- but also gender-specific) are extrapolated into the future, using a constant annual real growth rate and a discount rate. The projection of future net tax payments for cohort members is then multiplied in a third step with the number of cohort members: the higher the number of net contributors and the lower the number of net recipients in the demographic structure of a country, the better ceteris paribus the long-term financial situation of this country. Financial stability translates into a sustainable situation in which there will be future benefits for future citizens of the country in question. This method can thus measure fiscal sustainability on the macro level.[8]

As illustrated in the Lexis diagram, it is the comparison between full life cycles of different cohorts that matters for judgements about cohort justice. If the future individual will pay more (or less), the financial policy is called 'fiscally unsustainable' (or sustainable) in the economic literature.[9]

This 'fiscal gap' leads to important insights with regard to intergenerational justice of public policy. The indicators traditionally used in national budgeting refer only to the current year or the results of past development. They are 'past-looking'. While fiscal gap accounting adds to this the forward-looking perspective (and the concrete amounts) of the 'implicit national debts', it has (like every method) its own limitations. Methodologically, proponents of fiscal gap accounting tend to assume that the persons alive in the base year will enjoy the advantages of the current financial policy all their lives, despite the fiscal gap, while succeeding generations will start closing that gap, which they deem fiscally unsustainable (intertemporal budget restriction of the state; for a formal illustration see Benz and Fetzer 2006, 370). According to this theoretical premise, cohorts that are currently close to dead are able to 'escape' from this system without penalty, while future generations inevitably will have to pay the price. But the next generation can, in theory and practice, pass on its debts to the second-next. Thereby the next generation is just as well off in terms of implicit debt as their predecessors that created the debt. This 'game' is quite different from a chain letter game or Ponzi game[10] as these fraudulent games always fail because eventually the later buyers are the last buyers. But there will always be a following generation, as far as we know.

We should therefore note that proponents of fiscal gap accounting need to show that governments are really unable to run permanent primary deficits without breaking the intertemporal budget constraint. The point that 'the markets' will penalise countries with high fiscal deficits still needs to be made: for instance, the US federal government has a massive fiscal gap, roughly $200 trillion, but it still has a good rating from the rating agencies. Another methodological limitation of fiscal gap accounting is that the financial policy, the demographic situation, and the economic situation in the base year are assumed to be constant over the projection horizon. Setting the key input variables of the base year as representational is risky – and usually counterfactual. While demography is quite stable, public policy legislation sees significant changes almost in every legislature.[11]

Table 37.1 displays some recent findings from the EU Sustainability Ranking 2016 (Peters/Raffelhüschen/Reeker 2017). Regarding the long-term perspectives of the public budgets of the EU member states almost all countries have an implicit deficit (in addition to their explicit debt) in percentage of their GDP.

Table 37.1 International comparison of public debt (in % of GDP) in 2016

		Explicit debt	Implicit debt	Total debt
1	Croatia	83	−95	−12
2	Bulgaria	29	35	64
3	Sweden	42	43	85
4	Latvia	41	59	99
5	Denmark	38	67	105
6	Portugal	130	−7	123
7	Italy	132	−2	130
8	Estonia	9	134	144
9	Germany	68	78	146
10	Poland	54	103	157
11	Czech Republic	37	141	177
12	Malta	58	140	198
13	Hungary	74	133	206
14	France	97	153	249
15	Austria	84	177	260
16	Slovak Republic	52	228	280
17	Cyprus	107	181	288
18	Lithuania	40	248	288
19	The United Kingdom	88	210	298
20	The Netherlands	62	247	309
21	Greece	181	145	326
22	Finland	63	342	406
23	Romania	38	380	417
24	Belgium	106	383	489
25	Slovenia	79	412	490
26	Spain	99	520	619
27	Ireland	73	624	697
28	Luxembourg	21	895	915

Source: Peters, Raffelhüschen, and Reeker (2018, 20) (data from European Commission reports and their own computations). Available at: www.stiftung-marktwirtschaft.de/wirtschaft/themen/generationenbilanz.html.

Age group and cohort inequalities in comparison

As noted earlier, one widely shared assumption in theories of intergenerational justice is that it is not *prima facie* problematic that at one given point in time different age groups receive an unequal treatment from the state. But if, even after taking into account socio-economic controls and reasonable income growth over time, such inequalities are perpetuated across different birth cohorts over the entire life cycle, then we end up with intergenerational inequities. In other words, age group inequalities are not necessarily objectionable (but see McKerlie 2013; Bidadanure 2016), while inequalities over the entire life cycle between birth cohorts are prima facie objectionable. If they occur there will be generations (in the sense of cohorts) that take advantage of other generations.

What insights do methods like the EBiSS and Fiscal Gap Accounting add to this view? As stated by Figure 37.1, Poland, Greece, Italy, Slovakia, and the Czech Republic have high

EBiSS levels. These states spend on average between 5.5 and 8.5 times as much on every elderly citizen as on every non-elderly one. Now, those who are old now were once young and those who are now young will once be old. As long as a specific EBiSS value stays relatively stable over time, it need not necessarily create inequalities between people's complete lives, as everyone belongs in turn to each of the age groups. Rather, we would have a case of welfare states based on 'Spartan childhoods for luxury old age' trade-offs for all cohorts in, say, Poland or Greece. Thus there would be no prima facie intergenerational injustice *if* and only if every successive Polish cohort could count on roughly the same EBiSS value also in the future.[12] If, however, as seems more likely than not given recent policy developments in both countries, today's young or working-aged Greeks and Poles will later be confronted with a significantly lower EBiSS, then we would have a strong indication of intergenerational injustice.

Age group measures like the EBiSS are most informative if they cover a long time horizon and if the analysis is repeated often. If those countries that have a high EBiSS in 2010 had a low one 40 years ago, age group inequality would turn into cohort injustice, for this means that people who were in their twenties and thirties 40 years ago profited a lot from state benefits in *all* stages of their lives. One of the few studies on how different generations have fared under the social welfare policies of governments since the 1930s is that of David Thomson (1991), who argues that in New Zealand, 'the big winners (. . .) have been (. . .) those born between about 1920 and 1945. Throughout their lives they will make contributions which cover only a fraction of the benefits' (Thomson 1991, 3).

Especially in view of recent and near-future expected demographic ageing developments, it would stretch the limits of credibility to argue that the high Polish, Greek, or Italian EBiSS values truly reflect democratically desired 'Spartan childhood for luxury old age' trade-offs, *and* that such values have been – and will remain – relatively stable over time. There is growing evidence that, even after taking into account socio-economic controls and reasonable income growth over time, such inequalities are not balanced over the entire life cycle for succeeding cohorts, especially for countries in Southern and continental Europe, such as Spain, Italy, and France. In these countries, even after taking into account reasonable income growth over time for all cohorts, the baby boom generation born after World War II has been significantly better off in terms of post-tax-and-transfer disposable income than cohorts born both beforehand and afterward (Chauvel and Schröder 2014; see also Chauvel 2010). We then end up with lucky and unlucky generations – or insider and outsider cohorts – within the same country.

As it happens, mounting evidence indicates that younger age groups today increasingly doubt the intergenerational equity of current policy patterns – with good reason. For instance, Sabbagh and Vanhuysse (2010) studied more than 2,000 undergraduate university students from eight democracies across four worlds of welfare, using the fair balance of benefits-*relative*-to-contributions yardstick set out earlier. They found that young adults aged 18–35 were systematically perceived to get a worse deal of rights and obligations from society than either older working-age adults or the elderly (Sabbagh and Vanhuysse 2010). Moreover, in all European countries, public transfers already tend to flow from non-elderly to elderly groups today (Lee and Mason 2011; Gal et al. 2018).

We now turn to the inequalities between cohorts that are measured by generational accounts – and the question of whether they create injustices. At first glance, high implicit debts (>500% of GDP) seem utterly unfair. But one must not forget that intergenerational justice verdicts cannot be derived from looking at only one cohort-generation. A present cohort with a high implicit debt might seem to have a deplorable fiscal lot, but if previous and succeeding cohorts have had and will have a similar implicit debt, one cannot say that the present generation is treated unfairly. This is probably the main conceptual difference to the concept of 'sustainability' which establishes an absolute standard.[13] From the correct statement that countries like Ireland have a problem with their fiscal sustainability one cannot infer that one newborn Irish person is treated unfairly with regard to previously born Irish persons. Of course, this does not justify the reverse conclusion that intergenerational injustices do not exist in Europe. In certain countries and certain sectors, these injustices undoubtedly exist. In Germany, for instance, the younger cohort's yield out of their mandatory contributions to the pay-as-you-go pension scheme will be significantly lower than that of earlier generations (Wilkoszewski 2008; Tremmel 2009, 32).

Early human capital investment and other policy reform proposals

Combatting the inherent present bias of voters and politicians in democracies is needed to safeguard the opportunities of future generations in ageing welfare states (Boston 2016; Ricoy-Gonzalez and Gosseries 2016; Vanhuysse 2015b; Tremmel 2015). On the policy supply side, seemingly 'obvious' measures that merit a new look in light of this perspective include fiscal and social security benefits or credits to reward family members for raising children and caring for the elderly (often expending substantial private cost for societal benefit), the adjustment of official pension ages and pension benefits to rising life expectancy, and ecologically motivated tax frameworks, such as carbon taxes and phasing out nuclear energy.

There is a particularly strong case for mobilising political coalitions for spending more on high-quality *early childhood* education and similar social investment policies that increase the human capital of the smaller-sized younger generations in ageing societies, and thus bolster the fiscal basis of their welfare states in the process (Francesconi and Heckman 2016; Heckman 2013; Vanhuysse 2015b). Such investments are a way to boost the skill levels of young people preparing to enter future labour markets. They are a readily available way to marry economic efficiency (in the form of very high social returns throughout the later life cycle) with intergenerational justice (in the form of levelling the playing field for all citizens across barriers of class and cohort). As Folbre (1994) puts it, children are significant *public* goods, predominantly privately paid for. More precisely, children are *deliberately socialised* goods whose future benefits are rival and excludable (Olsaretti 2013). Parents bear the lion's share of the cost of raising their own children – in cash and time, both directly and in terms of opportunities foregone. These costs are in part socially imposed by ever-stronger legal obligations for continuity of adequate care (Folbre 2008; Alstott 2004). Yet, to the extent that children subsequently become productive tax- and social security–paying adults, they create positive externalities that benefit all of society (Gal et al. 2018). They will finance, for instance, future public pension and health and long-term care benefits, all of which will also benefit non-parents.[14]

In other words, children's future benefits are heavily socialised, but their current costs only marginally so. The resources involved in raising children need to be increasingly socialised to safeguard the sustainability of ageing welfare states. Asset-based predistributive policies, such as stakeholder grants or baby bonds, to be set up by government for each newborn baby and potentially topped up by parents, which could be made accessible with compound interest rates upon reaching legal voting age, are one example of an intergenerationally progressive policy (Ackerman and Alstott 1999). What such proposals have in common is the idea that they might partly counter the often high pro-elderly bias of public spending in favour of the currently elderly in a way that would be more explicitly youth-oriented and comparatively cheap (possibly even long-term self-financing) from a macro-fiscal perspective.

Against the backdrop of the growing numerical weight of pensioner-voters, could changes in voting schemes create room for intergenerational justice with regard to public policy? Different proposals have been discussed. For instance, proposals for (proxy) voting rights for parents (Demeny 1986, 1987; Van Parijs 1998) extend the scope of the franchise. Specifically, they suggest giving each parent (or caretaker) one-half extra vote, to be used on behalf of each underage child until that child reaches legal voting age (for empirical effects of this changed voting scheme, see Goerres and Tiemann 2009; Vanhuysse 2013, 2014). Opponents see advocacy voting rights for parents as a violation of the fundamental normative principle of democracies: one person, one vote. But proponents note that children are persons too, that democratically no longer capable very sick or very old persons are not systematically disfranchised either, and that proxy votes would reward parents for the public good they produce for society in raising children.

Many opponents of parental proxy voting argue for a general lowering of the minimum voting age as an alternative. They point to the fact that young adults and older children can hold different political opinions and thus prefer different parties than their parents. Tremmel and Wilhelm (2015) advocate a 'flexible voting age' building on the willingness of minors to participate in elections. This proposal takes into account that babies, little children, and many younger adolescents have no interest in political participation anyway. The 'flexible voting age' proposal contains a need for adolescents to register in voting lists and must thus be strictly distinguished from proposals that come under the name of 'voting from birth on' or 'voting age zero'. Lowering the voting age is a worldwide trend that can be monitored since the advent of modern democracies in the eighteenth century, and it is likely to continue in the future.

Conclusion

We end by noting that there is a remarkable asymmetry in the socialisation of intergenerational transfers in modern societies. Working-age people pay taxes and social security contributions to institutionalise care for older persons *as a generation*. But they invest significant amounts of private resources in cash and in time to raise *their own* children, often with large social returns (Gal et al. 2018). This key socialisation asymmetry has important implications for both inter- and intra-generational justice in pro-elderly welfare states that are simultaneously child-oriented societies. Pro-elderly *policy* constellations may derive from rational (as opposed to strongly egoistic) reasoning by the electorally key group of older voters. These voters, as (grand)parents, may correctly assume that they are more reliable and more concentrated sources of resource transfers to their *own* (grand)children than the state (which, by definition, also favours other people's [grand]children). And the fact that it is families, not states, who shoulder the major burden of investing in children-as-public-goods in Europe shows why policies are needed to combat intra-generational problems of class.

Equality-of-opportunity enhancing policies such as early human capital investment in particular seem a promising way forward. They are doubly progressive on the outcome side, in that they are also especially likely to boost the cognitive and non-cognitive skills of *young* children born in *disadvantaged* families (Vanhuysse 2015a). Current policy constellations in many countries seem to put a heavy and disproportionate burden especially on the *poorest members* of the younger generations, because they do not receive as many public resources as the poorest members of the older generation and their parents and grandparents cannot transfer as many private resources as can wealthier parents and grandparents (Gal et al. 2018). Significant early human capital investment policies are thus also a way to marry inter- and intra-generational justice.

Notes

1 Theories of justice that are designed for other policy areas – say, environmental policy or ducation policy – will have other currencies, but these are different debates in which we do not enter here. We do not make the claim that monetary units/indicators are the most adequate currency for all conceptions of justice – only that they are an adequate currency for conceptions of intergenerational justice within the realm of public policy (without denying that monetary transfers impact important policy goals, such as well-being, quality of life, and human capabilities). On the adequate equalisandum in theories of egalitarian justice, see Otsuka (2011).

2 One factor that also impacts the well-being of a current generation is the size of it in relation to the size of the predecessor generation; see Easterlin (1980).

3 The EBISS is one dimension within Vanhuysse's four-dimensional Intergenerational Justice Index; see Vanhuysse (2013, 2015a). Another example of the 'assessing impact' approach is Leach et al. (2016).

4 A hypothetical construct illustrates this aspect of the EBiSS: in country A, the population at t1 is divided evenly in elderly and non-elderly citizens. Public expenditure is likewise distributed evenly between these two groups. The value of the EBiSS is therefore 1. Between t1 and t2, the population of country A ages, and at t2, elderly people make up two-thirds and non-elderly people just one-third. If public expenditure is distributed with the same ratio (two-thirds for the elderly, one-third for the non-elderly), the EBISS does not change. It remains at 1. But if the elderly are now a political majority get more than two-thirds of public expenditure, the EBISS will rise above 1.

5 For instance, in the first seven years of democracy alone, literally hundreds of thousands of working-age Hungarians and Poles, but not Czechs, were incentivized to exit into early and disability pensions by means of more generous and better protected pension benefits relative to 'younger' programs, such as unemployment and family benefits (Vanhuysse 2006).

6 In the terminology of Tremmel (2009), 'justice between age groups' is synonymous to 'temporal generational justice'.

7 Out of the three possible umbrella terms – fiscal gap accounting, fiscal sustainability accounting, generational accounting – we generally use the first term.

8 Benz and Fetzer (2006, 372): 'In contrast, the OECD method employs two different ways of projecting revenues and expenditures. The first projection method, used for all revenues and for so-called non-age-specific expenditures, increases these aggregates at the same rate as is employed for the GDP, which necessitates an additional GDP projection. The second projection method, applied to all future age-specific expenditures, varies between different studies, along with which of the expenditures are assumed to be age-specific'.

9 Tax policy must address three fundamental questions: what is taxed, who is taxed, and how tax burdens are allocated among taxpayers. This chapter examines the ethical dimensions of these questions, including the merits of income taxation, consumption taxation, and Pigouvian taxes, the tax treatment of families and of corporations, the justification of progressive taxation, and tax competition. It considers theories of tax fairness grounded in taxpayers' ability to pay and in the benefits taxpayers receive from government as well as the perspectives of utilitarians, egalitarians, and public choice theorists.

It is worth noting that fiscal gap accounting is an umbrella term that encompasses quite diverging methods (for an overview, see Benz and Fetzer 2006). One method rests on the methodological assumption that all cohorts currently alive are entirely exempted from helping eliminate a country's fiscal gap. They assume an infinite time horizon. Often, the term 'generational accounting' (or classical generational accounting) is reserved for this method; see Raffelhüschen (1999) and Bonin (2001). Another method reflects the increase of contributions/reduction of transfers by/to currently living cohorts in order to leave no deficit behind that needs to be paid by future generations. Here, the presently living generations alone balance the account. A third indicator assumes the currently living and future generations together will close the fiscal gap. The time horizon cannot be infinite here, but the choice of a certain number of years is quite arbitrary. The European Commission reports' period under review extends until the year 2060.

When it comes to calculating the fiscal gap for a specific social system in a specific country, the devil lies in the details. For instance, some approaches take into account that statutory pay-as-you-go schemes have a yearly adjustment of contributions before restoring the fiscal deficit (surplus); some take account of the fact that some national laws establish an upper ceiling for contributions, and so forth.

10 A Ponzi game is an investment operation in which the operator generates returns for the first investors through revenue paid by succeding investors, rather than from legitimate business activities. It is considered a fraudulent scheme as the agent (an individual or a corporation) offers very high short-term returns for early investors that cannot be sustained for later investors.
11 A comparative analysis in several consecutive base years is necessary to reduce this methodological problem. In the European Union, fiscal gap measures are calculated every three years for all its member states (European Commission 2015).
12 For elaborations on this argument, see, for example, Daniels (1988), McKerlie (2013), and Bidadanure (2016).
13 The well-known sustainability definition issued by the Brundtland Commission demands that present needs of present people be satisfied. The needs of future people are a secondary, auxiliary condition. This makes sustainability a 'sufficientarian' account of intergenerational justice. While relational accounts of intergenerational justice compare the state of one generation to another generation in order to arrive at justice statements, a 'sufficientarian' (=non-relational) account of intergenerational justice forgoes any comparisons between two or more different generations.
14 For an analysis of the ethics of child-rearing and families, see Gheaus in this volume.

References

Ackerman, B. and Alstott, A. (1999), *The Stakeholder Society*. New Haven: Yale University Press.
Alstott, A. (2004), *No Exit: What Parents Owe Their Children and What Society Owes Parents*. Oxford: Oxford University Press.
Auerbach, A., Gokhale, J. and Kotlikoff, L. (1991), Generational Accounts: A Meaningful Alternative to Deficit Accounting. *Tax Policy and the Economy*, 5, 55–110.
Auerbach, A., Gokhale, J. and Kotlikoff, L. (1994), Generational Accounts: A Meaningful Way to Evaluate Fiscal Policy, *The Journal of Economic Perspectives*, 8(1), 73–94.
Benz, U. and Fetzer, S. (2006), Indicators for Measuring Fiscal Sustainability – A Comparison of the OECD-Method and Generational Accounting, *Finanzarchiv*, 62(3), 367–391.
Bidadanure, J. (2016), Making Sense of Age-Group Justice: A Time for Relational Equality? *Politics, Philosophy & Economics*, 15(3), 234–260.
Blanchard, O. et al. (Eds.). (1990), *The Sustainability of Fiscal Policy: New Answers to an Old Question*. OECD Economic Studies 15. Paris: OECD Publishing.
Blanchard, O. (1993), Suggestions for a New Set of Fiscal Indicators, in: Verbon, H., and van Winden, F. (Eds.), *The Political Economy of Government Debt*. Amsterdam: North-Holland, 307–325.
Bonin, H. (2001), *Generational Accounting – Theory and Application*. Heidelberg: Springer-Verlag.
Boston, J. (2016), *Governing for the Future: Designing Democratic Institutions for a Better Tomorrow*. Bingley: Emerald.
Chauvel, L. and Schröder, M. (2014), Generational Inequalities and Welfare Regimes, *Social Forces*, 92(4), 1259–1283.
Chauvel, L. (2010), Comparing Welfare Regime Changes: Living Standards and the Unequal Life Chances of Different Birth Cohorts, in: Tremmel, J. (Ed.), *Young Generation under Pressure? The Financial Situation and the "Rush Hour" of the Cohorts 1970–1985 in a Generational Comparison*. Heidelberg: Springer, 23–36.
Daniels, N. (1988), *Am I my Parents' Keeper? An Essay on Justice Between the Young and the Old*. Oxford: Oxford University Press.
Demeny, P. (1986), Pronatalist Policies in Low-Fertility Countries: Patterns, Performance and Prospects, *Population and Development Review*, 12, 335–358.
Demeny, P. (1987), Re-Linking Fertility Behavior and Economic Security in Old Age: A Pronatalist Reform, *Population and Development Review*, 13, 128–132.
Easterlin, Richard A. (1980), *Birth and Fortune: The Impact on Numbers on Personal Welfare*. New York: Grant McIntyre.
European Commission. (2015). *Fiscal Sustainability Report*. https://ec.europa.eu/info/publications/economy-finance/fiscal-sustainability-report-2015_en
Folbre, N. (1994), Children as Public Goods, *American Economic Review*, 84(2), 86–90.
Folbre, N. (2008), *Valuing Children*, Cambridge MA: Harvard University Press.
Francesconi, M. and Heckman, J. (2016), Child Development and Parental Investment: Introduction, *Economic Journal*, 126, F1–F27.

Gál, R. I. and Monostori, Judit. (2016), *Indicators of Economic Sustainability and Intergenerational Fairness.* AGENTA Research Reports. www.agenta-project.eu/Jacomo/upload/publications/d-6.1-submitted. pdf

Gal, R. I., Vanhuysse, P. and Vargha, L. (2018), Pro-Elderly Welfare States Within Child-Oriented Societies, *Journal of European Public Policy*, 25(6), 944–958.

Goerres, A. and Vanhuysse, P. (2012), Mapping the Field: Comparative Generational Politics and Policies in Ageing Democracies, in: Vanhuysse, Pieter and Goerres, Achim (Eds.), *Ageing Populations in Postindustrial Democracies*, Abingdon: Routledge/ECPR Studies in European Political Science.

Goerres, A. and Tiemann, G. (2009), Kinder an Die Macht? Die politischen Konsequenzen des Stellvertretenden Elternwahlrechts, *Politisches Vierteljahresschrift*, 50, 50–74.

Gonzalez-Ricoy, I. and Gosseries, A. (Eds.). (2016), *Institutions for Future Generations.* Oxford: Oxford University Press.

Gosseries, A. (2002), Intergenerational Justice, in: LaFollette, Hugh (ed.), *The Oxford Handbook of Practical Ethics.* Oxford: Oxford University Press, 459–484.

Gosseries, A. and Meyer, L. H. (Eds.). (2009), *Intergenerational Justice.* Oxford: Oxford University Press.

Heckman, J. (2013), *Giving Kids a Fair Chance.* Cambridge, MA: The MIT Press.

Kotlikoff, L. J. and Burns, S. (2012), *The Clash of Generations.* Cambridge, MA: The MIT Press.

Leach, J., Broeks, M., Østensvik, K. S. and Kingman, D. (2016), *European Intergenerational Fairness Index: A Crisis for the Young.* London: Intergenerational Foundation.

Lee, R. and Mason, A. (Eds.). (2011), *Population Aging and the Generational Economy: A Global Perspective.* Cheltenham: Edward Elgar.

Lynch, J. (2006), *Age in the Welfare State.* Cambridge: Cambridge University Press.

McKerlie, M. (2013), *Justice Between the Young and the Old.* Oxford: Oxford University Press.

Olsaretti, S. (2013), Children as public goods,' *Philosophy and Public Affairs* 41(3), 227–258.

Otsuka, M. (Ed.). (2011), *On the Currency of Egalitarian Justice, and Other Essays in Political Philosophy/G. A. Cohen.* Princeton, NJ: Princeton University Press.

Peters, F., Raffelhüschen, B. and Reeker, G. (2017), *Ehrbare Staaten? Update 2016. Die Nachhaltigkeit der öffentlichen Finanzen in Europa.* www.stiftung-marktwirtschaft.de/wirtschaft/themen/generationenbilanz.html

Peters, F., Raffelhüschen, B., and Reeker, G. (2018), *Ehrbare Staaten? Update 2017. Die Nachhaltigkeit der öffentlichen Finanzen in Europa.Argumente zu Marktwirtschaft und Politik* 139(Jan), 20.

Preston, S. H. (1984), Children and the Elderly: Divergent Paths for America's Dependents, *Demography*, 21(4), 435–457.

Raffelhüschen, B. (1999), Generational Accounting: Method, Data and Limitations, in: European Commission Directorate General for Economic and Financial Affairs (Ed.), *Generational Accounting in Europe, European Economy, Reports and Studies*, 6(99), 17–28.

Sabbagh, C. and Vanhuysse, P. (2010), Intergenerational Justice Perceptions and the Role of Welfare Regimes: A Comparative Analysis of University Students, *Administration & Society*, 42(6), 638–667.

Sanderson, W. and Scherbov, S. (2007), A Near Electoral Majority of Pensioners, *Population and Development Review*, 33(3), 543–554.

Sinn, H-W. and Uebelmesser, S. (2002), Pensions and the Path to Gerontocracy in Germany, *European Journal of Political Economy*, 19, 153–158.

Tepe, M. and Vanhuysse, P. (2009), Are Aging OECD Welfare States on the Path to Gerontocracy?' *Journal of Public Policy*, 29(1), 1–28.

Tepe, M. and Vanhuysse, P. (2010), Elderly Bias, New Social Risks, and Social Spending: Change and Timing in Eight Programs Across Four Worlds of Welfare, 1980–2003, *Journal of European Social Policy*, 20(3), 218–234.

Thomson, David. (1991), *Selfish Generations? The Ageing of New Zealand's Welfare State.* Wennlington, NZ: Bridget Williams Books.

Tremmel, J. (2009), *A Theory of Intergenerational Justice.* London: Earthscan.

Tremmel, J. (2015), Parliaments and Future Generations – the Four-Powers-Model, in: Birnbacher, Dieter and Thorseth, May (Ed.), *The Politics of Sustainability. Philosophical Perspectives.* London: Routledge/Earthscan, 212–233.

Tremmel, J. and Wilhelm, J. (2015), Democracy or Epistocracy? Age as a Criterion of Voter Eligibility, in: Tremmel, Jörg, Mason, Antony, Dimitrijoski, Igor and Godli, Petter (Eds.), *Youth Quotas in Ageing Societies.* Dordrecht: Springer, 125–147.

Vanhuysse, P. (2006), *Divide and Pacify: Strategic Social Policies and Political Protests in Post-Communist Democracies*. Budapest: Central European University Press.

Vanhuysse, P. (2013), *Intergenerational Justice in Aging Societies. A Cross-National Comparison of 29 OECD Countries*. Gütersloh: Bertelsmann Stiftung.

Vanhuysse, P. (2014), Intergenerational Justice and Public Policy in Europe, *European Social Observatory (OSE) Paper Series*, Opinion Paper No.16, March.

Vanhuysse, P. (2015a), Progressive Social Policies for Intergenerational Justice in Aging Societies: Demography Is Not Destiny, in: Diamond, Patrick and Chwalisz, Claudia (Eds.), *The Pre-Distribution Agenda: Tackling Inequality and Supporting Sustainable Growth*. London: I.B. Tauris, 47–62.

Vanhuysse, P. (2015b), Skills, Stakes and Clout: Early Human Capital Foundations for European Welfare Futures, in: Manin, B. (Ed.), *The Future of Welfare in a Global Europe*. Alderschot: Ashgate, 267–296.

Vanhuysse, P. and Goerres, A. (Eds.). (2012), *Ageing Populations in Post-Industrial Democracies*. Abingdon: Routledge.

Van Parijs, P. (1998), The Disfranchisement of the Elderly, and Other Attempts to Secure Intergenerational Justice, *Philosophy & Public Affairs*, 27(4), 292–333.

Wilkoszewski, Harald. (2008), Demographic Pressure and Attitudes Towards Public Intergenerational Transfers in Germany – How Much Room Left for Reforms? in: Tremmel, Jörg (Ed.), *Demographic Change and Intergenerational Justice*. Heidelberg: Springer, 175–205.

38

DEVELOPMENT AND CLIMATE ETHICS

Darrel Moellendorf

This chapter discusses the relationship between two projects of fundamental importance to the international community. The first project, recognised as the first of the United Nations Sustainable Development Goals, is to end poverty in all of its forms everywhere. Experience suggests that doing so will require states to pursue sound national development strategies under propitious international conditions. These conditions include access to inexpensive energy. Historically, states have relied on the burning of fossil fuels to achieve human development aims. The second project is recognised as Sustainable Development goal 13, to take urgent action to combat climate change and its impacts. Combatting climate change requires drastically reducing, and eventually within the course of this century completely halting, CO_2 emissions. There is the clear potential for conflict between these goals. Yet the right to sustainable development recognised by the United Nations Framework Convention on Climate Change (UNFCCC) aims to constrain acceptable mitigation policies by development interests of poor states. The Paris Agreement of the UNFCCC offers hope that these aims can be reconciled. But realising the Paris Agreement would require minimising collective action problems and encouraging appropriate technological development.

This chapter begins by discussing the justification of human development as a moral aim. It proceeds to discuss the moral requirement to mitigate climate change and clarifies how these two morally mandatory projects might conflict. It then rejects arguments from those who would minimise the problem of the climate change. These arguments offer a false resolution to the tension between human development and the mitigation of climate change. The chapter discusses the collective action problems that bedevil the effort to achieve a binding and ambitious agreement on climate change. The chapter closes by discussing the promise of the Paris Agreement as a way to move forward in the face of these difficulties.

Human development and energy consumption

The United Nations Human Development Programme (UNHDP) has developed a Human Development Index (HDI) that ranks states on a scale of 0 to 1. The UNDP describes the HDI as 'a summary measure of average achievement in key dimensions of human development: a long and healthy life, being knowledgeable and have a decent standard of living' (UNDP 2015a). Somewhat more precisely, the HDI of a country is the geometric mean of the three measures. One is the life expectancy at birth; another is the per capita national income; the final one combines the mean years of schooling for adults and the expected years of schooling for children just starting school. The most recent HDI classifies countries into the following four groups: Very High Human Development (0.800 and above), High Human Development (0.700–0.799), Medium Human Development (0.550–0.699), and Low Human Development (below 0.550) (UNDP 2015b). The four classifications are merely quartiles of the class of all countries listed (Nielsen 2011). Hence, the difference between, say, a ranking of 0.799 and 0.800 does not correspond to a more significant development difference than the difference between 0.798 and 0.7999. Still, given the importance of three main components that compose the HDI, there is reason to value improvements along the scale.

Why is human development valuable? John Rawls famously claims that 'Justice is the first virtue of social systems, as truth is of a system of thought' (Rawls 1999: 3). Rawls thinks of justice in terms of how well institutions secure basic liberties, equalise opportunities, and promote the well-being of the least advantaged. One can imagine two countries with institutions doing roughly equally well in satisfying justice, but with one at a much higher HDI rank than the other. Although both countries are nearly equally just, there is good reason to think that the country with higher HDI rank is *ceteris paribus* morally superior. That is so in virtue of the value of human development. The UNDP reports the purpose of developing the HDI as follows: 'The HDI was created to emphasize that people and their capabilities should be the ultimate criteria for assessing the development of a country, not economic growth alone' (UNDP 2015a). The HDI directs focus on the well-being of people. Although two countries might be approximately equally just according to a Rawlsian conception of justice, the aggregate well-being of the people may still vary. And that would be morally significant.

Amartya Sen argues for taking 'development as a process of expanding the real freedoms that people enjoy' (Sen 1999: 36). According to Sen, development consists in the expansion of real or substantive freedoms, which are powers to act in morally valuable ways. Better health and education and more income increase these powers. When a country makes progress with respect to indices of education, income, and health, according to this view, the citizens are substantively freer. The value of developmental progress for a country then is that such progress consists in greater freedom for its citizens. Moreover, although not a component of the HDI, Sen contends that political participation and dissent (ibid.) are also constitutive elements of development because they are parts of real freedom. Sen's view entails that the HDI measures freedom, and is therefore more important than conceptions of development focusing only on economic growth. Development is valuable then because it is constitutive of the expansion of real human freedom.

Sen does not consider that there may be value to health, income, and education apart from being constituents of freedom, but an account of the value of human development would be incomplete without clarifying these other kinds of value. Health is instrumentally valuable in the pursuit of valuable ends and meaningful projects. It seems also to be valuable for its own sake, apart from being a constitutive element of freedom or necessary for the pursuit of valuable ends and meaningful projects. A prisoner, or some other person of limited freedom and sharply restricted aims, still has reason to value her health. Education is also valuable in pursuit of ends and projects. The knowledge that education can yield serves to promote other values, such as health. But knowledge is valuable for its own sake as well, regardless of the use to which it is put. And finally, income is valuable as an all-purpose means. A great deal of what we have reason to value in modern society is traded for money. An increase of income for most people means they are able to have more of what they value. Hence, the value of human development consists not only in the expansion of human freedom but also in the achievement of better health and educational outcomes, and the greater income constitutive of development as well.

Human development is very energy-intensive. There is a strong correlation between energy access and human development. The International Energy Association (IEA) has developed an Energy Development Index composed of the following four measures: the percentage of the population with access to electricity and per capita residential consumption, the percentage of modern fuels (excluding electricity in residential fuel consumption, per capita public sector electricity consumption, and the percentage of economic activities in the total final consumption. Each factor is scored on a 0 to 1 scale, and the EDI is the arithmetic mean of all four (IEA 2012). That scale is devised for ease of comparison with the HDI. The comparison reveals a strong correlation between HDI value and EDI value (ibid.: 547). The direction of causation is disputed. It is unclear whether increased energy consumption causes human development progress or whether human development causes energy consumption to grow (D. Stern 2016: 18–19). Either increased use of modern energy promotes human development or human development increases the demand for such energy. Either way, on balance the evidence suggests that progress in human development involves expanding energy access and use very considerably.

Overcoming the desperate poverty that shackles billions of people is a fundamental moral duty, and one of highest importance. Even philosophers who deny that duties of global justice exist (Nagel 2005) affirm the basic moral importance of poverty eradication. Recent experience suggests that proper national development strategies are a necessary part of making human development gains. Some states have shown impressive success in poverty relief, but they have done so at the cost of increasing their CO_2 emissions dramatically. According to the World Bank China reduced the number of people living in poverty from 1981 to 2001 by 400 million people. During that time the poverty rate dropped from 53 to 8 per cent (World Bank 2016). Meanwhile, however, total CO_2 emissions from the consumption of energy in China increased from 1,599.51 million metric tons to 3,913.89 million metric tons (EDGAR 2015a). And per capita emissions increased from 1.6 metric tons in 1981 to 3.0 in 2001 (EDGAR 2015b). Poverty-eradicating human development has up to now involved a massive increase in CO_2 emissions. That poses a serious challenge to the aims of climate change mitigation.

Climate change mitigation aims

Climate change is driven primarily by the concentration of greenhouse gases in the atmosphere (IPCCC 2014: 6). These concentrations raise the risks of various devastating events. The poor are especially vulnerable to these events. Food security will be threatened, especially certain stocks of marine animals and the growth of wheat, rice, and corn in temperate and tropical regions could be especially affected (IPCC 2014: 13). Summarising recent scientific data the Intergovernmental Panel on Climate Change (IPCC) expresses with high confidence the claim 'that climate change is expected to lead to increases in ill-health in many regions and especially in developing countries with low income, as compared to a baseline without climate change' (IPCC 2014: 15). And the IPCC's survey of the scientific studies leads it to project that climate change will produce

> increased risks for people, assets, economies and ecosystems, including risks from heat stress, storms and extreme precipitation, inland and coastal flooding, landslides, air pollution, drought, water scarcity, sea-level rise, and storm surges (very high confidence).

These risks are amplified for those lacking essential infrastructure and services or living in exposed areas.

(IPCC 2014: 15)

The IPCC also has medium confidence in projected lower economic growth in impoverished countries, resulting in slower poverty reduction and the creation of new poverty traps and "Hotspots of hunger" (IPCCC 2014: 16). Climate change mitigation efforts seek to reduce the occurrence of these negative effects in the future by reducing and then halting CO_2 emissions.

CO_2 concentrations in the atmosphere have been built up by the emissions of generations going back to the beginning of the Industrial Revolution. For example, about 40 per cent of the CO_2 emitted since 1750 remains in the atmosphere today (IPCC 2014: 4). But about half of all CO_2 emissions have occurred in the last 40 years (IPCCC 2014: 4). The combination of historical contribution but recent amplified contribution must be taken into consideration when considering the nature of the duty to mitigate climate change on behalf of future generations. The duty to mitigate cannot only be conceived as guided simply by a principle demanding that we rescue future people from a harm caused by our predecessors, for recent emissions are also a significant part of the problem. Nor, however, is the moral requirement captured entirely by a principle of refraining from causing harm since our mitigation is required in part because of what others have done. Mitigation policy is required because of the risks inherited from distant earlier generations *and* those that have come to be as a result of the currently living and recently dead. Setting aside certain complications about duties to future generations and the existence of competing duties, the duty to mitigate can be understood in the first instance in terms of the duty not to compound already existing risks (Moellendorf 2017). The compounding of risks requires that there be pre-existing risks and that present agents can augment them. Since compounding is a kind of causing, the duty not to compound existing risks is a species of the duty not to cause undeserved suffering, adjusted to the increased risk of doing so as a result of the actions of others.

Globally CO_2 emissions continue to grow. The growth is driven primarily by emissions in the developing world (USEIA 2016). The IPCC's summary of existing science finds that,

> Globally, economic and population growth continued to be the most important drivers of increases in CO_2 emissions from fossil fuel combustion. The contribution of population growth between 2000 and 2010 remained roughly identical to the previous three decades, while the contribution of economic growth has risen sharply. Increased use of coal has reversed the long-standing trend of gradual decarbonization . . . of the world's energy supply.
>
> *(IPCC 2014: 5)*

Coal has been used by rapidly developing countries because of its price competitiveness.

The short-term aim of any credible mitigation policy has to effect a reduction in global emissions. Merely reducing emissions is not enough, however. Halting temperature increase at any particular temperature requires stopping net CO_2 emissions and possibly even withdrawing CO_2 from the atmosphere. The atmospheric concentration of CO_2 and other greenhouse gases drives global temperature increase. Due to the long residence time of CO_2 in the atmosphere, the atmospheric concentration is a function of cumulative historic emissions. For any particular warming limit target, there is a budget of total cumulative emissions (IPCC 2014:8). For example, the carbon budget to limit warming to 2°C has already been over half spent (Trillionth-tonne.org). Hence the ultimate goal of a mitigation policy that seeks to constrain warming to any temperature level is to phase out and then stop global anthropogenic CO_2 emissions completely. Pursuit of that goal will probably need to occur along with employing technology to remove a portion of CO_2 from the atmosphere.

The duty not to compound the undeserved suffering of future generations requires phasing out all CO_2 emissions over the course of this century. But the morally mandatory aim to eradicate global poverty requires that national development strategies aimed at doing so not be retarded. Pursuit of climate change mitigation then must be constrained by the requirement that human development policies not be hampered. This presents a major moral challenge for international climate change policy.

Denial and democracy

In the previous two sections I argued that although global poverty eradication and climate change mitigation are morally mandatory projects, they potentially stand in conflict with one another insofar as poverty eradication happens fastest through fossil fuel–intensive human development strategies. There would be no such potential conflict if the expected problem of climate change were less severe than the mainstream scientific position summarised by the IPCC projects. There are various versions of climate change denial that hold that view. And in some countries versions of denial have considerable public credibility. One of the first acts of the current president of the United States, Donald Trump, was to remove references to climate from official government websites (Davenport 2017).

Both warming and the increase of CO_2 in the atmosphere are well established by careful and multiple measurements made by scientists all around the world. To deny either of these would involve appealing to the systematic falsification of scientific evidence. That is wildly implausible to most people. The door to denial is opened slightly more when it comes to projections of future warming. Humans have known for well over 100 years that CO_2 is a greenhouse gas. So, barring intervening factors, one would expect the global mean temperature to increase as the concentration of CO_2 in the atmosphere increases. But the climate system is remarkably complex, and there are possible feedback mechanisms that could serve either to amplify or reduce the warming to be expected by increasing the atmospheric concentration of CO_2. Those that increase warming are known as *positive feedback mechanisms*, while those that decrease it are referred to as *negative feedback mechanisms*. Climate scientists do not fully understand the multiple positive and negative feedback mechanisms in the climate system. That produces a range of uncertainty about how much warming will be produced by an increase in the atmospheric concentration of CO_2.

The term *climate sensitivity* refers to the global mean temperature increase produced by a doubling of the atmospheric concentration of CO_2 since pre-industrial times. From the measurement of CO_2 in ice cores scientists have determined that at the dawn of the Industrial Revolution the concentration of CO_2 in the atmosphere was approximately 279ppm. Climate sensitivity then refers to the mean global temperature increase above the pre-industrial era produced by 558ppm of CO_2 in the atmosphere. The predominant view among climate scientists, as summarised in IPCC reports, is that the temperature increase would be in the range of 1.5–4.5°C. The midpoint is then 3°C. One important reason that a more precise figure cannot be given is due to uncertainty about the feedback role of water vapour in the atmosphere. As the temperature increases, more water evaporates, causing increased cloud formation. Water vapour is a greenhouse gas. So evaporation can be expected to create a positive feedback contributing to warming. But how much will the warming be offset by the cooling caused by the shade of the clouds? The degree to which water evaporation will function as a positive feedback mechanism is uncertain. The IPCC report before the most recent one observed that the feed-back role of clouds is the biggest source of uncertainty (IPCC 2007). The uncertainty about climate sensitivity ripples across other projections. For example, increased temperature causes thermal expansion in the oceans, resulting in sea-level rise. But thermal expansion varies as the temperature varies. Moreover, significant sea-level rise would be caused by the collapse of land-based ice sheets in Antarctica or Greenland. Such collapse, however, is due to melting, which also varies with warming. One contrarian climate scientist even maintains that rain drainage from clouds will reduce cloud cover and allow more heat to escape, resulting in a much lower value for climate sensitivity than the IPCC's range (Lindzen 2008).

The vast majority of citizens of any country do not have sufficient scientific expertise to judge on its scientific merits either the case for climate change represented by the IPCC or the case for some alternative account. Yet in democracies citizens have a voice to influence climate policy. The expression of that voice will ultimately rely on trusting the scientific analyses of others. What rational grounds are there for ordinary citizens either to affirm or to deny the seriousness of climate change?

Ordinary citizens and policy-makers not trained in science have two good reasons to trust the consensus scientific position summarised in the IPCC, even though there is a very small minority of scientists in the contrarian camp (Moellendorf 2014). The first reason is precisely that it is the consensus position. Citizens and policy-makers are not in an epistemic position that allows them rationally to assess the merits of the case. In such a circumstance it makes sense to go with the mainstream scientific position on the grounds that it has won the allegiance of more people who are in a position to rationally evaluate the arguments and evidence. Just as a patient making a health care choice has reason to prefer the therapy recommended by the medical con-sensus over alternative therapies, so does the citizen have reason to trust the mainstream posi-tion. The second reason to trust the consensus position of the IPCC is that the costs of being wrong when adopting policy guided by that view are far less than the costs of being wrong if policy were adopted based on a view that underestimates the threat. To base policy on the latter recommendation is to leave future generations exposed to very serious climatic effects, possibly even catastrophes, if the projections are wrong. The danger of wrongly basing policy on the projections of the consensus scientific position is to very slightly slow global growth. Nicholas Stern cites studies suggesting the investments required would be in the range of 1 to 3 per cent of the global GDP per year (N. Stern 2015: 38–39). And with these costs come benefits, such as much cleaner air and reduced pollutions costs.

Some hostility to climate change mitigation comes not from denying the danger of climate change outright but from the argument that the greater danger to the poor of the world is pov-erty and insofar as climate change mitigation would divert attention and resources away from poverty reduction it is not money well spent with an eye to improving the well-being of the poor (Lomborg 2008). The idea is that the first priority should be human development. Pursuit of fossil fuel–intensive human development efforts will make the next generation wealthier and their societies more resilient in the face of climate perturbations. Adaptation later is a better use of resources than mitigation now.

The most significant problem with that position is that it fails to take seriously the carbon budget discussed in the previous section. Not to attend to climate change mitigation now would result in increasing cumulative emissions and raising the temperature at which the system finally achieves equilibrium. Failure to mitigate would likely lock in warming of around 4°C by the end of the century (IPCC 2014: 11). That's a temperature that far exceeds any during the time in which human civilisations have developed. But the speed of that warming is more important than the magnitude. In the past when the Earth has warmed that much it has taken

5,000 years to do so. The rate of warming that failure to mitigate would bring about would be at least 20 times faster than previous warming of that magnitude on Earth (NASA 2010). Ecosystems and communities would be put under such immense pressure that it is by no means certain that adaptation would even be possible. The rapid temperature rise would also be occurring simultaneously with what is expected to continuous growth in the global population, at least up till 2050 or 2060 (New et al. 2011). Providing for a growing global population presents serious challenges in any case. These are simply magnified by the stress to agricultural systems and water resources that climate change can be expected to cause. The threat of mass hunger seems realistic. Hence, with the well-being of the poor in particular in mind, waiting to address climate change by means of adaptation is a bad idea.

The right to sustainable development

The United Nations Framework Convention on Climate Change (UNFCCC) is the treaty instrument that serves as the basis of international climate change negotiations under the auspices of the United Nations. Parties to the UNFCCC meet each year at a Conference of the Parties (COP) to discuss various means by which to pursue 'the ultimate objective' state of the treaty, stated in Article 2, to 'prevent dangerous anthropogenic interference with the climate system' (UNFCCC 1992: 4). The UNFCCC contains other important norms that constrain negotiations and policies in pursuit of the ultimate objective.

One norm that is especially important to the theme of this chapter appears in Article 3, the right to sustainable development:

> The Parties have a right to, and should, promote sustainable development. Policies and measures to protect the climate system against human-induced change should be appropriate for the specific conditions of each Party and should be integrated with national development programmes, taking into account that economic development is essential for adopting measures to address climate change.
>
> *(UNFCCC 1992: 5)*

The right to sustainable development acknowledges the importance of access to energy sources needed for human development and the threat that mitigation could pose to that access. The agreement reached in Paris at COP 21 in 2015 alludes to these considerations as well in Article 2: 'This Agreement, in enhancing the implementation of the Convention, including its objective, aims to strengthen the global response to the threat of climate change, in the context of sustainable development and efforts to eradicate poverty' (UNFCCC 2015: 3).

I noted earlier that recent experience suggests that proper national development strategies are a necessary part of making human development gains. But international agreements can either give license to or constrain national development strategies. An international climate change mitigation agreement that raises the price of energy by limiting fossil usage can constrain efforts to pursue human development. At present, however, the least developed and developing countries have reason to prevent such increases in the cost of energy, as that would hamper efforts to eradicate poverty. The right to sustainable development, therefore, is best understood as a moral claim that developing and least developed states have on industrialised ones that policies to limit climate change not harm their prospects of economic development. The nature of the demand is disjunctive. Either least developed and developing states have a liberty to pursue energy-intensive human development even it that involves the use inexpensive fossil fuels, or they have claim on developed states for financial assistance in making the transition to more expensive renewable energy in a manner that does not slow development. Because mitigation policy must aim to phase out fossil use completely, the use of the right in a rational mitigation policy would have to move from the liberty to the claim right over the relatively short term, assuming that fossil fuels remain less expensive than renewables.

Two compelling justifications of the right to sustainable development both invoke non-controversial and widely shared moral principles, rather than more controversial accounts of global justice (Moellendorf 2015). The first justification rests on the principle of promise keeping. The party-states who signed original 1992 United Nations Framework Convention on Climate Change treaty pledged to respect the right to sustainable development. That pledge creates a promissory obligation to do so. Promises must not always be kept. But to be morally excused from fulfilling the obligation a promisor needs a compelling lesser evil justification. If there are economic and social costs to developed countries caused by meeting their promissory obligation, they are surely not sufficient to support the claim that the lesser evil would be to break the promise to respect the right to sustainable development. Promissory obligations are widely understood and recognised. Hence, in the context of international negotiations the justification of the right to sustainable development on grounds of a promissory obligation has considerable practical appeal.

There is also a justification of the right to sustainable development that does not rest on the contingent fact that developed states have pledged to honour it. Climate change mitigation is a cooperative endeavour serving the good of all state parties engaged in the effort. There are moral constraints on cooperative projects aiming towards mutual advantage. Fairness is one such constraint. Fairness requires that parties not be assigned devastatingly burdensome duties merely to relieve a fairly minor burden for other parties. It would also be unfair to insist that a party assume a burden that would prevent them from pursuing a moral mandatory aim, unrelated to the cooperative pursuit, in order to allow other parties to benefit even more. Among the possible ways to achieve the aim, some are ruled out on grounds of fairness even if they would otherwise equally well serve the aim. Preventing or slowing parties' pursuit of human development is ruled out on grounds of both the weight of the burden of forestalling human development and its interference with the morally mandatory aim of pursuing human development.

Collective action problems

In the social sciences efforts to achieve a stable international climate change mitigation regime are often characterised as hobbled by a tragedy of the commons collective action problem. Ensuring commitment to an agreement is difficult because although all parties have an interest in an effective agreement to mitigate, many parties may lack sufficient interest in acting as the agreement demands even if all the other parties do. The lack of interest in abiding by a mitigation agreement is due to the short- to medium-term cost of effecting a transition to an economy based on renewable energy. As long as the levelised costs (the full costs of generation, including infrastructural development) of renewable energy are greater than those fossil fuels, parties will have an interest in burning fossil fuels. The problem appears even more vexing, however, if the parties have high discount rates vis-à-vis the interests of future persons. Then the problem looks more like what Stephen M. Gardiner calls the intergenerational storm (Gardiner 2001). Each generation has an interest in the previous reducing its emissions, but not in reducing emissions itself. Once again this is due to the comparative cost of transitioning to renewable energy.

It is unclear that much additional work in explaining the problems of reaching an international agreement is done by the intergenerational storm analysis. For one thing the tragedy of the commons seems better suited to explain why states would try to game agreements since it takes the relevant agents to be states, whereas the intergenerational storm takes the agents to be generations. Now the intergenerational storm analysis can explain why an agreement would likely lack ambition and be toothless. No generation has an interest in assuming heavy burdens. But the tragedy of the commons account would also maintain that no state has an interest in being held accountable to a strong agreement so each will seek to insure either a lack of ambition or high ambition but a lack of enforcement capacity. But the two analyses would seem to largely converge in any case if the tragedy of the commons assumes that state negotiators strongly discount the future costs and benefits. In that case their motivations coincide with that of generations in the intergenerational storm analysis.

According to both analyses of the collective action problem, lack of an ambitious and binding agreement is driven by the costs of transitioning from fossil fuels to renewable energy. As long as fossil fuels are cheaper, the assumption of the costs of transitioning to renewables disincentivises acting on a mitigation plan. But the severity of the collective action problem decreases as the cost of renewable energy in comparison to fossil fuels falls. And in the case of climate change mitigation that provides some reason for hope.

The cost of renewable energy in comparison to fossil fuels is falling. One reason for this is that the absolute cost of renewable energy, solar power and wind in particular, is dropping quickly. Although the levelised cost of coal is often estimated to be less than solar, the costs of solar are steadily falling (IEA, NEA and OECD 2015). Solar energy has doubled its market share seven times in the last 15 years. And every time solar's share of the market doubles, costs fall 24 per cent. In contrast to solar's growth, coal consumption is dropping in OECD countries; and coal consumption also seems to be flattening out in China (Randall 2016). As the price of solar falls, the gap between the comparative price of solar and coal narrows.

Coal is also significantly more expensive than has been appreciated since its market price does not fully incorporate its costs, which include environmental and health costs. By some estimates these costs amount to nearly 4 per cent of global GDP (IMF 2015). One recent study estimates that fossil fuel combustion in energy plants and industrial facilities is responsible for 3 million premature deaths each year (IEA 2016a). Insofar as the real price of fossil fuels is higher than previously appreciated, the gap between the costs of renewables and fossil fuels is less wide than previously calculated.

Movement in both directions is closing the price gap between renewable energy and fossil fuels. Solar is becoming cheaper, and fossil fuels are more expensive than we have reckoned. Some studies now indicate that solar and wind are even cheaper than coal and gas in certain markets (Carbon tracker 2016). Insofar as a collective action problem driven by the cost of transitioning to renewable energy threatens to undermine an ambitious and binding mitigation agreement, the closing of the gap between the cost of renewable energy and fossil fuels is a sign of hope. Moreover, new mitigation policies can be expected to raise the price of fossil fuels. So, the competiveness of renewables should strengthen. The bad news is that none of this is necessarily sufficient to remove the collection action problem. This is because insofar as action is guided by beliefs rather than facts, the collective action problems are belief- and not fact-sensitive. That creates the space for parties with an interest in fossil fuel consumption to engineer beliefs conducive to their interests.

Recent studies indicate that one-half to two-thirds of all remaining fossil fuels reserves cannot be exploited if we are to have a reasonable chance of limiting warming to 2°C (IEA 2016b). Thus, the fossil fuel industry has a strong incentive to discourage mitigation efforts and falsify climate science, which it has been doing (Oreskes and Conway 2010). These campaigns can affect public opinion. Employees in the fossil fuels industries, communities dependent on their income, and representatives whom they elect are particularly susceptible to falsified science. Where political systems allow fossil fuel companies to exercise political influence on legislation directly, there is a strong incentive to do so. One study finds that the fossil fuel industry spent almost $351 million donating to, and influencing, the 113th Congress of the US. Perhaps not coincidently the fossil fuel industry received nearly $42 billion in federal production and exploration subsidies (Oil Change International 2016. Hence, even if the factual basis for the collective action problem is vanishing, the problem will not necessarily simply go away. Reasonable hope of limiting warming to 2°C will require not only that the costs line up in favour of renewable energy but also that public opinion and political will do so as well. Achieving that in many countries will require public education, political struggle, and adequately addressing the vulnerability of workers in the fossil fuel industry.

Assessing the Paris Agreement

The agreement reached at the COP 21 of the UNFCCC in Paris seems to have brought new optimism to the negotiating process that had been in doubt ever since the COP 15 in Copenhagen in 2009 failed to produce the robust treaty. The Agreement aims to limit warming to well below 2°C, possibly as low as 1.5°C (UNFCCC 2015). The Paris Agreement was made possible in part because the process of making emissions reduction pledges was decentralised. Two years before Paris at COP 19 parties were called upon to prepare Intended Nationally Determined Contributions (INDCs) (UNFCCC 2013). The INDCs were pledges made independently by states, not the product of diplomatic wrangling. Although these pledges were to be devised independently, they were supposed to take into consideration both sufficient ambition to limit warming by 2°C and fairness (UNFCCC 2014).

The decentralised process that gave rise to the Paris Agreement encouraged broad participation. Since no state was compelled to make pledges against its will there was little reason not to participate. Moreover, it served as a procedural safeguard to the substantive claim of the right to sustainable development. Once again no state was compelled to make a pledge that would frustrate its efforts to pursue poverty-eradicating human development. Still the process did not, and seemingly could not, ensure that the sum of the pledges is sufficient to hit the stated goal of limiting warming to well below 2°C. Independent analyses of the pledges made in Paris provide reasons to think the total emissions that they allow would considerably overshoot the temperature goal. One recent report projects that the warming that would occur if the pledges were honoured would be in the range of 2.6°C to 3.1°C (Rogelj et al. 2016). At the high end, that is more than double the 1.5°C that is also mentioned in the agreement as a desired goal.

The need for states to increase their mitigation ambition was predicted by the Paris Agreement. Article 4, paragraph 3 of the Agreement states that 'Each Party's successive nationally determined contribution will represent a progression beyond the Party's then current nationally determined contribution and reflect its highest possible ambition' (UNFCCC 2015: 4). Subsequent pledges by states are expected to be more ambitious than the state's previous pledge. The agreement envisions a survey of progress in achieving the aims of the agreement occurring at five-year intervals beginning in 2023 (UNFCCC 2015). After each review, pledges would be expected to be renewed and increased. Due to the limit on cumulative emissions, if warming is to be limited to 2°C, delaying the first survey till 2023 will require subsequent pledges to be very ambitious because eight years will have gone by in which parties were pursuing pledges the sum total of which was inadequate to limit warming to 2°C.

The lack of ambition of the pledges may not be the biggest concern about the Paris Agreement. Probably more important is whether states can be expected to keep even the inadequate pledges that they have made. Relevant to this question is whether the price for renewable energy continues to fall. If renewable energy were to remain significantly more expensive than fossil fuels over the period until the first survey, effort to mitigate might be undermined by a collective action problem. Although each state has an interest in having warming limited so as to reduce the risks of climate change, it could be the case that no state has an economic interest in assuming the costs necessary to keep its pledge.

In light of the danger of such a collective action problem there is need for transparency in reporting activities so that it would be discernible when states are shirking. The Paris Agreement takes note of that need. It says in Article 4, paragraph 3 that 'Parties shall account for their nationally determined contributions. In accounting . . . Parties shall promote environmental integrity, transparency, accuracy, completeness, comparability and consistency, and ensure the avoidance of double counting' (UNFCC 2015: 4). Stating the norm is important, but it is unclear whether it will be honoured. If honoured, states would have some additional incentive to honour their pledges since they will accrue reputational gains by doing so and that could recompense some of economic loss. The importance of seeing other parties making good on their proposals for purposes of building trust and reducing the tendency to seek competitive advantage is well understood in the study of collective action problems (Ostrom 2015).

An effective mitigation regime also requires an authoritative body that could promote compliance with the pledges. In Article 15, paragraphs 1 and 2 the Agreement declares that

> A mechanism to facilitate implementation of and promote compliance with the provisions of this Agreement is hereby established. The mechanism . . . shall consist of a committee that shall be expert-based and facilitative in nature and function in a manner that is transparent, non-adversarial and non-punitive.
>
> *(UNFCCC 2015: 19)*

The representation structure of the Compliance and Implementation Committee has been established, but its membership remains to be determined (Voigt 2015). The inclusion of a Compliance and Implementation Committee shows recognition of the problem of the incentives not to comply that could undermine the success of the agreement. However, the language stating that the committee should be non-adversarial and non-punitive raises concerns about its effectiveness and suggests the persistence of the collective action problem. Widespread compliance is good, but each state would also like to avoid sanctions. The problem of establishing enforcement mechanisms is a second-order collective problem. The primary problem of keeping the agreement can be solved only by assurance that parties will comply (Ostrom 2015). That assurance is fostered by enforcement of the agreement, but establishing the incentive to enforce presents its own problems.

In addition to overcoming the collective action problems of international climate negotiations, attaining the Paris Agreement's goal of limiting warming to well below 2°C will require technological progress. Most of the scenarios surveyed by the IPCC that would make it more likely than not the warming would be limited to 2°C assume the deployment of atmospheric carbon dioxide removal (CDR) technology (IPCCC 2014). By some estimates around 17 per cent of the mitigation burden will have to be carried by such technology by 2050 (IEA 2014). Currently the technology is not sufficiently advanced to be deployed on that scale. So, a great deal of innovation seems to be required within a relatively short time frame.

The Paris Agreement offers hope that climate change might be mitigated within the constraint of recognising the right to sustainable development. Whether that hope is fulfilled will depend on several factors: political efforts to counter the entrenched interest that seek continued exploitation of fossil reserves; favourable market conditions, in particular on the continued decrease in the costs of renewable energy in comparison to fossil fuels; and the development of scalable technology to remove CO_2 from the atmosphere. Absent the political efforts and improved market conditions it is unlikely that the collective action problems associated with achieving a binding agreement to move to renewable energy will be overcome. But moving to renewable energy alone is unlikely to be enough. Technological innovation in CDR technology seems likely also to be necessary.

Conclusion

There is a fundamental tension at work in making progress in the international pursuit of climate change mitigation. On the one hand, parties to the United Nations Framework Convention on Climate Change (UNFCCC) have agreed to the imperative of limiting emissions so as to prevent dangerous anthropogenic interference in the climate system. Mainstream science tells us that regardless of the particular limit set on warming above pre-industrial levels, halting mean temperature increase will require stabilising concentrations of greenhouse gases in the atmosphere. Because of the long residence time of carbon dioxide in the atmosphere, stabilising concentrations greenhouse gases requires completely eliminating emissions. The lower the temperature limit, the lower the atmospheric concentrations and the sooner emissions must stop. But they must stop for any temperature limit. On the other hand, the path to human development in developing and least developed countries requires economic growth and a massive expansion of energy consumption. To date, development has been fuelled primarily by means of fossil fuels because they have been cheaper than the alternatives. The parties to the UNFCCC have also recognised the right to sustainable development. Arresting warming stands in tension with the historic means by which development has been pursued.

Mitigating climate change risks pitting the interests of future generations in a stable climate system against the interests of the poor in the present generation in poverty-eradicating human development. International and domestic public policy must find an acceptable means of resolving this potential conflict. The 2015 Paris Agreement under the auspices of the UNFCCC holds some promise of making progress in that regard. The voluntary nature of the pledges that countries made in Paris has served the aim of wide participation and has provided insurance that no developing or least developed country could be coerced into making commitments that would detract from its development aims. But the sum of all pledges fails to achieve what is necessary to limit warming to no more than the 2°C limit affirmed in Paris. So, it will be very important to find policy means by which ambition can be increased. Increased ambition, however, is insufficient. Progress must be monitored and states must be held accountable. The Paris Agreement recognises the importance of all three of these matters. But finding the policy tools to realise them will be a major challenge.

Additionally mainstream climate science suggests that simply reducing emissions is unlikely to achieve the stabilisation of atmospheric concentrations of greenhouse gases at a level that would be likely to limit warming to 2°C. Achieving that aim will require removing carbon dioxide from the atmosphere and storing it. So, another important aim of international public policy is to encourage the appropriate testing and development of the needed technology.

References

Carbon Tracker Initiative. 2016. "The End of the Load for Coal and Gas." www.carbontracker.org/report/the-end-of-the-load-for-coal-and-gas/

Davenport, Coral. 2017. "With Trump in Charge, Climate Change References Purged from Website." *New York Times*, January 20.

EDGAR. 2015A. "CO2 Time Series 1990–2014 per Region/Country." http://edgar.jrc.ec.europa.eu/overview.php?v=CO2ts1990-2014&sort=des9

EDGAR. 2015B. "CO2 Time Series 1990–2014 per Capita for World Countries." http://edgar.jrc.ec.europa.eu/overview.php?v=CO2ts_pc1990-2014

Gardiner, S.M. 2001. *A Perfect Moral Storm: The Ethical Tragedy of Climate Change*. Oxford: Oxford University Press.

IEA. 2012. "World Energy Outlook." www.iea.org/publications/freepublications/publication/WEO2012_free.pdf

IEA. 2014. "Energy Technology Perspectives." www.iea.org/publications/freepublications/publication/energy-technology-perspectives-2014.html

IEA. 2016a. "World Energy Outlook." www.worldenergyoutlook.org/publications/weo-2016/

IEA. 2016b. "Can CO$_2$ Capture and Storage Unlock 'Unburnable Carbon'?" May. www.ieaghg.org/exco_docs/2016-05.pdf

IEA, NEA and OECD. 2015. "The Projected Costs of Generating Energy 2015 Edition." www.oecd-nea.org/ndd/pubs/2015/7279-proj-costs-electricity-2015-es.pdf

IMF. 2015. "IMF Working Paper: How Large Are Global Energy Subsidies?" www.imf.org/external/pubs/ft/wp/2015/wp15105.pdf

IPCC. 2007. "Climate Change 2007 Synthesis Report and Summary for Policy Makers." www.ipcc.ch/publications_and_data/ar4/syr/en/spm.html

IPPCC. 2014. "Climate Change 2014 Synthesis Report and Summary for Policy Makers." www.ipcc.ch/pdf/assessment-report/ar5/syr/AR5_SYR_FINAL_SPM.pdf

Joeri Rogelj, et al. 2016. "Paris Agreement Climate Proposals Need a Boost to Keep Warming Well Below 2 °C," *Nature* 534.

Lindzen, R.S. 2008. "Is the Global Warming Alarm founded on Fact" in Ernesto Zedillo ed. *Global Warming: Looking Beyond Kyoto*. Washington, DC: Brookings Institute Press.

Lomborg, B. 2008. *Cool It: The Skeptical Environmentalist's Guide to Global Warming*. New York: Alfred A. Knopf.

Moellendorf, D. 2014. *The Moral Challenge of Dangerous Climate Change: Values, Poverty, and Policy*. Cambridge: Cambridge University Press.

Moellendorf, D. 2015. "Taking UNFCCC Norms Seriously" in Dominic Roser and Jennifer Heyward eds. *Climate Change and Non-Ideal Theory*. Oxford: Oxford University Press.

Moellendorf, D. 2017. "Justice in Mitigation After Paris" in Colleen Murphy, Pablo Gandoni, and Robert McKim eds. *Climate Change and Its Impacts: Risks and Inequalities*. New York: Springer.

Nagel, T. 2005. "The Problem of Global Justice," *Philosophy and Public Affairs* 33: 113–147.

NASA. 2010. "Global Warming." https://earthobservatory.nasa.gov/Features/GlobalWarming

New, M. et al. 2011. "Introduction: Four Degrees and Beyond: The Potential for a Global Temperature Increase of Four Degrees and Its Implications," *Philosophical Transactions of the Royal Society A* 369: 6–19.

Nielsen, L. 2011. "Classifications of Countries Based on Their Level of Development: How It Is Done and How It Could be Done." IMF Working Paper. https://pdfs.semanticscholar.org/bc7f/5b086b8db9adaa3f51645896fda5d1e46659.pdf

Oil Change International. 2016. "Fossil Fuel Funding to Congress: Industry Influence in the US." http://priceofoil.org/fossil-fuel-industry-influence-in-the-u-s/

Oreskes, N. and Conway, E.M. 2010. *Merchants of Doubt: How a Handful of Scientists Obscured the Truth from Tobacco Smoke to Global Warming*. New York: Bloomsbury.

Ostrom, E. 2015. *Evolution of Institutions for Collective Action*. Cambridge: Cambridge University Press.

Randall, T. 2016. "Wind and Solar Are Crushing Fossil Fuels," *Bloomberg*, April 6. www.bloomberg.com/news/articles/2016-04-06/wind-and-solar-are-crushing-fossil-fuels.

Rawls, J. 1999. *A Theory of Justice*, rev. ed. Cambridge, MA: Harvard University Press.

Sen, A. 1999. *Development as Freedom*. New York: Alfred A. Knopf.

Stern, D. I. 2016. "The Role of Energy in Economic Growth" in Lakshman Guruswamy ed. *International Energy and Poverty: The Emerging Contours*. London and New York: Routledge.

Stern, N. 2015. *Why We Are We Waiting? The Logic, Urgency, and Promise of Tackling Climate Change*. Cambridge, MA & London: The MIT Press.

Trillionthtonne.org. www.trillionthtonne.org/

UNDP. 2015a. "Human Development Index." http://hdr.undp.org/en/content/human-development-index-hdi

UNDP. 2015b. "Technical Note." http://hdr.undp.org/sites/default/files/hdr2015_technical_notes.pdf

UNFCCC. 1992. "United Nations Framework Convention on Climate Change." http://unfccc.int/files/essential_background/background_publications_htmlpdf/application/pdf/conveng.pdf

UNFCCC. 2013. "Report of the Conference of the Parties on Its Nineteenth Session, Held in Warsaw from 11 to 23 November 2013." http://unfccc.int/resource/docs/2013/cop19/eng/10a01.pdf#page=3

UNFCCC. 2014. "Intended Nationally Determined Contributions of Parties in the Context of the 2015 Agreement." http://unfccc.int/resource/docs/2014/adp2/eng/7drafttext.pdf

UNFCCC. 2015. "Conference of the Parties, Twenty-first session (Paris Agreement)." https://unfccc.int/resource/docs/2015/cop21/eng/l09.pdf

USEIA. 2016. "International Energy Outlook 2016." www.eia.gov/outlooks/ieo/emissions.cfm

World Bank. 2016. "Fighting Poverty: Findings and Lessons from China's Success." http://econ.worldbank.org/WBSITE/EXTERNAL/EXTDEC/EXTRESEARCH/0,,contentMDK: 20634060~pagePK: 64165401~piPK: 64165026~theSitePK: 469382,00.html

Voigt, C. 2015. "The Compliance and Implementation Mechanism of the Paris Agreement," *Review of European Community and International Environmental Law* 25.

39

THE ETHICS OF WASTE POLICY

Ivo Wallimann-Helmer

Introduction

Human beings produce waste, and this waste must be handled in some way or other. In modern societies, it is depolluted or recycled. Depollution and recycling of waste require facilities for reclaiming, incineration, or storage, such as aluminium processing plants, incinerators, and repositories for nuclear waste. For efficiency, technical, and security reasons, these facilities cannot be equally distributed across society. Ideally, however, their distribution would not lead to an unfair burdening for any social groups in society. The unjust distribution of waste facilities was a major driver at the beginning of the environmental justice movement in the United States. Proponents of this movement found an unequal burdening of the socio-economically disadvantaged with waste facilities and landfills and argued that this was unjust. Since then, research on waste policy has most often been conducted within the framing of environmental justice. That is why this essay on the ethics of waste policy focuses on the environmental justice issues arising from waste facilities and associated risks. It is divided into four sections.

The bulk of research on environmental justice is empirical. The aim of this essay is to investigate its ethical implications. The first section provides an overview of the most important aspects to consider when assessing whether inequalities in exposure to waste facilities are unjust. It explains the relevance of distinguishing between empirical findings and their ethical evaluation. At first sight, avoidable unequal burdening of the socio-economically disadvantaged seems to be unjust. The second section discusses how such an evaluation may be warranted and shows why it is often problematic for efficiency, technical, and security reasons. This is why policy issues about waste facilities should not only concern the fairness of their geographical distribution. The third section discusses the conditions of procedural justice – that is, democratic participation – in policy decisions about the siting of waste facilities and about compensation for increased environmental risks. Since appropriate involvement of all affected by a waste facility should play a crucial role in decisions about waste facilities, the essay closes with two challenges of inclusion. The first challenge concerns the conditions of equal citizenship, the second challenge the appropriate extension of the decision-making body.

While the first section is mainly concerned with conceptual issues, the three sections that follow deal with three different kinds of justice considerations. In so doing, I follow Schlossberg, who claims that considerations of environmental justice can be divided into three categories

(Schlosberg, 2007): distributive justice, procedural justice, and justice as recognition. In the case of waste facilities, distributive justice concerns the geographical distribution of risks due to these facilities. In the environmental justice literature, procedural justice defines the fairness conditions for the democratic processes of making policy decisions. Finally, justice as recognition aims to go beyond the distributive and procedural frameworks (Young, 1990). In environmental justice debates, justice as recognition considers forms of disrespect towards ethnic minorities and the socio-economically disadvantaged. It is often concerned with securing effective political participation of all affected.

Empirical research and ethical evaluation

The environmental justice movement and environmental justice research are relatively young; both emerged only in the 1970s. One important landmark of their emergence was protests in Warren County in North Carolina against the siting of toxic waste in the predominantly black and low-income community (Johnson, 2009). During these protests, more than 500 protesters were arrested. Even though not successful, the protests gave rise to the formation of a nationwide movement against environmental injustices in the United States. Waste policy was an important issue at the beginning, but neither the political movement nor environmental justice research has been concerned purely with waste policy and waste facility siting: both have also investigated such issues as exposure to pollution, flooding risks, and more recently the adverse effects of climate change (Schlosberg, 2013). Nonetheless, unfair waste policy is still one of the main topics in empirical research on environmental justice. This research often finds a strong statistical correlation between unequal exposure to waste facilities and socio-economic disadvantage, which is commonly interpreted as an injustice (Agyeman et al., 2016). To interpret such a correlation as indicative of an injustice, however, it is necessary to be clear about what supports such an evaluation.

In the following, I first introduce the main indicators investigated by empirical environmental justice research to determine an injustice in the statistical correlation between unequal exposure to waste facilities and socio-economic disadvantage. I argue that these indicators are insufficient to assess whether an injustice is at issue; they only indicate inequalities. In order for such inequalities to indicate injustices, it must be shown that exposure to waste facilities constitutes a normatively relevant disadvantage. Furthermore, socio-economic disadvantage must be shown to increase risks in a normatively significant way. Finally, principles of justice are required as an ethical standard against which these inequalities can be assessed as injustices.

Inequality in exposure is defined by several indicators (Evans and Kantrowitz, 2002). The simplest is geographical proximity. The closer one lives to a waste facility, the more likely one is to be exposed to any threats it poses. Another indicator of this type concerns the nature of the facilities that individuals and communities may be exposed to. It makes a difference whether a waste facility is a recycling facility, an incinerator for non-hazardous or hazardous waste, a waste dump, or a repository for nuclear waste. The kind of facility one is exposed to affects the evaluation because the threats posed by the by-products of a facility determine the severity of the exposure. These threats may also be increased by the kind of waste being recycled or depolluted, which thus makes a difference for the assessment of exposure as well. The more dangerous the waste recycled or depolluted, the more severe is the exposure. A final important indicator is how long the waste will remain dangerous. Living near a nuclear waste repository is obviously more significant than living close to a bottle bank.

Incorporating all these indicators leads to geographies of exposure, which map out inequalities in exposure to waste facilities (Jerrett and Finkelstein, 2005). However, these geographies do not themselves display any injustices (Walker et al., 2007). They do so only if they display a normatively relevant disadvantage, such as risks for health or other potential harm due to exposure to waste facilities. The nexus between proximity to waste facilities and health is perhaps the most prominent indicator of a normatively relevant disadvantage (Martuzzi et al., 2010). If the by-products of waste facilities like toxins and pollution increase health risks for those living nearby, then exposure to these facilities displays a normatively relevant disadvantage. Another normatively relevant disadvantage concerns the risk of accidental harm. Depending on the waste processed in a facility, such risk can range from contamination of water and land to the destruction or loss of valued assets. Other normatively relevant harmful by-products of waste facilities include increased noise and air pollution due to the operation of a facility or transportation of waste to or from facilities (Fernandez Rysavy and Floyd, 2016).

At the beginning of empirical environmental justice research in the United States, the strong statistical correlation between race and exposure to waste facilities led researchers to claim that in the US there is environmental racism (Bullard and Johnson, 2000). However, other studies argue that the broader category of socio-economic class rather than ethnicity is better suited to capturing these differences in disadvantage (Krieg and Faber, 2004). According to these studies, the relevant socio-economic differences concern education, social and cultural circumstances, and economic capacities rather than differences in ethnicity. While for the United States the relevance of ethnicity for environmental injustice is still debated (Bullard et al., 2008), in many European countries differences in ethnicity are less relevant. However, an important exception concerns the environmental discrimination of Roma communities (Harper et al., 2009).

Similarly to exposure itself, a strong statistical correlation between exposure to waste facilities and socio-economic disadvantage must be shown to be problematic in a normatively relevant sense as well. It must be shown why socio-economic disadvantage increases the risks related specifically to the exposure to waste facilities. This is why empirical environmental justice research often investigates not only the statistical correlation between socio-economic disadvantage and exposure but also how socio-economic disadvantage aggravates the negative side effects of waste facilities (Martuzzi et al., 2010).

One normatively relevant factor that aggravates risks arising from socio-economic disadvantage and exposure to waste facilities concerns social gradients in health (Brulle and Pellow, 2006). Socio-economic disadvantage has been shown to be accompanied by increased vulnerability to ill health. For this reason, exposure to waste facilities that increases the risk of ill health is more problematic since it tends to exacerbate the vulnerability of those already at higher risk. Other normatively relevant circumstances aggravating risks concern economic capacity. Lower economic capacity diminishes the ability to insure valued assets against loss and damage as a consequence of the failure of waste facilities. Lower economic capacity also limits opportunities to move from a neighbourhood and thus binds the socio-economically disadvantaged to the place they already inhabit. Moreover, some empirical studies have shown that areas exposed to waste facilities tend to attract poorer people since waste facilities and their accompanying environmental drawbacks lower rents nearby (Pastor et al., 2001).

Taken together, social gradients in health and differences in economic capacity establish geographies of vulnerability that signal normatively relevant unequal distributions of aggravated risks due to waste facilities. The highest environmental risks occur where geographies of exposure and geographies of vulnerability overlap. This is so because in these neighbourhoods the most vulnerable face the highest risks due to waste facilities. Mapping out these overlaps, geographies of risk or 'risk-scapes' can be argued to display environmental injustices, since they indicate a geographically unfair unequal distribution of environmental risks (Morello-Frosch et al., 2011).

Whether such unequal distributions in fact signal injustices, however, depends on the normative principles employed for their evaluation. This is so for two reasons. First, the fact that the risks accompanying waste facilities are distributed unequally is not an injustice per se. There may be reasons that justify these inequalities. Second, if communities agree to have waste facilities in their neighbourhood under the condition of being compensated for the increased risk, for example, this is a legitimate reason warranting a heavier exposure to environmental risks for these communities. These two reasons are the focal perspectives of the next two sections that follow.

Distributive justice and feasibility constraints

Empirical environmental justice research often considers cases of unequal burdening of disadvantaged social groups as instances of injustice. However, these inequalities do not necessarily display any injustice. For such a claim of injustice to be valid it must be shown that an unequal distribution of burdens conflicts with some principle of distributive justice (Schuppert and Wallimann-Helmer, 2014). In case of waste policy, principles of distributive justice define the conditions under which the geographical distribution of waste facilities in society can be deemed just. At least three principles of just outcome distribution may become relevant here (Watson and Bulkeley, 2007).[1] First, the principle of equality demands that all members of society should be equally exposed to waste facilities. Second, the polluter-pays principle demands that exposure to waste facilities should be in proportion to the waste produced by individuals or communities. Third, the beneficiary-pays principle demands that exposure to waste facilities should correlate to the differing amount of benefits extracted from waste production.

In empirical environmental justice research, the most prominent principle is that of equality. According to this principle, waste facilities should be distributed equally across society (Walker, 2012). A correlation between socio-economic disadvantage and the unequal geographic distribution of waste facilities is often taken to be sufficient to claim an injustice. However, whether the distribution of waste facilities can indeed be deemed unjust depends not on their geographical distribution alone but on the distribution of the overall risk they engender. As argued earlier, an unequal geographical distribution of waste facilities is unjust only if the environmental risks are actually distributed in a way that aggravates normatively relevant disadvantage. This is especially the case if a distribution of waste facilities places a heavier burden on parts of society that are already more vulnerable due to increased health risks and lower economic capacity. Thus, it is more plausible to demand that the risks of exposure and vulnerability are distributed equally rather than the waste facilities themselves.

One common argument in defence of the principle of equality is the presumption of equality. According to this presumption, the default distribution when distributing goods and burdens is equality (Gosepath, 2015). This is so because an equal distribution of goods and burdens is the only pattern of distribution which is not in need of justification. However, this presumption can be questioned in the case of waste facilities. Our different lifestyles do not all produce equal amounts of waste, and we tend not to produce the same kinds of waste. Therefore, it seems more plausible to demand that environmental risks of waste facilities be distributed in accordance with the differing production of waste. This is where the polluter-pays principle comes in (Gardiner, 2004). According to the polluter-pays principle, a just distribution of waste facilities is one that distributes them so that those producing the most and the most dangerous waste are those that face the greatest risks. Whereas the principle of equality seems to presume that the production of waste is equally or similarly distributed all over society, the polluter-pays principle takes inequalities in the production of waste as the starting point for defining a just outcome distribution of waste facilities.

The polluter-pays principle has some intuitive appeal. Most believe that those who produce a mess have the duty to tidy it up; in the case of waste, this means that they should accept the higher risks of depollution (Shue, 1999). However, waste often accumulates not only in the use of goods but also in their production. Consequently, those consuming the goods do not directly produce the waste. If understood this way, the polluter-pays principle can foster injustices, since the affluent are usually those who consume more goods but do not work in the production of these goods and thus do not directly produce the waste. The consumers of goods often only benefit from others, who are most often the socio-economically disadvantaged, producing waste, as they create the goods that others subsequently consume. According to a third principle of distributive justice, the beneficiary-pays principle, it is therefore not those who produce the waste that should face higher environmental risks but those who benefit from the production of goods leading to waste (Page, 2008). The affluent consuming the most waste-intensive goods should be most exposed to waste facilities and their associated risks.

According to all three principles of distributive justice mentioned thus far, an unequal burdening of the socio-economically disadvantaged seems to be unfair. Higher environmental risks due to an unequal distribution of waste facilities are deemed unfair either if the socio-economically disadvantaged face unjustifiably higher risks than the affluent or if they face risks disproportionate to the waste they produce or the benefits they extract from waste production. As plausible as these claims of injustice might seem at first sight, they can be challenged, because due to feasibility constraints a just outcome distribution of waste facilities is difficult if not impossible to achieve.

The most obvious of these constraints on feasibility are those of efficiency (Nakazawa, 2016). Logistically, it is simply more efficient to gather waste in a small number of facilities than to have many facilities in many neighbourhoods and backyards. Logistical reasons also justify siting waste facilities in regions that are easily accessible for waste transportation. Furthermore, large incineration plants and recycling facilities are better suited not only to processing larger amounts of waste more efficiently but also to ensuring better security for the surrounding neighbourhoods. Security and technical reasons are especially important in the cases of nuclear waste and other hazardous and toxic wastes (Krütli et al., 2015). The danger of contamination of land and water by these kinds of waste is very high, and storage is possible only under specific geological conditions. These considerations show that strict outcome justice in the distribution of waste facilities is difficult if not impossible to achieve. Consequently, it is necessary to consider how injustices in the distribution of waste facilities can be legitimised or made socially acceptable to those exposed to waste facilities.

Although efficiency, technical, and security reasons may become relevant, they must be weighed against considerations of outcome justice and vulnerability, since they take into account neither the distribution of overall environmental risks nor the differences in producing waste or in benefiting from waste. Thus, communities living in geographical regions that allow more efficient waste depollution or more secure and technically more feasible storage of waste cannot simply be said to be better able to accept waste facilities. Such claims would amount to another principle of justice, the ability-to-pay principle (Caney, 2010). However, this principle seems to be implausible in the case of waste facility siting.

Risk and the importance of procedural justice

From the previous section, it appears that due to efficiency, technical, and security reasons it is highly probable that a just outcome distribution of the risks from waste facilities cannot be achieved, at least not in the foreseeable future. Two further considerations of justice can correct this kind of injustice – that is, they can legitimise and increase the social acceptability of such unjust siting: procedural justice and compensatory justice. Procedural justice, to wit democratic participation in policy decisions about waste facility siting, could help legitimise the unequal burdening of certain parts of society. Compensating the neighbourhoods of waste facilities would allow the unjust distribution of overall environmental risks due to waste facilities to be rectified. In the following, I argue that procedural justice must be guaranteed not only in policy decisions about the siting of waste facilities but also in decisions about what kind of compensation is just for increased environmental risks.

Empirical environmental justice research not only detects injustices in the outcome distribution of waste facilities. In many cases, it also finds that the communities exposed to waste facilities have not been properly involved in the political processes leading to their siting. For instance, it has been shown that in Eastwick only after the socio-economically disadvantaged gained influence in policy decisions more just results in land-use could have been reached (Sicotte, 2010). Before that, land-use decisions discriminated against local residents in favour of industry displacing many residents from their homes. Coordinated protests by locals allowed for more influence in these decisions leading to the abandonment of several waste disposal facilities, including facilities for nuclear and hazardous waste.

The lack of involving those potentially affected by waste facilities in policy decisions is problematic for at least three reasons. First, failing to appropriately involve those affected means discriminating against their interests unjustifiably. According to the all-affected principle, it is illegitimate to deny a voice in policy decisions to those who have an interest at stake (Goodin, 2007). Second, it is unacceptable to expose others to risks if they have not had the possibility to consent (Hansson, 2013). This is especially important when more hazardous risks are at stake because the potential harm is more severe. Third, there is an empirical argument why democratic involvement is important: social-psychological justice research on nuclear waste repository siting in Switzerland has shown that transparency and involvement of those affected can substantially increase social acceptance (Krütli et al., 2015).

These three arguments indicate three conditions of procedural justice applicable to policy decisions about the siting of waste facilities. Firstly, according to the all-affected principle, all those exposed to waste facilities should be involved. Secondly, it is important to secure appropriate scientific information for all affected since it is only those affected who can decide how to evaluate the risks they face (Wallimann-Helmer, 2016). Thirdly, to increase the social acceptance of siting decisions, it is important to make the rules for decision-making as transparent and as inclusive as possible. Taken together, these three conditions can be said to define the core of what it means to ensure procedural justice in waste facility siting but also in many other occasions in which the increased imposition of environmental risks is at issue.

In fact, many waste facilities have been sited without ensuring appropriate democratic involvement of those affected, and in many protests relevant for the formation of the environmental justice movement claims for more involvement in policy decisions were part of the campaigning (Johnson, 2009). In these kinds of cases, communities were often faced with increased risks to their health or damage to and loss of valued assets. To remedy such injustice, compensation seems to be the most appropriate course of action. Those facing increased environmental risks of waste facilities must find themselves in circumstances as if the increased environmental risk had never occurred. Similarly, given appropriate democratic involvement in siting decisions, those potentially facing increased risks due to the future siting of waste facilities will most probably demand some kind of compensation for the fact that they will be burdened more heavily with environmental risks. However, what compensation is appropriate in these kinds of cases is not as straightforward as it might seem (O'Neill, 2017). It depends not only on how the environmental risks can be determined empirically but also on the individual assessment of those facing these risks. This is for the following reasons.

Generally speaking, the goal of compensation should be that those affected subjectively feel as well off as before they were injured (O'Neill, 1987). The meaning of this claim is most straightforward in cases of monetisable harm. If someone is harmed and must be compensated, then it is appropriate that that person receives enough money to be able to pursue the same ends as before. In Goodin's words, this is means-replacing compensation (Goodin, 1989). In this case, money allows the means damaged or lost to be repaired or replaced. However, not all harm is monetisable, and it is not even clear in all cases of monetisable harm what amount of money makes good for the damaged or lost assets. And in some cases, the assets lost cannot be replaced at all. The ends usually realised by these assets must be modified. According to Goodin, this demands another kind of compensation: ends-displacement compensation (e.g., assistance in changing livelihood due to contaminated agricultural land).

This distinction between two kinds of compensation is especially important if waste facilities increase health risks or other risks of harm not readily monetisable. It is not straightforward what amount of money makes good for bad health or an increased risk thereof. It is difficult to say what amount of money appropriately compensates for the loss of livelihood due to, for instance, contamination of agricultural land. In these kinds of cases, it might be better not even to try to replace means but to compensate by helping those affected to change their valued objectives. That is, the best goal of compensation might be assisting in modifying ends so that those being compensated no longer depend on the means damaged or lost to feel subjectively as well off as before.[2]

These considerations show why involvement of legitimate claimants for compensation in policy decisions is key. They should not only assess the tolerability of the environmental risks they face but also determine what compensatory measures are most appropriate and, in order to avoid paternalism, in what way they want to modify their valued objectives. Admittedly, democratic involvement of all affected cannot outweigh an unjust outcome distribution of waste facilities, even if accompanied by appropriate compensation. At best, it can legitimise an unjust distribution of waste facilities and, if fair and transparent decision procedures are applied, increase the social acceptability of a facility in a neighbourhood. However, since efficiency, technical, and security reasons render a just outcome distribution unfeasible, in many cases this will be the best approximation to justice reachable.

But, as discussed previously, higher socio-economic vulnerability tends to reinforce environmental risks from waste facilities. Therefore, procedural justice and appropriate compensation seem to be especially important in these cases. Since members of vulnerable communities tend to be less well educated, capacity building in these neighbourhoods becomes particularly important. Only under conditions of adequate capacity can members of vulnerable communities appropriately influence the policy decisions to be taken, whether it is about the siting of waste facilities or about compensating for increased environmental risks. This is one of the issues that concerns justice as recognition, to which we now turn.

Recognition, citizenship, and inclusion

Following the argument thus far, unequal exposure of parts of society to the higher environmental risks of waste facilities can become acceptable if all affected have been appropriately involved in policy decisions, in deciding either about the siting of waste facilities or about the compensation for increased risks. This condition demands that those affected can have an effective voice in the decisions concerning waste facilities. Too much socio-economic inequality undermines this condition, because voicing one's beliefs about increased environmental risks demands at least some basic social and economic capacities. However, social and economic capacities for information gathering and campaigning tend to be significantly lower for the socio-economically disadvantaged than for the affluent. Consequently, to ensure an effective voice for all affected it becomes necessary to reduce socio-economic inequalities.

This requirement to reduce socio-economic inequalities incorporates one of the two issues I discuss in this section. The first issue concerns the conditions of effective and equal voice in policy decisions about waste facilities. I argue that, depending on how these conditions are defined, not only must socio-economic inequalities be reduced to a greater or lesser extent, but also the inequalities that are acceptable in the distribution of environmental risks vary. The second issue is the appropriate extension of the decision-making body. This is the question of who should be involved in policy decisions related to waste facilities and their siting. While at first sight, these challenges might seem clearly distinct from each other, they are usually discussed in environmental justice research as part of the third category of justice mentioned at the beginning: justice as recognition. Among other things, appropriate recognition means granting all those affected by waste facilities an effective voice in the policy process leading to their siting or to agreements on compensatory measures for increased environmental risks (Walker, 2009).

Many different approaches could be deemed relevant to evaluating the requirements for appropriate recognition of those affected by the siting of waste facilities. What I take to be a promising approach is to look at different understandings of democratic citizenship through the lens of justice (Schuppert and Wallimann-Helmer, 2014). This lens makes it possible to show why it depends on our understandings of democracy and citizenship that more or less deviation from a just outcome distribution in waste policy is acceptable. We can think of democratic citizenship as a formal or a substantial requirement of justice.[3] Formal and substantial requirements demand different conditions for citizens to secure effective and equal voice in policy decisions. In doing so, they demand more or less extensive reduction of socio-economic inequalities. It is this demand that defines the space for unequal yet legitimate distributions of waste facilities and accompanying environmental risks.

According to the formal requirement, citizenship is defined by the formal and legal rights every citizen enjoys (Downs, 1957). These include the right to vote, the right to life, and all other rights usually considered basic rights. Following this account, once formal rights to vote have been given, any policy decision is acceptable if it does not undermine these basic rights. This means that policy decisions about the siting of waste facilities and potential compensatory claims are acceptable as long as all citizens affected had a formal right to participate in the processes leading to these decisions. This account faces two challenges. First, the socio-economic inequalities between the parties involved in policy decisions need not be counterbalanced. Although these inequalities most probably increase the unfairness in waste policy decisions, according to the formal requirement of citizenship the right to vote is enough to ensure legitimate decisions. Second, under the condition that the resulting policy does not infringe upon basic rights, it is deemed acceptable irrespective of how bad the consequences are for those exposed and most vulnerable to environmental risks.

The substantial requirement of citizenship can remedy these unfavourable implications by demanding that policy decisions are acceptable only if citizens are substantially equal in their powers during policy-making and remain so thereafter. According to this account, unequal distributions of waste facilities and associated risks would be acceptable only to the extent that they do not undermine substantial conditions of justice (Van Parijs, 2011). However, while the formal requirement leaves great leeway for inequalities, such a stringent substantial requirement is far too demanding. It claims that policy decisions are acceptable only if they are in line with comprehensive conditions of outcome justice. In the case of the siting of waste facilities, their unequal geographical distribution would be acceptable only if their associated environmental risks could be distributed according to principles of distributive justice. As argued earlier, however, efficiency, technical, and security considerations render this infeasible. Therefore, for the siting of waste facilities to be possible the substantial requirement of citizenship should not be interpreted too restrictively.

What seems to be needed is a middle-ground position that incorporates both requirements of citizenship. One version of this position could be called the social-egalitarian account (Anderson, 1999). It allows for inequalities in the siting of waste facilities and associated risks but demands that, to be fair, policyprocedures presuppose substantial conditions of free and equal citizenship. These conditions should not be undermined by any inequalities resulting from the siting of waste facilities. If these conditions are not undermined, any inequalities in the distribution of environmental risks resulting from appropriate decision procedures are acceptable. I take this conception of citizenship to be attractive because it secures at least some basic substantial equality between citizens while leaving enough space for acceptable policy decisions not fully aligned with the principles of just outcome distribution (Schuppert and Wallimann-Helmer, 2014).

But, just as with any other account of citizenship, it remains silent about the second challenge of inclusion mentioned before. The question about the appropriate extension of the decision-making body incorporates two aspects. First, exposure to waste facilities and vulnerability to their associated environmental risks are not restricted to the boundaries of a jurisdiction or a state. Second, risks from waste facilities do not exclusively concern those living at the time of policy decisions about waste facilities; generations living far in the future are affected too (e.g., in the case of nuclear waste this is thousands of years). The first aspect deals with the relevance of geographical proximity to waste facilities and how to recognise interests beyond the boundaries of given jurisdictions and states. The second aspect concerns the inclusion of future generations in the policy decisions of those living today. Similarly to the geographical challenge of inclusion, the interests of future generations tend to be ignored by those actually involved in policy decisions today. Consequently, both aspects of inclusion investigate whether the policy-making body should be expanded, and if so how.

The geographical challenge of inclusion may plausibly be answered by involving all those geographically exposed to the consequences of policy-making irrespective of boundaries (Valentini, 2012). However, although not so difficult to imagine, such a solution is quite unusual for states as we know them today, because their boundaries of jurisdiction usually remain stable and do not vary depending on the policy issue. The lack of inclusion of future generations cannot be overcome by varying the decision-making body as currently constituted. What would be needed for their inclusion is some kind of proxy representation in the policy-making process and corresponding changes in institutional structures (Wallimann-Helmer et al., 2016).

However, in most countries, institutional change for both challenges of inclusion as envisaged here needs more time than is available to deal smoothly with pressing policy issues like the siting of waste facilities. As a consequence, those deciding about the siting of waste facilities and probable compensatory measures should be ready to recognise that the people potentially vulnerable to these facilities are not only those officially involved in the decision-making process but also born or unborn others beyond the jurisdiction or the state concerned.

Conclusion

In this essay I argued that the ethics of waste policy mainly concerns three different kinds of justice considerations. First, it concerns the just geographical distribution of environmental risks from waste facilities. Second, the fair procedural involvement of all those potentially affected is key because due to efficiency, technical, and security reasons waste facilities cannot be distributed in a way fully corresponding with principles of outcome justice. Third, recognition of all those potentially affected by waste facilities, either to be involved in the decision-making process on fair terms or being legitimate claimants of compensation, demands securing an effective voice and careful consideration about the extension of the decision-making body. However, to assess whether inequalities in exposure and vulnerability can be deemed injustices, it is necessary to clarify whether they are normatively significant.[4]

Notes

1 Proponents of the environmental justice movement and empirical environmental justice researchers are often not very explicit about the principles they invoke to warrant injustices in the distribution of waste facilities. This differs from the debate about climate justice in which the principles discussed here are more prominent (Gardiner et al., 2010).
2 This reasoning faces at least two challenges I cannot comprehensively discuss here. First, assisting people to modify their ends readily tends to be overly paternalistic, since helping changing ends involves directives from those who assist. This is one important reason why I believe that regarding compensatory issues procedural justice is of key importance. Second, the costs of monetisable compensation are clearly restricted by the amount of money lost. In the case of revising ends, the limit for resources to be spent on assistance is not as clear-cut as in the first case. Here letting only those affected decide about the compensatory measures to be taken might be more problematic.
3 In political theory, the distinction between liberal and republican conceptions of citizenship is common. I use the distinction between formal and substantial requirements of citizenship because I believe that the social-egalitarian account I favour cannot be captured by distinguishing between liberal and republican accounts of citizenship only.
4 I would like to thank Leandra Bräuninger, Annabelle Lever, Simon Milligan, Andrei Poama, Fabian Schuppert, Stefan Wallaschek, and participants of the Colloquium "Politische Philosophie" in Zurich for comments and feedback on early and earliest versions of this essay.

References

Agyeman, J., Schlosberg, D., Craven, L. and Matthews, C. (2016), "Trends and Directions in Environmental Justice. From Inequity to Everyday Life, Community, and Just Sustainabilities", *Annual Review of Environment and Resources*, Vol. 41 No. 1, pp. 321–340.
Anderson, E. (1999), "What Is the Point of Equality?" *Ethics*, Vol. 109 No. 2, pp. 287–337.
Brulle, R.J. and Pellow, D.N. (2006), "Environmental Justice: Human Health and Environmental Inequalities", *Annual Review of Public Health*, Vol. 27, pp. 103–124.
Bullard, R.D. and Johnson, G.S. (2000), "Environmental Justice: Grassroots Activism and Its Impact on Policy Decision Making", *Journal of Social Issues*, Vol. 56 No. 3, pp. 555–578.
Bullard, R.D., Mohai, P., Saha, R. and Wright, B. (2008), "Toxic Wastes and Race at Twenty: Why Race Still Matters After All of These Years", *Environmental Law Review*, Vol. 38, pp. 371–411.
Caney, S. (2010), "Climate change and the Duties of the Advantaged", *Critical Review of International Social and Political Philosophy*, Vol. 13 No. 1, pp. 203–228.
Downs, A. (1957), *An Economic Theory of Democracy*, Harper and Row, New York.

Evans, G.W. and Kantrowitz, E. (2002), "Socioeconomic Status and Health: The Potential Role of Environmental Risk Exposure", *Annual Review of Public Health*, Vol. 23, pp. 303–331.

Fernandez Rysavy, T. and Floyd, A. (2016), "Dirty Recycling Systems Are Trashing Communities of Color", *Green American Magazine*, No. Summer.

Gardiner, S.M. (2004), "Ethics and Global Climate Change", *Ethics*, Vol. 114, pp. 555–600.

Gardiner, S.M., Caney, S., Jamieson, D. and Shue, H. (Eds.) (2010), *Climate Ethics: Essential Readings*, Oxford University Press, Oxford, New York.

Goodin, R.E. (1989), "Theories of Compensation", *Oxford Journal of Legal Studies*, Vol. 9 No. 1, pp. 56–75.

Goodin, R.E. (2007), "Enfranchising All Affected Interests, and Its Alternatives", *Philosophy and Public Affairs*, Vol. 35, pp. 40–68.

Gosepath, S. (2015), "The Principles and the Presumption of Equality", in Fourie, C., Schuppert, F. and Wallimann-Helmer, I. (Eds.), *Social equality: On what it means to be equals*, Oxford Univ. Press, Oxford, pp. 167–185.

Hansson, S.O. (2013), *The Ethics of Risk: Ethical Analysis in an Uncertain World*, Palgrave Macmillan, New York.

Harper, K., Steger, T. and Filčák, R. (2009), "Environmental Justice and Roma Communities in Central and Eastern Europe", *Environmental Policy and Governance*, Vol. 19 No. 4, pp. 251–268.

Jerrett, M. and Finkelstein, M. (2005), "Geographies of Risk in Studies Linking Chronic Air Pollution Exposure to Health Outcomes", *Journal of Toxicology and Environmental Health. Part A*, Vol. 68 No. 13–14, pp. 1207–1242.

Johnson, G.S. (2009), "Environmental Justice. A Brief History and Overview", in Steady, F.C. (Ed.), *Environmental Justice in the New Millennium: Global Perspectives on Race, Ethnicity, and Human Rights*, Palgrave Macmillan, New York.

Krieg, E.J. and Faber, D.R. (2004), "Not so Black and White. Environmental Justice and Cumulative Impact Assessments", *Environmental Impact Assessment Review*, Vol. 24 No. 7–8, pp. 667–694.

Krütli, P., Törnblom, K., Wallimann-Helmer, I. and Stauffacher, M. (2015), "Distributive Versus Procedural Justice in Nuclear Waste Repository Siting", in Taebi, B. and Roeser, S. (Eds.), *The Ethics of Nuclear Energy: Risk, Justice and Democracy in the Post-Fukushima Era*, Cambridge University Press, Cambridge, pp. 119–140.

Martuzzi, M., Mitis, F. and Forastiere, F. (2010), "Inequalities, Inequities, Environmental Justice in Waste Management and Health", *European Journal of Public Health*, Vol. 20 No. 1, pp. 21–26.

Morello-Frosch, R., Zuk, M., Jerrett, M., Shamasunder, B. and Kyle, A.D. (2011), "Understanding the Cumulative Impacts of Inequalities in Environmental Health: Implications for Policy", *Health Affairs (Project Hope)*, Vol. 30 No. 5, pp. 879–887.

Nakazawa, T. (2016), "Politics of Distributive Justice in the Siting of Waste Disposal Facilities. The Case of Tokyo", *Environmental Politics*, Vol. 25 No. 3, pp. 513–534.

O'Neill, J. (2017), "The Price of an Apology. Justice, Compensation and Rectification", *Cambridge Journal of Economics*, Vol. 41 No. 4, pp. 1043–1059.

O'Neill, O. (1987), "Rights to Compensation", *Social Philosophy & Policy*, Vol. 5 No. 1, pp. 72–87.

Page, E. (2008), "Distributing the Burdens of Climate Change", *Environmental Politics*, Vol. 17 No. 4, pp. 556–575.

Pastor, M., Sadd, J. and Hipp, J. (2001), "Which came First? Toxic Facilities, Minority Move-In, and Environmental Justice", *Journal of Urban Affairs*, Vol. 23 No. 1, pp. 1–21.

Schlosberg, D. (2007), *Defining environmental justice: Theories, movements, and nature*, Oxford Univ. Press, Oxford.

Schlosberg, D. (2013), "Theorising environmental justice. The expanding sphere of a discourse", *Environmental Politics*, Vol. 22 No. 1, pp. 37–55.

Schuppert, F. and Wallimann-Helmer, I. (2014), "Environmental Inequalities and Democratic Citizenship: Linking Normative Theory with Empirical Research", *Analyse & Kritik*, Vol. 36 No. 2, pp. 345–366.

Shue, H. (1999), "Global Environment and International Inequality", *International Affairs*, Vol. 75 No. 3, pp. 531–545.

Sicotte, D. (2010), "Don't Waste Us: Environmental Justice through Community Participation in Urban Planning", *Environmental Justice*, Vol. 3 No. 1, pp. 7–11.

Valentini, L. (2012), "Justice, Disagreement, and Democracy", *British Journal of Political Science*, Vol. 43 No. 1, pp. 177–199.

Van Parijs, P. (2011), *Just Democracy: The Rawls-Machiavelli Programme*, ECPR press essays, ECPR Press, Colchester.

Walker, G. (2009), "Beyond Distribution and Proximity. Exploring the Multiple Spatialities of Environmental Justice", *Antipode*, Vol. 41 No. 4, pp. 614–636.

Walker, G. (2012), *Environmental justice: Concepts, evidence and politics*, Routledge, London.

Walker, G., Mitchell, G., Fairburn, J. and Smith, G. (2007), "Industrial Pollution and Social Deprivation. Evidence and Complexity in Evaluating and Responding to Environmental Inequality", *Local Environment*, Vol. 10 No. 4, pp. 361–377.

Wallimann-Helmer, I. (2016), "Differentiating Responsibilities for Climate Change Adaptation", in *Archiv für Rechts- und Sozialphilosophie*, Beiheft 149, pp. 119–132.

Wallimann-Helmer, I., Meyer, L. and Burger, P. (2016), "Democracy for the Future: A Conceptual Framework to Assess Institutional Reform", *Jahrbuch für Wissenschaft und Ethik*, Vol. 21, 197–222.

Watson, M. and Bulkeley, H. (2007), "Just Waste? Municipal Waste Management and the Politics of Environmental Justice", *Local Environment*, Vol. 10 No. 4, pp. 411–426.

Young, I.M. (1990), *Justice and the Politics of Difference*, Princeton University Press, Princeton, NJ.

40

THE ETHICS OF BEHAVIOURAL PUBLIC POLICY

Robert Lepenies and Magdalena Małecka

What is behavioural public policy?

Insights from the behavioural sciences, such as cognitive psychology and behavioural economics, are currently reshaping much of public policy around the world. Behavioural approaches are drawn upon in a variety of policy fields, such as in health and environmental policy, labour regulations, and consumer protection law. The first nudge unit, the Behavioural Insights Team (BIT), was established in 2010 under David Cameron's coalition government in the UK within the cabinet office. It has since become a quasi-privatised company ("Behavioural Insights Limited") with more than 150 employees that consults and tests policy innovations for the UK government and abroad. The BIT serves as a model for many other behavioural insights teams worldwide: in the US, Germany, France, the Netherlands, Australia, Japan, and Singapore, which all have recently created nudge units. Similar behavioural policy units can be found at the World Bank and at different teams within the United Nations, at the OECD, and the European Commission (Joint Research Centre). A peak point in behavioural sciences applied to policy was reached when President Obama issued, in 2016, an executive order entitled "Behavioral Science Insights Policy Directive" (EO 13707 2015: 56365) that aimed at developing 'strategies for applying behavioural science insights to programs and, where possible, [to] rigorously test and evaluate the impact of these insights'. Shortly before, the White House had created a Social and Behavioral Sciences Team (SBST), which was influenced by the tenure of Cass Sunstein as head of the Office of Information and Regulatory Affairs during the Obama administration. The take-up of psychological insights by public actors is noteworthy as it often presents a far-reaching change from the status quo of the contemporary design, formulation, implementation, and evaluation of policy (Halpern 2016).

The first normative defence of behavioural public policy (BPP) was spelled out in the writings on libertarian paternalism (Thaler & Sunstein 2003) and in *Nudge* (Thaler & Sunstein 2008). Ethicists of public policy have, for now more than a decade, meticulously engaged with the framework formulated by Thaler and Sunstein, creating a large and sprawling literature, which we would like to divide into "general philosophical", "topical", and "discipline-specific" bodies of work. Most *general* philosophical treatments can be found within moral and political philosophy (Hausman & Welch 2010; Wilkinson 2013). For instance, the defensibility of libertarian paternalism has been called into question (Mitchell 2004; Rebonato 2012), while conceptual debates have sought to define nudging (Saghai 2013; Hansen 2016) and related notions such as choice architecture (Vallier 2016). At the same time, distinct *topical* discussions about the ethics of nudging have emerged independently from within fields in which nudges have been applied. Examples include debates in sub-fields such as public health (Ménard 2010) and bioethics (e.g., in clinical contexts when discussing nudging by physicians, see Cohen 2013; Gorin et al. 2017), ethics of artificial intelligence and big data (Helbing et al. 2017; Yeung 2017), environmental nudges (Schubert 2017b), and charitable giving (Hobbs 2017) and development (Berndt 2015). Here, debates are specific to the field of application and rarely discuss the ethics of nudging across fields in general terms.

In addition to general and topical debates about the ethics of nudging, we find reflections about the theoretical and methodological compatibility of behavioural approaches for a given scientific discipline. Examples include debates in law and legal theory (Alemanno & Sibony 2015; Kemmerer et al. 2016), economic methodology and welfare economic theory (Sugden 2017; Whitman & Rizzo 2015), development studies (Reddy 2012), health policy (Quigley 2013), cognitive and social psychology (Gigerenzer 2015; Hertwig & Grüne-Yanoff 2017), and marketing (French 2011; Chriss 2015). The discipline-specific body of literature about the ethics of nudging shows that not just policy but also the social sciences are being 'behaviouralised' as experimental methodology and behavioural insights are spreading throughout academia (Małecka & Lepenies 2018).

Yet, the contributions mentioned earlier mostly take Thaler and Sunstein's framework and concepts not just as the starting point but also as the end point of their engagement. The current debate on ethics of nudging is focused on defending or criticising this initial theoretical framework.

We here want to argue that ethicists of public policy must look elsewhere in the future: they should ask how public policy is actually undertaken – that is, how behavioural policy is institutionalised and argued for in practice, and – being aware of its intellectual origins and context – begin to reflect on the justification of behavioural interventions if these are to become more widespread. It is helpful in this regard for ethicists of public policy to take note of incipient research *on* BPP (whether in the sociology of BPP or in the epistemology and intellectual history of the behavioural sciences).[1] We will focus on three aspects of BPP – namely, the instruments it uses, the organisational forms it involves, and the view on (behavioural) science it presumes. BPP poses different problems in democracies: it is hard to make it compatible with deliberative and participatory approaches in research and implementation, it often relies on instruments that impact the behaviour of citizens without necessarily relying on reason-giving, and it instrumentalises science for practical use, potentially eroding public trust in science and scientists.

The chapter is structured as follows: We begin by contrasting behavioural public policy with evidence-based policy-making, describing the former as an increasingly institutionalised policy movement. Then, we describe how behavioural public policy invokes "science" while justifying behavioural interventions. We then consider the challenges to democratic ethics posed by behavioural policy instruments, behavioural organisations, and its relation to science before concluding.

Behavioural public policy and evidence-based policymaking

The phenomenon of behavioural public policy is closely related, though not identical, with that of evidence-based policymaking (EBPM), which is an approach to policy broadly encouraging a principled grounding of its decisions on the best available scientific evidence. BPP, like EBPM, aims to ground policy design, its formulation, implementation, and evaluation on scientific insights. BPP restricts these to scientific insights about human behaviour won from the "behavioural sciences", whereas EBPM is not limited to scientific insights stemming from a specific domain or set of scholarly approaches. Both BPP and EBPM accept the 'specific hierarchy of scientific methods, with randomised control trials (RCTs) and meta-analysis/ the systematic review of RCTs (published in high-status peer-reviewed journals) at the top' (Cairney 2016: 3). In practice, this is expressed particularly in the endorsement of experimental methodology (especially through RCTs) and meta-studies.[2]

What matters to us here is that EBPM is most commonly described as a 'vague, aspirational term, rather than a good description of the policy process' (Cairney 2016: 1). This distinguishes BPP, which represents both a novel intellectual approach to policy and a policy movement with increasingly well-defined contours. For a good example of this behavioural proposition, see the call for bridging the 'divide between behavioral science & policy' in Fox and Sitkin (2015). Proponents of BPP aim to change the way in which academic scholars influence policy, and understand themselves as a 'growing movement among social scientists and leaders within the public and private sector, dedicated to grounding important decisions in strong scientific evidence' (Behavioral Science & Policy Association 2017).

BPP is increasingly institutionalised, networked, and embedded in governance practices: it has become a policy movement. Studies of networks of behavioural change agents show the spread of a transnational network of BPP proponents with a distinct rhetoric, journals, and associations alongside and beyond new governmental "nudge units" that are created around the world (Jones et al. 2013; Pykett et al. 2016; Strassheim & Korinek 2016; Whitehead et al. 2014). With varying zeal, entrepreneurial proponents of behavioural policy push towards bringing behavioural insights to policy (John 2014), making sophisticated calculations comparing the relative effectiveness of behavioural instruments to alternative policy measures (Benartzi et al. 2017).[3] While doing so, traditional (non-behavioural) approaches to policy are commonly labelled as not being rigorous enough. Hence, it has become a frequent strategy for behavioural insights teams to quantify and monetise their achievements in terms of how the application of the behavioural scientific findings leads to tax dollars saved, pollution avoided, accidents prevented, lives saved, and happiness increased. Indeed, using behavioural science is defended as a moral imperative. As one of the leading behavioural analysts of the French prime minister's Centre for Strategic Analysis argued, 'No one would accept that a new drug would be developed only by economists and lawyers and launched without the proper trials. We should not tolerate this in policy-making either' (Oullier 2013: 463). Because of these normative assumptions of BPP, ethical reflection is needed.

Intellectual underpinnings of behavioural public policy

All key behavioural publication outlets are keen on discussing the ethics of behavioural policy, with frequent invitations to ethicists and applied moral philosophers to comment (in addition to frequent inclusion of such perspectives at behavioural conferences). On the key tenet, however, proponents of behavioural public policy are not swayed: the consensus is that choice architecture is inevitable; there is no way not to nudge. For example, Sunstein argues,

> It is pointless to raise ethical objections to nudges and choice architecture. [. . .] No government can avoid some kind of choice architecture. We can object to particular nudges, and particular goals of particular choice architects, but not to nudging in general [. . .] government is nudging even if it does not want to do so.
>
> *(Sunstein 2016: 15–16)*

Indeed, in the "age of the behavioral sciences" (the title of Sunstein 2016) it would be irresponsible not to use science for the greater societal good.

Yet, little has been said about what it means that policy is informed by the "behavioural sciences". What counts as a behavioural science in this movement? BPP is drawing on a specific subset of disciplines that has historically included some but not other strands of understanding human behaviour (Heukelom 2014; Thaler 2015). BPP is consciously interdisciplinary, but selectively so (Lepenies & Małecka forthcoming). Put a bit provocatively, BPP itself has a selective science bias. Only certain approaches are being received that share the methods and styles of inquiry of BPP: those that heavily draw on behavioural economics (which itself developed out of cognitive psychology – e.g., Tversky & Kahneman 1975 or Kahneman & Tversky 1979) and use experimental methodology (see Małecka & Nagatsu forthcoming on the variety of approaches within the behavioural sciences). BPP is almost entirely influenced by a specific strand of study of human behaviour (cognitive psychology with experimental evidence, but not, for example, evolutionary psychology), but there is no real pluralism in the types of psychology that BPP draws upon. The relationship between BPP in practice and other disciplinary approaches is hence what we could describe as one of select interdisciplinarity. This select interdisciplinarity does not acknowledge considerable diversity within the contributing disciplines in advocacy of behavioural applications.

From "nudge" to behavioural practice

The lesson to draw from this is that ethicists of public policy should be aware that behavioural public policy comes with novel claims about what behavioural sciences *are* and what they are *for*; it also comes with (implicit) claims about the role of science in policy, together with novel institutional configurations (nudge units) and organisational interests that bring these changes about. Therefore, for ethicists to make adjudications on behavioural policy, it is necessary to understand the empirical reality of the practice they want to evaluate. Informed by this approach, we highlight three sets of challenges BPP poses in democracies through the specific (1) *instruments* it uses, the (2) *organisational forms* it involves, and the (3) *values* that scientific behavioural research is permeated with.[4] These facets are not necessary features of BPP but are historically grown and therefore contingent features that characterise the currently dominant variant of bringing "psychological insights to policy".

The purpose here is hence not to claim irreconcilability of behavioural approaches with democratic principles on a general level, but to investigate some contingent practices insofar as they stand in tension with democratic principles. In the case of behavioural *instruments*, the behaviour of citizens is impacted without policy-makers necessarily relying on reason-giving, and by relying on non-participatory research methods. In the case of behavioural policy *organisations*, policy is made in a setting that is not under direct democratic control, and administrative interventions have thus far preferred administrative interventions over legislative actions. Lastly, regarding *values embedded in scientific research*, BPP's emphasis on the practical use of behavioural scholarship confronts policy-makers with only a partial and narrow view of how a science of human behaviour may benefit public policy, which might undercut BPP's ability to provide fora for scrutinising these values in democratic procedures. Such an analysis might also be of constructive value, helping policy-makers to make behavioural practice more transparent, accountable, and attentive to different inter- and intra-disciplinary inputs.

Instruments

Nudging has become the most prominent example of behavioural public policy as articulated by Thaler and Sunstein in their best-seller *Nudge* (2008). Nudges are gentle non-coercive policy solutions, explicitly justified by the normative framework of libertarian paternalism: they are social interventions that are choice-preserving but welfare enhancing for individual citizens and can be applied in a range of policy fields.

> A nudge [. . .] is any aspect of the choice architecture that alters people's behaviour in a predictable way without forbidding any options or significantly changing their economic incentives. To count as a mere nudge, the intervention must be easy and cheap to avoid. Nudges are not mandates. Putting fruit at eye level counts as a nudge. Banning junk food does not.
>
> *(Thaler & Sunstein 2008: 6)*

Sunstein is covering many responses to critics of these debates in subsequent works (2015a, 2015b), most recently in his *The Ethics of Influence* (2016). Here, he carefully defends nudges on a variety of ethical grounds (from traditional "perspectives" of autonomy, self-government, dignity), and in particular, welfarist perspectives. Each of these defences has been challenged. Our focus here will lay on instrument-specific issues that are less often discussed. Nudges are difficult to capture with traditional typologies of policy instruments (Howlett 1991; Vedung 1998; Loer (forthcoming)). Some have claimed that especially those nudges which have non-cognitive characteristics are unlike other instruments of command and control, incentives or information and persuasion. Here, some nudges violate a criterion of democratic publicity: how can a polity endorse instruments that "work in the dark", and which citizens are not aware of (Hausman & Welch 2010)? More problematically, does a widespread application of behavioural policy not undercut reason-giving in democracies, as behaviour is impacted based on knowledge about behavioural regularities, but not through normative argumentation (Lepenies & Małecka 2015)? Proponents have attempted to counter these worries by pointing to empirical acceptance of nudges (Reisch et al. 2017) or by saying that public nudge-for-good might be necessary to counterbalance corporate nudges-for-bad (see Schmidt 2017) or by arguing that some nudges are trivially uncontroversial (e.g., simplified tax forms).

Proponents usually endorse, implicitly or explicitly, a welfarist stance. Correspondingly, nudge units argue they have positive social impact and that they "nudge for good". We feel, however, that this focus on nudges misses the point: behavioural practice has moved on. When new behavioural units are being set up today, it is not libertarian paternalist principles that are invoked, but rather, it is the discourse of a more scientifically oriented approach to policy that is being used (which means, at times, more "realistic", "rigorous", "evidence-based"). Behavioural instruments are now not primarily offered via a normative defence (freedom-of-choice-preserving, non-coercive) or an economical one (cheap) but through a scientific one. Shafir, in the introduction to the landmark *Behavioural Foundations of Public Policy Handbook*, writes that

> a rich body of research conducted over the past three to four decades [. . .] has changed the way we understand people [. . .] our new understanding, this *new view of the human agent*, might help design and implement better public policy.
>
> *(Shafir 2012: 9, our emphasis)*

Behavioural reports by nudge units frequently play down the role of nudges as representing only one behavioural instrument among many (Sousa Lourenço 2016), and that "behavioural science" provides insights beyond the normative frame of libertarian paternalism. Rather than looking at one new instrument (nudge), behavioural policy crucially alters the way that tools are selected compared to alternative policy approaches. Behavioural policy tools differ from traditional policy tools (carrots, sticks, sermons: material incentives, command-and-control measures, persuasive techniques) not because of their inherent characteristics but because of the procedures that have brought them into the policy process. In the case of behavioural instruments, they were chosen as part of an experimental methodology and their presumed effectiveness in changing citizens' behaviour alone.

For ethicists of public policy, this means entering new territory, as behavioural policy reorders the ways in which tools are being selected. Effectiveness alone matters for tool selection, which means that tool-intrinsic qualities are not considered as relevant by policy-makers anymore (e.g., it makes no normative difference for proponents whether a ban, tax, or psychological cue is getting people to smoke less, where in the past, aspects other than effectiveness played a role in tool selection). However, the focus on effectiveness simplifies the purpose of such instruments to only one dimension – the impact on citizens' behaviour.

Organisational forms

Today, there are BPP proponents working on issues from 'behavioral finance, labor contracts, philanthropy, and the analysis of savings and poverty, to eyewitness identification and sentencing decisions, racism, sexism, health behaviours, and voting, health, environment, and nutrition, to dispute resolution, implicit racism, and false convictions' (Shafir 2012: 1). The portfolio of nudge units mirrors this broad range of topics. Take the most prominent example of the Behavioural Insights Team, which to date has published hundreds of behavioural trials in the UK and abroad. These trials are not done in secret: the BIT is extraordinarily transparent in its policy work as it brings norms of academia into policy. This is true for many larger behavioural insights teams, where trials are pre-registered, null findings are reported, and there is a close cooperation with academic institutions as well as in transdisciplinary projects with NGOs or private companies. In addition, BPP engages openly with their own "behavioural failures", as will be pointed out ahead. Yet, other aspects of BPP are considerably less transparent: how, for example, do nudge units choose their areas of engagement? Behavioural policy units in different countries seem to prioritise quite differently here, choosing different organisational forms (centralised, networked; bottom-up or top-down; academic or administration-driven). They range from Danish grassroots organisation INudgeYou to purely governmental units in Germany (Projektgruppe "Wirksam Regieren") or Japan, to policy initiatives at the international, local, or regional level. The most influential team, the UK BIT, was actually semi-privatised and became a so-called social purpose organisation, with several offices around the world. Others went from a higher involvement of private actors in looser networks to a more public status (Nudge France), or went from being federally organised (SBST in the US) to a more decentralised format (behavioural projects at the Department of Defense, as well as on municipal and city level). At the same time, new behavioural consultancies are being created in the private sector (e.g., at Nestle, Deloitte, Ogilvy).

Yet some organisational forms are more problematic than others. How legitimate is it for behavioural public policy to become a private consulting service? Should behavioural policy units be as public as possible in terms of ownership structure? We think that publicly owned nudge units enable them better to fend off exploitative commercial behavioural practices ("counter-nudges"). An important question going forward here is to figure out which organisational form best accommodates a variety of voices (from different scientific fields and beyond) in behavioural policy practice.

This becomes particularly pressing as BPP units develop their own political economy (Schubert 2017a): teams face resistance from within government and from industry and corporate lobby groups, and constantly have to persuasively present their findings in order to gain political credibility. In practice, this has turned behavioural units into political and strategic actors themselves that have to balance accountability and institutional survival. Fox and Sitkin (2015: 5), for example, argue for the need to 'learn several lessons from the unrivaled success of economists in influencing policy. We highlight three: Communicate simply, field test and quantify results, and occupy positions of influence'. This shows, in accordance with predictions from organisational theory in political science, that once behavioural institutions exist, they need a reason to sustain themselves. As mentioned earlier, BPP constitutes a transnational movement to renew policy (Pykett et al. 2016; Jones et al. 2013), where this institutionalisation is coordinated and strategic.[5]

BPP requires a high level of expertise. Here, convincing sociological explanations of the importance of individual proponents of BPP have been put forward (John 2014; Strassheim et al. 2015; Strassheim & Korinek 2016).[6] These individuals are often a hybrid of researchers and policy-makers themselves. Maybe, in the case of BPP, we should cease to speak dichotomously about policy-makers, policy-takers, and scientists somewhat on the outside. Cairney (2016) suggests usage of the term "policy community" to denote that decisions about policy are made by those who influence informally, and those who bear formal responsibility. In the case of BPP, what is also novel is the direction in which "behavioural knowledge" is travelling in the policy community. It is not just from established findings into practice, but just as often, knowledge is co-produced not because policy-makers and behavioural scientists are participating but because members of nudge units are frequently researchers and policy-makers at the same time who have acquired "behavioural expertise" (as Strassheim and Korinek call it), as well as strategic knowledge about policy processes.

General questions on the place of experts in democracies have been well rehearsed elsewhere (Fischer 2009). Yet, there is at least one additional challenge when relying on behavioural experts in democracies that is posed by the involvement of highly specialised experts (so-called choice architects or *planners*) in organisations that are capable of translating findings from the *behavioural* sciences to policy. For behavioural insights to be applied, at the beginning, there is the diagnosis of a policy problem. In the case of BPP, this usually involves identifying stable cognitive biases in the target population and counteracting them through behavioural interventions (which could be heuristics-triggering or heuristics-blocking interventions). By doing this, however, experts necessarily have to endorse a view of what the target population would reasonably want if they were free from the cognitive bias that experts have diagnosed.[7] Here, behavioural expert opinion is used to diagnose behavioural biases in the target population and implements remedies without necessarily using deliberative fora of democratic institutions of collective will formation. Instead, nudge units act by attempting to identify the "real" but hidden preferences of citizens when choosing interventions. This is hotly debated in economic methodology (Sugden 2017). But the practical challenge is put by the existence of nudge units directly: how can behavioural experts influence policy without forestalling democratic procedures of collective will formation? There have always been ethical challenges of experts (see Philip Tetlock's 2017 critique of political expertise, on epistemic democracy in the 'good judgment' project), and there has always been the technocratic critique of the idea of engineering good societies, but what is new here is the institutionalised form of bringing like-minded experts together in well-structured organisations that reference, and draw authority from, a new influential science of human behaviour. Our hypothesis is that proponents of BPP are not merely recipients of findings from an established body ("the" behavioural sciences) but rather the first actively to bring into existence new research in the behavioural sciences (e.g., through studies set up by nudge units) and therefore both recipients and participants in the scientific endeavour they draw upon, and draw legitimation from a field that they partially create themselves through the design of experiments, tests of new interventions, and new policy ventures. By invoking (self-created) behavioural science as a justification, practitioners thereby assume political and epistemic authority to be one and the same thing.

With unconventional policy tools at their disposal, systematic preference of administrative discretion rather than legislative action, and without full democratic control and oversight, politicised behavioural insights teams may unduly[8] blur the borders between politics, policy, and science.

Values in behavioural research

We have seen how the attempt to bring the behavioural sciences to policy finds specific contours as it moves from theory to practice. The idea of using knowledge about the regularities and tendencies of human behaviour to make policies effective (i.e., to bring about desired effects) presumes a rather simplified view of science (in this case, the behavioural sciences) as a repository of facts or findings that are then being applied in the practical context (see Jolls, Sunstein, Thaler 1998; Shafir 2012; Sunstein 1997). An important insight from the contemporary discussions in the philosophy of science is that political, social, and ethical values cannot be kept separate from the processes of knowledge production, and interfere with what makes (behavioural) knowledge reliable and, as such, suitable as a basis of policy applications (Douglas 2009). Proponents of BPP have not yet discussed what this could mean for their project.[9]

Values have an indispensable role in scientific research (Douglas 2009; Longino 1990; Kourany 2010; Wylie & Nelson 2007; Solomon 2001). Once we recognise and acknowledge this role, we quickly see that the relationship between behavioural findings and their practical use in the policy contexts is complex. Values are entering the very process of producing knowledge within the behavioural sciences already; they do not appear only at the stage of *applying* this knowledge outside science – that is, in policy. It is perceived as relatively uncontroversial to state that non-epistemic values, such as normative and emotive commitments that concern moral and social life, can influence the choice of topics and of goals that research is expected to serve. The real challenge arises with the question whether there is any type of influence of these values on the acceptance of hypotheses and theories. As scientists have to decide whether the evidence is sufficient to support a claim/hypothesis, non-epistemic values are a necessary part of hypothesis testing and theory choice – particularly in the behavioural and social sciences. They help in assessing the consequences of making a mistake while making judgements about the evidential support for a hypothesis (Rudner 1953). Furthermore, in order to assess the evidential warrant of a hypothesis, scientists have to decide what kind of evidence is relevant for the hypothesis – at least in some cases this decision can be value-laden (Longino 1990). Longino also points out that moral and social values are allowed to enter into decisions concerning the background assumptions of scientific reasoning (Longino 1990).

Generally, it is believed that the best the scientific community can do is to make values explicit and to work out the procedures and approaches for discussing them (Longino 1990, Longino 2002). This, of course, is difficult to achieve with BPP as it is not directly a subject of democratic control in its current state. This is complicated through the use of experimental methodology in all nudge units around the world: choice architects have biases – this much behavioural proponents recognise. But citizens themselves, who are partaking in experiments, cannot be choice architects at the same time.[10]

When confronted with the question of what should follow from the realisation that values infuse scientific practice, one common suggestion is to democratise science. The proposal here is that the public receives the chance to legitimately contest (1) the direction of scientific research effort, (2) the legitimacy and acceptability of expertise, and (3) the institutional structures for science (public assessment of research agendas, of expertise, of science's institutions) (Douglas 2009). Currently, BPP does not offer democratised structures on any of these three aspects.

What does the foregoing discussion mean specifically in the context of BPP? Behavioural scientists, as all scientists, are also making inferences in the face of uncertainty. Therefore, while making judgements about which evidence is sufficient for supporting or rejecting a hypothesis, behavioural scientists rely on values when it comes to reasoning about possible consequences of making false positive or false negative errors.

Furthermore, in a paper that has not thus far attracted attention of the field, Lacey argues that behavioural scientists are making value judgements when deciding 'which strategy to adopt' (Lacey 2003: 209). Lacey claims that value judgements have an indispensable role during the 'adoption of strategy' during the research process. Adoption of strategy means to '*constrain* the kinds of theories (hypotheses, regularities) that might be entertained in a given domain of inquiry, thus to specify the kinds of possibilities that may be explored in the course of the inquiry' Lacey (2003: 212). Gaining empirical knowledge depends on the strategy scientists adopt, which means that the type of strategy chosen influences what phenomena scientists gain empirical knowledge of. Lacey argues that the involvement of values during the adoption of strategy is especially important in the behavioural and cognitive sciences.

In the behavioural and cognitive sciences scientists confront the choice of adopting, for instance, behaviourist, cognitivist, or sociobiological strategies. The behaviourist strategy constrains hypotheses to those that concern lawful relations between behaviours and environments, whereas the cognitivist strategy does so to those that concern representations of mental structures and computational accounts of mental processes. Lacey points out that 'radical behaviorist approaches are partly motivated by the value of furthering our capability to exercise control over human behaviour, and some cognitive psychology approaches are motivated partly by highlighting the values of rationality and freedom' (p. 219). He argues for a pluralism of strategies employed within the behavioural sciences and claims that attempts to extrapolate and generalise one strategy, for instance, in a form like 'all behavior is explicable in terms of behaviorist categories', or 'all mental phenomena are computable' mean in fact the endorsement of metaphysical claims sustained by the fruitfulness in guiding research and, thus, by value commitments.[11]

We have hypothesised earlier that while BPP is programmatically interdisciplinary in its references to the behavioural sciences, it does not allow for such a pluralism as Lacey describes. Proponents of BPP claim to rely on a particular body of research within the behavioural science, for instance: cognitive psychology and behavioural economics. With behavioural trials, they themselves contribute to co-produce this field, while not taking into account alternative approaches within the behavioural sciences – for example, the socio-economic studies and social epidemiology or non-mainstream psychological schools. Favouring one approach over another can be related, as suggested by Lacey, to the practical aim and attempt of controlling behaviour, or steering it into more rational directions.

There are two main lessons to be learnt from understanding the role values play in science, and specifically in the behavioural sciences. First, we see that the knowledge on the basis of which BPP formulates its policy solution can be value-laden in the sense explained and elaborated earlier. Values that enter the behavioural research can influence the ways in which this research is being applied to policy. For instance, we observe that certain approaches in behavioural sciences become more influential than others, which is related to the ways in which epistemic and non-epistemic values and interests (e.g., in controlling human behaviour) are entangled.[12] Second, BPP is an approach to policy that lacks full integration with democratic institutions (parliaments, scientific oversight committees) and, as such, poses challenges, or threats, to the possibility of a democratic control over behavioural policies. This becomes problematic also when we account for the role that values play in the behavioural research. One important way of making these values explicit and subject to critical scrutiny is by exposing scientific research to public criticism through democratic engagement. Scrutinising values embedded in behavioural research can have significant impact on the ways in which this research is applied within BPP; it can also allow for more diversity of approaches informing BPP.

Conclusion

The contemporary phenomenon of behavioural public policy is an innovative and increasingly influential approach to public policy which raises unique concerns about its compatibility with democratic ideas, processes, and institutions. We survey a selection of such problems by analysing the instruments it uses, the organisational forms it has brought about, and the role that values play in behavioural research. BPP poses different problems in democracies: it is hard to make compatible with deliberative and participatory approaches in implementation, it often relies on instruments that impact the behaviour of citizens without necessarily relying on reason-giving, and it instrumentalises science for practical use which might occasionally undercut its reliability as a legitimate source of knowledge.

Funding information

The work of Magdalena Małecka is sponsored by Academy of Finland grant no. 308682.

Notes

1 We follow here an approach to ethics of public policy which is inductive in the sense that we start from empirical observations about changes in the practices of public administration in democracies. We have explored an institutionalist perspective on behavioural policy elsewhere (Lepenies & Małecka 2015). Here, our approach is similar to Thompson (2005) in that we propose to avoid excessive individual framings ("How to nudge for good?") and instead focus on themes of institutional responsibility. Indeed, we think that the value of social institutions cannot be appraised by referencing their contribution to the achievement of outcomes that have a single dimension (here: effectiveness). Without spelling out an account of the intrinsic normativity of (certain) social institutions, we take here the more minimal position of arguing against their instrumentalisation.

2 For behavioural public policy, see especially how academics and policy-makers collaborated in the influential policy report endorsing the "Test, Learn, Adapt" framework (Haynes et al. 2012).

3 With impressive results: the automatic savings plan "Save More Tomorrow" by Benartzi and Thaler (2013) has boosted retirements savings in the US by more than $7.4 billion annually, according to their own calculations.

4 We must leave out here the fascinating discussion about whether behavioural instruments should be used to support democratic processes. Sunstein (2016) discusses examples of how behavioural insights might be used to, for example, encourage electoral turnout.

5 For example, the UK Behavioural Insights Team (BIT) has introduced a mnemonic ('APPLES') with which it advises international partners on how to best convince policy makers to establish nudge units. APPLES stands for: the necessity of networking within Administration, support from Politics, well-recruited People, close physical Location to sources of power, a culture of scientific Experimentation, proximity to universities and other institutions of Scholarship.

6 '[A]gency as well as structure plays an important role in the adoption and diffusion of the ideas from the behavioural sciences' (John 2015). John here notes that critics often assume too linear a view of the policy process, and that behavioural ideas and evidence are 'more limited and less uniform' in their use as commonly assumed.

7 Sunstein suggests that no ethical problems arise for experts if citizens have clear self-control problems, have voiced their preferences beforehand, or can be shown to be ex-post content with behavioural interventions (2017).

8 This relies on a normative view of what these borders ought to be. Our position here is what we would call anti-instrumental institutionalism: we generally believe that societal institutions (whether law, politics, science, or others) have value independently of their capability to achieve a specific outcome (i.e., to be effectively achieving a one-dimensional goal).

9 This section draws on ideas developed in Lepenies and Małecka (forthcoming).

10 For an exception, see John et al. (2011) for attempts to complement nudge with participatory "think" approaches.

11 See also Johnson and Orr in this volume.

12 The interpretation of how disciplinary values might impact policy is contested: Schubert (2017a) finds, for example, a systematic bias within regulatory agencies in favour of scientific information that seems to support extending regulation.

References

Alemanno, A. and Sibony, A.L. eds., 2015. *Nudge and the law: A European perspective.* Oxford: Hart Publishing.

Benartzi, S., Beshears, J., Milkman, K.L., Sunstein, C.R., Thaler, R.H., Shankar, M., Tucker-Ray, W., Congdon, W.J. and Galing, S., 2017. Should governments invest More in Nudging? *Psychological Science*, pp. 1041–1055.

Benartzi, S. and Thaler, R.H., 2013. Behavioral economics and the retirement savings crisis. *Science*, *339*(6124), pp. 1152–1153.

Berndt, C., 2015. Behavioural economics, experimentalism and the marketization of development. *Economy and Society*, *44*(4), pp. 567–591.

BSPA, 2017. Behavioral Science & Policy Association Website. #Mission. Available at: https://behavioralpolicy.org/about/#_mission [Accessed August 7, 2017].

Cairney, P., 2016. *The politics of evidence-based policy making.* Springer.

Chriss, J.J., 2015. Nudging and social marketing. *Society*, *52*(1), pp. 54–61.

Cohen, S., 2013. Nudging and informed consent. *The American Journal of Bioethics*, *13*(6), pp. 3–11.

Douglas, H., 2009. *Science, policy, and the value-free ideal.* Pittsburgh: University of Pittsburgh.

Exec. Order No. 13707, *Federal Register*, 80(191), 56365–56367 (2015) of Sep. 15, 2015.

Fischer, F., 2009. *Democracy and expertise: Reorienting policy inquiry.* Oxford: Oxford University Press.

Fox, C.R. and Sitkin, S.B., 2015. Bridging the divide between behavioral science & policy. *Behavioral Science & Policy*, *1*(1), pp. 1–12.

French, J., 2011. Why nudging is not enough. *Journal of Social Marketing*, *1*(2), pp. 154–162.

Gigerenzer, G., 2015. On the supposed evidence for libertarian paternalism. *Review of Philosophy and Psychology*, *6*(3), pp. 361–383.

Gorin, M., Joffe, S., Dickert, N. and Halpern, S., 2017. Justifying clinical nudges. *Hastings Center Report*, *47*(2), pp. 32–38.

Halpern, D., 2016. *Inside the nudge unit: How small changes can make a big difference.* London: Random House.

Hansen, P.G., 2016. The definition of nudge and libertarian paternalism: Does the hand fit the glove?. *European Journal of Risk Regulation*, *7*(1), pp. 155–174.

Hausman, D.M. and Welch, B., 2010. Debate: To nudge or not to nudge. *Journal of Political Philosophy*, *18*(1), pp. 123–136.

Haynes, L., Goldacre, B. and Torgerson, D., 2012. *Test, learn, adapt: Developing public policy with randomised controlled trials.* Cabinet Office.

Helbing, D., Frey, B.S., Gigerenzer, G., Hafen, E., Hagner, M., Hofstetter, Y., van den Hoven, J., Zicari, R.V. and Zwitter, A., 2017. Will democracy survive big data and artificial intelligence. *Scientific American*, Feb 25.

Hertwig, R. and Grüne-Yanoff, T., 2017. Nudging and boosting: Steering or empowering good decisions. *Perspectives on Psychological Science*

Heukelom, F., 2014. *Behavioral economics. A history*. Cambridge University Press.

Hobbs, J., 2017. Nudging charitable giving: The ethics of nudging in international poverty reduction. *Ethics & Global Politics*, *10*(1), pp. 37–57.

Howlett, M., 1991. Policy instruments, policy styles, and policy implementation. National approaches to theories of instrument choice. *Policy Studies Journal* 19(2): 1–21.

John, P., Cotterill, S., Hahua, L., Richardson, L., Moseley, A., Smith, G., Stoker, G. and Wales, C., 2011. *Nudge, nudge, think, think: Using experiments to change citizens' behaviours*. London: Bloomsbury.

John, P., 2014. Policy entrepreneurship in UK central government: The behavioural insights team and the use of randomized controlled trials. *Public Policy and Administration*, *29*(3), pp. 257–267.

John, P., 2015. Behavioural Science, randomized evaluations and the transformation of public policy: The case of the UK government (November 2, 2015). Available at: http://dx.doi.org/10.2139/ssrn.2685049

Jolls, C., Sunstein, C.R. and Thaler, R., 1998. A behavioral approach to law and economics. *Stanford Law Review*, *50*, p. 1471.

Jones, R., Pykett, J. and Whitehead, M., 2013. *Changing behaviours: On the rise of the* psychological *state*. Cheltenham: Northampton.

Kahneman, D. and Tversky, A., 1979. Prospect theory: An analysis of decision under risk. *Econometrica: Journal of the Econometric Society*, pp. 263–291.

Kemmerer, A., Möllers, C., Steinbeis, M. and Wagner, G. eds., 2016. *Choice architecture in democracies: Exploring the legitimacy of nudging*. Nomos.

Kourany, J.A., 2010. *Philosophy of science after feminism*. Oxford University Press.

Lacey, H., 2003. The behavioral scientist qua scientist makes value judgments. *Behavior and Philosophy*, pp. 209–223.

Lepenies, R. and Małecka, M., 2015. The institutional consequences of nudging – nudges, politics, and the law. *Review of Philosophy and Psychology*, *6*(3), pp. 427–437.

Lepenies, R. and Małecka, M., forthcoming. Behaviour change: Extralegal, apolitical, scientistic? In: Beck, S. and Strassheim, H. (eds), *Handbook of Behavioural Change and Public Policy*. Cheltenham, UK/Northampton, MA: Edward Elgar.

Loer, K., forthcoming. The enzymatic effect of behavioural sciences – What about policy-maker's expectations? In: Beck, S. and Strassheim, H. (eds), *Handbook of Behavioural Change and Public Policy*. Cheltenham, UK/Northampton, MA: Edward Elgar.

Longino, H.E., 1990. *Science as social knowledge: Values and objectivity in scientific inquiry*. Princeton: Princeton University Press.

Longino, H.E., 2002. *The fate of knowledge*. Princeton University Press.

Małecka, M. and Nagatsu, M., forthcoming. How behavioural research has informed consumer law: The many faces of behavioural research. In: Purnhagen, K., Sibony, A. and Micklitz, H. (eds), *Research handbook on methods in consumer law*. Edward Elgar Publishing.

Małecka, M. and Lepenies, R., 2018. Is the behavioral approach a form of scientific imperialism. In Maki, U., Walsh, A. and Fernández Pinto, M. (eds), *Scientific Imperialism: Exploring the Boundaries of Interdisciplinarity*. London: Routledge.

Ménard, J.F., 2010. A 'nudge' for public health ethics: Libertarian paternalism as a framework for ethical analysis of public health interventions? *Public Health Ethics*, *3*(3), pp. 229–238.

Mitchell, G., 2004. Libertarian paternalism is an oxymoron. *Nw. UL Rev.*, *99*, p. 1245.

Oullier, O., 2013. Behavioural insights are vital to policy-making. *Nature*, *501*, pp. 463–463.

Pykett, J., Jones, R. and Whitehead, M., 2016. *Psychological Governance and public policy: Governing the mind, brain and behaviour*. Oxon: Routledge.

Quigley, M., 2013. Nudging for health: On public policy and designing choice architecture. *Medical Law Review*, *21*(4), pp. 588–621.

Rebonato, R., 2012. *Taking liberties: A critical examination of libertarian paternalism*. Palgrave Macmillan.

Reddy, S.G., 2012. Randomise this! On poor economics. *Review of Agrarian Studies*, *2*(2), pp. 60–73.

Reisch, L.A., Sunstein, C.R. and Gwozdz, W., 2017. Beyond carrots and sticks: Europeans support health nudges. *Food Policy*, *69*, pp. 1–10.

Rudner, R., 1953. The scientist qua scientist makes value judgments. *Philosophy of Science*, *20*(1), pp. 1–6.

Saghai, Y., 2013. Salvaging the concept of nudge. *Journal of Medical Ethics*, *39*(8), pp. 487–493.

Schmidt, A.T., 2017. The power to nudge. *American Political Science Review*, *111*(2), pp. 404–417.

Schubert, C., 2017b. Green nudges: Do they work? Are they ethical? *Ecological Economics*, *132*, pp. 329–342.

Schubert, C., 2017a. Exploring the (behavioural) political economy of nudging. *Journal of Institutional Economics*, pp. 1–24.

Shafir, E., 2012. *The behavioral foundations of public policy*. Princeton University Press.

Solomon, M., 2001. *Social empiricism*. Cambridge, MA: The MIT press, p. 186.

Sousa Lourenço, J., Ciriolo, E., Almeida, S.R. and Troussard, X., 2016. Behavioural insights applied to policy: European report 2016. *Brussels: European Commission*.

Strassheim, H., Jung, A. and Korinek, R.-L., 2015. Reframing expertise. In *Moments of valuation*. Oxford: Oxford University Press, pp. 249–268.

Strassheim, H. and Korinek, R. 2016: Cultivating 'nudge': Knowing behavioural governance. In: Freeman, Richard and Voss, Jan-Peter. (Hg.), *Knowing governance (Palgrave Studies in Science, Knowledge and Policy)*. Houndmills: Palgrave Macmillan, pp. 107–126.

Sugden, R., 2017. Do people really want to be nudged towards healthy lifestyles? *International Review of Economics*, *64*(2), pp. 113–123.

Sunstein, C.R., 1997. Behavioral analysis of law. *The University of Chicago Law Review*, *64*(4), pp. 1175–1195.

Sunstein, C.R., 2015b. The ethics of nudging. *Yale Journal on Regulation*, *32*, p. 413.

Sunstein, C.R., 2015a. Nudges do not undermine human agency. *Journal of consumer policy*, *38*(3), pp. 207–210.

Sunstein, C.R., 2016. *The ethics of influence: Government in the age of behavioral science*. New York: Cambridge University Press.

Sunstein, C.R., 2017. Nudges that fail. *Behavioural Public Policy*, *1*(1), pp. 4–25.

Tetlock, P.E., 2017. *Expert political judgment: How good is it? How can we know?* Princeton University Press.

Thaler, R.H., 2015. *Misbehaving: The making of behavioral economics*. New York: WW Norton & Company.

Thaler, R.H. and Sunstein, C.R., 2003. Libertarian paternalism. *The American Economic Review*, *93*(2), pp. 175–179.

Thaler, R.H. and Sunstein, C.R. 2008. *Nudge: Improving decisions about health, wealth, and happiness*. New Haven: Yale University Press.

Thompson, D. F., 2005. *Restoring responsibility: Ethics in government, business and healthcare*. Cambridge: Cambridge University Press.

Tversky, A. and Kahneman, D., 1975. Judgment under uncertainty: Heuristics and biases. In: *Utility, probability, and human decision making*. Springer Netherlands, pp. 141–162.

Vallier, K., 2016. On the inevitability of nudging. *Georgetown Journal of Law & Public Policy*, *14*, p. 817.

Vedung, E., 1998. Policy instruments: Typologies and theories. In: *Carrots, sticks, and sermons: Policy instruments and their evaluation*, *5*, pp. 21–58.

Whitehead, M., Jones, R., Howell, R., Lilley, R. and Pykett, J., 2014. Nudging all over the world: Assessing the global impact of the behavioural sciences on public policy. *Economic Social & Research Council Report*. Swindon, UK.

Whitman, D.G. and Rizzo, M.J., 2015. The problematic welfare standards of behavioral paternalism. *Review of Philosophy and Psychology*, *6*(3), pp. 409–425.

Wilkinson, T.M., 2013. Nudging and manipulation. *Political Studies*, *61*(2), pp. 341–355.

Wylie, A. and Nelson, L.H., 2007. Coming to terms with the value (s) of science: insights from feminist science scholarship. In: Harold Kincaid, John Dupre and Alison Wylie (eds), *Value-free science? Ideals and illusions*. pp. 58–86

Yeung, K., 2017. 'Hypernudge': Big Data as a mode of regulation by design. *Information, Communication & Society*, *20*(1), pp. 118–136.

41

ETHICS, NEUROSCIENCE, AND PUBLIC POLICY

A case study of raising neuroscientists' awareness of the problem of dual use

Simon Whitby and Malcolm Dando

Introduction

This chapter notes that innovation in neuroscience raises new ethical problems and dilemmas. It argues that such problematics are best addressed through collaborative initiatives involving scientists, professional associations, state-level security and policy-makers, ethicists, and educators. In the light of concern about dual use emerging at the international level, and with reference to calls from professional science societies that such challenges should be met, it considers a European state-level project on the societal impact of innovation in neuroscience, and it identifies the value of active learning approaches as a means to engage the wider neuroscience community in awareness-raising and education initiatives that address innovation.

Scientific and technological revolutions inevitably produce results that lead to difficult ethical problems. The current revolution in neuroscience is no exception, as has been pointed out by a number of authors recently.[1] Moreover, it is clear that these problems extend to issues of national and international security – for example, by providing opportunities for those with hostile intentions to develop novel forms of chemical and biological weapons.[2] The recognition by important states, such as the United States, China, Japan, and the European Union, that advances in neuroscience are likely to lead to significant improvements in dealing with pressing problems of mental illnesses has also led to the initiation of a series of well-funded new research programmes in neuroscience[3] that are certain to accelerate the rate of discoveries and therefore potentially generate ethical problems that will have to be dealt with in the end by public policy.[4]

While they do not, of course, bear all of the responsibility for dealing with the ethical problems their benignly intended work produces, scientists, because of their special expertise, must take some part in helping society to find acceptable solutions. Nowhere is this clearer than in regard to the problem of dual use: the aspect of potential misuse related to the possible development of novel chemical and biological weapons based on advances in our understanding of the operations of the central nervous system.[5] As the Scientific Advisory Board of the Organisation for the Prohibition of Chemical Weapons noted in 2012,

> [T]he types of chemicals and pharmaceuticals known to have been considered as incapacitants from open-literature sources were discussed. Most are centrally acting

compounds that target specific neuronal pathways in the brain. All of them emerged from drug development programmes undertaken from the 1960s to the 1980s.[6]

Unfortunately, it is clear that practising neuroscientists remain largely ignorant of the problem of the possible misuse of their work for hostile purposes. Thus, in order to engage their expertise in seeking solutions to this problem the first step has to be to raise their awareness that there is a problem that needs their attention. As the United Kingdom Royal Society recommended in 2012,[7]

> There needs to be fresh effort by the appropriate professional bodies to inculcate the awareness of the dual-use challenge (i.e. knowledge and technologies used for beneficial purposes can also be misused for harmful purposes) among neuroscientists at an early stage of their training.

As explained ahead, the fact that the general level of awareness of the dual-use challenge among life scientists has not improved much during the last decade despite the clear concerns of state parties to the Chemical Weapons Convention (CWC) and the Biological and Toxin Weapons Convention (BTWC) indicates that achieving the objectives set out by the Royal Society will not be an easy task. One reason for the difficulty has been found to be that lecturing ethics to scientists is not often successful. Scientists are used to seeking clear answers to explicit questions, not to thinking about questions that have different answers depending on the ethical framework within which they are approached. Thus, more active forms of learning which aim first to engage the participants are usually required.[8]

Some of the state-level brain projects have components covering ethical issues. The European Union Human Brain Project (HBP), for example, includes consideration of the impact of advances in neuroscience on society through its Ethics and Society work packages on: Foresight Analyses and Researcher Awareness; Neuroethics and Philosophy; Public Dialogue and Engagement; Ethics Management; and Scientific Coordination.[9] The HBP also has an education programme run by a group at the Medical University Innsbruck, which has three main objectives: to provide young European scientists with transdisciplinary knowledge and skills; to connect young researchers within the HBP and beyond; and to build awareness of the project's work and results.[10] As part of its work the programme has produced a series of open online courses, one of which deals with ethical issues and within that course one of us (Dando) contributed a video lecture on the problem of dual use.

Following on from making that video lecture we were asked if we would contribute another lecture on dual use to the 1st HBP Curriculum Workshop, entitled *Research: How to Deal with Animals and ICT in Science – An Ethical Approach, Ethics and Societal Impact: Responsible Research*. This workshop was organised by the Karolinska Institute and Linnaeus University at the Karolinska Institute in Stockholm and the EU Human Brain Project's Education Programme Office on July 10–12, 2017. We were also asked if we would like to supplement the lecture with a team-based learning (TBL)[11] exercise on dual use. This seemed to be an important opportunity to see if TBL would be a useful way in which to help raise the awareness of young practising neuroscientists about dual use, so we were happy to take up the opportunity. What follows in this chapter is therefore an account and analysis of what we did in Stockholm. We will explain ahead why we think this should be seen as a hard test of whether TBL can be used in such circumstances and of what further might be done with this method of awareness raising for neuroscientists.

Background to the TBL

We were involved in a research project that followed the attempts to strengthen the Biological and Toxin Weapons Convention[12] during the 1990s.[13] When that effort failed in 2001 state parties began a process of annual meetings in which they attempted to reach agreement on more tractable issues, and among these issues was the role and responsibilities of life and associated scientists in relation to the Convention at a time of rapid scientific and technological change.

We therefore thought it worthwhile to find out what scientists thought about the issue. So, in collaboration with Brian Rappert (University of Exeter) we sought the views of UK scientists working on acetylcholine. This seemed a sensible point to start given the importance of nerve agents in the arsenals of major states during the Cold War.[14] We discovered to our surprise then that few practising scientists knew much about the BTWC or the recently agreed Chemical Weapons Convention (CWC). A series of grants from the UK Economic and Social Research Council and the Carnegie Corporation of New York allowed us to show that this lack of knowledge was pervasive both in the UK and in 15 other countries around the world.[15]

So before 2010 we began to develop material that might be used by university lecturers to include some BTWC/CWC related topics in their courses for life scientists. We produced an education module consisting of a series of lectures in PowerPoint slides with explanatory notes and references in cooperation with colleagues at Japan's National Defence Medical College under funding from the British Council and a great deal of supporting material with funding from the UK Wellcome Trust. Most of the debate on dual use has concerned microbiology/immunology, but we also produced some similar PowerPoint slides and supporting material in lectures specifically for neuroscientists in collaboration with colleagues at the University of Manchester. All of this material was made openly available on the Internet, but our estimation is that the take-up and use of this material, and similar material produced by other groups, remain limited.[16]

For the reasons explained earlier we became convinced that part of the reason for the limited use of such material was that scientists find non-scientific subjects (e.g., ethics) far from easy to deal with unless active learning techniques are used. So when we recently finished editing the set of essays on dual use for the UK and Canadian governments titled *Preventing Biological Threats: What You Can Do*,[17] Tatyana Novossiolova, one of the authors and editors, also developed a set of team-based learning exercises for each of the chapters.[18] When we were asked to include an exercise in addition to our lecture for the meeting in Stockholm it therefore seemed a good idea to run a TBL based on the introductory chapter in *Preventing Biological Threats*, which deals with the debate on gain-of-function experiments[19] in microbiology and dual use in recent years,[20] and ask participants for feedback on how it might be improved. TBL exercises take considerable work to design, but a major advantage we believe is that once designed they can be used repeatedly to help raise awareness of quite large groups of people without the need for extensive training of the organisers of the exercise. These exercises have been used extensively in university courses and in efforts to raise the awareness of dual use among microbiologists in a number of countries.[21] If found to be effective for neuroscientists, TBL could therefore be an efficient method of beginning to engage them in helping to protect their work from hostile misuse.

Organising the TBL

Team-based learning has been used extensively in a variety of subjects in university-level courses. Usually students are grouped into small teams of five to seven people and remain in those teams throughout the course. This has been found to encourage engagement of all students in the course as teams are marked, in part, according to the work of the whole team. Electronic systems are used in many courses so that individual students and the teams can report their answers back to instructors immediately, and the instructors can follow the performance of students in order to make effective interventions to facilitate learning by the students. Two concepts are clearly stressed in the literature – first that design of the exercise is centred on starting with the key learning objectives and then working out how to present material to the students to achieve these objectives, and second that the instructor is there to facilitate the students' understanding of the key learning objectives, not to tell them what they should learn.[22]

Clearly, we did not have established teams for the TBL exercise in Stockholm nor did we have an elaborate electronic system at our disposal. However, we knew that it is possible to work with groups in such circumstances from previous studies[23] even if we were unsure that it would be possible with the very diverse practising scientists – ranging from molecular biologists to information technologists – that have now become involved in neuroscience. We did not know the participants in advance, nor did they know us.

In these circumstances, we made a number of adjustments to the standard form of a TBL exercise to help familiarise participants with what was being undertaken. Normally, as described ahead, students are required to familiarise themselves with some pre-reading and then their knowledge of this material is tested by them completing an iRAT (individual readiness assurance) test. Then each team is required to answer the same questions in a tRAT (team readiness assurance) test informed by a prior group discussion of the questions and answers within the group. It is expected that the rate of correct answers will increase in each team as they debate their different views. After that there are two application exercises, each followed by a discussion that allows students to apply and debate their answers to more complicated questions, and this is followed by an essential wrap-up discussion (de-brief) of the whole TBL exercise (see the section ahead on running the TBL exercise). Throughout this process the instructor has to keep the key learning objectives in mind and find ways of highlighting these for the students. We varied this standard structure first by giving students a one-page summary based on the previous section of this chapter as a backgrounder on who we are and what the exercise was about as they entered the room for the exercise, and we started the exercise with a brief overview of the exercise in a PowerPoint presentation. The first slide in this presentation attempted to clear up the distinction we needed to make between laboratory-based biosafety and biosecurity and the dual use problem we were addressing. The slide stated that

> Biosecurity and Biosafety (and Biorisk Management) make vital contributions to a wider concept of 'biological security' that is made up of a web of integrated and complementary elements that reinforce each other . . . [This] refers to a 'web of prevention' that locates biosafety and biosecurity in the context of a range of 'biological security' measures that go beyond the laboratory door that include: *international and national prohibitions, disease detection and prevention, effective threat preparedness, export controls, oversight of life science activities, and biosecurity education and codes on conduct,* the latter ensuring that all those engaged in the life sciences whether in government, industry or academia are aware of their responsibilities to protect their work from misuse to counter the threats to humans, animals, and plants posed by states, non-state actors or other entities.

In this initial presentation, we made every effort to ensure that participants understood that the TBL was concerned with this wider view of biological security and not just with laboratory biosafety and laboratory biosecurity by stressing the aspects and giving examples of measures shown in italics in the slide just described from our presentation. We also made clear in a PowerPoint slide that our key learning objectives were that participants should at the end:

1   Understand the meaning and impact of the concept of dual use research;
2   See and understand how this concept of dual use research is applied in a concrete case;
3   Get insight into and understand the ethical, legal, and social responsibilities of scientists; and
4   Get to know different and divergent arguments as well as the interests of involved parties (scientists, government, citizens).

Running the TBL

As we had to run the TBL entirely with paper copies of questions and answers we were much dependent on our colleagues at the Medical University Innsbruck, who provided all the paper material, and our colleagues at Linnaeus University, who helped us by analysing the answers so that they could be quickly and effectively fed back to the participants. Only the pre-reading chapter from *Preventing Biological Threats* was sent out digitally in advance to participants, and even that was also provided in hard copy at the start of the TBL.

Unfortunately, a number of the expected participants were unable to attend the workshop because of delays with their visas. However, 13 attendees, about half of whom were members of the HBP and half not, took part in the TBL. The group was also roughly divided into half male and half female, and their ages ranged from mid-twenties to early fifties. The countries represented were Germany, Ireland, Netherlands, Portugal, Sweden, Switzerland, and the UK. Standard practice in TBL exercises is to try to make each team as diverse as possible to encourage debate between different perspectives within the teams, and we attempted to do this in advance from the information available about the background disciplines of the participants. We had received pictures of the room where the exercise was to be carried out in advance and had agreed how teams would be arranged around tables to encourage discussion within groups and debate later between different groups. Participants were informed of which team they were in as they entered the room for the exercise. We were fortunate that three members of the group of speakers for the workshop volunteered to take part in the TBL, and we therefore had five teams taking part in the exercise overall.

The TBL took place on the afternoon of the first day of the workshop, and as participants had been given two lectures in the morning session we decided to run the TBL first and then give our lecture on dual use after the TBL. Experienced users of TBL exercises stress the need to keep to the designated timetable in order to allow participants to have time to contribute effectively. So, in a departure from standard practice we set out our intended timetable clearly in a slide in our initial introductory presentation (Figure 41.1).

We kept closely to this timetable, although the break between the two exercises for refreshments gave us some flexibility with the time for discussions of the exercises. To help participants we also had PowerPoint slides relevant to each of the stages of the exercise in the initial presentation, and we put these up on the screen at appropriate times during the exercise.

The exercise began with participants being asked to complete the iRAT question forms. These questions related to the pre-reading material as shown in Figure 41.2.

It will be noted that the questions were not intended to be straightforward, as this one asks what is false. Additionally, a research-informed approach to learning and teaching dictated that we would need to present course participants with questions that challenged received knowledge

Formation of Groups and Introduction (1:30–2:00)
iRATs (2:00–2:15)
tRATs (2:15–2:30)
Feedback and Discussion (2:30–2:50)
First Application Exercise/Discussion (2:50–3:30)
Tea Break (3:30–4:00)
Second Application Exercise/Discussion (4:00–4:30)
Review by Participants (4:30–5:00)

Figure 41.1　Timetable for the TBL

---

1 Which statement about gain-of-function experiments is FALSE?

a)　There are strict international guidelines on how information about such experiments involving influenza has to be conducted and communicated.

b)　Such experiments are generally daily practice in the modern life sciences, and are not, in themselves, a cause for concern.

c)　Studies that seek to enhance the biological properties of biological agents, such as virulence and transmissibility, are examples of gain-of-function experiments.

d)　The creation of mammalian-transmissible H5N1 virus in 2011 constituted a gain-of-function experiment.

Figure 41.2　iRAT/tRAT Question 1

Source: Novossiolova, Biological Security Education Handbook, chap. 2.

they possessed about their subject. This was done through the adoption of a 'threshold concepts' approach and through the inclusion in the subject matter, and in the orientation of the questions, of concepts that have the potential to be 'transformative', 'irreversible', 'integrative', 'bounded', and 'troublesome'. Indeed, Meyer and Land[24] recognise that certain concepts are often central to the mastery of a subject. An example of a threshold concept for a biologist would be Darwin's ideas on evolution by natural selection. Once this is understood it really is difficult to see the world in any other way. It could be argued that in trying to raise awareness of the challenge of dual use we are attempting to get neuroscientists to see their work in an entirely different way. The concept of 'biological security' set out earlier is perhaps an obvious example of a threshold concept that is relevant to neuroscience and to the area of dual use. The available evidence clearly indicates that the vast majority of practising life scientists, including neuroscientists, do not consider the wider social implications of their work. Thus, getting them to engage with these wider implications, particularly the possibilities of hostile applications of the results of their work, can be seen as using biosecurity (as defined) as a threshold concept. The inclusion of questions specifically oriented to lead TBL participants to address both the consequences of their work and their duties as responsible life science practitioners can, we argue, facilitate the engagement of neuroscience practitioners in applied ethical discussions leading to an introduction to, and an appreciation of, some of the main schools of thought (consequentialist and deontological approaches) that are often involved in ethical deliberation. That is not just to induce some caution about what is done, but additionally to take up a serious responsibility towards how advances in neuroscience are implemented by society. Indeed, to see the Biological and Toxin Weapons Convention and the Chemical Weapons Convention as 'their' conventions, towards which their expertise can be applied, requires that they have a special responsibility.[25]

There were five questions on the iRAT and we allocated 4 marks to each correct answer. In total, the *participants* scored 58 per cent correct answers on the iRATs. When the process was repeated with the *teams* each answering the same questions on the tRATs (Figure 41.3) the correct answers rose to 80 per cent, thus indicating a reasonably high level of understanding of the essential pre-reading material that they needed to be familiar with in order to undertake the application exercises.

This finding is in line with what is expected as the teams share their answers to the questions and argue out the correct answers. However, we asked teams to reveal their answers to each of the questions simultaneously. That provided a means of opening up a cheerful discussion[26] that further helped to ensure that everyone was familiar with the pre-reading material (Figure 41.4).

The first application exercise presented a much different challenge by giving teams the following instructions:

> This exercise involves choice of one option from a list.
>
> You need to agree, write down and submit your best answer for the task AND your rationale for the answer e.g. why you have chosen an option, the criteria for your choice, or the points you considered when reaching a decision.
>
> You need to nominate a spokesperson, who will speak for the team during the feedback time. This role should be shared around the team as much as possible. Reveal your answers as directed.

The question and options available to the participants are set out in Figure 41.5. The aim of this application exercise was to show that there were a range of other stakeholders involved in

Figure 41.3   Team 5 working together on the tRAT

Source: © Lisa-Marie Leichter, HBP Education Programme Office.

Figure 41.4 Answers to the tRAT

Source: © Lisa-Marie Leichter, HBP Education Programme Office.

Based on the H5N1 controversy described in Chapter 2, identify which of the following stakeholders bears the chief burden of responsibility for the prolonged debate?

A   The media who spread panic following the initial report on the findings presented by Ron Fouchier at the conference in Malta in September 2011;

B   The funding agencies who should have demanded that the applicants submit a detailed risk-benefit analysis of the proposed studies related to biosecurity;

C   The local institutional biosafety committees that should have insisted that scientists conduct thorough risk assessments with regard to biosecurity prior to, during and after the experiments;

D   The scientists who should have ensured that measures were in place to address any potential biosecurity concerns likely to arise from the experiments, before submitting their funding proposals;

E   The National Science Advisory Board for Biosecurity (NSABB) who should have allowed the publication of the manuscripts after having reviewed them in December 2011;

F   The security community who should have developed guidelines for what kind of life science research should be subject to restrictions in terms of publication;

G   The editorial boards of *Science* and *Nature* who should have published the papers without consulting the US Government and the NSABB;

H   The US Government who should have classified the manuscripts when the editorial boards of *Science* and *Nature* consulted them.

Figure 41.5 Question for and possible answers to the first application exercise

Source: Novossiolova, Biological Security Education Handbook, chap. 2.

the debate besides the scientists and that they had differing views on what should be done and by whom.

The teams were asked to reveal their answers simultaneously as in the responses to the tRATs. Clearly the answers varied, with the teams voting as follows: Team 1:A, Team 2:C, Team 3:F, Team 4:F, and Team 5:E. These different results provoked a vigorous discussion, both about the answers and about the precise meaning of the questions. As might be expected given that the participants were mainly practising life scientists, there was little use of overtly stated ethical arguments in the discussion.

The second application exercise attempted to focus directly on the question of biosecurity responsibilities outside of the laboratory by posing the following question:

> As noted in Chapter 2 [the pre-reading], scientists have broader responsibilities to society to ensure that their work does not pose unnecessary risks.
>
> The figure presents a timeline with the different stages of a research process – from the conceptual phase of the research to its final publication. For each stage identify the responsibilities of the life scientists conducting the research with regard to biosecurity, and suggest at least one action that could be taken to address any potential biosecurity concerns.

The figure mentioned in the question set out the stages of the research process as shown in Figure 41.6.

It is quite clear from the list in Figure 41.6 that participants were required to think about possible actions well beyond the laboratory door. The teams were encouraged to make posters and to present their answers in sequence to the rest of the teams. As shown in Figure 41.7 the teams did not confine themselves to the initial stages of the research process but attempted to engage with the problem of minimising misuse across the full range of the stages.

Our only major problem with the whole exercise was that we could have done with much more time for these final presentations and to have a more extended discussion of the implications of the suggestions for action that participants had made. However, we tried to address some of these issues in the following lecture on dual use, particularly in regard to the dangers that advances in neuroscience will open up possibilities for novel chemical and biological weapons and how the CWC and the BTWC might be strengthened to help prevent such dangers to society.

Stage 1: Project Concept and Design
Stage 2: Funding Application and Award Process
Stage 3: Institutional Approval
Stage 4: Ongoing Research
Stage 5: Development of Manuscript and Other Research Product
Stage 6: Publication of Manuscript or Other Research Product

Figure 41.6 Stages of the research process

Source: Novossiolova, Biological Security Education Handbook, chap. 2.

Figure 41.7 Presentation of application exercise 2

Source: © Lisa-Marie Leichter, HBP Education Programme Office.

Lessons learnt and implications of the exercise

Clearly, we were pleased with the TBL in Stockholm in that a diverse group of people was able to take part and engage in the exercise and that we were able to complete the intended sections in the time available. We did not ask specifically for written feedback, but our impression was that participants found it interesting as well as enjoyable and in assessing the whole workshop six people mentioned the TBL specifically: one found it "difficult"; one "enjoyed it a lot"; one said it was a "great activity"; and two found it "excellent".

So, we return to the key learning objectives of the exercise, which we set out as follows:

1   Understand the meaning and impact of the concept of dual use research;
2   See and understand how this concept of dual use research is applied in a concrete case;
3   Get insight into and understand the ethical, legal, and social responsibilities of scientists; and
4   Get to know different and divergent arguments as well as the interests of involved parties (scientists, government, citizens).

It might be argued that there was a good chance of participants going away with an understanding of some of these objectives. However, we think that only an initial beginning had been made on objective 3 for many of the practising scientists involved in the exercise if the wider societal impacts of advances in neuroscience are considered.

In our view, therefore there are some obvious conclusions to be taken into account if this exercise is repeated for neuroscientists. First, of course, there needs to be the development of some specific dual-use TBLs for neuroscientists to follow on from this type of more general dual-use material. Secondly, much more specific questioning has to be developed to make full use of the second application exercise, where broader societal questions are in focus. We felt that much more could have been made of the excellent presentations made by the participants in the second application exercise – for example, by raising questions about the different ethical approaches that could be taken to dealing with their responsibilities. Indeed, it might have been a better idea to have two TBLs separately at the workshop, with one near the beginning going through to the first application exercise and discussion and then a separate session later on, dealing specifically with the second application and a much broader discussion. Given that the workshop was in an ethics series this might also have been an opportunity to bring some specific ethical reasoning into the debate.

If more time was available a better idea, perhaps, would be to have a short course in which four linked TBL exercises were run in sequence. This sequence could begin with the dual-use TBL used successfully in Stockholm, but then followed up with more specific examples of the misuse of neuroscience. For example, the paper on the hijacking of benignly intended neuroscience research in the development of the novel and very dangerous spice cannabinoids could be used to ask more generally about the responsibilities of neuroscientists.[27] That could be followed with a specific example of dual use by focusing on the confirmation of the use of derivatives of the opioid fentanyl[28] to break the Moscow theatre siege in 2002, with the loss of over 120 of the hostages' lives because of the effects of the fentanyl.[29] Finally, the general issue of the responsibilities of scientists could be dealt with by finishing with the TBL in the *Biosecurity Education Handbook* on Chapter 3 of the *Preventing Biological Threats* that deals in detail with advances in science and technology and the evolution of bioweapons capability and describes in considerable detail how civil work in the life sciences has been used in the last century to develop novel chemical and biological weapons.[30]

So far so good then, but what lessons have been gained besides the knowledge that a one-off TBL on dual use can be carried out within a neuroscience workshop? More importantly how does this help us with the task of widespread raising of awareness of the dual-use challenge set out in 2012 by the Royal Society report *Neuroscience, Conflict and Security*? The longer-term aim must be to bring the challenge of dual use into the regular university training of all neuroscientists as part of their consideration of responsible conduct in the global neuroscience enterprise.[31] The Stockholm TBL might best be seen as a small step along that road.

We have long argued that team-based learning can be an effective and efficient means of awareness-raising and education about the problem of dual use for scientists,[32] but that there is also a need for coordinated national, regional, and international action[33] to achieve the level of awareness implied by the UK Royal Society in *Neuroscience, Conflict and Security*. Exactly what needs to be done was set out by the Ukraine and the UK in their joint proposal of language for inclusion in the report of the 8th Review Conference of the BTWC in 2016. As they put it,[34]

> 18. The Conference should therefore adopt the following language in the Final Declaration text for Article IV:

> > The Conference stresses the critical importance of biosecurity education and awareness-raising in achieving effective implementation of the Convention, which should be put into effect through national implementation measures, as appropriate, in accordance with the constitutional process and practices of each State Party.

19. The Conference notes that such measures could include:

(a) encouraging the promotion of a culture of responsible science among those working in the biological sciences and other relevant scientific disciplines;

(b) promoting among those working in the biological sciences, and other relevant scientific disciplines, awareness of the obligations of States Parties under the Convention, as well as relevant national legislation and guidelines;

(c) promoting the development and implementation of training and education programmes as well as training guides, handbooks and course materials, including raising awareness of the implications of dual use research and technology, for those granted access to biological agents and toxins relevant to the Convention, and especially for those with the knowledge or capacity to modify such agents and toxins;

(d) encouraging the development, adoption and promulgation of codes of conduct to promote awareness among relevant professionals in the private and public sectors and throughout relevant scientific and administrative activities.

This along with many other good ideas for strengthening the convention were lost in the failure of the conference to agree much other than to meet again in late 2017 to see if it was possible to find agreement on such issues. Fortunately, in the December 2017 follow-up meeting of state parties to the BTWC it was agreed that the annual meetings through to the next Review Conference in 2021 would have a working group on science and technology[35] and that this working group would have as one of its topics '[D]evelopment of a voluntary model code of conduct for biological scientists and all relevant personnel, and biosecurity education, by drawing on the work already done on this issue in the context of the Convention, adaptable to national requirements'.[36] Thus, there is a real chance that progress can be made in raising the awareness of neuroscientists about the problem of dual use and further engaging them in dealing with the problem in coming years and that TBL exercises can be useful in that regard and in opening up more detailed ethical deliberations about this issue in the scientific community.

Notes

1 Blank, R. H. (2013) *Intervention in the Brain: Politics, Policy, and Ethics*. The MIT Press, Boston, MA.
2 Moreno, J. D. (2006) *Mind Wars: Brain Research and National Defense*. Dana Press, New York.
3 For an account of these programmes in, for example, the EU, the US, China and Japan see the special issue of the journal Neuron volume 92, November, 2016.
4 One such set of problems concerns how to maintain and develop the international agreements – the Chemical Weapons Convention (CWC) and the Biological and Toxin Weapons Convention (BTWC) – that ban the use of chemical and biological weapons of mass destruction. Changes to these conventions will require agreements to be reached at the international level and then implemented within nation states.
5 Australia (2014) Weaponisation of Central Nervous System Acting Chemicals for Law Enforcement. C-19/NAT.1, OPCW, The Hague, 19 November.
6 OPCW, Report of the Scientific Advisory Board on Developments in Science and Technology for the Third Special Session of the Conference of the States Parties to Review the Operation of the Chemical Weapons Convention, RC-3/DG-1, OPCW, *The Hague*, 29 October 2012, 1–31, p. 4.
7 Royal Society (2012) *Brain Waves Module 3: Neuroscience, Conflict and Security*. The Royal Society, London.
8 See, for example, Immersing students in responsible science through active learning pedagogies: lessons from educational institutes in the MENA region, by Lida Anestidou and Jay Labov, and Interactive

biosecurity: Team-Based Learning in action by Tatyana Novossiolova in Preventing Biological Threats: What You Can Do. Available at www.brad.ac.uk/social-sciences/peace-studies/research/publications-and-projects/guide-to-biological-security-issues.

9 For details see www.humanbrainproject.eu/en/open-ethical-engaged.

10 See https://education.humanbrainproject.eu/web/hbp-education-portal/about.

11 Team-based learning is a special form of collaborative learning that uses a specific sequence of individual work, group work, and immediate feedback to create a motivational framework whereby the focus is shifted from conveying concepts by the instructor to the application of concepts by student teams.

12 The Biological and Toxin Weapons Convention (BTWC) adds a series of prohibitions, for example, on the development of biological and toxin weapons, to the ban on use embodied in the 1925 Geneva Protocol. The convention was negotiated in the 1970s, and although its prohibitions are sweeping in concept it suffers from serious deficiencies in implementation despite decades of efforts by state parties to strengthen it – for example, by improving its verification provisions and organisational support.

13 See, for example, Wheelis, M., Rozsa, L., and Dando, M.R. (Eds.) (2006) *Deadly Cultures: Biological Weapons Since 1945*. Harvard University Press, Cambridge, MA.

14 Chemical weapons of increasing lethality were developed and used during the First World War. In the 1930s chemists doing civil work on pesticides discovered the first of the nerve agents and these were weaponised but not used by Germany in the Second World War. Then during the Cold War even more deadly nerve agents were developed, again after discoveries by civil scientists, and huge stocks of these agents were built up particularly by the United States and the Soviet Union. These agents were also used, for example, in the 1980s Iran-Iraq War and recently in the Syrian Civil War.

15 In total, we discussed the problem of dual use with several thousand practising life scientists in universities in 16 different countries. We used a form of focus group to structure the discussions. It was very unusual for us to find anyone who had knowledge of the problem. This finding has been replicated and reported in official papers and statements at meetings of the BTWC and the CWC.

16 See SBTWC: Web of Prevention Clearing House at www.opbw.org.

17 Whitby, S., Novossiolova, T., Walther, G., and Dando, M. R. (Eds.) (2016) *Preventing Biological Threats: What You Can Do*. Available at www.brad.ac.uk/social-sciences/peace-studies/research/publications-and-projects/guide-to-biological-security-issues.

18 Novossiolova, T. (2016) *Biological Security Education Handbook: The Power of Team-Based Learning*. Available at www.brad.ac.uk/social-sciences/peace-studies/research/publications-and-projects/guide-to-biological-security-issues.

19 Since the beginning of the century there has been increasing concern about experiments with dual-use implications, such as those with the mousepox virus and highly pathogenic influenza. The experiments to make the highly pathogenic influenza virus contagious by the airborne route became known as gain-of-function experiments.

20 Van der Bruggen, K. (2016) *Biosecurity challenges in the 21st Century: The Case of Gain-of-Function Experiments*. Available at www.brad.ac.uk/social-sciences/peace-studies/research/publications-and-projects/guide-to-biological-security-issues.

21 For details see Chapter 20 on Interactive biosecurity: Team-Based Learning in action by Tatyana Novossiolova in Preventing Biological Threats: What You Can Do. Available at www.brad.ac.uk/social-sciences/peace-studies/research/publications-and-projects/guide-to-biological-security-issues.

22 Charles Gullo, Tam Cam Ha and Sandy Cook (2015) Twelve tips for facilitating team-based learning, *Medical Teacher*, 37:9, 819–824, DOI: 10.3109/0142159X.2014.1001729.

23 Novossiolova, T. (2018) The Role of the Non-Governmental Life Science Community in Combatting the Development, Proliferation and Use of Chemical Weapons. Chapter 18 in M. Crowley, M. R. Dando and L. Shang (Eds.), *Preventing Chemical Weapons: Arms Control and Disarmament as the Sciences Converge*. Royal Society of Chemistry, London (in press).

24 Meyer J.H.F. and Land R (2003). Threshold Concepts and Troublesome Knowledge – Linkages to Ways of Thinking and Practising. In C. Rust (Ed), *Improving Student Learning – Ten Years On*. OCSLD, Oxford.

25 The problem of dual use is complex and will require a diverse set of solutions. In some instances, experiments could be of such concern that they should not be carried out, but these will likely not be frequently encountered, so legally banning experiments is unlikely to solve the problem in itself, particularly as we all want civil work intended to help people who are ill to be carried out. Therefore, lesser restrictions, such as codes of conduct and effective education throughout a scientist's career, seem

more appropriate, but given the complexity of the science the expertise of scientists and their professional organisations will be needed to help decide what best can be done. Moreover, what is best to be done could change quite rapidly given the pace of advances being made in neuroscience.

26 A video of the whole TBL is available at: https://education.humanbrainproject.eu/web/1st-hbp-curriculum-ethics/workshop-media. Team Based Learning Exercise – Social, ethical and legal responsibilities of life sciences, 1st HBP Curriculum Workshop Series – Research, ethics and Societal Impact, 10–12 July 2017, Karolinska Institutet, Stockholm, Sweden. Video recorded by the Human Brain Project Education Office. Tutors: Shamin Patel, Linnaeus University, Sweden, Malcolm Dando, Simon Whitby, Bradford University, UK. YouTube: https://youtu.be/EFvraNKU1UE.

27 Wiley, J. L. et al. (2011) *Hijacking of Basic Research: The Case of Synthetic Canabinoids.* Methods Rep RTI Press, November; 2011. doi:10.3768/rtipress.2011.op.007.1111.

28 Fentanyl is a synthetic chemical with actions similar to morphine, but it is much stronger in its effects. Again, this chemical was developed by civil scientists for benign purposes, but then used for other purposes in the theatre siege.

29 Riches, J. R. et al. (2012) Analysis of clothing and urine from Moscow theatre siege casualties reveals Carfentanil and Remifentanil use. *Journal of Analytical Toxicology*, 36, 647–656.

30 Novossiolova, T. (2016) *Biological Security Education Handbook: The Power of Team-Based Learning.* Available at www.brad.ac.uk/social-sciences/peace-studies/research/publications-and-projects/guide-to-biological-security-issue.

31 InterAcademy Partnership (2016*) Doing Global Science: A Guide to Responsible Conduct in the Global Research Enterprise*, Princeton, NJ: Princeton University Press.

32 Novossiolova, T., Mancini, G. and Dando, M.R. (2013) *Effective and Sustainable Biosecurity Education for those in the Life Science: The Benefits of Active Learning. Briefing Paper No 7 (Third Series)*, University of Bradford, June.

33 Novossiolova, T. and Pearson, G.S. (2012) *Biosecurity Education for the Life Sciences: Nuclear Security Education Experience as a Model. Briefing Paper No 5 (Third Series)*, University of Bradford, October.

34 Ukraine and the UK (2016) Awareness-raising, education, outreach: An example of best practice. BWC/CONF.VIII/WP.10. United Nations, Geneva, 19 October.

35 Convention on the Prohibition of the Development, Production and Stockpiling of Bacteriological (Biological) and Toxin Weapons and Their Destruction (2017) *Report of the Meeting of States Parties.* United Nations, Geneva, December.

36 Ukraine and the UK, Awareness-raising, education, outreach, 6.

INDEX

Note: Page numbers in *italics* indicate figures and page numbers in **bold** indicate tables.